The
BOOKER T. WASHINGTON
Papers

The

BOOKER T. WASHINGTON

Papers

VOLUME 6

1901–2

Louis R. Harlan
and
Raymond W. Smock

EDITORS

Barbara S. Kraft

ASSISTANT EDITOR

University of Illinois Press

URBANA · CHICAGO · LONDON

Library of Congress Cataloging in Publication Data (Revised)

Washington, Booker Taliaferro, 1856–1915.
  The Booker T. Washington papers.

  Includes bibliographies.
  CONTENTS: v. 1. The autobiographical writings.—
v. 2. 1860–89.—v. 3. 1889–95.—v. 4. 1895–98.
—v. 5. 1899–1900.—v. 6. 1901–2.
  1. Washington, Booker Taliaferro, 1856–1915.
2. Afro-Americans—History—Sources. 3. Social
reformers—United States—Correspondence.
E185.97.W274   301.45'19'6073024   75–186345
ISBN 0–252–00650–X (v. 6)

To the Memory of
Amanda Ferguson Johnston

CONTENTS

CONTENTS

CONTENTS

CONTENTS

CONTENTS

Contents

ILLUSTRATIONS

INTRODUCTION

In this volume Booker T. Washington fully arrives on the national stage, ready to play his role as the most powerful black figure of his age. Because relatively little of his outgoing correspondence was preserved, however, the volume documents the events in which he participated more than his own private thoughts and concerns.

Early in 1901 Washington's autobiography, *Up from Slavery*, appeared in book form, fixing his image on the national consciousness as the American success hero in black and as the man with a practical solution to race problems. A month later a whole trainload of philanthropists in Pullman cars left New York for the Conference for Education in the South, which moved from its original meeting place at a mountain retreat in West Virginia into the heart of the New South, Winston-Salem. Out of it grew the Southern Education Board, which employed Washington as its agent for blacks in a regionwide educational campaign, but never allowed him to attend its meetings. Out of the Southern Education Board grew John D. Rockefeller's General Education Board, which sponsored higher education for southern whites and industrial education for southern blacks. Tuskegee's new Carnegie Library and Rockefeller Hall symbolized the shift in philanthropic support of Tuskegee from the church- and abolitionist-oriented philanthropy of New England to the business philanthropy of New York and later Chicago.

It was in the political sphere, however, that Washington's life saw its greatest expansion. Coinciding with Washington's meteoric rise to become a counselor of presidents, black political rights in the South plummeted through disfranchisement and a worsening racial

climate. In September 1901, on the very day that President Mc-
Kinley died of an assassin's bullet and Theodore Roosevelt became
President, the latter telegraphed Washington inviting him to a
conference on southern appointments. On Washington's advice,
Roosevelt appointed as an Alabama district judge not a white Republican but a conservative Gold Democrat who had befriended
black voting rights in Alabama. Soon afterward, also on Washington's advice, the President appointed one of Washington's Tuskegee neighbors, Joseph O. Thompson, the postmaster, as collector of
internal revenue for Alabama and the principal referee for political
appointments in the state. Soon afterward he extended the referee
system to Mississippi, where Washington's white Gold Democrat
friend Edgar S. Wilson became the President's kingpin for the state.
Washington also secured appointment or retention in office of his
black friends throughout the South, usually on the ground that
they were men who had succeeded at some business or profession
rather than being the allegedly venal professional black politicians
of the past. This course of action reached its climax with the non-
controversial appointment of Robert H. Terrell as a judge in the
District of Columbia and the highly controversial appointment of
the black physician William D. Crum as collector of the port of
Charleston.

On October 16, 1901, Washington dined at the White House
with President Roosevelt, his family, and an old friend from Colorado. This was the first time in history — and the last time for many
years — that a black man had dined at the White House, though
in past administrations blacks had attended receptions there. The
southern press and political leaders seized the opportunity to denounce the action in hysterical language; and the white South never
again completely trusted Washington, though he soon took the
edge off their anger by conservative words and actions. Neither
Washington nor Roosevelt publicly commented on the dinner for
almost a decade. The occasion had little importance for Roosevelt,
who never repeated the indiscretion and omitted mention of it in
his autobiography. For Washington, and for all the blacks who
would never be invited to the White House, the dinner had great
symbolic importance as a sign of his arrival at the heart of power in
America. The vicarious experience of the dinner incident bound

Washington's black followers to him in a way that rhetoric or ideology never could.

In Alabama, however, events were taking a somber turn. The Alabama constitutional convention met with the avowed purpose of disfranchising black citizens. Washington and other Alabama black leaders sent a mild and ineffectual petition to the convention asking it not to discriminate against blacks. The constitution, however, had many devices for excluding all but a few thousand of the black citizens of the state from the ballot box. Washington did not openly oppose ratification of the constitution, and the registrars in his county sent him a special invitation to qualify for his lifetime voting certificate. In the deepest secrecy, however, he engaged a New York black lawyer, Wilford H. Smith, for a challenge to the Alabama grandfather clause. To conceal Washington's involvement, Emmett J. Scott and Smith carried on their correspondence about these suffrage cases under the assumed names of Ajax and Filipino and then R. C. Black and J. C. May. In 1902 a faction of the Republican party in Alabama known as the "lily whites" used the disfranchisement laws as the grounds for a move to exclude blacks from membership in the party. At the party's state convention black delegates were barred from the meeting hall, even those who were registered voters. Thus began Washington's long-time battle for racial equality in the southern Republican party, with aid from Roosevelt and his chief liaison with black Republicans, General James S. Clarkson, collector of the port of New York.

As Washington's star rose, that of T. Thomas Fortune declined. Fortune's excessive drinking and his determination to be a gadfly to the Roosevelt administration often made him an embarrassment to Washington. Though Washington continued to use and subsidize Fortune and his newspaper, the New York *Age*, he turned to others as his lieutenants in the leading northern cities, as the Tuskegee Machine extended its web of influence in the first years of the new century. In New York it was Charles W. Anderson who emerged as Washington's principal agent, not only in politics but in all aspects of black public affairs. In Boston William H. Lewis had formerly been one of the Tuskegean's sharpest critics, but Theodore Roosevelt had known Lewis through Harvard University, where Lewis had once coached the football team. Through

Roosevelt's influence and Lewis's ambition, Lewis was persuaded to turn coat and join Washington's team. Once decided on this course, he followed it wholeheartedly and with great ability. In Chicago the lawyer S. Laing Williams was Washington's chief contact. In Washington, D.C., it was Whitefield McKinlay, the black realtor, and Robert H. Terrell, the school principal and later judge. Washington's critics were by no means silent in these years, and those in Boston worried him enough to cause him to subsidize a newspaper there to compete with William Monroe Trotter's Boston *Guardian*. The opposition was as yet unfocused and unorganized, however, and Washington was easily able to dominate racial affairs through his National Negro Business League, effective control of the Afro-American Council, and publicity in the white press that kept him constantly in the public spotlight as spokesman of the race.

There are also a number of minor themes in the volume. A candid exchange of views begins between Washington and the black novelist Charles W. Chesnutt. Washington's book review attacking William Hannibal Thomas's racist book is interesting not only in its content but in the fact that Washington used spies to gather damaging information about Thomas. Washington's daughter Portia entered Wellesley College for a year in 1901, encountered academic difficulty, and the following year entered Bradford Academy. The volume also contains letters recounting Frances Benjamin Johnston's visit to Tuskegee to photograph the campus and its people, and her subsequent involvement in a racial fracas at Ramer, where a Tuskegee graduate was conducting a "little Tuskegee" but was forced to abandon his school and flee from the town when local whites objected to a white woman riding in a black man's buggy at night. A selection of her Tuskegee photographs of 1902 are included in the volume. Washington used the photographs extensively as illustrations for magazine articles and at exhibits to promote a positive image of Tuskegee Institute and industrial education.

Staff members who made valuable contributions to the volume are Janet P. Benham, Patricia A. Cooper, Janet E. Hartman, Sadie M. Harlan, Geraldine McTigue, Denise P. Moore, Judy A. Reardon, William M. Stowe, Jr., Jerry Thornbery, and Thomas E. Weir, Jr.

We are grateful for the assistance of R. Hunt Davis, Mary A. Giunta, Sara D. Jackson, Alfred A. Moss, Jr., and Sylvia L. Render.

The editors acknowledge with thanks the continued aid and encouragement of the National Endowment for the Humanities, the National Historical Publications and Records Commission, and the University of Maryland.

SYMBOLS AND ABBREVIATIONS

STANDARD ABBREVIATIONS for dates, months, and states are used by the editors only in footnotes and endnotes; textual abbreviations are reproduced as found.

DOCUMENT SYMBOLS

1. A — autograph; written in author's hand
   H — handwritten by other than signator
   P — printed
   T — typed

2. C — postcard
   D — document
   E — endorsement
   L — letter
   M — manuscript
   W — wire (telegram)

3. c — carbon
   d — draft
   f — fragment
   p — letterpress
   t — transcript or copy made at much later date

4. I — initialed by author
   r — representation; signed or initialed in author's name
   S — signed by author

Among the more common endnote abbreviations are: ALS — autograph letter, signed by author; TLpI — typed letter, letterpress copy, initialed by author.

REPOSITORY SYMBOLS

Symbols used for repositories are the standard ones used in *Symbols of American Libraries Used in the National Union Catalog of the Library of Congress,* 10th ed. (Washington, D.C., 1969).

ATT	Tuskegee Institute, Tuskegee, Ala.
DLC	Library of Congress, Washington, D.C.
DNA	National Archives, Washington, D.C.
GEU	Emory University, Atlanta, Ga.
LND	Dillard University, New Orleans, La.
MB	Boston Public Library, Boston, Mass.
MeB	Bowdoin College, Brunswick, Me.
MH	Harvard University, Cambridge, Mass.
MNS	Smith College, Northampton, Mass.
MU	University of Massachusetts, Amherst, Mass.
NcGU	University of North Carolina at Greensboro, N.C.
NN	New York Public Library, NYC
NN-Sc	Schomburg Collection, New York Public Library, NYC
ViHaI	Hampton Institute, Hampton, Va.
ViU	University of Virginia, Charlottesville, Va.
WHi	State Historical Society of Wisconsin, Madison, Wis.

OTHER ABBREVIATIONS

BTW	Booker T. Washington
Con.	Container
NNBL	National Negro Business League
RG	Record Group
Ser.	Series

Documents, 1901–2

From John Edward Bruce

New York   5 Jan 01

Dear Sir   I have another occasion to write, same as before. I hate to; it seems mean. But it isn't; you have a right to it.

In your *Outlook* paper, this date, you say: "We tried several locations before we opened up a pit that furnished brick clay."

"Opened up" is bad. Again: "By this time, it had gotten to be pretty well advertised throughout the state that every student who came to Tuskegee, no matter what his financial ability might be, must learn some industry."

I think "gotten" is bad. I cannot say with sure knowledge that it is so; but I feel confident of it. Got is a good word; in my judgment, gotten is not. Gotten has been rated as obsolescent; it is more in use now; but, I think, not by very good writers in general; and it is decidedly in general use by poor writers. I think it a word to be avoided, as almost unclean; but my feeling outruns my knowledge.

My admiration for your writing grows; but that is decidedly second to my feeling that writing is by no means of first consequence to you. You are entitled to the feeling that makes big head. I see not the least sign of it. It is almost absurd to speak of it; not quite. Big head afflicts some very considerable persons.

I heard you speak once; have not known very much of your work; enough to have an impression of it. Now I have an opinion.

I said of you the other day: He seems to me as important as anybody. I have held, till lately, that E L Godkin was the most important man in U S. I fear his work is done. I am not sure that you don't come next. Yours truly

J E Bruce

ALS   Con. 206   BTW Papers   DLC.

From Hamilton Wright Mabie[1]

New York   January 8, 1901

My Dear Mr. Washington: You know, I presume, something about the new work of Thomas[2] on The American Negro, just published

3

by The Macmillan Company: it is, I suppose, the most important book on the subject which has been written. We are very anxious to have you review it for our columns over your own name, and we should be glad to give you any space you want — from one to two thousand words, or even longer.[3] Any word from you on this whole question would be read with the deepest interest by our readers, and would be extremely valuable. May I send you the book? Of course the usual check would be sent on receipt of the review.

May I tell you how profoundly interested we are in your auto-biography, and how glad we are that it came in our way to print it. It is in my opinion one of the most important human decuments which has come to light in this part of the world for many years. Yours sincerely,

H. W. Mabie

TLSr Con. 204 BTW Papers DLC.

1 Hamilton Wright Mabie (1845?–1916) was an editor of the *Christian Union* (re-named *Outlook* in 1893) from 1879 to 1916.

2 William Hannibal Thomas.

3 See A Book Review in *Outlook*, Mar. 30, 1901, below.

From Edgar Gardner Murphy

Montgomery, Alabama. January 11th, 1901

Dear Mr. Washington: The fate of the Conference[1] has been some-what in the balance, but at the last meeting of the executive com-mittee the program committee was unanimously ordered to go ahead; and we will have it if we can get the men we want (and I do not want a Conference that would be made up of inferior men — for that is a kind of failure we could not live down).

We have had powerful forces against us, for there are many men who want no open discussion of the subject at all; but the way is now clear. The program (as projected) includes men like St. Clair McElway,[2] of the Brooklyn Eagle; Mr. Andrew Carnegie;[3] Mr. McIver;[4] Gov. Sayers; Gov. Samford; Senator D. B. Hill[5] of New York; Clark Howell; and possibly Mr. Mabie of the Outlook. There will be no speeches like those of Barringer and Graves; and perhaps no such strong advocacy of your cause as the speech of Dr. Curry;

the whole discussion will be more "even" in temper. I do not mean that all these men have accepted, but we are going ahead in the hope of getting most of them.

I should like to talk the matter over with you as soon as possible, for I personally wish you to know just what we are about. In the meantime there is a very decided favor which you can do for me, if you are so inclined. President McKinley is coming South about the first of May — and we earnestly wish him to attend the Conference and speak to it — if only for a few minutes. I have certain friends who will act for us in Washington; but I believe you will have as much weight with him as anyone. He will probably pass right through Montgomery — and it would cost little in time or trouble for him to stop. We will not fix our date precisely till we have consulted his convenience. May 1st 2nd or third would suit us admirably. I think his presence here will do great good, and he may say little or much — just as he prefers, and a hearty welcome will be accorded him.

If you can see your way clear to write him, your letter will serve two purposes. In the first place it will assure him that men of sincerity and personal standing are behind the Southern Society. In the second place it will assure him that the movement is not dreaded by the wiser leaders of the Negro Race, and that we have no narrow or unworthy purpose at heart. My friends all over the country have been surprised at the breadth of the discussion as printed in our official Report, after reading the press despatches at the time; for the press largely ignored men like Dr. Curry and Dr. Frissell, and gave most of the space to the sensational matter of other addresses. If you can write to Mr. McKinley in such a way as to put him right on the subject, kindly do so at once. If for any reason you cannot do so, you need not think that I shall have any personal feeling in the matter whatever.

From the forces that have *opposed* us, I feel the Negro would be one of those who would lose something, if the Conference should be abandoned. Wise men can usually tell whom a movement is helping, by noting the men who are opposed to it. Nothing would more certainly assure the success of the undertaking than the presence of the President of the United States. Always Sincerely,

Edgar Gardner Murphy

TLS Con. 206 BTW Papers DLC.

1 This was to be the second annual conference of the Southern Society, which had sponsored the Montgomery Race Conference in May 1900. Murphy's plans, however, failed to materialize.

2 St. Clair McKelway (1845–1915) was editor-in-chief of the Brooklyn *Eagle* beginning in 1884. He championed Grover Cleveland in his gubernatorial and presidential campaigns, but often took stands independent of party affiliation. McKelway fought for clean city government in Brooklyn and was nationally known as a speaker on educational topics.

3 Andrew Carnegie (1835–1919), the Scottish-born steel manufacturer and philanthropist, showed but little interest in BTW or Tuskegee when first approached about 1890, but in 1900 he agreed to give $20,000 for a Carnegie library at the institute. Paying a visit of inspection, he was amazed at the ability of BTW to construct such a large building for so little money, by using student-made bricks and student labor. In 1903 he gave $600,000 in U.S. Steel bonds to Tuskegee Institute, including $150,000 to BTW and his family as a personal gift. The latter sum the trustees insisted should be invested by them, the interest to be used to pay his salary. Carnegie also privately subsidized the NNBL and the Committee of Twelve for the Advancement of the Negro Race. He agreed at Washington's request to give a Carnegie library to Fisk University, and made similar gifts to other black schools. He frequently referred to BTW as the black Moses, or a combination of Moses and Joshua, and in his letter of gift in 1903 he said: "History is to tell of two Washingtons[,] one white, the other Black, both Fathers of their people." (See Andrew Carnegie to William Henry Baldwin, Jr., Apr. 17, 1903, below.) Carnegie's money and prestige gave BTW the opportunity to develop several important institutions of his Tuskegee Machine. Carnegie refused, however, to support a proposal drafted by Washington and his subordinates for a Carnegie Foundation on the Negro, an ambitious proposal for a research institute on race problems.

4 Charles Duncan McIver (1860–1906) was, with Edwin A. Alderman, the founder of the southern educational campaign which later took organized form as the Southern Education Board. In 1889 he and Alderman, both graduates of the University of North Carolina, were appointed state conductors of weekly teachers' institutes. Moving county by county through the state, they sought not only to improve the quality of instruction but to promote interest in the cause of public education. In 1892 McIver persuaded the state legislature to found a school for the training of white women teachers, the State Normal and Industrial School. He became its first president, serving until his death. In 1901 he and other southern white educators joined the Conference for Education in the South, and later that year he became a member of the Southern Education Board, the executive body for a regionwide public educational campaign. McIver was an engaging public speaker, enlivening his pleas for education with humorous anecdotes. An ardent Bryanite, he died of apoplexy while on the "Bryan Special" campaign train on its tour of North Carolina.

5 David Bennett Hill (1843–1910) was governor of New York from 1885 to 1891 and U.S. senator from 1891 to 1897.

From William Jennings Bryan

Lincoln, Nebr., Jan. 11, 1901

Dear Sir: I take pleasure in enclosing a check for five dollars, which may be of some little assistance to your school.[1] I regret that it is not more but at this time my account for charity and education is very much overdrawn.

Appreciating the work that you are doing, I am, very truly yours,

W. J. Bryan

TLS Con. 704 BTW Papers DLC.

[1] On at least one other occasion Bryan contributed a small amount to Tuskegee. On Dec. 23, 1899, Bryan's wife Mary sent a donation to BTW. She asked that "no public mention be made of this contribution as a public announcement brings us dozens of similar requests and proves very embarrassing." She told BTW that Bryan gave "ten per cent of his income for church, charity and education." (Con. 150, BTW Papers, DLC.)

A Sunday Evening Talk

Tuskegee, Ala., January 13, 1901

INFLUENCING THE HOME LIFE OF THE PEOPLE

There is one thing to which I want to call your attention before I begin my talk; to a custom which largely prevails in the South, and which also, I am sorry to say, largely prevails among our people. I mention the useless and abominable habit of carrying concealed weapons.

I think that all of you understand that it is against the rules and the policy of this institution for any student to have concealed weapons, pistols or guns, of any kind, about them. I speak of this because we want to get out of the habit of feeling that it is necessary to carry about weapons to defend yourselves. It indicates a civilization that is not of the highest character. Among people who represent the highest civilization, among people who represent the highest intelligence, and among people who are really refined, you do not find the habit of carrying concealed weapons. Among other reasons, it is a useless expense. You cannot afford to get into the habit of carrying an instrument of death. It is, as I said, a useless expense, for it costs from $5 to $10. You must not get into the habit of carrying about your person a weapon that is likely at any time to get you into a difficulty, into trouble of a kind for which you will be sorry all your lives. The carrying of concealed weapons, gets a person into trouble ten times, where it saves his life one time. I repeat, I believe the habit of carrying concealed weapons gets an individual into trouble ten times, where it results in saving his life one time. It is needless. You do not want to get into such a habit. Make up your minds that you are not going to disgrace yourselves. It is unnecessary for you to carry a weapon upon your person. Some of the students here received, I remember, during the holidays, as presents, pistols and other weapons from their parents. Think of a parent sending to one of these young men a pistol for a Christmas gift. You do not want to go out from here with the idea that it is necessary for you to carry weapons to defend yourselves. Let your parents present you a book or a number of books. Let them present you something that is going to result in your higher growth, instead of something that is going to lower your civilization and that might be the means of getting you into trouble.

Now, most of you are going out from Tuskegee sooner or later, to exert your influence in the home life. You are going to have influence in homes of your own, you are going to have influence in homes of your mothers and fathers, or in the homes of your relatives. You are going to exert an influence for good or an influence for evil in the homes wherever you may go. Now, the question how to bring about the greatest amount of happiness in the home, is one that should concern every student here. I say this because I want you to realize that each one of you is to go out from here to exert an influence. You are to exercise this influence in the communities where you go; and if you fail to exercise it for the good of other individuals, you have failed to accomplish the purpose for which this institution exists.

In the first place, you want to exert all your influence in the direction that will bring about the best results, and that will present to the people the highest forms of home life. Very often I find it, and especially the more I travel about among our people, that many of them have the idea that people cannot have comfortable homes unless they have a great amount of money. Well, now, some of the happiest and most comfortable homes I have ever been in, have been homes where the people had but little money; in fact, they might well be called poor people. But, there was a certain degree of order and convenience, that made you feel that you were in the homes of persons of great wealth. Now, I want to speak plainly. In the first place, there must be promptness in connection with everything in the life of the home. Take the matter of meals, for instance. It is impossible for a home to be properly conducted unless there is a certain time for each of the three meals. It is important that our people have a certain degree of promptness in this respect. In some homes the breakfast may take place at six o'clock one morning, eight o'clock the next morning and, perhaps, at nine o'clock the next morning. Dinner may be served at twelve, one, or two o'clock, and supper may be served at five, six or seven, and then one-half the members of the family are absent when the meal does take place. There is useless waste of time and energy, and an unnecessary amount of worry. It saves time and it saves a great amount of worry to have it understood that there is to be a certain time for each meal and that all the members of the family are to be present at that time. In this way the family will get rid of a great deal of worry, and the useful, precious time will be saved and can be used in reading, or in some other useful direction.

Then, as to the matter of system. No matter how cheap your homes are; no matter how poverty-stricken you may be in regard to money, it is possible for each home to have its affairs properly systematized. It is possible for a certain amount of system to exist in your homes. I wonder how many housekeepers can go into their homes the darkest night there is, and put their hands on the box of matches without difficulty? That is one way to test a good house-keeper. If she cannot do it, then there is a waste of time. It saves time, and it saves worry, too, if you will have a certain place for the matches to be kept, and if you will teach the members of the family that those matches are to be always placed there. Oftentimes you find the match box on the table, in the corner of the room, on

9

the floor, and sometimes here, and sometimes there. In many homes, five or ten minutes are wasted during the day on account of the negligence of the housekeeper or wife in this little matter.

Now, as to the matter of the dish cloth. You should have a certain place for your dish cloth, and put it there every day. The persons who do not have a place for it, are the persons who are found looking in doors and out of doors, from five to ten minutes, when ever it is needed, for it. They will be saying, "Johnny, where is it; where did you put it the last time you had it?" and all that kind of thing. Now, I am speaking very plainly to you here. The same kind of thing is true of the broom. In the first place, in the home where there is system, you do not find the broom on the wrong end. I hope all of you know which the right end of the broom is. You do not find the broom on the wrong end, and you always find that there is a certain place for it, and there it is kept. When these things are out of place and you have to look for them, you are not only spending time, but you are spending strength that should be used in some more profitable way. There should be a place for the cloak, for the hat and, in fact, a place for everything in the house. Then, the people who have a place for everything, are the ones who will find time to read and who have time for recreation. Why, you wonder sometimes how the people in New England can afford to have so much time for reading books and newspapers, and still have sufficient funds to send here to this institution to be used in our education. These people find time to keep themselves intelligent with all that takes place in the world, because everything is so systematized about their homes that they save the time which you and I spend in worrying about something we should know all about. I do not know that I have ever gone into a boarding house kept by our people and found the lamp in its proper place. When you go into the house they will have to look for the lamp; then when they find it, it is not filled; somebody forgot to put the oil in it in the morning; then they have got to go and hunt a wick and then they must get a chimney. And when they get all these things, they must then hunt for the matches, with which to light it.

I wonder how many girls there are here now that can go into a room and fix it for an individual to sleep in. That is, provide the proper number of towels, the soap and the matches, and have everything that should be provided for the comfort of the individual who is to use it. I would be afraid to test some of you. You must learn to prepare a room for an individual before you leave here, in order that you may be of some use to yourself and to others as well. If you are not able to, you will be a disappointment to us.

Tuskegee Student, 13 (Jan. 19, 1901), 1, 4.

Margaret James Murray Washington to Ednah Dow Littlehale Cheney

The Oaks   Tuskegee   1-13-1901

My dear Mrs. Cheney: I am very grateful indeed to you for your gift. My mothers are too. You have no idea how these women are cheered in their home life by these meetings. With all of my school work, I often grow tired and feel that I must give up these meetings, these outside interests, but when I look into the faces of these children and women, I just pick up the threads and go on. I have not had at any one meeting this fall less than fifty or sixty, until yesterday when it had been raining a week and there were even then two women who came in from seven miles around. It is the one bright spot in their lives. I am thinking of putting in a bathing apparatus where we carry on the sewing classes for the girls. They seldom get a *real* bath. Our Night School in the village is doing good work. It is helping many of the boys and men who can not get into any Day School. It is a comfort to work for those who need it, and who appreciate it. I shall use some of the money for seed, garden seed. Last year I helped them in this way and now so many have at least one thing to eat, collards, or turnips. I have "raced" with them as to gardening — you understand that these people are undeveloped children and one has to try the same art in helping teaching them.

The Colored women here in the South have just closed a meeting in Atlanta which Mrs. Lowe[1] visited. She said she was interested in all we did and wanted to help?

It may be that I shall come to Boston in Februa[r]y on a little business — if I do I hope to see you.

11

Again thanking you for your great interest in *us* I am yours
Sincerely

Margaret J Washington

ALS   Ednah Dow Cheney Papers   MB.

1 Rebecca Douglas Lowe.

To William McKinley

[Tuskegee, Ala.] January 14, 1901

Dear Sir: You will receive soon an invitation from the officials of
the Southern Race Conference which is to assemble again in Montgomery sometime during the month of May, to visit this Conference for a brief moment at least, on your way through Montgomery
to California. I very much hope that you can see your way clear to
accept the invitation. In doing this you will be giving encouragement to one of the most important movements that has been started
since the war that has for its object the improvement of the condition of both races in the South. This Conference is in the hands of
some of the strongest, most cultured and influential white men in
the South, and I believe that it is going to prove a great medium
for the final proper solution of the race problem. Yours truly,

Booker T. Washington

TLS   William McKinley Papers   DLC.

To Emmett Jay Scott

[Tuskegee, Ala.] January 14, 1901

Mr. E. J. Scott: Please be very careful to see that all electric lights
in your Department are shut off whenever they are not actually
being used. By giving attention to this, you will save the school
quite a good deal.

B. T. W.

TLI   Con. 216   BTW Papers   DLC.

An Item in the *Tuskegee Student*

Tuskegee, Ala., January 19, 1901

Mrs. Booker T. Washington and Mrs. Edgar Penney, of the Normal School, recently conducted a Pledge Service at the night school. Although it was cold and the rain pouring down, the ladies met them. After the rendition of a program by the students, they took charge of the exercises. A majority of the young men took the pledge not to drink, lie, gamble, or steal. It was a happy occasion.

Tuskegee Student, 13 (Jan. 19, 1901), 3.

A Menu

The Aldine Association [New York City] Monday 21 January MCMI

"One of my earliest recollections is that of my mother cooking a chicken."

Grape Fruit — Tuskegee Fashion

———

Consomme Hampton

———

Olives   Almonds   Celery

———

Whitebait à la Tallapoosa River

———

Filet of Beef Armstrong

———

New South Sprouts   Dixie Potatoes

———

Outlook Sherbet

———

Chicken à la Kanawha Log Cabin

———

Lettuce Salad

———

Tuskegee Bricks of Ice Cream
         Auld Lang Syne Ginger Cakes

———

Coffee

"At that time those ginger-cakes seemed to me to be absolutely the most tempting and desirable things that I had ever seen."

PD Lyman Abbott Papers MeB. The four-page menu contained a photograph of BTW and other quotations from *Up from Slavery*. The dinner was sponsored by the Outlook Co. to honor BTW for his biography, which was running serially in the *Outlook*.

To Emmett Jay Scott

Grand Union Hotel, New York. Jan. 24, 1901

Dear Mr. Scott: I have received your several letters and thank you for them. By the time I reach Tuskegee I wish you would have some mature plan by which we can get the names and addresses of the parties mentioned in the enclosed list. The plan is to send them each a copy of my book, The Future of the American Negro.

I was glad to see that several of the New York papers contained the associated press dispatch bearing upon the meeting of the next Negro Conference.

I have read Thomas's book carefully, and it is by far the worst thing that has been said about the Negro. It is worse by fifty per cent than anything that Dr. Barringer has said. Yours truly,

Booker T. Washington

TLS Con. 215 BTW Papers DLC.

From Giles Beecher Jackson

Richmond, Va., Jan. 24th. 1901

Dear Sir: Yours of the 22nd. to hand and in reply I will say that I will go to Washington next week and confer with Mr. Lawson, after which I will do the best I can in the premises.

It is true as I wrote you a few days ago that I have been so astounded at the decision of the Supreme Court, sustaining the infamous "Jim Crow Car Law," that I have felt as [if] I sustained an electric shock that has paralyzed my energy in the cause; however I have somewhat recovered and now stand enlisted to assist in making a final effort to remove the cause of these infamous legislations. I am only reminded that this was your suggestion last summer, hence Mr. Lawson and the others interested can rely upon me for my share of the burden.

As I am regarded by the local newspapers as a kind of bureau of information as to the acts and doings of the colored people of our City and State, I informed them that the Richmond Branch of the "National Business League" had invited you to lecture here on the 11th. or 18th. of February and that the said League had appointed me as a Committee of one to invite the Governor and Legislature of Virginia to be present on the occasion, hence the following appeared in all of our daily papers on the 22nd., which you will find on the slip of newspaper here enclosed.[1] Now as our people are aroused and enthusiastic over the thought of your coming, and from a poll of the Members of the Senate and the House of Delegates, every body is anxious to hear you speak; I will therefore promise you that the whole General Assembly, including the Governor, will be present, and since you promised me in a former communication that you would come in the near future from the date of that communication which was in early fall, I felt so certain of your coming that I have taken occasion to name certain dates upon which we desire you to come, ranging from the 4th. 11th. and 18th. of February and also the 25th. But our preference would be either the 11th. or 18th.

Your lecture at this time under the auspices of the Richmond Branch of the National Negro Business League would have more than local bearing and interest; it would be entirely a national affair and will result in future organization of Branch Leagues throughout the Country; and as our League will agree to give two thirds of the money realized after paying your expenses and other incidental expenses, to the cause represented by Mr. Lawson, Mr. Lyons, myself and others. Of course you are not interested and it will not be known to no one but yourself, Mr. Graham[2] and myself, as the published purpose of this lecture is for the interest of the Richmond

Branch of the National Negro Business League, under whose auspices it will be held; and again another reason we desire your presence here at this time is because the Legislature was called for the specific purpose of disfranchising the Negro by Constitutional enactments; this they will do at all hazards; but there is still a more serious matter; that is, it is being agitated among some quarters to separate the school fund to the end that the taxes paid by colored people shall be appropriated for their education and no more; of course we have the sentiment of the best white people against such a measure and it is they who think it is an opportune time for you to lecture before the Legislature on "The Past, Present and Future of the Negro," which would present our cause properly before, not only the Legislature of Va., but the Legislatures of the other Southern States now in session and dealing with the Negro problem. Of course you understand that your lecture will not be looked upon and regarded as a political one, but as coming from one who has studied the Negro problem and the one who is now engaged in solving the Negro problem, and being the author and the President of the "National Negro Business League," under whose auspices you are invited here to lecture.

Of course it is not necessary for me to say that the whole General Assembly including the Governor, are Democrats and desire to hear you speak.

Now you will see that the object of the lecture will be double-fold; First, to have you here in our midst; 2nd, to stimulate enthusiasm in the organization of Branch Leagues; Third, to inform the Legislature of Va. of the progress made by the Negro in business; Fourth, to more widely and thoroughly publish the purposes of our National League; Fifth, the proceeds after paying your expenses and incidental expenses, two thirds of which will go to a cause very dear to you and myself and every other Negro in the land, which cause is better known to you and I than to anyone else who will be interested in this lecture; for these and other reasons I respectfully ask you to accept this invitation and write me your acceptance at once in a shape so that I can publish it.

The two letters I wrote you several days ago, addressing them at Tuskegee, containing about what I am now writing you, except the cut from the Richmond Dispatch, our leading Daily Newspaper which seldom has a good word to say for a Negro. This cut will give you some idea of what our people are doing here, part of which may find mention in your lecture upon the present condition of the Negro in business.

Now hoping an immediate reply in the affirmative by letter or telegraph for publication, I am Dear Sir Your Friend and Admirer,

Giles B. Jackson

(Dict'd.)

TLSr Con. 201 BTW Papers DLC.

[1] The unidentified clipping was a general announcement that BTW would speak in Richmond in the near future under the auspices of the NNBL and that the event would be scheduled so the state legislature could be invited to hear the address.

[2] Wesley Faul Graham (b. 1858), president of the Richmond branch of the NNBL, was educated in Arkansas and also attended Wayland Seminary. He was ordained a Baptist minister in 1880 and had charge of a church in Richmond from 1892 to 1911. He was active in national Baptist affairs and was also a prominent black businessman in Richmond. He founded in 1894 the Richmond Beneficial Society, which absorbed several smaller groups including the American Beneficial Insurance Co., which Graham had founded earlier. Graham was a director of the Mechanics' Savings Bank in Richmond and chairman of the board of trustees of Virginia Theological Seminary and College. He later resided in Philadelphia.

From James Hulme Canfield[1]

New York January 25th, 1901

Private

Dear President Washington: Have you seen — you must have seen — "The American Negro," by William Hannibal Thomas, just published by the Macmillan Company.

It is a terrible book — terrible if false, and far more terrible if true. I instinctively feel that it is a mass of exaggerations, rhetorical and otherwise. But even then its publication must be disastrous in more ways than one.

I wish you would write me very frankly and confidentially about it. I shall be asked about its statements, by those who ought to be set right. I feel very sure that it will come up in the International Y.M.C.A. Under all these conditions I certainly need your most frank and detailed advices.

No — I am not in a panic at all: but when a blow like this is struck, one must be quickly on guard. Hastily but   Very cordially yours,

James H. Canfield

TLS   Con. 193   BTW Papers   DLC.

1 James Hulme Canfield (1847–1909) was an educator, writer, and public speaker who served as librarian of Columbia University from 1895 until his death.

From H. T. Johnson[1]

Philadelphia, Pa., Jan., 26th, 190[1]

My dear Mr. Washington: Your confidential letter just at hand. I had just written to Mr. Thomas for a copy of his extraordinary book on the strength of a letter received from Dr. Ward of the Independent concerning the same on yesterday. If the book is what I believe you truthfully characterize it as being, I may have something quite interesting to say as to its author. I know Rev. Wm. Hannibal Thomas quite well. The Recorder will deliver its soul on this Judas of the race in its next issue.

I leave for Tuskegee next week. Should you be kind enough to advise me when you pass through I will gladly call and meet you at the station or your stopping place. Yours truly,

H. T. Johnson

TLS   Con. 201   BTW Papers   DLC.

1 H. T. Johnson was the editor of the *Christian Recorder*, the official organ of the A.M.E. Church, from 1892 to 1912. He was born in South Carolina and attended the University of South Carolina, Howard University, Lincoln University, and Boston University. During his career as editor, Johnson's views on racial matters occasionally vacillated between conservatism and militancy. In 1895 he was critical of BTW's Atlanta Exposition address, but two years later he supported the Tuskegean wholeheartedly. Johnson even praised William H. Councill, who was more of an accommodationist than BTW. By 1905, however, Johnson had moved away from accommodationism and endorsed the Niagara Movement and the strategy of militant protest. Despite his ideological shift, he remained personally loyal to BTW. (Meier, *Negro Thought*, 233.)

To George Bruce Cortelyou

Grand Union Hotel, New York. Jan. 27, 1901

My dear Sir: I hope it is not improper for me to remind you that when I saw the President some weeks ago he very kindly asked you to take a note of the fact that I had asked him to place Major Manly Curry, who is now in the Paymaster's Department, on the permanent list of army officials after the passage of the bill for the reorganization of the army. Now that this bill has passed, I very much hope that you can see your way clear to call this matter to the attention of the President.

Major Curry is the son of Dr. J. L. M. Curry as you know. No single individual has done more since the war in his praiseworthy efforts to educate and lift up all classes of people at the South than Dr. Curry. He has been especially helpful in his educational work to my race and to the bringing about of helpful relations between the two races. It would be a beautiful and fitting tribute to the services of Dr. Curry to honor his son in the way that I have suggested. Yours truly,

Booker T. Washington

TLS   William McKinley Papers   DLC.

From Portia Marshall Washington

[Tuskegee, Ala.] Sunday. Jan. 27—1901

My dear papa: I recieved your letter Friday and I was delighted to hear from you. I am so sorry that you have been sick. I guess you had some Tuskegee Lagrippe. So many of the students have it.

Papa is there any way that we may have a *grand piano* for the chapel. If we can only rent one for this year. The music in the chapel is so very *poor* I shall be sorry for the Conference singing if there is not any improv[e]ment. Please see if we can rent one just for this year — and then prehaps we could buy one.

We all miss you so much — but are glad that you will soon return again.

Here is something that was sent me to day.

I guess it was sent because my name is Marshall. Prehaps you know more about it than I.

Mamma is cooking dinner to day. Baker and Dave are both up and full of mischief as ever.

Please do not forget the piano. A *Grand* — is the best. Lovingly yours.

Portia

ALS   Con. 215   BTW Papers   DLC.

From William Henry Baldwin, Jr.

Brooklyn Heights. [N.Y.] Jan. 27, 1901

Dear Washington. I spent an hour with Mr. Gates* today. He is getting interested again. He is reading the Outlook. He wants you to spend an evening (possibly the night) at his house just as soon as you return.

He will ask you all about finances, and you should have your statements in your pocket and the principal points in your head.

I have just read your last Outlook article. It is good.

My regards to Mrs. Washington. Faithfully yours

W. H. Baldwin Jr

*Mr. Rockefeller's Gates. Gates ajar.

ALS   Con. 792   BTW Papers   DLC.

From Emily Howland

Sherwood, N.Y. Jan. 27. 1901

Dear friend   Some weeks or months ago you wrote asking me if I would like to add a new machine to your shop for iron working. I replied not then, "perhaps the 1st of April, I should feel like doing it." I decide that I will do it before, at once. I enclose toward the lathe, a draft herewith, for $240.00. I do not remember exactly the required sum, I think it was $312.00. I returned a letter to you that contained the estimate I believe, your own letter does not give the price. When I hear from you, I will remit the remainder of the sum.

We are all enjoying your autobiography immensely. My opposite neighbor, a very strict Friend not given to indulging enthusiasms, says that she is so interested that she can scarcely wait for the next paper. I subscribed for the "Outlook" to get it and, it was not sent at the beginning of the Chapters, to my chagrin, so I lost them, and must await the appearance of the whole in a book, if I cannot borrow the missing papers.[1] It is admirably written and will be a book that will live I think.

I remember once urging you to write your life & you said, if you could find the time you would. I am rejoiced that time or no time, it is getting itself written.

The book will last, not only for its own merits, as fascinating reading, but because your career began in the most interesting and complicated period of our nation's history, when it was casting out slavery, and that you are one of the most important factors in the working out [of] the problem of reconstruction.

The Queen deservedly honored of all the world whose reign covered in length, the lives of the largest part of humanity rests from her labors. Are we not glad that we saw her! What an interesting occasion that Windsor Castle event was! Cordially

Emily Howland

ALS Con. 197 BTW Papers DLC.

[1] BTW sent Howland the early *Outlook* installments of *Up from Slavery* and remarked: "I have been very greatly surprised at the wide attention my Outlook articles have attracted. I had no idea before I began writing that they would arouse one hundredth part of the interest they have aroused. They seem to be read by all classes and conditions of people." (Feb. 5, 1901, Emily Howland Papers, NN-Sc.)

From Kelly Miller

Washington, D.C., Jan 27 1901

Dear Sir: I am informed by Mr Calloway that you have read the recent work on the American Negro by one, William Hannibal

Thomas. Altho' this book does not rise above the level of low black guardism, yet I fear that by means of the imprint of so reputable a house as that of McMillan Co, it will do much to fix an evil reputation upon the colored race.

It seems to me to be the plain duty of those colored men who are leaders of the people to devise some means of counteracting its baleful effect.

It occurred to me that it might be well if a number of influential colored men would join in a protest to McMillan Co. against issuing such a vile and attrocious document.

On first reading the work I was impelled to indite the accompanying note to the publishers, but on sober reflection I concluded that a more deliberate and perhaps a more dispassionate proceedure might be more effective. I suggest, therefore, to your wise discretion, that you formulate a plan by which the desired object can be accomplished. Yours truly,

Kelly Miller

ALS Con. 235 BTW Papers DLC.

From Emmett Jay Scott

Tuskegee, Ala., Jan. 28, 1900 [1901]

Dear Mr Washington: Our friends and we, too, have reason to fear the effect of the Thomas book. It is a terrible indictment — exaggerated and I fear malicious. I attach advertisement from NY Tribune.[1] It will be referred to by every man who would malign the race or defend the iniquities that have been visited upon the Negro. I also enclose a letter[2] from Mr Canfield, the Librarian of Columbia University. I hope your trip is proving satisfactory & that we shall soon have you here with us. Yours very truly

E J Scott

ALS Con. 209 BTW Papers DLC.

[1] The advertisement cited favorable reviews that Thomas's book had received and quoted at length from the Boston *Transcript*, which stated: "He certainly is a deeper thinker than Mr. Washington, and the ideas he presents are more orderly than those contained in Mr. Washington's recent volume." (New York *Tribune*, Jan. 27, 1901, 10.)

[2] See Canfield to BTW, Jan. 25, 1901, above.

From Giles Beecher Jackson

Richmond, Va., Jan. 28th., 1901

Dear Sir: In reply to yours of the 25th., in which you said you could accept our invitation to lecture here either the 12th. or 13th. of February, and I immediately wired you that the 12th. would suit us, but after consultation to-day with the Manager of the Academy of Music, the largest Theatre in the City and from which platform no colored man has ever spoke, I find that it has been engaged for the 12th., but I can get it for the 11th., which is on Monday, and a more appropriate day for the lecture.[1] Of course if you can't possibly come on the 11th., we will hold on to the 12th, but on account of this being the 1st. time that this Hall has been let to colored people for such an occasion, I wish to enjoy this distinction in having you to lecture in this Hall to a mixed audience, with the colored people occupying seats other than the "Jim Crow Gallery," which the Manager has agreed with me to let them do. All of this will add to the success of your visit; of course I have all of the colored Halls and Churches at my disposal and will have to utilize the largest and best of them if you cannot come on the 11th. instead of the 12th., which is the only day I can get the White Hall. And since the white people are as anxious to hear you as the Colored, and since the colored people are so enthusiastic over the fact that I have secured the consent of the white people for them to hear you in a Hall heretofore refused them, which Hall is the most aristocratical Theatre in this City and since there is only the difference of a day in securing this Hall, I hope you will, if any way possible, give us the 11th. instead of the 12th. Don't wait to write but wire on receipt of this letter if you haven't already wired in reply to my telegram of this day; and if you have wired in the negative, please reconsider and wire in the affirmative, as the single word "11th." means a great thing for Richmond and Virginia, so far as the Negro is concerned. Yes, the word 11th. will be a great day; while of course, as I said, if we cannot get the 11th. we will hold on to the 12th., rather than lose all. Now as all eyes are looking to see and all ears are waiting to hear from me, I shall hope for an answer in the affirmative at once. Very Respectfully,

(Dict'd.)   [Giles B. Jackson]

TL Con. 201 BTW Papers DLC.

1 BTW accepted Feb. 11 as the day he would speak. Jackson wrote BTW that receiving his telegram was "one of the happiest moments in my life." (Feb. 5, 1901, Con. 201, BTW Papers, DLC.) BTW spoke before a full house that included many members of the state legislature. Blacks were segregated in the gallery seats while whites occupied the floor. The Richmond *Times* described BTW as "a born orator. He is a man whose personal appearance would not attract any attention from those who would pass him on the street. He is a bright-skinned colored man of about the average stature.

"Washington's earnestness of purpose impresses an audience at the outset. He is at times in his remarks eloquent, pathetic, argumentative and humorous." BTW's speech was typical of his many utterances that stressed education and economic striving as the solutions of the race problem. (Richmond *Times*, Feb. 12, 1901, 1; see also Richmond *Dispatch*, Feb. 12, 1901, 7.)

From Robert Wesley Taylor

Boston, January 29, 1901

Dear Mr. Washington: Before I received your letter I had started on the trail of that unnameable scoundrel[1] and I followed it up yesterday with the results herein stated.

He has been around Boston for the last twelve or fifteen years and up until about nine years ago he lived with a woman whom he made believe was his wife and by whom he had a child. She was a poor, ignorant creature who had earned a little money by working out to SERVICE and as soon as he went through with all she had he cast her off — telling her that the marriage ceremony they had was a mock one. While he was living with this woman another came on from Washington to marry him — Miss Barbara Pope, by name — but she was saved from his clutches through the intervention of Mrs. A. C. Sparrow of this city. Failing in his effort to get Miss Pope he married the woman with whom he now lives about nine years ago. This is all that is definitely known about his domestic life around here but it is believed that he has several illegitimate children in South Carolina, all now grown.

His only visible means of support is the pension that he gets from the U.S. Government. He has no Law Office and so far as is known he is not a lawyer. How he got his title of "Colonel" nobody knows. The general opinion is that he assumed it, and Mr. Wolfe the colored Lawyer of this city who is the Attorney General of the Grand Army of the Republic of the United States shares that opinion.

He is a man who has tried to live by his wits — preaching, lecturing and representing himself as an agent of some Southern School. I have learned from the very best authority that he beat Mrs. Mary Stearns of West Medford out of a snug sum of money. He also subscribed for the Library of the World's Best Literature and the Company had to put its bill against him in the hands of a Lawyer who, failing to collect, authorized the Company to seize the books. I know the Lawyer quite well and this information he gave me himself. Whether the Company has seized them or not he could not say.

Thomas lives in a very modest way on Tylerson Street, Everett in a house containing eight rooms and a bath. The rent is fifteen dollars per month and he sub-lets a part of it for eight dollars per month. He has but little dealings with colored people except as he can use them to his own selfish and damnable ends. Not one good word have I heard concerning him, but he is universally decried as a low, mean, contemptible cur.

I shall continue my investigation and if I learn more I shall let you know. It has been whispered that he is mentally unsound, but I believe that he has studiedly and maliciously taken advantage of the present state of the public mind to betray his race into the hands of its enemies. This blow, I fear will do us irreparable harm. "He is a colored man and therefore speaks authoritatively," say those of the Tillman ilk. Nothing conceivable could come at a more convenient time for our enemies and at such an ill time for us. "The die is cast." Yours very truly,

Robert W. Taylor

TLS   Con. 213   BTW Papers   DLC.

1 William Hannibal Thomas.

From James Nathan Calloway

Lome   Togo W.A. Feb 3rd 1901

Dear Mr. Washington   Your letter of Dec. 8th. reached us Jan. 22. At the same time each of us received a copy of Southern Letter. These gave us great delight since we have not seen an American paper since Nov. 3rd.

We had a rather pleasant trip out from Hamburg and reached our first point in Africa Dec. 10th. This was Bissao a Portugu[e]se settlement about 1000 miles up the coast from Lome. Bissao is 50 miles up the Geba river and was at one time [a] slave trading post. The natives in this colony are kept in their original state.

Leaving this point we stopped frequently along the coast and went ashore among the natives. The next point at which our vessel stopped was Conakery[1] a French Colony. Here we found the natives as clerks, costum officers, and traders. We visited a little church for the English speaking natives and found it filled with nicely dressed natives and a native preacher conducting the services. Many of these natives have come here from S[i]erra Leone.

Our next stop was at Monrovia Liberia. Here to our sorrow we had only one day. The 6 or 8 hours we had on shore were spent in viewing the town and visiting the Senate which was in session at this time. This body consists of about 22 members. About half of this number were natives or native born. The debate was filled with words of wisdom and showed some statesmanship. This little republic is exerting a great influence upon the natives along the coast below. The Negro here from America must work and thus he teaches the natives to work. These natives are sought by the European vessels for laborers and carried down the coast. In this way they are being used for most [of] the important labor along the west coast. Manual labor is more dignified here than in other colonies. The masters work here.

In the English Colonies we found the natives especially the boys quite improved in education but not inclined to manual labor. They seek to immitate their masters and become English Gentlemen.

Lome, Togo was our first and only stop in German territory. Here the German exactness is in evidence. The natives are made to do their work in order and promptly. They are made to build good roads and to keep them in good condition. They are encouraged to have farms, and markets are formed in the little town on certain days that they may sell their produce. New enterprizes are encouraged to come among the natives for the improvement of the colony.

We have located our farm and have 150 laborers clearing it off. In our next letter we will speak of our plantation.

Regards to Mrs Washington & children. Young men send regards.

J N Calloway

ALS Con. 213 BTW Papers DLC. The letter appeared in the *Tuskegee Student*, 13 (Mar. 23, 1901), 1.

1 Conakry or Konakri.

From Alice Mary Robertson[1]

Muskogee, Ind. Ter., February 6, 1901

Dear Mr. Washington: I have under my supervision in addition to fifty Indian schools, twenty-five schools — three boarding and twenty-two day schools — for the Creek freedmen, these schools being supported from the Creek Indian funds. There is so much room for improvement in these schools that I am very anxious to obtain all the practical knowledge possible to be used in efforts toward bettering present conditions. It has occurred to me that nothing could be more helpful than to attend your approaching Conference. I have applied to the authorities at Washington for permission to leave my post of duty here long enough to go to the Conference. I write now to ask you whether in the event of my being granted permission to go I can find a boarding place and also whether there are any special rates on railroads. While I have a generous salary I came into my present position with a burden of debt which makes me desirous of economizing wherever it is practicable. I really can not afford the trip but I am just going to make it any way if the Department grants me leave to go.

One thing I am very anxious to do is to find out the probability of our being able to get some good teachers from you. We do need some very, very much. I suppose there is no place on the face of the globe where the negro has so good an opportunity as here and he is letting it slip. In property rights, in political power the negro is placed on a par with the Indian. Land, School privileges, even books are absolutely free. With all this the large majority live in hovels and eke out a hand to mouth living. What are we going to do about it? I think we need men imbued with your spirit. That is why I want to come to Tuskegee.

I am the daughter and grand-daughter of missionaries to the Indians and my people came to this country with the Indians from the "Old Nation." You know Tuskegee is a Creek name.

Hoping for a reply at your early convenience, I am, Very truly yours,

Alice M Robertson

TLS Con. 208 BTW Papers DLC.

1 Alice Mary Robertson (1854–1931), born in Indian Territory, the daughter of missionary parents, worked for the U.S. Department of the Interior as school supervisor for the Creek Nation. She was a participant in the Lake Mohonk Indian Conferences from 1889 to 1892, and was a friend of Theodore Roosevelt, whom she met at the conferences. In 1920 she was elected for one term to Congress as a Republican from the second congressional district of Oklahoma, and was the only woman in Congress at that time.

From James Hulme Canfield

New York   February 8th, 1901

Dear President Washington: I am under many obligations to you for yours of February fourth. There is no abating, I think, the *force* of Thomas's book. What I suspect is that someone else has put it together for him — for it is certainly scholarly and logical and extremely strenuous: beyond almost any other book that I have read for many a day.

But the distrust which at once attaches to its exaggerated statements is quickened and strengthened by a knowledge of the life and habits of the author. I think it will do great harm, but not as much harm when all the facts are known.

At the same time I can well understand that to make any open attack upon him will be to advertise the book and secure its wider circulation. It would be better to let it die — unless a quiet movement could induce the publishers to withdraw their imprint: as the Scribners did in the matter of a certain history of Williams College written by Professor Perry.[1]

When I go before the International Y.M.C.A. Committee — and elsewhere for that matter — I shall quote freely what you have written me: though of course not disclosing my authority. Cordially yours,

James H. Canfield

TLS Con. 193 BTW Papers DLC.

[1] Arthur Lathan Perry, *Williamstown and Williams College* (1899).

From William Hayes Ward

New York   Feb. 8, 1901

My dear Mr. Washington: I thank you very much for the letters you have sent me including this last one from Tuskegee with its enclosure from Boston. It lets in a startling light upon the character of Mr. Thomas, at the same time it is not of the kind that can be used. I had hoped that I might somehow get some statement as to whether he was arrested in connection with the Wilberforce matter, but I have had no answer from Wilberforce; and also what the schools were that he was agent for, but it seems that he is a common swindler.

The notice of the book will appear I presume in our next week's issue.[1] Yours very truly,

William Hayes Ward

TLS Con. 215 BTW Papers DLC.

[1] The unsigned review, written by Ward, appeared in *The Independent*, 53 (Feb. 14, 1901), 393–94. Highly critical of W. H. Thomas for writing such a book, Ward cast doubt on Thomas's evaluation of himself as an important figure during Reconstruction in South Carolina. "Why a negro should write such a book is a problem in psychology," he wrote. On Feb. 21, 1901, Ward wrote to Francis J. Grimké: "I have a communication this morning from Dr. Johnson, editor of the A.M.E. Review [actually

the *Christian Recorder*], and from Booker T. Washington thanking me for the review. I hope that some of the negro papers in Washington or elsewhere will look up pretty carefully Mr. Thomas's record and give it as far as they can. I am getting a good many hints on the subject." (Woodson, *Works of Francis J. Grimké*, 4:69.)

From Frederick Taylor Gates

New York. February 9th., 1901

My dear sir: I am in receipt of your esteemed favor of February 5th. I am desirous of seeing you to confer more broadly than I have yet been able to do on the general subject of Colored education in the South and to get your views as to the best plan for conducting the work on perhaps a larger scale than any single institution could contemplate. The leisure and quiet of my home would afford a much better opportunity for conference than my office. It would gratify Mrs. Gates and myself therefore if we could have you as a guest at our home when you can find release for a few hours from your pressing duties and engagements. I shall be at home at Montclair, N.J. — reached either by the D.L. & W. Ry. or the Erie Ry. — on to-morrow the 10th., and so far as I now know I shall be at home on the first of March. If you can come to-morrow on receipt of this, we will be delighted to have you do so. If possible please arrange to spend the night with us. If your engagements will not permit this, you will gratify us if you can arrange for a little visit on your next return to New York. If you will let me know in advance I will advise you of any absence or sickness in our family to prevent. My home in Montclair is #172 Union Street. Yours very truly,

F. T. Gates

P.S. Montclair is about 35 minutes ride from Jersey City via the Erie Ry or Hoboken via the D.L. & W. Ry.

TLS Con. 189 BTW Papers DLC.

From George Madden Martin[1]

Louisville, Ky. Feb 10th, 1901

Dear Sir: It is because I feel the subject to be of decided present moment and future significance that I write to you.

It is upon the question of the admission of Colored Woman's Clubs to The General Federation of Woman's Clubs, that I very much desire to have your advice.

Through Bishop C. C. Penick,[2] I have become very much interested in all concerning the Negro race. Your own position, attitude, work and success, I am following closely. May I state how much I respect the just and wise acceptation, the fair, patient and strong spirit revealed in your Autobiography?

I am a Southern woman, granddaughter and daughter of slave holders. Yet I believe I am nearer in understanding, touch and sympathy with the people who once were slaves, than are my Northern Club sisters.

I have a vote in two clubs which send delegates to the Federation. I have pondered the question until I cannot decide. I may have some influence in my clubs by a decided stand. What shall I do?

To force a situation on Southern white women will induce an antagonism, similiar to that you state as having been possible at the time of The Atlanta Exposition, had the *North* clambered for Negro representation at that exposition.

To refuse admission to the Massachusetts deligate, i.e. to Colored Clubs — will cause the whole New England representation to withdraw, and thus bring back the old sectional dislike, distrust, antagonism and separation of Northern and Southern women.

Personally the only inferiority I recognize, I honestly believe, is mental and moral inferiority. Caste of race or color finds no sympathy with me. Social inferiority it seems to me is the inevitable reward and outcome of the mental and moral inferiority. But one cannot force personal opinions on others. I hold that outward conditions will change as inward conditions change.

What do you counsel? Is there any tolerant, middle course, to bring about that state of patience, in which the matter may be allowed to work itself out naturally? Time is going to adjust all these things, even the question of color in the South.

I beg that you will consider this letter of grave enough importance to merit an immediate reply. After February 20th, it can be of no specific avail, the vote being cast on that date.

I am late in writing, but it is a final condition of personal indecision of the wise, yet broad & just, stand that urges me to seek your advice. Very truly yours

George M. Martin

ALS   Con. 204   BTW Papers   DLC.

1 George Madden Martin (Mrs. Attwood Reading Martin) wrote novels and short stories for magazines in America and England. She was active in club work in Louisville.

2 Charles Clinton Penick (1843–1914) was a bishop of the Protestant Episcopal Church. He did missionary work in Africa and also among blacks in the southern United States. He wrote *Hopes, Perils, and Struggles of the Negro in America* (1893).

From James Alexander Ross[1]

Buffalo, N.Y. Feby 11 1901

Dear Sir   I desire to have your permission to manufacture a cigar to be known as the Booker T. Washington.[2] If this is satisfactory to you I should like to have a Photo that you would like to have on a box. Very Respectfully

Jas A Ross

Fortune[3] is manufacturing the B. K. Bruce, The Fred Douglass and the La Fortune.

ALS   Con. 208   BTW Papers   DLC.

1 James Alexander Ross, born in Kentucky in 1866, was a Buffalo, N.Y., editor, lawyer, and businessman. Educated in Catholic and public schools in St. Louis, Mo., and Carbondale, Ill., he taught school in southern Illinois and Arkansas before moving to Buffalo. There he ran a cigar business and, on the same street, operated another office that published the monthly *Gazetteer and Guide*. He also practiced law and was in the real estate and mortgage loan business. Ross was in charge of the Negro exhibit at the Pan-American Exposition in 1901 and fought successfully for the appointment of a black commissioner to the exposition. He was active in Democratic party politics beginning about 1900 and later was president of the Colored Democratic Association. Beginning in 1911 he published a journal, *The Reformer*, from Detroit.

2 It is not certain whether BTW gave Ross permission to use his name on a cigar. BTW received several requests to use his name in this way. W. C. Johnson, Jr., of St.

Louis, president of the Shryock-Johnson Manufacturing Co., had asked to use BTW's name in 1899. (Johnson to BTW, Mar. 6, 1899, Con. 161, BTW Papers, DLC.) In 1902 BTW wrote to Charles F. Bacon of Grand Rapids, Mich., that he had given no cigar company permission to use his name, and that he was "very much grieved and shocked" that his name and picture had been used on billboards in Grand Rapids. (See BTW to Bacon, May 5, 1902, below.) A black-owned cigar firm, A. Eichelburger and Co., of Boston, did produce a Booker T. Washington cigar during BTW's lifetime. In 1915 the NNBL *Official Souvenir Program* described the firm as "Manufacturer of the Famous Booker T. Washington Clear Havana Cigars."

3 T. Thomas Fortune was a partner of T. L. Douglas and R. R. Mathews in the cigar-manufacturing business of Douglas, Fortune & Co., on Cedar Street in New York City. Roscoe Simmons, a nephew of BTW's wife, was also involved in the business. The enterprise proved a failure and only added to Fortune's financial difficulties. (Thornbrough, *T. Thomas Fortune*, 213.)

From William Edward Burghardt Du Bois

Atlanta, Ga., Feb 11, 1901

Dear Mr. Washington: I shall probably attend the Tuskegee conference this year again.[1] I have been thinking that perhaps I could do a service there in taking a personal census of all the visitors, especially the farmers &c. — number, property owned, age, history, crops, improvements, &c., &c. If you could furnish me 3 or 4 or 5 reliable clerks I could probably do the work & present results to the final meeting. This plan occurred to me, and I mention it to you. Very Sincerely,

W. E. B. Du Bois

ALS   Con. 195   BTW Papers   DLC.

1 Du Bois arrived at Tuskegee on Feb. 19, 1901. He wrote BTW asking to have some badges printed for the farmers to aid in his census. (ca. Feb. 15, 1901, Con. 190, BTW Papers, DLC.)

From Hayes Robbins[1]

New York   February 11th, 1901

Dear Sir: We want to use your article[2] as the opening contribution in our March number and would very much like to receive, by return mail, one of your latest and best photographs to use as the frontispiece in that number. I hope you will not disappoint us in this as we shall hold the Magazine open for it.

There is a matter which comes right into the heart of the subject of your article but which I find is not discussed in it: namely, the apparent failure of the negro as a factory operative in the South. We have recently seen a report that a large cotton factory in one of the southern states, either North Carolina, Georgia or South Carolina, I cannot recall which, which has been trying for some time to use negro labor has had to close up entirely and discharge all hands. When Professor Gunton[3] and I were in the South we found this universal complaint regarding the negro as a steady factory hand. We think it would very greatly strengthen your article and add to its quotability in the press if you could send us two or three paragraphs discussing the reasons for this apparent failure as contrasted with the success of the negro in the industrial lines along which you are developing him. I wonder if you cannot do this and let us have it by next Tuesday or Wednesday, February 19th or 20th, at the latest. A comparatively brief discussion of the point would answer in case you have no time to do anything else. At any rate I would be glad if you will let me know by return mail whether you can send this so that I may know whether to hold the article for it. Yours very truly,

Hayes Robbins

TLS Con. 208 BTW Papers DLC.

1 Hayes Robbins (b. 1872) of Mt. Vernon, N.Y., was an editor of *Gunton's Magazine*.

2 See An Article in *Gunton's Magazine*, Mar. 1901, below.

3 George Gunton (1845–1919) was an English-born economist and student of American labor who edited the *Social Economist* (changed to *Gunton's Magazine* in 1896) from 1891 to 1904. Gunton championed shorter hours and a higher standard of living for workers.

From Elkan Naumburg[1]

New York, February 13, 1901

Dear Sir: About five years ago I made a tour of observation through the south with a dozen gentlemen in connection with large interests in cotton mills which most of the party had. I remarked to Capt. J. H. Montgomery, the Superintendent of two or three of the largest cotton mills in South Carolina and one of the ablest men in that line: "Captain, the day is not very far off when we will have to employ colored labor in the cotton mills." Captain Montgomery said: "You can never make a success with colored labor." To my great surprise and rejoicing this very gentleman together with a few others bought a mill about two years ago in the city of Charleston, S.C., and employed colored labor exclusively. The outcome of it no doubt you saw in the various newspaper reports: that it was a failure and that they had to abandon the buildings and move the machinery to Georgia where they have white labor exclusively.

You have made a life-long study of this question, and since I take a great interest in this matter and if I can serve you in solving it, I should be very happy to do so.

Hoping to hear from you at your convenience, I remain, Yours very truly,

E Naumburg

TLS   Con. 205   BTW Papers   DLC.

1 Elkan Naumburg (1834–1924), a prominent clothing manufacturer, in his late fifties switched businesses and founded the Wall Street banking firm of E. Naumburg and Co., which he ran until 1909. Naumburg was a patron of music in New York, promoting free concerts.

From Frederick W. Moore[1]

Brooklyn N.Y. Feb 14, 1901

Dear Sir: I have read with no ordinary pleasure your life's account in the Outlook. But surely you have forgotten yourself, when you penned the words about English servants and masters.[2]

Can you for a moment forget that slavery bespeaks the most awful "deference" to "masters?"

What is your Tuskegee work for if it isn't to lift people out of that very condition personified by the English servant?

Mens souls need to be fired with the dignity of their worth, the curse of your race is its menial condition.

The term "master" is an insult to any man with free blood in his veins. Yours truly

F. W. Moore

ALS   Con. 235   BTW Papers   DLC.

1 Frederick W. Moore, born in Iowa in 1861, lived with his widowed mother and two brothers in Brooklyn, N.Y. The 1900 census reported him as "out of work." His brother, Henry Hoyt Moore, was on the staff of the *Outlook* for many years as a printer, illustrator, and writer and was president of the Brooklyn Ethical Association from 1897 to 1899.

2 See above, 1:367.

From Lawrence Fraser Abbott

New York   February 15, 1901

My dear Mr. Washington: I am very glad to know from Mr. Thrasher that you are willing to give us an article on Chickens and Pigs for our Recreation Number. Anything that we can do here to interest people in wholesome and useful country life, we want to do. Many of our most serious social and political evils come from the huddling together of great masses of men and women in the cities. There are, I am convinced, hundreds, and I venture to say thousands of men and women earning their bread and butter in New York City to-day who would like to live in the country and earn it there, if they knew how. I am one of them myself. But if I had to live on the eggs that I could make my hens lay, I should starve to death in short order.

Of course our motive in asking you to prepare this article is two-fold. We have the desire to be helpful and to turn the minds of our city readers toward the country, and to encourage our country readers to stay where they are, but we also want to make a picturesque, readable, and perhaps somewhat personal article. As Mr. Thrasher has told you, I think, we hope to arrange to have Mr. Clifton Johnson[1] go down to Tuskegee to take some photographs of you with your pigs and chickens. I am sure you will be interested to meet Mr. Johnson. He was born and brought up on a farm in Massachusetts, in fact his home is still in old Hadley, which is one of the most beautiful towns of the Connecticut River valley. So many of us, particularly young men among us, are apt to think that bankers and lawyers and merchants produce the wealth of this country, and so many of us lose sight of the fact that agriculture — no I prefer to call it as you do, plain farming — is the foundation of our National life. I sometimes wonder if the man who can hatch eggs and make hens lay, and at the same time read a few good books, hear a little good music, and bring up his family to be kindly, useful and sound citizens of the Republic, is not doing more for his race than the newspaper editor who sits at a roll-top desk and tries to tell his fellowmen how they should think.

Looking forward with great interest to the article, which should be not more than three thousand words in length, and for which we should be glad to send you our check for $75, on receipt of the manuscript, I am   Very sincerely yours,

Lawrence F. Abbott

P.S. In view of the extra length of your "Up From Slavery" serial, and of the additional labor which you have put upon it since we made the original contract with you, we feel that you ought to receive an additional payment, and I therefore take pleasure in enclosing our check for two hundred dollars. I need hardly add again expressions of gratification on the part of the entire staff of The Outlook at the success which has attended the publication of "Up From Slavery."

TLS   Con. 261   BTW Papers   DLC.

1 Clifton Johnson of Hadley, Mass., was a writer and photographer who specialized in country, travel, and nature themes. Many of his stories and illustrations appeared in the *Outlook*. In 1901 he visited Tuskegee to do the photographs for BTW's article, "Chickens, Pigs and People," which appeared in the *Outlook*, 68 (June 1, 1901), 291–300. He also wrote a vivid description of Tuskegee entitled "Tuskegee: A Typical Alabama Town," *Outlook*, 72 (Nov. 1, 1902), 519–26.

From Charles Francis Adams, Jr.[1]

Boston. February 15, 1901

My dear Mr. Washington: I some days since received your favor of the 7th inst.

I am glad to hear that you are turning your attention to the question of habits of thrift among your people. As a rule on this subject, as I said to you when we met in my office, it seems to me our people have got the cart before the horse. They insist upon education as fundamental, rather than on thrift. Now, as I told you when we met, I consider thrift, the saving habit, the accumulating instinct, as the foundation on which educational and all other forms of development must be based. Mere technical, or other, education, unless starting from the habit of thrift, will lead to no satisfactory results.

The difficulty with your position, and the African race in this country, is that, through slavery, they have for centuries been educated in a spirit of improvidence and waste. How long it will take to get them out of it I do not know; I fear a very long time. Meanwhile, the first thing in the way of progression is to make a commencement.

It is, therefore, with very great pleasure I hear that savings institutions are being established among those of African blood in the South. I regard a savings bank established by those people on their own account, and managed by those of their own color, as more important than any school, college or university. Believe me, etc,

Charles F. Adams

TLS   Con. 188   BTW Papers   DLC.

1 Charles Francis Adams, Jr. (1835–1915), of the distinguished Boston family, was a railroad manager, historian, and reformer. Adams sought to combine business management with social reform by training a corps of executives who shared his ideals. A star trainee, William H. Baldwin, Jr., was one of BTW's closest associates. BTW forwarded Adams's letter to Baldwin with a note: "You will be interested in seeing the enclosed letter from Mr. Adams. We must hold onto Mr. Adams and cultivate his interest." Baldwin agreed, and he wrote back on the same letter: "B. T. W., Noted with great pleasure WHBJr." (Feb. 19, 1901, Con. 188, BTW Papers, DLC.)

From Elizabeth Cady Stanton

[New York City] Feb. 15th 1901

Dear Sir, In reading "The Outlook," from week to week, I always turn first to your deeply interesting "Reminiscences."

There is a mistake in the last number which I hope you will be sure to correct in the published volumn. My son's name is Theodore, who graduated a few years ago from Cornell University; a far younger man than *Edwin* Stanton, Secretary of War in Gen. Grant's cabinet, a name more familiar to you. *Theodore* is very proud of his name, given him in honor of Theodore Dwight Weld, one of the distinguished pioneers in the anti-slavery struggle. Mr. Weld married Angelina Grimké of South Carolina, who emancipated her slaves and lectured extensively in the North on the slavery question, she was very eloquent, and attracted large crowds to her meetings. Edwin Stanton was a cousin of my husband's. As a family we are proud of our anti-slavery record, and hence tenacious as to our right names. When next you chance to be in New York, I hope you and Mrs. Washington will honor me with a visit. Your struggles and triumphs are a grand character study for all young men of either race. My son Theodore will be proud to have his slight attentions and acquaintance with you in Paris mentioned in your book.

With kind regards for Mrs. Washington and yourself   Cordially Yours

Elizabeth Cady Stanton

HLSr   Con. 210   BTW Papers   DLC.

A Sunday Evening Talk

Tuskegee, Ala., February 17, 1901

The old idea of life used to be that it was something to be gotten rid of as soon as possible; that it was something to be shaken off, and was not connected in any large degree with the life that is to come. More and more we are learning, however, that the new idea of life is that we are a continuous being; that the life in this world is as important as the life in the next world; that we simply continue to live after we pass from this stage of being into another stage of being. In a word, the idea is becoming more and more emphasized that life is something to be retained; that life is something to be made great; something to be improved, and it seems to me that as students, you ought to learn to get all you can out of life here in this world. I believe that it is impossible for a person to live a high life, a noble life in the future world, who does not live a high life in this world. I don't believe that individuals who are mean, low and ungrateful in this life, are tranferred into another life and made higher beings. I believe that, very largely, in another life we are what we are in this life. We are certainly preparing ourselves here for what we are to be in another life; so we should practice the habit, day by day, of trying to get all we can out of life. Be sure we get the best things in this life, be sure we do the best things in this life, be sure we learn the higher things in this life. The person who has learned to love trees, to love corn, to love flowers, or has learned to get enjoyment and pleasure out of rain, out of sunshine — out of everything, in a word, that is put here by our Creator for our enjoyment, is the person who is happy and contented. Perhaps there are many things we have not yet discovered, but I do not believe there is a thing put on this earth that is not meant for our use; to give us enjoyment and comfort. The more we learn to love trees, the more we learn to love corn, the more we learn to love sunshine and rain, the more we learn to get out of nature, the nobler we shall be growing day by day. And so, I want you to get the idea that each day brings to you a serious responsibility. You should try to get as much out of the twenty-four hours in each day as is possible for an individual to get out of twenty-four hours. Learn to get out of each day, out of the twelve hours of each day, just as much as is possible for one to get. Learn to get out of every hour, every year, as much as it is possible for you to get. You have only one life to live; remember you pass through this life but once, and if you fail, you fail, perhaps, for all time. You should consider closely the serious obligation you have upon you to live properly through a day, through a year, and you should try to get everything that is best out of that day, out of that year.

Suppose you have only a dollar to spend during the year, would you spend every cent during the first six months of the year? Now, you have only one life that you may shape as you will. You will not have it tomorrow again. How careful then you should think as to how to spend each moment, each hour, each day of your life!

My experience has been that one gets out of life what he puts in it. If he puts hard, earnest study and effort into his life, he gets pleasure, satisfaction, enjoyment out of it. As I have said, if an individual puts hard, earnest work into his life, he will get out of it strength. On the other hand, if he is indifferent, reckless, you will find such an individual continually complaining, finding fault, seeking another place — you will find such an individual unhappy, and at the same time, making every one about him unhappy, too. He is simply living on the outer edges of his work, instead of entering into the life of it. An individual gets happiness out of his study, out of his work, in proportion as he puts hard, earnest work into whatever he has to perform. You find an individual who is constantly complaining that the world has no love in it, and you will find an individual who is cold and hard-hearted himself, doesn't love the people in the world — he is not loved by the other people; he gets out of life just what he puts in it. You find an individual who is constantly complaining of those about him being selfish and cold in their treatment of him; you examine into the cause of that individual's complaint and you will find that he is cold and selfish himself. We get out of every department of life just about what we put in it.

Life should give to us opportunity for the highest mental, physical and spiritual enjoyment. The old idea that people used to practice, and practice it even to this time, that in order to get happiness one has got to punish the physical man, has largely passed away. Out of the earth, out of nature, out of everything with which we come in contact we should learn to get the highest physical, mental and spiritual enjoyment if we would learn to look at life in the right way. You want to learn, in a word, to fill your lives with all that is best in the world. Fill your life with all that is best by continually seeking out what is best, what is noblest, what is highest and best in men, in books, in nature so far as the treasuries of nature have been discovered, and you will find with all of these highest and best things in life your lives will be successful.

Tuskegee Student, 13 (Mar. 2, 1901), 1.

From John Roach Straton

Mercer University   Macon, Ga., 2/18/'01

My Dear Prof. Washington, I take the liberty of sending you the MS. of a book on the Race Problem which I am just completing. If you can find time to read it and give me a word of comment, it will be of value in getting my facts and thoughts upon the situation before the thinking people of the country. The comment will be used in connection with expressions from Mr. Cleveland, Senator Morgan, Dr. Curry, etc., etc.

I trust that you will give the conclusion reached your earnest consideration. I become more convinced with each passing year that the hope of your people is in the direction indicated at the close of my book. Though looking primarily at the interests of my own race, I am driven more and more to this conclusion as a friend of the Negro.

For your personal information, I hand you herewith some observations upon your review of my June North American paper. I thought once of using the remarks in another paper shortly to appear, but concluding that it is now to[o] late to refer to the matter in the reviews, I content myself with handing you the thoughts upon the question of the Negro's status in the island of Jamaica.

Though differing from you as to the possibility of finding the *ultimate* solution of the problem through the elevating of the Negro race, you will observe that I am in hearty sympathy with the efforts looking to Negro betterment or a tentative programme. And especially am I in sympathy with your wise and beneficent efforts for your people. I cannot strongly enough express my admiration for your earnestness, wisdom, and conservatism — and I only regret that the conditions, as they appear to my mind, will not allow me to enjoy an optimism akin to yours touching the final outcome. In any event, however, I join the conservative men of the nation in regarding you as the Moses of your people — and I earnestly hope, therefore, that you will ultimately be led by your thinking to an acceptance of some proposition looking to racial separation.

If you can get the MS. back to me within two weeks, it will be time sufficient.

With kind regards, I am, Very Sincerely Yours,

John Roach Straton

ALS   Con. 213   BTW Papers   DLC.

From a Friend of the Race

Chicago, Illinois. February 25, 1901

Dear Sir: As I see that you advise the Negroes of this country to go into business I would like to call your attention to a weekness among colored men when they do go into business. You take the average colored man and let him go into business and he always runs a Negro business and solicits only Negro trade; something that has never been known to make any money. The writer knows two colored men who manufacture two first-class articles but both of these men make the sad mistake of putting their Negro portraits on each and every bottle and package that they send out and that confines their sales almost entirely to colored people. Now the writer knows that one of the largest stores in the United States has refused to handle one of these article[s] simply because the man who manufactures the articles refuses to take his Negro portrait off of the bottles. If you would advise the colored people to keep their pictures off of the article[s] they make they could sell them and make money but they can never make any money running a Negro business for Negroes but must run business as men[,] American citizens and gentlemen. Yours Truly,

A Friend of the Race

AL   Con. 214   BTW Papers   DLC.

43

From Mary Lawton[1]

Washington, D.C. February 25th, 1901

My dear Sir: Allow me to say you have probably had no more interested and approving readers than my mother and myself. From a moral and scientific standpoint your work excites the deepest enthusiasm; from an artistic, the early chapters remind one of Alphonse Daudet at his best. But I should not intrude upon your busy day with praise and thanks alone. I add thereto a suggestion to which coming as it does from the capital of the Nation, I trust you will give thoughtful attention.

At the Library of Congress there is a Reading-room for the Blind where every day someone reads aloud for an hour. I hope you will kindly contribute to this quiet entertainment if ever you have the leisure, as did Mr. Dunbar last year.

Lately speaking of rich people, one of the blind girls said "Of course, we only meet the good; only good people come here." It occurs to me that this idea might in a measure be applied to your situation.

Without wishing to lessen your splendid optimism, I cannot refrain from speaking of discouraging conditions existing here where they are most conspicuous and where temporary sojourners from all parts of our country, I may say, the world, find material on which to base unfavorable testimony touching your race. Is it not possible that "only the good," in a large degree, come to your notice — the liberal-minded, the courteous and kind-hearted among the whites, the industrious and reasonable among the colored? Granting this, still doubtless you have been sorely tried, but I think it likely you may be unaware of the attitude of the whites in the District of Columbia towards their darker fellow-citizens and the reasons therefore. I have been pained on countless occasions by hearing from members of all classes of society, utter contempt and skepticism expressed as to "darkies." I have often replied that in my experience connected with the management of a little improved real estate, I have found so much fraud and stupidity in the whites that I could not say they were better than the colored. Yet I remember reading several years ago that the better class of colored people in the District had met to investigate the causes of the percentage of crime being so much higher with their race than with the whites.

You say graduates are going out from the Institute, carrying the good seed to barren wastes. Surely the capital should be among the first of the wastes to be reached. There is nothing like your work, I believe nearer than Manassas, where an industrial school has been established through the eloquence of Jennie Dean.[2] A very dear friend, Mrs. C. B. Hackley[3] of N.Y. has taken a warm interest in this school. But it is too far to affect the situation here.

I am a native of Washington, of New England ancestry, a D.A.R. and a member of the Society of Mayflower Descendants. Our family has always been Democratic — my grandfather was in Buchanan's Cabinet, but he stood by the Union, and again in '96 he was a partisan of McKinley's. My pastor, Doctor Alexander Mackay-Smith of St. John's, (the most influential Episcopal church here) preached in St. Luke's (colored) several years ago, after the death of Dr. Crummell, and I heard him then say there was no church in Washington in which he felt a greater interest.

You will appreciate my motive in addressing you and in speaking so frankly. Believe me   Sincerely Yours

Mary Lawton

ALS Con. 203 BTW Papers DLC.

[1] Mary Lawton was born in the District of Columbia in 1864. She lived with her widowed mother, Annie A. Cole.

[2] Jennie Dean (1852–1913) was the founder and guiding light of the Manassas Industrial School for Colored Youth at Manassas, Va. Born in slavery as Jane Serept Dean at Sudley Springs, Va., she worked as a cook and maid in Washington, D.C., after the Civil War. A person of great energy, she organized several Baptist churches and Sunday schools in northern Virginia. In 1891 she traveled to New England to solicit funds for a school for black children. Her first real benefactor was Edward Everett Hale, who endorsed her work and thus opened the purses of the New England donors to black education. The school was incorporated in 1894. Always in financial difficulty, Jennie Dean asked Oswald Garrison Villard in 1905 to assume the presidency of the school and through his influence gained increased support from northern philanthropists. Villard's absentee rule of the school from 1905 to 1927 guaranteed the school's financial survival, but it was a source of some bitterness to local blacks, including Jennie Dean, who found their influence in school affairs waning. Villard turned often to BTW for advice on running the school and seldom consulted local opinion in Manassas. Jennie Dean remained active, however, despite failing health, in the annual farmers' conferences that were held at the school.

[3] Frances A. (Mrs. Caleb B.) Hackley of Tarrytown, N.Y., was the founder of Hackley School in 1899. She was a regular donor to Tuskegee and other black schools in the South. She died in 1913 at the age of ninety-three.

From Edgar Gardner Murphy

Montgomery, Alabama. February 25th, 1901

Dear Mr. Washington: I have ignored Thomas's book, because I have not wished to call attention to it; but I find it given the leading review of the Literary (Saturday) edition of the New York Times, and I feel therefore that silence is no longer wise.[1] I hoped that Mr. Ogden, with his great influence in the office of the Times, would be able to prevent so favorable and conspicuous a review of it in that journal. But it probably slipped by him. At any rate I have just sent a very earnest letter to the Times upon the subject, and I hope they will print it. I have pointed out some contradictions that I think will destroy it as a serious authority, and I shall take great pleasure at the thought that the first conspicuous repudiation of the book may come from a Southern white man. But there may have been other criticisms that I have not seen. You may be sure that I said a word for you and for Dr. Curry! Always Sincerely,

Edgar Gardner Murphy

TLS   Con. 235   BTW Papers   DLC.

1 The New York *Times* praised Thomas's book and said that, next to BTW, Thomas was probably the best authority on the Negro. Since the book was written by a black, the *Times* reviewer surmised, it had a ring of authority and sincerity, and because Thomas was black he could say things that whites could not without being accused of race prejudice. (New York *Times, Saturday Review of Books and Art,* Feb. 23, 1901, 113–14.)

Murphy's reply to the review appeared the following Saturday. "The book is a calamity," he wrote; "the general acceptance of its spirit and its method would be little short of a catastrophe." Murphy attacked Thomas for failing to refer even once to BTW and Tuskegee. Even in his attempt to attack a racist book, however, Murphy could not check his own feelings. "The later generation of negroes," he lamented, "has presented some disappointments. It has disappointed many of the friends of the race in its failure to preserve the happy simplicity and the quaint piety of the old-time slave." Most of Murphy's letter consisted of quotations of Thomas's most inflammatory statements, which only gave them wider circulation. Murphy concluded: "A dependent race, like a dependent flower or a dependent child, can grow better only in the sunshine." (New York *Times, Saturday Review of Books and Art,* Mar. 2, 1901, 141.)

From Frederick W. Moore

Brooklyn, N.Y. Feb. 26th, 1901

Dear Sir: At your suggestion I have read the paragraph, to the sentiment of which I have taken objection, over several times. It is not simply to the terms "master" and "mistress" that I object, and to which you seem not to seriously object or abhor, but to your calling attention to the deference of the English servant with a mild satisfaction on your part as to his behavior.

There is no question as to the fact; the English servant is deferential. But what I say is that that deferentialism is an abomination. Do I want to go through the world to have men who are my equals in every respect accost me with that deferentialism which was so conspicuous with the slave? No; I wish to see men act as free men, as though they could all trace their lineage back to the Mayflower.

You yourself have called attention to what the negro has done for the South, then ought he not to hold himself up, not as a fine specimen of servant but as an equal? He has done the work, he has plodded through the mud and grime and sweat. And your profound mistake is in not recognizing the relationship existing between slavery and the servant, and in not condemning most heartily and severely this lack of a true appreciation of themselves which is shown by this spirit of deferentialism.

I think you ought to acknowledge your fault, and henceforth never equivocally state your feeling as to servitude in any form, but to regard the servants of the world wherever found as only typical of slavery, and, as a system, to represent a most miserable travesty on justice.

Mr. Washington, the servant is a servant because he feels and believes that to be his proper sphere. Let him appreciate what he has accomplished; let the worker know who is the producer in this world, and your servant will rise because of an inherent power in his own soul.

Slavery may be over, but its essential point of injustice still largely exists; and through the servant, white or black, we have a retention of much of its barbarity, whereby the worker receives but

a tithe of his earnings and no proper meed of respect and consideration as the most useful part of the human family. Yours truly,

F. W. Moore

TLS Con. 235 BTW Papers DLC.

From Walter Hines Page

New York   March 4th, 1901

Dear Mr. Washington: The publishers of your first Autobiography,
we notice are advertising the book in The Outlook, offering it by
mail for 95 cents. Our understanding was that these gentlemen had
the right to sell this book by contract with you, only by subscription. Are we wrong in supposing that your contract with them gave
them only the subscription field and not the book trade, just as
your contract with us gives us the book trade and keeps us out of
the subscription field except by their consent? If the book be kept
practically in separate channels there will be no confusing conflict;
but if these publishers are at liberty to offer their book in the way
they have now done in The Outlook, there will inevitably arise
confusion of one book with the other. Please let us know what your
contract with them is. Very truly yours,

W H Page

TLS Con. 206 BTW Papers DLC.

From Jesse Lawson

Washington, D.C. March 5, 1901

My dear Sir: We collected at the church this afternoon just one
hundred dollars, the required amount to complete the retainer fee
for Mr. Romain of Louisiana, and I am very glad that we will not
be compelled to draw on you for that amount. You have done more

than anybody else for the cause that should be dear to the heart of every American citizen.

Will write you as the case progresses. Hoping that you are well, and that I may hear from you at your convenience, I remain, Yours truly,

Jesse Lawson

TLS   Con. 203   BTW Papers   DLC.

Margaret James Murray Washington to Lyman Abbott

The Oaks   Tuskegee   March 12, 1901

Dear Sir: My only apology for thus intruding upon your time is to thank you for the kindly interest you have shown in my husband who is an exceedingly timid man but who appreciates very much your friendship and interest.

It is this sort of interest that makes it possible for him to carry the heavy burden which has fallen to him.

I want to thank you for the Autograph Menu Card which you sent me some time ago.[1]

Our great hope is that we shall be worthy of your continued friendship. Yours very respectfully,

Margaret J. Washington

HLS   Lyman Abbott Papers   MeB.

[1] See A Menu, Jan. 21, 1901, above.

To Paul Brandon Barringer

Grand Union Hotel, New York City. March 13, 1901

My dear Sir: Since we met in Chicago I have thought much concerning your earnest words, and the more I consider what you said the more I am sure that on the vital points connected with the elevation of our race there is not so much difference between us as I feared there was. I am very anxious to get better acquainted with you and your views. I feel that in working together we can accomplish much towards the solution of the problem which is so dear to the hearts of all of us. The whole matter weighs upon me heavily day and night.

The suggestion which you made of a conference between Northern and Southern people where the whole matter can be studied not from a sentimental standpoint but where the cold hard facts can be carefully weighed, will accomplish much good and I hope that you can see your way clear to encourage such a conference.

I have asked my publishers to send you a copy of my book, "Up from Slavery," which I hope you will find [time] to glance through. Yours truly,

Booker T. Washington

TLS   Paul B. Barringer Papers   ViU.   By permission of Anna Barringer.

From Emmett Jay Scott

Tuskegee, Ala., March 13, 1901

Dear Mr. Washington: I want to suggest that you have Dunbar come to New York Monday morning early or Sunday evening for the reason that I find that he is still keeping up in a greater or less degree his old habit of drinking. It would be very unfortunate if he should reach you not in proper condition.

Sometime since he was to be at a church entertainment in Chicago and the church paper roasted him unmercifully for coming to them in such condition that he could not read. Yours sincerely,

Emmett J Scott

TLS   Con. 209   BTW Papers   DLC.

From Charles Waddell Chesnutt

Cleveland, O., March 13, 1901

My dear Mr. Washington: I arrived safely home, after a roundabout trip with numerous stops, and have brought with me many pleasant impressions of Tuskegee, and of the great work you have under way there. I have put some of my impressions in the shape of letters to the *Boston Transcript*, which will no doubt see the light, unless I have delayed them too long.[1] I hope they may please you.

But, personally, I don't like the South. I couldn't tell the people any better place to go to, and I hope they may work out — a happy destiny there; you are certainly doing a great deal to help them to that end. I hope to meet you sometime at the North, and meantime I remain, Yours cordially

Chas. W. Chesnutt

ALS Con. 193 BTW Papers DLC.

[1] In an article entitled "The White and the Black," in the Boston *Transcript*, Mar. 20, 1901, 13, Chesnutt contrasted the "busy note of industry" at Tuskegee Institute with the "air of scholastic quiet" at Atlanta University. He wrote that blacks needed both industrial training and higher education. He also wrote at length upon the injustice of Jim Crow cars, and concluded the article with an attack on William Hannibal Thomas for writing *The American Negro*. He said that his trip to the South had convinced him that blacks were acquiring property, gaining in education, and developing in culture and character, despite the pessimism of Thomas's book.

To Frederick Taylor Gates

Grand Union Hotel, New York, March 19, 1901

Dear Sir: Last year Mr. Rockefeller very kindly gave us $10,000 towards current expenses; $5,000 towards paying off obligations created prior to last year and $5,000 toward last year's current expenses.

Herewith I hand you our Auditor's report as of December 1st., 1900. While I could have prepared for you a later report, I find that conditions have not materially changed, which means that we have held our own since December 1st.

For several reasons our indebtedness is larger at the present time. First, we have devoted a large part of our time and strength during the last twelve months to increas[ing] our endowment fund, and have succeeded in increasing it from about $100,000 to $227,000. Second, we have found it necessary for efficient work, to purchase supplies for our various departments in larger quantities, and as the Auditor's figures show our indebtedness is largely represented by stock in trade. Third, demands on my time are made more and more from both north and south for the general cause of education in the South and this has prevented me from giving as much time as heretofore to the solicitation of funds.

What we owe ourselves (about $15,000) is to be provided for as soon as we can make a sale of the 25,000 acres of land in Alabama, given to us by Act of Congress.

What we need most, just now, is the money to clear off all indebtedness and place the school upon an absolutely cash basis; in other words, our need is largely for a working capital. Towards this end, I am glad to say that we have been offered by some ladies in Brooklyn $10,000, if $25,000 more shall be raised in New York within the next thirty days. Of this amount $11,630 has been received to date, leaving $13,370 to be raised to secure the $10,000 gift. We have, therefore, received, or been promised, as stated above, $21,630, leaving about $26,000 to be raised to wipe out all our cash indebtedness of $48,000 as shown on the statement enclosed.

As for the expenses for the remainder of the present school year, I see no reason why if those who contributed last year will give an equal amount this year, we should not be able to pay off all of our current bills. With the removal of the debts referred to, we shall be in a far better condition for good results than ever before, and I personally shall be much encouraged. Yours truly,

[Booker T. Washington]

TLc   Con. 215   BTW Papers   DLC.

From Paul Brandon Barringer

Charlottesville, Va. Mar. 20th, 1901

Dear Sir: Your kind letter of recent date came duly to hand and this a.m. I had the pleasure of receiving from your publishers the book you were good enough to send me. Allow me to thank you for this work and to add that I will read it with great pleasure, having already seen parts of it in the Outlook.

Let me also say that I believe that in the solution of this problem we are largely agreed as to the general principles. How best to apply them is a matter to be worked out step by step, on the ground, here in the South. I see no immediate prospects of improvement. Another generation will have come before any serious change is made in the present situation. We can only influence the sentiment of the future. You did not exactly understand me in regard to a conference. We had best go very slowly in this matter for one or two ill-timed speeches at such a conference would do more harm than good. Of this I will write you again.

Hoping that some fair, equitable and christian solution of this problem may be speedily attained for the benefit of all, I remain
Very respectfully yours,

P. B. Barringer

TLS Con. 191 BTW Papers DLC.

From Edgar Gardner Murphy

Montgomery, Alabama. March 20, 1901

Dear Mr. Washington: I have your kind letter inviting me to come to Tuskegee at the time when you receive your visitors in April, and I shall probably be able to do so. It may be that I can be of assistance by manifesting the interest which is felt in Tuskegee by the better classes of the white people of the state. I have been gratified with the number of expressions which have reached me on the subject of my letter in the Times, and I hope that in some small degree I may have removed the impression that the South would be delighted with Thomas's book. I have seen one or two important reviews in which the statement was made that that book represented the view of the Negro which is entertained at the South.

I have not yet heard definitely from Mr. McKinley, but I believe that he will miss a great opportunity should he decline our invitation. The platform adopted by the Democratic Convention on yesterday was most discouraging in its tone,[1] and for Mr. McKinley to have an opportunity in the very city where that platform was adopted to say a few wise, reasonable words in favor of a just conservatism, is of more significance than he perhaps can realize; particularly as the invitation is extended by a body of representative Southern men. I earnestly hope that he will come. I wrote to Secretary Herbert at once, as you suggested, but I am not sure just what action he has taken. I know that he has written to the President, and I hope that he has called upon him personally.

As to the platform of the Convention yesterday, it may be well for me to say that it sounds a great deal worse than it is, and that it has an inside history. The best men of the state are most anxious to secure a new Constitution, but they realize that there is little popular interest in it, and that in the rural districts especially, there is such a dread of white disfranchisement, that it is going to be very difficult to secure its passage at all. They have had to make it a distinctive party question, and to strengthen it by an appeal to the democratic party in order to give it the ghost of a chance. Even now, they are much concerned as to its fate. Remarkably enough, the opposition to the Convention is coming from the free silver, Negro-hating element in the state. These men know that the Negro has much less chance under present conditions than he would have under any possible constitution. He not only does not vote where his vote is regarded as dangerous, but upon the contrary, his vote is usually *"counted,"* wherever it is needed, upon the side of democratic candidates. They would rather count the Negro *in* as a democrat than count him *out* as a republican.

The platform, therefore, makes its appeal for support to the narrowest element in the state, but the Convention itself will be made up of our best men. That men like Gov. Jones,[2] Gen. Oates,[3] Mr. White[4] and Mr. Knox[5] should come from the state at large, is almost incredible in view of the platform. The members of the Constitutional Convention will represent the very best that Alabama can do upon the subject, and from this standpoint, the outlook is encouraging. I can talk to you more fully and freely upon this subject when I see you. All this, of course, is in confidence.

The holding of the Conference will depend very largely upon the acceptance of Mr. McKinley. Practically, it would be a relief to me if it should be postponed until another Spring. I have recently ascertained that under a standing order of the Convention of the Diocese of Alabama, the Annual Council of our Church in the whole state meets in Montgomery on the 8th, 9th, 10th and 11th of May. As the whole burden of hospitality will fall on me, the handling of two meetings at approximately the same time, will be a frightful strain. Our projected dates for the Conference are May 1st, 2nd and 3rd, but the gatherings come so nearly at the same time, that all the details of the work will have to be handled together. I do hope you had a successful meeting the other evening in New York. Very Sincerely yours,

Edgar Gardner Murphy

TLS Con. 261 BTW Papers DLC.

1 The Alabama Democratic party reaffirmed earlier pronouncements that made the calling of a constitutional convention a party cause. The Democrats endorsed a constitutional convention that would disfranchise black voters, and the platform upheld the dual concept of white supremacy and honest elections. (Hackney, *Populism to Progressivism in Alabama*, 174–75.)

2 Thomas Goode Jones (see above, 3:60), a supporter of BTW, was among the minority of delegates at the Alabama constitutional convention of 1901 who urged equal qualifications for voters regardless of race. This no doubt influenced BTW's decision to endorse Jones for a federal judgeship in 1901.

3 William Calvin Oates.

4 Francis Shelley (Frank) White (1847–1922) was a former Confederate soldier and lawyer who served in the Alabama House during the 1880s. He was president of the Democratic state convention in 1900 and a delegate to the state constitutional convention in 1901. White stated the real purpose of the constitutional convention when he said, ". . . time has demonstrated that the negro has no capacity to rule, but a great capacity to ruin. The negro . . . was disfranchised years ago by fraud and the purpose now was to do it by constitutional enactment." (Hackney, *Populism to Progressivism in Alabama*, 175.) White, however, was among the minority who opposed the adoption of a grandfather clause at the convention. In 1902 he was chairman of the Farmers', Merchants', and Laborers' Committee (known as the White Committee), which spearheaded the movement for railroad regulation in Alabama and fought political control of the state by outside railroad interests. This earned White a leading place in the development of progressivism in Alabama. From 1908 to 1910 he was chairman of the executive committee of the Democratic party in Alabama, and from 1914 to 1915 he was U.S. senator from Alabama, filling the vacancy caused by the death of Joseph F. Johnston.

5 John B. Knox, a railroad and corporation lawyer, was a prominent Democrat in Alabama. He was president of the Alabama constitutional convention of 1901 and chairman of the rules committee. In his presidential address he stated that it was within the limits of the U.S. Constitution to establish white supremacy in Alabama. Knox also advocated the disfranchisement of illiterate whites, but was more cautious on this controversial issue. (Hackney, *Populism to Progressivism in Alabama*, 191, 210–11.)

From William Hayes Ward

New York   March 21, 1901

My dear Mr. Washington: I presume the Albany man referred to by Mr. Fortune is John Edward Bruce,[1] of 97 Orange St., Albany, who has written a blatherskitey article about Thomas to the *Star of Zion.* I have written to him for any information he may give me. I am a little suspicious of him because he says that he lost his arm by its being cut off in a saw-mill, which I think is hardly probable considering that he is living on his pension; and Thomas is well reported of by the colonel of his regiment.

Thank you for the information. I presume I shall see Mr. Fortune soon. Yours very truly,

William Hayes Ward

P.S. I have an answer this morning from Mr. Bruce, who says that he was associated with Thomas in Boston for about three weeks in the conduct of a magazine called "The Negro." He says that he does not know of his own knowledge that Thomas's arm was cut off in a saw-mill, but that the information was given to him by some one in Boston prior to his meeting Thomas.

W. H. W.

TLS   Con. 215   BTW Papers   DLC.

1 Bruce was outraged by William H. Thomas's book and wrote BTW: "It occurs to me that the best thing to do with a viper like thomas is to show the white people who are quoting him that Titus Oates, is a saint compared with him. Testimony against a whole race from a man who consorts with courtesans[,] jumps bail for debt, dishonors his notes; and lives on the earnings of women to whom he is not married, will not be seriously regarded by serious men." He went on to say: "He is the worst onion, that ever came out of the loins, of the black race." (Mar. 20, 1901, Con. 190, BTW Papers, DLC.)

From Theodore Roosevelt

Oyster Bay, N.Y. Mch. 21, 1901

My dear Mr. Washington: Mrs. Roosevelt[1] is as much pleased as I am with your book. I shall not try to tell you what I think about it, my dear sir, for I do not want to seem to flatter you too much. You know I have always been afraid that you might succumb to the flattery you have received; and that would be a great misfortune, for I do not know who could take your place in the work you are doing. I wish I could see you to talk with you more at length than I was able to at the Century.

With hearty regards and many thanks, Very sincerely yours,

Theodore Roosevelt

TLpS Theodore Roosevelt Papers DLC.

[1] Edith Kermit Carow Roosevelt (1861–1948) married Theodore Roosevelt in 1886.

From Elizabeth Bartlett Grannis[1]

New York, March 21st., 1901

Dear Sir: I am just as deeply interested in your work and successes for the Negro Race, as when I first learned of you through the public prints, and your first Address which attracted such public attention, surprise and approval!

I have no doubt in my own mind that from the little you know of me, you have unjustly decided that I have made an unwise record in behalf of the Negro Race.

I have never been so thoroughly impressed with your sagacious wise policy as a shrewd politician, working for what you believe to be of the highest good for your people, as I was last Monday evening in Concert Hall, Madison Square Garden. With all that I have read in the daily papers of your sayings, and the policy you have pursued, my judgment has been confirmed along the line, that you suppressed much that you would like to say in defense of your people to curry favor with the wealthy citizens of the Southern States, as well as those of the Northern, from whom you would be most likely to secure funds for the benefit of your College, and the Colored People.

I have felt on many occasions in reading the reports of your Addresses in the Evening Post, that you either showed the "white feather" to the detriment of your own people, or, you were wiser than any of the Children of Light, in securing money, or that I was defective in ability to grasp your motives, and that to decide which, I must simply watch and wait!

I have a Piece of Property in this City, which I hope to sell in the near future; then I shall send a small contribution to the Tuskegee Institute, as I have had it down on my list for a number of years. I never place my poor little hard-earned dollars in any great Enterprise, to any considerable extent. I have put in over $14,000 into the "National Christian League Home for the Benefit of Self-Supporting Women," during the past six years. This money I have earned according to your teaching and practice, and I have willed the home in which I live to the "National Christian League for the Promotion of Social Purity."

I do not wish you to repeat the anecdote to another audience which has been read and reread, about the Dairyman who addressed you as "Mr. Washington," because that has been printed too many times in New York Papers, and you have hundreds of equally interesting ones which have *not* been repeated! The Young Woman's Faithfulness whom you commended, to whom you refused the Diploma, was one of the most helpful anecdotes which I have heard you repeat.

When Mr. Morris K. Jesup, complimented your work, and told of his experience at the Negro Sale in Virginia, and closed his sensible remarks with the declaration that he would not say that the Negroes would eventually be equal, or on an equality with the Whites, I doubt if many people in your position, and with your ability, would have failed to improve the opportunity to reply to that remark![2]

If I were ever to have the opportunity, and you the time to answer, I should like to ask you, if you could give any explanation why the Heavenly Father having no respect of persons, arranged only about one-fourth of his family to have their being in the Caucasian Race, *if* the Anglo-Saxons are superior to all other Peoples of the Earth! Why should we not receive a hint concerning the explanation from a member of one of the so-called inferior races in view of the fact that no Caucasian Theologian Writer has attempted to solve this problem.

Is it not a fact that each Race is superior to every other race in certain possessions by natural talents and vice versa! Is not each Race defective as compared with others in talents or natural gifts! The Head of the Church, the Founder of Christianity, the Only Begotten of God the Father, placed the heart of a Nation above its intellect, as truly as the heart of an individual above the head. What of the universal heart of the Negro Race, and what concerning its development under applied Christianity!

Who is the Judge — save the Creator of Nature? Is the talent which develops the greatest Mathematician, Accountant and Accumulator of Wealth, etc., superior to the qualities which have achieved most in Fine Arts? Who is to estimate the ability in Scientific Discovery, Mechanical Inventive Genius in reference to the value to the whole human race when compared with many other talents especially exercised and developed by their Sister Races and Nationalities?

I was never present at a Convention when I realized that any person or persons were so thoroughly justified in blowing their own Race Trumpets, as at the International Negro Convention held in London, England, last July! The Eloquence of Delivery, with the Quality of Matter which was listened to on this occasion, would certainly have astonished the best types of the Ante-Bellum-Masters of their Slaves. And you were not there! The year before I learned that your Wife was present at one of the Sessions of the International Council, but *I* neither met or saw her!

I consider the Ex-Representative from Texas,[3] gave the most helpful Address last Monday night.

I was much disappointed in Mr. Dunbar's Selections. From what I have read of his published poems, I could not see that he selected those best adapted to his audience. He impressed me much as Pastors and Ministers do in their After-Dinner Speeches at Social Functions when they attempt to come down to their audiences from their dignified positions by giving themselves to silly anecdotes and witticisms, which they imagine suitable to the occasion!

If you have neither the time or inclination to send me a line in reply to this letter, I shall in no sense be disappointed, and my friendship and esteem of your people will remain just the same in practice. Faithfully

Elizabeth B. Grannis

TLS Con. 261 BTW Papers DLC.

[1] Elizabeth Bartlett Grannis (1841?–1926) of New York edited the *Church Union* for more than twenty-three years beginning in 1873. She was a friend of the poet William Cullen Bryant, and his poems often appeared in the *Church Union*. About 1885 she organized the National Christian League for the Promotion of Social Purity. The league sought to instill higher moral values in men and women and also promoted the idea that women should develop independent careers to avoid dependence on men. The league also did social welfare work among the poor and had hospital auxiliaries in many countries. For more than twenty years before women won the right to vote, Grannis would march to the polls on registration day and demand to be reigstered on the grounds that she was a "female man," defining "man" generically and biblically. In 1920 she refused New York police the right to tap wires on her building to gain evidence against a nearby gambling house.

[2] Morris K. Jesup presided at the meeting of the Armstrong Association on Mar. 18, 1901, and introduced BTW. The reference to the "Negro Sale in Virginia" is unclear, since the newspaper accounts of the meeting did not report all of Jesup's remarks. (New York *Times*, Mar. 19, 1901, 9.)

[3] Robert Lloyd Smith.

To Emmett Jay Scott

Grand Union Hotel, New York. March 22, 1901

Dear Mr. Scott: Please say to Mr. Logan that Mr. Dunbar will be at Tuskegee sometime in April, and that I want him taken good care of. Give him a room somewhere where he will be comfortable. I want him to read to the students several times, and perhaps he might do some work with one or two of the classes in literature while there. Yours truly,

Booker T. Washington

The enclosed letter from Secy. Long I think you might use in the Southern Letter, omitting the name of Dr. Gordon to whom it is addressed.[1]

B.T.W.

TLS Con. 215 BTW Papers DLC.

1 John D. Long, Secretary of the Navy, wrote George A. Gordon, a member of the Tuskegee board of trustees, that he had the "highest respect" for BTW. He wrote: "I regard Booker T. Washington as one of the benefactors of the time — a worthy successor of the sainted Armstrong." (*Southern Letter*, 17 [Apr. 1901], 3.)

From Charles W. Parmenter[1]

Boston. March 22, 1901

Dear Sir: I was very glad to receive, this morning, your note of March 21, 1901, because it gives me an opportunity to draw your special attention to your son's school work.

In consideration of the noble service which you have rendered to the nation, the Committee on Manual Training of the Boston School Board granted my request for permission to receive your son[2] into my school as a *special student*. This concession would not have been made to the son of any man in Massachusetts. My teachers have freely given the boy a large amount of time and special attention, but I am sorry to say that the results are not as encouraging as it seems to me that they ought to be; and I am, therefore, very anxious to have you come to the school and have a conference with me before you return to your home. As a result of your experience you may be able to suggest methods that I can employ calculated to arouse the boy's ambition. He appears to have little comprehension of the value of the advantages which have been given him. His power to concentrate his mind upon a given task is very slight. If he had come from a Boston grammar school, I should call him provokingly lazy, but I am by no means sure that I understand him, and it is quite possible that such a statement would do him great injustice. Very simple directions must be repeated many times before he appears to comprehend them, and he forgets in a few minutes what has been told him. It has seemed to be necessary to use considerable pressure to secure any genuine effort on his part. He makes many mistakes which seem to be due to inexcusable carelessness, but his unfailing good-nature leads me to think that, at heart, he desires to please his teachers.

I have been astonished at his lack of judgment concerning very simple matters. The enclosed registration slip is a case in point. When I gave him the blank to fill out, I told him, as plainly as I could, what to write on each line and placed special emphasis upon the importance of writing plainly his street and number in Boston. I find it difficult to comprehend the state of mind that made it possible, under the circumstances, for him to write merely the number, which is, of course, of no possible use to me. I am very anxious to be of service to you, and will do all that I can for your son. The boy is at a critical stage in his development, and his future success will depend, in large measure, upon the forces that can be brought to bear upon him just now. I do not know what to do, and I feel that I need very much the light which you may be able to throw upon the situation in a conference with me.

With renewed expression of my high esteem, I am   Very sincerely yours,

C. W. Parmenter

TLS Con. 261 BTW Papers DLC. Addressed to BTW at the Grand Union Hotel, New York City. The enclosure mentioned is no longer attached.

1 Charles W. Parmenter was born in Vermont in 1852. He was headmaster of the Mechanic Arts High School in Boston.

2 BTW Jr.

To Francis James Grimké

Grand Union Hotel, New York, March 23, 1901

My dear Dr. Grimké: I am very glad that you are pleased with "Up from Slavery," and when you have time to read it carefully I shall be glad to get your further opinion of the book. I have had wholly in view the accomplishment of some good for the race in the writing of this book.

I am very sorry that of recent years I have not been able to see much of you in Washington, it has been however, almost wholly owing to the fact that in some way I cannot stand the atmosphere of Washington and always get out just as quickly as I can. I think I never was in a place where there are so many people that are continually after one to secure them a place of some kind as is true of Washington and the office seeking atmosphere which seems to pervade the whole city disgusts me so very much that I can rarely stay there longer than I am absolutely compelled to do so.

I hope at some time that we can have you at Tuskegee again and that Mrs. Grimké can accompany you. I want you to see something of the improvements that have been made there, not only in physical directions but I believe in real life. Yours very truly,

Booker T. Washington

PL   Carter G. Woodson, ed., *The Works of Francis J. Grimké* (Washington, D.C.: Associated Publishers, Inc., 1942), 4:70.

From Pambani Jeremiah Mzimba[1]

Entabeni   Box 4, Alice, Cape Colony [South Africa] 23 Mar 1901

Sir   I have heard very imperfectly of your most important Institute for the education and improvement of coloured young men & young women who desire to better their condition but have not the means financially to pay for college training. Your Institute meets such by giving such young men to help themselves by learning a trade and receive good education as well.

In South Africa there are many young people who are anxious for education but have not means to pay for college training but who would be thankful to learn a trade and be able to receive higher education as well. We would be much obliged to you, if you could [write] fully and even to the smallest particulars about your noble Institution's and the conditions which would be required from such young men or women. The sons of Africa are crying to the Africans in America "Come over & help us." We have about 12 young men & 6 young women anxious to go at once. I am, Sir Yours faithfully

P J Mzimba

ALS   Con. 235   BTW Papers   DLC.

1 Pambani Jeremiah Mzimba (1850–1911) of Cape Colony, South Africa, attended Lovedale Institution and was ordained a minister in the Free Church of Scotland in 1875. Feuds with white missionaries over the building of a new church at Lovedale

led Mzimba to resign his ministry in 1898. He then founded the Presbyterian Church of Africa to avoid the conflicts that arose from white missionary control. His church, popularly known as "Mzimba's Church," had more than 13,000 members in thirty-three congregations by the time of Mzimba's death.

Mzimba preached a doctrine of economic self-help similar to BTW's. He eschewed politics in favor of building black schools and churches and believed that race prejudice would end through the development of education and the acquisition of wealth.

The first students from South Africa to attend Tuskegee appeared in the 1903–4 school catalog. These were Vice Joel Kwatsha and Hamilton Samuel Luzipo, in the A preparatory class, and Edward Blekie, Enoch Silolo Massingo, and Alfred Nkomo, in the B preparatory class. It is not clear if any of these students arrived in America through the efforts of Mzimba.

Jane E. Clark[1] to Emmett Jay Scott

Oberlin College. Oberlin, Ohio. Mch-24-'01

Dear Mr. Scott, In reply to your letter of March 14th inquiring as to my nationality I would say most emphatically that I am *colored*.[2] I am not a little surprised to think that I could be mistaken for anything else. Very sincerely yours,

Jane E. Clark

ALS   Con. 194   BTW Papers   DLC.

[1] Jane E. Clark was lady principal and then dean of the woman's department at Tuskegee from 1902 to 1907. In 1907 she married Leslie Pinckney Hill, a Tuskegee faculty member, and the Hills moved to Manassas, Va. During her tenure at Tuskegee Jane E. Clark was an outstanding member of the faculty and a good friend of the Washington family. She accompanied Portia Washington as her chaperone when Portia toured Europe in 1905.

[2] Jane E. Clark first wrote BTW about a teaching position on Jan. 31, 1901. (Con. 194, BTW Papers, DLC.) As it was not clear from her letter whether or not she was black, BTW requested a photograph of her. The picture apparently did not clearly reveal her race, since she was light-skinned, so Scott had to end the subterfuge and ask her the question directly.

From John C. Leftwich

Montgomery, Ala., March 25th, 1901

My dear Sir — I thought that I would write you and let you know that I am in the land of living, for some time I have been sniffing the winds to see if I could hear from you, but my anxiety has about waned. I can now & then hear of your success in the north and the good things you are doing. I am still tugging at the same old thing, that is I am trying to follow your example and the many things that I have gleaned from your speeches so you can say that you have one poor devil in our state, who is trying to do just as you say, about trying to build up, so far I am succeeding very well. I can now see the importance of industrial education, I have a large black-smith shop in Klondike, Ala., and I wrote to your school and tried to get a smith, but failed, so far I have been unable to get one at any price. I also wanted a wheel wright, but failed to get one, again I have a fine Academy in Klondike, and need a first class hustling Principal, I tried to get one at Tuskeegee, but failed. I wanted a first class-farm-manager, tried to get one from Tuskegee, but failed. I have built a large store at Klondike, and is putting in about five thousand dollars worth of goods, I tried to get a first class book-keeper and clerk from your school, but failed, pray tell me what become of your students, I am anxious to give your boys a chance in my town, but I can not get the material. I hope that you are get-ting along allright in the north, you know I had a little taste of it last summer.

Klondike is on a boom, and if any one should inquire about my little town, tell them that we are building right along, that we have five new buildings going up, that I have a large store and two more in course of erection, that I have a large blacksmith shop, that I have organized a firm known as the Klondike-Mercantile, Farmers and Real-Estate Co., with a Capital of $25,000, which is doing a rushing business. I am also running a large farm, seven head of gray stock, and twenty five hands, this farm is known as the "Klondike Gray Horse Farm," she is a dandy, I wished that you could see the same in operation. I simply call your attention to these things, that you may know that I am alive, and still a great deciple of yours. I am still in Uncle Sam employee, but do not know how long, but I hope to continue, and will want you at the proper time to whisper in his ear to retain me for four more years, I know that you will do this for me.

I will not worry you any longer with this long dry letter, but I asked Mr Carnegie to give me a library for Klondike, I have not heard from him yet, I told him that I did not expect to get it, and I am not disappointed.

When you have time and get to thinking about your old friend in this city, please drop me a line to encourage my weary mind and droopy soul, because I am almost crazy, studying about getting rich, and with the ambition of being the largest negro farmer in the world. I am yours,

John C. Leftwich

TLS Con. 203 BTW Papers DLC. Written on stationery of the Department of Interior, U.S. Land Office.

From Theodore Roosevelt

Oyster Bay NY Mar 26 1901

Could see you next Monday four twenty two Madison Avenue four pm

Theodore Roosevelt

HWSr Con. 541 BTW Papers DLC.

From Ethel Perry Chesnutt[1]

Smith College, Northampton Mass. March 27, 1901

My dear Mr. Washington, Of the courses which are taught at Tuskegee I have studied physics, civics, mathematics, philosophy, history, grammar, elocution and of course I have been through all ordinary grade work. I should prefer to teach mathematics, philosophy and history.

The salary would be perfectly satisfactory. Would I have to teach at night? Would I have a room alone? My father does not particularly approve of my going into the South but he does not understand yet that I am grown up, capable of taking care of myself, and not worried in the least by many of the questions which worry him. When I have convinced him of these facts, he will withdraw his objections. If you give me the position, you could let me know by summer what branches you would want me to teach, could you not? Hoping this will be satisfactory, I am, Very sincerely,

Ethel Perry Chesnutt

ALS Con. 194 BTW Papers DLC.

[1] Ethel Perry Chesnutt, a 1901 graduate of Smith College, was one of four children born to Charles Waddell and Susan Utley Perry Chesnutt. She taught history at Tuskegee during the 1901–2 school year. In Nov. 1902 she married Edward C. Williams, the librarian of Adelbert College in Cleveland, Ohio, who later taught at Howard University.

From Will Marion Cook[1]

New York City– Mch 29/01

My dear Sir: In accordance with our talk of last Thursday I wish to submit the following proposition to you:

That I shall organize a company of nine (9) — eight singers and a pianist — who shall be known as "Tuskeegee's Real Negro Singers." There aim shall be to demonstrate just how much the Negro has done to cultivate and develop the plantation melodies. The progra[m]me shall consist of twelve numbers. Four (4) the pure melodies of the uncultivated slave such as swing low etc. Four numbers of slightly developed melodies by Taylor,[2] of London, Burleigh[3] and myself; and four numbers of a rather ambitious character which would display the range of voice and musical cultivation of the singers. In this manner the following purposes would be served. Namely: The fact would be proved that there is an abundance of musical material in the themes of the Southern Negro capable of thorough development and may form a basis for the growth of a music which shall be called truly American; further — the compositions of the three Negroes mentioned may be taken to show that the Negro himself is to play some part in the development of this music (a fact not hitherto conceded); and lastly, the Negro voice loses none of its tenderness and sweetness when carefully cultivated. These are the artistic arguments. The financial possibilities seem to be very good. A company that could give its initial concert at the

Waldorf-Astoria, and be subjected to the thorough criticism of the New York press would, if the entertainment proved unique and successful, be something of a sensation and would draw largely at Concerts, at homes etc. I wish to organize such a company. The power of your name and that of Tuskeegee would gain us a respectful hearing.

I offer to furnish the company and devote one half of the proceeds resulting from its entertainments to the advancement of the glorious work you are doing at Tuskeegee. The only obligations resting upon you will be those of "the name," "advice," and that you understand and encourage the musical efforts.

Trusting that you will pardon my writing at such length   I am Yours very respectfully

Will Marion Cook

ALS   Con. 194   BTW Papers   DLC.

1 Will Marion Cook (1869–1944) was born in Washington, D.C., the son of John H. Cook, a professor at Howard University. He attended Oberlin Conservatory of Music and, in 1895, studied for a time under Anton Dvořák, then head of the National Conservatory of Music. Cook wrote many popular songs and musical plays. He did the music for Paul Laurence Dunbar's "Clorindy, the Origin of the Cakewalk," which appeared on Broadway with an all-black cast in 1898. He composed music for the famous black vaudeville team of Bert Williams and George Walker. Among his tunes that were popular around the turn of the century were: "Exhortation," "The Rain Song," and "The Casino Girl." His wife, Abbie Mitchell Cook, was a well-known black actress. There is no evidence that BTW agreed to Cook's proposal, probably on the ground that there was already a quartet of singers touring the North in behalf of Tuskegee.

2 Samuel Coleridge-Taylor (1875–1912), the Afro-British composer, was best known for his choral works, *Hiawatha's Wedding Feast* (1898), *Death of Minnehaha* (1899), and *A Tale of Old Japan* (1911). Portia Washington was particularly fond of Coleridge-Taylor's arrangements of Negro melodies, and her piano concerts almost always included his work, especially her favorite, "Sometimes I Feel Like a Motherless Child."

3 Harry Thacker Burleigh (1860–1949), born in Erie, Pa., was a black singer and composer who did much to preserve the traditions of the Negro spiritual. Burleigh's formal training was at the National Conservatory of Music under Anton Dvořák, who became Burleigh's personal friend. James Weldon Johnson recalled that Burleigh had a reputation among New York black musicians of the time for being the "final authority" on all questions of musical theory. (Johnson, *Along This Way*, 173.) In 1917 Burleigh was awarded the NAACP's Spingarn Medal.

A Book Review in *Outlook*

[Mar. 30, 1901]

THE AMERICAN NEGRO

In his introduction Mr. Thomas makes it known that he is partly a negro, though throughout the book he refers to the race as if he were not a part of it. One gets the feeling that he is making the most of the fact that he has enough blood connection with the race to enable him to speak from the inside, yet he is not proud of being a negro, and never once refers to the race as "our race" or "my race." Mr. Thomas acknowledges that he was a "carpetbagger," that he fought in the Civil War, and afterwards was elected by the colored vote in South Carolina to the State Legislature, and still later held a judicial position in that State. Still later he claims to have been engaged in educational work in the South, though diligent inquiry so far fails to bring us accurate information as to where he was engaged in the work of education. At any rate, it is clear that the last twenty years of Mr. Thomas's life have been spent mainly in the North near Boston, away from the great bulk of the race and out of direct touch with the tremendous constructive forces which have been at work during the last twenty years for the regeneration of the black man.

We have seldom seen a "carpetbagger," black or white, who did not take a gloomy view of the future of the South and of the negro. So long as the negro, by his vote, was able to keep the carpetbagger in office, the negro was all right; when he ceased to do this the future became very dark. On the other hand, men like the late S. C. Armstrong, of Hampton, and the late Dr. Cravath, of Fisk University, who were soldiers, and remained in the South after the war, not for the purpose of getting office, but of lifting up the negro and the white man, have always taken a hopeful view of the future.

One strain that runs through Mr. Thomas's book from first to last is his insistence that the negro get land and education. This, however, is not new, for this is the thing that most of the educators in the South for more than thirty years have been insisting upon. More recently the importance of land-getting has been emphasized through the medium of the Tuskegee Negro Conference and the various local conferences that have grown out of it and are now scattered throughout the South. There is no mistaking the fact, though, that the main object of the book is to show, in a word, that the negro so far has been a failure from a material, mental, and moral point of view. Over against many of the bold, unsupported statements made by the author of "The American Negro" as to the lack of material progress, we want to place a few facts that will tend to show whether or not the efforts of negro schools in the South have been fruitless, and whether or not the negro has stood still or gone backward. First, let us take the State of Virginia, where the colored people have been under the direct influence of the great Hampton Institute as well as of other schools. The Hampton Institute and its work, however, Mr. Thomas strangely omits altogether, or brushes it aside as being of no consequence. The official figures in relation to the negro's ownership of land in Virginia for the past year are as follows:

> The negroes now own one-twenty-sixth of all the land in Virginia. They own one-sixteenth of all the land in Virginia east of the Blue Ridge; one-tenth of all the land in twenty-five counties in the State; one-seventh of Middlesex County, one-fifth of Hanover County, and one-third of Charles City County. The negroes of Virginia are acquiring land at the rate of about fifty thousand acres a year. Their real estate holdings would appear much larger if there were added the farms for which they have contracted, upon which they are making payments, but have not received the title.

In regard to the negro's material progress in the State of Georgia, the State Comptroller has recently given out the following figures, which are reliable in every respect:

> The aggregate of property owned by negroes in Georgia is $14,118,720, as against $13,560,179 last year. Of this $4,361,390 is city and town property, and $4,274,549 is represented by farm lands. They own $72,975 worth of merchandise, have $93,480 in cash solvent debts and $469,637 in plantation and mechanical tools. The total number of acres of land owned by negroes is 1,075,073, and there are 110,985 negro voters in the State, as shown by the digest. Their property returns show a flattering increase for every year since 1879, when they returned for taxation only $5,182,398 worth of property. In 1889, ten years later, they had doubled their possessions, returning for taxation at that time $10,415,350 worth of property.

Other Southern States could make as good a showing, and yet Mr. Thomas would have us believe that practically no material progress has been made. According to the theory advocated in his book, he would have us throw a wet blanket over all this splendid advance through individual effort, and have the General Government enter into a scheme of buying and selling lands to the negro much on the old "forty acres and a mule" plan. He would have the negro trained to look to Washington for everything, instead of depending on himself or his State, and have the whole South flooded again with Federal officers.

A fair idea of the value of Mr. Thomas's economic ideas can be obtained by reading the passage in his book wherein he criticises such men as ex-President Hayes, Morris K. Jesup, William E. Dodge, and Dr. J. L. M. Curry for not following his advice to invest the John F. Slater Fund of a million dollars in Southern lands. According to his theory, which he outlines with much detail, if his advice had been followed, instead of that of bankers like Morris K. Jesup, the million dollars would have yielded the *first year* an interest amounting to four hundred thousand dollars, and the *second year* it would have yielded five hundred thousand dollars. Clearly, according to this showing, Mr. Thomas's rightful place is in Wall Street, rather than in the field of book-writing. It is perhaps true that no single agency has accomplished more in stimulating and guiding the education of the negro along proper channels than the John F. Slater Fund. At least this is the opinion of experts and of men of National reputation in the educational world.

The author of this book condemns practically every method that has been used for lifting up the negro; everything is wrong except that which he advocates, but which he himself, it seems, has failed to put into practice anywhere in the South. He advocates industrial education all through his book, yet condemns it as it now exists in many negro schools at the South. He goes so far as to outline a curriculum for the teaching of agriculture to the negro. We have recently placed this curriculum by the side of that of one of the largest industrial schools in the South, and find that what he condemns the educators of negro youth for not doing is actually being done in several schools, and is fast spreading all through the South.

Mr. Thomas devotes much space to a contention that the fundamental mistake in the education of the negro is in educating him along Anglo-Saxon lines, and yet, at the end of his long contention, it is almost pitiful to see how he knocks the foundation from under his own logic by stating that a certain literary college in Kentucky, where there is almost no attempt at industrial education, and where the bulk of the students are white — only a small proportion being negroes — is the only institution in the South that is educating the negroes along correct lines. How can a college that exists mainly for white people educate along anything but Anglo-Saxon lines? And in what respect is the curriculum of Berea College — a very worthy institution — different from that of Fisk University and Atlanta University?

But, plainly, the main point of the book is to discount the morals of the negro. In this respect many of Mr. Thomas's statements are so extreme and so entirely unsupported by evidence, except his own bare assertions, that much that is good and valuable in the book will be discounted. We believe that no one would be quicker to refute many of these unreasonable statements than the Southern white people themselves. A writer, who is unknown and almost unheard of, who makes such statements with expectation of being believed, should be careful to fortify himself by giving names, places, and dates, and not deal so largely in generalities and statements taken merely from his own head. He speaks constantly of having received his information from a "certain Governor" or a "certain physician" or a "certain teacher."

For example, does the author of "The American Negro" expect himself to be taken seriously by intelligent and thoughtful people when he says, "The consequence is that there is no school of prominence in negro training which has not had among its pupils young freedwomen sustaining immoral relations with white men, whose school expenses have been, in many instances, defrayed by such persons with the knowledge and consent of the school authorities?" It would be hard to make any of our readers believe that such a statement would apply to men like Dr. Frissell, of Hampton, the late Dr. Cravath, of Fisk University, Dr. Bumstead, of Atlanta University, the President of Wilberforce University, and numbers of institutions under the control of the Congregational, Methodist, and Baptist denominations at the South.

In another statement he says: "We shall, however, in view of all the known facts at our command, be justified in assuming that not only are fully ninety per cent. of the negro women of America unchaste, but the social degradation of our freedwomen is without a parallel in modern civilization." A little later on, Mr. Thomas seems to have forgotten this outrageous statement regarding negro women, and says, when speaking of the whole race: "It is correct to say that fully ninety per cent. of the freedmen are reasonably law-abiding, and, apart from an instinct for petty pilfering, are fairly honest in deportment. They have the confidence and support of orderly white society, and are rarely molested by its lawless class."

In another case he says: "For instance, the negro's ethical code sternly reprobates dancing, theater attendance, and all social games of chance." A few pages further on he forgets this statement, and adds: "It is as much a quest for physical excitement as the promise for pecuniary gain which impels the negro to indulge in petty gambling, and makes him the chief 'policy player' of the community, in every city, North and South."

In another instance he states that the high death-rate and low birth-rate of the negro people shuts out any possibility of their attaining formidable proportions in this country. A little further along in the book he speaks of the "ever-increasing millions of negro citizens."

In still another statement he speaks of the South being overrun with incompetent, illiterate doctors, among other classes of professional men. Now, what are the facts? In Alabama, for example, no man, black or white, can enter the medical profession without passing a very severe examination. Perhaps with the exception of the State of Virginia, the examination in Alabama is more severe than that of any other State in the Union. In that State a diploma from no college is accepted. No one can enter the medical profession without taking the regular State examination, and it is very rare that any man can pass this examination inside of ten days. The code of medical ethics in the South perhaps is higher than it is in the North; no man of any race would, for a single day, be tolerated in the profession of medicine who did not lead a correct, moral life and was not well prepared professionally for his work. In Alabama there are about twenty-five negro physicians, and we have facts that warrant us in saying that, almost without a single exception, these men are highly educated, are successful in their practice, are respected by their white brother physicians, and have high moral and business standing in their communities. There are nearly seven hundred thousand negroes in Alabama, and it is bordering on the ridiculous to speak, for example, of that State being overrun with negro physicians, when there are only twenty-five to practice among seven hundred thousand people. What is true of Alabama is in an equal degree true of other Southern States. No set of individuals have made a higher record professionally and otherwise since the war than the negro physicians.

Further on Mr. Thomas enlightens us again in the following statement: "The preacher in charge of the moral training of his people, and the teacher engaged in their mental instruction, will steal from each other and from the whites as readily as the most indigent freedman." This statement will include such ministers as the Rev. Dr. J. W. E. Bowen, of Gammon Theological Seminary, the Rev. Dr. F. J. Grimke, of Washington, D.C., and such teachers as Dr. W. E. B. Du Bois, of Atlanta, Ga., Professor Hugh M. Browne, of the Hampton Institute, and Mrs. B. K. Bruce, woman principal of the Tuskegee Institute, and Miss Maria Baldwin, Principal of the Agassiz public school of Cambridge, Mass. It has remained for Mr. Thomas to inform the public that such persons will steal from one another and from the whites.

He further proceeds with the statement that the more intelligent the negro is, the more does his disposition to theft enlarge. In answer to this, some years ago, a careful investigation was made, and it was found that not a single man or woman who had graduated from one of the larger institutions in the South was to be found in a State prison.

Mr. Thomas says: "There are, in all of the large cities, North and South, among the race, so-called voudoo and conjure doctors to whom vast throngs go for amulets to ward off disease, and for treatment when sick." As a practical test of much that the writer says in this book, we should be interested in having some one interested in sociological conditions in Boston or New York ask Mr. Thomas to lead him to one of these voudoo and conjure doctors to whom "vast throngs" go for treatment. We venture the statement that no such "vast throngs" can be found, and that few if any voudoo or conjure doctors can be found in our Northern cities; at any rate, we hope some of our readers will put Mr. Thomas to the test. The following statement is equally unworthy of belief: "It is, therefore, almost impossible to find a person of either sex, over fifteen years of age, who has not had actual carnal knowledge."

We have not been slow to point out the weaknesses of the negro race nor to condemn the negro's follies. We know that the race at many points is weak and needs to make itself strong, but at the same time we are convinced, through direct and reliable evidence, that there never was a time in the history of the race when so much real progress is being made materially, educationally, and morally as is true at the present time. This progress is slow, but it is steady and sure, and no one need become discouraged or lose hope for the negro race. Mr. Thomas, on the other hand, would, it seems, lift the race up much as one would build a house. This cannot be done. If the author of "The American Negro" had spent his time during the last ten or twenty years in going through the South, speaking directly to the colored people in their schools, their churches, conventions, and associations, about the weak points that he brings out in his book, and this book had been the natural result of his efforts in this direction, we confess that we should have more respect for him and for what he says. The people in the United States do not have a very high regard for a man who goes to England to make known the weak points in the life of Americans. The people of Boston do not have high regard for an individual who goes to New Orleans to condemn Boston. The citizens of Atlanta do not have much respect for an individual who goes to New York to condemn the people of Atlanta. The men of the white race will not have high regard for a writer who seems to withdraw himself from his own race and goes outside of it to emphasize its weak points before an audience of another color.

The remedy for such an extreme case of the blues as Mr. Thomas evidently has is to be found in going right into the field among the people and entering into hard, earnest work for their uplifting. So long as the men and women who are actually engaged in a first-hand manner in the lifting up of the negro do not become discouraged, so long we shall have great faith in the future. It is sad to think of a man without a country. It is sadder to think of a man without a race; and this, we fear, is about the position in which Mr. Thomas may be described as having voluntarily placed himself through the medium of his book.

[Booker T. Washington]

Outlook, 67 (Mar. 30, 1901), 733–36. An autograph draft appears in Con. 215, BTW Papers, DLC. It makes clear that the statistical data on Virginia are from the Richmond *Dispatch*.

An Article in *Gunton's Magazine*

[March 1901]

THE NEGRO IN BUSINESS

The conference of the National Negro Business League, which assembled in Boston in August of 1900, was unique. For the first time since the negroes were freed an attempt was made to bring together, from all over the United States, a company of representative business men and women of the race. Over three hundred delegates were present. They came from thirty states, and from an area which extended from Nebraska to Florida and from Texas to Maine.

Many of these men once were slaves. Others were younger men, born since the civil war and educated in the industrial schools and colleges; but they were almost all alike in one respect, that they had come up from the bottom and had gained whatever of property and position which they possessed by their own efforts. The business enterprises which they represented were manifold; their range and the success which these men have attained in them were object-lessons to the country. Another lesson, no less striking, was the conduct of the conference itself.

The New Orleans riots occurred while the preparations for the conference were being made. The streets of New York resounded to the cries of a negro-hunting mob just at the time when many of the delegates were leaving their homes to come to Boston. When the conference assembled, on the morning of August twenty-third, the newspapers were filled with accounts of the disturbances at Akron. And yet, throughout sessions which occupied two days and two evenings, in which at least two hundred persons spoke, there was not one single reference to the riots or to the conditions which gave rise to them. These were business men, come to Boston for a definite purpose with which politics had no connection, and they attended strictly to business. Nor was this the result of fear or intimidation. The position of the promoters of the league had been plainly stated beforehand and the policy of the gathering outlined.

I quote from one of the most widely published announcements of the meetings: "Those who are interested in the success of the league do not underestimate the importance of seeing to it that the negro does not give up any part of the struggle for retaining his citizenship. They are against the repeal of the fifteenth amendment, and they believe that election laws throughout the country should be made to apply with equal justice to black and white alike. They believe that if the franchise is restricted in any state it should not be done in such a way that an ignorant white man can vote while an ignorant black man cannot. At the same time they recognize the fact that to retain citizenship and the respect of the nation there must go with the negro's demands for justice, tangible, indisputable proofs of the progress of the race, or, briefly, that deeds and words must go together. They believe that helping the negro along commercial lines will help his political status. This is not a political meeting. It is a business gathering. Politics and other general matters pertaining to the race are dealt with at the sessions of the national Afro-American Council."

I think that a paragraph in an editorial in one of the Boston papers, printed just after the conference adjourned, described the tone of the gathering admirably. It said: "There was no politics in this gathering. There was no clamoring for rights. There was as little sentimentality as in a meeting of stock jobbers or railroad directors. . . . Wanton, insane cruelty of white men was something which colored men, minding their own business, could not reasonably cause, nor effectually rebuke. With a perfect dignity they left the matter to those whom it concerned. . . . Their conduct was a sign of power, equal to any other that the conference gave witness of, the supreme power of manliness that is recognized in self-restraint."

It had seemed to me for some time that an organization was needed which would bring together the colored business men and women of the country for consultation and to obtain information and inspiration from each other. As I had traveled through the country, especially in the South, I had often been impressed and repeatedly surprised to see how many colored men were succeeding in business enterprises, often in small, out-of-the-way places where they are never heard of, but where they are doing good work not only for themselves but for the race. I do not mean that the men and women who are in business in the cities are not doing equally well, but their work is better known because it is more obvious. How much I wish that our race might be judged by these people and by its students and teachers instead of, as is too often the case, by those who are in the penitentiaries and idle on the street corners. Other races are judged by their best. Why not the negro?

Unless one has given some consideration to the subject he will be surprised to learn how widely the colored people have gone into business. There were present at the meeting in Boston the representative of a colored cotton factory, a bank president, the president of a negro coal mine, grocers, real-estate dealers, the owner of a four-story brick storage warehouse and the proprietor of a trucking business operating forty teams, dry-goods dealers, druggists, tailors, butchers, barbers, undertakers, the owner of a steam carpet-cleaning business, manufacturers of brooms, tinware and metal goods, hair goods, etc., a florist, printers and publishers, insurance agents, caterers, restaurant keepers, general merchants, contractors and builders, the owner and proprietor of a brick yard (in North Carolina) which turns out several million bricks a year, and in fact representatives of almost every industry which can be suggested.

Two men who were present at the conference were the mayors of negro towns which they have built up in the South. One of these men, Mr. Isaiah T. Montgomery, was once a slave of Jefferson Davis.[1] Fifteen years ago he began to colonize a tract of land in the valley of the Yazoo River, in Mississippi. Colored people now own 12,000 acres there. In the town of Mound Bayou, which is the nucleus of the settlement, Mr. Montgomery said there are ten stores and shops owned by colored people, doing a business of at least $30,000 a year. Mr. J. C. Leftwich, of Alabama, owns over a thousand acres of land not far from Montgomery, where he is building up a town which he has named "Klondike." All the business is in the hands of colored people, even the postmaster being a colored man.

Three of the best addresses were made by women, one of them, Mrs. A. M. Smith,[2] the president of a colored business woman's club and employment agency in Chicago; one by Mrs. A. Thornton,[3] a dermatologist, of Cincinnati, and one by Mrs. A. A. Casneau,[4] a dressmaker, of Boston. The last named woman is the author of a book upon dressmaking which has been quite widely used. She told of an interesting experience with a white woman who came to Boston to take some additional lessons from her, suggested from the book, and who did not know that the woman she was coming to see was a colored woman. For this to be understood I must first relate an incident which occurred to one of our Tuskegee Institute students, because it was to this incident that Mrs. Casneau referred.

Among the other industries taught at Tuskegee Institute is that of dairying. We have a herd of over one hundred good dairy cows, and classes of young men and women are constantly receiving practical instruction in this industry, doing all of the work of the dairy at the same time. There came to our knowledge the fact that the owners of a certain creamery were looking for a competent superintendent. We had just graduated a man whom we knew to be thoroughly competent in every way, but he was just about as black as any one could possibly be. Nevertheless we sent him on to apply for the position. When the owners of the creamery saw him they said: "But you are a colored man. That would never do. We cannot hire a colored man."

Our candidate politely intimated that he had not come there to talk about any color except butter color, and kept on talking about that, while the owners kept talking about his color. Finally something which he said so caught their attention that they told him he might stay and run the creamery for a fortnight, although they still insisted that it was out of the question for them to hire a colored man as superintendent.

When the returns for the first week's shipment of butter made by our man came back, it was found that the butter had sold for two cents a pound more than any product of the creamery had ever before sold for. The owners of the establishment said: "Why, now, this is very singular"; and waited for the next week's report.

The second week's returns showed that the butter had sold for a cent a pound more than that of the week before, three cents more than before the colored man had taken charge of the work. That time the owners did not stop to say anything. They simply hired the man as quickly as they could. The extra three cents on a pound which he could get for his butter had knocked every particle of color out of his skin so far as they were concerned.

Mrs. Casneau, in her address before the league, said that when she received a letter from her customer saying that the woman was coming to Boston to call upon her at a certain time, her courage failed her because she knew that this customer had no idea that she was to meet a colored woman as the author of the book which she had been studying. When the day came, and the bell rang, and she was told that this woman had arrived, she was at first almost tempted to send in word that she was ill and could not see her, when suddenly there came into her mind the story of the Tuskegee graduate who had declined to discuss any question of color except the butter color which pertained to his business. "I went into the room as bravely as I could," she said, "and, although the woman looked and acted just as I felt sure she would, I would not let myself take any notice of it, but went on talking business as fast as I could. The result was that we made a business engagement, through which, afterwards, other work came to me."

This meeting not only showed to the country what the colored people are doing, but it gave the delegates, especially those who came from the South, an opportunity to see something of the business methods employed by northern people. I think it will have something of the same good effect on them that the bringing of the Cuban teachers to the United States may be expected to have on the Cubans.

If a record of the business enterprises operated by colored men and women in the United States were available it would be interesting and instructive, but such information has not yet been very generally reported.

From the published reports of the valuable studies of Professor W. E. B. Du Bois I make a few extracts bearing on the subject. In his book, "The Philadelphia Negro," Dr. Du Bois deals chiefly with the colored people of the seventh ward of that city. The author says that this particular ward is selected because it "is an historic center of negro population and contains one-fifth of all the negroes in the city." The negro population of Philadelphia in 1890 was 40,000, and over 8,000 lived in this ward. Both these numbers will undoubtedly show an increase when the figures of the census recently taken are available. In this ward Dr. Du Bois found the following-named business establishments operated by negroes: 39 restaurants, 24 barber shops, 11 groceries, 11 cigar stores, 2 candy and notion stores, 4 upholsterers, 2 liquor saloons, 4 undertakers (two of these were women), 1 newspaper, 1 drug store, 2 patent-medicine stores, 4 printing offices.

There were 83 caterers in the ward, but some of these Dr. Du Bois reports as doing a small business, and others as engaged in the business only a part of the year, being otherwise employed the rest of the time. The business of catering by negroes in Philadelphia has always been remarkable for the ability and success with which it has been conducted. Several men of the race in that city have been famous for their work in this line. Dr. Du Bois, in writing of the caterer, reports "about ten who do a business of from $3,000 to $5,000 a year."

In addition to these there were at the same time in other parts of the city, among the negro business establishments, 49 barber shops, 8 grocery stores, 27 restaurants, 8 coal and wood dealers. There was a successful florist, a large crockery store, and successful real-estate dealers.

From the reports of other studies of Dr. Du Bois, in the South, I make some extracts. I do not quote his lists in full, but give only a few of the leading enterprises reported:

Birmingham, Ala. — 8 grocers, 6 barbers, 4 druggists, 4 tailors. Montgomery, Ala. — 6 grocers, 2 undertakers, 2 drug-store keepers, 1 butcher. Vicksburg, Miss. — 2 jewelers, 2 tailors, 2 drug-store keepers, 2 newspapers, 2 dry-goods dealers, 1 undertaker. Nashville, Tenn. — 9 contractors, 6 grocers, 2 undertakers, 2 saloon keepers, 2 drug stores. Houston, Tex. — 11 grocers, 10 real-estate dealers, 5 contractors, 6 barbers. Richmond, Va. — 2 banking and insurance men, 2 undertakers, 2 fish dealers. Tallahassee, Fla. — 3 groceries, 2 meat markets. Americus, Ga. — 12 groceries, 1 drug store, 1 wood yard. Seattle, Wash. — 1 real-estate dealer, 2 barbers, 3 restaurants. I do not have available a list of enterprises in the city of Pensacola, Fla., but there are at least two groceries there, conducted by colored men, doing a business of $10,000 a year each, and successful restaurants, contractors, drug-store keepers, shoe-makers and tailors.

Much has been said and written about the fitness of the negro for work in cotton factories. Until the negro is given a fair trial under encouraging conditions I shall be slow to believe that he is not fitted for profitable work in factories. For years the colored man has been the main operative in the tobacco factories of the South, and, aside from this, he operates in very large measure all the cotton-seed oil mills in the South and is engaged in every avenue of mechanical work. I think those who hold to the theory that the negro cannot be depended upon as a laborer in factories will find their theory exploded in a few years very much in the same way that dozens of other theories regarding him have been exploded.

The failure of the Vesta Cotton Mills, in Charleston, S.C., has been laid to the door of the negro. Those who have written on this subject seemingly forget, however, to state that these same mills failed once, and I think twice, under white labor and that these mills have never had colored labor exclusively in them. When I visited Charleston a few months ago and made a careful inspection of these mills, I found at least one-third of the operatives were white people, the remaining two-thirds being colored. The colored people, as I remember it, occupied two floors and the whites the other floor, so that the failure cannot be wholly ascribed to colored labor.

Few cotton mills North or South have succeeded in large cities where there is no opportunity to segregate and control the labor. If the negro is given a fair trial in a small village, or in a country district where he is so situated in his home life that the operators can control, as they do in the case of the white laborer, the life of families, I believe that the negro will succeed in the cotton factory equally as well as the white man. Until such fair trial is given him it is unfair and misleading to make sweeping statements regarding his reliability in this respect.

In further proof of my statement that the negro can succeed in factory work if given a fair opportunity, I refer to the employment of colored persons in the silk factory at Fayetteville, N.C., a small town where conditions are much more conducive to factory life than in Charleston. Mr. H. E. C. Bryant, a white man and one of the editors of the Charlotte *Daily Observer,* published at Charlotte, N.C., recently visited this silk factory in Fayetteville and after his visit said in his paper:

"It is the most unique and interesting manufacturing plant in the state, if not in the entire South. It is managed by Rev. T. W. Thurston,[5] a mulatto, born in Pennsylvania and educated in Philadelphia, and who is highly respected by the white and colored citizens of Fayetteville."

Mr. Bryant further remarks:

"It has proved a signal success. Its continued success will mean much to the negro of the South. The building is of brick, three stories high, and the mill has 10,000 spindles and employs 400 operatives, mainly boys and girls between 10 and 18 years old. The first floor contains the reeling department over which Mr. J. H. Scarbough, a young German, is foreman; the second is devoted to winding and doubling, and Gertrude Hood[6] (colored), daughter of Bishop Hood, is in charge; and the third, weaving, with Mr. Harry Fieldhouse, an Englishman, as foreman. The mill has the appearance of a well-regulated school. The operatives are thoroughly organized and work with perfect system. I found order and neatness on every hand. The children did not seem frightened but satisfied and ambitious. None but the best class of boys and girls are employed at the silk mills. The employment of colored labor has not caused racial trouble. It takes the young negro from the streets and makes a good citizen of him and turns loose about $4,000 a month to spend for food and clothing."

Despite these evidences of progress, it has been said, sometimes, that negroes cannot come together and successfully unite in holding such meetings as that of the National Negro Business League, and that this is a proof of their business incapacity. I think such a meeting as that of last August disproves that theory. What gave me the most encouragement was the manly and straightforward tone used in all the papers and discussions. There were no complaints. At the next session I believe that there will be still larger numbers and stronger support. I believe that as a race we shall succeed and grow, and be a people, with our due representation in business life, right here in America. We must not be discouraged, and we must watch our opportunities and take advantage of them. There is no force on earth that can keep back a brave people that is determined to get education and property and Christian character. They never can be defeated in their progress.

Gunton's Magazine, 20 (Mar. 1901), 209–19. A copy is in Con. 977, BTW Papers, DLC.

1 Actually, he was the slave of Joseph E. Davis, Jefferson Davis's brother.

2 Albreta Moore Smith, born in Chicago in 1875, graduated from Armour Institute of Technology in 1894. In 1896 she worked as a stenographer for the Afro-American National Republican Bureau. Active in women's club work, she founded the Colored Women's Business Club in Chicago and served as its president. BTW invited her to attend the first meeting of the NNBL, where she was elected one of the vice-presidents.

She was an organizer for the NNBL in the Midwest. In Nov. 1900 she became the Chicago correspondent of the *Colored American Magazine* and wrote a monthly column on black affairs in Chicago.

3 Anna Thornton, born in Kentucky in 1856, was a "scalp specialist" according to the 1900 census. Her letterhead stationery described her business as: "MRS. A. THORNTON'S PARLOR OF DERMATOLOGY," specializing in scalp disorders and facial massage. The letterhead also stated: "CURES FOR ALL FACIAL BLEMISHES, Black Heads, Pimples, Freckles, Sallowness. Wrinkles prevented, and ladies advised how they may preserve a youthful appearance unto old age. Scrawny necks and busts Developed, and their faces restored to healthy beauty by Massage. Sulphur, Milk and other baths. You are invited to consult family physicians concerning my method of treatment." Mrs. Thornton sent her son Charles to Tuskegee Institute, where he was listed as a senior in the 1904–5 school catalog. (See Anna Thornton to BTW, Mar. 14, 1904, Con. 295, BTW Papers, DLC.)

4 Alice A. Casneau, a black woman, was born in Virginia in 1866. The 1900 census does not report her occupation, but shows her in the household of her husband, Elmer E. Casneau, a Boston barber.

5 Thomas Wellington Thurston, Jr., was born in West Virginia in 1866, and was ordained a Baptist minister in 1894. In 1895 he entered the field of silk manufacturing and established over the next decade mills in Columbia, Pa., Fayetteville, N.C., and Kinston, N.C. Later he became manager of the W. H. Ashley Silk Co. in North Carolina.

6 Gertrude Hood of Fayetteville, N.C., was the daughter of Bishop James Walker Hood, a distinguished clergyman of the A.M.E. Zion Church. During Reconstruction James Hood served in the North Carolina constitutional convention of 1868 and also held the post of superintendent of public instruction.

An Excerpt from the Journal
of Florence Ledyard Cross Kitchelt[1]

[New York City] April 3–1901

Last night went to dinner of the Social Reform Club[2] at Clarendon Hotel, given in honor of Mr. & Mrs. *Booker Washington*, both of whom spoke.[3] Mr. Chas. Sparr[4] spoke of Mr. Washington as the Benj. Franklin of his race — a splendid comparison, as they both are especially noted for their *common sense*. Mrs. Washington is lighter than he and has beautiful features, arched brows, blue (?) eyes, a Grecian nose, and a poise of the head like a Gibson girl. Her hands are white as mine and beautifully shaped. But her hair is kinky. Mr. W.'s speech was mostly from that he already has written in his biography. I hear he raised $47,000 — at the meeting at Madison Garden a few weeks ago.

AM Sophia Smith Collection MNS.

1 Florence Ledyard Cross Kitchelt, born in Rochester in 1874, was a graduate of Wells College. In the late 1890s she became a social worker, particularly among Italian immigrants. She also actively promoted trade unionism, woman suffrage, and socialism. From 1900 to 1902 she was with the College Settlement in New York City. Later she was the head social worker at the Little Italy House in Brooklyn for a year, and head social worker with the Italian settlement in Rochester from 1907 to 1910.

2 The Social Reform Club of New York City was founded in 1894 on the suggestion of Felix Adler that workingmen and representatives of other groups needed an organization to study the causes of the strikes of the early 1890s. Once organized, however, the club moved in another direction. It saw as its object "to consider, advocate, and forward such practical measures for the improvement of the industrial and social condition in the city of New York as can be undertaken in the immediate future with fair hope of success." Though many of the members were followers of Henry George, the single-tax advocate, the club's rules barred consideration of "general theories of society" and "social panaceas." Its members were required to have an active interest in the elevation of the wage-earner. They met on Tuesday evenings to discuss such questions as contract labor, municipal ownership of public utilities, tenement conditions, and so on.

3 The topic of the evening was "The Industrial Condition of the Negro." Besides the Washingtons, William H. Baldwin, Jr., and others spoke. In his address, BTW noted that the Negro often had difficulty in getting good treatment from his employers. He might even fail to get work despite an industrial education. Slavery had taught Negroes to despise labor, and in the early days of freedom they often looked on education as a way to escape from labor, he said. They were now changing, however, from being office-seekers to being taxpayers. (*Tuskegee Student*, 13 [Mar. 30, 1901], 2; New York *Times*, Apr. 3, 1901, 9.)

4 Charles Barzillai Spahr, a former president of the club.

From Pinckney Benton Stewart Pinchback[1]

Washington D.C., Apr 5, '01

Dear sir: Some days ago I received a letter from Mr. Charles Green, a general prisoner in the military prison at Alcatraz Cal., seeking my intercession with the government in his behalf, and he enclosed a letter from you dated March 18, 1901, as his warrant for writing to me. In your letter among other things you say: "I wish to refer you, however, to Hon. P. B. S. Pinchback, Washington D.C., who makes a specialty of handling such matters."

I am utterly amazed that you should write such a statement to that unfortunate fellow, or any one else, and you will pardon me if I ask upon what authority you wrote it? I am quite sure you are aware that I am not in criminal or any other kind of practice, and have been in practical retirement ever since I have resided in Washington, for I told you so myself the last time we met.

The statement is not only untrue but unkind to that unfortunate man, annoying to me, and unworthy of a man of your high standing in the country. I repeat, it utterly amazed me. Very respectfully,

P. B. S. Pinchback

ALS   Con. 207   BTW Papers   DLC.

1 Pinckney Benton Stewart Pinchback (1837–1921), a prominent figure in Louisiana Reconstruction, was born in Macon, Ga., to Eliza Stewart and her white master, William P. Pinchback. The Mississippi planter freed Eliza and her children and sent them north to Cincinnati, where Pinchback attended school. His father's death and the subsequent victory of white relatives in the contest over the paternal estate cut short the boy's formal education. Beginning as a cabin boy on Ohio riverboats, Pinchback became a steward on the luxury steamers cruising the Mississippi. In 1862 he ran the blockade at Yazoo City, reached New Orleans, and formed a Union Army company in the second regiment of Louisiana Native Guards. But in 1863 Pinchback resigned from the army to protest the unequal treatment of black soldiers.

Active in Reconstruction politics from the beginning, Pinchback was the only black in New Orleans to head a Republican ward club; he also served on the party's state committee from 1867 on. As a member of the 1867–68 constitutional convention, he drafted the new document's civil rights article. Elected to the state senate in the fall of 1868, he became president *pro tempore* in 1871, and acting lieutenant governor when the incumbent died. Thus, during Henry Clay Warmoth's impeachment, Pinchback served as acting governor of Louisiana for forty-three days in 1872–73. He had meanwhile run for Congress in the fall of 1872 and was declared the victor, but his Democratic opponent contested the election and ultimately won the seat. Pinchback's senatorial aspirations were similarly crushed. The Louisiana legislature elected him to the U.S. Senate in Jan. 1873; three years later, in a close vote, Congress decided against him.

Pinchback also served as a New Orleans school director from 1871 to 1877. The Redeemer governor in 1877 rewarded him for his accommodation to the new regime with a position on the state board of education. Pinchback represented Madison Parish in the 1879 state constitutional convention. The *Weekly Louisianian*, a black journal he had started in 1870, ceased publication in 1881. From 1882 to 1885, Pinchback was the surveyor of customs for the port of New Orleans. He then studied law for a year at Straight University (1887).

Worried by the deteriorating racial atmosphere, Pinchback founded the American Citizens' Equal Rights Association early in 1890, but the organization never flourished. About 1891 he moved north, first to New York City, where he worked briefly as a federal marshal, then to Washington, D.C., where he settled permanently. Pinchback practiced law for a time, then lived in semi-retirement in the national capital.

A close friend of Whitefield McKinlay in Washington, Pinchback was an adviser to BTW on national capital affairs and made frequent visits to the White House and to congressional committees in BTW's behalf, particularly in patronage matters.

From Barrett Wendell[1]

Harvard College, [Cambridge, Mass.] April 12, 1901

My dear Sir: Will you allow me to express the pleasure which your book, Up from Slavery, has given me. For about twenty years a teacher of English, and mostly of English Composition, I have become perhaps critical as to the matter of style. Certainly I have grown less and less patient of all writing which is not simple and efficient; and more and more of a style which does its work with simple, manly distinctness. It is hard to remember when a book, casually taken up, has proved, in this respect, so satisfactory as yours. No style could be more simple, more unobtrusive; yet few styles which I know seem to me more laden — as distinguished from overburdened — with meaning. On almost any of your pages, you say as much again as most of men would say in the space; yet you say it so simply and easily that one has no effort in reading. One is only surprised at the quiet power which can so make words do their work.

The story you tell is a stimulating one — a stirring new phase of the world — old per aspera ad astra. The chief reflection which it excites in me goes deep in human nature. By what might commonly be held a lucky chance, I have happened in this world to be singularly free from hardship. The most severe moral efforts I have known, then, have been those needful to keep me at work in spite of need. I wonder whether you yourself quite understand the great, if disguised, opportunity which has been yours. It is the needful effort which has strengthened you to pierce the hardships and see the star-light. Sincerely yours —

Barrett Wendell

TLSr Copy   BTW Papers   ATT.

[1] Barrett Wendell (1855–1921) taught English at Harvard from 1880 to 1921 and was influential over the whole field of English and American literature.

From Pinckney Benton Stewart Pinchback

Washington, D.C., April 12, 1901

My Dear Sir: Your favor of the 8th inst. received, explanation noted and accepted and I will close the incident on my part by saying: There was no offense in referring the man to me. I objected to the assertion, that, I made the "handling of such cases a specialty." I never handled such a case. It was a gross misrepresentation. Of course I do not believe that a wrong was intended and it may seem to you like making a "mountain of a mole hill" but I am extremely sensitive about being misrepresented for the following reasons: When the legislature of the State of Louisiana in January 1873 elected me United States Senator for the term beginning March 4, 1873 my political enemies and opponents determined to oppose my admission to the Senate and began a villainous and systematic attack on my personal character by hired mercenaries through the press of the country which for unadulterated mendacity never had a parallel in political history. These attacks which were kept up until my final defeat in the Senate by a vote of 31 noes to 29 yeas after a three year contest, charged me with nearly every crime in the decalogue and were replete with misrepresentations. And for years after, periodically, extraordinary stories, full of gross misrepresentations concerning me — which were not calculated to enhance my character — continued to make their appearance in some of the leading papers throughout the country. These misrepresentations shrouded me in mystery and beclouded my reputation to such an extent as to make an unfavorable impression of me upon many persons who never saw and knew nothing about me. I dare say you yourself were not entirely free from such an impression before we met. They have been not only a source of great annoyance but positive injury as well.

In the past, guided by pride and conscious of my rectitude, I have treated my defamers with silent contempt and trusted to the correcting agencies of time and the impartial historian of the future to "speak of me as I am"; but I fear this has been a mistaken course, for, even now, after the lapse of over a quarter of a century and standing the test of the searchlight of an unfriendly public press and when I am entering the borders of old age and nearing the dread command, "dust to dust," the baneful influence of the infamous work of my detractors still casts its shadows about me. Is it any wonder, then, that I am sensitive about being misrepresented?

I believed you were my friend. I am your friend. Of all men living you were the last one I could permit to misrepresent me without an emphatic protest. Hence my request for an explanation of your letter to that prisoner.

I have watched your career at Tuskegee from its inception, been concerned about the success of your work and sorry, as I have told you, that my limited fortune prevented me from attesting my friendship by financial assistance. I have, however, did the next best thing by publicly and privately commending you and your great undertaking. I rejoice over your success thus far and hope it may ever continue no matter what the status of our relations, which, I trust, however, will always be friendly. Yours very truly,

P. B. S. Pinchback

DICTATED

TLS Con. 207 BTW Papers DLC. Written on stationery of Whitefield McKinlay, real estate, loans, insurance, and notary public.

From Edward Dana Durand[1]

Washington, D.C., April 13, 1901

Dear Sir: The Industrial Commission has directed me to renew its request that you appear before it as a witness concerning conditions of the negroes in the South.[2] The Commission recognizes that you are very much occupied and that it has doubtless been impracticable for you to come to Washington hitherto in response to our request. I may say, however, that we expect to complete our testimony in the months of May and June, and that we are exceedingly anxious to have you give evidence before the close of the investigation. We have had very interesting testimony from a number of educators in the South. Among these have been President Wright, of the Georgia State Industrial College, President Dabney, of the University of Tennessee, Mr. Frisbee,[3] and various others. We feel that the importance of your work makes it exceedingly desirable that our reports should contain a description of it, which can be laid before Congress and distributed more or less widely through the country. The Commission is also anxious itself to have information and opinions from you as an aid in preparing its conclusions and recommendations.

Will you not accordingly try to arrange your plans so as to be in Washington at some time in May or June. We should prefer to hear you on some day between May 7th and 18th, but we could probably arrange for a hearing after May 18th. The regular June session will probably last from June 4th to the 22nd. If you can name a definite date in advance, we should be very glad; if not, we can arrange to hear you on very short notice if you will write or wire at our expense. While we do not wish to bring undue pressure upon you, we trust that you will consider this a matter of public duty. Very truly yours,

E. Dana Durand

TLS Con. 193 BTW Papers DLC.

1 Edward Dana Durand (1871–1960), an economist and statistician, was secretary of the U.S. Industrial Commission. From 1909 to 1913 he was director of the U.S. Census.

2 Apparently BTW did not appear before the U.S. Industrial Commission. In the final volume of the commission's report in 1902 are listed all those who testified, and BTW's name was not among them.

3 Probably Hollis Burke Frissell.

From Olivia Egleston Phelps Stokes

Summit N.J. April 15th 1901

My dear Mr Washington   In reference to the services at Tuskegee, I wanted to say that "Dorothy" is a name know[n] in our family for nearly three hundred years, we having had several grandmothers bearing the name and a sister Dora, for this reason my sister[1] had asked that the new building be known as Dorothy Hall,[2] and I was glad to write in the suggestion.

My sister intends making every effort to reach Tuskegee Monday about noon, though she fears other engagements will prevent her remaining more than a few hours.

I will ask you to telegraph me hour decided on for services in Chapel on Monday. I am exceedingly sorry not to be able to be present at the opening exercises of the new building, in which I am deeply interested. I trust the building will prove helpful and that perfect work done there will develope perfect character.

As there will be several clergymen in this party coming to Tuskegee whose words would be especially helpful to the young men preparing for the ministry I should be very glad if some opportunity was arranged for their speaking directly to these young men of Phelps Hall.

It has occurred to me that to [serve?] a meal in the large dining hall, if some table could be conveniently reserved for them there, might possibly be an interesting feature of a visit to Tuskegee.

With kind regards to Mrs Washington and yourself in which my sister joins   I am sincerely yours

Olivia E. P. Stokes

ALS   Con. 210   BTW Papers   DLC.

1 Caroline Phelps Stokes.

2 Dorothy Hall, the girls' industrial building at Tuskegee Institute, was dedicated on Apr. 22, 1901. The $15,000 brick building contained 535,000 bricks, all made at the school. In his remarks, the principal speaker, Dr. E. Winchester Donald, rector of Trinity Church of Boston, said the building was "the achievement of the brains, skill and muscle of the school itself," and that it exemplified "the national fame and public confidence, which are the secure possessions of the Institute to-day." Robert C. Ogden, John D. Rockefeller, Jr., Mr. and Mrs. William H. Baldwin, Jr., and Caroline Phelps Stokes were among those present, and Paul Laurence Dunbar, visiting Tuskegee at the time, wrote a special poem for the occasion. (*Tuskegee Student*, 13 [Apr. 27, 1901], 1, 3, 4.)

From William Edward Burghardt Du Bois

Atlanta, Ga., April 17 1901

Dear Mr. Washington: Mr. Mosely[1] of the Inter-State Commerce Commission has advised me to retain Mr. W. C. Martin,[2] a colored lawyer of 503⅓ D St. N.W., Washington, for my interstate commerce case & to bring it thus to a regular trial with sworn witnesses &c. What do you think of this?[3] Do you know Martin? I shall write for his charges — I do not want to get too deeply involved financially. Very Sincerely,

W. E. B. Du Bois

ALS Con. 195 BTW Papers DLC.

1 Edward Augustus Moseley (1846–1911), the first secretary of the Interstate Commerce Commission, was a lawyer and former member of the Massachusetts legislature. Moseley was an expert on railroad safety practices, and wrote several works on the subject. He also helped draft Cuban railway laws and was appointed by Theodore Roosevelt as assistant recorder of the Anthracite Coal Strike Commission.

2 William C. Martin was born in Virginia in 1857.

3 On a letter of Du Bois to BTW on the same subject (May 16, 1901, Con. 195, BTW Papers, DLC), Scott penciled a note, presumably at Washington's dictation: "will help if go ahead." Apparently after a few preliminary steps Du Bois did not pursue the case. (See Du Bois to BTW, Nov. 22, 1902, below.)

An Account of a Speech in Atlanta[1]

Atlanta, Ga. [Apr. 21, 1901]

Professor Booker T. Washington was introduced to follow Dr. Frissell. In the introduction Dr. Proctor stated that some time ago when Professor Washington came to this city he had been compelled to ride all night in half a smoking car because of the intense race prejudice and that when he arrived in this city he was unfit for any exertion and unfit for appreciation of the honors that had been paid him.

"I came from Tuskegee to Atlanta in a Pullman car," said Professor Washington to begin with. He referred pleasantly to the efforts of his white friends in his behalf, and then continued:

"I came here for two reasons. The first was to welcome Mr. Ogden and his party to the south and to thank him, and the gentlemen with him, for their courtesy and kindness and to show them that their efforts on behalf of the negro are appreciated. Besides this I am here for a selfish reason. A few weeks ago Mr. Ogden told me his party would spend a day in this city and, therefore, I come now to be sure that the party gets out of Atlanta. Atlanta is interested in all parts of the world, but is mostly interested in Atlanta."

Here to Live It Out

Referring to the negro question, he said: "Some time ago I heard it said that the negro is going back, fast going back, to barbarism. I see no signs of barbarism here. After seeing this remarkable assembly I see no reason for forming a negro state, as has been spoken of. I think we have about made up our minds to settle down here and live it out. We have religion enough and patriotism enough."

Following this utterance there was a remarkable outburst of applause from the congregation. It continued for a minute before it was stopped, when Professor Washington raised his hand and said reverently: "This is church."

"Sometimes," he continued, "it may be that we don't go forward fast enough to please us, but I believe that God in His own way will work out this problem to please all. We are slowly but surely learning. Compare this assembly with conditions in the south forty or fifty years ago. This meeting would have been impossible. This meeting alone proves that we are going upward and forward."

Professor Washington closed with an appeal to all for less prejudice, more fellow feeling between races and more mutual help. Several times he was interrupted by applause, an unusual demonstration in church, and was forced to stop his hearers by raising his hand.

Atlanta *Constitution*, Apr. 22, 1901, 1.

1 The Atlanta *Constitution* described the interracial meeting held in the black First Congregational Church as "one of the most remarkable ever held in the South." Prominent whites had front-row reserved seats but the overflow crowd forced people to sit where they could find room. "The color line, for the time being at least, was completely obliterated," the *Constitution* reported. The meeting featured, in addition to BTW, Charles H. Parkhurst, J. L. M. Curry, William H. Baldwin, Jr., and Hollis B. Frissell. Parkhurst told the audience that this was the first time he had spoken to a congregation including blacks. "When it comes to the resurrection," he said, "I presume we will all be the same color." (Atlanta *Constitution*, Apr. 22, 1901, 1.)

The meeting was part of Robert C. Ogden's tour of the South with thirty-five industrialists and philanthropists in a special six-car train. The Conference for Education in the South had met at Winston-Salem, N.C., Apr. 18–20, 1901. After this stop in Atlanta the group went on to Tuskegee.

From Theodore Roosevelt

Oyster Bay, N.Y., April 23rd, 1901

My dear Mr. Washington: I have your letter of the 20th inst. Your invitation is very attractive. Would you need me to give you a definite answer now? The time that would be most convenient for me would be immediately after election — that is about November 12th. Would that suit you? Sincerely yours,

Theodore Roosevelt

TLS Con. 208 BTW Papers DLC. Written on stationery of the Vice-President's Chamber, Washington, D.C.

From Belton Gilreath[1]

Birmingham Ala   At Home   April 24/1901

My Dear Sir   I received your letter some days ago & have been waiting to answer untill such time as I could write soundly. I am as before stated anxious to do something to help you in your work. I am not certain that my motives are of the highest. I sometimes fear that pride and desire for praise of men is lurking behind my actions. I have held my self back in great measure because of this distrust of my self or motives. But I cannot get the matter off my mind & feel now that, as I will have to deal with the matter sooner or later; it is probably better to take it up at on[c]e; *gradually* at least.

I desire for this district to buy a lot of your books & to raise some money for your school. Enough at least at the start to get them interested in your institution, *and* to take a pride in it & look on it as our own. I beleive that I can get the large Coal & Iron operators to cooperate & am forming some plans in my mind which I would like to discuss with you before putting them into effect.

I have been thinking of going to Tuskeegee to see you *but* have not been able to get off. It has occurred to me this morning to get Dr Pettiford or some prominent Colored friend of mine to go to see you and lay my plans before you, *for* your consideration and suggestions. What do you think of this, & when & where could he see you if you approve of the idea.

I have finished reading your book & I enjoyed it & it was more interesting than any book I have ever read with the single exception of part of the life of Abraham Lincoln. He too is my ideal Saint.

I desire to mention also that I was much impressed with the character of Dr Armstrong,[2] *as* pictured by you. My deepest love & sympathies (like his), are for the struggling poor whites & blacks of the South.

I am running 3 mines with large number of both classes of them working there & I have built them school & churches & never loose an opportunity to give them my time and money wherever I feel that I can be of real service to them.

But I must now close, *as* I will have to leave for one of the mines in a few hours. This letter is written very hastily from my library at home and in my own hand as an evidence of my sincerity & love. Tru[ly] yours

Belton Gilreath

ALS Con. 198 BTW Papers DLC.

[1] Belton Gilreath of Birmingham was one of BTW's most outspoken southern white admirers and with a $500 gift the largest southern contributor to Tuskegee before 1907. He was the president and general manager of the Gilreath Coal and Iron Co., which operated two mines in Jefferson and Walker counties. Sincerely interested in black education, he established schools at both of his mines. In his efforts to raise money for Tuskegee in Birmingham, he gave away many copies of *The Future of the American Negro* to friends and business acquaintances. He followed BTW's lead in many matters, joining the American Peace Society, serving on the Anna T. Jeanes Foundation, and contributing to the Republican campaign in 1908. He was a trustee of Tuskegee Institute from 1907 until after BTW's death.

[2] Samuel Chapman Armstrong.

To J. L. Nichols and Company

[Tuskegee, Ala.] April 26, 1901

Dear Sirs: Please forgive me for my delay in answering your letter of April 18th. We have had a large number of important visitors here during the last two or three days and they have occupied all of my time. I am very glad to hear that you have sold so large a number of the copies of my book.

In regard to the Outlook advertisement I have this to say. I have a very strong feeling that in the end it pays from a business standpoint as well as from other points of view to do nothing that might in any way indicate that one was trying to give the wrong impression. When I prepared the "Story of My Life and Work" for you I was aware of the fact that you did your business mainly if not wholly through agents and that your main territory for the sale of my book would be in the South among the colored and white people, consequently my book was written for those readers, I mean the colored and white people in the South.[1] A book to be effective[?] is very much like an address; if it is prepared for one audience and then delivered to another it becomes non-effective and non-interesting. The book which you published was not prepared for Northern and Eastern readers where the Outlook mainly circulates, and to have it circulated in these localities places me in rather an awkward position and brings criticism, a statement which several letters I have already received will confirm. The advertisement which you proposed placing in The Outlook and which has already been placed in several other publications is to my mind misleading in that it seeks to give the readers of The Outlook the impression that the book which you have published is made up from the series of papers which have passed through The Outlook, and I cannot get the consent of my conscience to give my assent to any such misleading of the public. The line which I quote from your advertisement, "now in book form" is especially likely to mislead the public and will do both yourself and myself an injustice. Doubleday, Page & Co., who have published "Up from Slavery," made an early application to me to be permitted to sell their book through agents and I refused telling them that I felt quite sure that this would be an injustice to you. I am just as much interested in the sale of your book as I am in the sale of "Up from Slavery" but at the same time I cannot agree to anything that I do not think is absolutely proper. Yours truly

[Booker T. Washington]

TLp   Con. 282A   BTW Papers   DLC.

[1] John A. Hertel of the Nichols firm wrote to BTW: "The fact that you wrote THE STORY OF MY LIFE AND WORK expressly, as your letter seems to imply, for the

southern people is *news to us*. Our contract does not intimate anything of this kind and if an important thing of this kind was intended it would certainly, it appears to us, have been brought out in the terms of our agreement. If that was your original intention and idea in writing for us this book you made a serious mistake." He also told BTW, "It would be a gross injustice to us and a violation of the terms of our contract for you to authorize Doubleday, Page & Co. to sell their book by subscription. These people have written us this morning again intimating that we should confine our advertisements to the Southern States and they even go so far as to dictate the price at which we should sell." ([ca. Apr. 30, 1901], Con. 205, BTW Papers, DLC.)

From Jabez Lamar Monroe Curry

Washington, D.C. April 26, 1901

My dear Sir: The pressure of your engagements which you met with such success, and the hurry of leaving, prevented me from thanking you for sending for me to Chehaw, and for the kind letter you wrote, and the kinder acts you did with reference to Major Curry.

The Conference at Winston, and the excursion were a wonderful success. I must say that I never had a week away from home, of more delightful enjoyment. The high character of the men and women, the unusual intelligence, their enthusiasm and spirit with which they entered into every thing, made the week an era in the life of all of the company. I need not say that their visit to the Institute was one of the chiefest pleasures. Please accept assurances of my increasing regard, and believe me, Yours sincerely,

J.L.M.Curry

TLS Con. 194 BTW Papers DLC.

From Charles Waddell Chesnutt

Cleveland, O. April 27, 1901

My dear Mr. Washington: Permit me to congratulate you on the cordial reception which the press & the public have given your autobiography. It is worthy of all praise, has made you many friends, and I hope may make you some money; for I believe the laborer is worthy of his hire.

As I came along up from my visit to the South — I am only just now recovering from the illness I contracted in your interesting section — I mentioned to a great Washington daily certain things I had learned about William Hannibal Thomas. They, rather carelessly, published them. Thomas asked them for the source of their information; they fell back on me, and I set on foot certain inquiries which resulted as set out in the enclosed statement, to which, by the way, I have called the attention of Thomas's publishers, raising the question whether they fully appreciated certain statements in the book, and whether publishing ethics or common decency ever demanded the withdrawal of a book from sale. My correspondence with them has been on the quiet, as I do not intend to advertise the book thereby.

I know that your own work absorbs most of your time; but you will undoubtedly be met by questions raised by this book. I do not know a better answer to any disputed statement in the book than to say that the word of Thomas, at least, can have no weight one way or the other, since he is a man without character & not entitled to credit. This information, if you do not possess it already, will enable you to make that statement. My regards to Mrs. Washington. It is pleasing to note the recent honors of which you have both been the recipients. Cordially yours,

C. W. Chesnutt

ALS Con. 223 BTW Papers DLC.

From James Nathan Calloway

Lome   Togo W.Africa   April 30. '01.

Dear sir   Your letter of Mar 1st with Mr Baldwin's inclosed reached me by recent mail. I am glad you gave me this notice of the lost part. I should not have missed it until I unpacked our gin next autumn. Now it will reach us in time for our use. We have left the gin at the coast for the present.

Our horses and oxen have begun to work quite well now. We will leave the coast tomorrow with our wagons loaded with cotton seed and iron. The road has been especially prepared for our wagons and are very good from here to Plantation. I have written Berlin Komitee to forward instructions to Mr. Baldwin concerning the condenser. They will take up the matter. The young men are quite well at present. Mr. Burks does not keep so strong as the rest of us. Our work looks quite promising at present and we believe that we will make cotton. To the present time we have had very little rain. We hope the climate is better than we at first thought. We are planting some cotton now but will plant most of our crop in May and June.

With best regards to your family   I am yours

Jas. N. Calloway

ALS   Con. 213   BTW Papers   DLC.

From John Elmer Milholland

"Pentwynn"   Freshwater Bay, Isle of Wight. April 30th, 1901

Confidential

My Dear Mr. Washington, I think I told you at one of our interviews that for the last two or three years I have been trying to find the right man to go through the South for the purpose of writing the situation there as it actually exists at present. I wanted a man big enough to grasp the question comprehensively, energetic enough to gather the enormous mass of data required, scientific enough to classify this data properly, and with sufficient insight to interpret the matter aright. To you it would be superfluous to elaborate this point. You know what has to be done; you understand the various factors that enter into the problem, and hence the difficulty there is in securing one brainy enough and yet so judicially minded as to make the work profitable and effective.

I thought I had the right man in New York, and I was about to send him into the South, but I found that, after all, his point of view was not satisfactory. You suggested Professor Bryce,[1] and we are both still favorably disposed towards him, but whether he will go or not I am unable to say. I think he will dine with me in a few days, and perhaps I can then tell better. But time has become a very important factor in the case. I wonder if you really appreciate this sentence. Do you realise that the opportunity is at hand to do more towards a satisfactory settlement of the Southern question than has been afforded in years? I refer of course to Gorman's[2] reckless work in Maryland, and how it has brought home to the people of the United States the true inwardness of this cruel crusade against the Negro. A reaction is at hand; the public mind which has been impassive, if not impervious, to all appeals on this question of late years will be as wax when Congress gets together, assuming the Republican programme to be carried out. The people will listen. Have we our story ready to tell? That is what I am seeking for now with more zeal than I have at any time during the last few years, and I do not think I have been idle or indifferent.

A few weeks ago, I met at Bishop Colenzo's son's[3] house a Mr. Tobias, whom I believe you know. He talked so intelligently, so progressively, and with so much originality that I asked him to dine with me the following week. He came. I suggested that he go into the South and gather the material. He took time to consider it; dined with me again in London last week, and agreed to decide the question on Saturday. I enclose his decision. You will notice he does not see his way to go, and while I thoroughly respect his position, I am a little disappointed; disappointed because the time is short.

Now what can you do in this matter? Can you not, with your wide acquaintanceship, find me the right man or men? I offered to pay Tobias' expenses while he was doing the work, no matter how long it required, I am ready to do the same for any man who can do the work properly but I want to get at *facts*, I want to know all about the convict labor question, the chain gangs, the way in which the census returns work unjustly in regard to the crime statistics, the partisan bias of parties and juries, *the real facts*, the thousand and one matters pertaining to lynchings, the progress, the prosperity and the poverty of the people, and so forth, and so forth.

What have you to suggest in the matter? We ought to get this data together and the book published before Congress assembles in December. Can it not be done? And if not, why not? The hour has come to accomplish a great work; *we must do it.* The obstacles in the way are only things to be overcome.

Another matter: I have been on the point of writing to Mr. Baldwin, your treasurer in New York. I have begun to think very highly of him, but I have never met him personally, and perhaps he might not understand my suggestion, which is that a special effort be made to raise enough money to take care of Tuskegee Institute, and so give you a free hand towards organising similar institutes throughout the Southern States. It is absurd to keep you running round the country with your hat in your hand for the sake of half a million dollars. I have a practical suggestion to make on this point, which I think can be as successfully carried out as was another that I had the honor of suggesting two years ago along other lines.

Your friends, Mr. & Mrs. Unwin are very well, and heartily reciprocate your kind expressions. I was dining there the other night with the Committee representing the Pan-African Association. I found the organization was in rather a bad shape for lack of funds and proper management. Having in mind what you said, I suggested that they identify themselves with this great International Union which we have started over here, and which I think is ultimately to be a great factor in human affairs. I think I sent you a pamphlet about it. I send you another, under separate cover. I will talk more about this when I see you, because it has a direct bearing upon our Southern problem.

Your purchase of the 80 acres of land near the school is, to my mind, a very sensible step. It enables you to keep an eye on the experiment when you come to try it.

I am glad my farmer is a practical man. Sanctified common sense is one of the precious attributes that we appreciate more and more as we get along in life. I have every confidence in his success. When I visit your Institute, as I hope to when I return in a few weeks or months, you must bring me into relations with this young man. Of course I should feel terribly cut up if my friend Cockran's farmer should prove the better of the two.

Finally, you understand that I do not expect you to be personally identified with this work that I want to do in the Southern States. I want you to get me a man, or men, and I want to give the press of the country *facts, facts, facts!*

Write me at my London address until June. I am down here at the Isle of Wight for a short time to enable Mrs. Milholland to recover from a very severe illness. Sincerely yours,

Jno. E. Milholland

P.S. What you tell me about money going into the South in big blocks for Educational purposes is most gratifying. But you must spend it — JEM

TLS Con. 1 BTW Papers DLC.

1 James, Lord Bryce.

2 Arthur Pue Gorman (1839–1906) controlled the Democratic party in Maryland from 1872, when he became president of the Chesapeake and Ohio Canal Co., until his death. He was U.S. senator from 1881 to 1899 and from 1903 to 1906. Gorman strongly endorsed a Maryland election law in 1901 providing for a secret ballot on the ground that it would prevent Republicans from aiding illiterate voters at the polls. Gorman argued that "the colored population has had ample opportunity to learn to read and write . . . and if after these years of honest effort on the part of the white people in supporting these schools at their own expense there are, as is claimed, 26,000 of them who cannot read or write the fault can only be attributed to their lack of desire to obtain knowledge. If they prefer to remain in ignorance there is no way to compel them to learn, unless the incentive to vote may hereafter encourage them to attend the schools." (Baltimore *Sun*, Apr. 1, 1901, 7.) Gorman conducted an openly racist campaign for election to the U.S. Senate in 1902, using a campaign button depicting BTW and Roosevelt at dinner as an example of what could be expected of the Republican party.

3 John William Colenso (1814–83) was the Anglican bishop of Natal from 1853 until his death. The son referred to here was probably Francis E. Colenso, who resided in England, rather than his other son, Dr. Robert Colenso, who lived in Durban, Natal, after 1880.

To Wallace A. Rayfield[1]

[Tuskegee, Ala.] April 30, 1901

Mr. Rayfield: One of the members of the Executive Council reports that he met you smoking on the streets on the public road not far from one of the school buildings a few evenings ago. I hardly need to say that such conduct is contrary to the rules and wishes of the school. The policy of the school is to have no smoking on the part of teachers or students on or near the school grounds or in town.

Booker T. Washington

TLpS Con. 282A BTW Papers DLC.

1 Wallace A. Rayfield taught architectural and mechanical drawing in the industrial department at Tuskegee from 1899 to 1908.

From George Foster Peabody

New York City. May 2, 1901

My dear Mr. Washington: While at Waycross waiting between trains I took a drive with a very bright mulatto, who gave me his name as James Murdock, and his residence as 21 James street, Waycross, Georgia. He said that he was only 16 years old, as he understood it, but I think he must be over 20. He seems to be a capable business man, as he has already saved money with which he bought the house he lives in, and another which he rents, six acres of land being included. He owns a hack and a couple of little horses which he takes care of, and is evidently wide awake and keen respecting money matters. He told me that he has a young sister and an older brother, the latter married. I suggested to him that when his sister is a little older he make inquiry respecting her going to Tuskegee and getting a suitable education. I was the more impressed with this because I fear he is in a fair way to have his morals permanently upset, particularly respecting the proper use of property; for I fancy that his good wages, (he told me he was able to make $35 a week) are in large part because of his being so fully aware that many traveling men who stop over at such places pay larger prices to be taken to immoral houses. This was particularly impressed upon me because he asked me if I wanted to go to a "sporting house" when I told him I wanted to drive around the place.

I do not know whether you have an organization which would reach out for such a young man as this, but if there is anyone near there who could get hold of this young man and have him study nights and realize the moral basis of life, I believe he has some capacity for usefulness. Yours very truly,

George Foster Peabody

TLS Con. 206 BTW Papers DLC.

From James Earl Russell[1]

New York   May 4th, 1901

My dear Mr. Washington: In reply to your letter of the 27th inst I want to extend to you a very hearty invitation to spend a day or two with me in order that we may go over the ground covered in your letter more thoroughly. Please let me know when you are coming to the city so that I can arrange to be as free as possible at the time.

Meanwhile, however, let me say that I was intensely interested in your work. It is certainly a great inspiration to anyone to see what you have accomplished in the past 20 years and to note how excellent is the foundation which you have laid. The industrial side of your work appealed to me very strongly. You certainly have fine ideas of what to do and how to do it, and I want to add my testimony to the many congratulations you have justly deserved from this work.

There are, however, some phases of your work which did not impress me so favorably. Your academic work is certainly considerably behind the industrial; not that you have poorer teachers necessarily, because you have some very excellent teachers in this department, but rather because of a lack of coördination and of adaptability to the needs of your pupils. You have, as most schools have, a good many teachers who do not know how to teach, but what is the more noticeable is the fact that you apparently have no one who is able to bring these poorer teachers up to a satisfactory standard and to harmonize the work of all departments in such a way as to make it efficient. You need a strong organizer in this department who shall know his trade as thoroughly as the men do who are responsible for your industrial department.

As for your normal department, I think that is very bad. When I get the chance I want to tell you how I think you can apply in this work precisely the same ideas you are using in your trade work. The art of teaching must be acquired by your teachers in precisely the same manner as the art of blacksmithing. You do not ask your blacksmith apprentice to rely exclusively upon a few lessons in the class room, nor are you satisfied with his skill as a mechanic after sending him to the shop to observe the work of some one else. No more can you make teachers after this fashion. You have an opportunity, I am sure, of doing the same thing for those who are to be teachers that you do for those who are engaging in trades, and I am sure that a plan can be devised whereby the necessary time can be found in addition to the necessary subjects of the academic and industrial course.

I beg you will not misunderstand my criticisms. I speak frankly because I have every reason to believe you are in a position to overcome these defects. Some other schools that I visited would seem to me to be almost beyond hope. You are doing a magnificent work, and because it has in it real vitality I know it will grow and overcome any minor defects that may now be apparent.

Please give my kindest regards to Mrs. Washington and to Dr. Kenniebrew who entertained us so kindly during our stay at Tuskegee. I am   Very sincerely yours,

Jas. E. Russell

TLS   Con. 208   BTW Papers   DLC.

[1] James Earl Russell (1864–1945) was dean of Teachers College of Columbia University from 1897 to 1927.

From Robert Curtis Ogden

New York, May 6, 1901

Dear Mr. Washington: Your favor of May 1st, and the clippings concerning Gov. Candler's alleged remarks are very interesting.[1] He has denied the violent utterances; nevertheless correspondence that comes to me from many directions indicates that there are some people who think that he was intoxicated when he made the remarks, and others that do not credit the denial.

I am sorry for the denial or recantation. To my mind nothing could be finer than some such utterances on the part of the ignorant and prejudiced element of the South, that the wise, conservative and progressive people would be compelled to combat and oppose. The best people in the Southern country have no common standing ground. Such opposition as Gov. Candler's, would compel them to integrate and cohere and thus develop a sound public opinion.

I know perfectly well that if Gov. Candler did make the remarks attributed to him, he did not represent the best intelligence and refinement of his section of the country. I am not in the least disturbed. A better day is coming, and its dawn is very near. Yours very truly,

Robert C. Ogden

TLS Con. 205 BTW Papers DLC.

1 The Atlanta *Constitution*, Apr. 25, 1901, 2, reported that Governor Allen D. Candler said that he was opposed to "the use of Yankee money for the education of the Negro," and that he did not think much of Ogden's party of northern philanthropists. He said that BTW was "a good negro," and he understood that it was in BTW's interest to gain the support of wealthy northerners. "I do not believe," Candler said, "in the higher education of the darky." He thought that blacks should receive only industrial education, for "when he is taught the fine arts he gets educated above his caste and it makes him unhappy."

From Martin Grove Brumbaugh[1]

San Juan Porto Rico   May 7th, 1901

My dear Sir: The Legislature of Porto Rico has recently made provision to send from this Island to your school and to Hampton, Va., and to other similar institutions, twenty boys and girls, who will be able to leave this Island as soon after July 1st. as you advise in view of the conditions at your school. How many of these twenty can you receive, and at what cost per capita, and under what conditions would you be willing to accept them? It is my desire to send as many to you as you can conveniently accommodate, as I believe you are doing the best work for the colored race that is now being done anywhere in the United States.

It has occurred to me that in order to break up their Spanish language we might scatter some of them into other similar institutions; upon this subject, however, I am not clear and I write to you in perfect frankness for your advice. Would you recommend any other schools besides your own and Hampton for these colored children? If so, will you be kind enough to give me the name and address of such institutions in order that I can take up the question with them?

I write thus frankly to you because I know that you have the interests of the race at heart and my whole purpose is to do the largest good for these twenty children.

Awaiting your immediate reply, I am, Very sincerely yours,

M. G. Brumbaugh

ALS Con. 189 BTW Papers DLC.

[1] Martin Grove Brumbaugh (1862–1930) was the first U.S. commissioner of education of Puerto Rico, serving from 1900 to 1902. A graduate of Juniata College, he studied at Harvard and Jena and received a Ph.D. from the University of Pennsylvania. Among his principal public offices were superintendent of the Philadelphia public schools (1906–15), Republican governor of Pennsylvania (1915–19), and president of Juniata College (1895–1906, 1924–30).

From John Eaton

Washington, D.C., May 11, 1901

My dear Sir: I have just finished reading "Up From Slavery," and am much pleased with its unaffected naturalness. Its style is excellent; it gives yourself; fiction cannot approach it. It realizes what I have long desired, the life of a colored man of merit, rising above all difficulties described, in a realistic, unaffected manner; you have given both. You have furnished the needed example, and you have described it in a style that must receive approval. Since, in the fall of 1862, Grant ordered me to care for the colored people coming within his lines in northern Mississippi, I have felt that the colored man, for his encouragement needed such an example before him; indeed, that both white and colored needed this solution of life, and its description in literature.

I look to see great results from it, and trust the Lord will guide you, and help you, and that his better plans for your race may not be interrupted. Sincerely yours,

John Eaton

TLS Con. 272 BTW Papers DLC.

From John C. Burrowes[1]

Charlotte, N.C., May 12, 1901

Dear Sir: Yours of the 1st instant relative to granting Mr. H. G. Maberry permission to ride on Dining Cars for the purpose of observing methods of serving, etc., he rendering such services as he can to cover cost of being on train. Please note attached letter from Mr. Chas. A. Wickersham President and General Manager of the A. & W.P. R.R. and the Western Ry. of Ala. Note particularly what he says in case accident, railroad cannot be held responsible for any injury that might be sustained. Kindly advise me on this line and I will send letter for Mr. Maberry to present to Conductor of Dining Car running between Atlanta and Montgomery. I think that this will be the best car for him to ride on for reason that we serve Breakfast a la carte and Dinner table d'hote, and he will be able to get a good idea of both kinds of service. You will understand why I did not reply to your letter before, reason being that this was a matter I had to take up with Mr. Wickersham, and time has been consumed in this way.

We will be glad to assist this young man in any way that we can. I note that your letter is addressed to Pullman Dining Car Service. I will ask leave to correct this point, noting heading above. Yours truly,

Jno. C. Burrowes

TLS Con. 261 BTW Papers DLC.

[1] John C. Burrowes was the superintendent of dining cars for the Southern Railway Co. in Charlotte, N.C.

From Jesse Lawson

Washington, D.C. May 13, 1901

My dear Sir: I send you one hundred and fifty copies of The Washington Post[1] of this date containing an article by myself relative to the work of testing the validity of the Louisiana constitution of 1898.

Senator McEnery's[2] letter, quoted in the article above referred to, makes the Democrats in the U.S. Senate committed to the view that the "grandfather clause" is unconstitutional.

Our lawyers are not willing that we publish in the newspapers just what they have done, nor the method employed by them in getting at the issue for fear that it might make it more difficult for them to get the matter through the courts in Louisiana.

Hoping that you are well, and that I may hear from you at your convenience, I remain, Yours truly,

Jesse Lawson

TLS Con. 203 BTW Papers DLC. Written on stationery of the headquarters of the National Afro-American Council.

[1] Lawson's letter to the editor condemned the grandfather clause of the Louisiana Constitution and reported that the National Afro-American Council would test the provision before the Supreme Court. He wrote that blacks would accept voting qualifications if they applied equally to whites and blacks. (Washington *Post*, May 13, 1901, 10.)

[2] Samuel Douglas McEnery (1837–1910), a former governor and judge in Louisiana, was U.S. senator from 1897 to 1910. Jesse Lawson's letter to the Washington *Post* quoted from a letter that McEnery had written to the New Orleans *Times-Democrat* in 1898 in which the senator had declared that the grandfather clause was unconstitutional and that, if adopted, it would cause Louisiana to lose representation in Congress.

To J. L. Nichols and Company

[Tuskegee, Ala.] May 14, 1901

Dear Sirs: Complying with my promise to write you further upon my return to Tuskegee. I will not take up in detail all of the points raised in your correspondence as my letter from New York seemed to cover them pretty well, but I think we might as well understand each other on this point, that no threats of withholding the royalties or anything of that kind will have the least bearing upon my actions pro or con. I intend to do the proper thing by you and would stand by a promise just as faithfully if no royalty were involved as if royalty were involved.

In order to refresh your memory as to whether or not I am simply trying to gouge you or anybody else for the sake of getting money,

I remind you of the following points: In the first place, I suffered you to charge $1.50, $2.00 and $2.75 for the book when the contract said the book was to be sold at $1.00. This you understand reduced my royalty very materially. Secondly, when a firm in Chicago brought out a book in which I had written a chapter bearing upon the conduct of the Negro soldiers in the Spanish-American War, a subject which had no relation whatever to our contract, and when this firm tried to deceive the public by making it believe that this book was written by me, at my own expense I hired a lawyer and had this deception stopped. Third, later on you made another request that I permit my royalty to be reduced to 4 cents in order [to] enable you to make a special sale of 2,000 copies of the book. This [I] consented to do. It seems to me that this action on my part might indicate to you clearly that I am not actuated by selfish or mere financial considerations.

If you get hold of any specific instances in the future showing that Doubleday, Page & Co. are selling my book by subscription I wish you would let me know and I will place the matter clearly before the firm. I feel quite sure that this firm will be guided by my wishes in the matter. Yours truly,

Booker T. Washington

TLpS   Con. 282A   BTW Papers   DLC.

From Shepherd Lincoln Harris

Lome, Togo West Africa, May 15, 190[1]

My Dear Principal: More than one time I have thought of leting you hear from me, but I have been puting it off until now.

We left America as you know on the 3rd., third of Oct. last for the above named place. After many hard ships on the ocean we at last got to the long looked for place where we saw and are still seeing strange things.

As for my work here I am geting along very well. I find it very hard here to get matirial to work with. This country like all other unsettled countries is yet without modern machinery, the saw mill, the cotton gin and in fact all of them yet to be introduced, some of which we hope to have in operation before our time is out here, or before [we] come away.

Whe[n] we reached Lome we thought we were at the end of our journey, but we had yet 100 miles to go in the "bushes" as they call it here. It may sound hard, but a part of us had to walk this distance carrying with us such things as we thought would supply our needs until we could get settled. The trip was made in (4) four days.

By the 14th of Jan. we had about settled where our farm is now, or where we thought then we would try to make it. We began work on the clearing away with the help of the natives, and in a short while the site for our new home was selected.

I know to some it will sound like too much praise, but since we have been here, we have done more and better work than any other company here at work. There are a good many here. Some doing the same kind of work we are doing, and others doing different things, but all those who know any thing about either put our work in the lead.

We have cleared away more than 100 acres of land, and a part of the same is planted in cotton, corn, peanuts and other things, and some of the cotton has more fruit on it now than many of the farmers will make on their whole crops in America. There is no doubt about the growing of cotton here, for it has been demonstrated already. Six months ago the place where men were seen to pass and not even turn their heads; for it was nothing but a field of bushes and elephant grass — but to day one is attracted at the number of buildings, the growing of cotton, and other products, also the pulling of plows by horses and men guiding them.

While Mr. Burks & Robinson are busy with their farm I am at work trying to get the gin house ready to gin the cotton when it is gathered. In front of the shop on this cut will be seen a part of the gin house and other things I made by the help of these young men on the picture.

I find the Natives like to work and will work if they get plenty of "chop" as they call it, but they are not able to do much hard work. They soon give out.

I feel safe in saying that we all are doing all that there is in our power to reflect credit upon our race in America, and above all; credit upon Tuskegee our dear old Al.

I hope some one will be ready to come take my place, for when my time is out or soon as I can I hope to come home.

Our health has been very good, but we have a little sic[k]ness some times. The rainy season has started which will last six months the people say.

I will send a small contribution to the school soon as I can make it posible to do so.

Messrs Burks, Robinson and Mr. Calloway wish to be remembered.

Remember me very kindly to Mrs. Washington. I remain most truly,

S. L. Harris

ALS Con. 199 BTW Papers DLC. An edited version of this letter appeared in the *Tuskegee Student*, 13 (July 13, 1901), 3.

From George T. Robinson[1]

Nashville, Tenn. May 17 1901

My kind Sir: Your kind favor of the 14 received for which I thank you very much. I believe with your endorsement, together with others, I will land.

I am reading your autobiography with much interest. My early experience was very similar to your early ones. I only wish the similarity were kept up to this day. But you have out stripped us all. I congratulate you and my prayer is that you may soar still higher. I count myself fortunate to be able to number you among my friends. Your readiness in complying with my request begets a deeper interest in you on my part. I rejoice that the files of my paper, The *Nashville Citizen*, show some complimentary things about you, and that your likeness adorns its pages more than once. You occupy a very high place in my estimation. I wish your name was Washington T. Booker, as there was an illustrius Washington before your day. As it is, we sometimes have to explain which one is meant.

We can't say we have had only *one Washington*, but if it were otherwise, we could say we have only one Booker.

Howeve[r], all America is proud of Washington the 2nd, just

the same — the man more highly honored than any Negro America ever produced.

God bless you, your family and your great work. I pray that your sons may prove worthy of their illustrius sire.

I have the honor to be yours truly

Geo. T. Robinson

ALS Con. 208 BTW Papers DLC.

1 George T. Robinson, a black lawyer and editor of Nashville, was born in Kentucky in 1854.

An Address at the Dexter Avenue Baptist Church

[Montgomery, Ala., May 19, 1901]

The subject of which I am going to speak to you for a few minutes, "The Gospel of Service," may not on first hearing strike a very popular chord, but when I assure you that I have nothing but the highest and best interest of the race at heart in speaking to you upon this subject I believe that I shall have your confidence.

The word "service" has been too often misunderstood, and has consequently carried with it a meaning in too many cases indicating degradation. Every individual in some capacity serves another or should do so. Christ said he who would become greatest of all must become the servant of all; that is, he meant that in proportion as one renders service he becomes great. The President of the United States is a servant of the people because he serves them; the Governor of Alabama is a servant because he renders service to the people; the greatest merchant in Montgomery is a servant because he renders service to his customers; the school teacher is a servant because it is his duty to serve the best interests of his pupils; the cook is a servant because it is her duty to serve the interests of those for whom she works; the housemaid is a servant because it is her duty to care for in the best manner the property intrusted to her care; and so, in one way or another, every individual who amounts to anything is a servant. The only man or woman who is not a servant is one who accomplishes nothing.

It is very often true that a race, like an individual, does not appreciate the opportunities that are spread before it until the opportunities have disappeared. Before us as a race in the South today there is a vast field for service and usefulness which is still in our hands, which I fear will not be ours very much longer to the same extent that it has been unless we change our ideas of service; put new life, dignity and intelligence into it. Perhaps I am right in saying that in no department of life has there been such great progress and such changes for the better during the last ten years than is true in the department of domestic service, or housekeeping. The cook who does not make herself intelligent, who does not learn to do things in the neatest and cleanest manner, will soon find herself without employment, or at least find herself a "drug on the market," instead of being sought after and paid high wages. The woman who does not keep up with all the latest methods of decorating and setting her table and putting the food on it properly, will find her occupation gone within a few years. The same is true of general housekeeping, laundering, and nursing. All of these occupations are at present in our hands, but I repeat that very great progress is being made in every part of the world in all of them, and we will find that we will lose them unless our women go forward and get rid of the old idea that such occupations are only fit for ignorant people to follow.

At the present time there are scores of books and magazines being published bearing upon every branch of domestic service. People are learning to do things in an intelligent and scientific manner. Sometime ago I sat for an hour listening to a lecture delievered on the subject of dusting. It was one of the most valuable hours that I have ever spent. The person who gave this lecture on dusting was a highly cultured and educated woman and her audience was composed of wealthy and cultured people. We must bring ourselves to the point where we can feel that one who cooks and does it well should be just as much honored as the person who teaches school.

What I have said in relation to the employments which concern our women is equally true of those occupations which are followed by our men. It is true that at present we are in a large degree cultivating the soil of the South, but if other people do this work more intelligently, learn more about labor-saving machinery and become more conscientious than we, we will find our occupation departing.

It used to be, in many parts of the North, the Negro was the coachman, but in a very large degree in cities like New York and Philadelphia, the Negro has lost the occupation, not because, in my opinion, he is a Negro, but because in many cases he did not see that the occupation of coachman was constantly improving, that more and more of it was being lifted up and brains and skill put into it until it has almost become a profession. The Negro who expects to remain a coachman should learn the proper dress for a coachman and learn how to care for horses and vehicles in the most approved manner. What is true of the coachman is true of the butler. In too many cases, I fear, we use these occupations merely as stepping stones, holding on to them until we can find something else to do, in a careless and slipshod manner. We want to change all of this and put our whole souls into these occupations and in a large degree make them our life work. In proportion as we do this we will lay a foundation upon which our children and grandchildren are to rise to higher things. But the foundation of every race has got to be laid in the common everyday occupations that are about our doors. It should not be our idea to see how little we can put into our work, but how much; not how quickly we can get rid of our work, but how well we can do it. I often wish that I had the means to put a large training school for giving instruction in all lines of domestic service in every large city. Few things will add more to the fundamental usefulness of our race than would such a school.

Perhaps it may be suggested that my argument has relation only to our serving white people. It has reference to doing whatever we do in the best manner, no matter whom we serve. The individual who serves a black man poorly, will serve a white man poorly. Let me illustrate what I mean. In the city of Birmingham a few days ago I found a large hotel run by colored people. It is the cleanest and best and most attractive colored hotel that I have found in any part of the country. In talking to the proprietors, I asked them as to what were the greatest obstacles that they had to overcome, and they replied that it was finding colored women who would do their work well and systematically; who, in a word, would keep the rooms in every department of the hotel thoroughly swept and cleaned. I found that this hotel had been opened three months, and during that time the proprietors said that they had had fifteen different chambermaids and that they had gotten rid of a large proportion of these fifteen simply because they were determined not to have anybody in their employ who did not do their work well.

One weakness pertaining to the whole matter of domestic employment in the South at present, is this: It is too easy for our people to find work. If there was a rule running through every family of those who employ persons to the effect that no man or woman could be hired unless he brought a letter of recommendation from the person in whose employ he was last, we would find that the whole matter of domestic service would be lifted up a hundred per cent, but so long as an individual can do poor work for one family and perhaps be dishonest at the same time, and be sure that he or she will be employed by some other family, without regard to the kind of service rendered the last employer, so long will domestic service be poor and unsatisfactory.

And then it seems to me, that those who employ our people should, in a very large degree, try to protect their moral life. No people can become the best servants whose bodies are not kept clean, whose moral life is impure. A great many of our men are ruined because of the fact that they get the greater portion of their living from the back door of some white man's kitchen. The colored woman who supplies them with this food is responsible for a great deal of idleness among our people. The employers should see that this source of supply is cut off, and then a great many of the men who lounge about the streets will be forced to go to work. All that I have tried to say to you is a very serious matter for our race, not only for our race, but for both races. Many white people seldom come in contact with the Negro in any other direction except that of domestic service. If they get a poor idea of our service in this respect, they will judge that the entire life of the Negro is unsatisfactory from every point of view. We want to be sure that wherever our life touches that of the white man, that we must so act that the white man will get the best impression of us.

In addition to what I have tried to say in this regard, we must learn more and more to draw the line between the good and bad; between the pure and impure. Let the line be drawn strictly, no matter who is ostracised or does not like it. We must place a stamp of reward upon right living and a stamp of condemnation upon wrong living. More and more we must learn to save our money;

get a bank account. Every colored man and woman in Montgomery should have a bank account. No race of people can ever be respected until it learns to save money and own their own homes and live cleanly and respectably. I am glad to say that a large proportion of the colored men and women in Montgomery are doing this. Notwithstanding all the fault that I have found, I recognize that no race under similar circumstances, has made greater progress within thirty-five years than is true of the Negro race. I have spoken to you thus plainly and frankly, that our progress in the future may be still greater than in the past.

Tuskegee Student, 13 (June 1, 1901), 1, 4. A typed extract of this speech is in Con. 215, BTW Papers, DLC.

Minutes of a Meeting in Montgomery

Montgomery, Ala., May 20, 1901

Upon a call from Mr. B. T. Washington a number of representative col. men assembled to lay before the Constitutional Convention an address.[1] After stating the object of the meeting more fully on motion of Mr. Washington, Mr. Ad Wimbs[2] of G'boro was chosen Chm'n. Dr. C. O. Booth[e] offered prayer. On motion of Mr. Adams[3] R. B. Hudson[4] was choes secretary. The address as prepared by the Sub-Com. was read by the secretary. After the reading on motion the address was unanimously adopted.

M. H. Adams	Uniontown
Wm Watkins,[5]	Montgomery
V. H. Tulane[6]	Montgomery
Elijah Cook[7]	Montgomery
J. L. Thomas[8]	Union Springs
Booker T. Washington	Tuskegee
Moses Davis	Waugh
H. A. Loveless	Montgomery
A. J. Wilborn	Tuskegee
A. J. Woods,	Benton

J. W. Adams	Montgomery
R. E. Lee[9]	" "
John N. Brown[10]	" "
C. F. Stears[11]	Montgomery
Wm Wadkins[12]	Montgomery
Sidney Ross[13]	" "
Ad. Wimbs	Greensboro
Chas. O Boothe	Selma
W. R. Pettiford	B'ham
W. H. Council[l]	Normal
R. B. Hudson	Selma

HDSr Con. 865 BTW Papers DLC. Written on stationery of J. W. Adams's dry-goods store, perhaps in the hand of R. B. Hudson, the meeting's secretary.

[1] See A Petition to the Members of the Alabama Constitutional Convention, May 28, 1901, below.

[2] Addison Wimbs, born in Alabama in 1860, spent most of his adult life in Greensboro, Ala., where he engaged in a number of occupations. In the 1900 census he gave his occupation as "private bookkeeper," perhaps of Edward de Graffenried and R. B. Evins, law partners whose stationery he habitually used. He also owned some farmland, and had a grocery and general merchandise store, in partnership with J. R. Graham in 1903 but as sole owner in 1907. He was also an undertaker. Though he maintained a personal independence in his relation to BTW, he generally agreed with BTW's conservative approach to race relations. He went further than Washington when he endorsed the Alabama Constitution of 1901. In the early years of the twentieth century Wimbs was an active Republican, aiding BTW in his battle against lily-white Republicans. He was a member of the Republican state executive committee for several years. He tried twice without success to secure appointment as postmaster of Greensboro. In 1909 he was president and general manager of the Colored Fraternal Farm Improvement Association at Greensboro, designed to aid local farmers through model farms, farmers' institutes, and an agricultural school, and to help tenant farmers to secure land. In 1927 Wimbs was at Scott, Miss., where he edited a weekly newspaper, *The Cotton Farmer*.

[3] Probably J. W. Adams of Montgomery.

[4] R. B. Hudson, a former schoolteacher, was a successful coal and wood dealer in Selma and an active member of the NNBL.

[5] William Watkins, a prosperous black contractor. See above, 2:326.

[6] Victor H. Tulane, a black merchant in Montgomery, was born in Alabama in 1873. He was a trustee of Tuskegee from 1905 until after BTW's death in 1915.

[7] Elijah Cook was a black undertaker in Montgomery. He was born in Alabama in 1835.

[8] John L. Thomas, a black grocer in Union Springs, was born in Alabama in either 1858 or 1863, according to the 1900 census.

[9] Robert E. Lee, a black man born in North Carolina in 1865, was a railroad brakeman living in Montgomery.

10 There were four black John Browns in Montgomery, three of them farm laborers. Probably the man listed here was a hotel cook born in Alabama in 1850.

11 Charlie F. Sterrs, born in Virginia in 1849, was a cabinetmaker in Montgomery.

12 Possibly William Watkins, already listed above. There was, however, a farmer living in Montgomery County named William M. Wadkins. He was born in Alabama in 1849.

13 Sidney Ross was a black drayman in Montgomery, born in Alabama in 1855.

From Alice J. Kaine

[Milwaukee, Wis.] May 20-1901

Dear Mr Washington. I thank you for Dr Murphy's circular letter. I admire his fearlessness and I do think he wants to be fair. It is such a difficult thing for a Southern man or woman to see justice when it comes to the Negro but I am constantly encouraged at the growth of sentiment in the right direction. I shall watch anxiously for the result of the Convention which opens in Montgomery tomorrow.

I am utterly suspicious of Southern men on the colored question. They were so determined at the Race Conference to take the question in their own hands without considering the North, the Nation or the Negro and they know they must play a shrewd game or the Government will interfere. (Although so far as McKinley is concerned I think they may feel secure.)

Their methods are wiley and unjust and there is an element that stands ready to prevent the growth of liberality.

I honor Dr Murphy so far but I should want continued proof of his sincerity. He may wish to be fair but the environment may prove too strong for him. I am an optimist on most questions but on the Southerner I think all the slow, sceptical German in me rises to the surface and bids me be cautious.

I suppose you are reading Miss Kellors articles in the Arena.[1] I met her at Tuskegee last year and had a very interesting talk.

The bill for placing women on the State Board of Control was killed in the assembly after having passed the senate by a large majority. I thought you would be interested to know the outcome.

I know how busy you all are and wish I could be present at the Commencement.

Kindest regards to Mrs. Washington and the children as well as yourself. Very sincerely

Alice J. Kaine

ALS Con. 20 BTW Papers DLC.

1 Frances A. Kellor wrote a series of eight articles on "The Criminal Negro" that ran in *Arena* beginning in Jan. 1901. Kellor concluded that crime among blacks was due to environment and did not represent a deterioration of the race. She believed that blacks should be trained to be small farmers, and that educated blacks did not become criminals. Part of her study used some Tuskegee students as a control group against which she compared black criminals.

From Allen Caperton Braxton[1]

Staunton, Va., May 21, 1901

Dear sir: As a member of the Constitutional Convention about to assemble in this State, I am deeply interested in the proper solution of the problems which will be presented to that body in connection with the public school system of this State. There is a large element here earnestly in favor of a division of the school fund between the whites and the blacks, appropriating to the public schools of each race only that portion of the school fund contributed by the members of that race. Many honest men in this State are enthusiastic advocates of this scheme. I have never had occasion before to give any particular study to the subject, and therefore I am diffident, at this time, about expressing my views, which doubtless will strike you as very crude. I have, however, a most earnest and sincere desire to act in this matter with wisdom and prudence, and to that end I wish to avail myself as much as possible of the superior knowledge and experience of other men who have devoted their lives to the study of this subject.

With this object in view I have taken the liberty of writing you this letter, in the hope that you may have the opportunity and inclination to favor me with some suggestions as to the proper solution of this problem.

I cannot bring myself to believe that ignorance is beneficial to any race or condition of men; and yet it seems to be a fact that such education as many of the colored children now get at our public schools is either utterly wasted or positively detrimental to them. The reason, as I am led to believe, is, that we do not give them the proper kind of education. As it seems to me, the vast majority of our primary colored public schools should teach only such elementary branches as reading, writing, and common arithmetic, and that in addition to these the education given should be in the nature of manual training, calculated to fit them for the practical business of life to which 99% will have to look for a living. I am sure that you will fully agree with me in the great advantages that will result from such manual training, rather than from a vain attempt to educate these children in the higher branches of so-called "book learning." I believe that they should all be taught to read and write and make simple arithmetical calculations. With this as a basis, they can readily carry on their studies to the fullest extent that their capacities, tastes, and subsequent necessary environment, will justify. It would doubtless be well to have a few graded schools where the higher branches could be taught, to those few, to be selected from the various primary schools, who may show some unusual capacity for such learning; but the vast majority of the pupils, as I believe, would not desire, and would surely not be benefited by, this higher learning, which unquestionably tends to unfit its possessors for the humbler walks of life, where physical labor and manual training are the necessary requisites for success.

I fear, however, that there would be much practical difficulty in maintaining the manual schools, even of a very simple character, in those numerous districts in the eastern part of the State, where the population is so poor and sparse. Whether the idea is a practical and feasible one, or not, is a question. It has occurred to me, however, as a possible answer to the argument which is often adduced, that public school education, as we now have it, tends to unfit the colored children for the only kind of work that 99% of them are destined for, without in any way enabling them to better their position; thus feeding the ranks of the idle and vicious, who crowd our cities and towns and make their living largely by criminal and vicious practices, while looking down with contempt upon anything like physical labor, however honest or respectable.

Knowing that you have had much experience and given much time and thought to these questions, I have hoped that you may have the goodness to assist me in arriving at a wise and practical solution of this problem which our Convention will soon have to dispose of. Anything that you may be pleased to write me in reply to this letter will be received and treated as strictly confidential, unless you desire it to be made public. Thanking you by anticipation for your reply, I am, Yours very respectfully,

A. C. Braxton

In substance my idea is to introduce your "Tuskegee Plan" into our public school system at least for colored children. Is the idea a practical one? That is the question.

TLS   Con. 261   BTW Papers   DLC.

1 Allen Caperton Braxton (1862–1914), a lawyer, represented the city of Staunton and Augusta County in the constitutional convention of 1901. He played a minor role in the convention but was a member of the committee on final revisions.

From Margaret James Murray Washington

[Tuskegee, Ala.] May 22-1901

Mr. Washington: The more I think about it the less inclined I am to accept a man in the Laundry. I believe if we have the necessary things to carry on this work properly (which we have never yet had) it could be better done by two women.

Next year the Laundry will be in the Girl's Trades Building and I think it will be better managed. First, because there is more room. Second, because it is a greater distance from Alabama Hall and surrounding influences and third, because of the personal attention I shall be able to give it being in the building myself. Yours truly,

Mrs W

TLI   Con. 215   BTW Papers   DLC.

From Grace W. Minns[1]

S.S. Seguranca—for Cuba   May 24th 1901

My dear Mr. Washington, I had the pleasure of meeting you last November or December, at the house of Mr. Henry L. Higginson, in Boston, on the occasion of a reception given to the honor students of Harvard College. After the reception you staid a little while, and a few of us had supper together. I recall this as an introduction to you, before proposing what I have very much at heart. This is that your autobiography — "Up from Slavery" — should be translated into Spanish for the purpose of introducing it into Cuba.

I spent most of last winter in Cuba, to visit the charitable institutions there, & also the orphans placed in families, & reported to the Department of Charities. I am now returning there to continue the same work for another three months.

In this way I have come to know something of the people. The condition of the Colored population there is not very unlike that of our own colored people after the war — or perhaps worse. Most of them are very ignorant — not only of all education but of all decent ways of living. The land — which is very fertile — is much undercultivated, & there are practically no industries except the manufacture of cigars & sugar. All of the arts which make good homes, & in which such emphasis is laid at Hampton & Tuskegee, are practically unknown to the rank & file of the people.

In industries & agriculture lies the hope of the elevation of the race, & of the development & prosperity of the Country. Many colored children — who seem bright & eager to learn — are going to the Public Schools, started about a year & a half ago. These schools are of course very elementary, & practically teach only reading, writing, arithmetic & geography. The only industrial & agricultural education is given in the State Industrial & Reform Schools — still in their infancy. To go there, a child must be enrolled as destitute or delinquent. Good as these schools are in their place & indispensable, you will easily see the menace to good citizenship while they are the only means for such education for the growing generation.

I have written you at this length, because I have wanted to show you why it seems to me that the soil in Cuba is ready for the seeds from Tuskegee & Hampton to be planted. I have also written to

Dr. Albert Shaw, editor of the Review of Reviews — Astor Place, New York — telling him of my hope that you may approve of publishing your book in Spanish, & asking if his own article on Hampton — published as a pamphlet — "Learning by Doing" — with illustrations, could also be put into Spanish for the same purpose. Perhaps there is a similar pamphlet about Tuskegee? I thought a catalogue perhaps rather technical for wide distribution.

I am not familiar with the method to be pursued in translating a book, nor whether the expense and risk is one which the publishers are likely to take. If you approve of this, I wish very much that the trustees of Tuskegee and Hampton could be interested, and with their sanction & help, if money is needed, I believe it could be raised.

Mr. Homer Folks,[2] the Secretary of the State Charities Aid Association — 105 East 22nd St. New York — knows the conditions in Cuba — & if you should happen to be in New York, would I know, be very glad to tell you more of them. Mr. Folks, at General Wood's invitation, very ably organized the Department of Charities in Cuba. He spent six weeks there, & is greatly interested in these problems.

The desire which one feels in Cuba, to help to raise the people out of the depth in which they rest, must be my excuse for troubling you. I believe also that your book should be read in Mexico, & South America, & perhaps also the Philippine Islands — & not only English speaking peoples. The development of the Spanish speaking people, bound up as it is in many cases, with that of Negroes & Indians — could not it seems to me, fail to be benefitted by learning the ideas & ideals of Hampton and Tuskegee. Would you kindly write me to the address below, & tell me what you think of this? I hope that you may approve. Very truly yours,

Grace W. Minns

[P.]S. Would you be so good also as to mail me some reports of Tuskegee?

ALS Con. 204 BTW Papers DLC.

[1] Grace W. Minns completed the translation of *Up from Slavery* into Spanish by the spring of 1902, and it was published by D. Appleton and Co. by arrangement with Doubleday, Page and Co. She wrote BTW in 1903: "One thousand copies of your book are now spread all through Cuba, and it will be read by the children in the

public schools, in the orphan asylums, by patients in the hospitals, by old men and women in the almshouses, by employees in the cigar factories, and by a large number of persons who are interested in the administration of the schools, the charitable institutions, and in public affairs." (Jan. 10, 1903, Con. 236, BTW Papers, DLC.)

[2] Homer Folks (1867–1963), a social worker, was secretary of the New York State Charities Aid Association from 1893 to 1902.

A Sunday Evening Talk

Tuskegee, Ala., [May 26][1] 1901

We have come to the close of another school year. Some of you will go out from among us now, not to return. Others will go home for the summer vacation and return at the end of that for the next school year.

As you go out, there is one thing that I want to especially caution you about. Don't go home and feel that you are better than the rest of the folks in your neighborhood because you have been away at school. Don't go home and feel ashamed of your parents because you think they don't know as much as you think you know. Don't think that you are too good to help them. It would be better for you not to have any education, than for you to go home and feel ashamed of your parents, or not want to help them.

Let me tell you of one of the most encouraging and most helpful things in connection with the life of our students after they leave this institution: I was in a Southern city, and going about among the homes of the people of our race. Among these homes I noticed one which was so neat looking that it was conspicuous. I asked the person who was with me, "How is it that this house is in such good condition, looks so much better than some of the others in the neighborhood?" "It is like this," said the man who was accompanying me, "the people who live there have a son whom they sent to your school, at considerable self-denial to themselves. This young man came home from school a few weeks ago. For some time after he came back, he did not have work to keep him busy, and so he employed his spare time in fixing up his parents' home. He fixed the roof and chimney, put new pailings in the fence where they were needed and did such things as that. Then he got a stock of paint and painted the house thoroughly, two coats, outside and in. That is why the place looks so neat."

Such testimony as that is very helpful. It shows that the students carry out from here the spirit which we try to inculcate.

Another thing. Go home and lead a simple life. Don't give the impression that you think education means superficiality and dress.

Be polite; to white and colored people both. It is possible for you, by paying heed to this, to do a great deal toward securing and preserving pleasant relations between the people of both races in the South. Try to have your manners in this respect so good that people will notice them and ask where you have been, at what school you learned to be so polite. You will find that politeness counts for a great deal, not only in helping you to get work, but in helping you to keep it.

Don't be ashamed to go to church and Sunday school, to the Young Men's Christian Association and the Christian Endeavor Societies. Show that education has only deepened your interest in such things. Have no going backward. Be clean, in your person, your language and in your thoughts.

Be economical. Save your money. If you are earning only three dollars a week, don't pay two dollars of that sum to hire a horse and buggy to take some girl riding on Sunday. And you, young women, if the young men haven't got enough common sense to not do such a thing as that, tell them you have got too much to let them do it. They will respect you all the more for your frankness, and you will be doing them a real kindness.

Tuskegee Student, 13 (June 29, 1901), 1.

[1] Reported as the last Sunday Evening Talk before commencement, which was held on May 30.

From John Winfrey Robinson

Tove Plantation, Lome, Togo, West Africa   May 26th, 1901

Dear Mr. Washington: Knowing how anxious you are to keep in touch with those who have been with you and have gone through the mills of the Institution, and now bear the label "Tuskegee";

and knowing also, how interested you are in the work done by such individuals, I feel no reluctance what ever in attempting to tell you in a brief way what we are doing in this far away country; yes, far away indeed, but still it is our own dear "fatherland."

I was very anxious to give you a detailed account of our trip from Tuskegee, Ala. To Africa, and in fact the account is before me in pencil form but we have been so closely engaged and the work from the start, has made such an urgent and exact demand upon our time that I have never found opportunity to complete it. Now the occasion is so far passed I shall fore go the pleasure and proceed to tell you at once of our efforts here in the wilds.

After nearly two months of weary sailing; we landed at Lome, Togo Dec. 30, 1900 with a distance of nearly 100 miles to be made on foot to the interior. Of course we brought wagons and quite a bit of cargo with us carried from America, but there were little accomodation afforded by such vehicles where there are no means of conveyance. The natives expressed an eager desire to take the wagons on their heads but that method of locomotion would have been alright for the wagons no doubt, but meant nothing to us, for we could not be so disected and distributed around in parcels to be carried on the heads of natives, so we stored the wagons with the heavy cargo at the shore — took the balance with a hundred or more carriers and started for the "bush." I cannot say the trip was very agreeable with in a few degrees of the equator — beneath a parching sun, after such a prolonged ride from America, any way after four days and a half travel — all foot sore lame and weary we reached our destination — Missahoa.[1] After three days we went out to locate the place of action and on the fourteeenth Jan, 1901, we made a desperate attack upon the mighty African forest.

The beginning was significant only in that it came near smothering the ray of hope that had constantly shot across our mental horizon since we left American shores.

For days we toiled away, silently meditating over the giant forest with its mammoth trees some 20 feet in diamiter or over the tangled jungle of elephant grass some 15 ft. high — deep and strongly rooted and so closely inter-woven as to render it impenitrable, all in dumb silence which was the only alternative to words of disparagement.

In March we received from the district some 200 miles above us,

20 horses and 20 cows. The former had never tasted a bit and the latter had yet to learn that the yoke was easy and the burden light. Well, we were very glad for this additional force but you will see what a miserable plight we were in when I tell you that many of the laborers had never seen a horse or cow — 50% had never seen such common empliments as an axe, hoe or pitch-fork ½ of 1% had never seen a plow wagon or harness, to say naught of knowing how to use or manipulate them. They were as afraid of a horse or cow as a common American youth is of a "mad dog" and worst still, you could not understand a word they spoke nor they you. It is no uncommon occurence even now, for six or eight of these men to leave you at the risk of your life with two of the most vicious and bison looking bulls that Africa has ever produced. Yes, really take to heels at the very first rebelious move of the beast, and no utterance that you are able to make will return them to your relief until you have succeeded in calming the beast. The time passes on and you get a few "boys" trained, to some extent, then they begin to disappear then you have to take a new set. It is common now to find a boy with the collar and harnes tied around the girth of his horse the bridle on backward and plowing up your cotton. Of course that isnt just what we want and a continual repetition of the which is certianly far from being agreeable, so much so, that we trust we are excused for the blue flames of English that occasionally escape our lips.

Never-theless we are still hopeful — and with the old Tuskegee idea of persevearence, thoroughness and mastery in one's undertakings, we have ploded on, and to day, away to the interior of Africa — a little to the North East of the highest point of the Gulf of Guinea nestled near the foot of the Argu mountains upon the banks of the Argu river,[2] we have s[u]cceeded in transforming some 75 acres of this teaming forest and tangled jungle into varied fields of cotton and still continue to fell the forest primeval.

The picture here in, represent[s] the force of cows, horses and boys trained to help with the tecnical part of the work. I speak of them together for I am quite sure that it was more difficult to train the boys than it was to train the horses.

A few Sundays ago we reached home with the wagons stored at Lome, drawn by our cows and horses; this was quite an event in all German Togoland — at every native town the people gathered to look and having done so, went and fetched their brothers crying, "come and see."

We are getting on as well as can be expected being so far removed from civilization. There are only ten really civilized persons with in a radius of 50 miles or more, and as for that matter, there are only 107 whites out of the 2½ millions of inhabitants of Togoland and that 107 are found principally along the coast.

We are not always well but as well I suppose as is probable under extreme tropical conditions. We wish to thank you kindly for "The Student" and "Southern Letter" which find their way to us constantly. Messrs. Calloway, Burks and Harris join in best greetings to you, family and friends of Tuskegee. I am sincerely yours

John W. Robinson

ALS Con. 215 BTW Papers DLC.

1 Misahöhe.
2 Possibly the Ogou River.

A Petition to the Members
of the Alabama Constitutional Convention

[Montgomery, Ala.] May 28, 1901

Since it is true that our race numbers in this State about 800,000 and there is no member of the race a member of your body, who can speak directly for us in an official capacity, we do not think that you will misunderstand the object and spirit of this communication, for it is not sent to you in a dictatorial, fault-finding spirit, but with an earnest desire to be of some assistance in the performance of a grave and perplexing task. We make ourselves all the more bold to send you this communication because members of your body in nearly every part of the State have expressed a desire to hear from us.

It could not be expected that the 800,000 colored people in this State would not have some interest in the deliberations of a body that is to frame the fundamental law under which both races are to be governed in this State, perhaps for all future time.

Your petitioners are not stirrers up of strife between the races, but we feel that the questions with which you are to deal are above and beyond party politics. Each of us, in some calling, is a hard-working, tax-paying, and we trust law-abiding citizen, and we believe that we represent in a large measure the feelings and desires of the masses of our people in the State.

We beg of your honorable body to keep in mind, in dealing with the problems that grow out of our presence, that, as a race, we did not force ourselves upon you, but were brought here, in most cases, against our will; but nevertheless, we recognize that since being here we have been vastly benefitted. We have gotten habits of industry, the English language, and the Christian religion, and at the same time we have tried, in an humble way, to render valuable service to the white man in clearing the forests, building the railroads, cultivating the lands, working the mines, as well as in many forms of domestic service and in other activities. Our fathers and mothers have helped nurse you and your children, and when the male members of the family were away from home fighting in a war that might have meant our continued enslavement, we remained at home, working your farms, supporting and protecting your helpless wives and daughters. When we have been called to perform any duty of citizenship, whether fighting a foreign foe, working the public roads, or any other duty, we have tried to do our best.

We beg of you to bear in mind that for more than twenty years the Negro in this State has not, as a rule, been a disturbing or offensive element. Immediately after the war we made mistakes just as would have been true of any people placed in the same position, but we have learned our lesson from those mistakes and they are not likely to be repeated.

The changes wrought by time and the providence of God, it seems to us, place your body in a peculiarly responsible position. You assemble at a time when your actions will not be directed or restricted by any pressure from the Federal Government or elsewhere. The North is almost unanimous in its agreement that the future of the Negro in a large degree rests with the South. Almost for the first time since freedom came to us a law-making body assembles in the South, bearing the supreme law-making power of the State, and is left free to act entirely untrammeled by outside influence. Almost for the first time the Negro is to rest his future in a large degree upon the conscience and intelligence of a great law-making body of a great Southern State. You have the power. The world will watch while you act.

It requires little thought, effort or strength to degrade and pull down a weak race, but it is a sign of great statesmanship to encourage and lift up a weak and unfortunate race — destruction is easy; construction is difficult.

There are those among your petitioners who have persistently urged the Negro to learn to trust his future with his Southern white neighbor, and that when the supreme test came he would receive justice at his hands. This is a crucial hour for those who have thus advised our race, but we do not believe that our faith in you will be misplaced. We believe that the possession of great power will deepen your sympathy for the weak and dependent elements of our population.

It seems to us, on the whole, that the relations of the two races in this State are reasonably satisfactory, and we tremble and fear lest something will be done to disturb these relations and to bring discouragement and demoralization to our race.

Of the greatest importance is the economic consideration. The greater portion of our people are settled upon the plantations in the cotton raising districts. These people are occupying and cultivating land that is largely owned by white people or operating other industries owned by white people. Still, others are buying homes and thereby contributing to the welfare of the State. In most cases they are a contented, producing, law-abiding people. Already, alarm is beginning to spread among them and their fears are being worked upon by emigration agents and exodus associations, who are telling them that under the new constitution the Negro's citizenship will be taken from him and that his schools will virtually be blotted out. These agencies expect, in one way or other, to reap gain by reason of something that you will do in your convention.

Anything that will unsettle and cause excitement of people at the present time when more than ever, in all parts of the State, the race is beginning to improve, to settle down to habits of thrift, economy and common sense, will not only prove injurious to our race, but to yours also. The history of all races proves that a contented, intelligent, friendly working class is the greatest possession of any State.

The Negro youth must have some incentive for right and useful living held out to him. Let the Negro youth feel that no matter how intelligent or useful he makes himself, that there is no hope of reward held out to him, and there will be danger that he will become a beast, reveling in crime and a body of death about the neck of the State. In a thousand ways the ignorant, shiftless, criminal Negro will retard the progress of the white race.

The Negro is not seeking to rule the white man. In this State, the Negro holds not a single elective office. Whenever he votes, he usually votes for some white man. There is in the last analysis a feeling of tenderness, good will and sympathy existing between the two races, in this State, which the outside world can hardly understand or appreciate. We pray that that relation may not be disturbed.

The Negro does ask, however, that since he is taxed, works the roads, is punished for crime, is called upon to defend his country, that he have some humble share in choosing those who shall rule over him, especially when he has proven his worthiness by becoming a tax-payer and a worthy, reliable citizen. While the amount of direct taxes paid by the Negro is small, all will acknowledge that he is a large factor in enabling some one else to pay taxes; for the Negro who rents a farm or a house not only pays the rent, but indirectly, the taxes, also.

We rejoice in that we have reached a period in our development when we can speak in frank but friendly terms of the subject of your convention, the chief aim of which is, we trust, the wise and just government of all the people of Alabama. In this high purpose your petitioners agree and sympathize with you. We are all owners of property and tax-payers and have the same interest in good government that you have. We know that the task before you is a delicate, trying and perplexing one. In this connection, we desire to add that, in our humble opinion, while there may be doubt and uncertainty in many directions, one thing is absolutely and unmistakably clear — that nothing that is not absolutely just and fair will be permanently successful.

Any law which will merely change the name and form of fraud, or can be interpreted as meaning one thing when applied to one race and something else when applied to another race, will not in our opinion improve our present condition, but may unsettle the peace and interfere with the thrift of our people and decrease the wealth and prosperity of Alabama.

While you deliberate and act, be assured that you will have the prayers and good wishes of thousands of black people in every part of our State.

Respectfully submitted:

(Signed)

Chas. O. Boothe,	R. E. Lee,
V. H. Tulane,	Ad. Wimbs,
Elijah Cook,	S. S. H. Washington, M.D.,
John L. Thomas,	C. F. Sterrs, Sr.,
Booker T. Washington,	Wm. Watkins,
M. H. Adams,	Henry Todd,
Moses Davis,	S. Ross,
H. A. Loveless,	R. H. Herron,
A. J. Wilborn,	W. R. Pettiford,
A. J. Wood,	W. H. Councill,
J. W. Adams,	R. B. Hudson,
Jno. N. Brown,	Alfred C. Dungee, M.D.

PD Con. 865 BTW Papers DLC. The petition also appeared in the Montgomery *Advertiser*, May 29, 1901, 11. A draft in BTW's hand is in Con. 215, BTW Papers, DLC.

From Benjamin Strong[1]

New York. May 29th 1901

Dear Mr. Washington. I have the a/c just received from Small, Maynard & Co., in which they state that they have printed & sent out 7208 copies of the Future of the American Negro as proposed by the Slater board, thus leaving on hand 2792 copies to be distributed. You will remember you sent me a list of members of the Alabama convention & were to send a list of the members of a Virginia convention, it has not yet arrived. Had we not better retain the balance of this edition for any names that may turn up in the near future as this is all the Trustees have as yet authorised printed. Yours respectfully.

Benj. Strong

TLS Con. 211 BTW Papers DLC. Written on stationery of Morris K. Jesup.

1 Benjamin Strong (1872–1928), a banker, was a clerk with Cuyler, Morgan and Co. of New York before becoming secretary of several banks and president of the Bankers Trust Co. In 1914 he became a governor of the Federal Reserve Bank of New York.

An Article in *Outlook*

[June 1, 1901]

CHICKENS, PIGS AND PEOPLE

I have always been intensely fond of outdoor life. Perhaps the explanation for this lies partly in the fact that I was born nearly out-of-doors. I have also, from my earliest childhood, been very fond of animals and fowls. When I was but a child, and a slave, I had close and interesting acquaintances with animals.

During my childhood days, as a slave, I did not see very much of my mother, since she was obliged to leave her children very early in the morning to begin her day's work. The early departure of my mother often made the matter of my securing breakfast uncertain. This led to my first intimate acquaintance with animals.

In those days it was the custom upon the plantation to boil the Indian corn that was fed to the cows and pigs. At times, when I had failed to get any other breakfast, I used to go to the places where the cows and pigs were fed, and make my breakfast off this boiled corn, or else go to the place where it was the custom to boil the corn, and get my share there before it was taken to the animals.

If I was not there at the exact moment of feeding, I could still find enough corn scattered around the fence or the trough to satisfy me. Some people may think that this was a pretty bad way in which to get one's food, but, leaving out the name and the associations there was nothing very bad about it. Any one who has eaten hard boiled corn knows that it has a delicious taste. I never pass a pot of boiled corn now without yielding to the temptation to eat a few grains.

Another thing that helped in developing my fondness for animals was my contact with the best breeds of fowls and animals when I was a student at the Hampton Institute. Notwithstanding the fact that my work there was not directly connected with the stock, the mere fact that I saw the best kinds of animals and fowls day after day increased my love for them, and made me resolve that when I went out into the world I would have some as nearly like them as possible.

I think that I owe a great deal of my present strength and ability to work to my love of outdoor life. It is true that the amount of time that I can spend in the open air is now very limited. Taken on an average, it is perhaps not more than an hour a day, but I make the most of that hour. In addition to this I get much pleasure out of the anticipation and the planning for that hour.

I do not believe that any one who has not worked in a garden can begin to understand how much pleasure and strength of body and mind and soul can be derived from one's garden, no matter how small it may be; the smaller it is, the better, I think, in some respects. If the garden be very small, a man can have the gratifying experience of finding out how much can be produced on a small plot carefully laid out, thoroughly fertilized, and well cultivated. And then, when the garden is small, but the vegetables and plants large, there springs up a feeling of kinship between the man and the plant, as he tends and watches the growth of each individual plant from day to day. Each day there is some new development. The rain, the dew, the sunshine, each causes some new growth.

The letter or the address that one began writing the day before never budges or moves forward one iota until you return and take up the work where it was left off; not so with the plant. Some change has taken place during the night; there is the appearance of bud or blossom or fruit. This sense of newness, of expectancy, brings to me a freshness, an inspiration for each day, that it is difficult to describe.

It is not only a pleasure to grow good vegetables for one's own table, but I get much satisfaction from sending some of the best specimens to some neighbor whose garden is backward, or to some one who has not learned the art of raising the best or the earliest varieties, and who is therefore surprised to receive some new potatoes two weeks in advance of any one else.

When I am at my home at Tuskegee, I usually find a way, by rising early in the morning, to spend at least half an hour in my garden, or with my fowls, pigs, or cows. As far as I can get the time, I like to find the new eggs each morning myself, and when at home am selfish enough to permit no one else to do this in my place. As with the growing plants, there is a sense of freshness and newness and of restfulness in connection with the finding and handling of newly laid eggs that is delightful to me. Both the anticipation and the realization are most pleasing. I begin the day by seeing how many eggs I can find, or how many little chickens there are that are just beginning to peep through the shells.

Speaking of little chickens coming into life, a few days ago one of our students called my attention to something in connection with the chickens owned by the school itself that I had not previously known. That was that, when some of the first little chickens came out of their shells, they began almost immediately from the outside to help others not so forward to break their way out. It was delightful to me to hear that the chickens raised at the school had, so early in life, caught the Tuskegee spirit of helpfulness for others.

I am deeply interested in the different kinds of fowls, and, aside from the large number grown by the school in its poultry house and yards, I grow at my own home common chickens, Plymouth Rocks, Buff Cochins, and Brahmas, Peking ducks, and fan-tailed pigeons.

The pig, I think, is my favorite animal. I do not know how this will strike the taste of my readers, but it is true. In addition to some common-bred pigs, I keep a few Berkshires and some Poland Chinas; and it is a real pleasure to me to watch their development and increase from month to month. Practically all the pork used in my family is of my own raising.

Speaking of pigs, and of the Tuskegee spirit, I heard a story of one of our graduates not long ago that gave me great satisfaction.

A man had occasion to go to the village of Benton, Ala., in which Mr. A. J. Wood, one of our graduates, had settled ten years before, and gone into business as a general merchant. In this time he has built up a good trade and has obtained for himself a reputation as one of the best and most reliable business men in the place. While the visitor was there, he happened to step to the open back door of the store, and stood looking out into a little yard behind the building. The merchant, joining him there, began to call, "Ho, Suke! Ho, Suke!" and finally, in response to this calling, there came crawling out from beneath the store, with much grunting, because he was altogether too big to get comfortably from under the building, an enormous black hog.

"You see that hog," the man said. "That's my hog. I raise one like that every year as an object-lesson to the colored farmers around here who come to the store to trade. About all I feed him is the waste from the store. When the farmers come in here, I show them my hog, and tell them that if they would shut their pigs up in a pen of rails, and have the children pick up acorns in the woods to feed them on, they might have just such hogs as I do, instead of the razor-backs they have now running around wild in the woods.

"Perhaps I can't teach a school here," the man added, "but if I can't do that, I can at least teach the men around here how to raise hogs as I learned to raise them at Tuskegee."

In securing the best breeds of fowls and animals I have the added satisfaction at Tuskegee of seeing a better grade of stock being gradually introduced among the farmers who live near the school.

My favorite cow is the Jersey. The Jersey, when properly taken care of, not only repays one in her yield of milk and butter, but she soon becomes a great pet. I get much satisfaction in leading these cows around, and in holding them by a rope in the yard while they eat a tempting portion of green grass or oats.

After I have gathered my eggs, and have at least said "good-morning" to my pigs, cows, and horse, the next morning duty — no, I will not say duty, but delight — is to gather the vegetables for the family dinner. There are no peas, no turnips, no radishes, no beets or salads, that taste so good as those which one has raised and gathered with his own hands in his own garden. In comparison with these all the high-sounding and long-named dishes found in the most expensive restaurants seem tame and flavorless. One feels, when eating his own fresh vegetables, that he is getting near to the heart of nature; that is, not a second-hand, stale imitation of something, but the genuine thing. How delightful the change, after one has spent weeks eating in restaurants or hotels, and has had a bill of fare pushed before his eyes three times a day, or has heard the familiar sound for a month from a waiter's lips: "Steak, pork chops, fried eggs, and potatoes!"

As I go from bed to bed in the garden, gathering my lettuce, peas, spinach, radishes, beets, onions, and the relishes with which

137

to garnish the dishes, and note the growth of each plant since the previous day, I feel a nearness and kinship to the plants which makes them seem to me like members of my own family. When engaged in this work, how short the half-hour is, how quickly each minute goes, bringing nearer the time when I must go to my office! When I do go there, though, it is with a vigor and freshness and with a steadiness of nerve that prepares me thoroughly for what perhaps is to be a difficult and trying day — a preparation that I could not have had but for the half-hour spent in my garden.

All through the day, too, I am enabled to do more work and better work because of the delightful anticipation of being permitted to have another half-hour, or perhaps more than that, in my garden after the office work is done. I get so much pleasure out of this that I frequently find myself beseeching Mrs. Washington to delay the dinner hour that I may take advantage of the last bit of daylight for my outdoor work.

The time spent in my garden in the evening is usually devoted to laying out new beds, planting new vegetables, in hoeing the plants, or in pruning my peach-trees.

While I am fond of shrubbery and flowers, I must confess that they do not possess enough of the industrial or economic element to particularly appeal to me, and all that part of the gardening I leave to Mrs. Washington.

My own experience in outdoor life leads me to hope that the time will soon come when there will be a revolution in our methods of educating children, especially the children in the schools of the smaller towns and rural districts. I think that it is almost a sin to take a number of children whose homes are on farms, and whose parents earn their living by farming, and cage them up, as if they were so many wild beasts, for six or seven hours during the day, in a close room where the air is often impure.

I have known teachers to go so far as to frost the windows in a school-room, or have them made high up in the wall, or keep the curtains to the windows down, so that the children could not even see nature. For six hours the life of these children is an artificial one. As a rule, the apparatus which they use is artificial, and they are taught in an artificial manner about artificial things. To even whisper about the song of a mocking-bird or the chirp of a squirrel in a near-by tree, or to point to a stalk of corn or a wild flower, or to speak about a Holstein cow and her calf, or a little colt and its mother grazing in an adjoining field, is a sin for which they must be speedily and often severely punished. I have seen teachers keep children caged up on a beautiful, bright day in June, when all nature was at her best, making them learn — or try to learn — a lesson about hills, or mountains, or lakes, or islands, by means of an artificial map or globe, when the land surrounding the school-house would be full of representations of these things. I have seen a teacher work for an hour with children, trying to impress upon them the meaning of the words lake, island, peninsula, when a brook not a quarter of a mile away would have afforded the little ones an opportunity to pull off their shoes and stockings and wade through the water, and find, not one artificial island or lake, on an artificial globe, but dozens of real islands, peninsulas, and bays. Besides the delight of wading through the water, out in the pure bracing air, in this way they would learn more about these natural divisions of the earth in five minutes than they could learn in an hour by the book method. A reading lesson taught out on the green grass under a spreading oak-tree is a lesson that one has to use little effort to get a boy to pay good attention to, to say nothing of the sense of delight and relief that comes to the teacher.

I have seen teachers make students puzzle for hours over the problem of the working of the pulley, when not a block from the school-house there would be workmen with pulleys in actual operation, hoisting bricks with which to construct the walls of a new building.

I believe that the time is not far distant when every school in the rural districts and in the small towns is going to be surrounded by a garden, and that it will be one of the main objects aimed at by the course of study to teach the child something about real country life, and about the occupations that his parents are engaged in. As it is, a very large proportion of the subjects taught in the schools have to do more or less directly with city life. Since the greater part of the child's education bears upon city life, as soon as he gets old enough, he naturally goes to the city for occupation and for residence.

I am glad to say that at the Tuskegee Institute we now have in process of erection a new school-house in and about which, so far as we can do so, the little children of the town and vicinity will be taught, in addition to books, the real things which they will be called upon to use in their homes. Since Tuskegee is surrounded by people who earn their living by agriculture, there will be about this school-house three acres of ground on which the children are to be taught to cultivate flowers, shrubbery, vegetables, grains, cotton, and other crops. In addition they are to be taught cooking, laundering, sewing, sweeping, and dusting, how to set a table, and how to make a bed — the things by which they are to live. I have referred to this building as a "school-house," but we are not going to call it that, because the name is too formal. We are going to call it "The Children's House."

Also, in the training of the negro ministers for our people, especially those who are to work among the people who live in the smaller towns and country districts, where in the Gulf States, eighty-five per cent. of our people reside, I wish that something of the real conditions these ministers are to meet might be kept in mind.

In this, as in too many other things, the negro minister is trained to meet conditions that exist in New York or in Chicago — in a word, it is too often taken for granted that there is no difference between the work to be done by negro ministers among our people after only thirty-five years of freedom, and that to be done among the white people who have had the advantages of centuries of freedom and development.

The negro ministers, except those who go to the large cities, go among an agricultural people, as a rule — people who, of course, lead an outdoor life. They are poor, without homes or ownership in farms, without proper knowledge of agriculture, in most cases people who are able to pay their minister but a small and uncertain salary — such a small salary that no one can live on it honestly and pay his bills promptly.

During the three or four years that the minister has spent in the theological classroom, scarcely a single subject that concerns the every-day life of his future people has been discussed. He is taught more about the soil of the valley of the Nile or of the valley of the river Jordan, than about the soil of the State in which the people of his church are to live and to work.

What I urge is that the negro minister should be taught something about the outdoor life of the people whom he is to lead. More than that, it would help matters immensely if in some more practical and direct manner this minister could be taught to get the larger portion of his own living from the soil — be taught to love outdoor work, and to make his garden, his farm, and his farm-house object-lessons for his people.

The negro minister who earns his living in a large part on the farm is independent, and can reprove and rebuke the people when they do wrong. It is not so with the one who is wholly dependent upon his congregation for his bread. What is equally important, an interest in agricultural production and a love for work tend to keep a minister from that idleness which, in the case of some men not so employed, proves a cause for their yielding to temptation.

To me there is nothing more delightful and restful than to spend a portion of each Sabbath afternoon in the woods with my family, near some little stream where we can gather wild flowers and listen to the singing of the mocking-birds and the ripple of the water. This, after a good sermon in the morning, seems to take us very near to nature's God, and prepares me not only for my evening "talk" in the chapel to our students and teachers, but also for the week's work.

At least once a week I make it a practice to spend an hour or more among the people of Tuskegee and vicinity — among the merchants and farmers, white and black. In these talks with the real people I can get at the actual needs and conditions of the people for whom our institution is at work.

When talking to a farmer, I always feel that I am talking with a real man and not an artificial one — one who can keep me in close touch with the world as it actually exists. When talking with a simple, honest cultivator of the soil, I am sure of getting first-hand, original information. I have secured more illustrations that I have found useful in public addresses in a half-hour's talk with some white or colored farmer than from hours of reading books.

If I were a minister, I think I should make it a point to spend a day in each week in close, unconventional touch with the masses of the people. A vacation spent in visiting farmers, it seems to me, would often prepare one as thoroughly for his winter's work as a vacation spent in visiting the cities of Europe.

Outlook, 68 (June 1, 1901), 291–300. The article contained eight illustrations by Clifton Johnson.

From James Nathan Calloway

Lome   Togo W.A. June 2nd '01

Dear sir   Your very welcome and encouraging letter reached us about May 1st. We were indeed glad to hear of your success in money getting. We hope the amounts to be given under conditions may come to us.

If you could see this land and know these people you would have even a greater zeal for your work. If Africa is ever reclaimed it will be through such missionary work as is done in school, shops and farms at Tuskegee. The people are more willing to work than they get credit for. They lack most in knowledge and skill.

We have gone right on with our plantation. About 75 acres have been cleared off and about 50 acres of it planted in cotton. Some of the cotton 4 ft high now and looks as though it will make a heavey crop. We are trying an experiment on American, Native and Egyptian cotton. With some of each we try fertilizers and will note the result. This information we hope to be able to send you when complete. At present the Komitee wishes us to say nothing in a public way about our work here.

I shall send a picture of our first trip out from Lome with wagons. I shall ask Mr[s] Calloway to forward this to you as soon as she receives it. It can be published with some letter from [the] young men if you wish. We shall leave tomorrow morning for interior (Tove) with our one-horse wagon drawn by 4 oxen. You probably know we have this wagon made by the school. I am now in Lome for supplies and money for our work. The papers which you are so kind as to send us from time to time have been a great source of pleasure. Someone sends us (the youngmen) a few copies of Magizenes every month. These we suspect come from Mr Baldwins house. Anyhow they are fine reading for us all. I dont write as much as I hoped to from the fact that a person is lazy here and if he tries to overcome this by work he gets fever. I have just bought $5.00 worth of quinine today and hope to keep well for 2 months on that. We have small fevers often but none are serious.

Many thanks for the clipping of New S.S. line to Africa. This line however does not come within a thousand miles of us. The distances here are very much greater than we in America can think. Best regard to Mrs Washington & children.

I hope to write at least once per month here after. Yours truly

Jas. N. Calloway

ALS   Con. 213   BTW Papers   DLC.

To Thomas Wilkes Coleman[1]

[Tuskegee, Ala.] June 4, 1901

Dear Sir: Since I saw you I have thought considerably about the suggestions which you made regarding getting something into the constitution that might prove a constant and direct incentive to industry — but I must confess that I am unable to formulate anything that will answer that end and at the same time be reduced to such form as could be embodied into law.

Since I saw you I have had a meeting with about twenty-five of the most substantial and influential colored people representing different portions of the state, and I find that either of the conditions for voting expressed roughly on the enclosed sheet, will prove satisfactory to our race.

The property qualification, it seems to me, is the nearest thing to your idea and it meets my endorsement. I find that when a member of my race secures property it stimulates industry, economy, leads to conservatism and good character, and besides makes him a supporter of his state government. The exhibit of the tax receipt would admit of no debate as to one's right to vote.

This will be handed you by Mr. J. W. Adams, who is a successful Montgomery merchant and one of our most reliable men.

I shall hope to see you within a few days. Yours truly,

[Booker T. Washington]

TL Copy   BTW Papers   ATT.

1 Thomas Wilkes Coleman (1834–1920) was an Alabama judge who was educated at Princeton and the University of Alabama Law School. He practiced law at Eutaw in Greene County before the Civil War. An officer in the Confederate Army, he was a

delegate to the Alabama constitutional convention in 1875 and served in several judicial posts before becoming associate justice of the Alabama Supreme Court in 1891. In 1901 he was a delegate to the constitutional convention, the only person to have served in both 1875 and 1901. Coleman was chairman of the committee that drafted the restricted suffrage provisions in the Alabama Constitution.

From William Henry Baldwin, Jr.

[New York City] June 4th 1901

Dear Mr. Washington: I have your letter of the second. I think you do well in attending to the Constitutional Convention. If you can succeed in helping to bring about a conservative result in their action, you will be in still better shape to get the necessary funds for your Institution. I should not let that worry me. I am very much delighted to know that you feel that the conservative element is getting the upper hand.

With kind regards, I am, Yours very truly,

W. H. Baldwin, Jr.

TLS Con. 792 BTW Papers DLC.

From George Washington Campbell

Tuskegee, Ala., June 4 1901

Friend Washington: I have thought some about this Constitutional question as to the disfranchisement of the negro, & have come to the conclusion that you have done everything that ought to be required of you to have the matter brought before the Convention, *dont be too persistent* in this matter. I am fearful you may overdo the thing, I do not know that you propose doing any more than you have done, I mearly make this suggestion.

See article in Atlanta Journal of June 3rd headed "Alabama Negroes Threaten Whites"[1]   very Truly yours

G. W. Campbell

ALS Con. 193 BTW Papers DLC. Written on stationery of the Macon County Bank.

1 The Atlanta *Journal* reported that two black preachers in Mobile, Ala., had published a demand for fair play from the Alabama constitutional convention, and warned that if blacks were not properly treated there would be trouble in the future. The *Journal* stated: "It is believed that the violent tone of the article will do much to destroy the good effect and favorable impression created by Booker Washington's and W. H. Councill's appeal in behalf of the race in convention made a few days ago." (Atlanta *Journal*, June 3, 1901, 1.)

From Bradford Lee Gilbert[1]

New York, June 4th, 1901

My dear Mr. Washington: I have your letter of the 1st and also photographs which you sent (for which accept my thanks) and which I will use for the purposes already referred to.

I have one of the most clever Sculptors working on an original figure[2] to be placed in the Court of your Building on the Natural-Section at the Exposition Grounds, Charleston. Mr. J. Q. A. Ward,[3] Prest. of the National Sculpture Society and Mr. Charles R. Lamb,[4] President of the Arts Club, will pass on this group, and I really believe it will be one of the finest on the grounds, and these gentlemen above mentioned stand at the topmost limit of their profession as Sculptors. They are highly enthused over the subject and are taking the greatest interest in working it out successfully.

The central figure of the group is a young Negress poising on her head a full basket of cotton and standing up in a most dignified and effective manner. At the right is a typical figure of a muscular and well-formed man holding a plough, as indicative of agricultural pursuits, in which such a large field lies open for success, and it is in this figure that I propose to have designed as an ideal a likeness of yourself, as the recognized and acknowledged leader of your Race today, and I pray God you may never do anything which shall place you in any other position. On the left, with a leather working apron round his loins and the tools of a mechanic lying at his feet, is a young man resting at noon-time on a bale of tobacco or cotton with a banjo which he is intently examining and playing. The whole group while in repose is full of life, is dignified and shows everyone occupied with some special industry and the design can be viewed from all sides, standing as it will in the central court of your building on the axis line of the principal entrance to this section from the hill in front of the old Homestead on the Wagener tract in the shadow of the enormous live oaks; with the figures eight feet in height and standing on a pedestal eight feet above the ground, you can form some idea of its effectiveness and beauty when completed. We have four other original groups — one typical of Colonial days, one of the Huguenots, another of the Spanish and Aztecs and one of the Aborigines or Indians, executed at a similar scale.

The Exposition Directors have asked me to accomplish almost an impossible feat by providing a building twice the size of the sketch submitted at practically the same cost, but I have practically accomplished this result by changing the style and architecture of the building, using replicas of certain staff ornamentation which will give a most effective and beautiful structure, carried out in strong Renaissance motif.

I told Dr. Crum[5] while last at Charleston that "if you would set a date, at any time you please, for the laying of the corner stone of this building, if you gave us about two weeks' notice, we would be ready for you." I thought it would be a good idea if you had a photograph of the Negro Building, also of the original group in the Court or Patio, if you could write an article for some one of the best known magazines it would cause widespread comments and favorable criticisms and might be the means of bringing in a large revenue from your own people, as well as others. I feel confident also that the Exposition magazine in the next number would be delighted to publish these photographs and such an article also. I trust you will take the matter in hand personally, as I believe in my best judgment you are the only man who can handle this theme successfully.

I had a most delightful trip with President Baldwin of the Long Island Railroad, to his home yesterday evening, and had a very pleasant chat about this matter. Anything I can do toward helping you to make a success of the Negro exhibit at the Charleston Exposition, will simply be a pleasure. Very truly,

B. L. Gilbert
ARCHITECT IN CHIEF

TLS   Con. 209   BTW Papers   DLC.

1 Bradford Lee Gilbert, a prominent New York architect, specialized in public buildings, particularly railroad stations. In 1898 he was the architect for the enlargement of Grand Central Station in New York City.

2 For the controversy among blacks over the statuary outside the Negro Building, see Thomas J. Jackson to BTW, Oct. 9, 1901, below.

3 John Quincy Adams Ward (1830–1910), a leading American sculptor, best known, perhaps, for *Indian Hunter*, one of the first statues in Central Park in 1868, and the equestrian statue of General George H. Thomas in Washington (1878). In 1865 he produced the popular statuette *Freedman*, a seated figure of a black man looking at the shackles from which he has been released.

4 Charles Rollison Lamb (1859 or 1860–1942), a New York architect with a special interest in church architecture, was a founder of the National Arts Club.

5 William Demosthenes (or Demos) Crum (1859–1912), a black physician and Republican party leader in Charleston, S.C., was born free in Charleston. His paternal grandfather (originally Krum) had emigrated from Germany early in the nineteenth century. William's white father, Darius, inherited a large plantation near Orangeburg and about forty slaves. He and his black wife, Charlotte, had seven children. At the end of the Civil War the father had died and the family fortune was depleted, so the elder sons migrated to the North in search of employment. They aided their younger brother William to attend Avery Normal Institute, an American Missionary Association school in Charleston, where he graduated in 1875. After studying for a time at the University of South Carolina, he entered the medical school of Howard University, graduating in 1880. He set up practice in Charleston, and in 1883 married Ellen Craft of London, a child of the famous fugitive slaves William and Ellen Craft.

By 1900 Crum had achieved a place of prominence in the Charleston black community. He was head of the local black hospital, an active member of the A.M.E. Church, a trustee of Avery Institute, and active in local business enterprises. White promoters of the South Carolina Interstate and West Indian Exposition recognized his standing by appointing him head of the Negro Department of the exposition. He was a suave and deferential interracial diplomat rather than a person remarkable for his achievements. Crum was active also in Republican politics, serving for twenty years as chairman of the party in Charleston County. He was a delegate to every Republican national convention from 1884 to 1904. In 1892 President Benjamin Harrison sought to reward his party services by appointing him postmaster of Charleston, but local whites were so vociferous in their opposition to a black postmaster that the President withdrew the nomination. Two years later the Republicans chose Crum to make the hopeless race against Benjamin R. Tillman for the U.S. Senate. Though Crum lost the election, his nomination was a victory for the black faction of his party. The blacks during the McKinley years controlled the party machinery in South Carolina, but the lily whites secured the federal patronage.

When Theodore Roosevelt became President, it was partly because of BTW's endorsement but also because of pressure from South Carolina blacks for a prominent federal appointment that the President nominated Crum collector of the port of Charleston. As Charleston was one of the leading southern seaports, this was an important post. Among the leaders of opposition to the Crum appointment were the same business leaders who had recently placed Crum at the head of the Negro Department of the Charleston Exposition. The vehemence of white Charlestonians' opposition shocked the President. They enlisted the support of Senator Tillman, who invoked senatorial courtesy to block the Senate's confirmation of Crum. The President continued to submit Crum's name to a recalcitrant Senate, meanwhile keeping him in office on interim appointments, until the Senate finally ratified the nomination in

1905. Meanwhile, Washington and his friends throughout the country carried on a letter-writing campaign for Crum among the senators.

Throughout the Roosevelt administration, Crum performed his duties as collector efficiently, and Washington was able to point to him as the type of black federal office-holder he sought as replacement for the older professional politicians. Crum was never able to win the confidence or friendliness of Charleston's whites, however, and they made things hot for him and Roosevelt. Among President Taft's first actions on winning the presidency in 1908 was to notify BTW that he intended to remove Crum at the beginning of his term. Through BTW he offered Crum two alternatives. If Crum would voluntarily resign the collectorship, he would find Crum another office of distinction outside of the South. If Crum refused to resign, he would dismiss him without another office. BTW persuaded Crum to resign, and in 1910 Taft appointed him minister to Liberia. Never a robust man, Crum contracted malaria in Monrovia and soon died. The Crum case was the last major effort to maintain black political patronage in the South after disfranchisement, and its ultimate failure was a sign of the worsening times in the Taft years that led toward the federal segregation policies of the Wilson administration.

From James Earl Russell

New York   June 5th, 1901

My dear Mr. Washington: As a result of the Ogden tour, I have had several special Scholarships, of five hundred dollars each, placed in my hands for the benefit of Southern teachers. In this list I suppose we should include Mr. Macy's[1] promise to you to support a teacher whom you might send to us. I have also a tentative promise of two other Scholarships which may be used in case there seems to be an especially good opening. If you know of a thoroughly good person, either a college graduate or a well trained normal school graduate, who has demonstrated superior teaching ability, I shall be glad to have you make a nomination to me. The idea is that these persons, after a year or two of special study, should return to the South, prepared to do administrative or normal school work. Some such person as Miss Porter, head of your Normal Department, is the one I am looking for. If she were free to come next year, I think it would mean much for your Normal Department thereafter.

With best wishes for your continued success, I am, Very sincerely yours,

Jas. E. Russell

TLS Con. 213 BTW Papers DLC.

1 Valentine Everit Macy (1871–1930), a wealthy New York philanthropist who gave substantially to Teachers College of Columbia University, the Metropolitan Museum of Art, and the National Child Labor Committee. Macy attended the Conference on Education in the South in 1901 and also toured Tuskegee Institute.

From Robert Curtis Ogden

New York. June 6th, 1901

Dear Mr. Washington: You will recall our conversation concerning a gentleman residing in Atlanta for membership in the committee which, as President of the Southern Educational Conference, I am to form for the continuous prosecution of educational ideas in the South. You will remember that your impression was that he was not available on account of personal, professional and political antagonisms.

Yesterday I had a conference with Dr. Dabney and Messrs. Page, Baldwin and Doubleday upon the composition of the committee. The name in question was very fully discussed, all the pros and cons considered, and the unanimous advice of these gentlemen was that the party named would be a very desirable member of the committee. Before proceeding to send him an invitation, I desire to submit the matter to you again for your further advice.

The committee, as it now rests in my mind, would be composed as follows: Drs. Dabney, Alderman,[1] McIver and Frissell and Mr. George Foster Peabody; also the gentleman under discussion from Atlanta. For the remaining appointment probably a Baptist Clergyman. The choice for the latter appears to lie between Mr. Buttrick,[2] of Albany, and Dr. Eager, now of Chicago, and formerly of Montgomery, Alabama. Mr. Murphy has been here and I have consulted with him considerably. It is his opinion that the Committee would be strengthened by a good broadminded member of the Baptist

communion. Mr. Baldwin shares the same view. Hence the foregoing suggestion, concerning which I have asked the advice of Mr.
Rockefeller, Jr.

There are many important considerations that bear upon each
one of these appointments, too many for me to recite in the course
of a letter.

I am extremely interested in Dr. Dabney's intelligent energy.
His soul is on fire with this question of the universal popular education in the South, and he is also under very severe criticism in his
own part of the country, because of his advanced notions upon
education and the courage with which he gives the actual facts to
the world.

I will welcome very cordially the utmost frankness on your part
concerning this matter. The present seems to me a critical period.
If intelligence, industry and courage are now applied, much good
may be wrought, especially in the creation of an improved public
sentiment in the South. Yours very truly,

Robert C. Ogden

TLS BTW Papers ATT.

1 Edwin Anderson Alderman (1861–1931) was one of the principal southern founders
of the Southern Education Movement. Graduating from the University of North
Carolina, he became a teacher and then superintendent of schools of Goldsboro, N.C.
After serving as conductor of teachers' institutes and professor at the Normal and Industrial School for Women at Greensboro, Alderman became professor of education
at the University of North Carolina in 1893 and its president in 1896. Serving four
years there and four years as president of Tulane, Alderman became president of the
University of Virginia in 1904. Combining the New South spirit with the manner of
the southern gentleman, Alderman found his niche at Virginia, where his gifts of
oratory and diplomacy cajoled adequate state funds from the Martin-Byrd political
machine. One of the original members of the Southern Education Board, he was one
of the few southerners who, by their urbanity and intersectional diplomacy, managed
to become members of the more powerful General Education Board. He served there
from 1906 to 1928. Though he presided over BTW's address to a mixed audience in
New Orleans in 1902, Alderman as a member of the Southern Education Board was
reluctant to risk a campaign for black schools that might jeopardize the board's
standing with white southerners.

2 Wallace Buttrick (1853–1926), a graduate of Rochester Theological Seminary,
was a Baptist minister for almost twenty years before becoming executive secretary
of the General Education Board when it was established with funds from John D.
Rockefeller in 1902. Buttrick had previously worked with Frederick T. Gates, Rockefeller's adviser on philanthropy, on the Baptist Educational Board. The General
Education Board had an overlapping membership with the Southern Education
Board, and Buttrick worked closely with the latter in its efforts to improve southern

public education. The chief contribution of the General Education Board in this area was the promotion of southern white rural high schools through the appointment of professors of secondary education in the state universities, with the responsibility of promoting high schools. An affable man who avoided at all costs the alienation of southern whites, Buttrick did nothing to prevent the gross neglect of black schools in the General Education Board's philanthropic grants in the South. His influence on black education was increased when he became a member of the Southern Education Board and secretary and member of the Slater Fund board. As the Rockefeller philanthropies expanded, he was a trustee of the Rockefeller Foundation, member of the International Health Board, and chairman of the International Education Board.

To Hollis Burke Frissell

Tuskegee, Ala., June 7, 1901

Dear Dr. Frissell: I very much hope that you and others are maturing some plans by which to influence the members of the Virginia State Constitutional Convention both on the question of education and the question of the suffrage. As you know, the Alabama State Constitutional Convention is now in session and I am dividing my time pretty nearly equally between that convention and the school and I consider it an important part of our work. I believe that we are facing about the same conditions in Alabama as you are in Virginia and I think that if you can get together in some quiet way as we have done in this state, the most substantial colored men for a conference it will be helpful.

There was at first in this state quite a radical element both in regard to the franchise and the division of the school fund, but I am glad to say that we have practically won the fight against the division of the school fund so much so that I do not believe the question is going to be seriously debated in the convention. I understand on good authority that the committee on education is most unanimously opposed to any division.

I am also glad to say that by united and constant effort the spirit of the convention regarding the franchise has been very much modified, so much so that I believe we are going to get a rather decent election law.

I have tried to put every white man in Alabama that I could get my hands on who is at all favorable to our side to work, and this in addition to what the colored people have done has been quite helpful. Yours truly,

Booker T. Washington

TLS   BTW Folder   ViHaI.

From Hilary Abner Herbert

Washington, D.C. June 7, 1901

Dear Sir: I am in receipt of yours of June 4th. in which you express the hope that, in case it comes in my way, in the address I am to make before the Alabama State Bar Association on the 28th instant, to say anything bearing on the work of the present State Convention, I will be as liberal as I can regarding the treatment of your race.

I do not now know whether I shall touch directly upon the question of suffrage or not, but think it quite probable I may. I shall certainly deal unsparingly with the question of frauds at elections, and insist that the votes of qualified voters shall be counted as cast.

In the meantime, permit me to say that I have to some extent already anticipated your request. In reply to two members of the Convention who have written me on the subject, I have urged upon them the necessity of treating your race liberally, stating that while I thought a large proportion of them should be disfranchised, yet that quite a number of them ought to be allowed to vote, and that it would certainly be a great wrong to deprive the negro of the hope of bettering his condition by proper conduct, politically, financially and socially. From one of these gentlemen I received a reply, stating that he agreed with me fully; the other did not respond.

I also stated in my letter, that in view of our past experience negro domination under any well considered and fair system of suffrage was not to be feared.

I read very carefully your Memorial to the Convention, and I wish to say that I have seen no document more pathetic, touching or forceful. I certainly hope, from what I have heard and seen, that this Memorial will meet with a proper response.

I am also in receipt of your little book, The Future of the American Negro, which I shall take great pleasure in reading at the first opportunity. Permit me to thank you for it. Yours truly,

H A Herbert

TLS   Con. 193   BTW Papers   DLC.

To Hollis Burke Frissell

Tuskegee, Ala., June 8, 1901

Dear Dr. Frissell: Mr. Calloway has resigned as principal of the school at Kowaliga. Without going into details I wish to say that I am sure that things are in a bad condition at that school and I do not feel that it is right under the present circumstances for the school to bear our endorsement. Since however, it is very largely dependent upon our endorsement for its support I think the present may be a good opportunity to put the institution into some kind of decent shape and that is by insisting that we name the man who is to take Mr. Calloway's place. I do not write for the purpose of asking you to act at present on this suggestion but to think about it and reach some conclusion if possible by the time we meet. Yours truly,

Booker T. Washington

TLS   BTW Folder   ViHaI.

To William McKinley

Washington, D.C. June 10, 1901

Dear Sir: Hearing that our friend, Hon. C. W. Thompson, Member of Congress from this district, was going to Washington, I have taken the liberty to write you through him to remind you that it was at Mr. Thompson's house that you were entertained while in Tuskegee. Mr. Thompson has been of great service to our institution and is a friend to our race. I have thought that you might like to renew the acquaintance.[1] Yours truly,

Booker T. Washington

TLS   William McKinley Papers   DLC.   Written on Tuskegee Institute stationery.

[1] BTW gave Thompson a letter of introduction to carry to the President's secretary, George B. Cortelyou. He requested that Cortelyou arrange a meeting between Thompson and the President "at as early a moment as possible and at a time when he can see the President to the greatest advantage." (June 10, 1901, William McKinley Papers, DLC.)

From Thomas Goode Jones

Montgomery, Alabama. June 10th 1901

Personal

Dear Sir. I am obliged for your letter. The positions taken in the letter to which you refer, have been my life long views; and if I can enforce them to any extent in solving our problems I will feel that I have accomplished something for the good of our state. The educational assault on the negro I feel sure, has now been effectually killed. You have doubtless seen the resolution I offered, and the little interview I had in the Advertiser, on that subject.[1] One of the complements I valued most, regarding my administration of the office of Governor, was from a very intelligent negro, who once said to me "your election brought no terror to any negro cabin."

You are going through a very trying experience; for when you are doing what is wisest and best for your race, there are fools with pens who assail your fidelity to it, and advocate policies which give your race and its friends double obstacles to overcome in getting a wise solution of our troubles. Such a man is the negro editor in Mobile.[2] In all proper ways I will cooperate with you—though I think it wise policy, as far as you can, to move others rather than appear to move yourself. I still hope for a fair Constitution, and I hope in the end both races will be bettered. Yours truly

Thos. G. Jones

ALS   Con. 201   BTW Papers   DLC.

1 In the Montgomery *Advertiser*, June 4, 1901, 4, Jones argued against disfranchise-ment based on race. He did support, however, educational and property qualifications for voting. "Any scheme," he said, "no matter how fair on its face, which is adminis-tered so as to discriminate in favor of the white man and against the negro as such, is vicious, and sooner or later liable to bring the State in collision with Federal cor-rective measures, both by the courts and Congress, and in some instances, with the judicial power of the state itself."

2 A. N. Johnson.

A Press Release[1]

New York City, June 17th, 1901

Mr. Booker T. Washington, while in the City, said in reference to the Alabama State Constitutional Convention, which is now in session, that it is composed of some of the strongest and most con-servative and wisest men in the State of Alabama; and it is my opinion that the men composing this Convention are essentially seeking to find a way to do the best and wisest thing for the interests of both races in the State.

The main questions which called the Convention together were those of Education and the Franchise. There was an element in the State in favor of dividing the school fund in proportion to the taxes paid by each race, but the sentiment of the Convention seems strongly opposed to any such division. No plan has as yet been ma-tured concerning the Franchise; but it is my opinion that Alabama will have a much more satisfactory Constitution than any of the Southern States that have recently held such conventions. The members of the Alabama Convention appreciate the fact that Ala-bama is a State of diversified industries, and is quite different in its resources and opportunities from such a State as Mississippi. The members of the Alabama Convention also appreciate the impor-tance of encouraging outside capital to come into the State, and they know that capital is shy of any State that does not have the best and most just laws. So far as I can learn, the question of the Fran-chise is being approached from a different point of view in Alabama than has been true of any other Southern State. Something will be done, in my opinion, that will hold out an incentive for both races to make the best and most conservative citizens. The members of the Alabama Convention also appreciate the fact that the prosperity of the State depends largely upon having a happy, contented and friendly class of laborers instead of a class of laborers that is restless, resentful and unhappy, seeking on every occasion to go to fields that are more inviting.

The Committee in charge of the Franchise is not permitting itself to be hurried, but is seeking light from every source. While I may be disappointed, my own feeling is, that we are going to get in Alabama the most satisfactory Constitution that any of the Southern States have recently made, perhaps with one exception.

TM   Con. 215   BTW Papers   DLC.

1 BTW sent the statement to Edward P. Clark, editor of the New York *Evening Post*, with a note: "As I did not have time to call at your office or to let one of your reporters know that I was here, I send enclosed something in the shape of an interview, which you can use, if you think it wise." (June 17, 1901, Con. 215, BTW Papers, DLC.) The newspaper did not publish the statement.

From Margaret James Murray Washington

[Tuskegee, Ala.] 6-19 [1901]

Mr. Washington: You remember that I spoke to you just before you left with reference to Julian working in the afternoons for cash. He is a boy now thirteen and it is most natural that he wants to have a little money. It seems to me that you might allow him fifteen cents for every half day that he works. I would suggest that you put him under Brown[1] on the farm as the boy is so delicate and grows so slowly. It would be very much better if all of the Cubans were worked in the afternoons and paid for it, for these boys have so much time to walk into mischief. And besides it is a great temptation to find yourself without money.

Mrs. Washington

TLSr   Con. 214   BTW Papers   DLC.

1 Joseph B. Brown taught truck gardening at Tuskegee beginning about 1902 and continuing until 1906.

From John Willis Baer[1]

Boston, June 21, 1901

My dear Mr. Washington, The chairman of the Entertainment Committee for the coming convention at Cincinnati informs me that he is arranging for your entertainment while in Cincinnati in private homes and he will notify you of this fact, giving full information a little later.

An explanation is due you. We had expected that you would be entertained with the Board of Trustees at the Grand Hotel in Cincinnati. The hotel people decline to enter into the arrangement and we protested but without success. Several letters and telegrams passed backward and forward. The officers and trustees of the United Society are the guests of the Cincinnati people and are obliged to fall in with their plans for hotel arrangements, but we do it under protest for we should have been very glad indeed as in the past to have had you with us at our hotel.

And understand, we draw no color line in our conventions and if we were paying this Cincinnati hotel bill, we would not go to that hotel unless you could go as our guest and have exactly the same treatment as we shall expect, but as I have said we are the guests of the Cincinnati people who are paying this hotel bill.

You will accept this letter we know in the spirit in which it is offered, but we desire you to have a perfectly frank statement of a matter that has been displeasing to us.

Enclosed please find a platform ticket and let me know when you will arrive in Cincinnati. Yours cordially,

John Willis Baer

TLS Con. 261 BTW Papers DLC.

[1] John Willis Baer was general secretary of the United Society of Christian Endeavor in Boston.

To Andrew Carnegie

Tuskegee, Ala. June 22, 1901

Dear Mr. Carnegie: I thought that perhaps in your far away Scotland home you might like to glance at a picture showing our students at work in the erection of the library building which you have so kindly provided for us. I am sorry that we were not able to get a better photograph. I send the photograph by this mail. Yours truly,

Booker T. Washington

TLS   Andrew Carnegie Papers   DLC.

From Robert Wesley Taylor

Ithaca, N.Y. June 24, 1901

Dear Mr. Washington: I have your favor of June 20th with reference to the Dining Car incident on the Southern Road June 6th.

The whole affair arose over the fact that the Conductor spoke to me as a *"bully"* instead of as a gentleman. I told him that I should report the matter to Mr. Hardwick and that, no doubt, is why he concocted the infamous false[hood] he did. He the wronged Saint, I the wrong-doing Sinner.

Enclosed herewith I send you a copy of the last letter written to Mr. Hardwick.

I am not unduly sensitive, neither do I look for trouble, but imposition without provocation is decidedly indigestible. Yours very truly,

Robert W. Taylor

ALS   Con. 212   BTW Papers   DLC.

From John Davison Rockefeller, Jr.

New York. June 25th, 1901

Dear Mr. Washington: I am in receipt of your favor of June 22nd consenting to speak to the Bible Class of our Church on October 17th. I heartily appreciate your kindness in arranging to be present with us on this occasion and shall be very glad indeed to have the members of the Class meet you and hear you speak. Very truly,

John D. Rockefeller, Jr.

TLS Con. 709 BTW Papers DLC.

From George Foster Peabody

New York, June 26, 1901

My dear Mr. Washington: I have yours of the 22nd with reference to your being in New York. I do not think that I shall be able to be in New York on Monday the 15th, but if you advise me definitely that you will be in New York on the 16th, and not on the 17th, I will arrange to meet you on the 16th, and would prefer the afternoon. I should be glad to have the meeting at my office, if convenient.

I also have your letter with reference to the female college for white women at Tuskegee,[1] and would say that I shall be glad to have my subscription stand for that at $2,000. provided they raise as much as $10,000., or at $1,000. provided they raise as much as $6,000.; although I question the wisdom of getting into debt of this character. I am not inclined to help denominational colleges, but in view of what you say of this one, and your judgment in the matter, I am glad to make an exception in this case.

I am, Yours very truly,

George Foster Peabody

TLS Con. 208 BTW Papers DLC.

[1] Alabama Conference Female College.

From Alexander Walters

Du Quoin Ill, June 27—1901

My Dear Friend: Your good letter of 21 inst has been forwarded to me. I was delighted to hear from you and to learn that you were pleased with the Indianapolis interview. You have won first place on your merit and I think we all ought to be generous enough to give it to you.

I am greatly pleased with your work and have long ago decided to do all in my power to advance your interest. Believe me when I tell you that I do so cheerfully. I have ordered Mr Thompson[1] treasurer of the Afro-American Council to pay over to Mr Birney the $200.00 need[ed] to make up $500.00 but Mr Fortune stopped the payment, and informed me that he would consult you about the matter. What about it? I am of the opinion that we had better pay the $500.00 and push the case.

Dont fail to be present at the Phil Meeting ~~July~~[2] 7–10. We hope to collect a $1000.

Accept my congratulations on your efforts to check the Convention of your State in its work of disfranchisement. May heaven continue to bless you with health and great success.

I remain yours sincerely,

A. Walters

ALS Con. 215 BTW Papers DLC.

[1] John W. Thompson of Rochester, N.Y., was reported in the 1900 census as a superintendent of dining rooms. He was born in 1863. The Afro-American Council named him treasurer at its first meeting in Dec. 1898. In Mar. 1901 Thompson invited BTW to give an address to celebrate the emancipation of the slaves and to commemorate the third year of the Douglass monument in Rochester. (Thompson to BTW, Mar. 23, 1901, Con. 212, BTW Papers, DLC.)

[2] Walters struck out July but failed to write August, the month of the National Afro-American Council meeting in Philadelphia. BTW did not attend despite Walters's urging that if BTW did not appear "I am afraid that the enemy will use it against us." (Walters to BTW, July 27, 1901, Con. 214, BTW Papers, DLC.)

From Thomas Goode Jones

Montgomery, Alabama. June 28th 1901

Personal

Dear Sir. If my word had a more far reaching influence than I supposed, I am gratified.[1] I have received scores of letters from all over the State giving praise to the speech, far beyond any thing I thought it deserved. The question came up suddenly on Saturday evening, and I was not prepared to make a set speech.

There are two virtues in the Constitutional provision which I framed — *one* was to take the impeachment out of the county, where the mob dominates, and put it in the Supreme Court where the *State* can have a fair trial — the other is auxilliary to it, allowing the judge's[?] mean time to suspend. Already it has stirred up the Sheriffs who are *protesting*. I am sure it is the beginning of the end of lynching.

I am not a candidate for anything — have no ambition, and am not in any bodys way; yet I can not be blind to the fact that there is some jealousy of me among many politicians. For these reasons, I concur in your view, that it is better to let this matter wait until after the suffrage question is settled. Yours truly

Thos. G. Jones

ALS   Con. 200   BTW Papers   DLC.

[1] On June 22, 1901, Jones spoke extemporaneously before the Alabama constitutional convention in support of a provision declaring that a sheriff could be impeached if he allowed a prisoner to be taken from his jail for the purpose of lynching. He made a ringing appeal to end mob violence in Alabama. The convention approved the measure, and the Alabama newspapers praised Jones's speech. (Montgomery *Advertiser*, June 23, 1901, 1; Birmingham *Age-Herald*, June 23, 1901, 1; Mobile *Daily Register*, June 23, 1901, 2.)

From Robert Curtis Ogden

New York. June 29, 1901

Dear Mr. Washington: My financial cow has about gone dry. Nevertheless, I will be glad to be counted in for $100 on the matter of the library for the Alabama Female College. When well-intentioned people are coming out into the light it is a good thing to help them to see the "glory of the coming of the Lord." Yours very truly,

Robert C Ogden

TLS Con. 208 BTW Papers DLC.

From Lillian Marion Norton Ames Stevens[1]

Portland, Me., 1 July 1901

My dear Mr. Washington: I have read your Autobiography "Up From Slavery" with deepest interest. I read it too as one who has always been interested in your people, and who has recognized them as *our people*, and can unhesitatingly say I consider it one of the greatest books of the day. Much more I might say did I think it necessary.

I am going to beg the privilege of asking you a few questions, and I do not ask them in the spirit of criticism, but because I have a vital and living interest in the temperance cause, because I know the drink evil is the curse of all races and that it is confined to no one class. May I ask why you make no allusion to the drink evil in your book? Why, in speaking of your honored wife's connection with the Federation of Clubs do you not mention her connection with the largest organization of women in the world, the Woman's Christian Temperance Union? While you make fitting mention of that great woman, Susan B. Anthony, why do you not mention that greater woman, the greatest woman of the century, Frances E. Willard? And the first and only woman whose statue has ever been ordered to be placed in Statuary Hall, at the Nation's Capitol. Your race never had a more loyal friend, and I am sure no kinder, broader recognition could have been given Mrs. Washington than has been accorded her by Frances Willard on our public platform. I have heard her speak of you and describe your work as she saw it at Tuskegee, and I can but wonder if in any way you have misunderstood her, if you have misunderstood her great work and the work of the W. C. T. U. which is still going on with marked success.

Because of your nobility of soul I feel that you will receive this letter in the same spirit in which it is written, and I sincerely hope that you will favor me with a reply in order that I may answer the questions that are being asked me in regard to the matter.

Please remember me with kindest regards to Mrs. Washington, and with best wishes for the success of your work which God has so signally helped, I am, Very sincerely yours,

Lillian M. N. Stevens

TLS Con. 211 BTW Papers DLC.

[1] Lillian Marion Norton Ames Stevens (1844–1914) was a crusader for temperance and women's rights. She was a founder of the Maine Woman's Christian Temperance Union in 1875 and served as treasurer and then president from 1878 until her death. She became president of the National WCTU in 1898 and vice-president of the world organization in 1903.

From John Willis Baer

Boston, July 1, 1901

My dear Mr. Washington, Unless you hear from us to the contrary, either by letter or by wire, immediately upon your arrival in Cincinnati go to the Grand Hotel. We think that we have brought pressure to bear to change the hotel people. At any rate, we hope so, and feel confident that you will not be subjected to any humiliation. Of course, when you register you are not supposed to know anything about the friction that we have had. Yours cordially,

John Willis Baer

TLS Con. 189 BTW Papers DLC.

From Belton Gilreath

Birmingham, Ala. July 3rd. 1901

My dear sir: I received your letter some days ago and intended answering sooner, but have been very busy and have also been out of the city a part of the time.

I am glad you sent me the half dozen copies of your book. I needed about that number to complete the number of names on my list to whom I wanted to present your book.[1] I note that you state that you will send me a few more copies if needed. In this connection, I would state that I could use half dozen more, I think, with advantage.

I have just sent your publishers check for $18.00 for payment of a dozen copies bought by myself; and if you will furnish me with a dozen copies I think I can, with these 24 books, put some good men and women in harmony with you and your work.

In this connection, I might state that I hope your publishers will publish a cheap paper edition of this book that can be sold to the general public and on railway trains at low prices. This would enable many people to read it that could not buy an expensive edition. Furthermore, it will enable some of us who are interested in your work to buy more copies for our employees to read at our mines. However this is a suggestion for your consideration only. If you have reasons for not doing this, satisfactory to yourself, you will of course leave it off. It may be that others may know of your work in other ways than by reading your book; but, I must say as far as I am concerned, that reading this book impressed me more and put me in deeper sympathy with you and your plans than any other agency could possibly have done.

I am putting these books in the hands of the ablest and most liberal men of our district, and I believe that these people reading them will get in sympathy with you, and give your school such proper aid and encouragement in future as is their duty to do. I feel exactly as I did at the start; that this district ought to help you, and will do so if they can get the matter properly put before them. I now have the faith that this will be done since my recent talk with you in Montgomery. I was impressed with your statement, in this conversation, that you had great confidence in faith and patience as a means to secure a good end. This must undoubtedly be true, as our great men and teachers who have gone before us laid down this principal.

In thinking over the magnitude of your work and heavy expense I have thought the South would probably have to come to your rescue at no distant day. While I think the Northern people will continue to stand by you, yet I think some subscriptions from the progressive and best people of the South; and their sympathies also will be needed in order that you may get the best results from our friends living in the North.

These are the thoughts that have passed through my mind in the past, and in reading the sentiments of the Northern people, and press; and the Southern people also I have no reason as yet to change my views. But however that may be, I am working a large number of your people at my different mines and I propose, as far as I can, to do my duty by them in the matter of paying them liberal wages; and dividing my gifts with them and in supporting their institutions; and also giving them my time and advice at such time and place as they call on me, whenever I feel that I can be of real service to them. Yours truly,

Belton Gilreath

P.S. Please excuse length of this letter. I did not intend to write so much, but while on the subject thought I would give you my feelings in the matter.

BG

TLS Con. 189 BTW Papers DLC.

[1] Gilreath gave more than thirty copies of *The Future of the American Negro* to prominent businessmen, editors, and clergymen in Birmingham. He told BTW that he presented most of the books personally and that many recipients expressed their hearty endorsement of BTW's work. Gilreath especially wanted the Birmingham coal operators to read the book "because they work a great many of your race; and I thought it could do the most good that way." (Gilreath to BTW, June 8, 1901, Con. 198; Gilreath to BTW, Jan. 21, 1902, Con. 228, BTW Papers, DLC.)

From William Edward Burghardt Du Bois

Atlanta, Ga., July 3 1901

Dear Mr. Washington: I shall be delighted to accept your kind invitation of the 26th ult. to camp in West Va.[1] My summer address is Sea Isle City, N.J. I enclose a letter from Martin.[2] Very Sincerely,

W. E. B. Du Bois

ALS Con. 195 BTW Papers DLC.

[1] See An Item in the Washington *Colored American*, Sept. 14, 1901, below.
[2] William C. Martin.

To Charles Eliot Norton[1]

Tuskegee, Ala., July 6, 1901

My dear Dr. Norton: I thank you very much for your generous view of my failure to fill my engagement in August. When the Convention met it was the intention of the more radical element to not only stop the Negro from voting but at the same time to divide the school fund in proportion to the amount of taxes paid by each race. While the majority report of the franchise committee is not satisfactory, I am glad to say that it is much better than the law which Louisiana, Mississippi and North Carolina have and I think is going to be still further improved before it is finally passed. The effort to divide the school fund is completely dead, so much so that I do not believe it will be even debated in the Convention. It has taken considerable work, however, on the part of some of us to bring about these conditions. The danger, however, is not fully passed and I feel that I must stand by with the exception of a few days until the Convention adjourns; when it will adjourn no one can tell. Yours truly,

Booker T. Washington

TLS   Charles Eliot Norton Papers   MH.

1 Charles Eliot Norton (1827–1908), a distinguished editor and teacher, was one of the founders of *The Nation* in 1865. He taught at Harvard from 1873 to 1897. Norton sponsored a series of annual dinners from 1879 to 1903 which featured prominent men of the day who spoke on various movements of social reform including reform of the civil service and the tariff, anti-imperialism, and promotion of education for blacks.

From Addison Wimbs

Greensboro, Alabama. July 6th 1901

My Dear Sir: If the Committee's Suffrage report goes through intact I am of the opinion that at least a part of the Negro problem in Alabama has been solved. It concedes the rights of some Negroes whereas a large part of the white men of Alabama believe that the Negro has no political rights however competent. We can not get all the concessions at once. While the Grand Daddy clause on its face discriminates in favor of the white man yet I see no reason why we should raise any objection to that favoritism, so long as we get out of the mill something. As conditions are now no Negro in Alabama has any real political power whereas if after this constitution is adopted, if adopted, we will have at least a respectable minority of Negroes votes in Alabama. The way I figure we will under the temporary board, if we manage right, get a goodly number of our present voters registered for life and when the permanent plan is put in operation we will then get considerable more, so that in the end we will gather together on the list at least 60000 Negro voters and the way I reason I would rather have even 25000 than none as at present. This minority of Negro voters should certainly have sense enough to form with an element of the white voters working arrangements for the benefit of both. I have no fears on that line.

I am greatly encouraged with the situation and do not look upon it as some, that our labors have been in vain. The First section of the report is a concession made that but few men expected for it was thought that the disfranchisement would be sweeping.

It is true that under the temporary plan a great deal will depend upon the administration of the law and all or nearly all of the Negroes could be excluded from the roll, but I reason we should have sufficient sagacity to get a goodly number of our people on the roll and this can be done if proper work is quietly pushed, especially in the Black Belt.

If this Committees report, is adopted, when it comes to the appointment of the registrars for the counties let us quietly look after the personnel of these boards as best we can and then if we should not get such men appointed as we would like to have, then let us make prayerful terms with the Registration Boards of the various counties where ever we can. My plan is to get the best we can out of this convention and then meet them as best we can by seeing that the machinery works properly. If this report goes through, I am of the thorough conviction that the thing for the Negroes to do is to meet the enemy with the olive branch and beat them at their own game. The profession[al] ballot box thief will be loath to rob himself of all power and if such are made registrars they will in my opinion register as many Negroes as they can and then after we get them registered we can then join with those of the citizens who want honest elections and force honest count. My plan is first to use the "boys in the trenches" to get our folks registered and then after they are registered use the "Amen corner pure election members" to force a fair and honest count of these registered voters. I may be dreaming but I believe it would work.

This letter is personal. I do not want my views made public. I simply give them to you for what they are worth and for you to consider them in connection with your thoughts in this matter. Yours truly

Ad. Wimbs

P.S. If all should fail we would be as well off as now politically.

TLS Con. 216 BTW Papers DLC.

An Announcement of
the National Negro Business League

[Tuskegee, Ala.] July 6, 1901

After full consideration and consultation with officials of the National Negro Business League and friends throughout the country, it has been decided to call the next session of the League to meet at Chicago, Ill., Wednesday, Thursday and Friday, August 21, 22 and 23.

It is generally conceded that the meeting held in Boston last August was one of the most successful gatherings ever held in the history of the race, and that it gave an encouragement and impetus to the race in all lines of business in a way that is now apparent in all parts of the country. It is earnestly hoped that the meeting in Chicago will even surpass the Boston meeting in point of attendance, in interest and in permanent value.

The citizens of Chicago are enthusiastic over the prospects of the meeting and stand ready to give those who attend it a cordial welcome. Aside from the matter of special reduced rates over the various railroads, reduced rates granted in connection with the

Buffalo Pan-American Exposition will offer unusual opportunities to reach Chicago at small expense.

Any person engaged in any commercial enterprise or properly delegated to represent any individual or individuals engaged in commercial enterprises, is entitled to membership under such regulations as may be adopted. Women as well as men engaged in business should be represented.

It is strongly urged that Local Business Leagues be established in every part of the country where no such leagues now exist and those already organized be strengthened wherever necessary, and that these local leagues send delegates, as far as possible, to the National organization, and keep in close touch during the year with the officers of the National organization; that these local organizations hold meetings monthly as far as practical; that everything possible be done in these local organizations to discourage complicated and useless parliamentary machinery, and that parliamentary and technical discussions be avoided, as far as possible, with a view to concentrating time and strength on the real objects of the organization.

Every one engaged in business owes it to himself to take a week or more of vacation each year for the purpose of rest and recreation and for the purpose of getting new ideas.

It is the desire of the officers of the League to make a large exhibit of photographs at Chicago of the places of business of our people as well as of the persons engaged in business. These photographs should show both outside and inside views as far as possible, and they should be forwarded to the President of the League at Tuskegee, Ala., as early as convenient.

The proceedings of the Boston meeting have been published in book form by Mr. J. R. Hamm, 46 Howard Street, Boston, Mass. A copy of this volume should be in the hands of every Negro in the country who is engaged in business, or who is expecting to enter business.

The time has come for the race to take a long step forward in establishing itself permanently and more generally in the business of the community where it resides.

Let no legislation or attempted legislation discourage or dishearten us. There should be no doubting or halting. Every move should be a forward one. To gain recognition and success we may have to struggle harder and longer than others, but out of the very struggle we shall gain a strength that we can get in no other way. The influence and power of intelligence, high character and high standing in the business world are sure to place the race in the end in a position where it will be honored and treated with justice in every part of the land. Let our watchword constantly be, "FORWARD."

Booker T. Washington
President, Tuskegee, Ala.
T. Thomas Fortune
Chairman, Executive Committee,
No. 4 Cedar Street, New York.
E. E. Cooper, Secretary,
459 C Street, N.W.
Washington, D.C.

Indianapolis *Freeman*, July 6, 1901, 6.

From Henry Floyd Gamble

Charleston, W.Va., July 8 1901

My Dear Mr Washington, Yours of a few days ago gladly received and contents noted with care and pleasure. I can help you in securing and arranging your outing if you deside to come. It will be impossible to secure a house. Up Elk is sparsely settle[d] and houses and accom[m]odations are so poor they would be intolerable. I have secured a large tent that will accommodate ten or twelve and it is at your disposal with out any cost. I can get you a good cook for $1.25 to $1.50 per day. You should also have a large boy to assist. For a party of 6 or 8 the cost of living ought not cost more than $3.50 to $5.00 per day for board, this depend[s] however on taste etc etc. As to location up Elk I would say that fishing is very poor within four or five miles of Charleston, because the constant floating out of logs, and the great quantity of sawdust from the very many mills for a distance of 40 miles up elk, make it very disagreable for fish, in fact the sawdust in the river gets into the gills of the fish and is very destructive to them hence the fish go above these disturbances. The best fishing is above Yankee Dam near Clay Courthous[e], 45 or 50 miles above Charleston; The Charleston Sportsman Club House is located near that point for the reasons stated.

With a good tent and a good cook you might locate at any suitable point along the river for hunting and rest and while fishing may not be so good near the city yet you might find enough for past time and pleasure.

I have been to some pains and have taken some time to secure these facts and am ready to assist and serve you in this matter in any way you may determine.

I am   Yours very sincerely

H. F. Gamble

ALS Con. 198 BTW Papers DLC.

From Theodore Roosevelt

Oyster Bay, N.Y. July 9th, 1901

My dear Mr. Washington: I am just in receipt of your letter of the 5th inst. You could not do anything that would please me more than to have Mr. Baldwin and Mr. Riis[1] accompany me. They are the very two men of all others that I would have chosen had you asked me. I think it would be a good thing to have the Chambers of Commerce at Atlanta and Montgomery receive me. I had not thought of visiting Montgomery, but had been intending to visit Atlanta, as I want to stop off and see my mother's old home at Roswell which is near there. I think it would be a first class thing for me to visit both cities. Moreover, I believe to have me received by the two chambers of commerce of these two capitals, when I have come down to speak at your institute would be excellent for the very purposes you have in view, and with which I so cordially sympathize — the purpose of fitting the Colored man to shift for himself and of establishing a healthy relation between the Colored man and the White man who lives in the same states.

Exactly what dates am I expected at Tuskegee, Atlanta and Montgomery? Sincerely yours,

Theodore Roosevelt

TLS Theodore Roosevelt Papers DLC.

1 Jacob August Riis (1849–1914), a Danish immigrant, was a police reporter in New York City from 1877 to 1899. Through his writings and his photographs he vividly exposed the life of poor people in the slums of New York in *How the Other Half Lives* (1890). His autobiography, *The Making of an American*, appeared in the same year as BTW's *Up from Slavery* (1901). In Sept. 1904 Riis guided BTW and the Archbishop of Canterbury on a tour of New York's East Side. He visited Tuskegee in Feb. 1905 and endorsed BTW's work and his gradualist philosophy of racial advancement. (See Lane, *Jacob A. Riis and the American City*, 176–78.)

From Emmett Jay Scott

Montgomery, Ala., July 9th 1901

My Dear Mr Washington: I came down this morning & went at once to see Mr M.[1] As I have wired you today, he thinks the situation practically unchanged since he saw you. The Convention yesterday finally finished what is called "The Bill of Rights," & is today considering the question of "Local Legislation." He thinks that this & extraneous matters will more than cover the time which will elapse during your absence. I do not think he seemed quite as cheerful & hopeful as usual. He says nobody can tell what will be done as regards the Suffrage matter. He said to me what he has doubtless said to you: that the Education Report is being delayed till after consideration of the Franchise. He thinks if the latter report is unfavorable that the Educational report will go through without material change, as he feels the Convention would be ashamed to deal harshly if it had acted wrongfully in the Franchise matter. On the other hand, he feels the Education report will be hard hit if a favorable Franchise law is finally secured. He praises Mr Graham[2] unstintedly & says his Committee has prepared a good report.

He is preparing an article which he will send to News at Birmingham, or to Advertiser, he did not indicate trend of article. Gov. Jones has prepared a good strong speech in defense of the Minority

report. He does not feel that opposition is weakening at all, & yet
he does not feel that adverse sentiment is particularly pronounced.
I have sent you a copy of Age-Herald containing a number of interviews, etc. in opposition. It is the Sunday issue & perhaps has
already been seen by you. I go to Tuskegee tonight & am to wire Mr
M. Thursday as to advisability of coming down again to see him so
as to make you a report. Personally, he does not think any further
good can be done by you, thinks you have done more than your
part & that harm can now be done by pushing matters. Of course
this does not mean that you should not keep advised as to the progress of events, but that he does not see how you can personally do
any more.

I hope your reception at Cincinnati was as cordial as ever & that
you are feeling quite well. I hope also you have found Mrs Washington bearing up well under the strain incident to the Federation meeting.[3] "Mr Adams knows nothing of interest." He asks
to be remembered to you. Yours Very Sincerely

Emmett J Scott

ALS   Con. 188   BTW Papers   DLC.   Written on stationery of J. W. Adams's
dry-goods store.

[1] Edgar Gardner Murphy.

[2] Joseph Brown Graham (1864–1903) was superintendent of schools of Talladega
County. In 1900 he was president of the state Democratic convention. A delegate to
the state constitutional convention in 1901–2, he opposed the racial division of public
school funds. As the Alabama field agent of the Southern Education Board he helped
to organize the state local tax campaign in 1902.

[3] See An Editorial in the Cleveland *Gazette*, July 20, 1901, below.

From Emmett Jay Scott

Tuskegee, Ala., 7, 12, 1901

Dear Mr. Washington: Herewith I beg to hand you copy of Southwestern Christian Advocate for current week with marked note
regarding the Business League. I wrote this in the form of an editorial and sent to all of the colored newspapers. If it should appear
in all or in a great majority of them it will do much to stir interest.
I am sending out a similar one again this week and shall keep some-

thing in all of the colored newspapers from now until the meeting of the League. We have to date written more than 800 letters and none of these letters, with very few exceptions, have been returned, evidencing that they have been received by the persons to whom they have been written. Somehow, however, the returns do not seem to be quite as flattering as I should like to have them. There shall be no relaxation of effort, however, at this end, and I shall be getting out a second letter to be sent to the whole number of 1200 names which we have on our list in a few days.

The Advertiser which I am sending you today contains a letter which is signed Jeffersonian which is by Mr. Murphy. I have just talked with him over the telephone and he tells me that the caucus to which you will find reference made is not meeting with favor. He says that Gov. Jones and all whom he can control are not going to attend the caucus and be bound by it, in fact they look upon it as a means of preventing an honest expression of opinion. I should not be surprised now to see the whole thing go up in the air as there seem to be determined men on both sides of this controversy. I do not believe that the minority will permit itself to be stifled and yet it is quite hard for Democrats to resist an appeal for caucus. This caucus will be held Monday night and I shall advise you at once as to what comes of it. I shall see Mr. Murphy and shall let you know at once what he thinks about it.

Your reception at Cincinnati was a splendid one and we are all glad to learn that such an ovation was extended you. I hope the meeting at Boston was equally successful.

It is very, very hot here. Yours truly,

Emmett J. Scott

TLS Con. 209 BTW Papers DLC.

1 Murphy's long letter signed "A Jeffersonian" appeared in the Montgomery *Advertiser*, July 12, 1901, 5. It criticized the constitutional convention's committee on suffrage reports, particularly the grandfather clause and the clause giving the registrars of each county, appointed by the governor and his staff, arbitrary power over registration. This would allow registrars in black counties to continue to use a controlled black vote, he claimed.

A Book Review by William Edward Burghardt Du Bois

Atlanta University, Atlanta, Ga. [July 16, 1901]

The Evolution of Negro Leadership

In every generation of our national life, from Phillis Wheatley to Booker Washington, the Negro race in America has succeeded in bringing forth men whom the country, at times spontaneously, at times in spite of itself, has been impelled to honor and respect. Mr. Washington is one of the most striking of these cases, and his autobiography is a partial history of the steps which made him a group leader, and the one man who in the eyes of the nation typifies at present more nearly than all others the work and worth of his nine million fellows.

The way in which groups of human beings are led to choose certain of their number as their spokesmen and leaders is at once the most elementary and the nicest problem of social growth. History is but the record of this group leadership; and yet how infinitely changeful is its type and history! And of all types and kinds, what can be more instructive than the leadership of a group within a group — that curious double movement where real progress may be negative and actual advance be relative retrogression? All this is the social student's inspiration and despair.

When sticks and stones and beasts form the sole environment of a people, their attitude is ever one of determined opposition to, and conquest of, natural forces. But when to earth and brute is added an environment of men and ideas, then the attitude of the imprisoned group may take three main forms: a feeling of revolt and revenge; an attempt to adjust all thought and action to the will of the greater group; or, finally, a determined attempt at self-development, self-realization, in spite of environing discouragements and prejudice. The influence of all three of these attitudes is plainly to be traced in the evolution of race leaders among American Negroes. Before 1750 there was but the one motive of revolt and revenge which animated the terrible Maroons and veiled all the Americas in fear of insurrection. But the liberalizing tendencies of the latter half of the eighteenth century brought the first thought of adjustment and assimilation in the crude and earnest songs of Phillis and the martyrdom of Attucks and Salem.

The cotton-gin changed all this, and men then, as the Lyman Abbotts of to-day, found a new meaning in human blackness. A season of hesitation and stress settled on the black world as the hope of emancipation receded. Forten and the free Negroes of the North still hoped for eventual assimilation with the nation; Allen, the founder of the great African Methodist Church, strove for unbending self-development, and the Southern freedmen followed him; while among the black slaves at the South arose the avenging Nat Turner, fired by the memory of Toussaint the Savior. So far, Negro leadership had been local and spasmodic; but now, about 1840, arose a national leadership — a dynasty not to be broken. Frederick Douglass and the moral revolt against slavery dominated Negro thought and effort until after the war. Then, with the sole weapon of self-defense in perilous times, the ballot, which the nation gave the freedmen, men like Langston and Bruce sought to guide the political fortunes of the blacks, while Payne and Price still clung to the old ideal of self-development.

Then came the reaction. War memories and ideals rapidly passed, and a period of astonishing commercial development and expansion ensued. A time of doubt and hesitation, of storm and stress, overtook the freedmen's sons; and then it was that Booker Washington's leadership began. Mr. Washington came with a clear simple programme, at the psychological moment; at a time when the nation was a little ashamed of having bestowed so much sentiment on Negroes and was concentrating its energies on Dollars. The industrial training of Negro youth was not an idea originating with Mr. Washington, nor was the policy of conciliating the white South wholly his. But he first put life, unlimited energy, and perfect faith into this programme; he changed it from an article of belief into a whole creed; he broadened it from a by-path into a veritable Way of Life. And the method by which he accomplished this is an interesting study of human life.

Mr. Washington's narrative gives but glimpses of the real struggle which he has had for leadership. First of all, he strove to gain the sympathy and coöperation of the white South, and gained it after that epoch-making sentence spoken at Atlanta: "In all things that are purely social we can be as separate as the fingers, yet one as the hand in all things essential to mutual progress" (p. 221). This conquest of the South is by all odds the most notable thing in Mr. Washington's career. Next to this comes his achievement in gaining place and consideration in the North. Many others less shrewd and tactful would have fallen between these two stools; but as Mr. Washington knew the heart of the South from birth and training, so by singular insight he intuitively grasped the spirit of the age that was dominating the North. He learned so thoroughly the speech and thought of triumphant commercialism and the ideals of material prosperity that he pictures as the height of absurdity a black boy studying a French grammar in the midst of weeds and dirt. One wonders how Socrates or St. Francis of Assisi would receive this!

And yet this very singleness of vision and thorough oneness with his age is a mark of the successful man. It is as though Nature must needs make men a little narrow to give them force. At the same time, Mr. Washington's success, North and South, with his gospel of Work and Money, raised opposition to him from widely divergent sources. The spiritual sons of the Abolitionists were not prepared to acknowledge that the schools founded before Tuskegee, by men of broad ideals and self-sacrificing souls, were wholly failures, or worthy of ridicule. On the other hand, among his own people Mr. Washington found deep suspicion and dislike for a man on such good terms with Southern whites.

Such opposition has only been silenced by Mr. Washington's very evident sincerity of purpose. We forgive much to honest purpose which is accomplishing something. We may not agree with the man at all points, but we admire him and coöperate with him so far as we conscientiously can. It is no ordinary tribute to this man's tact and power, that, steering as he must amid so many diverse interests and opinions, he to-day commands not simply the applause of those who believe in his theories, but also the respect of those who do not.

Among the Negroes, Mr. Washington is still far from a popular leader. Educated and thoughtful Negroes everywhere are glad to honor him and aid him, but all cannot agree with him. He represents in Negro thought the old attitude of adjustment to environment, emphasizing the economic phase; but the two other strong currents of feeling, descended from the past, still oppose him. One is the thought of a small but not unimportant group, unfortunate in their choice of spokesman, but nevertheless of much weight, who represent the old ideas of revolt and revenge, and see in migration alone an outlet for the Negro people. The second attitude is that of the large and important group represented by Dunbar, Tanner, Chesnutt, Miller, and the Grimkes, who, without any single definite programme, and with complex aims, seek nevertheless that self-development and self-realization in all lines of human endeavor which they believe will eventually place the Negro beside the other races. While these men respect the Hampton-Tuskegee idea to a degree, they believe it falls far short of a complete programme. They believe, therefore, also in the higher education of Fisk and Atlanta Universities; they believe in self-assertion and ambition; and they believe in the right of suffrage for blacks on the same terms with whites.

Such is the complicated world of thought and action in which Mr. Booker Washington has been called of God and man to lead, and in which he has gained so rare a meed of success.

The Dial, 31 (July 16, 1901), 53–55. A review of *Up from Slavery.*

An Editorial in the Cleveland *Gazette*

Cleveland, Ohio, July 20, 1901

Mrs. Booker T. Washington certainly met a Waterloo in last week's annual convention of the National Association of Colored Women.[1] According to the dispatches to the daily newspapers Mr. and Mrs. Washington saw fit to ignore a reception being held by the association in order to attend the one held in her honor by a prominent club of white women in Buffalo, with the result noted above. If this is true, our ladies in the convention who brought about her defeat when a candidate for the presidency of the organization, did a very proper thing. It may be all right from a financial standpoint, as far as Booker T. Washington and Tuskegee Normal and Industrial institute are concerned, for Mr. and Mrs. Washington to "place the white people first," but it is not all right for the manly person, male or female, of our class, to stand it, especially whenever there is an opportunity to rebuke such mistreatment.

It is, too, both aggravating and amusing to note the unflagging persistency with which the white people of this country endeavor to make Afro-Americans accept Mr. Washington as their "Moses" and leader when his work and position make such a thing or condition, as far as he is concerned, absolutely impossible. We do not mean to say that he is not a leader in the industrial movement along educational lines, and concede him the credit for the great work he is doing in his school at Tuskegee, Ala. We are also mindful of the fact that some of the methods he pursues to accomplish his wonderful results are very hurtful indeed to the Afro-American of the north.

Cleveland *Gazette*, July 20, 1901, 2.

[1] At the convention of the National Association of Colored Women in Buffalo on July 9–12, 1901, both Margaret M. Washington and Josephine Bruce were candidates for the presidency. When they both attended a white club meeting during the convention instead of one held for the candidates by the Phyllis Wheatley Club of Buffalo, on the ground that they had already accepted the white club's invitation, so much bitter feeling was aroused that both were defeated by Mrs. J. S. Yates of Kansas City, Mo. (Washington *Colored American*, July 27, 1901, 1, 5.)

To Thomas Wilkes Coleman

[Tuskegee, Ala.] July 22d, 1901

My dear Sir: In order to be sure not to mislead or misrepresent anything to you, I have taken some pains since I saw you to get more fully the sentiment of our committee as well as that of other colored people, and I find that while they are most grateful to your committee for incorporating into your report several of the suggestions which the committee made and they feel that there is much in the report to stimulate our people to industry, and to acquire property, yet they ask me to say to you that they hope you can see your way clear to modify or leave out the plan providing for a board of registrars and also what is known as the "grand-father clause." It may be that further discussion and explanation on the floor of the convention may change their views. While I have not had time to call the full committee together, still I am satisfied that if these two changes are made the whole plan would prove reasonably acceptable to the colored people. Yours truly,

Booker T. Washington

TLSr Copy Con. 194 BTW Papers DLC. BTW sent a similar letter to John B. Knox on July 23, 1901, BTW Papers, ATT.

To Warren Logan

[Tuskegee, Ala.] 7, 25, 1901

Mr. Logan: In an organization so large as we have I think in the future it wise when you go away to be away during my absence that some more definite arrangements be made regarding the conduct of the school. It seemed uncertain when I came as to who was in charge of the school during your absence. In an indefinite way it seems that Mr. Scott understood that he was in charge but no one else knew this. I think it well in such cases not only to explain to the one definitely who is in charge but also inform the other heads of departments so that they may know to whom to look in case of emergency.

There seems to be uncertainty also as to who is to do the buying during your absence. Mr. Driver says that one or two orders were handed him but aside from that he says he has no understanding as to who was to do the buying.

The same uncertainty prevails as to who was to act as treasurer. Mr. Gibson says that nothing was said to him about acting in your stead and I cannot find that anything was said to anyone else. Several matters have come up which should be acted upon by the one definitely appointed by you to act in your stead as treasurer. The school is too large and there is too much involved to leave such important matters to mere chance.

Booker T. Washington

TLS BTW Papers ATT.

To Jacob August Riis

Tuskegee, Alabama. July 27, 1901

My dear Sir: Vice President Roosevelt is planning to visit this institution during the month of coming November, and I write to invite you to accompany him; it will be pleasing not only to me but also to Mr. Roosevelt. Mr. Wm. H. Baldwin, Jr. is also to be a member of the party. I am quite sure that you will find much at Tuskegee to both interest and please you, but what is more than that it will give us a good opportunity to know you.

Will you kindly let me hear from you at your convenience as to whether you think it will be possible for you to accept this invitation. Yours truly,

Booker T. Washington

TLS   WHi.

From Henry Floyd Gamble

Charleston, W.Va., July 29th 1901

My Dear Mr Washington: Yours of a few days ago received. I have select and engaged a good man for your company's cook. I will see to it that you have all the tents you need for your comfort.

Last night I saw Mr S. D. Collins a very wealthy lumber dealer who is operating seven or eight sawmills up Elk; he is a very excelent gentalman and a friend of mine. He told me last night that if there were only two or three in your party he would be delighted to have you come up to his place as his special guest, but it would be imposible for him to entertain a large party, his quarters being limited. He says he has and will make arrangements for everything you and your party need. Mr. Collins is a whole soul man and will do all he says.

About cotts and bedding. My furniture man can order the regular army canvis cotts at a cost of $1.00 should you need as many as 7 or 8. I will find out if Mr Collins will supply bedding if so you will not need to be supplied with the extra burdens and expense.

If you prefer the wire spring cott they can be rented, delivered at the depot for shipment and rehauled, at 50 cts each for the season. But with these it would be necessary to have mattresses etc etc materially increasing the bulk and burden of camp fixtures.

I regard it a great honor to have an invitation from you to accompany you and your friends on your outing and I would be delighted to take the advantage of the opportunity to be with you on this occasion, but the condition of my wife's health is becoming so serious that I can make no plans for the future that will take me away from her bed side.

I shall gladly notify you of any advantages that may develope affecting your interest and stay on this proposed West Va trip. Holding my self in readyness to serve you at any time I am more than pleased to repeat my self   Your sincere friend

H. F. Gamble

ALS   Con. 198   BTW Papers   DLC.

From Albert Enoch Pillsbury

Boston   July 30, 1901

Dear Mr. Washington: I shall be very glad to receive ex-Governor Jones' address on the Grandfather clause, and any and all other literature of that subject which you may send me — the more the better, as I am especially interested to get a comprehensive southern view of this provision.

You undoubtedly know that our Louisiana case is begun.[1] It is attended by some difficulties, and I think that to reach the root of the mischief we must also bring a suit directly calling in question the right to vote of some poor and illiterate white who has registered and is voting under the Grandfather clause. It was, of course, necessary to have a suit brought by a poor and illiterate negro who is actually disfranchised by the discriminating operation of this provision; as he alone is directly aggrieved by it, and the general rule is that only one who suffers by the alleged unconstitutional provision has a right to attack it in court. But if we stand on this case alone, I can see a way in which the court may possibly evade the whole question. They may say that even if the Grandfather clause is void for unlawful discrimination between the races, it is separable from the educational and property qualifications, which can stand without it, and which by themselves disqualify our plaintiff Ryanes, so that he is not entitled to vote whether the Grandfather clause is or is not unconstitutional. Of course, we attack the whole scheme of suffrage qualifications, as one scheme, which, we say, must fall if any part of it is unconstitutional and void. If we can get the court to go this length, which we are attempting in Ryanes' case, we shall be completely successful; but in view of the character of the subject and the disposition of the court to evade precipitating political issues by judicial decision, this is hardly to be expected. If we cannot do this, we must at least compel the court to finally decide upon the validity of the Grandfather clause. Apparently the only way in which we can be sure of compelling such decision is by a suit directly attacking the right to vote of some poor and illiterate white who is voting under it. If this also is done, it will drive the court to a decision of the validity of this clause. It seems impossible that the court should sustain this clause by itself. If overthrown, the only necessary result is to disfranchise the poor and illiterate whites who are voting under it, without opening the suffrage to the negroes. But this is at least a sentimental victory, and may be all that it is possible to accomplish. Several of our most intelligent colored men here have said to me that they would be satisfied with this, as it would at least establish equality of right.

I presume you will be interested in this brief statement of the situation and prospects as I view them, and as you are frequently in contact with those who are interested in the cause, you ought to be fully informed upon it. Very truly yours,

A. E. Pillsbury

TLS BTW Papers ATT.

1 *State* ex rel. *Ryanes* v. *Gleason*, 112 La. 612 (1903). David Jordan Ryanes, born in Tennessee in 1841, was a resident of New Orleans beginning in 1860. The case had a disappointing conclusion after four years of wrangling over strategy between the Afro-American Council lawyers, George H. White and Fredrick L. McGhee, and the three white lawyers, A. E. Pillsbury, A. A. Birney, and Armand Romain. The case was dropped without an appeal to the federal courts. BTW was somewhat disillusioned by the long struggle and never used a committee of lawyers again. (Harlan, "Secret Life of BTW," 397.)

To Matthew T. Driver

[Tuskegee, Ala.] 8, 1, 1901

Mr. Driver: I wish you would bear in mind what I told you sometime ago, and that is to give Mr. Adams all the trade that you consistently can; I mean buy anything that he can supply without loss to the institution.

Booker T. Washington

TLpS Con. 282A BTW Papers DLC.

From Walter N. Wallace[1]

Boston, Aug. 6, 1901

My dear Sir: I am about to make a disclosure to you which is strictly confidential, asking your indulgence of a careful perusal and advice. The future affairs of the COLORED AMERICAN MAGAZINE are in a critical condition. As organizer and general manager of the concern I can see shoals ahead which if taken in time can be shunned.

The *Magazine* has taken a gigantic stand even for my sanguine expectation, and is being watched with fervor by friend and foe, black and white. It within itself is an indisputed success as set forth by its accomplishment of $15,000 worth of business from its inception, May 1900 to May 1901. It has always been self sustaining but through the ill advice of a party who has had fifteen years experience in the publishing business, we have dabbled in the publishing of books (an expensive luxury) from the surplus proceeds of the magazine to such an extent that we find the summer dullness upon us with no sinking fund to meet increased expense. A second fault has been made plain to us through experience, that is we are beginning to place all Agents under security; since even with money expended upon book publishing would not interfere with our business if our agents were prompt with their remittances.

We have outstanding accounts and notes which would cover every cent of indebtedness ($1000).

Stock sales are slow for various reasons. Representative men throughout the country are waiting to see the business built up before taking Stock, not realizing that WE NEED THE MONEY NOW when the concern is in its infancy. Within ten days we need at least $500 which will successful[ly] tide us over the dullness; as October is the beginning of our fall campaign, which I have outlined extensively.

It would truly be a blow to the Negro's professed advancement for our enemies to believe that the race is not far enough advanced to appreciate a high-class periodical, run upon the lines we have followed in the past year. Fully one third of our subscribers are white.

(1) You can save us by an investment of $500.

(2) A loan with interest upon the Company's note or

(3) giving us notice of a backing for that amount (without expending a cent). This (3) statement would suffice by giving us more time in which to receive delayed receipts from Agents.

Rather than consider the complete failure after reaching this advanced stage; would consider allowing affairs to run to the limit and rescue the magazine from the debris (at an expense of $1000) with a change of affairs and to move on from where it left off.

Let me know if there is anything suggestible to alleviate this difficulty. You can address me personally as I have not as yet made mention of my appeal to you.

To the public, with our finely apportioned offices, surroundings, etc. it appears as a Gibraltar of strength, may it continue so through your advertence of pending difficulties.

All communications strictly confidential and I give you my word as a man, I believe on oath that every cent received or expended by the Company has been used for (what the Directors thought was) the good of the Company. Our circulation at present, actual output (post-office receipts to substantiate) between 15,000 and 16,000 per month.

Shall be willing to open our books to any Attorney you may name for your benefit.

MAY YOU SEE FIT TO AID US.

We remain, Ever yours for the Race through the magazine.

Walter N. Wallace

TLS Con. 194 BTW Papers DLC.

¹ Walter N. Wallace, born in Mecklenburg County, Va., in 1874, was managing editor of the Colored Co-operative Publishing Co. of Boston and published the *Colored American Magazine*. For BTW's involvement in the affairs of the magazine see Meier, "BTW and the Negro Press."

From Emmett Jay Scott

Houston Texas, Aug. 13/1901

My Dear Mr Washington: I reached Houston last night & found my mother alive. She has suffered a paralytic stroke & will hardly recover. The doctors have surrendered her twice but she is making a brave fight. I was so sorry not to be able to go to Canton for you, and am particularly sorry I shall not be at your Business League Convention. I am not morbid but the fates seem against me. I shall remain here for a week anyway & shall go on to Tuskegee as soon as I can leave. I should be greatly obliged if you would write to Mr. I. E. Gates & ask him to forward me here, 810 House St., Houston, Texas, a trip pass Houston to Montgomery. I am sure he can get a L & N pass if he wills. I do not feel that I ought to impose upon your generosity & continued kindnesses, but if [you] can favor me it will greatly help.

About the Council meeting: I do not feel that any particular good was accomplished but it served to emphasize the opposition to the disfranchising schemes. This opposition was violently expressed & got into the papers. Walters was re-elected. This brought on the only unpleasant feature of the Convention. Geo H White was a candidate & was slaughtered, & I think for the best as he only wanted it to use as a weapon to help him politically. In making his report, Mr Lawson did not use your name, but the initials X.Y.Z.¹ Whenever they were called cheers were given. I found the Convention most sympathetic in our direction. I am glad Mrs. Barnett was not there to complicate the situation. Her husband² in a speech referred to you as "the matchless orator & wise leader" & a burst of cheers greeted this. I am to be Chairman of the Business Bureau and am to bring the Business League & the Council into affiliation in promoting the business features of the organization. I hope I shall do some good. I trust your meetings are all they should be. Yours very sincerely

Emmett J. Scott

ALS BTW Papers ATT.

[1] Lawson wrote BTW: "The contributions made by you are credited to X.Y.Z., and those from other persons through you are noted as per X.Y.Z. I deem it wise to safeguard your interests in that way." (July 30, 1901, Con. 203, BTW Papers, DLC.)

[2] Ferdinand Lee Barnett, husband of Ida B. Wells-Barnett.

To Hollis Burke Frissell

Charleston, W.Va. Aug. 19, 1901

Dear Dr. Frissell: Since reaching New York and looking into matters I find that important developments are underway. I think a great responsibility devolves upon you and me in this connection. In the first place I think it wise that we keep in close and constant touch, in order to guide matters wisely. And in the second place that we take occasion very early together, to put matters plainly before Dr. Curry and perhaps Dr. Gilmore.[1] Mr. Rockefeller has just had another conference with Mr. Baldwin and has decided to act within sixty or ninety days. The amount Mr. Rockefeller thinks of spending will be much larger than the income of the Slater and Peabody Funds combined. It is now largely a question as to whether these two funds will permit themselves to become the foundation for the Rockefeller money, or whether they will permit Mr. Rockefeller to go it alone. In any case I believe that Mr. Rockefeller will insist upon Mr. Baldwin controlling his money. My own feeling is that you and I ought to get together again soon, before anything else is done. My address till next Thursday will be Palmer House, Chicago, after then at Tuskegee. Yours truly,

Booker T. Washington

HLS BTW Folder ViHaI.

[1] Daniel Coit Gilman.

A Statement in the Washington *Colored American*

[Washington, D.C., Aug. 24, 1901]

A PLAIN TALK AS TO SECURING NEGRO HOMES

Every colored man owes it to himself and to his children, as well, to secure a home just as soon as possible. No matter how small the plot of land may be or how humble the dwelling-place thereon, something that can be called a home should be secured without delay. A home can be secured much easier than many imagine. A small amount of money saved from week to week, or from month to month, and carefully invested in a piece of land, will soon secure enough land upon which to build a comfortable home. No individual should feel satisfied until he has a home. More and more the Southern States are making as one of the conditions for voting, the ownership of at least $300 worth of property, and persons who own homes not only reap the benefits that come from owning a home, in other directions, but such persons will also find themselves entitled to cast their ballot.

Care should be taken as to the location of the land. It is of little advantage to secure a lot in some crowded dark, filthy alley. One should try to secure a lot on a good street and one that is carefully and well worked, so that the surroundings of the home will be enjoyable. Even if one has to go a good ways into the country to secure a lot, it is much better than to buy land in an unsightly, undesirable alley. I believe that our people do best, as a rule, by buying land in the country rather than in the city, but in either case, we should not rest satisfied until we have secured a home, either in the country or in the city. No man has the right to marry and run the risk of leaving his wife at his death without a home.

I notice with regret that there are many of our people who have already bought homes; but after they secure the land, pay for it and build a cabin containing two or three rooms, they do not seek to go further in the improvement of the property. In the first place, in many cases the premises, especially the yards, are not kept clean. The fences are not kept in repair. Whitewash and paint are not used as they should be. After the house is paid for, the greatest care should be exercised that it is kept in first class repair; that the house and fences are kept neatly painted or whitewashed; that no "palings" are permitted to fall off the fence and remain off. If there is a barn or hen house, these should be kept in repair and should be made to look neat and attractive by paint and whitewash. Paint and whitewash add a great deal to the value of a house. If persons would learn to use even a part of the time they spend in idle gossip or in standing about the streets, in whitewashing or painting their houses, it would make a great difference in the appearance of the house, as well as add to its value.

Only a short time ago near a certain town, I visited the house — I could not call it a home — of a presiding elder, a man who had received considerable education and who spent his time going about over his district preaching to hundreds and thousands of colored people yet the home of this presiding elder was almost a disgrace to him and to his race. The house was not painted or whitewashed, the fence was in the same condition, the yard was full of weeds, there were no walks laid out in the yard, there were no flowers in it; in fact everything on the outside of the house and in the yard, presented the most dismal and disappointing appearance. There was around this house not a single vegetable so far as I could see, neither did I see any chickens or fowls of any kind. This is not the way to live, and especially is this true of a minister or teacher who is supposed to lead the people, not only by word but by example. Every minister and teacher should [make] his house, his yard and his garden a model for the people whom he attempts to teach and lead. I confess that I have no respect or confidence in the preaching of a minister whose home is in the condition of the one I have described. There is no need why, as a race, we should get into the miserable and unfortunate habit of living in houses that are out of repair, that are not whitewashed, that are not painted, that are not comfortable and houses that we do not own. There is no reason why we should not only make our houses comfortable, but attractive, so that no one can tell from the outside appearance, at least, whether it is occupied by a white family or a black family.

After a house has been paid for, it should not only be improved from year to year and kept in first-class repair, but as the family grows, new rooms should be added. The house should not only be made comfortable, but convenient. There should be as soon as possible, a sitting room, where books and papers can be found, a room in which the whole family can read and study during the winter nights. I do not believe any house is complete without a bath room. As soon as possible every one of our houses should be provided with a bath room, so that the body of every member of the family can be baptized every morning in clean invigorating, fresh water; such a bath puts one in proper condition for the work of the day, and not only keeps him well physically but strong morally and religiously.

Another important part of the home is the dining room. The dining room should be the most attractive and comfortable place in the house; it should be large and airy, a room in which plenty of sunlight can come, and a room that can be kept comfortable in both winter and summer.

These suggestions are made in the hope that a number of persons will see their way to put them into practice. All of them are suggestions that we, as a race, notwithstanding our poverty, in most cases can find a way to put into use.

Every suggestion made should be taken up by our ministers, teachers and others in church and school, as well as in the women's meetings.

[Booker T. Washington]

Washington *Colored American*, Aug. 24, 1901, 4.

From Hollis Burke Frissell

Hampton, Va. August 24, 1901

Dear Mr. Washington: Your letter of August 19th is at hand. I entirely agree with you as to the importance of our getting in touch with one another and keeping our hands on what is going on. I had a talk with Mr. Baldwin in New York and he expressed to me the same thought that he did to you in regard to the necessity of quick action. I have written to Dr. Curry as was suggested at Bar Harbor, giving him some idea of the general condition of affairs and making a plea for speedy action, and also trying to impress upon him the importance of our all pulling together.

I am expecting now to leave here tonight to get a few days with my wife at Castine and I could easily run over to Northeast and Bar Harbor to confer with President Gilman and Mr. Jesup. I shall probably at least see Dr. Gilman during my northern stay.

Mr. Ogden had a talk with Mr. Baldwin and suggested the possibility of making the Southern Educational Committee, which is composed as you know of Dr. Curry, Dr. McIver, Dr. Dabney, Dr. Alderman, Dr. Buttrick, Mr. Peabody and Mr. Ogden and myself, a basis for a larger committee, which should embrace men who were representatives of all the Boards, and of which Mr. Baldwin might be the Executive Officer. Of course, what his relation would be to Mr. Murphy, who has as you know been talked of as possible agent of that board, could be easily settled. There would be need of several workers in connection with such a committee, and one need not interfere with the other, but all would help. Very truly yours,

H. B. Frissell

TLS Con. 213 BTW Papers DLC. Addressed to BTW at the Palmer House, Chicago.

A Book Review by William Dean Howells[1]

[August 1901]

AN EXEMPLARY CITIZEN

If one were to name Paul Dunbar with Booker T. Washington, Frederick Douglass and Charles W. Chesnutt, one would have a group of Americans who, even if they were not known to be Afro-Americans (I did not invent the term, I am glad to say; but I am glad to use it, for it serves), would lift themselves far above our undistinguished average, white or black. The fact that they are Afro-Americans is not the chief fact concerning them. It was, indeed, the function of Douglass to be an Afro-American, and that is in a way the function of Mr. Washington. But when one reads what they have written or spoken, one no more feels a quality of Afro-Americanism in them than one feels it in the work of Mr. Dunbar or Mr. Chesnutt, whose function is to be literary artists. Mr. Dunbar is entirely black, and Mr. Chesnutt, to the unskilled eye, is entirely white. Mr. Washington, as Douglass was, is a half-blood. But they are all colored people, and it is only just to credit their mother-race with their uncommon powers and virtues, since, if they were weak or vicious, it must bear the blame and the shame of their shortcoming. So far as I can make out from the study of their minds in their books, they are of one blood with their fathers or forefathers. There is, apparently, no color line in the brain. One almost wishes there were, and that there were a region of thought-life, apart from ours, characterized by something strange, something different, some hint, even, of the ancestral Grand Custom. The ancestral Cakewalk seems to intimate itself for a moment in Mr. Washington's dedication of his autobiography to his "wife, *Mrs.* Margaret James Washington," and his "brother, *Mr.* John H. Washington"; but nothing is less characteristic of the author than the cakewalk, and its apparent flourish, in this instance, has a pathos to which, rightly seen, one wishes to uncover. It is part of the proud tenderness, the loving loyalty to family and race, which is one of the finest traits of this remarkable book and of this remarkable man.

I

Except for the race ignominy and social outlawry to which he was born, the story of Booker T. Washington does not differ so very widely from that of many another eminent American. His origin was not much more obscure, his circumstances not much more squalid, than Abraham Lincoln's, and his impulses and incentives to the making of himself were of much the same source and quality. He was born in slavery, but not in poverty much more abject, more absolute; and he was like another great American of his own color, in those conditions of his birth which forbade him to know his father or even his father's name. They each understood vaguely that he was a white man on a neighboring plantation; but they had never any reason to ascribe to him those gifts or talents which we are fond of attributing to the white half of a mulatto's origin when he shows them. The mother of Douglass died when he was a child. She could do nothing, in that hopeless period of slavery, to fit him for his wonderful career. He remembered her as a tall, straight young woman, handsome and proud, with "deep black, glossy" skin, and features like those of an Egyptian king in a picture he had seen. She was the only person of her color on the plantation who could read; yet Douglass no more learned of his mother to read than Booker Washington, whose mother could not have taught him from her own knowledge, but who was as ambitious for his education as if she could have led or followed him. There is nothing more touching in his book than the passages which record her devotion and her constant endeavor to help him find the way so dark to her. There is nothing more beautiful and uplifting in literature than the tender reverence, the devout honor with which he repays her affection. His birth was a part of slavery, and she was, in his eyes, as blameless for its conditions as if it had all the sanctions. The patience, the fearless frankness, with which he accepts and owns the facts, are not less than noble; and it is not to their white fathers, but to their black mothers, that such men as Frederick Douglass and Booker Washington justly ascribe what is best in their natures.

II

The story of his struggle for an education is the story of Booker Washington's life, which I am not going to spoil for the reader by trying to tell it. He has himself told it so simply and charmingly that one could not add to or take from it without marring it. The part of the autobiography which follows the account of his learning to read and write, in the scanty leisure of his hard work in the West Virginia coal mines, and of his desperate adventure in finding his way into Hampton Institute, is, perhaps, more important and more significant, but it has not the fascination of his singularly pleasing personality. It concerns the great problem, which no man has done more than he to solve, of the future of his race, and its reconciliation with the white race, upon conditions which it can master only through at least provisional submission; but it has not the appeal to the less philosophized sympathies which go out to struggle and achievement. It is not such interesting reading, and yet it is all very interesting; and if the prosperity of the author is not so picturesque as his adversity, still it is prosperity well merited, and it is never selfish prosperity.

Booker Washington early divined the secret of happiness as constant activity for the good of others. This was the first thing he learned from the example of the admirable man who became his ideal and his norm: he formed himself, morally at least, upon General Armstrong, and in a measure he studied his manner — his simple and sincere manner — oratorically.

This must be evident to any one who has heard both men speak. It was most apparent to me when I heard Mr. Washington speak at a meeting which had been addressed by several distinguished white speakers. When this marvellous yellow man came upon the platform, and stood for a moment, with his hands in his pockets, and with downcast eyes, and then began to *talk* at his hearers the clearest, soundest sense, he made me forget all those distinguished white speakers, and he made me remember General Armstrong, from whom he had learned that excellent manner. It was somewhat the manner of Salvini, when, in the character of another colored man, he defends himself to the Venetian Senate for having taken away Brabantio's daughter; and, perhaps, the poet was divining and forecasting the style of the race in the plain, unvarnished reasoning of Othello.

What strikes you, first and last, in Mr. Washington is his constant common sense. He has lived heroic poetry, and he can, therefore, afford to talk simple prose. Simple prose it is, but of sterling worth, and such as it is a pleasure to listen to as long as he chooses to talk. It is interfused with the sweet, brave humor which qualifies his writing, and which enables him, like Dunbar, to place himself outside his race, when he wishes to see it as others see it, and to report its exterior effect from his interior knowledge. To do this may not be proof of the highest civilization, but it is a token of the happiest and usefullest temperament.

III

The dominant of Mr. Washington's register is *business;* first, last and all the time, the burden of his song is the Tuskegee Industrial Institute. There is other music in him, and no one who reads his story can fail to know its sweetness; but to Tuskegee his heart and soul are unselfishly devoted, and he does not suffer his readers long to forget it. He feels with his whole strength that the hope of his race is in its industrial advancement, and that its education must, above all, tend to that. His people must know how to read and write in order to be better workmen; but good workmen they must be, and they must lead decent, sober, honest lives to the same end.

It was the inspiration of this philosophy and experience which enabled him, in his famous speech at the opening of the Atlanta Exposition, to bring the white race into kindlier and wiser relations with the black than they had known before. Social equality he does not ask for or apparently care for; but industrial and economic equality his energies are bent upon achieving, in the common interest of both races. Of all slights and wrongs he is patient, so they do not hinder the negro from working or learning how to work in the best way.

The temper of his mind is conservative, and, oddly enough, that seems to be the temper of the Afro-American mind whenever it comes to its consciousness. The Anglo-American of the South may be, and often has been, an extremist, but the Afro-American, so far as he has made himself eminent, is not. Perhaps, it is his unfailing sense of humor that saves him from extremism. At any rate, cool patience is not more characteristic of Mr. Washington than of Mr. Dunbar or Mr. Chesnutt or of Frederick Douglass himself. Douglass was essentially militant; he was a fighter from 'way back, from the hour when he conceived the notion that if the slave would always fight the man who attempted to whip him, there would be no whipping, and he did fight his master upon this theory, and beat him; his war with slavery was to the death. Yet he laid himself open to the blame of certain Abolitionists because he would not go all lengths with them, and he refused to take part in the attempt of John Brown, whom he loved with his whole heart. He kept amidst the tumult of his emotion the judicial mind, and he did not lose his head in the stormy career of the agitator.

This calm is apparently characteristic of the best of the race, and in certain aspects it is of the highest and most consoling promise. It enables them to use reason and the nimbler weapons of irony, and saves them from bitterness. By virtue of it Washington, and Dunbar and Chesnutt enjoy the negro's ludicrous side as the white observer enjoys it, and Douglass could see the fun of the zealots whose friend and fellow-fighter he was. The fact is of all sorts of interesting implications; but I will draw from it, for the present, the sole suggestion that the problem of the colored race may be more complex than we have thought it. What if upon some large scale they should be subtler than we have supposed? What if their amiability should veil a sense of *our* absurdities, and there should be in our polite inferiors the potentiality of something like contempt for us? The notion is awful; but we may be sure they will be too kind, too wise, ever to do more than let us guess at the truth, if it is the truth.

IV

Mr. Washington's experience of our race has been such as to teach him a greater measure of kindness for it than many of his race have cause to feel. His generous enterprise prospers by our bounty, which he owns, with rather more tolerance for the rich than the New Testament expresses. So far from bidding them "go to and howl," he is disposed to deprecate the censure which some of the public prints (perhaps in too literal a discipleship) heap upon them. With such open hands he believes there must go good hearts, and he finds not excuse only, but justification, for English aristocrats as well as American plutocrats. He does not know but there may be good reasons for the division of society into classes, and for the frank recognition of server and served, as in England. This may be because Mr. Washington's clock does not always strike twelve; and it may be because he and the nobility and gentry are right. In either case, it is interesting in itself and ingenuous in him. It makes assurance doubly sure that the negro is not going to do anything dynamitic to the structure of society. He is going to take it as he finds it, and make the best of his rather poor chances in it. In his heart is no bitterness. If his rights are taken away, he will work quietly on till they are given back. No doubt, it is the wisest way. If he keeps faithfully and quietly at work, he will presently be an owner of the earth and have money in the bank, and from such their rights cannot long be withheld. They can buy the strong arm that robs them; they can invoke the law to make the oppressor get off the land.

Mr. Washington's way seems, at present, the only way for his race, which has not even the unrestricted suffrage to its friend, as white labor has. Perhaps, if it had, it would make no more of it than white labor does. The ballot which was once supposed to

"execute the freeman's will
As lightning does the will of God,"

seems to operate tangentially, and not to carry with it the proof of a direct volition; but so does and does not the lightning, for that matter. What is certain is that Mr. Washington has entire faith in his plan, and that, while he is not insensible or indifferent to the unlawful disabilities of his people, he sees no hope in their making a fight against them, and further alienating the stronger race about them. By precept and by practice he counsels, not a base submission to the Southern whites, but a manly fortitude in bearing the wrongs that cannot now be righted, and a patient faith in the final kindliness and ultimate justice of the Anglo-Americans, with whom and by whom the Afro-Americans must live. He has seen the party which freed the slaves unable through forty years of interrupted power to keep them politically free or to make them socially equal with their former masters, and his counsel, enforced by his eminent example, has been for the Afro-American to forego politics, at least for the present, and to put from him indefinitely the illusive hope of associating with the Anglo-American.

If the Afro-American could only realize the fact that many Anglo-Americans are not worth associating with, it might help him put the vain desire from him. If he would reflect upon the fact, which must be perfectly obvious to him as cook, butler, waiter and coachman, that some of us Anglo-Americans will not associate with other Anglo-Americans, and that if we have "exaggerated incomes" we will not, according to Mr. Depew, admit Anglo-Americans "of distinction in art and letters," to our tables or ball-rooms or coaching parties, he will be still better able to console himself under his deprivation. Probably, he would be willing to consort with even such outcasts from exclusive white society; but, with his native love of splendor, I think he would prefer the exclusive society, and, upon the whole, he might be more fitted for it.

He is as likely to get into it as into any other white society, though I am not sure that he would be shut out from the very lowest, which sometimes embraces even Chinamen. At that level, he would find himself at home in the traditions of poverty, which are much the same, whether it is the poverty of the slave or of the freeman. Mr. Washington remembers, as one of the most significant features of the slave life to which he was born, that his people had no tables or beds where they ate or slept. They never sat down to meals, but caught up a bone or a crust and fed upon it wherever they happened to be. They never went to bed, but dropped down anywhere, and slept upon a heap of rags or the bare floor. But such conditions are not distinctive of slavery. If Mr. Washington were to go slumming, I will undertake that he should see on the East Side in New York very much the same conditions, very much the same usages. I myself have been received (without the express invitation of the hosts; one doesn't stand upon ceremony with such people) in tenements where they seemed to prevail, and I suspect that they prevail in a degree which would astonish the Afro-American sufficiently detached from the past of his race to view it objectively, and to realize the connotative facts.

V

White men rise from squalor almost as great as that which has left no taint upon the mind and soul of the born thrall, Booker T. Washington. But it must be remembered to his honor, and to his greater glory as a fighter against fate, that they rise in the face of no such odds as he has had to encounter. No prejudice baser than the despite for poverty bars their way. But the negro who makes himself in our conditions, works with limbs manacled and fettered by manifold cruel prepossessions. These prepossessions yield at certain points to amiability, to mildness, to persistent submissiveness, but at other points they yield to nothing.

In spite of them, though never in defiance of them, Booker T. Washington has made himself a public man, second to no other American in importance. He seems to hold in his strong grasp the key to the situation; for if his notion of reconciling the Anglo-American to the Afro-American, by a civilization which shall not seem to threaten the Anglo-American supremacy, is not the key, what is? He imagines for his race a civilization industrial and economical, hoping for the virtues which spring from endeavor and responsibility; and apparently his imagination goes no farther. But a less deeply interested observer might justify himself in hoping for it, from the things it has already accomplished in art and literature, a civilization of high aesthetic qualities.

As for the man himself, whose winning yet manly personality and whose ideal of self-devotion must endear him to every reader of his book, something remains to be said, which may set him in a true perspective and a true relation to another great Afro-American, whose name could not well be kept out of the consideration.

Neither by temperament nor by condition had Frederick Douglass the charm which we feel when Booker T. Washington writes or speaks. The time was against him. In that time of storm and stress, the negro leader was, perforce, a fighter. The sea of slavery, from which he had escaped with his bare life, weltered over half the land, and threatened all the new bounds of the Republic. By means of the Fugitive Slave Law, it had, in fact, made itself national, and the bondman was nowhere on American soil safe from recapture and return to his master. Frederick Douglass had to be bought, and his price had to be paid in dollars by those who felt his priceless value to humanity, before he could be to it all that he was destined to become.

It would have been impossible that the iron which had entered into the man's soul should not show itself in his speech. Yet, his words were strangely free from violence; the violence was in the hatred which the mere thought of a negro defying slavery aroused in its friends. If you read now what he said, you will be surprised at his reasonableness, his moderation. He was not gentle; his life had been ungentle; the logic of his convictions was written in the ineffaceable scars of the whip on his back. Of such a man, you do not expect the smiling good humor with which Booker T. Washington puts the question of his early deprivations and struggles by. The life of Douglass was a far more wonderful life, and when it finds its rightful place in our national history, its greater dynamic importance will be felt.

Each of these two remarkable men wrought and is working fitly and wisely in his time and place. It is not well to forget slavery, and the memory of Frederick Douglass will always serve to remind us of it and of the fight against it. But it is not well to forget that slavery is gone, and that the subjection of the negro race which has followed it does not imply its horrors. The situation which Booker T. Washington deals with so wisely is wholly different from the situation which Douglass confronted, and it is slowly but surely modifying itself. The mild might of his adroit, his subtle statesmanship (in the highest sense it is not less than statesmanship, and involves a more than Philippine problem in our midst), is the only agency to which it can yield. Without affirming his intellectual equality with Douglass, we may doubt whether Douglass would have been able to cope so successfully with the actual conditions, and we may safely recognize in Booker T. Washington an Afro-American of unsurpassed usefulness, and an exemplary citizen.

North American Review, 173 (Aug. 1901), 280–88.

1 Howells was supposedly reviewing three works, BTW's *Up from Slavery,* Frederick May Holland's *Frederick Douglass, the Colored Orator,* and Charles W. Chesnutt's *Frederick Douglass.*

From Portia Marshall Washington

The Oaks   Tuskegee   Sept. 4—1901

My dear papa: I am so disappointed about Lassell[1] but I am still in hopes that I can enter some school (preparatory). I send you these clippings — thinking prehaps you can telegraph them and find out if there is a possible openning. Prehaps I shall have to fall back on Wellsley. How do you like the idea of my going to Boston and studying under a private teacher until next year and then enter Lassell[?] I could take the course as it is laid down in the catalogue for the first year. I am very anxious to have the college preparatory work with the music. I am afraid that it is rather late to enter any desirable school. Mamma did not write to Wellsley saying that I was not to come. Lovingly yours.

Portia

ALS   BTW Papers   ATT.

1 Lasell Seminary for Young Women was founded in 1851 at Auburndale, Mass., by Edward Lasell, a chemistry professor at Williams College. Its music department had an excellent reputation. In 1932 it was renamed Lasell Junior College by the state legislature.

From Emmett Jay Scott

Tuskegee, Ala., Sept. 7, 1901

Dear Mr Washington: The McKinley tragedy[1] was so terrible that I thought it well to wire you as I do not know your distance from town, nor the possibilities in the way of the news penetrating to you. Mrs Washington sent Mrs. McKinley a very nice & tender message this morning, & thought you'd care to do the same thing.

Teachers & students are coming in. The former are being well cared for & well received. I understand Mrs Bruce comes tomorrow (Sunday) morning.

Everything seems in good shape & the School will go right off I believe, in good shape.

We still hope you are spending the vacation pleasantly. Yours sincerely

Emmett J. Scott

ALS   Con. 209   BTW Papers   DLC.

1 William McKinley was shot by an assassin on Sept. 6, 1901, while attending the Pan-American Exposition in Buffalo, N.Y. He died on Sept. 14, 1901.

From Theodore Roosevelt

Buffalo, [N.Y.] Sept. 7, 1901

My dear Mr. Washington: I am in receipt of your favor of the first inst. outlining the trip, and it is first rate in every respect. Jacob A. Riis writes me that he would be able to go the week beginning November 25th; but unfortunately I could not go at that time, as it is too near the convening of the Senate.

From one or two of my Chicago friends I learn of your kindness anent myself at the meeting of the Business Men's Association in Chicago.

I look forward to seeing you. Sincerely yours,

Theodore Roosevelt

Before you receive this, the President I am sure will be out of danger.

TL Copy   Con. 208   BTW Papers   DLC.

From William Calvin Oates

Montgomery, Ala., Sept. 7, 1901

Dear Sir: Your letter was duly received, carefully read and filed away, for it is one of the best of the many I received.

The Convention has adjourned and the Constitution will soon be submitted to the people for ratification. It is objectionable in several respects, but upon the whole, a better Constitution than the present or old one. Under the Suffrage clause, in my opinion, a larger number of your race will qualify and become voters within a few years than is generally apprehended. Your people will rapidly learn to read and write "any article of the Constitution of the United States," and any of them who own $300.00 worth of property and pays his taxes on that and poll tax $1.50, can vote whether they can read and write or not. And those who can read and write any article of the Constitution of the United States, can register and vote though they may not own any property. Very respectfully,

Wm C Oates

TLS BTW Papers ATT.

Extracts from an Address in Charleston, S.C.

[Charleston, S.C., Sept. 12, 1901]

I wish to thank the executive committee for arranging this meeting in the interest of the negro department of the South Carolina Inter-State and West Indian Exposition. This Exposition, which is open in December, will present a great opportunity for the negro to show to the world the progress he has made during the last thirty-five years. No race or individual ever got upon its feet without continual hard, earnest effort. We must pay the price for everything that we get. I understand and appreciate fully that there were those in this city and out of it, among my own race, people who objected to a separate negro department. Perhaps those who objected had good and reasonable grounds upon which to base their objection.

They were perfectly right in the beginning in stating frankly their objection to the separate department, but now that it has been definitely decided to have a separate negro department it seems to me that such objections should disappear and that there should be the completest unison and harmony to the end that the negro department of the Exposition may be made the most successful in the history of expositions. Every colored man who lives in Charleston or South Carolina should possess that local and State pride which should make him as anxious for the success of the department as could be true of any white man. I have little patience with any individual, black or white, who could never see anything good or praiseworthy in his own city or State. Charleston possesses some peculiarly gratifying advantages for a creditable negro exhibit. Perhaps in no Southern city can there be found so many creditable and industrious mechanics and skilled laborers of various kinds as is true of Charleston.

In the colored department we must make a specialty of exhibiting to the world the handicraft of these mechanics. We are to show what those who handle the saw, the hatchet, the trowel, and those who make dresses, can do. We want to show in the colored department also what the negro is doing in the lines of manufacturing. In all these directions Charleston possesses great advantages.

One other thing cannot be said too strongly and emphatically. It has been my privilege to come into contact with a good many expositions in various parts of the country, but in no case do I believe that we can find an instance where single-handed almost, without national aid and with little help outside the State and city, has such an Exposition been projected and carried so far to successful fruition as is true of this Exposition. Every large opportunity to exhibit our progress tends to solve what is called the race problem and to place the race upon its feet. We cannot lift ourselves up by mere complaint, adverse criticism and condemnation. We must exhibit to the world more and more each day tangible, visible, indisputable evidences of our progress and worth to the country. In order that we may succeed in doing this at this Exposition we must in the first place lose sight of self. We must be able to sink ourselves with interest to our great cause — that of building up our race, the State and city in which we live. Whatever helps the negro helps the white man; whatever is of benefit to the negro is of service to the white man; as one race goes up both go up. Whatever injures the negro injures the white man. We are bound together by a tie which we cannot break asunder. We cannot do our part in making this Exposition a success unless we are willing to sacrifice something — to sacrifice time, effort and money — and I believe that the citizens of Charleston and South Carolina are broad enough and generous enough to view the whole matter in this spirit. The negro department has now reached that point where there is no chance for it to fail. We are going to succeed and the only question is to what extent, with your help, we can make it the best Exposition of the kind that has ever been. We must show the people of this country what we are able to do; that we love it; that we are willing to work for it; that we are not aliens, but citizens, and as citizens willing to do our part manfully whenever the call comes. Through the medium of this Exposition we can show to the South and to the world that because of our usefulness we are indispensable to the progress and prosperity to the community in which we live. Usefulness in every line, in agriculture, in mechanics, in domestic services and education will constitute our highest and most potent protection. No individual who learns to do something as well or better than anyone else is ever left very long without proper recognition and reward.

We are planning to make the agricultural exhibit the best feature of our department. This is rightly so. The negro above all things else is an agricultural race. In every way possible we want to spread and emphasize the idea that there is a dignity, a beauty, an independence in agricultural life to such an extent that the educated negro will turn to the farm for his living and will not be tempted to idle about the street corners. This cannot be done without hard, earnest effort.

One of the things that weighs most heavily upon my heart, especially in our cities, is the large number of idle young men and women who loiter around. As a race we have no time for idleness. Idleness means crime and crime means the decay of the race. We all ought to emphasize the dignity and beauty of labor to such an extent that every boy and girl is made aware of the disgrace of idleness. I should strongly advise every mother and father to see to it that their sons and daughters are taught some useful occupation.

After considering what I have said I do not think any will doubt the tremendous progress that the negro race has made and is making in every part of this country. More and more we must be judged as a race by the best that we can produce and not by the worst types of the race. Some people are under the false impression that education injures the negro. After careful examination into facts I do not believe that one can find in the jails and penitentiary as many as one-half colored men and women who have been thoroughly educated in head, hand and heart. It is not the educated negro who commits crime, but the ignorant, idle and shiftless. It is sometimes said that the South is too poor to educate the negroes and every one of its citizens. We need not disturb ourselves too much about the relations that are to exist between the white man and the black man when the negro becomes a taxpayer and property holder. Education brings with it common sense, patience and forbearance to the negro; and the negro who is intelligent knows the only help for him is to possess a bank account and become a taxpayer and he becomes in every instance a stronger and more helpful person in his community.

Charleston *News and Courier*, Sept. 13, 1901, Clipping   Con. 1033   BTW Papers   DLC.

A Telegram to the New York *Herald*[1]

[Tuskegee, Ala., Sept. 14, 1901]

In my opinion, Wm. McKinley as a man, was our best example of the perfect American citizen. Both as a private citizen and as the nation's Chief Executive, he proved himself to be a sincere friend of my people and we join the nation in mourning the untimely removal of such a great and rare soul.

B. T. W.

TWIr Copy   Con. 182   BTW Papers   DLC.

[1] The New York *Herald* solicited the comment from BTW, asking for a brief statement "on McKinley as president & as a man." (New York *Herald* to BTW, Sept. 14, 1901, Con. 541, BTW Papers, DLC.) The telegram appeared along with other tributes in the New York *Herald*, Sept. 15, 1901, pt. 2:6.

From Theodore Roosevelt

Buffalo, N.Y., September 14, 1901[1]

My dear Mr. Washington: I write you at once to say that to my deep regret my visit south must now be given up.

When are you coming north? I must see you as soon as possible. I want to talk over the question of possible future appointments in the south exactly on the lines of our last conversation together.

I hope that my visit to Tuskegee is merely deferred for a short season. Faithfully yours,

Theodore Roosevelt

TLS   Con. 16   BTW Papers   DLC.

1 The date on which Roosevelt was sworn in as President of the United States.

An Account of the National Negro Business League Convention by Minnie R. Barbour[1]

Chicago, Ill. [ca. Sept. 14, 1901]

THE BUSINESS LEAGUE

CHICAGO AFRO-AMERICANS DESCANT ON THE CONVENTION AND TELL OF THEIR HOSPITALITY — WHAT THE COOK COUNTY LEAGUE DID — A FEW QUERIES — WISE AND OTHERWISE AND THE VIEWS OF A BRILLIANT WOMAN — HORN BLOWING, ETC.

The National Negro Business League which convened in Chicago recently is now a thing of the past, another page in the Negro history has been indelibly recorded. For more than a month the people of Chicago heard little else than the coming of this Convention. We were told by our business men, that it would be a great convention; it would benefit us as a people. We did whatever in our power lay to make the delegates happy in our city. Public receptions were ordered them; a visit to the great packing plant of the Armour Company was made, a trip on Lake Michigan enjoyed.

Teas, parties, dinners, stags and smokers were given in honor of the various delegates who had friends in our city. Chicago was hospitable. The Convention was held in Handel Hall, a beautiful, large, commodious building, conveniently and well located in the heart of our great city. The daily papers of Chicago gave space to every session, their reporters were ever present. Why all this? The Cook County League of Business Men is composed of some of our best citizens; men who have made their various business enterprises a success; men who have made thousands of dollars and who have saved their earnings; men whose word is not to be doubted and whose check is good at any bank; men of whom "colored Chicago" is justly proud and to whom "white Chicago" bows with friendly recognition. When such men as these were interested in the Convention and told us it was the right move we expected great things.

Were we disappointed? Was the Convention a success? Were Negro business men and women benefitted? Was the Convention a real benefit to any class of Negroes? These are questions the thinking people are asking themselves; asking each other; asking the members of the Negro Business Men's League of Cook County.

I am an ardent admirer of Prof. Booker T. Washington. I do not agree upon all points with Mr. Washington, oh! no. But I admire a man who has the courage of his convictions, who sticks closely to the path he believes to be right and best; and will not run here and there on "by ways" in order to please an opposition or win over to him self the flattery of an enemy; but who by his open, honest dealings shows the opposition its mistakes and gradually steadily brings those "by way" travelers into the main road and boldly leads on. This Mr. Washington has done. But when I saw Mr. Washington conducting the Business Convention I am forced to admit that my admiration of him received a little check. Because in this step I consider that Mr. Washington had left the main path he was wont to travel and was journeying in a "by way"; which path, I presume, Mr. Washington intends to bend into the big road by and by taking a big following of substantial business men.

The Business Convention was a sort of Methodist class meeting; and, perhaps, when the National League get their eyes open, they, like Johnnie with the Presbyterian-Methodist cats, of which the Reverend gentleman from Virginia told us, will declare the whole thing to have been a Baptist Convenant with Deacon Washington.

as Moderator. The National Negro Business League reminded me of the days when I was a "school-marm" and compelled to attend "Teachers' Meetings" and "State Teachers' Associations," some of which were presided over by the President of this Convention. In these Associations teachers told how they taught this branch of English or that Science, how they managed the department of Mathematics or Languages; how they governed and disciplined; how well they had succeeded or of their failure. These things, these experiences were discussed. These discussions were helpful to those who had failed and encouraging to all.

But when you enter a Business Convention conducted upon the same principal; hear business men up and air financial successes by extravagant exaggerations; talk of themselves and their importance, one naturally feels disgusted and cheapened. A delegate from Arkansas tells the Convention he is the only undertaker who owns his business in the city where he resides, that he is the proud owner of halls and houses and is so highly respected therefor, another of Missouri tells the Business Convention that he buries so many hundred dead in a year, and makes so many thousands of dollars thereby; then a man from Boston, poses as a diamond broker; a couple of bankers get the floor and tell a wonderful story of marvelous success and give large figures representing their wealth. Virginia arises in her glory with an Attorney-at-Law and Real Estate Dealer with his voluminous and statistical report of his financial success. Thus for three days these Business Men "blew their own horns," made and carried their own bouquets, each trying to blow louder than the other. Until we wished that successful business men were sensible, modest men as we had formerly thought them; that they knew as well what to say in public as they did how to make and save money.

We see no benefit from such a gathering. A union of business men would be a good thing no doubt if conducted differently; but a business convention conducted on the teachers' association platform, presided over by a school professor is to my mind a waste of time. What does not benefit, what does not reflect credit must at least cast a shadow.[2]

Washington *Colored American*, Sept. 14, 1901, 9.

¹ Minnie R. Barbour, a black woman born in Illinois in 1871, was a former school-teacher who contributed to several black publications regarding race affairs in Chicago.

² Two weeks after this criticism of the NNBL, the Washington *Colored American* ran another article that praised the convention and responded directly to the charges Minnie R. Barbour had made. It was written by BTW's friend Fannie Barrier Williams. (Washington *Colored American*, Sept. 28, 1901, 2.)

An Item in the Washington *Colored American*

[Washington, D.C., Sept. 14, 1901]

CAMPS IN WEST VA.

Charleston is soon to be visited by a company of representative Negroes, perhaps the most intelligent, the most cultured and the wealthiest in the United States.

The occasion is a proposed outing under the guidance of Professor Booker T. Washington, President of the Tuskegee Institute, of Alabama. He has invited and expects to have accompany him T. Thomas Fortune, author and associate editor of the New York Sun, Lloyd G. Wheeler and J. W. Smiley,¹ business men of Chicago, reputed to be the wealthiest colored men in this country, Prof. W. S. Dubois,² of Atlanta University, J. W. Durham,³ statesman and diplomat, of Philadelphia, E. E. Cooper, of Washington, D.C. and a number of others.

Here the party will be joined by Dr. H. F. Gamble, Phil Waters,⁴ B. Prillerman and others and a trip will be first made up the Elk to test the fishing spot of that stream and later the party will go to Gauley for a longer stay.

For the trip up the Elk river over the C. C. & S. railroad Superintendent McDermitt has placed a private car at the disposal of the gentlemen of the party and they will no doubt enjoy the novelty of the outing very much.

During his stay in this city Professor Washington has kindly consented to deliver an address on some appropriate subject at the opera house and an effort will be made to secure a large attendance of all classes.

This being Mr. Washington's home he is always ready and willing to address an audience of home folks and Charleston people are certain of a rare treat when they hear him.

Washington *Colored American*, Sept. 14, 1901, 9. Reprinted from the Charleston *Mail Tribune*.

1 Charles H. Smiley owned a successful catering business that served affluent white Chicagoans.

2 William Edward Burghardt Du Bois.

3 John Stephens Durham.

4 Phil Waters (1871–1918), a black lawyer in Charleston, W.Va., was educated at Howard University and the University of Michigan Law School. He campaigned for the Republican George W. Atkinson for governor in 1896 and was rewarded with an appointment as recording clerk in the secretary of state's office. He eventually became chief deputy clerk of the West Virginia Supreme Court of Appeals, a position he held until his death.

From Joseph Oswalt Thompson

Tuskegee, Ala. Sept. 16, 1901

Dear Sir, Can you appoint some hour today, to talk with me about a matter, in which you are very much interested?

Confidentially. You have no doubt noticed the movement inaugurated in Birmingham Saturday by certain influential Democrats, who oppose the ratification of the new Constitution.

The Rep. State Executive Committee, of which I have the honor to be a member, desires to move cautiously in the matter, and after having consulted with the chairman, we have a plan, of which I would like to speak to you. Respt.,

J. O. Thompson

ALS Con. 213 BTW Papers DLC.

From Timothy Thomas Fortune

New York, Sept 17, 1901

My dear Mr. Washington: I got home Thursday noon last and pinned down to hard work, plenty of which I found here. The death of the President upset everything for the time being, as it was really unexpected on the face of the doctor's report.

I want to see you and talk over the situation. I think that Roosevelt will be disposed to give me a good thing in the country so that you and I can engineer his campaign among our men. But it will depend very largely upon you, and just how you feel about it at this time I donot know. I want to pay for my home and get on my feet, and there is a reasonable chance to do so under the new conditions. How do you feel about it? Yours truly

T. Thomas Fortune

ALS   Con. 196   BTW Papers   DLC.

From William Henry Baldwin, Jr.

[New York City] September 18th, 1901

Dear Washington: I presume, of course, that your proposed trip with the new President must be considered off, and I regret it exceedingly. What a terrible calamity has come upon us in the death of the President. At the same time, how important it is now that Mr. Roosevelt is President that we bring to his attention the needs of your people in the South. I shall aim to make a special point of getting his co-operation on the general question of education of those who need it throughout the southern country. We cannot, of course, do anything now. We must wait some time. We must certainly keep it in mind. Yours very truly,

W H Baldwin Jr.

TLS   Con. 792   BTW Papers   DLC.

From William Vaughan[1]

Birmingham, Ala., Sept. 18, 1901

Personal

Dear Sir: A vigorous fight is being planned against the adoption of the new constitution which if perfected will in my belief defeat it.

I have conferred with a good many republicans as well as people of other political faith as to the course our party should pursue, as to time and methods. I have concluded that it will be better to let the proposed democratic organization against its adoption proceed and let the fight be thoroughly organized by them before the republicans begin actively their work, and I would be very glad confidentially to have your views on this subject, expressed as you prefer likewise in a confidential way to me. In my judgment three fourths of the white counties in the state will be adverse to the new measure, and I feel certain that some of the Black Belt counties, how many I do not know, will be found in the same column.

Our federal courts are now in session here and because of the illness of Judge Swayne[2] of Florida who was on the bench here nearly three weeks, the work has gotten considerably behind, however I shall endeavor to go to Tuskegee tomorrow morning for a short talk with you and my friend J. O. Thompson as to some work to be done in your section of the state, and incidentally about some other things in which all of us feel an interest. If the court work should not allow me to get off tomorrow morning I certainly hope very soon to be able to discuss these matters with both of you. Yours very truly,

Wm Vaughan

TLS Con. 213 BTW Papers DLC.

1 William Vaughan, born in Limestone County, Ala., in 1859, was a lawyer and Republican politician. With William J. Stevens, a black man, Vaughan headed the black-and-tan faction of Alabama Republicans in opposition to Robert A. Moseley, Jr., and the lily whites. The Vaughan-Stevens faction was seated in the 1896 national convention. Vaughan supported fusion with the Populists in Alabama, but the slate lost the gubernatorial election to Joseph Forney Johnston. In 1897 McKinley appointed Vaughan to the position of U.S. district attorney, and reappointed him in 1901.

2 Charles Swayne was U.S. district judge for northern Florida beginning in 1889.

From Amanda Ferguson Johnston

Malden. W.Va Sept 19. 1901

my dear brother   I recived the three boxes of things yu sent me they were all the things I needed   I thank yu so much for them. my

House is fine   there is Comers all the time to see it. brother the
gr[o]und on the Hill is $50.00 Dollars & acker   I am saveing peach
stones to plant   i[']ll Have & Orchard   tell me how much to get.
Then we will hafter have it Servade. Hope yu & all are well. We
are Sad abut Our Presedents deth. from yur Sister

Amanda Johnson

ALS Con. 201 BTW Papers DLC.

From Thomas Goode Jones

Montgomery, Alabama. Sept 20th 1901

Confidential

Dear Sir. I write this *in confidence*, not that I personally would object to its being known; but because the fact might arouse prejudices which might lessen my influence for good, if it became
known I had written you on such a subject.

You will see in the morning's paper the address of the Committee
in which I joined.[1] As you recall that I opposed the "grand-father"
clause, and did like the registrar clause, from whose action I wished
the jury trial, which was given, but the further right of appeal to
the higher courts, which was denied — you will readily understand
that I did not write that part of the address. I signed it because,
balancing all things, it occurs to me wisest and best that the Constitution go through.

If it fails of ratification it will only prolong an agitation and
bitterness which has already done harm, and in the end the outcome
will not be better. Balancing all things, I think a stride in advance
has been made. We have checked the tide of lynching, defeated the
division of school funds on race lines and poverty. The permanent
plan of suffrage will not in the end operate harshly on the negro
race; for coming up to its requirements will help to lift them up,
and all deserving people can come up to the requirements. Indeed,
the main opposition to this part of the plan comes from men like
Ex-Gov Johnston who insist that the qualifications should be made
more stringent against the negro — if they succeed in defeating

ratification it will only be to have a sharper instrument. All these considerations convince me that no permanent harm can come to the negro race from the adoption of the instrument — indeed that in after years it will operate fairly. Hence I believe it is wisdom and statesmanship all round to adopt it. I have not at all despaired of the disappearance of much of the unfortunate race antagonism, natural perhaps in the last thirty years; and believe the coming years will bring greater happiness and contentment.

For many years it has been my fortune to be considerably ahead of many of my associates in these questions. Twenty seven years ago I plead for the spirit of amity and concord, in a speech over the Confederate dead, like that which our dear departed president finally brought about. At that time, my views were considered not the proper thing for an Ex-Confederate. When I became Governor my inaugural, severely denouncing both the wisdom and the Constitutionality of a law apportioning taxes to schools according to the taxes paid by each race, drove from me very many of the extremists. The same element were bitter on me for my part as trustee in locating the colored university here, and defending the act and rebuking the hostility to it. I was elected to the Constitutional Convention against my wishes, and my course there has been not at all pleasing to the politicians. I have no political ambitions, and fully realize that all these things, and my stand against Bryan in 1896, would make it impossible to gratify them, even if I had future aspirations. I mention all these things simply to show that what I wish to urge upon you, if in your power, is entirely disinterested, and not urged by any personal or merely political consideration. I realize your difficulties in leading your own race, especially on such lines as this. I am free to confess my belief that your great work would be hindered if not destroyed, if you should actively engage in partisan politics of any kind. I would not have you do it.

It occurs to me, however, if you could exercise your influence to keep your people aloof from the contest over the ratification of the new Constitution, it would be a wise thing. If the Constitution should, possibly, be defeated by their efforts, it would only result in greater bitterness and a worse condition of things in the future. On the other hand, I would not ask them to join in its ratification, when some of the reasons, so intemperately urged in its favor, are based on such unreasoning passion against them as a race. In the end I do not believe the new Constitution will operate hardly on the negro. I am thoroughly convinced the course I suggest for them will promote their good in the end. Are you in position to do anything on this line?

For generations my family were slaveholders, and master and slaves always had an affection for each other. I remember my good old black mammy well, and my body servant during the war, who risked his life for me. One of my ambitions, the only one I have beside amassing a competency for myself & family, is to bring about a reign of confidence between the races, inculcate a spirit of justice to them, and have a part in happily solving the great problem we have, & which we can settle happily, if only we are brave and patient. Hence my earnestness in this private letter. Yours truly

Thos. G. Jones

ALS Con. 20 BTW Papers DLC. BTW sent the letter to George Washington Campbell with the comment: "Mr. Campbell: I thought it would not be a violation of confidence to let you read this letter. I agree fully in the Gov. Jones views and I think you will. I shall have nothing to do with any opposition. B. T. W."

1 The Montgomery *Advertiser*, Sept. 20, 1901, 9, reported on a committee of nine men who were assigned the task of explaining the new provisions of the constitution. The committee explained: "Those who framed the new instrument did not forget that it was the work of the dominant race, and should secure the just rights of the weaker race as well. They have not concealed from the world the conviction that the welfare of both races is secured and enhanced by keeping the control and direction of the government in the hands of that great race, whose blood and sacrifices founded our republic and gave free institutions to America. Neither have they builded a Constitution for a great State along the lines of race hatred or unworthy prejudices. The purpose of the new instrument is to protect the weaker as well as the stronger race."

To Thomas Goode Jones

Tuskegee, Ala. 9, 23, 1901

Dear Sir: I thank you for writing me so fully and frankly. Of course what I write is in confidence. I should have answered your letter more promptly but for the reason that I wanted to take plenty of time to consider your suggestions. After having done so, I want to say that even if my own heart and head did not agree with your views I should be strongly inclined to follow your suggestions so great is my faith in you and anything that you advocate. There is much in the new constitution I think that should be out and much out that should be in, but I earnestly hope with you that the new is a step towards better things. I confess that the thing that most grieves me regarding present conditions is the lack of honesty in enforcing laws. I think if we can get to the point where even a bad law will be honestly enforced we shall have made great progress. The want of respect for criminal law and law bearing upon elections is I think the saddest thing in our state. The thing I fear most about the working of our new constitution is not that some Negro votes are going to be cut off, but there is much in it that will tempt the white man to perjure and degrade his own soul by interpreting the law to mean one thing when a Negro is concerned and another when a white man is concerned — in a word I fear we shall have dishonesty — corruption protected and perpetuated by law. On the other hand largely owing to your brave words and actions there is much in the constitution that should encourage the Negro. This is especially true regarding lynching and schools.

I have been approached by several important parties to lend my influence in an effort to defeat the constitution. This I have refused to do and shall continue to refuse. I cannot find out whether those who oppose it want the Negro treated here harshly or more friendly. But in [any] case there is no consideration, financial or otherwise, that would tempt me to turn aside from my present work to enter politics. I presume that for the mere asking I could get from President Roosevelt almost any political office in reason but I should not think of yielding to such a temptation. I do not believe that there is going to be any active or serious opposition on the part of the colored people. There will be a little noise made by a few of not much importance. I shall use my influence judiciously in the direction that you suggest. I have the greatest faith in your deep interest in my race and my race as a whole honors you.

I shall hope to talk the whole subject over with you sometime soon. Yours truly,

Booker T. Washington

TLSr Copy   BTW Papers   ATT.

To the Editor of the Montgomery *Advertiser*

Tuskegee, Ala., Sept. 23, 1901

Editor The Advertiser: "Mob rule is destructive of all government." These are the words just spoken by the Hon. Adlai E. Stevenson.[1]

In the midst of the season of deepest grief, when the heart of a nation is shedding tears of sorrow as perhaps it has never before done for an individual, is it not a fitting time to stop to take our bearings that we may know whither we are drifting? With united voice we condemn the individual who was the direct cause of removing the, perhaps, most tenderly and universally loved President the nation has ever had. But in all sincerity, I want to ask, is Czolgosz[2] alone guilty? Has not the entire nation had a part in this greatest crime of the century? What is anarchy but a defiance of law and has not the nation reaped what it has been sowing? According to a careful record kept by The Chicago Tribune, 2,516 persons have been lynched in the United States during the past sixteen years and every State in the Union except five, has had its lynching. A conservative estimate would place the number of persons engaged in these lynchings at about fifty per individual lynched, so that there are or have been engaged in this anarchy of lynching nearly 125,000 persons to say nothing of the many organized bands of technically organized anarchists. Those composing these mobs have defied Governors, Judges, Sheriffs and helped create a disregard for law and authority that, in my mind, has helped to lay the foundation for the great disgrace and disaster that has overtaken the country.

We cannot sow disorder and reap order. We cannot sow death and reap life.

To check the present tendency, it seems to me there are two duties that face us: first, for all classes to unite in an earnest effort to create such a public sentiment as will make crime disappear, and especially is it needful that we see that there is no idle, dissolute, purposeless class permitted in our midst with which and among whom crime usually originates.

Second, for all to unite in a brave effort to bring criminals to justice, and where a supposed criminal is found, no matter what the charge against him is, to see that he has a fair, patient, legal trial. One criminal put to death through the majesty of the law does more, to my mind, to prevent crime than ten put to death by the hand of lynching anarchists.

At the present time, when governors, judges, the pulpit and the press in all parts of the country are condemning lynching and anarchy as never before, is the time to begin the reform.

When the practice of lynching was begun, it was said that lynching would be inflicted, but for one crime, but the actual facts show that so true is it that lawlessness breeds lawlessness, that more people are now lynched each year for other supposed crimes than for the crime for which it was begun.

Let us heed the words of our departed and beloved Chief, as he lay upon his dying bed, referring to his murderer: "I hope he will be treated with fairness." If William McKinley, as he was offering up his life in behalf of the nation, could be brave enough, thoughtful and patriotic enough to request that his assailant should be fairly and honestly tried and punished, surely we can afford to heed the lesson. The best way, it seems to me, to show our love and reverence for William McKinley is to reach the conclusion in every community, in every part of the country, that the majesty of the law must be upheld at any cost.

Booker T. Washington

Montgomery *Advertiser*, Sept. 24, 1901, 2. This also appeared, slightly edited, in the *Tuskegee Student*, 13 (Sept. 28, 1901), 3, and in other newspapers.

[1] Adlai Ewing Stevenson (1835–1914), Vice-President of the United States during Cleveland's second administration.
[2] Leon Czolgosz (1873–1901), McKinley's assassin.

From Theodore Roosevelt

[Washington, D.C.] September 24, 1901

My dear Mr. Washington: I have your letter, and shall expect to see you on either the 27th or 28th. I want to have a long talk with you. Come in at three P.M., on either of the days mentioned, letting me know a day in advance. Faithfully yours,

Theodore Roosevelt

TLS   Theodore Roosevelt Papers   DLC.

From Timothy Thomas Fortune

[New York City] Sept 26 1901

I will not see you tonight you will accept my resignation given at Chicago we are out of harmony and should seperate.[1]

Thomas Fortune

HWSr Con. 541 BTW Papers DLC. The telegram is marked "Received at Grand Union Hotel."

[1] Fortune and BTW quarreled during a committee meeting of the NNBL in Chicago. Fortune wanted to introduce a resolution condemning a brutal lynching in Atlanta and BTW opposed the measure and blocked it from getting to the floor of the convention. Fortune managed to speak out in spite of BTW's wishes, thus offending the Tuskegean. It is possible that Fortune had been drinking, and that BTW was afraid that he would repeat remarks he had made at the Philadelphia meeting of the National Afro-American Council on Aug. 7, 1901, when Fortune urged blacks to protect themselves from lynch law by using guns. (Thornbrough, *T. Thomas Fortune,* 218.) Two days later Fortune telegraphed BTW: "No reply to telegrams hope we may straighten matters satisfactorily." (Sept. 28, 1901, Con. 541, BTW Papers, DLC.)

From Timothy Thomas Fortune

Red Bank, N.J.   Sept. 29, 1901

Personal

Dear Mr. Washington: Your telegram of yesterday was received. Your letter of the 23rd, written at Tuskegee, reached me Friday morning last. I remembered that you said on the Gauley you expected to be in New York on the 26th. Having not heard from you since we parted at Montgomery, something very unusual with us, I was much worried and confused, and am so still, and called you up at a venture on Thursday. You seemed so uncertain about your own movements and our meeting that I decided to send the Thursday telegram. When your letter of the 23rd reached me Friday morning it explained matters somewhat, although it was not an answer and made no reference to the two letters I had sent you since we parted at Montgomery.

We have always worked with mutual understanding and sympathy, except at Chicago, where a misunderstanding arose through provoking remarks in the Palmer House by Dr. Courtney, who was officiously solicitous that I should say nothing about lynching and the like in the Convention — as if I did not know what to say and what not to say on such an occasion — and you seemed to take his view of the matter in calling a meeting of the executive committee without my knowledge and deciding that I should not speak in the regular order on the program. However, I concluded that the Chicago unpleasantness had been wiped out by our West Virginia trip. Your long silence after our separation rather upset that view of the matter.

I have simply been seeking an understanding since last Thursday, as I never could work with any one except in an honest and above board manner. There is nothing underhanded in my disposition or methods, and I have never found any in yours, and donot expect to find any.

I am anxious to get at the Roosevelt matter, about which I have written you, but I would not think of proceeding in it until you have defined your position, as I asked you to do in my former letter. With kind regards, Yours truly

T. Thomas Fortune

ALS Con. 196 BTW Papers DLC.

From Charles Harrison Tweed[1]

New York. Sept. 30, 1901

Dear Sir: I have received your letter of 24th inst. in reference to the treatment of colored passengers on the ferry which transfers passengers from New Orleans across the Mississippi River to the Southern Pacific road. This is a matter in respect to which I have no personal knowledge, and am writing today to New Orleans asking whether the objectionable features in connection with this transfer to which you call my attention cannot be obviated or at any rate in large degree ameliorated. Upon hearing from our friends in New Orleans in reference to the matter I will write you further on the subject. Yours truly,

Charles H Tweed

TLS Con. 210 BTW Papers DLC.

1 Charles Harrison Tweed (1844–1917) was general counsel and chairman of the board of directors of the Southern Pacific Co. From 1903 to 1907 he was a partner in the banking firm of Speyer and Co.

To Theodore Roosevelt[1]

[Tuskegee, Ala., Oct. 2, 1901]

My Dear Mr. President: I send you the following information through my secretary, Mr. Emmett J. Scott, whom you can trust implicitly:

Judge Bruce,[2] the judge of the Middle district of Alabama, died yesterday. There is going to be a very hard scramble for his place.

I saw ex-Gov. T. G. Jones yesterday, as I promised, and he is willing to accept the judgeship of the Middle district of Alabama. I am more convinced now than ever that he is the proper man for the place. He has until recently been president of the Alabama State Bar association. He is a gold democrat, and is a clean, pure man in every respect. He stood up in the constitutional convention and elsewhere for a fair election law, opposed lynching, and has been outspoken for the education of both races. He is head and shoulders above any of the other persons who I think will apply to you for the position.

I will give you more detailed information regarding other Southern appointments when I see you, which will be within a few days. Yours truly,

Booker T. Washington

P.S. — I do not believe that in all the south you could select a better man through whom to emphasize your idea of the character of a man to hold office than you can do through ex-Governor Jones.

Birmingham *Age-Herald*, Oct. 25, 1902, 1.

1 This letter was published in the Birmingham *Age-Herald*, about a year after it was written, as proof of BTW's role in the appointment of Thomas G. Jones to the federal bench. The Montgomery *Advertiser*, on the other hand, said that the letter was not proof that BTW had "secured" the position for Jones, but that it did represent the Tuskegean's "signal good judgment." The *Advertiser* stated that many persons, North and South, had recommended Jones to President Roosevelt. (Montgomery *Advertiser*, Oct. 26, 1902, Clipping, Con. 978, BTW Papers, DLC.) In North Carolina, the Wilmington *Messenger* reprinted the letter and said that it was proof that BTW was Roosevelt's "chief adviser and most trusted assistant in the matter of making appointments in the southern states and also that Washington prefers 'gold bug' democrats to negroes or white republicans when it comes to appointments to federal offices." (Wilmington *Messenger*, Oct. 28, 1902, Clipping, Con. 978, BTW Papers, DLC.)

2 John Bruce (1832–1901) was a U.S. district judge in Alabama beginning in 1875.

From William Calvin Oates

[Montgomery, Ala.] Oct. 2nd 1901

Strictly Confidential

Dear Sir. It is very rare that I ever write to any man in confidence but you are a man of so much good sense and reason that I write you a suggestion. A certain class of democrats are going to ratify the New Constitution. It will be so counted. You know that. I would not fight it because I knew before the Convention adjourned that there was no use. There is but one way. This morning I heard that Judge Bruce was dead. There are already before he is buried a host of applicants for the vacant Judgeship announced. With the impending sentiment among a large class of the white people in the south the greatest bulwark of protection to your race is to be found in the federal Judiciary. Those we have had and a majority of those we have now are not popular nor men of power and influence. Now is a most auspicious time for you to do a great work in Alabama on this line. You know that there is not a republican in the state of sufficiently high character and ability to exercise any greater influence in Bruce's place than the old man did which was nothing.

If you could induce the President to appoint a man, a conservative democrat of large influence[,] courage and a high sense of justice you would do the greatest good for your people and the Country. I have had a few gentlemen-democrats to approach me on the subject of applying for the appointment which I do not propose to do but it is a high position and takes a man out of politics. All that I have said her[e]in is for your own eye and by way of suggestion. There are other good men, better men perhaps than any named for that place. You are unquestionably the ablest man of your race and are doing more for it than any man who has ever lived and I honor you for it and sympathize with you in your efforts. Your friend

Wm C Oates

ALS   Con. 1   BTW Papers   DLC.

To Philander Chase Knox[1]

[Tuskegee, Ala.] Oct. 4, 1901

From best information I can get, Thomas R. Roulack[2] is Gold Standard Democrat. He is a man of high standing in his community and is well respected in the state. He lives outside of district where vacancy exists. Governor Jones is much better known throughout the state and has stood up bravely for education of all people against lynch law and justice to the Negro. It is my opinion that Jones has better qualifications than Roulack. Jones lives in Middle District where vacancy exists.

Booker T. Washington

TWSr   Con. 541   BTW Papers   DLC.

1 Philander Chase Knox (1853–1921) was U.S. Attorney General (1901–4), U.S. senator from Pennsylvania (1904–9, 1917–21), and U.S. Secretary of State (1909–13).

2 Thomas Ruffin Roulhac, born in Raleigh, N.C., in 1846, moved in 1870 to Greensboro, Ala., to practice law. In 1899 he moved to Sheffield, Ala., as attorney for the Sheffield Land Co. He was a state circuit judge from 1894 to 1898. In 1902 President Roosevelt appointed him U.S. attorney for the northern district of Alabama, but he was not reappointed when his term expired in 1906. As a Gold Democrat Roulhac was more acceptable to Roosevelt than a Bryan supporter would have been, but from BTW's perspective, there was no evidence of Roulhac's racial liberalism to strengthen the claim that his appointment would improve the federal service in the South. BTW

saw Roulhac's appointment, however, as a "slap to lily white element in Alabama," and he urged his lieutenants to congratulate Roosevelt on the appointment. (BTW to R. L. Smith, Oct. 8, [1902], Con. 275, BTW Papers, DLC.)

From Emmett Jay Scott

Washington D.C. Oct. 4/1901

My Dear Mr Washington: I called to see the president this morning. I found him all of cordiality and brimming over with good will for you. That pleased me much! He had received the telegram and had made an appointment for me. He read your letter, inquired if I knew the contents and then launched into a discussion of it. Wanted to know if Gov Jones supported Bryan in either campaign. I told him *no*. He wanted to know how I knew. I told him of the letter wherein he (Governor Jones) stated to you that he was without political ambition because he had opposed Bryan, etc. etc.[1] Well, he said he wanted to hear from you direct as to whether he had or not & asked me to wire you to find out. I am now awaiting that wire so as to call again on him. As soon as I see him again I will wire you & write you as to what he says. He is going to appoint Gov. Jones. That was made apparent. While I was waiting to see him Senator Chandler[2] with the Spanish Claims Commission called. They saw him first. I heard the talk however, which was mostly felicitation. Incidentally however Chandler said that the Commission was afraid it would lose one of its members because of the vacancy in Alabama, referring to W. L. Chambers who was present & who is a member of the Commission. The president laughed heartily, said the Senator always sprung recommendations unexpectedly & so forth & so forth. He did not inquire as to any of the others — the applicants — seemed interested only to find out about Gov. Jones. I have seen none of the applicants. There were many correspondents there at the door but I told them I was passing through to Buffalo, but had stopped over to invite the president to include Tuskegee in his itinerary when he goes South again. They bit! Dunbar, White,[3] Arnett[4] & others were waiting to see the president but failed. I will send the Blue Book tonight. It costs

$3.00. I go to Chicago via Buffalo Saturday tonight, & will be there Monday morning. Yours sincerely

Emmett J. Scott

Will write again when I see the president again.

ALS   Con. 209   BTW Papers   DLC.

1 Jones wrote BTW that he had opposed Bryan in 1896. (Oct. 2, 1901, Con. 201, BTW Papers, DLC.)

2 William Eaton Chandler.

3 George Henry White.

4 Benjamin William Arnett.

From George Bruce Cortelyou

Executive Mansion, Washington. October 4, 1901

Personal.

My dear Sir: In a recent personal communication to the President protest is made against the reappointment of Mr. Bingham[1] as Collector of Internal Revenue in Alabama.

The President will be glad to have from you, confidentially, a statement of your views on the subject. Very truly yours,

Geo. B. Cortelyou

TLS   Con. 193   BTW Papers   DLC.

1 Julian H. Bingham was U.S. collector of internal revenue for Alabama from 1897 to 1902. He was described by one newspaper as a "luke warm Republican" with Populist tendencies. (Birmingham *State Herald*, July 4, 1897, 1.) When he was removed from office the Montgomery *Advertiser* said, ". . . the President now sacrifices him on the altar of the negro vote." (Nov. 11, 1902, 1.) At the time of his release, Bingham, a lily white, was also Republican national committeeman from Alabama, and was replaced by BTW's friend Joseph O. Thompson. Emmett J. Scott wrote BTW: "Our folks are jubilant beyond measure because of Bingham's removal. The Washington correspondents of the State papers seem to be with the lily whites — but it is Satisfactory that they say he is removed because of activity in lily white movement. That will do good!" (Nov. 11, 1902, Con. 242, BTW Papers, DLC.)

From Charles Winston Thompson

Tuskegee Ala. Oct. 4/01

Dr. Sir: I am going to Washington to see the President in the interest of my Brother[1] and will thank you to give me a letter of introduction to him.

I will thank you to let him know that I have always been a friend to your school and that the colored people of this county voted for me almost unanimously.

I thank you very kindly for the letter you gave my Brother. Yours truly,

Chas. W. Thompson

ALS Con. 213 BTW Papers DLC. Written on stationery of the U.S. House of Representatives.

1 Joseph Oswalt Thompson.

From Thomas Junius Calloway

Washington, D.C., October 4, 1901

Dear Mr. Washington; Mrs. Calloway and I wish to thank you for the very excellent photograph of your home. We are sure that you and Mrs. Washington must be very comfortable in it. We are very glad that you directed Mr. Scott to our house and trust that you will honor us by coming to our modest home whenever you are passing through the city. We shall always be prepared for you at any time.

A matter that I have been seriously considering since you were here seems more important the more I think of it. It is, that you need here a representative, a sort of second self, in whom you can place confidence, and can serve you and the President as a go-between in matters political. Or to put it another way, a sort of "figurehead" to be used in working out knotty problems and rendering any assistance needed. In canvassing the field I have become convinced, without egotism I believe, that no one can serve both you and the President so well as I could. Having been associated with you intimately during the last ten years you will be at liberty to place in me your full confidence, and I have had such intimate opportunity to learn your ideas and to know your judgment that I believe I could serve you more faithfully than any other person. On the other hand, as I came into the Government service under the Civil Service Commission when President Roosevelt was a Commissioner, have never been a "politician" or made any attempts at the business, and the only public appointment that I have ever held, Special Agent to Paris, having been due to your influence as you know, President Roosevelt, it seems to me, would like just such a man to emphasize in his and your policy.

I had been thinking of this matter before Mr. Scott came, and was gratified that he suggested it to me before I had had occasion to discuss the matter with him.

Now if you think it advisable I should like to be considered in connection with an appointment by the President to a position that would enable me to serve you both. I should prefer to let him select or at least indicate his wish that a selection be made before asking for any particular position. My only preference would be that the position would be of sufficient prestige to enable me to serve you both to the highest advantage. I think I am sufficiently well known throughout the country because of my work in connection with Tuskegee, as having charge of the Negro exhibit to Paris, and otherwise, so that the public would not be surprised if I were appointed to a responsible position. In fact I believe that the press and the public would take to it with favor as an evidence of Civil Service promotion.

If appointed I would be in a position to serve the President's immediate and future political interests more, I believe, than the so-called politicians. As it becomes known that you are an adviser to the President you will be literally "swarmed" with "influence" hunters. You could refer them to me when you desire and in the meantime I could investigate them for you and secretly advise you as to their value.

I write you at this time so that you will have time to think over the matter before I see you. I shall appreciate your frank judgment in the matter, and assure you that I do not wish to take advantage of our friendly relations to embarrass you by becoming a candidate unless you think I can serve you both in doing so. Sincerely yours,

Thos. J. Calloway

TLS Con. 193 BTW Papers DLC.

From Emmett Jay Scott

Washington D.C. Oct 5, 1901

My Dear Mr. Washington: You have my telegram of today. I sent it as soon as I had seen the president. I had a three hours wait to see him & it was tiresome but I camped with them. When admitted to the general reception room the president met me & was cordial and asked me to wait awhile, till he could dismiss two (2) delegations, then he invited me into the office, or cabinet room & read very carefully the telegram received from you last night — Friday night.[1] His face was a study. He was greatly surprised to learn that the Governor voted for Bryan, and walked about considerably. At last he said, "well I guess I'll have to appoint him but I am awfully sorry he voted for Bryan." He then asked me who Dr Crum is and I told him that he was a clean representative character, and that he was favorably considered by Harrison for the Charleston post-mastership, etc. He did not know him & asked me what place was referred to. You had not discussed it with me, but I told him you most likely referred to the place made vacant by the death of Webster.[2] He then called Cortelyou into the office & asked him if he knew Crum. He said he didn't but that he had heard of him & always favorably. The president then asked Cortelyou what place a man named Blaylock[3] was being considered for & he said the place made vacant by Webster's death. He then turned to me & said that he was sorry, that he would certainly have considered [the] matter if he had had your word earlier. He asked me to tell you that if you wish Dr Crum considered for any other place that he will be glad to have you communicate with him. I then asked him what I should tell you in the Jones matter & he said — "Tell Mr Washington without using my name that party will most likely be appointed — in fact that I will appoint him — only dont make it that strong by wire." So I consider the matter closed. The other telegram came after I had gone to the White House, & I have only returned to find it. While there the Attorney General[4] came in & I saw him go in to see the president. The latter said nothing to me about Roulach & I had no chance to say anything & then I dont know Roulach & could have said nothing. I hoped you have wired substantially the same message regarding the two men to the Attorney General. I shall not annoy the president by going back again now that he has said he will appoint Governor Jones.

I hope I shall have your approval in this decision. I go from here tonight & shall be in Chicago Tuesday morning. I want to be in Buffalo Monday. I shall devote myself well to our matters in Chicago Tuesday and Wednesday.

The colored brethren here are scared. They dont know what to expect & the word has passed that you are the "Warwick" so far as they are concerned. I hope to find you well in Chicago. Sincerely yours,

Emmett J. Scott

ALS   Con. 272   BTW Papers   DLC.

[1] BTW wired Scott that Jones had indeed voted for Bryan in 1900 but did not publicly campaign for him. BTW also told Scott that Jones had "strongly and openly supported McKinley's expansion policy and was president of sound money club in ninety six. . . ." ([Oct. 4, 1901], Theodore Roosevelt Papers, DLC.)

[2] E. Alonzo Webster (1849–1901) was collector of internal revenue for South Carolina from 1889 to 1901, the state Republican boss, and a member of the Republican national committee. (Charleston News and Courier, Sept. 18, 1901, 1.)

[3] Loomis Blalock, a businessman in Newberry, S.C., switched from the Democratic to the Republican party only a short time earlier, perhaps in the campaign of 1900. It was first announced that he would be appointed collector of internal revenue for South Carolina, but President Roosevelt instead appointed a Gold Democrat, George R. Koester. (Charleston News and Courier, Oct. 11, 1901, 1.)

[4] Philander Chase Knox.

From James Lewis

New Orleans, La., October 5th, 1901

Esteemed Sir and Friend: Your very kind favor of the 3rd inst., is before me, and contents carefully noted. It found myself and little Regiment all well, and pleased to learn of the continued good health of yourself, and family. I note what you say regarding your reported interview, with the President, and I don't hesitate to say, that I don't see anything in it to condemn, or to compromise. It is a fact that the class of Men who are in control of the Republican Party Machine in the South, are not the best among the White, or Colored Republicans, and I think the President acted wise in calling you in Counsel, for no Colored Man in this Country knows the wants, and needs of his Race, better than you, your life is devoted to him, of the two letters received one blessing you, and the latter cursing you, the latter must have been from a played out Preacher, or Pot House Politician.

General Grant while President, always consulted with representative Colored Men in the respective Southern States, before making appointments, by this means worthy men received recognition, which is not so general now, among both White and Colored.

We have reputable and most worthy Colored Men all through the South that command the respect and confidence of the Community in which they reside, and I am with you to reach that class of our Citizens, I am also in accord with you regarding the cause leading to the death of our beloved President Wm. McKinley. Out side of a few office holders, your interview is approved. I note by the Morning Papers, friend Emmett Scott, is at the White House for the purpose of inviting the President to Visit Tuskegee, I hope He will accept.

While you were away, My Son received a letter from Mrs. Keever, now in England, for your Book, which was received through the kindness of Friend Scott.

Mrs. Lewis, and the rest of my Family Joins me in kindest regards to you, and your's, and a welcome to you and them whenever you come this way, Very truly yours,

James Lewis

TLS Con. 203 BTW Papers DLC.

From Oscar Richard Hundley[1]

Montgomery, Ala., Oct. 5th, 1901

My Dear Sir: I am an applicant for appointment to the office of U.S. District Judge, for the Northern and Middle Districts of Alabama, and I would most gratefully appreciate a letter from you in my behalf to the President. As you are aware, I was for four years a member of the Alabama House of Representatives, and eight years a member of the Senate, being Chairman of the Judiciary Committee of the latter body. I was also Commissioner to the World's Fair by appointment of President Harrison. You are also familiar with my ardent advocacy of the public schools throughout my public career, and I remember of helping you on several occasions while I was a member of the House and Senate. I have the strongest kind of endorsement from the Bench and Bar, and I take it that you are familiar with my standing generally as a citizen and lawyer. I have never *directly nor indirectly* been a party to the factional fights in the Republican Party in this State, but have been consistently advocating Republican principles, both in and out of this State since I became a Republican in 1896, at which time I received the unanimous nomination of the Republicans in my District for Congress. Now if there is anything in my career as a citizen and lawyer, which commends me to your favorable consideration, for this place, I assure you that your good offices in furtherance of the fruition of my ambition will ever be gratefully remembered and appreciated by me and mine.

I have the honor to remain, Very truly yours

Oscar R. Hundley

Address me at Huntsville, Ala, at your convenience.

ALS Con. 200 BTW Papers DLC.

[1] Oscar Richard Hundley (1854–1921) does not mention here that he was a Populist before switching to the Republican party in 1896, and that he was the sponsor of the unsuccessful Hundley amendment in the Alabama legislature in 1892–93, providing for the division of school tax revenues so that black schools would receive only the money collected from black taxpayers. (See above, 3:427.) In 1907, with endorsement from BTW, Hundley became U.S. district judge of the northern district of Alabama, serving until 1909.

From Timothy Thomas Fortune

Red Bank, N.J., Oct 6, 1901

My dear Mr. Washington: I have your frank but brotherly letter of the 3rd instant, and I appreciate every word you have said and am glad you have said what you have in the way you have said it. I feel that you have spoken the whole truth which I had not fully realized before, and I am going to prove to you, as I stated in my letter yesterday, that I have determined to justify your friendship and affection. I shall not give you cause for grief again on that score.

If we are disbarred from controlling the political situation in the way I have indicated, and we shall have to discuss that further, we shall have to find another way out, as I cannot go much further under present conditions.

But we shall talk over the situation on the 18th instant. Yours truly,

T. Thomas Fortune

ALS Con. 196 BTW Papers DLC.

To Theodore Roosevelt

Tuskegee, Alabama. October 7, 1901

My dear Mr. President: This letter will be handed to you by Mr. R. L. Smith of Texas, about whom we have talked several times. I thought that you might be glad to meet him personally and he can explain in person and in detail what the conditions are in Texas and what his own wishes are.

I have known Mr. Smith for a number of years and know him to be absolutely reliable and of the highest character, and further know that he has the respect and confidence of all classes of people in Texas. Yours truly,

Booker T. Washington

TLS Theodore Roosevelt Papers DLC.

To Theodore Roosevelt

Tuskegee, Alabama. October 7, 1901

My dear Mr. President: Your inquiry concerning Mr. Julian Bingham has been received and I have taken some pains to make a careful inquiry concerning him. My information has come from disinterested parties. Mr. Bingham has made a good record as a revenue officer in Alabama and stands high in both official and personal character. It seems that whatever opposition he has, is of a purely political nature. If I get further information on this point I shall write you.

If it should happen that you do not see your way clear to reappoint Mr. Bingham and you are in doubt as to a good man to appoint, I call your attention to Mr. W. R. Pettiford, the colored banker of Birmingham, Alabama. Yours truly,

Booker T. Washington

I think you already understand that Mr. Wm. Vaughan is the leader of one faction of the Republican party and Mr. Bingham is the leader of the other. Both men, however, stand above the average Republican politician.

B. T. W.

TLS   Theodore Roosevelt Papers   DLC.

To Emmett Jay Scott

Tuskegee Ala   Oct 7-01

Without letting them know I have made request wish you to arrange for me to meet separately editors of all chgo colored papers.

Booker T. Washington

TWSr   Con. 541   BTW Papers   DLC.   Addressed to Scott at the Palmer House, Chicago.

To Emmett Jay Scott

Tuskegee Ala   Oct 7-01

Conservator has vicious editorial[1] this week want to bring them into harmony if I can do so honorably.

Booker T. Washington

TWSr   Con. 541   BTW Papers   DLC.   This was sent about two hours after the previous telegram of this date.

[1] Perhaps a reference to Portia Washington, who reportedly experienced racial discrimination while at Wellesley. The St. Paul *Pioneer Press*, which often carried news from the Chicago *Conservator*, had such a story on Oct. 8, 1901, 6. It is possible that the *Conservator* was critical of BTW for sending his daughter to Wellesley in the first place.

To James Sullivan Clarkson

[Tuskegee, Ala.] 10, 7, 190[1]

Scott advises lily whites attempting to delay Roulhac appointment. I am sure they will not succeed as President has promised to appoint Roulhac at once. I have not wired President for that reason. Parties now urging delay have most shamefully humiliated our people and every Negro newspaper of influence is aroused. Am keeping them in line however on strength of promise something will be done this week. Any other course will greatly embarrass me. I am sure you feel with me that human rights and justice are most important than promise of a few uncertain votes.

Booker T. Washington

TWSr   Con. 541   BTW Papers   DLC.

From Charles Harrison Tweed

New York   Oct. 7, 1901

Dear Sir: Referring again to your letter of 24th ult., I have to say that I think there must have been some mistake made in connection with the suggestion to you as to the colored passengers being submitted to humiliation by waiting until after buggies, wagons, carts and cattle were permitted to land from our ferry transfer at New Orleans.

I am informed by the Assistant to the Manager at New Orleans that our boats are adapted to the handling of cars and foot passengers only and that they are not used for the passage of buggies, wagons, carts and cattle. It is quite likely that the features of ferry transfers at other points have led to the apparent mistake in respect to this matter, and I am very glad to learn that the Southern Pacific Company is not properly subject to the criticism referred to.

Of course you are aware that the separate accommodations laws in force in most of the Southern States have entailed quite a heavy expense upon all the railroad companies in those States, but we should not be held responsible for regulations which we are powerless to prevent or control and which involve a constant expense to us which we would be very glad to avoid. Yours truly,

Charles H Tweed

TLS Con. 210 BTW Papers DLC.

From Charles Waddell Chesnutt

Cleveland, O. October 8, 1901

My dear Mr. Washington: I have just requested my publishers to send you an advance copy of my new novel, "The Marrow of Tradition," which will be out in a week. It is by far the best thing I have done, and is a comprehensive study of racial conditions in the South, in the shape of what is said to be a very dramatic novel, which my publishers boldly compare with Uncle Tom's Cabin for its "great dramatic intensity and its powerful appeal to popular sympathies." It discusses, incidentally, miscegenation, lynching, disfranchisement, separate cars, and the struggle for professional and social progress in an unfriendly environment — and all this without at all interfering with the progress of an interesting plot with which they are all bound up. It is, in a word, our side of the Negro question, in popular form, as you have presented it in the more dignified garb of essay and biography.

If you feel moved, after reading it, to write a word or two, concerning it, I am sure it would be highly appreciated by my publishers and myself; or if you find it too strenuous for you to publicly approve, I feel pretty certain that in private you can do it almost as much good. I should like to feel that I had been able, in the form of a widely popular work of fiction, to do something tangible and worth mentioning to supplement your own work, and to win back or help retain the popular sympathy of the Northern people, which has been so sorely weakened by Southern deviltry in the past decade; for while the tolerance of the South is necessary to the progress of the colored race, and their friendship desirable, you know better than I can how absolutely essential is Northern sympathy to the work of Southern education.

I have read your utterances on the subject of the president's death, and its connection with national lawlessness; and I say amen to it. The country is suffering from blood-poisoning, and the South is the source of the infection. It is refreshing to note the growth of a small party of Southern whites who are beginning to perceive the truth. I see Mr. Page has been telling the North Carolinians some wholesome but unpalatable truths; my novel will tell them some more in the same strain. I hope they may profit by both.

My daughter[1] is very much pleased with Tuskegee. I hope she is making herself useful, and I am glad to be able to contribute through her, a little more work for the good cause.

With regards to Mrs. Washington, I remain, Cordially yours,

Chas. W. Chesnutt

TLS Con. 194 BTW Papers DLC.

1 Ethel Perry Chesnutt.

From Alfred Geiger Moses[1]

Mobile, Ala. Oct. 8th /01

Dear Sir; I have just laid aside a copy of your autobiography, "Up from Slavery," which has ingrossed my entire attention, although it is a very late hour. Your book has enthralled & captivated me. I cannot retire without gathering my impressions, and expressing my sentiments to you. "Up from Slavery" has read, like an inspired book, like another Bible. It is the story of your inner life, well told. I cried over certain portions, which smacked of the real bitter experiences of life. It has not only inspired deeper respect for your race, but also destroyed whatever prejudice lurked in my mind against the colored people. Belonging to a class, that has been oppressed, but risen, by its own merit & genius, in the world's esteem, I feel a sincere sympathy with your noble aims and lofty ideals to elevate your own people. Your condition, now, is almost analagous to the state, in which the Jews lived in Mediaeval Europe, for centuries. Under such wise & prudent leaders, as yourself, your race will work out its own salvation. I wish you godspeed in your glorious endeavors. Whenever I can be of service, to you, in helping the Tuskegee School, call upon me.

I have only lately come to the South & obtained the charge of the Jewish congregation in Mobile. The so-called "Negro Problem" has naturally interested me. I have resolved to study the question, impartially, & *not* by the prevailing prejudices. As a preacher, I feel morally bound to get at the truth, and, as a Rabbi, I have the opportunity of influencing the minds of the better class of Jewish people, as well as of the community at large.

I shall appreciate your kindness in sending me a catalogue of your school, and, in honoring me with a few personal lines.

Thanking you from the bottom of my heart, for the new light, you have given me through your classic autobiography, I remain, yours Resp'y

Alfred G. Moses

ALS   Con. 188   BTW Papers   DLC.

1 Alfred Geiger Moses (1878–1956), born in Livingston, Ala., graduated from the University of Cincinnati in 1900 and a year later received his rabbinical degree from Hebrew Union College. He was rabbi of the Shaarai Shomayim congregation in Mobile for many years beginning in 1901. He remained an admirer of BTW and "sat spell bound" when BTW gave an Emancipation Day speech in Mobile in 1906. "Your greatness makes me an optimist about the negro," he wrote BTW. "No race can produce a great man unless there is the ethnic material for his evolution. Be assured of my personal appreciation of your monumental work and call upon me whenever I can serve Tuskegee or yourself." (Jan. 2, 1906, Con. 328, BTW Papers, DLC.) Moses put BTW into contact with his brother, J. Garfield Moses, of the Educational Alliance, a settlement house on the East Side of New York. J. Garfield Moses invited him to the

house for a dinner and conversation with a group of Jewish intellectuals. "So surely as the Negro is persecuted and dealt unfairly with," he wrote BTW, "so surely will the status and the security of the Jews be the next object of attack. I have very little respect for a so called Christian who downs a fellow man and a fellow race, but for those Southern Jews who do the same, I have not only contempt but a hatred approaching almost a passion. I am a born and bred Kentuckian but the one man I honor most in this world is a Negro by the name of Booker T. Washington." (Jan. 14, 1906, Con. 809, BTW Papers, DLC.)

From Thomas J. Jackson

Charleston, S.C. Oct. 9, 1901

Dear Mr. Washington: We had an enthusiastic mass meeting in the interest of the Department last night. Many of the most prominent citizens were present and promised to do what they could to promote the work. There was considerable objection to the group of Statuary to be placed in front of the Negro Building and we may have considerable trouble in allaying the feeling of indignation aroused thereby.[1] I think you saw the statues when you were here. Aside from the objections to these statues the meeting was harmonious. We explained the statues by saying that it was the intention of the Company to have another group composed of yourself and others showing the contrast between this ignorant vicious type and the intelligent cultured type.

I have as yet heard nothing from the Board of Directors. If any communication comes today I will let you know. Yours very truly,

Thos. J. Jackson

TLS Con. 201 BTW Papers DLC.

1 Thomas E. Miller, one of the exhibitors in the Negro Building, wrote BTW: "I most earnestly call your attention to the group of statuary that has been placed through the kindness of heart of the Exposition Management in front of the main door of the Negro Building. The group is being condemned by every hopeful, aspiring, self respecting Negro of both sexes; and if it remains there it will bring our work into reproach and make the Negro end of this magnificent Exposition a loathsome thing and a byword." Miller urged BTW to look especially at the part of the statuary that showed a black youth with a banjo, which Miller described as a "blank idiot" rather than a true representation of plantation days. (Oct. 12, 1901, Con. 210, BTW Papers, DLC.) BTW tried to mollify disgruntled blacks in Charleston by pointing out that most members of the race were tillers of the soil or in menial positions and that the statue accurately reflected this. (Washington *Post*, Nov. 17, 1901, 8.)

From Jacob August Riis

New York, October 10th, 1901

My Dear Mr. Washington: Yes, we are both stumped on the trip with Roosevelt. He has other things to attend to now, and you and I both know — we all know — or if we do not now we will before he has finished his term — that they will be attended to right up to the handle, by a man as capable and honest and good, and splendid every way, as ever sat in George Washington's and Abraham Lincoln's chair. When we do meet we will all bear testimony to that and be happy together.

My love to all your people. Faithfully yours,

Jacob A Riis

TLS   Theodore Roosevelt Papers   DLC.

From Charles Emory Smith[1]

Washington, D.C. October 11, 1901

CONFIDENTIAL

My dear Sir: At the suggestion of the President I wish to advise with you in a private and confidential way respecting the Tuskegee post office. What you say to me in reply will be strictly confidential with the President and myself. We understand that you are favorable to the appointment of Mr. Thompson when a change shall be made and it is the President's purpose to appoint him then. But the term of the incumbent has not yet expired and our general policy is not to make changes until the expiration of terms. The Department has a letter from you, under date of September 7, expressing the hope that the incumbent may be left to serve out his term. Is this your judgment, or, do you privately feel that the change should be made at once? I know the pressure from different sources to elicit an expression from you and it is because the President wishes your judgment free from all such influences and entirely for private guidance that I write to you. Let me hear from you at your early convenience. Very truly yours,

Ch Emory Smith
Postmaster-General

TLS Con. 210 BTW Papers DLC.

1 Charles Emory Smith (1842–1908) was Postmaster General of the United States from 1898 to 1901.

To Emily Howland

Natchez, Miss. October 13, 1901

My dear Miss Howland: Your letter reaches me here in Mississippi where I am engaged in speaking at a series of meetings composed of both colored and white people in the interest of the cause which both of us have so near at heart. You can easily imagine that it is difficult for me to find much time in which to write. People seem so anxious for some word of advice and encouragement that I am overwhelmed by the crowds. Not the least encouraging feature of these meetings is the fact that so far they have been well attended by not only colored people but by white women as well as white men.

Now as to Lula Davidson.[1] While I have not had the opportunity of visiting and inspecting her school personally, several of our teachers have done so. All of them speak in praiseworthy terms of her work. I do not believe that you will make a mistake in helping her and I urge that you do so.

I suppose you saw in the newspapers what I said about the President's death. In a word, I stated that the lynchings which have been taking place recently in my mind led up logically to the murder of the head of the government. I am glad to find that here in Mississippi there is quite a growing sentiment against lynching and other forms of lawlessness. There is no doubt in my mind that the colored people are making slow but constant progress in all parts of this state.

I hardly know what to say about Smallwood. I presume the only thing is to let him run his course, of course exposing him whenever we can. I do not believe that anything that is not right will permanently continue to exist.

I am so glad to receive your letter because only a few days ago I was thinking of writing you.

Mrs. Washington has not been as well as usual this fall, otherwise she would have been with me on this trip.

I shall hope to see you sometime during the winter or spring. Will it not be possible for you to visit us at Tuskegee again? Yours very truly,

Booker T. Washington

TLS   Emily Howland Papers   NN-Sc.

1 Lula Julisees Davis Davidson was an 1896 graduate of Tuskegee Institute in nursing. She taught after graduation at Voorhees Industrial School, Denmark, S.C., and at Centerville, Ala.

From W. B. Jones[1]

Vicksburg, Miss., October 13 1901

Dear Sir & Bro   I write this to inform you that I had the pleasure of being one of the many that went to the Court House in this City last night to see and hear you. After list[en]ing to your enstructive and entertaining address, I must say that you have been misjudge[d] by a grate many of our People. Being a Bricklayer my self let me ask you not to lay so much stress on the Bricklayer as you did last night; because we can be over loaded with them just as we have been with Teachers & Preachers. My prayer is that you m[a]y live long and continue your good work.

If this do not find the way to the wast[e] basket I may write again. Yours for the advancement of the Race.

W B Jones

ALS   Con. 201   BTW Papers   DLC.

1 A black brickmason, born in Mississippi in 1868, Jones was a member of Bricklayers' Union No. 2 of Vicksburg.

From William Henry Lewis

Boston, Oct. 14, 1901

My Dear Mr. Washington: I am delighted to know that our minds were working in the same direction, as you had intended writing me before receiving mine of recent date.

I cannot tell you how pleased I am to know of your continued interest and good will. I agree with you that we can both work for the common end effectually, and without friction.

I shall be glad to see you when you are in Boston, and also in New Haven. I find I shall be in New Haven on the 16, 19th, and 22nd of this month. If convenient for you to see me, I shall be very glad to call.

It will perhaps, please you to know that I have received the Republican nomination for representative to the General Court from Cambridge. I am working, tooth and nail, to secure an election, as I believe it will help the cause.

I am sending this letter both to New Haven and to Tuskegee, to be sure of reaching you. With cordial regard until our meeting, Sincerely your friend,

William H. Lewis

TLS   Con. 203   BTW Papers   DLC.

From Peter Jefferson Smith, Jr.

Boston, Mass. Octo. 15—01

My dear friend: Your kind favor recent date reached me in due course. I thought you might find enclosed clipping interesting.

I beg to remind you that you have not yet sent to me the article on lynching. I've several persons waiting to see it.

John Ransom[1] and Clifford Plummer had a big fight with Forbes[2] and Trotter about some imaginary "wrong" you had done the Race. I am told that Ransom and Plummer won out amidst applause. O I forgot to say that the great and only Clement G Morgan had a hand in it too. It was at a meeting of that Swell literary society.[3]

I was not there, neither was Lewis in our talk about it a day or two ago, Lewis remarked that "those fellows are damn fools." I told him he had expressed a sentiment I had long entertained in that remark.

Excuse the above ink spot I am in such a hurry.

My regards to Mrs Washington and the children also Mrs Stewart and Carrie. Faithfully yours

P. J. Smith Jr

ALS   Con. 210   BTW Papers   DLC.

[1] John Ransom, a black railroad porter of Boston, Mass., was born in New York in 1857.

[2] George W. Forbes.

[3] Trotter was one of the organizers of the Boston Literary and Historical Association in Mar. 1901. The group became a center of militant opinion on racial matters in the Boston area and was often a forum for attacks on BTW.

To Theodore Roosevelt

Washington, D.C. October 16, 1901

My dear Mr. President — I shall be very glad to accept your invitation for dinner this evening at seven-thirty.[1] Yours very truly,

Booker T. Washington

HLS   Theodore Roosevelt Papers   DLC.

[1] For an account of the White House dinner, see Harlan, *BTW*, 304–24.

To the Editor of the New York *Evening Post*

Natchez, Miss., October 16 [1901]

Sir: I have been travelling through the State of Mississippi, and speaking at the large centers of population, at the request of the trustees of the John F. Slater Board. There are several things in relation to the life of our people in this State, and their relations to the white people, in which I think your readers will be interested.

My talks to them have covered mainly the subjects of the importance of securing land, building decent homes, cultivating habits
of economy, thrift, and industry. I have also spoken plainly on the
importance of education, correct moral habits, and proper relations
between the races. While I came into the State for the purpose of
speaking to the colored people, I have been surprised at every point
where I have spoken to note that my audiences have been very
largely composed of white people, as well as many colored people
as could crowd into the room. For example, here at Natchez, where
I have delivered two addresses, a large part of the audience-room on
both occasions was occupied by white men and women, and, the
same has been true at other points, notably at Vicksburg.

No one can look into the faces of the thousands of colored people
who crowd to these meetings, coming long distances in many cases,
and sitting for an hour or two hours, listening to a discussion of
matters pertaining to their welfare, without being convinced that
the race is slowly, but surely, making progress in every part of this
State. Evidences of progress can also be noted in the improvement
of the condition of the people, most especially in the number of
small, neat cottages which they own in the cities and towns. It is
also noticeable in the country districts that, whenever new buildings are erected, with few exceptions, the house contains two or
more rooms, instead of being the usual one-room cabin. The most
depressing, and I think serious, condition, regarding the industrial
and moral progress of our people is to be found on the large plantations where our people are, for the most part, renters. In speaking
of the improvement which has taken place, I must mention the case
of a colored man in whose home I was entertained. It has been my
privilege to see something of the homes of some of the best white
people in every part of the North and West, and I do not exag-
gerate when I say I have seldom been in the home of any white man
anywhere in the country where everything was so attractive, convenient, and comfortable. I had not been in this home five minutes
before the lady of the house asked me if I would not like to inspect
her kitchen and pantry, and I found everything in the kitchen as
neat and intelligently arranged as one would expect to find in a
home in New England. I confess that this home is much above the
average occupied by our people, but it is an indication of the

progress that is being made. The owner of the home to which I refer is Mr. Wesley Crayton,[1] who is a successful business man in Vicksburg.

Another thing that has rather pleased and somewhat surprised me is the fact that the railroads in Mississippi are beginning to provide better accommodations for their colored passengers. On the main lines of the large systems, while there is a separation of the races, I have noted that the colored people are given an entire coach, and in addition a smoking-car, and both compartments are equal. This improvement, I believe, will soon take place on all the roads. I think the railroads are beginning to see that it pays from a financial point of view to treat their colored passengers with justice.

In Greenville, Miss., I was surprised to find a colored man on the police force, and he has retained his position on that force for twelve or fifteen years. In the same town one of the largest book and stationery stores is owned and conducted by a colored man. Three-fourths of his customers are white people, and this colored man has more than once employed white clerks to assist in the conduct of his business. In Natchez by far the largest and most successful saddlery and harness store is owned and conducted by a negro by the name of Louis Kastor. I found a stock of goods in this large and attractive store that was valued at $6,000, and at least three-fourths of his trade is with white people. Every white man in the city with whom I spoke referred me with great pride to the success of this man. In several cases I find that colored clerks are employed by white merchants. There is a colored man not far from Natchez who sent to the market last year over 600 bales of cotton raised on his farm.

The relations existing between the two races in Natchez are the most satisfactory, I think, of any place that I have seen in the South. There have never been in the city of Natchez any of the horrible race outbreaks or lynchings. In the earlier days of reconstruction it seems that the colored and white people came to an understanding by which the county offices were to be divided between the races. In some way, however, most, if not all, of the offices have gotten out of the hands of the colored people. Still, I find that the same amicable relations exist. What I have said of Natchez in this regard will apply in a somewhat less degree to the relations of the races in

Vicksburg and Greenville. The fierce and unreasonable race difficulties for the most part occur in the smaller towns and in the country districts where ignorance is dense.

In both Vicksburg and Natchez I have found colored lawyers, who seem to be doing a successful business, and in both cities they told me that they feel their color does not prevent them from being treated with fairness in the courts.

It is difficult to speak with any degree of accuracy in regard to the negro vote, or to predict what is to take place in the future in regard to the franchise, but this much I believe I can say with a reasonable degree of safety: while the operation of the new Constitution cuts off the great mass of the negroes from voting, I have noticed, wherever I have investigated the subject, that in the cities to which I have referred, in the case of the colored man who owns the bookstore in Greenville, and in the case of the black man in Natchez who operates the largest saddlery and harness store, and including perhaps two dozen colored men of intelligence and character and business standing, such men cast their votes without question, and have them counted. I am led to believe that these few colored men really exercise more influence in politics than the masses who voted without restraint a few years ago, for the reason that their votes were in most cases freely counted out or in some way gotten rid of. I may be mistaken, but I am led to feel that gradually, as our people get property and intelligence, become conservative, and learn the lesson of casting their fortune in every honorable way with their neighbors, they are not going to be refused an opportunity to vote.

Notwithstanding the hopeful and encouraging indications to which I have referred, the fact must not be overlooked or smothered that there is an immense amount of work to be done in the direction of education in the broadest sense in this portion of the South, before conditions will be relieved from danger and anxiety. There never was a greater opportunity for people of wealth to do something that would lift up an entire section of country regardless of race than is presented in the South.

It means a great deal, I find, for our Southern States to have the right kind of Governors. Mississippi in the present Governor, Longino, has one of the bravest, wisest, and most just Governors. He has spoken out fearlessly in favor of education, and particularly against mob law, and has not only spoken against mob law, but has acted bravely and promptly. The influence of this man for all that is good can be easily seen and felt in every part of the State.

In Jackson the State officials very kindly tendered the use of the State Capitol for my meeting, but another audience-room was found larger than the Hall of the Representatives, and the meeting was not held in the State Capitol for this reason. At the meeting in Jackson there were as many people of both races on the outside of the house who could not get in as were on the inside, and my reception could not have been more cordial in New York or Boston than it was in the capital of the State of Mississippi.

In Jackson, as in the other cities that I visited, I found colored people engaged in nearly every kind of business. By far the leading bakery and confectionery store is in the hands of a black man, and I noticed that there were among his employees one or two white people. In Jackson the colored people own their own homes more largely than is true of any city I have visited. The colored man who does not own his home is the exception rather than the rule.

Taking it all in all, my eyes have been opened by my trip through Mississippi, and I have greater hope for the future of both races than I have ever had before.

Seven miles from Jackson there is located Tougaloo University, an institution founded some years ago for the education of colored people by the American Missionary Association. When I visited this university I was very glad to see many evidences which seemed to show that the white people in that vicinity hold that institution in high regard, and do not look upon it as a foreign institution, but one that is doing a work for the elevation of the whole South. When I spoke there, there were in my audience not a few Southern white men and women.

The condition of the colored ministry is a matter that has long interested the most thoughtful persons North and South. No one can now go through the South and keep his eyes open without being convinced of the fact that the ministry is improving, although there is still a great deal remaining to be done in this direction.

Booker T. Washington

New York *Evening Post*, Oct. 21, 1901, 4.

1 Wesley Crayton, a liquor dealer, was born in Mississippi in 1858. He was a delegate to the first convention of the NNBL in 1900.

A News Item in the Atlanta *Constitution*

Washington, October 16 [1901]

NEGRO GUEST ENTERTAINED BY ROOSEVELT

PRESIDENT HAS BOOKER T. WASHINGTON AT THE WHITE HOUSE FOR DINNER

ALL ROOSEVELT FAMILY PRESENT AT THE TABLE

WASHINGTON WAS IN EVENING DRESS AND HE WAS ONLY GUEST — PROBABLY THE FIRST NEGRO EVER ENTERTAINED AT THE WHITE HOUSE

Booker T. Washington, the well known negro educator, president of the Tuskegee, Ala., institute, was a guest of President and Mrs. Roosevelt at dinner at the white house tonight. Washington is probably the first American negro to dine with a president of the United States and his family, although it was reported that President Cleveland once entertained a negro friend at the white house board.

Since President Roosevelt occupied the white house there has hardly been a dinner or luncheon without its guests, and as the president has been so free with his invitations no special list of guests is prepared and the ushers do not know who the guests will be until they arrive. Tonight, just before 8 o'clock, a negro in evening dress presented himself at the white house door, and, giving his name, said that he was to dine with the president. Booker Washington has made several visits to the white house and his face is known there, so he was at once admitted into the private apartments and the president notified of his arrival. No other guest arrived and the dinner was soon served.

Dinner at the white house since the Roosevelts have occupied the mansion has been a family affair, Mrs. Roosevelt and the two children appearing at the table with father, mother and guests. After dinner the president takes his guests to the library, and there, over cigars, things political and otherwise are discussed.

Tonight the usual order of affairs was not disturbed on account of the color of the guest of honor, and Washington left the white house about 10 o'clock, apparently very much pleased with his dinner and his chat with the president.

Atlanta *Constitution*, Oct. 17, 1901, 1.

To Theodore Roosevelt

Grand Union Hotel, New York. Oct. 17, 1901

My dear Mr. President: Mr. W. E. Mollison,[1] Vicksburg, Miss., is a colored lawyer of intelligence and I think of high standing, he certainly has the confidence and good will of both white and colored people. He knows Mississippi conditions pretty thoroughly and I think you could get a good deal of information if you could see your way clear to have him come to Washington to confer with you. He is by profession a lawyer and I think has a good practice. Yours truly,

Booker T. Washington

The enclosed letter from Mr. Riis[2] I think any man in the world ought to be proud of.

B. T. W.

TLS   Theodore Roosevelt Papers   DLC.

[1] Willis E. Mollison, born in Mississippi in 1859, was a black lawyer, banker, and politician. He was educated at Fisk and Oberlin. Active in Republican politics, he was a delegate to the Republican national conventions from 1892 to 1908. In 1912 he joined the Progressive party.

[2] See Oct. 10, 1901, above.

To William B. Hoswell[1]

Tuskegee, Ala., October 17, 1901

My Dear Sir: I thank you very sincerely for your great kindness in placing with us the dressing gown and smoking cap worn by the late Frederick Douglass during his stay in Chicago during the World's Fair. I cannot tell you how very greatly it enriches our store to have this remembrance from you. It will be a constant reminder to us of Mr. Douglass, and also of his worth and great work for humanity. We shall place them in our new Carnegie Library Building among other articles of value as soon as it is completed.

I am glad to have had the opportunity of meeting you on the occasion of my recent visit to Chicago. Yours very truly,

Booker T. Washington

TLSr Small Collections Amistad Research Center LND. Signed in E. J. Scott's hand.

1 William B. Hoswell was president of the Hayden Brothers Lumber Co. in Chicago. A white man, he was born in Rhode Island in 1869. He and Frederick Douglass became friends during the time Douglass spent in Chicago as Haitian commissioner at the World's Columbian Exposition in 1893.

From Emmett Jay Scott

Tuskegee, Ala., Oct 17, 1901

My Dear Mr Washington: I congratulate you most heartily and sincerely on the especial mark of the president's favor shown by inviting you to have dinner with him and his family. It is splendid, magnificent! And you deserve it all. What pleases me more than all else is that the sometimes esteemed Atlanta Constitution has a long special about it and that it will get before our friends of the South in a way it might not ordinarily. The world is moving forward and I hope they will find it out sometime soon. My heart bubbles over, and I am so glad!

I have a letter from Mr. McKinlay[1] saying you could make his house your headquarters. I hope you have gone there and that you found the quarters pleasant and satisfactory. I hope you like him too. I think him a good man and one sincerely devoted to the cause you represent.

Again I want to congratulate you. I send Constitution. It is conspicuously displayed. Sincerely Yours,

Emmett J. Scott

ALS Con. 245 BTW Papers DLC.

1 Whitefield McKinlay, a black businessman and Republican politician, was a close friend and staunch supporter of BTW. He was born in Charleston, S.C., in 1857

and was educated at Avery Institute. He entered the University of South Carolina in 1874 and remained there for three years, until the school closed its doors to blacks. He taught school for a time in South Carolina before entering Iowa College at Grinnell, where he remained until 1881. He moved to the District of Columbia in the mid-1880s and worked in the Government Printing Office. In 1887 he entered the real estate and loan business in Washington and became a successful businessman who had both black and white clients. He was a director of the black Capital Savings Bank. McKinlay was active in black affairs in the District of Columbia and was a Republican stalwart. BTW often stayed at McKinlay's home when he was in Washington and McKinlay functioned as BTW's adviser on national political affairs and on black activities in the nation's capital. He frequently went to the White House on BTW's errands. McKinlay held two appointive offices. In 1907 President Roosevelt appointed him to a commission on housing for the poor in the District of Columbia, and in 1910 President Taft appointed him collector of the port of Georgetown, D.C. In early 1912 McKinlay was among the first to protest the segregation of federal employees, a trend that reached its fullest impact after Woodrow Wilson took office.

From Lawrence Fraser Abbott

New York   October 18, 1901

My dear Mr. Washington: Some time ago you wrote me saying that you had forwarded my copy of Prince Kropotkin's[1] "Fields, Factories and Workshops." Will you kindly let me know how you sent it, and to what address. It has not yet reached me.

Mr. Townsend, I believe, has already written you that we shall most willingly add the paragraph to Mr. Thrasher's article which touches upon your attitude toward political appointments in the South. Just when one is beginning to be encouraged about the race question in the South, isn't it a pity that the whole thing flares up again in a disagreeable and very obnoxious way. I refer to the dispatch from Washington in this morning's "Herald," which quotes from one or two Southern editorials, bitterly criticising Mr. Roosevelt because you were a guest at his table. I hope that such bigotry is only to be found in spots, so to speak.

When you come on to New York again, I wish you would give me the pleasure of coming in to take luncheon with me. Yours sincerely,

Lawrence F. Abbott

TLS   Con. 205   BTW Papers   DLC.

[1] Pëtr Alekseevich Kropotkin (1842–1921), the Russian anarchist.

From Amanda Ferguson Johnston

malden, W.Va   Oct. 18, 1901

my Dear brother   I did not know were yu was   Brother I have the prettist house in malden — it is given up by the best ones, is finished. george[1] sent the Bill to Tuskegee this weak.

Dont forget the land   mr Dickenson[2] Come to See me this last weak   I did not know where yu were. brother I read your Speeach in brooklin to many Persons they thought it grand. wr[i]te Soone from sister

Amanda Johnson

ALS Con. 201 BTW Papers DLC.

[1] Probably George Washington Albert Johnston.
[2] Probably John Quincy Dickinson, president of the J. Q. Dickinson Salt Works in Malden, or possibly his son, John Lewis Dickinson (b. 1870), a Charleston banker and businessman.

To Emmett Jay Scott

New York [ca. Oct. 19, 1901]

If any purported interviews[1] with me are published anywhere in the south telegraph my absolute denial as I have absolutely refused to talk with any one regarding Washington matter.

Booker T. Washington

TWSr Con. 541 BTW Papers DLC.

[1] A reporter for the Brooklyn *Eagle* claimed on Oct. 19 that he had interviewed BTW at length on the White House dinner on the occasion of BTW's address at the opera house in Huntington, L.I. He quoted BTW as saying that criticisms by the southern newspapers "represent a transient emotional sentiment on the part of a class of the white people of the South, but such feelings do not last, do not indicate the general feeling and opinion of Southern people." Of President Roosevelt he was reported to have said: "As far as I can learn of him he makes no distinction as to the color of a man's cuticle when he wants to get at facts, and is as ready to consult with the negro, Indian or Chinaman as he is with the Anglo-Saxon when he wants to get at the whole situation in any line of his work. I esteem him very highly as a man of sense and integrity." He was quoted as saying that two or three other guests were present and that he had been received in the homes of some of the best white

people of the South. (Brooklyn *Eagle*, Oct. 19, 1901, 1.) Though BTW denied that he had given any such interview, the Indianapolis *Freeman* quoted liberally from the *Eagle* on Oct. 26, 1901, 1. Other papers also carried the interview, or commented on it in editorials. On Oct. 23, 1901, BTW released a statement to the Associated Press denying the interview. See A Statement in the Atlanta *Constitution*, Oct. 23, 1901, below.

From Elwood W. Mattson[1]

Chattanooga, Tenn., Oct 19, 1901

Dear Sir: The severe criticisms of some democratic papers in Memphis and Chattanooga on President Roosevelt for his hospitality to you prompts me as editor of the Press, a republican paper in political harmony and sympathy with the administration, to ask you a question which I trust you will answer and grant me permission to publish. First, let me say, I was born in New Jersey, educated in Connecticut and have been in journalism here as editor of the Daily and Weekly Press for 14 years. I came South as a teacher under the direction of Dr. Rust[2] who was then Secretary of the Freedmen's Aid Society of the Methodist church. Therefore my sympathies are with the colored people, and having been born in the north I am free from those prejudices against them which prevail here. Knowing these facts, I think you will be free to answer my question. It is this: Have you not previous to dining with President Roosevelt, dined with Senator Morgan of Alabama, and sat at banquets in New York and elsewhere? If so, will you not please mention instances. I believe it is an ignorance of the facts, that has led papers like those I have mentioned, to criticise the President so severely for "violating all traditions" &c.

I have a great admiration for you as a man and esteem you highly for the noble work you have accomplished. I should be pleased to assist you in any way I can, and believe the publication of the truth would materially lessen the hostility which some rabid race haters on Southern papers are attempting to create against you.

Awaiting your favor, I am, Very truly yours,

E. W. Mattson

ALS Con. 206 BTW Papers DLC.

1 Elwood W. Mattson, born in New Jersey in 1857, was president of the Press Publishing Co. and editor of the Chattanooga *Press*.

2 Richard Sutton Rust (1815–1906), an abolitionist and Methodist Episcopal clergyman, was one of the organizers of the Freedmen's Aid Society in 1866.

From Walter Hines Page

Washington, D.C. 19 Oct. 1901

Dear Mr. Washington, Let me say that I am glad of this whole matter — I mean your dining at the White House and the whole pitiful hub-bub about it. It'll give some persons, who haven't yet found it out, a glimpse of what kind of man Theodore Roosevelt is. I told the President to-day that if he had invited you simply as a bit of Southern politics, he could not have done a better thing. [Of course he is the last man on earth to do such a thing for such a reason; but the effect will be wholly good — wholly good.]

And when I was talking with him there flashed on me the happiest thing that I've ever thought to say about the whole race question. Of course *you've* thought of it a thousand times, but it came to me to-day with enormous force; & it is this: The best test that can be made of the men to entrust public affairs to in the South is this — *Trust no man's judgment or courage in public affairs there except those who openly give the Negro a free & full chance —* those who willingly help to educate him & who would see him have an absolutely equal chance at the polls with the white man. That's the best test there is.

But the flare-up of these newspapers, I confess, somewhat astonishes me. Their "touchiness" has been made greatly more tender by these disfranchising campaigns. No such violently spoken sensitiveness would have been shown ten years ago — at least, not so generally shown. This disfranchising campaign has been waged on a cowardly discrimination, & those who have made it feel a fidgety need to defend it. The Nashville & Birmingham papers have a distinctly artificial ring in them. It is pumped-up — put-on: it isn't real. Consequently it'll pass the more quickly. The sudden violence of it shows its artificiality. But it does argue a desperation of mind that I am afraid of in the meantime, & I am a good deal concerned about it. It's the lynching temper brought to play in discussion.

Yet it's too infernally absurd to last a very long time. Sane men, in the South as well as everywhere else, have too much dignity & too much humor to do this foolish thing permanently. It's too childish.

Yet it does disturb me. Yet, again, the President's asking you to dine was a good thing for its political results: it gives all men a chance to measure him; & frank & brave Southern men honor him the more. Sincerely yrs

Walter H. Page

When he invites you again — go; make sure you go — let nothing keep you from going! It's worth 10 years' work for Southern liberalization.

ALS Con. 188 BTW Papers DLC. Brackets in original.

From James Carroll Napier

Nashville, Tenn., Oct. 19, 1901

My Dear Mr. Washington: Your letters were received on the 16th. instant. I thank you very much for them. I shall leave for Washington tonight at 7.30 and shall, at the earliest possible moment, present them respectively to Secretary Cortelyou and the President. I am with you heart and hand and shall do my utmost to make the most of my visit.

The politicians and yellow sheet newspapers are trying to make a Southern sensation of the dinner incident between yourself and Mr. Roosevelt, but it will all blow over and amount to nothing. Continue in the even tenor of your way and you will certainly come out victorious. I am sure the President will pay no attention what-ever to these unjust criticisms.

Again, I congratulate you upon this distinguished honor. Very truly yours,

J. C. Napier

TLS Con. 205 BTW Papers DLC.

From Edgar Gardner Murphy

Montgomery, Ala. October 19th, 1901

(Personal—Not Dictated)

Dear Mr. Washington: I have just received your telegram (at 10 P.M.) and I have put myself in touch with the local wires, and I find that there is nothing at this hour in the service of the Associated press. If there should be something of the sort, later on in the night, I think they will act in the right way about it. You may always depend upon my friendship.

You of course know enough about the situation here to know that this has been a trying week. I am not distressed at the bitterness of the narrow, but at the depression and discouragement of our best people. But the subject is too many-sided for a letter. I should like to talk to you on your return, if you can see me here. But I am sure you know me well enough to realize that I have no desire to intrude upon what, under one of its aspects, is a strictly personal matter.

But one of our burdens in this world (and one of the hardest) is the fact that when men come to represent something greater than themselves (the President in his Office and you in the leadership of your race) every act is representative, and carries, to the popular mind, a vast significance. It may be unreasonable, but it is inevitable. From this standpoint you know, I am sure, that I deplore the incident in question. But I acknowledge your telegram this evening, not in order to dwell upon that consideration, but to assure you that however much I may disagree with you as to questions of expediency and policy (and I do not know that I have ever questioned your wisdom before) you have, earnestly and always, my heartfelt confidence. Sincerely and Faithfully,

Edgar Gardner Murphy

TLS   Con. 261   BTW Papers   DLC.

From Jesse Lawson

Washington, D.C., October 20, 1901

My dear Sir: Enclosed[1] you will find a copy of a letter sent by your humble servant to President Roosevelt. I presume that he received it in due course of mail yesterday. Of course, you knew nothing about my sending it and can not object now that it has been sent. I also hope that strong letters will be sent to the President from all parts of the world congratulating him and sustaining him in the position he assumed in extending to you a certain courtesy on the 16th instant.

It matters not how just and righteous a cause may be, or how worthy the person upon whom a certain honor may be bestowed, race prejudice in America is so strong that it requires a great deal of moral courage for a man in public life, and of the dominant race, to give recognition to a member of our race when that recognition in anyway savors of social equality. President Roosevelt possesses that moral courage and heroism to a marked degree.

I shall also write Senators Foraker[2] and Mason[3] thanking them for their public utterances in support of President Roosevelt's position. I am personally acquainted with both of them.

Dr W. A. Croffut,[4] a white man, in addressing the lyceum of the Second Baptist Church, this afternoon, referred to the incident and was pretty severe upon the critics of the President. Dr. Croffut was, if I mistake not, the Secretary of the Anti-Imperialists during the last campaign. He is now an ardent supporter of the Administration. President Roosevelt has now the support of all classes of American citizens with the single exception of the bourbons, who like Ephraim of old "are joined to their idols."

Hoping that you are well, and that I may hear from you again soon, I remain, Yours truly,

Jesse Lawson

TLS Con. 203 BTW Papers DLC.

1 See Lawson to Roosevelt, Oct. 18, 1901, Con. 203, BTW Papers, DLC. Lawson told the President: "Your act in honoring him was a masterly stroke of statesmanship — worthy of the best minds this country has ever produced."

2 Joseph Benson Foraker (1846–1917), a Republican, was a U.S. senator from Ohio from 1897 to 1909.

3 William Ernest Mason (1850–1921), a Republican from Illinois, served in the U.S. Senate from 1897 to 1903.

4 William Augustus Croffut (1835–1915), a writer and journalist, was a founder and secretary of the Anti-Imperialist League in 1899.

From James Carroll Napier

Washington, D.C. Oct. 21st, 1901

My Dear Mr. Washington: I arrived here this morning and went at once, arriving at the White House about 11, to see the President. Your letters gave me immediate admission to an interview with him, although he had closed to visitors and was preparing to leave the City on a early train. My interview with him was satisfactory, pleasant and quite prolonged. I think that I made a favorable impression upon him and am sure that I was never more highly pleased and elated than when I left him.

He spoke of the dinner incident and said most positively that he did not care the snap of his finger what anybody thought or said about it. He said [he] proposed to do what was right and treat such gentlemen as yourself as they deserved without regard to criticism or praise. I cannot here tell you of all the details of my visit but shall reserve that until I see you. This I hope to do at a very early date. In my feeble way I tried to make known to him in how high esteem you are held by all classes and especially by our own people as the very first man and wise leader of the race.

I shall never cease to appreciate your favor in securing me this interview. Whenever I can in any manner return the favor do not hesitate to let me know and I shall be only too glad to serve you. Do not fail to inform me if you should again pass through Nashville. Very truly and sincerely your friend,

J. C. Napier

ALS Con. 205 BTW Papers DLC.

EQUALITY

DINNER GIVEN AT THE WHITE HOUSE BY PRESIDENT ROOSEVELT TO BOOKER T. WASHINGTON, OCTOBER 17th, 1901

Lithograph by C. H. Thomas and P. H. Lacey, 1903.
Smithsonian Institution

U. S.: "Well, where's the difference?"

From the Chicago *Inter Ocean*, Oct. 20, 1901, 1.

RUBBER!!

From the Brooklyn *Eagle*, Oct. 19, 1901, 5.

Booker T. Washington feeding chickens.
Outlook, 68 (June 1, 1901), 295

*CHICKENS, PIGS
AND PEOPLE*

By

Booker T. Washington

———

ILLUSTRATED WITH

PHOTOGRAPHS BY

CLIFTON JOHNSON

From the *Outlook*, 68 (June 7, 1901), 291.

PROF. BOOKER T. WASHINGTON.

Engraving of Booker T. Washington.
Indianapolis *Freeman*, Oct. 26, 1901, 1

Booker T. Washington at Yale University.

Clipping from the Buffalo *Express*, Nov. 3, 1901,
Booker T. Washington Papers, *Library of Congress*

Booker T. Washington on vacation in West Virginia.
National Magazine, 17 (Dec. 1902), 354

Booker T. Washington on vacation in West Virginia.
National Magazine, 17 (Dec. 1902), 355

Officers of the National Negro Business League, 1902.
Booker T. Washington Papers, Library of Congress

From Richard Robert Wright, Sr.

College, Ga., Oct. 21st, 1901

My dear Sir: Honors have fallen so rapidly upon you that I have not had the time between them to congratulate you upon any of the new ones which have come to you. Noticing to-day in Monday's paper an account of the speech of Prof. W. H. Councill at Dallas Texas and also the comments of some of the Southern papers on your reception at the White House, I could not refrain from writing the President thanking him for the consideration which he has shown the race through you, if that act is to be considered more than a personal one. I congratulate you upon having been the first one to receive so high a consideration. We all pray that you may continue to carry a level head over a good heart which shall permit you to feel and to do the best and wisest thing. Accept my highest consideration both for yourself and Mrs. Washington and my hearty good wish for the success of your work. I need not add that I feel as all feel that you did the proper thing and the only sensible thing which could have been done under the circumstances. Very truly,

R. R. Wright

P.S. Prof. Council[l] seems to be very much opposed to social recognition when the parties are of opposite race. His regard for the virtue of white ladies is very high.

W.

TLS Con. 216 BTW Papers DLC. The postscript is in Wright's hand.

From Emmett Jay Scott

Tuskegee, Ala., Oct. 21-1901

My Dear Mr Washington: I know just what you must be undergoing at this time! It all seems so pitiful and so pitiable. After all the years you have worked, to be misunderstood and traduced, must be a trial, but it has its compensating features. It gives the president a chance to see the inner, inner phase of Southern feeling, and also puts him on guard as to just what to expect here, and then too it gives a few papers and a few men — the very small few — to testify adversely in the midst of this terrible onslaught. The Constitution has not yet had a chance to say a word editorially, or rather it hasn't said a word. The Picayune is pronouncedly against the whole & says so as do also a number of individuals in different parts of the country. The Constitution is afraid that the "dough pan" will get away from them as note the Special from Washington on page 3 of yesterday's (Sunday's) paper & also the editorial. (I forgot that they did speak yesterday.) The Age-Herald of yesterday has the Brooklyn Eagle interview and Ned Brace (Barrett) comments on it.[1] I have sent Barrett absolute denial of the interview and have asked him to send it out to others. I hope he will do so. The Boston Transcript[2] & Evening Post article from Washington is good. It speaks for you & in splendidly arranged terms. You have seen them I am sure. I enclose in this package a magnificent letter from Mr. Page & also a cablegram from the Aid-Camp to Emperor Menelik.[3] You will desire to answer it on your private paper I am sure. Of course, you'll be very, very busy during this week, but I wish I might know how he felt over the general situation & as regards the reception of his appointment of Gov. Jones. I notice a letter from Mr. Napier & am sending it. Smith[4] also writes that he is getting ready to move on Washington. I hope them all success. Package of papers sent this mail. Yours sincerely

Emmett J. Scott

ALS   Con. 209   BTW Papers   DLC.

1 Ned Brace, pseudonym of Edward Ware Barrett (see above, 4:358), wrote: "Washington is a well educated negro — an eloquent talker. The temptation when President Roosevelt's invitation was extended him was great. Washington fell. He has injured his school and his life's work by this act on his part." He went on to say that Roosevelt made an even greater mistake by inviting BTW, and added: "His act will be construed as a desire on his part to bring about social equality among the races." (Birmingham *Age-Herald*, Oct. 20, 1901, 12.)

2 The Boston *Transcript*, Oct. 19, 1901, 1, denied that the White House dinner had anything to do with social equality. In an article signed "Lincoln" the author said he knew "of an occasion when a group of philanthropistic gentlemen were visiting Tuskegee Institute where Mr. Washington was the only person who could entertain them at dinner. They found the board well supplied and daintily spread; but no persuasion on the part of the guests without race prejudices could induce Mr. Washington or any member of his household to sit at their table. The host's excuses were as ingenious as any ever forged by an accomplished denizen of the great world; but behind

these was discernible that niceness of what he owed his cause – abstention from anything which could offend the prejudices of the white people of the section in which
he lived and labored."

³ Benito Sylvain cabled BTW from Paris: "Hearty compliments for President
Roosevelts reception." (Oct. 21, 1901, Con. 541, BTW Papers, DLC.)

⁴ Robert Lloyd Smith.

From S. D. Long

Brooklyn N.Y. Oct. 22, 1901

Sir! Referring to the article in the Brooklyn "Eagle," of Saturday
the 19th. inst. — why do you not request the Eagle to correct the
statement that you had been entertained at the houses of prominent
Southerners? Why do you request the Eagle to allow this terrible
misrepresentation to stand?

I am a native of Alabama and was born at Huntsville, in the
house of one of the Clay's. I know the aristocracy of Alabama[,]
Tennessee, Mississippi, Georgia and Louisiana, and their attitude
towards your race, and so do you, and you should, as a preacher,
and reformer (?) allow this to be corrected.

Of course, your school is a good thing to redeem your race from
idleness, but when you make the mistake to try to force social
recognition for them, you are indeed making a mistake and increasing the race feeling. You should be able to see that yourself.
These people up here *talk* a great deal about this question, but
they do not have to *live* it, as the Southern people do. They do not
all like even to employ colored help or eat the food prepared by
colored cooks, they shun your race in the trolley cars and it is *all talk*
about their admiration for them. You know this is the case, with
the masses here. In the South, place has been made for the negro
and the honest, faithful servant has all he can wish. It is the lawless,
ambitious negro, who seeks social equality with the white man and
tries to "be white," who causes all the race trouble. You know all
this. Why dont you *say* so.

I would treat you kindly and with consideration, but I would
never invite you to my house or *insult* you by mixing you up with
my race. No self respecting negro wants that, or seeks it.

Your actions have ruined Mr. Roosevelt, in the South, he probably has lost his career by it. All the work of our late President, to take the "seam out of the flag," is undone, by one selfish action. A great mistake! "Dont accept all the invitations you receive," is my motto. Very Truly

S. D. Long

ALS Con. 203 BTW Papers DLC.

A Statement in the Atlanta *Constitution*

[New Haven, Conn., Oct. 23, 1901][1]

I understand that some papers in certain parts of the country are printing alleged interviews with me. I want to state as emphatically as I can that I have given no interview and have refrained from any discussion of what occurred in Washington, although persistent efforts have been made to put words into my mouth.

[Booker T. Washington]

Atlanta *Constitution*, Oct. 23, 1901, 2.

1 BTW released the statement to the Associated Press while in New Haven.

From Edgar Gardner Murphy

Montgomery, Ala, 23 Oct—01

Reported here that you are to meet Roosevelt and daughter at Banquet this evening.[1] It is most difficult for me to speak for fear of misunderstanding but I earnestly hope you will not attend we are gradually getting the situation under control but effect of fresh excitement would be most unfortunate. The trouble is not superficial. The whole south has not been so deeply moved in twenty years. I think your whole past influence in the south and the very existence of Tuskegee are involved. This is strictly confidential.

Edgar Gardner Murphy

TWSr Con. 541 BTW Papers DLC. Sent to BTW in care of J. C. Schwab, New Haven, Conn.

1 Both BTW and Theodore Roosevelt received honorary degrees at the Yale University Bicentennial celebration. In the procession preceding the awarding of the degrees, both men marched together, and at the banquet afterward the President's daughter Alice sat near the Tuskegean. BTW was the guest of Morris F. Tyler, Yale's treasurer, on the evening of Oct. 21, at a dinner also attended by former Postmaster General Wilson S. Bissell. The Atlanta *Constitution* story, "NORTHERN WHITES FEED-ING WITH BOOKER WASHINGTON," commented that the invitations had been sent out and accepted ten days before BTW had dined with the President. (Atlanta *Constitution*, Oct. 24, 1901, 1.)

From Francis S. Shields[1]

New Orleans, La., October 23, 1901

Dear Sir: When Mr. Roosevelt became President, through the lamentable assassination of Mr. McKinley, conservative men like myself in this section openly expressed the fear that he would not be a safe man in the exalted position of President, especially for the South.

The South, just emerging from the nightmare which succeeded the destruction and desolation left by the Civil War, with its many intricate political, industrial, and social questions in process of slow solution along lines which time and conditions would indi-cate as wise, needs the continued and generally conservative poli-cy of Mr. Roosevelt's immediate predecessors, that it may work out its own difficult problems, more especially the burning na-tional problem, "the negro question," made essentially the prob-lem of the South not only because of present conditions, but because of all that has gone before in the century.

To you, Booker T. Washington, and men of your stamp and your methods, working hand in hand with the conservative men of all sections, but more particularly with those of the South, we are looking for the slow, but we hope eventual, working out of the "negro problem," the peaceful, absolutely separated, occupation of the same country by two distinct races ever so remaining. This means the gradual education of the two races and the properly directed influences of time and circumstances.

We feared that Mr. Roosevelt, with his impetuous nature and

his desire to bring about reforms by radical, and as it were, "short-cut" methods, would, by some ill advised rash act, or rather, act taken without advice, as to questions especially Southern, set back the wheel of progress which had dragged slowly through blood and tears and misery for thirty years.

When the fact that you had been entertained by Mr. Roosevelt at a private dinner at the White House was flashed over the wires the next morning, and the incident was being discussed by a party of business men and politicians, I stated that Mr. Roosevelt had made a great blunder and a sad mistake, possibly far reaching in its evil consequence, and that you, in a momentary loss of your remarkable level-headedness and good judgment, had, unwittingly, been a party to the setting back and undoing of your untiring good work for years past. I do not attribute motive nor purposes to this incident, nor is it my object to outline even the salient evil effects on both races leading back into the ills of the past.

I am instigated by the kindliest motives and good wishes toward you and your race and the great and good work which you are doing, which moves me to thus address you.

The friendly eye of one who stands without the whirl and spray of the waves can see the breakers ahead clearer than those struggling in the midst of the tempest.

It is not in the South alone that the evil effects growing out of this incident are to be actively felt, for I have said the "negro problem" is a national one.

The old abolition spirit of the north and east which cursed the whole country with the ten years of the re-construction, will be fanned into aggressive life by the criticism coming from the South. The spirit of conservatism which you and men of your stamp have labored long years to bring about, and the assurances which you have given that the South and the two races together could best work out their ultimate salvation, unaided by those unacquainted with conditions, will be, yea, are being, thrown to the winds.

Radical men will lead off; conservative men will lose their better judgment; a series of similar and other invitations will be extended, both as an endorsement of Mr. Roosevelt's action, and evidence of appreciation of your worth as a man and educator.

But your residence and your life's work is not in Washington, nor Harvard, nor Boston. Your home is in Tuskegee, Ala., in the "black belt" of a southern state. Your life's work is the education and elevation of your own race and indirectly the education up to your standard of thinking of the white race.

You are not only a remarkable man of your race but of the generation in which you are born and you have gone forward with a singleness of purpose and good judgment which have made us hopeful that you were strong enough to tread the narrow path which you must follow if you are to lay the bed rock on which the future welfare of your race is to be built up.

Are you strong enough, are you deeply enough wedded to your great work, to the betterment and elevation of your own race, and to the good that will through you result to the whole country?

Can you rise to the height of devotion to your cause and call a halt to those of the north and east who would be friends and tell them that it is not by ovations to you, which rouse the prejudice and go counter to the sentiments of the people among whom your lot and the lot of your people is cast, that good will come to them and to your cause and good work?

And then to retire quietly to your college and work and let the Washington and other similar incidents and criticisms they have aroused take their places in the things of yesterday, leaving the moral with us and hoping that no real harm or set-back may have been done to the cause in which we are all so vitally concerned.

To do all this requires an absolute self abnegation bordering on heroism, but your past course has naturally led up to it, and we watch with earnest interest that you do not disappoint the hope placed in you.

I should not be unknown to you. I sent you some months since a number of articles, clippings from the newspapers, protesting against the horrible lynchings which were perpetrated in various parts of our country.

I was one of the leaders and most persistent workers in the abolition of the penitentiary lease system in Louisiana, both individually and as a member of the Special Committee on legislation of the Prison Reform Association.

I have addressed you thus plainly because of my deep interest in the work you are doing and because of the high opinion in which you are held, and of the hope that your example and work will benefit your race and the South.

It is needless to say I am to the manor born for generations back. Yours, very truly,

F. S. Shields

TLS   Con. 1   BTW Papers   DLC.

1 Francis S. Shields, a white man born in Mississippi in 1860, was secretary of the New Orleans Sewerage and Water Board.

To Theodore Roosevelt

New York City. October 24, 1901

My dear Mr. President: I was unfortunate in my attempt to see you while you were in New Haven, but in any case I presume we could not have talked with any satisfaction there.

I write to say that I have left a list of colored men with the Attorney General as I promised, any two or three of whom I think would fill with credit the position of Civil Magistrate in the District of Columbia.

I am going to Tuskegee tonight where I shall remain for a week, and as I return through Washington I shall plan to see you. Yours truly,

Booker T. Washington

TLS   Theodore Roosevelt Papers   DLC.

To Philander Chase Knox

[New York City] Oct. 24, 1901

My dear Sir: At the suggestion of the President, I recommend for your consideration the following persons for appointment to the position of Civil Magistrate in the District of Columbia. I understand of course that the president is going to give but two or three of these appointments to colored people, but I have made the list large in order that you may make a selection. These are all good, clean, first class colored people and competent, and all of them are lawyers:

Mr. Jesse Lawson, 8011 Vermont Ave.
Mr. Robert H. Terrell, 609 F St., N.W.
Mr. Reuben S. Smith,[1] 715 3d St. N.W.
Mr. Joseph H. Bundy,[2] Howard University,
Mr. Joseph H. Stewart,[3] 609 F St. N.W.,
Mr. Fountain Peyton,[4] 303 D St., N.W.

In regard to Mr. Jesse Lawson, whom I put first,[5] I might add for your information that he is at present employed in the Pension Bureau and I think votes in New Jersey, but he has resided in the District for the last fifteen years and I think could be considered a resident for all practical purposes.

Mr. Robert H. Terrell, the second, is a present Principal of the Colored High School, but is a lawyer of high standing and is a graduate of Harvard University.

If I can serve you further in the matter please be kind enough to command me. I shall see the President within a few days and talk over the matter further in detail. Yours truly,

[Booker T. Washington]

TLc BTW Papers ATT.

[1] Reuben S. Smith, born in Jackson County, Fla., in 1854, taught in the Florida public schools. He was a delegate to the Republican national convention from Florida in 1876. He was a clerk in the U.S. Treasury Department while attending Howard University Law School, from which he graduated in 1883. Leaving the government service, he engaged in private law practice and business. He attended the Republican national convention in 1880 and was sergeant-at-arms at the 1900 convention. He was a participant in the first meeting of the NNBL in 1900.

[2] Probably James F. Bundy (1862–1914), secretary-treasurer of Howard University from 1890 until his death. Bundy had attended Oberlin College and had graduated from Howard University and its law school. He became an examiner in chancery of the supreme court of the District of Columbia, and from 1900 to 1906 he was a member of the school board of the District of Columbia.

[3] Joseph H. Stewart, born in Indiana in 1859, practiced law in the District of Columbia.

[4] Fountain Peyton (1861–1951), born in Stafford County, Va., moved as a child to Washington, where he worked as a newsboy. Graduating from Howard University Law School, Peyton practiced law in the District of Columbia until his retirement in 1921. He served from 1915 to 1921 on the District of Columbia school board.

[5] A week later BTW wrote Knox that he considered Robert H. Terrell to be his first choice. (Oct. 31, 1901, Box 200, RG60, DNA.)

From Theodore Wellington Jones[1]

Chicago, October 24, 1901

Dear Sir: Enclosed you will please find newspaper clipping,[2] which has prompted me in writing you at this time. While I do not arrogate to myself the office of guide or instructor for you, yet I wish to say in all candor that I hope you will not accept any political office, however much it may be urged upon you.

Office may make some men while it undoubtedly detracts from others; but it never added to the stature of one who was already great. As Booker T. Washington you may advise and assist in shaping the policy, not only of this administration, but of succeeding administrations, and your influence may widen and expand until it envelopes the North as well as the South and becomes national in its scope. As an office holder you would be expected to take the stump during campaigns in the interest of your party. This, in my opinion, would utterly destroy your influence and usefulness in the South where they are so sadly needed, and at the same time might not tend to strengthen them in the North. While it is meet and proper that some colored men should accept office, yet in your case I hold that it is preeminently wiser to decline it. As Booker T. Washington you are a bigger man than you ever could be as Secretary Washington. Admiral Dewey was a greater man before he yielded to the advice of misguided friends and became a candidate for political honors, than he may ever be again. Political office did not make Frederick Douglass great, but decidedly dwarfed him, although he very creditably filled every office to which he was appointed. But when he shall have been long forgotten as Minister to a foreign court, Recorder of Deeds, and Marshal of the District of Columbia respectively, he will yet be remembered as Frederick Douglass, the mouth piece of a people in the days when they could not speak for themselves, and the acknowledged leader of a once enslaved race.

Now, in closing, I beg to observe that your fame and reputation is of firm, steady growth, fairly earned by what you are, by what you have said, and by what you have done. Therefore, your influence, your wisdom and your genius, belongs not to any particular class or party, but should be the common property of all. Gifted with a knowledge of men, rare in itself, that knowledge, I trust will be used to the end that all may be benefited thereby. No official title can compare with that of Professor and no political honor can add to the honor of being the foremost educator of a race. It is far nobler to be known to future generations, not as a politician, but a great teacher; not as a stump speaker, but the one conspicuous champion of Industrial Education; not as an office holder, but the tireless toiler for the elevation of a down trodden race, and the never changing friend and defender of the rights of men.

Have sent you several newspapers commenting on the Washington incident. I thought you might like to know especially the sentiment of the Chicago Press. Under separate cover I mail two most excellent editorials in the leading Democratic paper of our city, which are particularly gratifying. Yours respectfully,

Theodore W. Jones

TLS Con. 201 BTW Papers DLC.

1 Theodore Wellington Jones, a black Chicago businessman, was one of the principal lieutenants of the Tuskegee Machine in Chicago. Born in Hamilton, Ontario, in 1853, he grew up in Lockport, N.Y. After attending Wheaton (Ill.) College, he founded a successful furniture-moving company on the South Side of Chicago. In 1895–96 he was a Republican member of the Cook County Board of Commissioners. An officer of the NNBL, he followed BTW's philosophy more closely than most northern blacks. He said in 1906 that "the Southern Negro's interest in the ballot is on the wane" and that "in those states where the disfranchisement laws are the most rigid, there thrift and repeated success has more than crowned the efforts of the Negro." (Chicago *Broad Ax*, Jan. 27, 1906, quoted in Spear, *Black Chicago*, 74.) Jones fell from power, however, and left Chicago under a cloud. He was reported in Kansas in 1908 facing a bigamy charge. In 1914 Jones was in Richmond, Va., where he was secretary-treasurer of the Negro Historical and Industrial Association, promoting the celebration of the fiftieth anniversary of emancipation. (Giles B. Jackson to BTW, Oct. 26, 1914, Con. 506, BTW Papers, DLC.)

2 The unidentified clipping cited the New York *Age* as hinting that BTW might succeed James Wilson as U.S. Secretary of Agriculture.

From William Reuben Pettiford

Birmingham, Ala., Oct. 24, 1901

My Dear Brother and Friend: I received your letters and telegrams at Washington and I obeyed the restrictions in letter and in spirit.

I found that your advice was exactly correct. I called to see the President on Saturday morning, and I never had a more cordial reception. His secretary presented me; and remarked that I was introduced by you. I handed him the letter, also after he had scanned it, repeated several times that he was proud, indeed, to make my acquaintance. He said that you had spoken very warmly of me to him. He spoke of the bank, and the appointment of Gov. Jones, and of his plan of getting information and using the best people of both races. At the same time he said [he] wanted to select some of the best specimens of our race to confer with him and wanted me to act in that capacity. He proceeded to find out my opinion as to the feelings of the better class of white people in this city towards myself. In my effort to inform him, I remarked that when I was applicant for revenue collectorship I was heartily endorsed by the better class of the whites, including judges, bankers, leading merchants and business men; also ex-Gov. Johnston and ex-mayor of this city. He asked me if I would let him see those papers, I consented and furnished him the papers on Monday.

I am now informing myself in a quiet and private manner so as to furnish him with the desired information. I was very much gratified and pleased with the reception accorded me and if it is possible, I shall be under greater obligations to you for your thoughtfulness in my interest than I was before. I know that you are my friend, because, of what I am trying to do for our people, and I shall ever feel thankful to you for the same.

Now as to the "White House" dinner, we negroes feel that you are greatly honored, indeed, and that you have done more to advance our interest in new territory than any living man. We believe also that it is not in the power of any living man to measure the significance of the "White House" incident as it relates to both races. I believe that this incident will serve in this age as the patriotic work of Frederick Douglass in the last, which called attention to the patriotic world to the wrong in the slavery institution. I believe the discussion of this matter relative to the conduct of the President inviting you to dinner will cause both north and south to look deeper into the merits of the negro for equal justice than anything that has happened lately. I regard you as our "Joseph" that with your intellectual and moral fitness have gone on in advance of us to save a people that are hopeless. As Joseph did, you may have to suffer somewhat, because of the wickedness of your surroundings, but afterwards, he was glad and expressed it in tears in the embrace of his brother's arms.

I heartily endorse your conduct in refusing to discuss through the papers the incident of the white house dinner to friend or foe. The unfavorable comment of the southern press on the president inviting you to his table is used here with the hope of being useful in ratifying the new Constitution.

My hope and prayer is, that the Lord may bless the discussion of the white house dinner to the good of both races.

Pardon long letter, I am happy over the comments of the Northern newspapers. I am yours as ever,

W. R. Pettiford

TLS   Con. 272   BTW Papers   DLC.

From Edgar Gardner Murphy

Montgomery, Alabama. October 24th, 1901

(Not dictated — Personal and Private)

Dear Mr. Washington: I have your letter of the 22nd inst, and I thank you for it. I quite agree with you that it is practically impossible to discuss this question by correspondence. I think, however, that my presence at Tuskegee just now would be a mistake from the standpoint of best usefulness to your work. My absence from Montgomery would be noted, and my presence there would be far more conspicuous than your presence here.

You must not feel that I am at all insistent about your coming to Montgomery, if it is not convenient just now to do so; but I think there can be no harm in your coming, and I shall be glad to have you come, as usual, directly to my study whenever you feel inclined to do so. There would be nothing about that for anybody to misunderstand. If you like, you can arrive on the train due here at 9:20 P.M., and leave on the train returning to Tuskegee at 6:20 the next morning. Governor Jones will probably be out of the city; but as his attitude and mine are identical I can give you a very clear idea of his impressions and suggestions.

I have strained every nerve in order to secure a wise attitude on the part of the Advertiser (the Journal is hopeless, but I have done what I could there). The Advertiser has not wholly risen to the occasion, but it has done better than I could have anticipated. If I can assure the paper that the incident at Washington is not the inauguration of a deliberate policy and that it will probably not be repeated, the Advertiser will gradually throw its whole strength to your support; but I have been most careful to guard the delicacy of your own position and to protect your own proper self-respect. The average man in the street can see nothing in the incident but a deliberate attempt on the part of the President and yourself to force the issue of inter-marriage and amalgamation! ! ! ! If the matter can drop into the background simply as an incident, and as an isolated incident, the man in the street can be answered and the situation will become full of hope. It is peculiarly unfortunate that this opportunity for the demagogue should have been afforded at the very hour when, thro the campaigns in Maryland, Virginia, and Alabama, the people of the South are brought so directly under the bitterest appeals of the politician.

You know that I think a mistake has been made; but I am sure you also know that there is no sacrifice I will not make if I can aid in the restoration of the hopefulness of the situation. I say this not in your interest alone, nor solely in the interest of your race; but rather in the interest of the whole South. The South has most to lose and nothing to gain through the weakening of your influence. If you need me, do not hesitate to speak.

I have not written of this matter to any of our Northern friends. I have kept silent about it, because I felt it to be fairer to you to speak directly to yourself; and I shall not speak of the matter there unless I can in some way be of service to some interest of yours. I have written a letter to the Advertiser, but I prefer not to publish it till you have seen it. I feel more than ever the critical necessity for the purchase of the paper here — to which I have often referred. The expenditure of $12,000 or $15,000, in that way, just at this time would be a strategic movement of great value. It is making money, and I think the investment would be secure. But I can speak of this further when I see you. Very Sincerely Yours,

Edgar Gardner Murphy

TLS Con. 261 BTW Papers DLC.

From Robert Lloyd Smith

Washington, D.C. Friday A.M. [ca. Oct. 25, 1901]

My dear Mr Washington, I want to express a few thoughts to you concerning the dinner at which you were the invited guest of the President.

Bear in mind these facts:

The incident will all be out of the papers in a few days.

You would have *ruined* yourself by declining.

The colored people who criticise you unfavorably are your enemies and would have jumped on you with "tooth and toe nail" if you had declined to go.

The hour is at hand to work the beginning of a new order for the race an era in which *sense* and *worth* and *work* will be recognized by the best of the land.

In God's providence you have been "called" to lead the way and you have obeyed.

What a sorry figure for the millions who look to you for representation would you have cut if you had declined because of racial antagonism!

You have acted *very* wisely in declining to discuss the matter. In no event say more than this for the public: Every good citizen regards the will of the Chief Magistrate as a law for himself in matters not against conscience.

The sober thought of the country is with you. You are all right. You will find that in a few more days this thing will all be over and I predict that you will yet be introduced down south as the Negro whom the *President* delighted to honor — I[']m with you   Your Friend

R L Smith

To my mind the greatest source of trouble is the foolish remarks of Negro papers.

ALS Con. 210 BTW Papers DLC.

To Theodore Roosevelt

Tuskegee, Ala., October 26, 1901

My dear Mr. President: I have refrained from writing you regarding the now famous dinner which both of [us] ate so innocently until I could get into the South and study the situation at first hand. Since coming here and getting into real contact with the white people I am convinced of three things: In the first place, I believe that a great deal is being made over the incident because of the elections which are now pending in several of the Southern States; and in the second place I do not believe that the matter is felt as seriously as the newspapers try to make it appear; and in the third place I am more than ever convinced that the wise course is to pursue exactly the policy which you mapped out in the beginning; not many moons will pass before you will find the South in the same attitude toward you that it was a few weeks ago. I hardly need make any such suggestion because I know that you are of such a nature that having once decided what is right nothing will turn you aside from pursuing that course. I hope to write you more fully within a few days on the same subject.

I shall be passing through Washington again before very long and shall see you. Yours truly,

Booker T. Washington

TLS   Theodore Roosevelt Papers   DLC.

Theodore Roosevelt to Herman Henry Kohlsaat[1]

White House   Washington. October 26, 1901

Personal.

My dear Mr. Kohlsaat: The President never gives letters, but I will have the Secretary of State give the letter you ask.

Some time I would like to talk with you over how things are going along here.

I am much saddened by the views of the South in reference to

Booker T. Washington. But of course it will not make me alter my policy. Sincerely yours,

Theodore Roosevelt

TLS   Con. 3   BTW Papers   DLC.

¹ Herman Henry Kohlsaat (1853–1924) made a fortune with a chain of lunch counters that sold fifteen-cent meals. He bought part ownership of the Chicago *Inter Ocean* in 1891 but sold it two years later. Subsequently he owned several other papers including the Chicago *Record-Herald*. In 1913 he returned to the editorship of the Chicago *Inter Ocean*.

A Sunday Evening Talk

Tuskegee, Ala., October 27, 1901

TWO SIDES OF LIFE

There are quite a number of divisions into which life can be divided but, for the purposes of this evening, I am going to try to divide life into two parts or two divisions; the bright side of life and the dark side of life. Now, in thought, in talk and in action, I think you will find that you can divide all of life into these two divisions — the dark side and the bright side, the discouraging side and the encouraging side; and there are two classes of people, just as there are two divisions of this subject. There is one class that is partially schooling itself and constantly training itself to look upon the dark side of life, and there is another class that is, consciously or unconsciously, continually training itself to look upon the bright side of life. Now, it isn't wise to go too far in either direction. The person who schools himself to see the dark side of life, is likely to make a mistake, and the person who schools himself to look upon the bright side of life, forgetting all else, is also apt to make a mistake; but notwithstanding this, I think I am right in saying that the persons who accomplish most in this world, the helpfulness to which this world looks most for service and are the most useful in every way, are the ones who are constantly seeing and appreciating the bright side as well as the dark side of life. I wish you to get it firmly fixed in your minds that there are two sides of life — the dark side and the bright side — and the experience of the world proves that it is wise, that it is better to school one's self to look upon the bright side of life rather than upon the dark side. You will sometimes find two persons who get up in the morning, perhaps a morning that is overcast with shadows — a damp, wet, rainy, uninviting morning, and one will speak of the morning as being gloomy, will speak of the mud-puddles about the house, about the rain and all of that. The second, who has schooled himself to see the brighter side of life, the beautiful things in life, will speak of the beauties that there are in the rain drops, of the beauty of the drooping birds, and will find something, notwithstanding the gloomy and general disconsolate appearance of things — will find out and see something in the gloomy morning that will cheer him.

You will see these two persons eat breakfast, and perhaps they will find out that the rolls are bad, but that the coffee is alright. If the rolls are miserable, it is a great deal better in such a case to get into the habit — and you will find that it pays from every standpoint — to get and grow into the habit that you will forget the miserable rolls for that morning, and let your thoughts dwell upon the fine and satisfactory coffee. Call the attention of your neighbor next to you to the satisfactory coffee. What is the result of that kind of schooling? You will grow up to be an individual whom the world will want to see and come in contact with constantly. You will grow up to be an individual whom the world will go to for encouragement, when the hours are dark and everything seems to be discouraging in the atmosphere, and so, when you go into your classrooms, when you recite your lessons, do not dwell upon the weak points or errors that your teachers make, or the mistakes in the presentation of the lessons. All teachers make mistakes, and it is the fine, excellent teacher who has courage enough when he or she has made a mistake to say frankly and clearly, I have made a mistake, or I don't know. It takes a very good and bright teacher to say I don't know. No teacher knows everything about every subject. The good teacher will say frankly and clearly, I don't know, I cannot answer that question. You will find it better when you go out to become teachers — as a large proportion of you will — that whenever you get to a point where a student asks you a question which you are not able to answer, or you are not well informed about, to say frankly and honestly, I am unable to answer your question, and they will respect you a great deal more for your frankness. Education is not what a person is able to hold in his head, so much as it is what a person is able to find. So each individual must get that kind of discipline, that kind of training so that he will know where to go and get hold of these facts, rather than holding these facts in his head.

I want you to go out from this institution so trained and so developed that you will be constantly looking for the bright, encouraging and beautiful things in life, instead of the discouraging things that are about us. It takes a strong individual to see the bright and encouraging things in life. It is the weak individual, as a rule, who is constantly calling attention to the other side and discouraging things in life. When you go to your classrooms, I repeat, try to forget the mistakes the teacher has made. Try and forget the weak points in the presentation of the lesson on the part of the teacher. Remember the consideration that has been given and the faithfulness, perhaps, with which that lesson was prepared, and the earnestness with which it was presented. Remember every good thing, every beautiful thing, every encouraging thing in connection with the presentation of that lesson; whether you are at work in the field under Mr. Carver or Mr. Greene,[1] or at work in the classroom, no matter where it is, try to seize hold of the encouraging things with which you come in contact. Try to remember the things that are encouraging, the things that are beautiful.

In connection with the personality of your teachers; it is a very unfortunate habit for students to grow into, that of continually finding fault with teachers and seeing nothing but the weak points about teachers that present themselves. Try to get into that atmosphere, that state of mind, where you will be constantly seeing and calling attention to the strong and beautiful things in connection with the life of your teacher. Grow into the habit just as much as it is possible. Grow into the habit of talking about the bright side of life. When you meet a fellow student, a teacher, or any body, when you write letters home, grow into the habit of calling attention to the bright side of life, to the things that are encouraging, to the things that are beautiful, that are charming, and just in proportion as you do it, you will find that you will not only influence yourself in the right direction, but that you will also influence others in the same direction. It is a very bad habit to get in of being continually growing moody and discouraged, and of making the atmosphere unpleasant for all of those about you or that come within ten feet of you. There are some people that are constantly looking for the dark side of life, who see nothing but this. Everything that comes from their mouth is unpleasant, about this thing and that thing, and they make the whole atmosphere gloomy for themselves from morning until night, and for every one with whom they come in contact, and such people are certainly undesirable. Why, I have actually seen people coming up the road who caused me to feel like going on the other side, as I didn't want to hear their tales of misery and woe. I had heard it so often that I didn't want to get into their atmosphere with them. It is often very easy to influence others in the wrong direction, and to grow into this moody, fault-finding disposition that one becomes so miserable that he is himself always unhappy, and is in such a condition that every one whom he touches becomes unhappy. The persons who live constantly by finding fault, by seeing the dark side of life, become negative characters. They are people who never go forward, who never suggest a line of activity, they are persons who live simply on the negative side of life. Now, as students, you cannot afford to grow that way. We want to send each one of you out from here, not as a negative force, but as a strong, positive, moving, helpful force in the world, and you will not accomplish the task unless each one of you go out from here, not with a moody, discouraging, fault-finding spirit, but with a heart and head full of hope and faith in the world, believing that there is work for you to do, believing that you are the person to accomplish that work.

The person who cultivates the habit of looking on the dark side of life, in nine cases out of ten, is the little person, the miserable person, weak in mind, heart and purpose. On the other hand, the individual who cultivates the habit of looking upon the bright side of life, of calling attention to the beautiful and encouraging things that are in life, in nine cases out of ten, is the strong individual, to whom the world goes for intelligent advice and support. I am trying to get you to see, as students, the best things in life. Be not satisfied with second-handed or third-handed things in life. Be not satisfied until you have gotten yourself into that atmosphere, where you can seize and hold on to the very highest and most beautiful things that there can be gotten out of life.

Tuskegee Student, 13 (Nov. 9, 1901), 1, 4.

1 Charles W. Greene.

A Resolution of the Young Men's Christian Lyceum

Guthrie, Oklahoma, Oct. 27, 1901

Whereas, His Excellency, Theodore Roosevelt, President of the United States of America, having in mind the general good and common welfare of all the American people whose servant he is, saw fit to extend special invitation to the peerless leader of the American negro, Booker T. Washington, that they might consider those measures which best subserve the advancement of a race, and more particularly to the end that the Chief Executive of the nation might be right in his official attitude towards the people whom his guest represented, and therefore just to all men, and

Whereas, the position taken by the President of the United States is one of wisdom, because it selects and consults the highest characters of a race for its true status, and to learn directly from those who know from contact, observation and sincerity, what the race's social maladies are and the most probable remedies for the same, and

Whereas, the motive which prompted the conference had for its object a correct adjustment of true Americanism, the suppression of all forms of anarchy by assuring all men that the sanctity of American institutions must be preserved by strict enforcement of laws, the increasing patriotism among all classes, and the perpetuity of the Republic, and

Whereas, the dining of Booker T. Washington, at the White House, with President Roosevelt, was simply a mark of courtesy due the learning, integrity and high standing of the guest, which in no measure excells the fealty and loyalty of the race he represents to the American Government, and not an effort emanating from the head of the nation to amalgamate the races, which would doubtless entail dangerous results to both races,

Be It Therefore Resolved: That the Young Men's Christian Lyceum, of Guthrie, Oklahoma, do most heartily endorse the stand taken by the President as wise, proper, courageous, generous and right, and as most fitly typifying the true spirit of American manhood, learning, citizenship and statesmanship; and it hereby pledges its unqualified support to him as the official head of this nation.

Put by the President and unanimously approved by the Young Men's Christian Lyceum, this 27th day of October, 1901.

George Thornton,[1] President

Attest: R. Emmett Stewart,[2]
Secretary.

TDSr Copy   Con. 210   BTW Papers   DLC.

[1] George Thornton, according to the 1900 census, was a black janitor, born in Tennessee in 1858.

[2] R. Emmett Stewart, born in Kentucky in 1864, practiced law in Guthrie, Okla. Later he became a judge in Muskogee, and in 1933, with the support of the state NAACP, he prepared a brief challenging the Oklahoma separate-school law.

From Samuel E. Courtney

Boston, October 27th 1901

My dear Mr. Washington, I have wanted to write you our congratulations since Dartmouth College did such a handsome thing for you. Mrs. Courtney and I rejoice with you in all the good things that have come to you recently. What a fine compliment the President has paid the race through you! We pray there will be no change of attitude to your work by the South, due to the thoughtless newspaper articles.

Guess you have seen by the Boston papers some of the cheap talk of Wm. M. Trotter, Geo. W. Forbes and that set of idiots. Trotter has been calling the President names for having *you* to dine with. Forbes so lost himself at a public meeting to say, "it would be a blessing to the race if the Tuskegee school should burn down &c." I think Mr. Forbes' remarks will cause him to lose his job in the public library. The colored people as a whole, are much incensed at the stand these fellows have taken. I have received one or two letters asking for a public meeting to denounce Trotter, Forbes &Co. Don't think it necessary to make them so prominent and give them the notoriety of such a meeting.

The Wendall Phillips Club, the leading colored organization, composed of the best people of the City, will have a banquet at one of the hotels to commemorate the birthday of Wendall Phillips, Friday, November, 29th. The Club is anxious to have you present. If you are in Boston on that date, it would be an excellent opportunity for you to meet and speak to a large number of the best people of Boston and vicinity. Mr. Smith[1] and I have talked the matter over, and we think you should be present if possible. Please let me know whether you will be in Boston about that time, and if it would be agreeable for you to meet the Club.

Portia has been in and spent Saturday and Sunday with us twice. Mrs. Courtney is glad to have her come, she seems to enjoy the change.

Our kindest regards to Mrs. Washington. Very truly yours,

S. E. Courtney

ALS   Con. 194   BTW Papers   DLC.

1 Peter J. Smith, Jr.

To Charles and Company[1]

[Tuskegee, Ala.] Oct. 28, 1901

Please send me by Adams' Express four bottles Burnt Island Scotch.

Booker T. Washington

TWSr   Con. 541   BTW Papers   DLC.

1 John C. Clark and Howard W. Charles operated a gourmet grocery store on the corner of 43rd Street and Vanderbilt Avenue in New York City, across the street from Grand Central Station. They also operated a chain of sandwich shops in the city. BTW ordered four bottles of Scotch from Charles and Co. again the following year. (Sept. 15, 1902, Con. 541, BTW Papers, DLC.)

From Alonzo Homer Kenniebrew

Tuskegee, Ala. 10-28 [1901]

Mr Washington   Jennie Harvey was admitted to girls hospital at noon with a crushed & burned hand rec'd at laundry. Compelled to amputate — I took the hand off a[t] wrist joint. She is doing well.

Last night 3 boys entered boys hospital with gun shot wounds rec'd while in a man's cane patch. Fortunately the shots were small and little harm was done. Only one had a painful wound — caused by 50 shots in the head — doing well. Yours

A H. Kenniebrew

ALS   Con. 202   BTW Papers   DLC.

1 Jennie Harvey of Beaufort, S.C., was a member of the B preparatory class in 1901–2.

From Isaac Newton Seligman[1]

New York. October 30, 1901

My dear Mr. Washington: I have received your kind note of the 28th instant, enclosing a copy of the last report to the board of trustees, which I shall read with pleasure.

I trust that the thoughtless and unjustifiable criticism by the Southern press incidental to the dinner given to you by President Roosevelt has now spent its force, and also trust that there will be no lasting injury to the people of the South or to the cause that you have at heart. Yours truly,

Isaac N. Seligman

TLS   Con. 209   BTW Papers   DLC.

1 Isaac Newton Seligman (1855–1917) was president of the New York banking firm of J. & W. Seligman & Co. from 1894 to 1917.

To Theodore Roosevelt

Tuskegee, Alabama. Oct. 31, 1901

My dear Mr. President: I know you have not had time to bother with many of the editorial expressions made regarding my dining with you, but I believe that it is worth your while to read the enclosed editorial which appears in today's Atlanta Constitution.[1] It is the first sign of returning common sense to the South and I think indicates a good deal. While I must confess that the outbreak over my dining with you was far beyond my expectations, I cannot help but feel that it was providential and that good is going to come out of it.[2] Yours truly,

Booker T. Washington

TLS   Theodore Roosevelt Papers   DLC.

[1] Atlanta *Constitution*, Oct. 31, 1901, 6. The editorial was entitled "Shall the Race Question Establish Anew the Mason and Dixon Line?" The *Constitution* stated that "social intercourse between the races would be destructive of race integrity and detrimental to social order," but urged tolerance for the opinions of both the North and the South. Concerning Roosevelt's proposed trip to Charleston, the *Constitution* supported the welcome issued by Charleston's mayor, but pointed out that the welcome was extended to Roosevelt in his role as President.

[2] Roosevelt replied that the whole incident had made him feel "melancholy" regarding the actions of his friends, but he assured BTW that the uproar would not have any effect on his policy. (Nov. 2, [1901], Theodore Roosevelt Papers, DLC.)

To Hollis Burke Frissell

Tuskegee, Ala., Nov. 1, 1901

My dear Dr. Frissell —   I am looking forward with a good deal of interest to the work in New York during next week and I do hope that the wisest and best thing may be done. I think you will have to bear in mind this point, while I think I realize as much as and as deeply as anyone could the importance of education of the white people in the South and am just as anxious for their broader education as any white man can be, at the same time I think you and others will have to watch carefully to see that nothing is done that would give the impression that Negro education is being shoved aside for white education, I mean that it is much easier to drift in the direction of least resistance. Of course Negro education means to those who are engaged in it a certain amount of trial, difficulty and ostracism that does not obtain in white education and for this reason the average man would yield to the temptation to go in the direction where there is the least hardship to be endured. The recent outbreak in the South regarding my dining with the President convinces me more than ever of the importance of broad liberal education for all the people regardless of race.

In regard to Mr. Murphy; he is in a very peculiar position and has got to make some decision for his future work within the next two or three weeks and I do hope something will be done that will give him definite information in regard to what he may expect. More and more I feel that we need a man like Mr. Murphy who is from the real heart of the South.

I have watched him pretty carefully during severe trials lately and I have more and more faith in him.

By this mail I send you a marked copy of the Atlanta Constitution which contains an interesting editorial. Yours truly,

Booker T. Washington

TLS BTW Folder ViHaI.

From William Henry Baldwin, Jr.

[New York City] November 1st, 1901

Dear Washington: I have your letter of 29th ult. I am delighted to know that there was no local feeling at Tuskegee on account of the Washington incident. I have no doubt that wherever your influence has really been felt directly that the public will be more generous and sensible, than at points where you are less known.

We must see to it now that good comes from this incident. It can be made of advantage. It will be helpful in the North, and will also help many people in the South to see more clearly the narrow prejudice which they possess in their misinterpretation of the act itself. I noticed that the Rev. Mr. Broughton,[1] of Atlanta, interpreted it correctly, saying that this invitation was made not as a recognition of social equality, but as a recognition of the work which you are doing. I imagine that perhaps the Rev. Murphy has had something to do with this expression.

It makes it very clear to my mind that you should be on the Committee for educational work in the South. That may be a point on which there will be a serious split, but it looks to me now as though that point should be insisted upon, and I certainly shall not give it up unless you say so. Yours truly,

W H Baldwin Jr

TLS Con. 792 BTW Papers DLC.

1 Leonard Gaston Broughton (1864–1936) was the founder and minister of the Atlanta Baptist Tabernacle and a popular writer of religious books. He had a D.D. degree from Wake Forest College and was ordained in 1893. He was unfriendly to the Conference for Education in the South on the ground that it brought the "godless" influences of the northern millionaires to the South.

From Shepherd Lincoln Harris

Lome Togo, West Africa, Novr. 3rd 1901

Dear Sir; I am glad to say that to day my time expiers here under the contract, but it is likely that I will be here until Christmas.

This letter I am sorry to say must be in a different tone from the other one I wrote you concerning the experement, yet I can say truthfully that there was a time when the prospects were bright as I told you. In regards to the growing of the cotton; very truly it did have the crop on it that I spoke of in my letter, but what skillful labor and nature produced, only nature the mighty power which no science of man can change has defaced the whole crop. We have harvested only (2) two bales of cotton from the whole crop. The experement so far has been a compleet failure, I mean in this section where we are. There are other places in the colony that are more suited for the purpose of growing cotton, but in spit[e] of the many objections made *the expert* stoped right here under the mountains where it has rained regular since March. Then too other farms were to be planted over the colony in order to find out just the better place for cotton, but not a one has been planted, so we only know best in regards to the growth of cotton where we are.

As for my work, which was the mechancial part, in my weak judgment I think it has been just as much successful as could be expected under the many disadvantages. Since I have been here I have had plenty of work to do, and have tried to do it in the best posible way, yet for the first time in my whole life I find it imposible to please the person I am now working under. The nearer the time is out here the harder the place seems.

I dont know the plans of the other young men, but as for myself I am only hopeing that my ticket may come on the next steamer.

I dont think I could stay here under any offer that might be made. I have the gin house up and ready to gin all the cotton that will be made here. So soon as I can get off, I am comeing home. I hope the school is geting along nicely. Remember me very kindly [to] Mrs. Washington, and friends. I remain most truly,

S. L. Harris

ALS Con. 213 BTW Papers DLC.

To Amy Nickerson[1]

[Tuskegee, Ala.] Nov. 4, 1901

Dear Madam: Replying briefly to your kind letter of October 30th I would say that I am glad to know that you are interested in the progress of my race, and that you contemplate visiting this part of the South sometime soon. We shall be delighted to see you at this institution and shall be glad to let you see something of the work that we are doing. We should also be glad to have you make any contribution that you might see fit towards the promotion of any of our departments.

In regard to the other questions raised by your letter I would say that I do not and cannot agree with the views that you seem to entertain. I cannot believe that any good would come to my race in the South or elsewhere by raising the question of social equality or attempting to encourage the colored people to obtrude themselves upon the white race from a social standpoint. All such attempts would be unwise and the result would prove harmful to both races. My own views on this subject I express fully in my address delivered at the opening of the Atlanta Exposition some years ago, and I take the liberty of enclosing you a copy of that address. I have never changed my mind the least on this subject since that time. Each race, in my mind, has its own peculiar work and its own peculiar destiny to work out. I believe that both races are to live in the South for all time side by side and everything possible should be done to foster friendly relations. Yours truly,

Booker T. Washington

TLpS Con. 282A BTW Papers DLC.

1 A resident of St. Louis, Mo.

From Henry McNeal Turner

Atlanta, Ga. Nov. 5 1901

Dear Sir: I have just learned that you are home in Tuskegee, and not caring to write when some one else would inspect your letters, I have waited for an opportunity to communicate with you directly. Not wishing to consume your precious time, I beg the honor of thanking, commending and adjulating you.

First, for the letter that you wrote and was published shortly after President McKinley died, and for all the conditions and circumstances connected with dining with President Roosevelt. You are about to be the great representative and hero of the Negro race, notwithstanding you have been very conservative. I thank you, thank you, thank you. God bless you, Respectfully,

H. M. Turner

ALS Con. 213 BTW Papers DLC. Written on stationery of the Colored National Emigration Association, of which Turner was listed as treasurer and chancellor. The letterhead proclaimed that the purpose of the organization was to purchase a ship "for emigrational purposes to any country where all men have rights regardless of their color."

From Charles Waddell Chesnutt

Cleveland, O. November 5, 1901

My dear Mr. Washington, Your kind favor of October 28th is before me. Replying first to a question that you ask me, I would say that I started to read "The Crisis"[1] but got switched off before I finished it. It is said to be quite a good novel, although the best critics say it lacks several of the elements of greatness. It is in the popular vein, which is sufficient to account in large measure for its popularity.

Yes, I have seen something of the storm that has been blowing down your way, and like you I think that everything of the sort will tend in the end toward the result which we seek. I think, however, that the feeling manifested by southern expressions concerning the little incident is very deep-seated. Underneath it all lies the fear of what they consider corruption of blood. But whatever they may call it or consider it, I think that it would be vastly preferable to the sort of thing toward which they are tending under the present condition of things.

I quite agree with you that the medium of fiction offers a golden opportunity to create sympathy throughout the country for our cause. It has been the writings of Harris[2] and Page and others of that ilk which has furnished my chief incentive to write something upon the other side of this very vital question. I know I am on the weaker side in point of popular sympathy, but I am on the stronger side in point of justice and morality, and if I can but command the skill and the power to compel attention, I think I will win out in the long run, so far as I am personally concerned, and will help the cause, which is vastly more important. I am really inclined to think from the reception so far accorded to "The Marrow of Tradition" that I may have "arrived" with this book. You and your machinery can do a great deal to further its reading.

For instance, your Mr. Robert W. Taylor called on me the other day while in Cleveland. I gave him a copy of the book. He writes me from Boston that he has read it with great interest and spoken of it widely, that a number have promised to buy it and that, in his opinion, it is bound to make a great hit. He has also dropped the suggestion here and there that I can be secured for lectures — for all which I am under obligations both to him and to Tuskegee.

I see that you received pronounced attentions at Yale College.

Everything that you accomplish, every upward step that you may take redounds to the credit and advances the interests of millions of people. I for one am most sincerely and unselfishly delighted at all of your successes. Very cordially yours,

Chas. W. Chesnutt

TLS Con. 193 BTW Papers DLC.

[1] *The Crisis* (1901), written by the American novelist Winston Churchill (1871–1947).

[2] Joel Chandler Harris (1848–1908) was a leading Georgia journalist, on the staff of the Atlanta *Constitution* for twenty-four years beginning in 1876. He was best known for his works using southern black folklore through the fictional character Uncle Remus.

To Theodore Roosevelt

Tuskegee, Alabama. November 6, 1901

My dear Mr. President: Your kind letter of November 2d is received and I thank you very much for it.

First, I want to say that if the reports are to any extent true that Mr. Koester,[1] I think it is, of South Carolina, took any part in a lynching or even by his presence approved a lynching, I hope that you can see your way clear not to let him continue in his office as Revenue Collector of South Carolina. It would clear the atmosphere wonderfully and serve as the greatest encouragement to our race if it could be understood that this man lost his position because of having taken part in a lynching; it would be a lesson that would do the whole South good.

I am very glad to know that you were so well pleased with my friend, R. L. Smith, of Texas. He is a fine fellow.

I wrote, at his request, the Secretary of the Interior yesterday regarding Dr. Crossland.[2] Dr. Crossland, so far as I can get information, is a clean, high toned man of ability, but is not known outside of the state of Missouri to any extent.

Hill[3] of Mississippi is one of the old time politicians, and I am sorry to say that he does not bear a very good reputation; whether there is anything very definite against him I do not know, but in some way he seems to be not in good odor, but when in Mississippi a few days ago I found that he seemed to be filling his office well.

I do not believe that the Bar Association is acting squarely with you in recommending Calvin Chase for any position. Granting that he was treated unjustly in that criminal libel matter, Chase does not bear a good reputation among the colored people of the District of Columbia nor among the colored people throughout the country as a whole. It is often true, I think you will find, that white men do not have an opportunity of knowing the real character and reputation of members of our race whom they recommend.

I would say that Cheatham on the whole is as good a man as Dr. Crossland and is much more widely known throughout the country among our people. One or two unfavorable things have been brought against Cheatham lately but I am not at all sure of the truth of the charges.

If you can get the time to do so, I think it would interest you as well as give you valuable information, to look over the papers of such a colored man as Rucker, of Atlanta, and see how some of the white people in that city have endorsed him. Many of the colored persons appointed to office in the South have the strongest endorsements of white people in their communities, and very often these endorsements are given to the colored man with a view of defeating the aspirations of some white man.

I shall call to see you when I am again in Washington. Yours truly,

Booker T. Washington

TLS Theodore Roosevelt Papers DLC.

1 George R. Koester (1871–1939), a newspaper editor, was born in Philadelphia and attended college in Greenville, S.C. He remained in South Carolina as a reporter and, in 1890, founded the Columbia *Record*. Acting upon Senator John L. McLaurin's recommendation, Roosevelt appointed Koester, a Gold Democrat, collector of internal revenue for South Carolina in 1901. Edmund H. Deas, the chairman of the state Republican executive committee, and Koester's other political enemies in Columbia lobbied in the U.S. Senate and circulated a charge that Koester participated in a lynching in 1893. Koester denied the charge, saying he was present only as a reporter and in fact restrained the mob from burning the victim alive. Koester's appointment, however, was not confirmed. In later years he was editor of the Greenville *Piedmont*.

2 John R. A. Crossland was born in South Carolina in 1864, and attended Shaw

University and Meharry Medical College before beginning the practice of medicine in St. Joseph, Mo. By 1901, after some years in Republican state politics, Crossland was a member-at-large of the Republican state committee and president of the Negro Republican State League. Eager for federal preferment, he recommended himself to Vice-President Roosevelt either to replace Henry P. Cheatham as recorder of deeds or to fill one of the traditional Negro consular offices, informing Roosevelt that he had the "entire endorsement" of the Missouri Republican party organization and that it had been more than thirty years since a western Negro had been given "a representative place." (Mar. 9, 1901, Theodore Roosevelt Papers, DLC.) In Jan. 1902, Roosevelt appointed Crossland as minister to Liberia, but after a scandal in which the diplomat was charged with housebreaking, fraud, assault, and wife-stealing, the Liberian secretary of state demanded his recall at the end of the year and Roosevelt complied. Crossland returned home, where he resumed his activities in state politics; in 1916 he was alternate delegate-at-large to the Republican national convention and an avid supporter of Roosevelt's nomination.

[3] James Hill, a black entrepreneur and Republican politician, was an associate of Frederick Douglass in the establishment of the abortive Freedom Manufacturing Co. in the 1890s. Hill then founded the Mississippi Cotton Manufacturing Co. In Jackson, Miss. He was at one time postmaster of Vicksburg and was a McKinley appointee to the U.S. land office at Jackson. He also held the position of receiver of public monies in Mississippi.

To Whitefield McKinlay

Tuskegee, Ala., 11, 6, 1901

personal.

My dear Mr. McKinlay: Referring to your letter again of November 1st[1] I would say that I have a letter this morning from the Attorney General acknowledging receipt of mine in which I recommended the two lawyers agreed upon by yourself and myself. I also stated in the letter that I should put first Mr. Robert H. Terrell provided he was eligible and asked him to give Mr. Terrell an opportunity to prove his eligibility. The Attorney General expressed his desire to see Mr. Terrell and consequently I telegraphed him today to call to see him.

I cannot agree with you, however, as to the wisdom of my going in any wholesale manner into securing such appointments; to do so in one case would mean that I meant to do so in a number of other cases.

I am sure that we put before the Attorney General the very best persons for this position and I have faith to believe that he and the President will do the proper thing by them. If Mr. Terrell proves his eligibility, the recommendations will then stand Mr. Terrell and Mr. Stewart. I hardly believe that the President would go outside of these three names at least without consulting me.

I am writing a letter to the President today in which I am cautioning him about giving too much attention to what white men say when recommending colored people. I am reminding him that in many cases white men do not know the character of colored men whom they recommend. I am doing this while answering a letter from him asking direct information about an individual whom you and I both feel is unworthy.

If you think of anything else I can do please write or telegraph me as the matter will be settled within a few days.

The President was immensely pleased with the visit of R. L. Smith. Smith made a fine impression on him.

I read your friend Leupp's[2] article in the New York Evening Post with a great deal of interest. I certainly want to meet him when I am next in Washington.

I do not believe that the President will appoint Ferguson[3] over Smith.

I am also under the impression that Crum, in case Koester is not appointed in South Carolina, is going to stand a very good chance. In case Koester is not appointed, it will give an opportunity for me to call attention again to both Dr. Crum and Col. Kaufman.[4] My understanding is that you know Kaufman well and can recommend him; is this so? Yours very truly,

Booker T. Washington

TLS   Con. 4   Carter G. Woodson Collection   DLC.

1 Whitefield McKinlay wanted BTW to use his influence with President Roosevelt to push for the appointment of Robert H. Terrell or Joseph H. Stewart. "I am thoroughly convinced," McKinlay wrote BTW, "that if the President in this matter could be reached and made to understand the very great importance of appointing only men qualified morally as well as intellectually, he would all the more appreciate our unselfish advice." McKinlay said he wanted to accomplish "such results as will reflect everlasting credit upon the race." (Nov. 1, 1901, Con. 261, BTW Papers, DLC. A draft with some minor variations is in Con. 4, Carter G. Woodson Collection, DLC.)

2 Francis Ellington Leupp (1849–1918) combined careers in journalism, reform, and public service. In 1885 he became a Washington correspondent of the New York *Evening Post,* and from 1889 until 1904 he was head of its Washington bureau, representing at the same time *The Nation.* A painstaking gatherer and checker of information, he was best known for his sharp characterizations of public men. Actively

interested in the Indians since the 1880s, Leupp became President Roosevelt's investigator in 1902 of charges against federal officials in charge of Kiowa, Comanche, and Apache Indians, and from 1905 to 1909 he was U.S. Commissioner of Indian Affairs. He befriended BTW, gave him advice on race strategy, and when he became Indian commissioner sought to adapt Tuskegee methods to Indian education. Leupp wrote a signed article in the New York *Evening Post*, Oct. 21, 1901, 7, entitled "The South and the Negro." He concluded that Roosevelt's dinner with BTW in the White House would help him politically in the North, whereas the South was lost to him anyhow, although Roosevelt "would have been the last man to think of this in entertaining Booker Washington."

3 Probably Henry C. or Charles M. Ferguson, mulatto brothers both active in Republican politics in Fort Bend County and in the state of Texas. Henry C. Ferguson was sheriff of the county for many years. Charles Ferguson was a delegate to the Republican national conventions in 1886, 1896, and 1900.

4 Abraham Charles Kaufman, born in Charleston, S.C., in 1839, was commissioner of public schools of Charleston from 1895 to 1903. An active Republican and a racial moderate, he was a trustee of Avery Normal Institute, a black school, beginning in 1901. He was a supporter of the Conference for Education in the South and the Southern Education Board.

From William Henry Baldwin, Jr.

[New York City] Nov. 6th., 1901

Dear Mr. Washington: We had a very important meeting of the Southern Conference Committee which met yesterday morning. Dr. Curry made a famous speech, as well as all the Southern members. In the course of Dr. Curry's remarks, I made a note of one statement which he made with all the fervor and power at his command. After saying many strong things about you, he said: "In twenty years laboring and associating with him under all kinds of trials and conditions, I never heard him say or do an imprudent thing."

The Southern Conference Committee had a meeting on Monday which lasted several hours; and again on Monday night when they asked me to come into their Board, and added also Walter H. Page and Dr. Shaw.

On Monday night, Mr. Jesup, Dr. Gilman, Dr. Curry and myself spent several hours talking over the possible program. It seemed to be the thought that a new Commission should be appointed with three representatives from the Peabody Board, three from the Slater

Board, and three from the Rockefeller Fund. This was to be taken up by Mr. Jesup with Mr. J. P. Morgan[1] to get his idea.

On Tuesday morning a meeting was had of the Southern Conference Committee, from ten o'clock to one o'clock at Mr. Ogden's office, and at one o'clock they met with Mr. Jesup, Dr. Gilman and Mr. Page and lunched at the Fifth Ave. Hotel, where many speeches were made and the general plans outlined. Mr. Jesup seemed to be very much interested in the plan of the Conference Committee.

The Conference Committee were to meet again this Wednesday morning at ten o'clock at Mr. Ogden's office, but I cannot be there. They meet again this evening at Mr. Peabody's invitation at the Metropolitan Club.

The point now is that there is to be a Committee of the Southern Conference to do the work outlined for it; and also it is planned to have a separate Commission to take up this whole work in its broadest aspect as a Treasury, a Clearing-house for information, etc., after the plans suggested above of appointing representatives from the different Boards of Trustees of the different Funds. The whole matter, however, is in the air, although it looks very encouraging.

I spoke to Dr. Curry and Mr. Buttrick first about your appointment on the Committee. They both approve of it. I wanted to wait until to-night's meeting before formally having your name presented, in order to get enough atmosphere created so that a Southern representative will suggest your name, — say Mr. Walter H. Page.

By the way, Mr. Page thinks that the President did exactly right in inviting you to Dinner, and that hc should pay no attention to the Southern clamor. "He has got to take that bull by the horns immediately." I shall not be able to give you any real information until after to-night's meeting. Question of Mr. Murphy, etc., has not yet come up. Yours truly,

W H Baldwin Jr

TLS Con. 792 BTW Papers DLC.

1 John Pierpont Morgan (1837–1913).

From Robert Heberton Terrell

Washington, D.C. Nov. 7, 1901

My dear Mr. Washington, I am in receipt of both your letter and telegram. I shall attend to the matter involved in them at once. I appreciate highly the good things that you have seen fit to say of me, as well as the kindly interest my friends have taken in me with regard to my appointment as one of the Magistrates for the District of Columbia. I am not a candidate for such preferment and I don't think that I would accept it if it came to me unsought. Not because I am ignorant of the honor and dignity of such a place, but because I am so thoroughly happy in school work for which I think I am better fitted than anything else. Of course I am an ambitious man and want a career. Can't I make it here? If I can I prefer the glory and satisfaction that come from being an Educator of the first rate.

I am pleased to know that one of your large experience and your acquaintanceship with men should not be fearful about saying a word in commendation of me. I am afraid, however, my friends here greatly overrate my ability in this matter of the judgeship. I am not so sure that I can fill the place with credit.

With kindest regards for Mrs. Washington and Mrs. Bruce, I am, Yours Sincerely,

R. H. Terrell

ALS   Con. 213   BTW Papers   DLC.

From Edward Elder Cooper

Washington, D.C., Nov. 7/01

Dear Mr. Washington: Your letter of the 25th inst. is to hand and I am glad you took time enough from your work to write me. The city of Washington, as well as the whole country, is agog talking about you. Mr. Fortune was down here last week, mixing with his friends and incidently putting in some blows for you. Editor Chase of The Bee is sore and kicking, but I have a private opinion that he would kick under almost any circumstances. I don't think he would have secured the appointment had you come out strong for him.

You are covering lots of ground and Prof. Robert H. Terrell and his friends are trying to plan some way to give you some evidence of their appreciation. I am not authorized to say this but I say it for I know how their pulses and their hearts beat.

I shall be glad to see you when you come through Washington and if you will accept my counsel, saw wood for the next few months and let somebody else do the talking as it will be a long time before they get to the heights that you have already climbed. Of course I would like to know when you are coming through again and if a man ever needed a blessing, if the elements are ever to open to one or, if Moses is ever to smite the rock, I can stand the whole thing at one time. In other words, I am as game as the pride of the farm-yard but as poor as Job's turkey. I think, as I have thought and written for ten years, that, Booker T. Washington is the greatest leader the race has ever produced.

That reminds me, have you received Judge Gibbs' MS.?[1] Write him a good introductory and send it back as soon as you can. He is a good soul but a little old and peevish and apt to draw conclusions. I have given him one copy each of your two autobiographies and he is delighted with them. I see by The World's Work that "Up From Slavery" is into its fifteenth edition.[2] You are not so bad after all. Yours very truly,

E. E. Cooper

TLS Con. 194 BTW Papers DLC.

1 Mifflin Wistar Gibbs, *Shadow and Light* (1902). See An Introduction to *Shadow and Light*, 1902, below.

2 Cooper apparently garbled the *World's Work* item in September, which referred to *Up from Slavery* as fifteenth in popularity as reported by librarians and sixteenth as reported by book dealers. In October the book was twelfth and in November sixteenth on the librarians' list but not among the top thirty as ranked by book dealers. (*World's Work*, 2 [Sept. 1901], 1227, [Oct. 1901], 1343, [Nov. 1901], 1451.)

From William Jennings Bryan

Lincoln, Nebr., Nov. 7, 1901

(Personal)

My dear Sir: Your favor at hand. I am in hearty sympathy with the effort which you are making to improve the members of your race. I believe that, because of race sympathies and race prejudices, a person like yourself can do more for the members of the negro race than a white man could. Your example is an inspiration to them, and your words are heeded by them. I have shown my interest in your work on former occasions, and I take pleasure in enclosing a small contribution now. Very truly yours,

W. J. Bryan

P.S. I take the liberty of enclosing an editorial in which I discuss the various phases of the negro question.[1] If you were the only member of your race in this country the incident referred to would have passed unnoticed, but I believe that the agitation of the question of social equality will estrange the races rather than bring them together.

TLS Con. 189 BTW Papers DLC. Docketed "10.00," the amount of Bryan's donation.

[1] In an editorial, "The Negro Question," *The Commoner*, 1 (Nov. 1, 1901), 1–3, Bryan called the dinner at the White House "unfortunate, to say the least." He thought blacks were entitled to the same legal and educational opportunities as whites, and claimed that their political rights were restricted only for a "probationary term," as were those of immigrants before naturalization. No political party, he said, had ever advocated social equality or "amalgamation." He thought that instead of trying to mix socially with whites, blacks should concentrate on their own "intellectual and moral development" in an atmosphere of race pride. He minimized the problems of American blacks as compared with peoples in the recently acquired U.S. colonies.

From Leonora Love Chapman Kenniebrew

[Tuskegee, Ala.] Nov. 8—'01

My dear Mr. Washington: At the outset, I wish to beg your pardon for taking *any* of your time, but I must remind you that you are to blame for it; for you have said publicly and privately that whenever we had anything to say, to say it to you, that you were never too busy to listen.

In reference to your letter [I] would say, that both what I have said and my motive have been misjudged or misunderstood. I have labored too long and too hard for Tuskegee to begin *now* at this late day to oppose its policy. And I do not think that you or any one else thinks I have done so.

As to only *"two* or *three"* being disgruntled and dissatisfied, you are *very much* mistaken. I could *name* to you *nearly* a *dozen* people who are dissatisfied to the extent that they say they do not mean to return here another year. These "two or three" whom you have in mind I presume are those who, like myself, have been unfortunate enough to take you at your word and be frank with you.

Again — you are quite right about its not costing any more to pay teachers who are in keeping with the school's policy than those who are not. However, I think you will find it vastly more expensive to employ mere *machines* or *parrots*.

Speaking to the matter in question — I could have ignored this outline completely and have said nothing, (and not used it either). Then perhaps I, too, could have been set down as "falling in line" instead of being judged as one "opposed to the policy of the institution." I preferred to be *honest* and *candid* with you. I had no other feeling than that expressed on the face of my note.

I know my teaching is not the best nor probably the best *I* can do. *None* of us knows it *all.* I hope I shall never reach that degree of ignorance and stupidity that I shall oppose any kind of improvement whatever and my *own* improvement especially. To this end, I have added to those I already had four books on teaching and I take *two* journals of my own and read others; am constantly looking for ways and means of bettering my work. When I have done this (and any other *live* teacher would feel the same) I object to *your* or any body's else treating me as if I were a mere *machine* or *parrot.* If you or "the school" is to lay down plans and make outlines for us to follow, then our money has been spent for books and papers which we do not need, as "the school" will do the studying and planning which we are supposed to do for ourselves. It is *this* I object to, — and in doing so, I do not think I am opposing the policy of the institution.

If in my work, I make mistakes, (and any one is liable to err) I have no objection to having those errors pointed out to me. At the same time, it would be a little encouraging if we occasionally hear some of the *good* points of our work, from you or "the school." As I have said before, if my work is not satisfactory to you, I am willing to quit, and shall feel that I have perhaps answered some one else's call to teach, and am not fitted for it. But I should dislike very much to give up my work on the charge of not being in sympathy with the policy of the institution, for that charge is as false as it is unjust. Very respectfully

Mrs. A. H. Kenniebrew

ALS Con. 555 BTW Papers DLC.

An Article in the *Tuskegee Student*

Tuskegee, Alabama, November 9, 1901

THE NEGRO AND THE SIGNS OF CIVILIZATION

There are certain visible signs of civilization and strength which the world demands that each individual or race exhibit before it is taken seriously into consideration in the affairs of the world. Unless these visible evidences of ability and strength are forthcoming, mere abstract talking and mere claiming of "rights" amount to little. This is a principle that is as broad and old as the world and is not confined to the conditions that exist between the white man and the black man in the South. We may be inclined to exalt intellectual acquirements over the material, but all will acknowledge that the possession of the material has an influence that is lasting and unmistakable. As one goes through our Western States and sees the Norwegians in Minnesota, for example, owning and operating nearly one-third of the farms in the State; and then as he goes through one of the cities of Minnesota and sees block after block of brick stores owned by these Norwegians; as he sees factories and street railways owned and operated by these same people, and as he notes that as a rule these people live in neat, well-kept cottages where there are refinement and culture, on nice streets, that have been paid for, he can't help but have confidence in and respect for such people, no matter how he has been educated to feel regarding them. The material, visible and tangible elements in this case teach a lesson that almost nothing else can. It may be said in opposition to this view that this is exalting too high the material side of life. I do not take this view. Let us see what is back of this material possession. In the first place the possession of property is an evidence of mental discipline, mental grasp and control. It is an evidence of self-sacrifice. It is an evidence of economy. It is an evidence of thrift and industry. It is an evidence of fixedness of character and purpose. It is an evidence of interest in pure and intelligent government, for no man can possess property without having the deepest interest in all that pertains to local and national government. The black man who owns $50,000 worth of property in a town is going to think a good many times before he votes for the officer who will have the liberty of taxing his property. If he thinks that a colored law-maker will use his taxing power wrongfully, he is not likely to vote for him merely for the sentimental reason that he is a black man. The black man who owns $50,000 worth of property in a town is not likely to continue to vote for a Republican law-maker if he knows that a Democratic one will bring lower taxes and better protection to his property. Say or think what we will there is but one way for the Negro to get up and that is for him to pay the cost, and when he has paid the cost — paid the price of his freedom — it will appear in the beautiful, well-kept home, in the increasing bank account, in the farm, and crops that are free from debt, in the ownership of railroad and municipal stocks and bonds (and he who owns the majority of stock in a railroad will not have to ride in a "Jim Crow car"), in the well-kept store, in the well-fitted laundry, in the absence of mere superficial display. These are a few of the universal and indisputable signs of the highest civilization, and the Negro must possess them or be debarred. All mere abstract talk about the possibility of possessing them, or his intention to possess them, counts for little. He must actually possess them, and the only way to possess them is to possess them. From every standpoint of interest it is the duty of the Negro himself, and the duty of the Southern white man as well as the white man in the North, to see that the Negro be helped forward as fast as possible towards the possession of these evidences of civilization. How can it best be done? Where is the beginning to be made? It can be done by the Negro beginning right now and where he finds himself. What I am anxious for is for the Negro to be in actual possession of all the elements of the highest civilization, and when he is so possessed, the burden of his future treatment by the white man must rest upon the white man.

I repeat, let the Negro begin right where he is, by putting the greatest amount of intelligence, of skill and dignity into the occupations by which he is surrounded. Let him learn to do common things in an uncommon manner. Whenever in the South, for example, the Negro is the carpenter, let him realize that he cannot remain the carpenter unless people are sure that no one can excel him as a carpenter. This black carpenter should strive in every way possible to keep himself abreast of the best wood work done in the world. He should be constantly studying the best journals and books bearing on carpentry. He should watch for every improvement in his line. When this carpenter's son is educated in college or elsewhere, he should see that his son studies mechanical and architectural drawing. He should not only have his son taught practical carpentry, but should see that in addition to his literary education that he is a first class architect as well — that, if possible, he has an idea of landscape gardening and house furnishing. In a word, he should see that his son knows so much about wood work, house construction, and everything that pertains to making a house all that it should be, that his services are in constant demand. One such Negro in each community will give character to a hundred other Negroes. It is the kind of effort that will put the Negro on his feet. What I have said of carpentry, is equally true of dozens of occupations now within the Negro's hands. The second or third generation of this black man's family need not be carpenters, but can aspire successfully to something higher because the foundation has been laid.

It is not only the duty of the Negro to thus put himself in possession of the signs of civilization, but it is also the plainest duty of the white man, North and South, to help the Negro to do so in a more generous manner than ever before. One-third of the population of the South is black. Ignorance in any country or among any people is the sign of poverty, crime and incompetency. No State can have the highest civilization and prosperity with one-third of its population down. This one-third will prove a constant millstone about the neck of the other two-thirds. Every one-room Negro cabin in the South, where there is ignorance, poverty and stupidity, is an adverse advertisement of the State, the bad effects of which no white man in the next generation can escape.

Tuskegee Student, 13 (Nov. 9, 1901), 3.

An Article in *Outlook* by Max Bennett Thrasher

[Nov. 9, 1901]

BOOKER WASHINGTON'S PERSONALITY

During the last five years I have been to Tuskegee, Ala., several times, in the course of my newspaper work, to report the sessions of the Tuskegee Negro Conference, or to write of the work of the Tuskegee Normal and Industrial Institute. I have also had the pleasure at certain other times of being associated with the Principal of the school, Mr. Booker T. Washington, in connection with newspaper and magazine work upon which I have been engaged. I propose, in what might perhaps be called an "anecdotal" article, to describe Mr. Washington as I have seen him, and his ways at work and at play.

To give some idea of the amount of travel which Mr. Washington's work requires of him, I copy a few entries from my diary, made in the fall of 1900, when I was doing some work with him in New York:

October 24. Mr. Washington arrived here from Tuskegee this morning. In the afternoon we went to Springfield, Mass., where he spoke before two great meetings of the American Missionary Association.

October 25. Came back to New York last night, reaching here at 7 A.M.

October 26. Went to Great Barrington, Mass., where Mr. Washington spoke in the evening before the High School.

October 27. Went by train from Great Barrington to Lenox and made some calls. Drove from Lenox to Pittsfield, and took train from there to Adams, where we were the guests of Mr. W. B. Plunkett.

October 28. Sunday. Mr. Washington spoke twice in the Congregational church.

October 29. Came back to New York.

October 30. Mr. Washington has gone to Norristown, Pa., to speak.

October 31. Mr. Washington back here to give final directions to the four Tuskegee men who sail to-day for Africa, under the auspices of the German Government, to teach cotton-raising to the natives in a German colony there.

November 1. Mr. Washington started to-day for Columbia, S.C., to attend a conference of officials connected with the Charleston Inter-State and West Indian Exposition.

From Charleston Mr. Washington went to Tuskegee, but he must have started again almost immediately, for I find under date of November 8, "Mr. Washington reached New York this afternoon to speak at the General Howard dinner at the Waldorf." On the evening of November 10 he was a guest at the dinner which the Lotos Club gave to Mark Twain, and on November 11 he started for Charleston, W.Va., his old home. On November 14 he was back in New York again, and the next day went to Boston to speak before a Catholic literary society. On Sunday, November 16, he had returned to New York, and on Monday evening spoke before the Congregational Club. November 21 he went to Boston again.

This is the story of less than a month, taken at random, and it is probably far from complete, for I had no idea at the time that I would have occasion to refer to the record, and so wrote down only such items as occurred readily to me.

Mr. Washington frequently has to put forth much effort to make his dates connect. I remember once coming with him from Tuskegee to Washington, when he was to speak in Washington one night and in Columbus, O., the next. It was only by having a carriage at the door of the church where he spoke in Washington that we were able to make the train which we must take to leave that city. Our train was due in Columbus at 7:45 P.M., and Mr. Washington was to speak at 8 P.M. before the General Conference of the African Methodist Episcopal Church — an audience of four thousand persons. At 7:30 P.M. we were still forty miles from Columbus, and

Mr. Washington came to me with a distressed face, looking at his watch, and asked me to send a telegram from the next station at which the train stopped, saying that he would be late. The conductor happened to pass through the car just then, and, seeing us looking at our watches, glanced that way himself, and then reminded us that we had forgotten to set the hands back an hour at Pittsburg, where the time had changed. We were saved. We reached Columbus just on time. Mr. Washington was rushed off by a reception committee to have some supper and change his clothes, while a good bishop went to the auditorium to — as he said — "keep the audience singing" until Mr. Washington could get there.

People sometimes comment on the great amount of work which Mr. Washington does — the number of meetings which he addresses — but few know how much he really does accomplish in this way. In the fall of 1899 I happened to be in New Orleans with Mr. Washington, who had gone to that city to speak before the Longshoremen's Protective Benefit Association, an organization composed of about five hundred colored men who work upon the wharves of the city. Mr. Washington did not reach New Orleans until 8 A.M., and was driven from the station to the home of one of the officers of the Association, where a breakfast was served to which several guests had been invited to meet him. Starting at 10 A.M., he visited in turn Leland University, the New Orleans University, the Southern University, and the famous "Thomy Lafon" School.[1] At all but one of these places Mr. Washington spoke to the assembled students, besides going over the buildings. He next went to the City Hall, where, by appointment, he called upon the Mayor, who was to introduce him at the evening meeting. From the City Hall he was driven to Straight University, and addressed the students there. From Straight he went to the Fisk School, which, like all the schools which he had visited, is for colored pupils. Here he spoke from a balcony to the children from all the rooms gathered in the yard below. After this came an hour's reception at the office of the President of the Association, a conference with a committee interested in establishing an industrial school for colored children in New Orleans, and then dinner, to which a number of guests were invited. At 8 P.M. he made the address for which he had come to the city, before a large audience, and after that was the guest of a local society at a reception and banquet, at which he spoke again, this being the seventh public address which he had made that day.

I remember that in one of these talks Mr. Washington, referring to his belief that the most profitable education of the people of his race required various methods, according to the needs of the people under different conditions, told a story of an old colored preacher who was endeavoring to explain to his congregation how it was that the Children of Israel passed over the Red Sea safely, while the Egyptians, who came after them, were drowned. The old man said: "My brethren, it was this way. When the Israelites passed over, it was early in the morning, while it was cold, and the ice was strong enough so that they went over all right; but when the Egyptians came along it was in the middle of the day, and the sun had thawed the ice so that it gave way under them, and they were drowned."

At this, a young man in the congregation, who had been away to school and had come home, rose and said: "I don't see how that explanation can be right, parson. The geography that I've been studying tells us that ice never forms under the equator, and the Red Sea is nearly under the equator."

"There, now," said the old preacher, "that's all right. I's been 'spectin' some of you smart Alecks would be askin' jest some such fool question. The time I was talkin' about was before they had any jogafries or 'quators either."

"That good old man," said Mr. Washington, "was just trying in his simple manner to brush away the cobwebs which stood in the way of his logic. By some such method the misconceptions which hamper the course of education for the colored people must be removed, before the best results can be attained."

One chief element of Mr. Washington's success as a public speaker is his ability to tell a story well, and to have his stories illustrate just the point which he wants to make. People who have heard him speak several times sometimes wonder where he can get so many good stories. He is on the watch for them all the time, and whenever he hears one which can be used to good advantage in his talks, he fixes it in his mind.

Once on board a train in Virginia the talk touched, in some way which I have forgotten now, the subject of the old-time Southern servants. A man whose dress showed him to be a clergyman, and who I afterwards learned was the rector of one of the oldest and most distinguished Episcopal churches in the State, said that he had taken charge of the parish where he was then located during the year previous, and had moved into the rectory which went with the church. His predecessor had died in office, after a long pastorate. When the new family came to the rectory to live, they found there an old colored man who had been employed about the grounds for many years, and hired him to remain with them and continue at this work.

"One day last summer," the rector said, "my wife decided that she would like a certain shrub in the garden better if it stood in another place, and the next morning told old John to dig it up and move it. Along in the middle of the day she was out in the garden, and, seeing that the shrub had not been transplanted, said, 'John, don't forget to move that bush there as I told you.'

" 'Yes, Marm,' said John.

"That afternoon my wife was away from home. When she returned, late in the day, she saw that the plant had not been disturbed. Annoyed at the man's disregard of her wishes, she called him to her and spoke to him rather sharply:

" 'Didn't I tell you twice to move that shrub there over to the other side of the garden?'

" 'Yes, marm, you certainly did.'

" 'And you told me you would?'

" 'Yes, marm, I surely did.'

" 'What do you mean, then, by distinctly disobeying me?'

"My wife said the old man laid down the hoe he had been using, and, coming up in front of her, took off his hat and stopped a minute before he answered, as if he was struggling between his sense of duty to her and his own feelings. When he finally looked up, she was astonished to see that the tears were streaming down his face.

" 'I hope you'll 'scuse me, marm,' he said, 'I surely hope you will; but I can't move that bush.'

" 'Can't move that bush! Why?' It was not a large one.

"The old man dropped his hat and clasped his hands together. 'Oh, marm,' he said, 'my old missis, what's dead now, planted that bush right there. I can't dig it up.' "

The bush was not moved.

Mr. Washington was to speak that night in the Opera House in Richmond. Both Houses of the Virginia Legislature attended in a body, as did also the officials of the city government. Besides these there were many other prominent white men present, so that, without doubt, the audience was representative of the most intelligent white citizenship of the State. In the course of his address Mr. Washington made an eloquent appeal in behalf of the people of his race that no change in the school laws of the State be made to the detriment of the colored schools, and told this story of the old negro gardener who could not move the bush because his dead white "missis" set it out. More than one strong man in the audience was brushing the tears out of his eyes before the story was done, and felt no sensitiveness about having his neighbor see him do it.

That a person who has as much on his mind as Mr. Washington has should be absent-minded at times is not strange. The only wonder is that instances of this do not occur oftener than they do. The students at Tuskegee still tell with delight of one Sunday last winter, when, at the close of the forenoon services in the school chapel, while the young men and women were still seated waiting for the beginning of the Sunday-school exercises, Mr. Washington rose, and, calmly spreading an umbrella which he had with him, deliberately walked across the great chapel with the umbrella poised over his head, quite oblivious to the fact that he had not yet reached the outdoor air where it would be needed.

It was only human that a ripple of laughter should have swept over the room after the Principal had gone out, and that more than one student should have nudged his neighbor and whispered, "Did you just see Mr. B. T.? If we had done that, the Major" — the military instructor and disciplinarian of the school — "would have given us more than one warning. We'd have got three warnings, sure."

The term "Mr. B. T.," by which the students almost universally designate the Principal of the school, is used, I think, partly because it unconsciously expresses more of affection and regard than the more formal "Mr. Washington" would do, and partly because the presence at the school of the Principal's two brothers makes "Mr. Washington" rather an indefinite designation here. As a result we have, almost constantly, except in direct address to the men themselves, "Mr. B. T.," "Mr. J. H.," and "Mr. J. B." Mr. Washington's two brothers followed him to Hampton, and after they had graduated there, years ago, came to help him here. Mr. J. H. Washington is at the head of the industrial department. Mr. J. B. Washington is the postmaster at the school.

A striking illustration of the affection which Mr. Washington's pupils have for him, and of the devotion to the school and its work which he is able to inspire, came to my notice one day quite by accident. I had called at the home of a woman who was one of the early graduates of the school, and who is now married and living in Montgomery. The woman's little boy — perhaps three years old — came into the room while we were talking, bringing with him a long white paper roll, and, leaning against his mother's knee, said, in his childish way, "I wants to see Mr. Was'in'ton." The woman unwound the roll — it proved to be one of the large lithographs of Mr. Washington such as are displayed in shop windows to announce his addresses — and held it up where the boy could look at it. A moment later she said, "Do you love Mr. Washington?"

The child took his eyes from the picture, and, turning them up to his mother's face, said slowly, "Ess, I do."

"That's right," said the mother. "When you are big enough, mother's surely going to send you to be a little Tuskegean."

The country colored people throughout the South speak of Mr. Washington among themselves very generally as "Booker," or sometimes, quite regardless of comparative ages, "Uncle Booker." A young man employed by the Institute to go about among the people and interest them in the Tuskegee Negro Conference told me of one old woman whom he tried to get to promise to come to Tuskegee to a session of this Conference.

"If I come," said she, "will I see Uncle Booker?"

"Yes," said the young man, "you will see Mr. Washington, and hear him make a speech."

"I don't care nuffin 'bout no speech," the woman, who was almost twice Mr. Washington's age, said. "All I wants is jest to set 'way back in some corner where I can peek out an' look at Uncle Booker."

I think that one of the very best characterizations of Mr. Washington that I ever heard was that of a colored preacher who made the opening prayer at a meeting in the Opera-House in Charleston, West Virginia, when Mr. Washington was to address a great audience there. He thanked the Lord for having given the race "a leader with such a consecrated character and so much practical common sense."

Mr. Washington has spoken so much in public that his personal appearance is quite generally known by this time, but the comments of people who see him for the first time are sometimes amusing. A colored school-teacher in Texas, who had read and heard much about Mr. Washington, but had never seen him, came to Tuskegee to attend a session of the Negro Conference. While he was here he wrote back to a paper published in his town a letter in which was this sentence: "At first sight Booker T. Washington is a little disappointing. When we hear of a man who is the talk of two continents, who has earned a degree from Harvard University, who is a student of economics and sociology, who controls and is the soul of the greatest institution for the race, we are apt to think of him as a striking personality, a magnificent animal, so to speak. Booker T. Washington is not a type of that class. He is not as striking a man in appearance as others whom you will see at the Tuskegee Conference, but, all the same, when the meeting is over, there is no doubt who is the master, and why it is so. Mr. Washington is an artist in the skill with which he handles crowds, makes them get down to business, and impresses upon them his own ideas. He is emphatically a business man. He has a large stock of patience, a quick wit, and a faculty of getting at the meat of the cocoanut every time."

Mr. Washington was once to speak in a large Southern city to which, previous to that time, he had never been. A young colored man who had arranged for the meeting went to the station to meet Mr. Washington, but not finding him, as he supposed, went back home. Afterwards, when he saw Mr. Washington, and learned that he had really come on the train on which he had been expected, this man confessed in his chagrin, "Why, yes, I saw that man. We walked around each other three or four times, looking for each other, I suppose. But somehow I was expecting to see a big man, with a tall hat, and perhaps gold spectacles, and a general air of fame."

Mr. Washington, on his own part, was equally misled. He had seen this young man at the station, but so youthful-looking was he that he had thought him only a boy, and had never supposed he could be the person with whom he had been corresponding, and who had made all the arrangements for what proved to be an exceptionally large and successful meeting. This young man, Mr. Emmett J. Scott, afterwards became Mr. Washington's private secretary, and in that position has proved such an efficient helper that Mr. Washington has repeatedly said that he could not begin to do the great amount of work he does if it were not for Mr. Scott's assistance.

It is impossible that a man who is before the public as much as Mr. Washington is should not suffer at times from misrepresentation, either unintentional or willful. One of the most recent instances of this was a statement, rather widely printed, that Mr. Washington, in reply to an inquiry of President Roosevelt, had advised that only the best class of white men be appointed to office in the South. Mr. Washington has studiously kept out of politics, having declined offers of positions which would have tempted most men; and such an error as this is therefore particularly annoying. I happen to know beyond any question of doubt that, so far as Mr. Washington has ever expressed an opinion on this subject, it was that, when men of either race are to be appointed to office in the South, only the best men should be appointed.

Outlook, 69 (Nov. 9, 1901), 629–33.

1 Thomy Lafon (1810–93), a black merchant, moneylender, and real estate dealer, left most of his estate of almost half a million dollars to charity. A public school and an orphanage were named after him.

From Theodore Roosevelt

[Washington, D.C.] November 9, 1901

Personal.

My dear Mr. Washington: I am already investigating that Koester incident. The allegations more than surprised me, because I had happened to know that Koester during the last few years had staunchly upheld the rights of the colored man, as McLaurin[1] has done, and the people who have now attacked him about the lynching were at that time attacking him because he had announced he should appoint George Washington Murray as his first deputy. However, I am going to look carefully into the thing and see what action can be taken. Sincerely yours,

Theodore Roosevelt

I am confident South is changing.

TLpS   Theodore Roosevelt Papers   DLC.

1 John Lowndes McLaurin (1860–1934), a pro-business Democrat, was U.S. senator from South Carolina from 1897 to 1903.

From William Henry Baldwin, Jr.

[New York City] November 9th, 1901

Dear Washington: I received your message last night and again a second message this morning, in which you leave to me the use of your name in connection with the Southern Education Board. It was the unanimous sentiment that, inasmuch as the Southern Conference originated with white people and had always been exclusively white, that it would not be wise, at least at present, to raise the other question, but that, the sentiment of everybody connected with the work being for universal education for both blacks and whites, and inasmuch as Hampton and Tuskegee were represented by four members on the Board, more could be accomplished by keeping the Directors white, and recognizing the colored people through special field agents to be appointed. This, of course, has nothing whatever to do with the larger plans of the Board to be finally appointed, on which, of course, you will sit. You will remember that I declined to serve on this Southern Educational Committee until this week, but find it quite necessary for me to do so under the circumstances.

I enclose a circular giving the names of the members of the Southern Education Board and the names of those who attended the dinner at the Waldorf last night. The whole affair was a most brilliant success. Addresses were made by Messrs. Dabney, Alderman, Frissell, McIver, Bishop Doane[1] and Dr. Edward Abott.[2] The opinions were all one way, that is, for universal education by taxation.

In short, the purpose of the Southern Executive Board is to start a propaganda throughout the South, Dr. Alderman to act as Field Director in Louisiana, Dabney in Tennessee, Frissell in Virginia, McIver in North Carolina, & Georgia to be common territory to be worked on some plan to be devised; you and Dr. Dickerman to do such work as you can, in short, just such work as you are doing.

Each person working in the field is to receive a small salary to defray expenses and in some cases to make it possible to hire other help to relieve the agents of their own regular work.

Forty thousand dollars is to be spent each year for two years, for carrying out this plan: twelve thousand dollars will be spent at Knoxville under the direction of Dr. Dabney in a Bureau for Statistics, etc. Five thousand dollars in each one of the States referred to above, and a salary for the Executive Secretary, to be appointed by Mr. Ogden. I suppose, of course, he will appoint Mr. Murphy. There has been extraordinary interest manifested in this plan. It is a strong combination; all of one mind.

The Slater Board has met twice this week, the Peabody Board once, the Southern Education Board six or seven times.

The result of the Peabody and Slater meetings was that a Committee of three from the Peabody Board, Mr. Jesup, Dr. Gilman and myself, and three from the Slater Board, Joseph H. Choate, Richard Olney[3] and Dr. Curry, were appointed to confer and agree on a plan such as we have talked over together. Mr. Jesup has been ready to move at any time in the matter. The Peabody Board, however, is very slow to act, due principally to the unwieldy membership of its Board. The Committee is very much interested, however, and ready to pursue the matter further. Mr. Rockefeller is willing to co-operate in any way that may be suggested that is reasonable. The exact situation to-day is that the two Committees above referred to, with the Committee from the Southern Education Board, consisting of Messrs. Ogden and Peabody, will meet in the near future, perhaps with Mr. Rockefeller, and some plan will be determined upon. It will be impossible for me even to outline in a letter all of the complications and difficulties that are in the way. Time and patience and education of ourselves in the matter will alone bring out the final result.

It is planned to have a large attendance at the Southern Conference meeting next April, and the meeting will probably be held at Knoxville, although Athens, Georgia, will be the place if sufficient accommodations there can be found.

A very interesting result of this Conference is shown in the suggestion of the Baptist Home Mission Society that they will be glad to co-operate with any new Committee to be formed and to carry out their work under its advice or suggestion, excepting in so far as their strictly theological schools are concerned. Of course we would not undertake to direct those anyway.

Out of all this, I hope you will get a general idea of the situation. I shall be glad to talk it over with you fully when I see you. Yours very truly,

W H Baldwin Jr

TLS Con. 261 BTW Papers DLC.

[1] William Croswell Doane (1832–1913) was the Protestant Episcopal bishop of Albany beginning in 1869. He was a trustee of the Peabody Education Fund.

[2] Edward Abbott (1841–1908), a Congregational and Episcopal clergyman, was editor of *Literary World* from 1878 to 1888 and from 1895 to 1903.

[3] Richard Olney (1835–1917), of Massachusetts, was U.S. Attorney General from 1893 to 1895 and U.S. Secretary of State from 1895 to 1897.

From Robert Heberton Terrell

Washington, D.C. Nov. 10, 1901

My dear Mr. Washington, I saw the Attorney General yesterday and had a long talk with him. Our meeting was a very pleasant one in every way. I soon satisfied him of my eligibility, though I told him that I was not a candidate for the place under discussion. Your recommendation of me impressed him so much, however, that he has sent my name to the President for appointment. I told him that I felt rather shaky about taking such a place, but my diffidence and hesitation seemed to be in my favor rather than against me. So I am in for it, and I hope that my work will be such that you will never have occasion to regret your indorsement.

Just how deeply I appreciate your interest in me and how greatly indebted to you I am I am unable to tell you. I trust, however, that the day will come when I can show you that I am not lacking in gratitude. Any time that you feel that I can be of any service to your great work at Tuskegee or your general efforts to help our race please command me.

I enjoy immensely your eloquent silence on the famous dinner. Faithfully Yours,

R. H. Terrell

ALS Con. 213 BTW Papers DLC.

From Ida Belle Thompson McCall

Normal School, [Tuskegee, Ala.] Nov. 11, 1901

Mr. Washington, I have considered this matter very carefully and have decided to give up my work, not because I am not in sympathy with the work of the school nor because I can't do the work but because I donot feel that I have been treated right. I think you are simply trying to make an example of me in order to cower the rest of the teachers. I donot bow down and fawn where I donot care to. I may go without a word of commendation. I donot believe that Miss Porter could say anything against my work.

You say that the work is improving when you have not been in one class. It seems to me that your opinions of matters here are entirely the results of what some one says. I don't think the teachers feel that they are doing better work. They are all dissatisfied, some of them are just afraid to say so.

Ida T. McCall

ALS Con. 235 BTW Papers DLC.

From Francis J. Lamb[1]

Madison, Wis., Nov. 11, 1901

Dear Sir: I have just read your account of your life and work "Up from Slavery" with great interest and satisfaction. Perhaps the relish was intensified by memories thereby stirred of my own experience in getting a moderate education unassisted. I reside as you see by this letter, at Madison, Wisconsin, and did so at the time the great National Teachers Association held its meeting here, to which you refer in your autobiography.

I was present and remember well the occasion, the meeting, and your appearance and that speech. I write this letter because of an incident immediately connected with your appearance and address, which, while not mentioned by you, I think you will remember.

A gentleman over six feet high, as it seems to me now, and a state officer, Superintendent of Public Instruction of Georgia[2] (I think), spoke at the meeting just before you did. It was understood he would answer questions in regard to the situation of the races in the south, and several questions were propounded to him on that subject. I, and others, thought he evaded, showed he did not intend to answer, some close questions, and finally, in what seemed impatience, he said in regard to the negroes, in substance,

"They have got here the best they can show. You will see him for yourself."

This was said, (as it seemed to me) sneeringly and in a spirit and tone of contempt for you and your race. This must have occurred in your hearing, and the words and manner, it seemed to me, were an unwarranted, ungenerous and unprovoked fling and a sting inflicted upon a representative of an unfortunate race.

Soon after that remark you came before the audience, and my memory is distinct that your address was straight-forward, plain, based on the fundamental thought in your Atlanta speech — but not so felicitous to be sure — but direct and practical.

Naturally we human beings at the time thought if any ability existed in you, the ability would find a way to resent decently the heartless attack upon you and your people.

But you did not, nor did you attempt anything of the kind.

Men of observation and experience of course understood that such a course as you took disclosed you in two ways, as either, (1.) a man who, if he ever had had any spirit or manhood had been cowed by a dominant and heartless race and had accepted servilely the estimate a southern white official assigned you to — or, (2) as a man so wise and strong and absorbed in his plan and mission, and confident in its success in time, that the mean insinuation and scarcely concealed scorn of the insidious attack, that you were not conscious of the sting, or were instantly able to rise above it — cast it effectually out of your mind and deliver your message totally ignoring the affront. So you see we were at the time puzzled and simply sorry for you, because the case at the moment did not seem to furnish evidence to us to justify applying the second standard just mentioned for estimating you or your course in the incident.

But the grand development of the basal idea you then had, and which you have worked out so strenuously through the years since that time, with the success of demonstration, enables us now to estimate, as we do, your course and reticence on that occasion as inspired by masterful wisdom and self-abnegation and a lofty purpose to endure the slur silently, rather than distract attention for one moment, from your setting forth to the audience the great aim and purpose you had even then so profoundly set before you for solving one of the most, if not the most, serious, difficult and delicate social, civic and racial problems that Christian men were ever called upon to deal with practically.

In conclusion let me say, your success has been marvelous; and permit me to suggest there is danger that you, like all human beings, may be endangered from two things, success and praise. Success is good and ought to make you strong, unless it should beget conceit. Praise is not so safe a thing. I will venture one exhortation to you. It is this. In your exalted and tremendously responsible position, hold fast to the Bible, not as mere literature, but as the inspired record of God's dealings with and revelation of himself and his will to men to guide them in all matters, embodying therein as St. Jude says (R.V.),

"The faith once for all delivered to the Saints."

With high regards and best wishes and prayers for your success, I am, Yours very truly,

F. J. Lamb

TLS   Con. 203   BTW Papers   DLC.

1 Francis J. Lamb, a white lawyer residing in Madison, Wis., was born in New York in 1825.

2 Gustavus Richard Glenn.

From John A. Hertel

Naperville, Illinois, 11/13/01

My dear Sir: On the 11th inst. we received a telegram[1] from you in which you beg to insist that your picture as guest of President Roosevelt be not used in the advertisement of the Rams Horn. You stated you would write us and we have been patiently waiting for your letter. We do not see what objection you could have to this advertisement, although we are very sorry to write you that as far as the Rams Horn is concerned your telegram reached us too late. The advertisement was printed all complete and about 150,000 copies of it run so that even if it would have been possible to eliminate it, it would have cost a couple thousand dollars to do it.

Now, Mr. Washington, in deference to your opinion regarding the White House episode I would gladly eliminate this picture, yet for the life of me I cannot understand why you should object to it when every paper of any note throughout the United States has commented on this incident. The Southern press, I notice, unmercifully criticised the President, but in nearly every instance had something good to say about you. By simply putting the same thought into a picture we certainly do not make it as strong as some of the Northern papers.

I wish further to add that your telegram has held us back on our advertisement very much. If we do not get your letter by morning we will miss our opportunity for three or four high class journals in which we intended to put full page ads. The advertisement in the Rams Horn cost us $250.00 for a single issue. We had about decided to put the same ad in the Outlook, in the Review of Reviews, in the Christian Herald and in the Interior — all high class papers and every paper of which is in sympathy with you and your work. As stated above, it is a great mystery to me why you should object to having us push your book to the front. The time is certainly ripe and it is our policy to strike while the iron is hot.

If you have not written us when you get this letter I hope you will wire immediately withdrawing all objections so that we will be able to catch at least some of these great journals at this opportune time.

Please bear in mind that before Christmas people buy three times, or perhaps ten times as many books as at any other season of the year. Yours very truly,

J. L. NICHOLS & CO.
by J A Hertel

TLS Con. 201 BTW Papers DLC.

1 BTW to J. L. Nichols and Co., Nov. 11, 1901, Con. 541, BTW Papers, DLC.

From Whitefield McKinlay

Washington, D.C., Nov. 13, 1901

My Dear Mr. Washington: Terrell told me that he telegraphed you last night that he had received his appointment, and I presume you have seen the same in the papers. All of the papers are giving you the credit for the appointment and I presume the same had been inspired by the President or the Attorney General. I am very glad that two appointments were made but I regret exceedingly that the President should have made the mistake to appoint so notoriously an unfit man as Hewlett.[1] Some body has imposed upon the President. There are at least ten men that I would have placed ahead of him. He does not measure up to the requirements of the position in any sense and is almost as ignorant as Chase. The fact that at present he is a Justice of the Peace means nothing, inasmuch as it is easy under the present code to take a change of venue from him or to go to other justices, but under the new code each justice will get a share of the work and hence Mr. Hewlett will be subjected to severe tests, and I am quite sure he won't give satisfaction. From those who know him I have not heard one favorable comment on his appointment whereas all speak highly of Terrell. It was exceedingly gratifying to me to hear the white attorneys speak so highly of Terrell.

You deserve the thanks of the community for the work you have rendered in this matter. I presume you have heard that the President frankly told Chase that he could not appoint any man with a jail record.

When I was up to the White House on Monday with Smith[2] the correspondent of the News & Courier told me that he learned on excellent authority that Cheatham would not be reappointed. Both Green[3] and Cheatham ought to be superseded by better and stronger men. Such men as Gov. Pinchback, Cong. White, John Durham, Napier and Settle[4] and a few others of their type are a credit to our race and I do not think you will make any mistake by keeping them before the President. Very truly,

W McKinlay

Dictated.

TLS Con. 261 BTW Papers DLC.

[1] Emanuel Molyneaux Hewlett, a black attorney in Washington, was born in Massachusetts in 1848. In Nov. 1901 he was appointed a justice of the peace of the District of Columbia.

[2] Robert Lloyd Smith.

[3] John Paterson Green.

[4] Josiah Thomas Settle, a black politician and businessman of Memphis, was born in 1850 of a slave mother and her white owner. Settle's father manumitted his mother, and she and her children moved to Hamilton, Ohio, while the father continued to manage his Mississippi plantation, returning to Ohio when possible. Josiah Settle entered Oberlin College in 1868, but the death of his father in 1869 forced him to withdraw. Moving to Washington, he entered Howard as a sophomore, graduating in 1872 and taking a law degree in 1875. He taught in the Howard preparatory school, Freedmen's Bureau schools, and Washington public schools. Moving to Sardis, Miss., he practiced law and entered local Republican politics, winning a seat in the Mississippi legislature in 1883. In 1885 Settle moved to Memphis, where for a time he was the chief city prosecutor. From 1876 to 1912 he was a delegate to every Republican national convention except that of 1880, when he was a presidential elector. In the 1890s he became attorney for and director of the Solvent Savings and Trust Co., a black-owned and operated bank in Memphis. One of BTW's loyal supporters, he arranged for BTW's speaking engagements in Memphis.

To William Jennings Bryan

Tuskegee, Ala., Nov. 14, 1901

My Dear Sir: I thank you most earnestly for your contribution to our school and want to assure you that we shall try to make every dollar of it do all the work possible.

I thank you also for your encouraging words. I do not think that the matter of dining with the President will have any permanent bad effect upon our work. Already I find that people in the South are beginning to view the matter from a very sensible standpoint.

Enclosed I send you an editorial published recently in The Tuskegee News, which is the white democratic paper of this county. I think this editorial will interest you. Very truly yours,

Booker T. Washington

TLS   Con. 27   William Jennings Bryan Papers   DLC.

To John A. Hertel

[Tuskegee, Ala.] Nov. 16, 1901

My Dear Sir: As I wrote you a day or two ago, I have determined not to exploit the matter of my dining with the President. It was a personal matter and not one to be publicly exploited. For this reason I hope you will respect my wishes as regards the advertisement. I have no objection to any part of the advertisement except the use of the cut of myself and the President at the dinner table. I am sure you do not mean your statement that I am trying to prevent the pushing of the book to the front. I simply have scruples about using an incident which is not public for gainful exploitation. Very truly yours,

[Booker T. Washington]

TLc   Con. 201   BTW Papers   DLC.

To Whitefield McKinlay

Crawford House, Boston, Mass. November 20, 1901

My dear Mr. McKinlay: I am in receipt of your letter of recent date and thank you very much for writing me so fully and plainly. I do not understand myself why our recommendations were not followed more closely, but I presume it meant a compromise with the political element and I suppose we ought also to be thankful for what we did get, though I am sorry that matters did not go through wholly as we had planned them.

I wish you would make a careful note of matters that you think should be brought to the attention of the President by the time I am in Washington again. I shall be there within a reasonably short time and shall try to notify you ahead of my coming, altho I do not wish it generally known that I am to be there. This will be my address for a week. Yours truly,

Booker T. Washington

TLS Con. 4 Carter G. Woodson Collection DLC.

From William Henry Baldwin, Jr.

[New York City] Nov. 21st., 1901

Personal

Dear Mr. Washington: I both lunched and dined with the President, and for a half hour to three-quarters of an hour I held the floor in the smoking room after dinner. Secretary Root[1] and Henry Cabot Lodge[2] were there, and I explained to them in a manner that you understand, just what the conditions are in the South, my special point being that we Northerners cannot draw conclusions based on our own process of thinking, but that we must recognize the foundation of ignorance from which public opinion in the South gets expression. This seemed to be difficult for them to understand, but I laid it very bare.

I also spoke particularly about the dinner at the White House. The President asserted that he had never dreamed of the effect one way or the other; in short, did not understand that it meant anything to anybody, except as a matter of convenience to himself and courtesy to you for what you have done. I told them frankly that I would not have invited you at that time, but would have aimed to do so at a later date, but that inasmuch as it had been done, I was glad of it, and that we would make good use of it in educating

321

the public to a clearer sense of conditions existing in the South. Secretary Root told me afterwards, privately, that he was very much interested in what I had to say on the subject. Yours very truly,

W H Baldwin Jr

TLS Con. 792 BTW Papers DLC. Written at the top of the letter in Baldwin's hand: "The Prest. is still worried about those Oyster Bay colored persons."

1 Elihu Root (1845–1937) was Secretary of War from 1899 to 1904, Secretary of State from 1905 to 1909, and U.S. senator from New York from 1909 to 1915. Despite Root's public approval of disfranchisement, BTW maintained a good relationship with him and used his friendship effectively in the Liberian financial crisis of 1908–9 and the establishment of the American protectorate. (See Harlan, "BTW and the White Man's Burden," 454–55.)

2 Henry Cabot Lodge (1850–1924) was U.S. senator from Massachusetts from 1893 to 1924.

An Interview with Portia Marshall Washington in the Birmingham *Age-Herald*

Wellesley [Mass.] November 23 [1901]

BOOKER WASHINGTON'S DAUGHTER IN SCHOOL

While Booker T. Washington has been one of the most talked of men in the country, public attention has naturally not been altogether withdrawn from his daughter, Portia, who recently entered college here as a special student. Soon after the Roosevelt dinner, Miss Washington, began indeed to be literally besieged by press representatives and curious folk who wished to "talk the whole matter out" with her. But a telephone message sent from New York to the embarrassed young girl, put a prompt end to this. "Do not talk to anybody sent out by newspapers," said her father's voice over the wire, "about the dinner at Washington, or about our opinions concerning the attitude of the whites in the matter of social intercourse with the negro."

Portia Washington has a very pleasant room with Mrs. Brio[1] in Howe street, just outside the college grounds and she takes her meals across the street with three professors of the college — Katherine Lee Bates,[2] the well known writer, Emily Balch,[3] a distinguished sociological essayist, and Katherine Coman,[4] president of the College Settlement Association of the United States — all women of culture who have been especially kind to this granddaughter of slavery, and child of the regenerate colored race.

The fact that Miss Washington was thus taken into the inner-circle of the faculty, inspired a mischievous rumor to the effect that the college was trying to rebuke the student body for drawing a color line in her case. But this seems to be wholly without foundation for Wellesley has had other colored students, and there is now in the college hall eating at the college table a colored girl about whom nobody thinks twice.

The real reason why a room in the college hall and a place at the table has not been given to Portia Washington is because as a special student she is not entitled to them. Moreover she herself prefers, she says, to live outside, because it is less distracting.

"I certainly have not had the slightest reason to feel that there might be such a thing as a color line here," she said. "Everybody has been as nice as possible to me, and I am having a very pleasant time. I am studying German, musical theory and the piano, and it is my great wish to make such progress that I may be really useful to my father at Tuskegee when I go back. I have already taught a little there, you know; but I felt a desire to be further educated myself before settling down to the teaching of others as a life work.

"Besides, my father has been very anxious to have me attend college. He believes in college education for girls where it is possible for them to have it; and my mother, you know, is a graduate of Fisk University. But for most of the girls at Tuskegee father sees that the industrial education and that which emphasizes the household arts is most needed. None the less, he encourages further study whenever it is possible for the student to get it. Of course, Tuskegee's great aim is to fit girls to teach others who have been without opportunity how to live higher and better lives. The mind of the negro woman, as we see it, takes more readily, though, to music and to domestic science than to the subjects which could be classed as more particularly academic, and the poor girls with whom we have to deal sorely need just such instruction as they are getting under my father.

"Direct teaching in manners and morals, like that given by Mrs.

Bruce, our dean, who is the widow of Senator Bruce, is also a very important factor in the uplifting of the people. The conditions out of which these students have, many of them, come are squalid and miserable beyond the imagination of Northerners. A large number of the girls have never known in their poor homes any of the refining influences. Perhaps their parents are living in sin. And the climatic conditions in the South, added to the temperamental laxity in manners that is undoubtedly a characteristic of the submerged negro woman, all tend to make the labors of Mrs. Bruce exceedingly valuable.

"Very often when the girls come to Tuskegee they lie atrociously. But Mrs. Bruce is especially stern about falsehoods, and the girl who does not very soon evince a desire to be truthful is sent back to her home. As for the statement recently made by a Northern writer to the effect the negro girls in the South are all shockingly immoral — that's a gross exaggeration. But heredity is a powerful factor for evil as well as for good and we have had too short a time at the work to have been able to educate the colored girl in every case out of a proneness to moral laxity.

"The educated negro woman who is good, however, has a conception of purity which seems to me to compare very favorably with that of the white girl of the same class. I have had ample opportunity to make observations from the inside of both a Northern and a Southern school for girls and I firmly believe that a colored girl of the South who has once realized with her heart and mind the sinfulness of sin and the beauty of womanly delicacy and restraint is often more pure in mind and deed than the Northern girl. I was at the practice school connected with the Framingham Normal School for three years and I saw there, of course, a great deal of boarding school life. It was at Framingham, too, that I received the only notion I have ever had in the North as to what a color line might be. And then the implied snub came from a Southern girl.

"The girl's home was in South Carolina and though she was civil to me she was never cordial as the other girls. And once when her brother came to visit her, he declared up and down, as I afterward learned, that he would not go to the table while I was there. He had never eaten at the same table as a colored person, he said, and he never would. But there was nothing for him to eat and his sister finally persuaded him, I was told, to come in and not make a scene. I didn't mind this at all, you know, for the Southern woman's feeling about social intercourse with colored people is a thing beyond her control. Education has not been so effectively directed to this weakness of hers that she is able to overcome it. For her to grow broad, as for the colored girl to grow delicate, will take time.

"It seemed to me last year when I went back home after a long absence and myself taught some of the classes at Tuskegee that there is not so very much, after all, to be said to the superior credit of the Northern white girl as compared with the poor colored girl of the South, when the difference in early environment and in heredity is taken into consideration."

Miss Washington wore a simple close-fitting walking skirt and a becoming shirt waist of green and pink organdie, trimmed with narrow white satin ribbon, on the day of this talk, and was herself so refined in appearance as to suggest quite naturally a question as to Tuskegee's influence upon the taste of the girls there graduated.

"The students soon become very careful about their clothes and most particular in the small matters of the toilet," she explained. "The uniform is dark blue percale, trimmed with red braid and it is made to fit very nicely with a shirt waist and a full skirt. The girls are early taught dressmaking, and they almost all, after they leave the school, make their own clothes and those of the family. I myself cut and make all my dresses. But the best work which springs from the school is undoubtedly that which comes as a result of the object lessons in neatness and social purity furnished by the consecrated lives of the graduates."

Miss Washington has a good many old friends among the girls at Wellesley, and she has received several invitations not ordinarily extended to special students. But she seems to feel, in spite of the cordiality which has everywhere been shown her, that college girls of the North are as a class inclined to be a bit selfish and rather thoughtless when they are themselves having a good time of the students who are not quite so much "in it" as are they.

"At Tuskegee," she remarked naively, "girls in the same school always speak to each other whether they have been introduced or not. And Southern girls are certainly in every case far less cold than are Northerners. I have no personal grievance, for I have been asked to many receptions, and everybody, as I have said, is kindness itself; but I have wondered a little why the very fact of common interest in an Alma Mater should not be a stronger bond from the very first than it seems to be here."

Portia Washington is 18 years old and her father's only daughter. She received her Shakespearian name because of Booker T. Washington's great admiration for the noble heroine of "The Merchant of Venice." To her the principal of Tuskegee is not at all a personage before whom to stand in awe. "We joke at home," she said, easily, "about father's silence. I suppose he is thinking always of the work when he sits so still, speaking not a word. But it is the public which sees him at his best. When he loses himself in his subject he is much more animated than in the family.

"I like his book, though, don't you?" she continued. "I, myself," this with eagerness, "want very much to write. Miss Chesnutt, the daughter of the well known colored writer, who graduated at Smith College last year, is now the teacher of English at Tuskegee, and I asked her not long ago if she thought she would ever write. She told me that she didn't believe any of her father's gift had come down to her! But I am all the time hoping some of my father's literary ability may fall to my lot. Above everything I would like that, though I am greatly interested in my music and practise two hours a day now. I'm working very hard on Bach's inventions for technique, but my favorite composer is Chopin.

"I differ from the rest of my family in that I am an Episcopalian. My father is not directly connected nowadays with any single denomination, but I came to be intensely interested while I was at Framingham in the Episcopal church and I was confirmed there. The music and the stately ritual strongly attracted me."

In manner Miss Washington is shy though very sweet and pleasant. Her resemblance to her father is marked. Like him, too, she becomes animated only when she is a little excited. But that she has a fine mind is evident and that she too is ardently devoted to the cause to which her parents are giving their lives there can be no doubt.

Birmingham *Age-Herald*, Dec. 1, 1901, 11. Written by a correspondent of the New York *Sun*.

1 Mrs. B. E. Brehaut.

2 Katherine Lee Bates (1859–1929) was a graduate of Wellesley who taught there from 1891 to 1925. She was the author of several volumes of poetry.

3 Emily Greene Balch (1867–1961), an economist and sociologist, was later international secretary of the Women's International League for Peace, and a 1946 recipient of the Nobel Peace Prize.

4 Katherine Coman (1857–1915), an economic historian and reformer, was a member of the Wellesley faculty from 1880 to 1913. She was the author of several texts in history and economics, and was active in social settlement work and the promotion of the rights of working women.

From John Stephens Durham

Philadelphia   Nov. 24, 1901

Dear Doctor Washington: If you can see your way clear to help me in an active way, I shall apply for reappointment to the diplomatic service. If, for any reason of your own, you cannot so help me, I think that I shall not apply. In reaching this conclusion, I have been impelled by two or three considerations. I think, first of all, that I can do the work better than any other public work. I speak German but weakly; still, I know enough to feel assured that in less than a year, I could work in the language. Spanish and French are familiar tools with me. I handle them vigorously though, I fear, with an awkwardness characteristically American. In international law, I have worked conscientiously several years. I have had practical experience in both the consular and the diplomatic branch of the foreign service. I would feel more confident, in view of these experiences, therefore, that my work would be satisfactory. Then, there is the consideration that, while one does generally apply for a post named, diplomatic appointments are often shifted around by the President. Then there is the thought that, perhaps, Mr. Roosevelt may, before he leaves office, so impress his ideas upon Congress as to open the way for a diplomatic career. In the foreign service, a colored man could work his way to distinction free from many of the inconveniences and real discouragements which baffle us when we try to do good work here at home.

It is a tradition in Washington that our President offered Mr. Douglass the Brazilian Mission. I think that Mr. Cleveland named Taylor to be Minister to Bolivia,[1] but that the Senate did not confirm. If these two nominations were proposed, then Mr. Roosevelt will not be without precedents.

I write to you, rather than wait to see you because I think the time intervening between now and my proposed trip to Boston precious. It may be that I will not get off at all. I have just been made a referee in a case of some importance and the fact that the agreement on a colored lawyer is an innovation requires that I do exceptionally judicious work. I have an ugly murder case next Monday and I will take up my hearings in the reference as soon as I get out of the criminal court. How long, the hearings will last, of course I cannot say. I want you to know about the reference though I am saying nothing about it here. The less fuss we make about "the progress of the race," the more progress, I think.

Pardon this long letter. Do give me as earnest consideration as you can. Very truly yours,

John S. Durham

ALS   Con. 195   BTW Papers   DLC.

1 In 1893 President Cleveland nominated the black Democratic leader Charles H. J. Taylor as minister to Bolivia, but the Senate refused to confirm him. Denying that he would be persona non grata in Bolivia on account of his race, Taylor wrote Cleveland: "I sincerely trust, Mr. President, that you will not allow certain Senators who are displeased with you about the Monetary question to take their spite out upon me and my people." (Nov. 9, 1893, Grover Cleveland Papers, DLC.) Cleveland decided, however, to appoint a white man, and he appointed Taylor recorder of deeds for the District of Columbia, a traditionally black position.

To Oswald Garrison Villard

Crawford House, Boston, Mass. November 25, 1901

My dear Mr. Villard: I have just been reading the addresses delivered on the occasion of the one hundredth anniversary of the Evening Post, and among the addresses I was deeply interested in the reference which you made to your father. It was very touching, and recalled to my mind his deep interest in Tuskegee and in all that concerned my race. What a satisfaction it would have been if he could have been present on that occasion to have witnessed the results of his efforts, but I am sure you will agree with me in saying that no effort put forth in the right direction is ever lost.

I hope to see you when I am in New York again. Yours very truly,

Booker T. Washington

TLS   Oswald Garrison Villard Papers   MH.

Edgar Webber to Margaret James Murray Washington

Guthrie O.T. Nov. 26 1901

Dear Mrs. Washington, I write to you in regard to a little personal matter to which I desire that you should call Mr. Washington's attention when it is convenient for you to do so. I always regarded you as one of my best friends at Tuskegee and I know I can depend upon you to bring this matter up.

Some time ago, my attention was called to a revised edition of "The Story of My Life and Work" one of the books which I assisted Mr. Washington to get in shape for the Publishers while I was at Tuskegee. I note that the revision cut out my picture which occurred in a group of Scott, Fortune and Webber and the would-be-picture of Laing Williams substituted in the place of my own.[1] While I *dont* care much about the circumstance of leaving my cut out of the book, still I am naturally curious to know why it was done. Then too it would not be so bad if the revisor or revisors of the book had also taken my name out of the list of illustrations. In the list of illustrations on page 9, of the book my name still appears as one of the group of Scott, Fortune, and Webber, but on turning to page 43 the noble face of S. Laing Williams greets you instead of that of Webber. This of course was an oversight of the revisors. I know it was an oversight because in the back in the index where the names of all persons mentioned in the book are given under the head of "W" I *find not* my name although Mr. Washington mentioned me three times in the text of the book, once in a footnote on page 13 and twice in chapter 9, page 113 and 114. It would appear from these that the revisor was determined to obscure me if possible. As I said before I am curious to know the reason of all this although I am not losing any sleep over the matter. To be frank, I am of the opinion that a little spite or envious work is being done against me for which Mr. Washington, I do not believe is responsible. The group illustration from which my "cut" was left out has this subscription at the bottom of the page: "A Trio of Brilliant Colored Americans, Enthusiastic Supporters of Mr. Washington." Now if I was left out because not thought brilliant like the other two, why well and good, but if I was left out because not thought to be still a supporter of Mr. Washington and his idea of industrial education then a grave mistake has been made. I have always, everywhere I have been since leaving Tuskegee, spoken in the highest terms of Mr. Washington and the work at Tuskegee. I believe in Industrial Education for the masses of our people. I have always believed in it since I first gave the subject any thought. It is a principle I believe in, it would be inconsistent for me to do otherwise than speak well of the work.

Mr. Washington and I did have a little dispute over a little account which he owed me, but I am sure he is not small enough to do spite work for that reason.

I am not like some, because I am away from Tuskegee, do all I can to run it down. I believe in the work and the good Mr. Washington is doing before I came there, while I was there, and ever since I left there. I never have spoken a word against the work always in praise of it, this I would have to do in order to be true to principle even if Mr. Washington and I should become to be personal enemies.

I realized more than anybody that my work at Tuskegee was finished when I was through with *MS* of that book. I have reason to believe that my work there was never allowed to appear to Mr. Washington in its true light by one of his close advisors and employees. I am doing nicely here in the Law practice, building up a practice among both white and colored. My health is much improved and still improving. Very truly

Edgar Webber

Kindest regards to yourself, family and friends.

E. W.

Would be glad if you would show Mr. Washington this letter.

ALS   Con. 246   BTW Papers   DLC.

1 See above, 1:xix.

From Henry Hugh Proctor

First Congregational Church, Atlanta, Ga. Nov. 26, 1901

My dear Mr. Washington: There is an attempt here to create a sentiment to remove the colored federal office-holders in Atlanta merely on the ground of their color. Of course we are all anxious that this should not be done. I am specially interested in the case of Hon. C. C. Wimbish, collector of the port, a member of my church, and whose office we visited when you were here. There seems to be considerable effort on the part of some white men to get his place. There is nothing against him. His office has been conducted in a throughly satisfactory manner even to the white public. He feels that there is need of alertness lest his opponents succeed, and he feels that a word from you to the President will do him great good.

I trust you will see your way clear to grant him this favor. It will be a kindness we will all remember, and a help to our race-cause. Yours very truly,

H. H. Proctor

ALS   Con. 206   BTW Papers   DLC.

From Robert Heberton Terrell

Washington, D.C. November 26, 1901

My dear Mr. Washington, I thank you very much for the letter from Mrs. Stearns. I hope you will allow me to keep it among my letters of congratulations. Mrs. Stearns was very, very kind to me when I was a student in Cambridge and I think of her always as one of the best of my friends.

I am very much gratified at the way that my appointment has been received throughout the country and I am especially proud of the fact that it was brought about through you and that the press has given you full credit for it. It means a great deal to our race to have a man of its own to speak for it in the matter of official preferment. Your advent into matters of this kind is a splendid thing

331

for educated young men. They should take on fresh hope and a new courage. The appointment of Mr. Hewlett and myself as Justices in an inferior court will surely be followed by the appointment of colored men to similar places in superior courts.

With best wishes for you and your work always, and a deep sense of gratitude for your unselfish interest in me, I am, Yours sincerely,

Robt. H. Terrell

TLS   Con. 261   BTW Papers   DLC.

From Edwin Anderson Alderman

New Orleans   November 27th, 1901

My Dear Sir: I have wanted to meet you for a number of years, and I have especially wanted to meet you and to see Tuskegee, since I have made my residence in Louisiana. Your sanity, and scholarship, and sympathy, and moral earnestness have appealed to me most genuinely. I feel that the education of the colored man in the right fashion is perhaps, our greatest question, and the wisdom with which we handle it will more effectively shape our life than any other thing. I have been willing to follow your guidance unreservedly. I want to see you, or to hear from you with reference to your ideas of the Southern Education Board, with the work which both of us have to do. I have just written to Dr. McIver, with the request that he ask you to meet us in Atlanta about the 10th of December. Very truly yours,

Edwin A. Alderman
President

TLS   Con. 188   BTW Papers   DLC.   Written on stationery of Tulane University. Docketed in E. J. Scott's hand: "Told him you'd be away until Jan. 12 '02, and that had forwarded letter to you. 11/29."

The Lyrics to a Song by Keith and Christian[1]

[Petersburg, Va., ca. November 1901]

TEDDY'S MISTAKE OR BOOKER'S RECEPTION
BY KEITH & CHRISTIAN

SUNG TO THE MUSIC OF COON, COON, COON

Rough Rider, Mr. Roosevelt, was searching out for fame,
Invited one black gent to dine, Booker Washington was his name;
  He took him to the dining hall where a sumptuous lunch was spread,
The paramount issues of the day were then in order read.
  Next came the negro problem; they agreed it must be solved:
Now Ted, said he, come let me see the amount that is involved;
  'Tis not a money question, but a social thing with me,
I'll show these white folks in the South who shall dine with me.

  CHORUS—For he is a coon, coon, coon, and Booker is his name,
        Coon, coon, coon, I need him in the game.
      Coon, coon, coon, now I am not to blame
        For being born a white man instead of a coon, coon, coon.

Teddy is good at shooting lions and riding a vicious horse,
He made a dandy soldier, but, he can't be a negro's boss,
  For he stands on a social basis with the whole of the African race;
Now isn't he a nice gentleman to fill McKinley's place.
  He is thinking of taking a Southern tour, but he must forget it soon,
For the South don't like a President that dines at home with a coon;
  He had better go West and show himself no more,
Because his finish we can see in nineteen hundred and four.

  CHORUS—Caused by a coon, coon, coon, and this coon has lots of fame,
        Coon, coon, coon, he is not to blame.
      If Ted could change his color he would be the same;
        He loves Booker Washington cause he is a coon, coon, coon.

Jeff Davis was our President, a noble man was he,
Abe Lincoln was the Yankey that set the coons all free;
  McKinley was a hero, he left us all too soon,
And Roosevelt, now our President, takes pride to dine a coon.
  No doubt he thought 'twould bring him fame, but his job will be the price,
Before he dines again with him he had better think twice,
  For he must remember he is still on American ground,
And the South will say to him, go way back and sit down.

333

CHORUS—He loves a coon, coon, coon, now do you think it's fair,
Coon, coon, coon, sitting in Teddy's chair;
From a coon, coon, coon, such things we must bear,
Just because this Rough Rider loves a coon, coon, coon.

PD   Con. 978   BTW Papers   DLC.

1 Keith and Christian, composers of comic songs in Petersburg, Va., sent this song to BTW on Dec. 17, 1901, with a cover letter that stated this was their "latest success in Coon Songs." They asked for fifty cents for the copy but said BTW could have it gratis. (Con. 978, BTW Papers, DLC.)

To the Editor of the Boston *Transcript*

Crawford House [Boston, ca. Dec. 2, 1901]

THE LATE MRS. GEORGE L. STEARNS

To the Editor of the Transcript: In the death of Mrs. George L. Stearns of Medford, Mass., my race loses one of the truest and wisest friends it has ever had. It has been my privilege to know Mrs. Stearns intimately for a number of years, and I never knew a sweeter or more generous soul. Her interest in the Tuskegee Institute began in 1882, when the institution was practically unknown. She had faith in the effort from the beginning, and never failed to manifest that faith until the time of her death. She lived day by day in the work that her noble husband did for freedom and the Union.

Even in the most trying period of the Negro's life as a freedman she never for a moment lost faith in the ultimate triumph of the right. I think no good cause that had for its object the helping of the South was ever turned from her door unhelped. Often when her departing physical strength could hardly permit it, she would make almost any sacrifice to hear about the progress of the work in the South. I have been often surprised at her intimate knowledge of institutions at the South, and equally surprised at the large number of these schools that she helped.

A few days ago a colored man, Mr. Robert H. Terrell, a graduate of Harvard, was appointed in Washington to a responsible judicial position. Soon after this appointment was made, I was surprised to learn that it had been largely through Mrs. Stearns's generosity that Mr. Terrell was enabled to go through Harvard. She had no bitter words for the South or for anyone.

One by one, those who were the first to assist my race to freedom and education pass away, but they leave the world richer and better for having lived. No one could spend five minutes in the presence of Mrs. Stearns without being made a better man or woman.

Booker T. Washington

Boston *Transcript*, Dec. 2, 1901, 8.

From Charles Hallock[1]

Jersey City, Dec 2, 1901

Dear Sir: Does Brer Washington know that a colored man (negro) is on the Peary Polar Expedition. He has been with that intrepid explorer since 1898, and is pronounced a "first class man" by his chief.

Now, who would have thought of an African son of the South going up to the North Pole, or have imagined that he could stand the cold? Why, it beats Hannibal crossing the Alps.

So, the above adds another laurel to the colored man's modern winnings. As I wrote you once last year, he makes a splendid follower to a competent leader. He bends readily to mental superiority. I would like to have the fact I mention about Peary more widely known. The colored mans name is Matthew Hanson.[2]

I shall be in Mobile by the end of this month, and am booked for a visit with Pres't Woodward of Birmingham Iron Company, later on. En route I mean to look in on your Tuskegee Institute, and will lecture to your students, if you care to have me do so, on my experience with the James City (N.C.) Negro colony during 1892–8. I could give some helpful suggestions, I know.

I am to be a guest of the Mobile Steamship men, Murray, Wheeler & Co., and the City Board of Trade. They want a magazine article written on their new boom. So, RR gives me transportation. Yours truly

Chas. Hallock

ALS Con. 201 BTW Papers DLC.

1 Charles Hallock (1834–1917) was an editor of several outdoor magazines, including *Western Field and Stream.*

2 Matthew Alexander Henson (1866–1955) accompanied Robert E. Peary on every trip except the first that the white explorer made in search of the North Pole. Born on a tobacco farm in Charles County, Md., Henson was working in a Washington, D.C., hat store when Peary hired him as his valet on an expedition to survey a Nicaraguan canal. Peary valued Henson for "his intelligence and faithfulness, combined with more than average pluck and endurance." (Peary, *Northward over the "Great Ice,"* 1:47.) Henson showed remarkable versatility as cook, barber, dog-trainer, sleigh-builder, and hunter, and he was the only member of the Peary expeditions who could interpret the Eskimo language. It was only fitting then that Peary selected Henson to accompany him and four Eskimo sled-drivers on the last dash to the Pole on Apr. 6, 1909. As a result of this exploit Peary was widely honored and retired with the rank of admiral; his black companion was given a dinner and a gold watch. After two years of odd jobs, he received appointment as a clerk in the New York custom house. He retired in 1936 on a pension of $1,000 a year. Four congressional bills to give him adequate recognition and compensation all failed. In his introduction to Henson's autobiography, *A Negro Explorer at the North Pole* (1912), xix–xx, BTW said too optimistically: "I am proud and glad to welcome this account of his adventure from a man who has not only honored the race of which he is a member, but has proven again that courage, fidelity, and ability are honored and rewarded under a black skin as well as under a white."

From Ralph Waldo Tyler[1]

Columbus, O. Dec. 3, 1901

Personal

My Dear Sir: Since you have placed the confidence that you have in me, and since it is generally accepted that you stand closer to the President than any other member of our race, I want to apprise you of a matter in confidence. I have no objection, however, to you relating the facts to the president, should perchance you meet again to talk over matters of interest to our race.[2] It is this:

Senator Hanna will be a candidate for president. As to this, just now, there is no possible chance for doubt. I have it straight, and further I have it that, so far as our people is concerned, his plans are pretty well formed.

Every colored office-holder, as you are doubtless aware, holds his appointment upon the recommendation of Senator Hanna, and every such one, at the proper time will work for his interests, this includes Cheatham, Lyons, Green, of Ohio, Powell,[3] of New Jersey, Adams,[4] of Illinois, et al., all of whom will be assisted by Bishop Arnett. The plan is, and they confidently bank on it, to go to the next National convention with a solid delegation from the South for Senator Hanna. I am confident that these men, at least those now in this country and holding office, already have their instructions, and while certain ones who are anxiously awaiting reappointments at the hands of President Roosevelt may be inactive pending their reappointment, as soon as reappointment, they will, in a quiet way, begin to exert their influence for Senator Hanna, for as you well know, with the possible exception of Minister Powell, all are professional politicians, selfish politicians, who consider their own interests first and those of the race as a secondary and unimportant matter.

In '96 I represented this paper at the National convention in St. Louis, and it was then that I became perfectly disgusted with the professional colored politician and office holder, who danced every time Mr. Hanna cracked the whip.

As a rule, I found that they were immoral and greatly over rated, and at the time I remarked to Mr. George A. Myers,[5] who had charge of the "influencing" of colored delegates, that my idols had been shattered; that colored men whom I had looked upon as the personification of greatness, were bar room patrons who frequently were in their "cups." Of the whole lot of "prominent" colored politicians who attended that convention, I observed but two who bore themselves with the dignity that reflected credit upon themselves and the race, and those two were Bruce and Lynch. And they, as perhaps you will recall, cut no figure at that convention.

I have every reason to know that the same influence? that was used by Senator Hanna in '96 to corral the brother in black for the late President McKinley, will prevail for the Senator's personal interests, and that a selfish policy, rather than a broad race interest and principle will actuate the colored men now in office, and whose appointments are due to the direct dictation of Senator Hanna.

I simply give you this for your own information, knowing that you have the interest of the whole race at heart. The only way to circumvent these colored politicians, and the power of the A. M. E. Church, which will be exerted through the influence of Bishop

Arnett, is to have "new faces at the window," new men — a higher type of Negro manhood, men who place race advancement far above [that] of temporary personal political gain. Very truly yours

Ralph W Tyler

TLS   Theodore Roosevelt Papers   DLC.

1 Ralph Waldo Tyler, a black journalist and politician, was born and reared in Columbus, Ohio, and began working for the white Columbus *Evening Dispatch* in 1884. He remained with the *Dispatch* for the next seventeen years, eventually becoming assistant manager and confidential secretary to the publisher, Robert Wolfe. From 1901 to 1904 Tyler was a reporter for the *Ohio State Journal*, also owned by Wolfe.

Tyler's active support of Theodore Roosevelt and opposition to Senator Joseph B. Foraker led to his appointment, at BTW's suggestion, as auditor for the navy in 1905, a position he held until the purge of black officeholders in 1913 during the Wilson administration. In the meantime he continued to write for several white and black newspapers.

Tyler was a shrewd politician whose main loyalty was to his own political career. He generally supported BTW, but often flirted with the Tuskegean's opponents as well. During the controversy over the Brownsville incident in 1906, Tyler bent over backwards to support Roosevelt and BTW and to blame some black critics for keeping the nation inflamed over the matter. In the 1908 Republican presidential campaign he was the "bag man," carrying Republican funds to black newspapers in the Midwest to win their editorial support of Taft. The Taft administration rewarded Tyler with an influence over black patronage appointments rivaling BTW's own, particularly after BTW became discouraged by Taft's steady removal of black officeholders in the South.

During World War I Tyler was associated with Emmett J. Scott when Scott became special assistant to the Secretary of War. Tyler went to France as a war correspondent and reported on the activities of black troops.

2 BTW forwarded the letter to Roosevelt and added: "The writer is a clean, clearheaded colored man who holds a responsible position on the Columbus Dispatch." (Dec. 8, 1901, Theodore Roosevelt Papers, DLC.)

3 William Frank Powell, born in New York in 1845, was district superintendent of schools in Camden, N.J., during the 1880s and introduced manual training into the curriculum. He later taught at the Camden High and Training School from 1886 to 1894. He was minister to Haiti from 1897 to 1905 and chargé d'affaires to Santo Domingo during the same period.

4 Cyrus Field Adams was born in Louisville, Ky., in 1858. He moved to St. Paul, Minn., in 1885, where he helped his brother John Quincy Adams edit the *Western Appeal* (later *Appeal*). In 1888 Cyrus Adams became manager of the branch office of the newspaper in Chicago. Although it was a St. Paul newspaper, the *Appeal* printed Chicago news and maintained the Chicago branch until 1913. Until the rise of Robert Abbott's Chicago *Defender*, it was probably the most successful black newspaper in Chicago. Adams was three-time president of the National Afro-American Press Association, succeeding his brother, who had held the position in 1880. He was active in the National Afro-American Council and claimed to be the only life member. In 1900 he was elected town clerk in Chicago, winning over the Democratic candidate

by appealing to ethnic voters in their own languages. That year he also became a member of the Republican National Advisory Committee and was a party stalwart. In 1901 BTW helped him gain appointment as assistant register of the treasury in Washington, D.C., a position he held until 1912, when he returned to Chicago as deputy collector of customs until his retirement in 1932.

5 George A. Myers (1859–1930), barber and Republican politico, was born in Baltimore, the son of a prominent free Negro, Isaac Myers, who, as owner of a shipyard, helped organize black workers and fought segregation in the labor movement. George Myers moved in 1879 to Cleveland, where he worked as a barber. In 1888 he became owner of the barbershop in the Hollenden Hotel, a gathering place of prominent white Clevelanders, including Mark Hanna. The barbershop was one of the most modern in America at the time. Telephones were even installed at the chairs for busy clients. The list of famous individuals who had shaves or haircuts from Myers included eight presidents from Hayes to Harding.

In 1892 Myers was a delegate to the Republican national convention, where he cast a key vote that gave victory to the Hanna-McKinley forces. Myers became Hanna's champion among black Republicans, even buying an important black vote to insure Hanna's election to the Senate. Frequently offered political spoils during the McKinley administration, including, at BTW's suggestion, control of the black organization of the Republican national committee, Myers chose to stay in Cleveland and run his lucrative business. After the deaths of McKinley and Hanna he played only a minor role as a Republican stalwart.

A conservative on racial matters at the national level, Myers worked against segregation in Cleveland businesses. Shortly after the death of BTW Myers wrote his friend, the historian James Ford Rhodes: "It was a very sad blow not alone to me but to the negroes of America to lose Dr. Booker T. Washington. There is no one to take his place before the American people. His work will go on at Tuskegee and that too perhaps better than ever, but as a leader we are without one. We were close personal friends."

Despite failing health Myers worked on as long as possible at the Hollenden barbershop because he knew that his thirty black employees would be replaced with whites the minute he retired. On Jan. 17, 1930, the day he was to announce the bad news to his employees, he died of a heart attack. (Garraty, ed., *The Barber and the Historian*, 36.)

To Edwin Anderson Alderman

Crawford House, Boston, Mass. December 4, 1901

My dear Sir: I thank you very much for your kind letter of November 27th. In reply I would say that I find it will be impossible for me to meet you and the other gentlemen to whom you refer any time in December as I shall be detained in the North and West until some time in January. I regret this exceedingly. If you can name another time I shall do my best to comply with your wishes.

May I add that almost nothing has given me so much encouragement during the last year as the deep interest which you, Dr. McIver, Dr. Dabney and other Southern men have manifested in education, I mean education for all the people of the South. I have read I think nearly everything I have seen from your pen and have always done so with interest and profit. Nothing that has been said regarding education in the South has so impressed me as the suggestions which you made in an issue of The Outlook some weeks ago in regard to the importance of having a sociological department endowed in several of the large white colleges in the South for the purpose of giving Southern white men the opportunity of making first hand investigations into the condition of the Negro. I was very much tempted at the time I read this suggestion to reenforce if possible what you had said by an article over my own signature in The Outlook, but I feared that such a plea coming from me might do harm rather than good. I have however, taken the liberty of speaking to wealthy men in the North about your suggestion. Only this week I called the matter to the attention of Mr. Baldwin and a day or two before that to the attention of Mr. Ogden. I am very anxious that this suggestion be carried out.

I thank you very much for your kind words regarding our work at Tuskegee and regarding me personally. There is a great work before us to be done in the South and we must lose sight of ourselves and pitch into it with all the strength and vigor that we can summon.

Sometime during the year I hope we can see you at Tuskegee. Yours truly,

Booker T. Washington

TLS   Edwin A. Alderman Papers   ViU.

From Charles Waddell Chesnutt

Cleveland, O. December 9, 1901

My dear Mr. Washington: Permit me to acknowledge receipt of your letter of December 5th, dated from the Crawford House, Boston, and to thank you very much for your cordial interest in

"The Marrow of Tradition," and your kindly effort to secure for it a wide reading. I imagine that such people as Mr. and Mrs. Trask[1] could do a great deal for a book among their friends and acquaintances; for, after all, it is the good word passed along from mouth to mouth which constitutes the best advertising for any book, or man, or cause.

"The Marrow of Tradition" is making its way gradually. It has not yet set the world on fire, but it is being read by a great many thoughtful people, and I hope, for several reasons that the number may increase. Mr. Howells paid his respects to it in the North American Review for December, and it has been widely and favorably commented upon by the newspaper press.

I had a letter from my daughter the other day, and she is still filled with enthusiasm, and seems to enjoy her work at Tuskegee very much indeed. Cordially yours,

Chas. W. Chesnutt

TLS Con. 194 BTW Papers DLC.

[1] Spencer Trask (1844–1909), a New York investment banker and philanthropist, was a partner of George Foster Peabody. His wife, Kate Nichols Trask (1853–1922), wrote poetry and novels under the name of Katrina Trask. She married George Foster Peabody in 1920.

From John M. F. Erwin[1]

Chicago, Ill. Dec. 9th 1901

Dear Sir; When I visited you at Tuskegee last February, I wanted to find out whether it would be advisable to employ some of your young men as managers in my various land schemes. I was highly pleased with all I saw at your school. I think you are doing a noble work and that you are turning out efficient workers. But I concluded that in the pioneer state of getting land settled and clearing land, experienced colored men would be better than your inexperienced young men. But my Louisiana settlement — I like that word better than "colony" — has reached the stage where your young men could do their best work. My people have learned all my present manager can teach them, and while I do not propose to discharge him, I am liable to promote him to the management of a larger new settlement. I now want to build in the Louisiana settlement the best school in that part of the country, and want your advice. By the end of next year there will be 65 families on the land we still own, and we have no room for any more there. There are besides, the small colored land owners to whom I have sold lands. I want you to select a young man who will go there at my expense and look the ground over and see what is needed and what the prospect is for building up a good school. We are business men, not philanthropists, and unless there is a prospect that with what aid we can get from the public fund, and what tuition the people will pay, the school will support itself, we would not care to start it. We would be willing however to guarantee to the teacher a salary for the first year so his living would be assured. We not to pay anything if he made more, and he of course to have all he could make. I believe the field is a good one.

Kindly let me hear from you about this.

I want to say that I thoroughly approve your work, but when you have such a struggle to get funds to maintain an institution for 1200 students, an institution generally admitted to be the best of its kind in the country, I think there is little hope of reaching the mass of negroes through philanthropy.

Philanthropy is necessarily of the few for the few. Greed is coarser but it has the elements of universality, perseverance, and "get-there." Convince the business men that there's money in putting the negro on forty acres of land, with incidental benefit to the negro, and the business man will not stop until that particular benefit has been offered to every negro in the land. There will be no lack either, of careful demonstration to the negro as to just where the benefit to him comes in. Very truly yours,

John M. F. Erwin

TLS Con. 272 BTW Papers DLC.

1 John M. F. Erwin, born in Greenwood, Fla., in 1864, described his family as "one of the 'old' families — several generations of slave holders. . . ." Erwin worked in the family store and later supervised black railroad laborers in southern Florida. He taught school in Georgia and was a National Educational Association officer in 1885 or 1886. He later attended the University of Virginia, graduating in 1889. He moved to Louisiana and became a land speculator, but lack of capital in the South caused him to move to Chicago, where he continued his land speculation and was a manufac-

turer's agent, according to a 1901 city directory. Erwin candidly wrote BTW: "I am a greedy business man trying to make money, and the good I may do the negro will be incidental." (Dec. 16, 1901, Con. 272, BTW Papers, DLC.)

To Emmett Jay Scott

Boston, Mass. 12, 12, 1901

Dear Mr. Scott: I notice that a great many people in Alabama get hold of my hotel address and bother me about matters that I do not care to be concerned with. As far as possible, I wish you would avoid giving people my address when I am away. Yours truly,

B. T. W.

TLI   Con. 214   BTW Papers   DLC.

From Theodore Roosevelt

[Washington, D.C.] December 12, 1901

Personal.

My dear Mr. Washington: Upon my word, it is very difficult to know what to do. I receive a number of letters like that which you enclose. For instance, the gentleman of whom you spoke to me, Mr. Wright, makes the most violent charges against Lyons and especially Rucker and Deveaux,[1] in Georgia. Various colored men assure me that all the colored men in office are against me personally, and what is much more important that they do no good to the race and are not very satisfactory officials. On the other hand, each and every one of these statements is specifically contradicted. I am at my wit's end to know what to do. As for the delegations from the southern states, I simply shall not consider them in making any appointment, for I believe if I once began to try to consider them or the effect my appointments would have on them, there would be an end to all effort to put in a fit and decent set of officeholders.

I wish I could cast off all my burdens as easily as I cast off the

343

consideration about the delegations. What gives me real concern is the impossibility of being sure as to the character of the men, particularly the colored men, who are in office in the south or apply for office from the south. Faithfully yours,

Theodore Roosevelt

TLpS Theodore Roosevelt Papers DLC.

1 John H. Deveaux, owner of the Savannah *Tribune*, was a long-time black politician in Georgia, beginning with a clerkship in the Savannah custom house in 1870. He was collector of the port of Brunswick from 1889 to 1893, and a McKinley appointee as collector of customs for Savannah.

From Edward Elder Cooper

Washington, D.C., Dec. 12, 1901

My dear Mr. Washington: I wrote you a letter last Saturday and put a postscript on it. You were in the city at the time I wrote the letter to you, but I did not know it until afterwards. I guess you have thought strangely of the tone of the letter and of my demand, and yet when I wrote the letter I meant every line of what I wrote, and said hastily then, what I shall say at more length now. It seems that some of the old guard, Pinchback, Lyons and others are a little chafed at the attention you are giving to the younger set, such as McCary, McKinlay and others, and the younger set just named are pouring it into the old heads and gloating over the fact that you seek them out when you come and all that kind of thing. Chase of the Bee is kicking like a wild steer and the colored lawyers are up in arms against Terrell for playing 'under cover', as they say. The fact of the matter is they[1] is fighting among themselves, but they make you the butt end of the argument. There is but one way to hold these fellows down and that is to let your old friends handle them as they have all along. Chase is a hard man to satisfy when he once learns that there is blood in the turnip. Confidentially, a number of the Anti-Washingtons are saying that Councill is right and all of that kind of thing. Thompson has just written a very nice article booming you for the head of the Negro department of the Louisiana Purchase Exposition at St. Louis. I have not used it this week, and do not intend to until I hear from you. If a fight is made for you for the place it will breed a crop of enemies among the so-called Negro leaders who are already beginning to say that 'Mr. Washington wants everything.' Let me know about this.

Fortune left the city last Wednesday morning for Red Bank. He and Paul Laurence Dunbar got on a "holy terror" last Wednesday and continued it up until just before the meeting of the Bethel Historical and Literary Association. Fortune came late and in no condition to speak. He had lost or mis-laid his manuscript and made an off hand talk in a rambling way very similar to the one he made at the Business League last August in Chicago. L. M. Hershaw[2] remarked to him after the meeting this, 'Mr. Fortune, I have heard some rank speeches, but yours tonight was the rottenest I have ever heard.'

Did you see the editorial in the Chicago Chronicle of December 6th? It is the best thing I have read on the situation in the South for a long time. The writer of the editorial evidently did not know that Councill was a colored man, and the way he poured it into Councill was a 'caution.' For fear you have not seen it, I enclosed it in this letter. Every thing is quiet down this way, and I hope you are prospering. Yours very truly,

E. E. Cooper

TLS   Con. 194   BTW Papers   DLC.

[1] Cooper originally wrote "there is" and then changed "there" to "they" but forgot to change the verb.

[2] Lafayette McKeen Hershaw (1863–1945), born in North Carolina, graduated from Atlanta University in 1880. After teaching for several years, he moved to Washington, D.C., in 1890 to become a clerk in the land office of the Department of the Interior. He later became a law examiner, after admission to the bar. Hershaw was active in the Bethel Literary and Historical Association, of which he was president, and a leader of black cultural life in Washington. A critic of BTW's philosophy and leadership, he was a charter member of the Niagara Movement in 1905. He assisted Du Bois in the publication of the magazine *Horizon*. He was a member of the Pen and Pencil Club of Washington and the American Negro Academy, and was a trustee of Atlanta University.

To Theodore Roosevelt

Crawford House, Boston. December 14, 1901

My dear Mr. President: I confess that I am greatly troubled about R. L. Smith, of Oakland, Texas. I appreciate, I think, in some degree, your difficulties because of the color feeling and your wanting to respect as far as possible the wishes of the regular organizations when they are in any degree decent.

The case of Smith is peculiar. You will perhaps recall that when we had our first talks in New York regarding the South, both of us referred to Smith as the type of a colored man to be recognized. Knowing Smith to be strong and clean and not in the hands of your enemies, I asked him to aid me in Texas and elsewhere in moulding influence for you. This he was doing effectively.

At present it is true that in Texas there is but one recognized organization, but until lately there have been two organizations and both contained some good men. Smith happened to be with the wing that was not recognized by Mr. Hanna. Smith has gotten practically all the endorsements that it was suggested he get except that of Mr. Hawley[1] and his element; this Smith said he could not get in the first place.

But the thing that is on my heart about Smith is this: His political enemies have brought all kinds of false charges against him, even going so far as to try to injure his moral reputation. This being true, for him not to be appointed will almost ruin his influence in educational and other work in Texas, among our people and the whites. His failure will be placed on the grounds that you believe these charges. It will seem like a recognition of the worst element of our people and a throwing down of the best. Smith's appointment will help *the race*.

Is it not possible to pacify the regular organization so that they will consent to Smith's appointment?

If you will give him the chance, I think that Smith can suggest a transfer of some of the white officers that will give satisfaction to most of those now opposing him.

I will not burden you with recommendations, but I hope you will read the two that are enclosed. Smith has scores just like these from colored people, white Republicans, and white Democrats. Mr. Ward[2] is the ex-Attorney General of the State.

I dislike so very much to seem to become a special pleader, and do not mean to become such in any case in the future.

This will be my address until December 19th, 1901, after that at Tuskegee. Yours sincerely,

Booker T. Washington

TLS Theodore Roosevelt Papers DLC. An autograph draft dated Dec. 13, 1901, is in Con. 214, BTW Papers, DLC.

[1] Robert Bradley Hawley (1849–1921), of Galveston, Tex., served in the U.S. House of Representatives from 1897 to 1901. In 1900 he organized and became president of the Cuban-American Sugar Co.

[2] Robert H. Ward, a white attorney of San Antonio, Tex., was born in Virginia in 1852. Ward served with R. L. Smith in the Texas legislature during the 1890s, and wrote a letter to Roosevelt on Smith's behalf in which he said that though he was a Democrat and Smith a Republican and though Smith was black and the legislature almost all white, Smith, "by reason of his individual merit and capacity, commanded the friendship of each member of the House." (Oct. 26, 1901, Theodore Roosevelt Papers, DLC.) Ward also wrote Smith: "If all the colored men in Texas were like you, the race problem would soon be settled." (Oct. 26, 1901, Theodore Roosevelt Papers, DLC.)

From Whitefield McKinlay

Washington, D.C., December 14, 1901

Dear Mr. Washington: For several days I have been debating with myself the wisdom of calling your attention to Fortune's spectacle before the Bethel Literary, which was so revolting that Dr. Grimkie left in disgust as soon as he realized the man's condition. I immediately followed Dr. Grimkie to his house to convince myself of my suspicions. I told the Doctor that I was glad that I could use him to you as a witness. Dancy told me that he and Pledger tried to sober him up so that he would be in condition to read his paper but that Dunbar took him off with the result that he not only could not read his paper but he was incoherent. He had a very good audience and hence you can infer how they felt.

The Chase incident and this affair confirm what I have stated to you; that for the sake of the race whose hopes are centered in you — you must diplomatically cut loose from these fellows and that at once.

Several very strong men have recently expressed surprise that you should associate with F. Dr. Grimkie said several of your white friends did the same thing. You must pardon me for being so frank but I feel that I would not be doing myself justice if I did not call your attention to this matter which unless heeded will sooner or later cause you endless embarrassment.

I trust that you will appreciate my unselfish advice by treating this with absolute confidence. Very truly,

W. McKinlay

Dictated.

P.S. Enclosed you will find 46 cts. stamps, as balance of the dollar you left with me.

I just learned through rumor that neither Cheatham nor Crossland will be appointed Recorder of Deeds. Dancy told me confidentially that Pritchard[1] told him that he wanted to crawl out but did not see his way clear as he had so strongly endorsed Cheatham but now that he is very much mortified to learn the facts.

TLS   Con. 261   BTW Papers   DLC.

[1] Jeter Connelly Pritchard (1857–1921), a lily-white Republican, was a senator from North Carolina (1895–1903), a justice of the District of Columbia Supreme Court (1903–4), and a judge of the U.S. Circuit Court of Appeals (1904–21).

To Whitefield McKinlay

Crawford House, Boston, Mass. December 16, 1901

My dear Mr. McKinlay: I am in receipt of your letter of December 14th and thank you for writing me so fully and frankly. I confess that the information which was referred to briefly in your last letter, and which seems to be fully confirmed in your present letter, causes me a great deal of pain. I confess that I hardly know what to do or say. One thing, however, is clear, and that is that while it may be necessary for me to be thrown from time to time into the company of people who are not right in their lives, I am determined that no such company or influence will ever make me swerve one iota from the path of right living as I see it.

I am all the more pained by the circumstances to which you refer because I had warned Mr. F. before he went to Washington about the class of people that he would meet and the temptations to which he would be subjected, and he made a promise that he would not be led astray. My position is all the more difficult and embarrassing because plenty of my friends are perhaps not broad enough to appreciate all the circumstances. It is impossible, as you know, to shake off at once the old time men and old time influences. Certain parties in Washington are already accusing me of giving more attention to what is called the "old crowd" who, in many cases, stood manfully in the earlier and darker days. Aside from this, it is very unfortunate, but it is also true, as you will appreciate, that public sentiment among our people, as is true of the white race, is very largely moulded and educated by the press. It will be impossible to use the press for the purpose of educating our people if one cuts loose entirely from those who control the press. I have wished many times that the press was in the hands of a different class of people, or that we had one good, strong organ that had behind it individuals who were clean in their private life and unselfish in their public utterances and influence.

I appreciate thoroughly the advice which you have given me and also the danger that there is to me personally in the present situation, and I assure you that wisely and I hope judiciously, I shall try to profit by what you have said, but after all the position is a trying one. I do not blame Dr. Grimke for his action on the night of the lecture, and I wish you would tell him that I appreciate his advice, also his kind interest in me.

I have just had rather a lengthy letter from the President, and he tells me that he is very much puzzled over the situation in the South. From every standpoint it is a trying one.

My address from the 20th to the 25th will be, Grand Union Hotel, New York City. Yours truly,

Booker T. Washington

TLS Con. 4 Carter G. Woodson Collection DLC.

From Thomas A. Cooper[1]

Oakland Calif. Dec. 16–1901

My Dear Sir   While I am an obscure atom of humanity, well along in the afternoon [of] life, I will close my career more peacefully by writing you my congratulations on your wonderful achievements. I am controverting with parties concerni[n]g you dining with President Roosevelt, and that act of his raised him still higher in my estimation. All great men are good, generous and just.

I claim that President McKinley and party were entertained by you at your home in 1898. Please inform me if I am correct and names of gentlemen present at the time. We have all one common origen. All are brothers. I care not for creed race color or former condition, it is the manly principle under the Skin I admire. I have publicly announced that I would rather set at table with Booker T. Washington all my life than one meal with such men as Thos. Platt,[2] Mat. Quay, Gorman, Crocker[3] and Hanna. All unscruplous politicians. I say that Booker T. Washingtons heart and record is lilly white compared to such men. Really I consider you one of the most wonderful men of our time. When we consider your envirniment, The adversities with which you have had to contend and the great work you have accomplished in a few short years, I say no other man has ever accomplished so much for him self and race as has Booker T. Washington. Men who love fairness, justice and equity, will stand by you, only narrow minded, prejudiced, bigots, will oppose, simply on color line. I am a native of the State of Georgia born in Walker County that State in 1838. I am for justice to all humanity and if there was a God who raised up Moses to lead his people, the same power raised a Lincoln to liberate your race and the same power selected, raised up Booker T. Washington to lead his race out of the wilderness of enforced ignorance and establish them on the high fertile plains of education progress and agricultural commercial prosperity. He who shapes and guides the course the destiny of men and Nations will sustain you in your noble work, your philosophy will yet solve the race problem in the South.

True manliness, education and wordly accumulations will command and receive due respect. Education is power, specially when allied with money. God speed your noble work and preserve your life to see your fondest hopes and ambitions realized. I will feel grateful for a letter from you. Yours fraternally and in the cause of justice and righteousness.

T. A. Cooper

ALS Con. 194 BTW Papers DLC.

1 Thomas A. Cooper was a carpenter, according to the 1900 census.

2 Thomas Collier Platt (1833–1910) was the Republican political boss of New York State. A member of the U.S. House of Representatives from 1873 to 1877, he was elected to the Senate in 1880 but resigned after two months in office following a patronage dispute with President Garfield. Platt was re-elected to the Senate in 1896 and 1902.

3 Charles Crocker (1822–88), the California railroad baron.

From Timothy Thomas Fortune

Red Bank, N.J. Dec. 16, 1901

My Dear Mr. Washington: I have your letter of the 13th, and am much discouraged by it. I accepted some social attentions in Washington, but for the most part drank seltzer water and milk. I made a special effort to keep in the middle of the road and am sure I did. I shall have hereafter to refuse all social business, as I find that I am misrepresented by the very people from whom I accept such. As a matter of fact I am now drinking nothing whatever. Like yourself I have plenty of enemies who profess to be friends who magnify everything I do and of which they are habitually guilty. I am sorry that these gossip items reach you, because there is little foundation in them, and the people who bandy them have axes of their own to grind. I shall have to cut out the entire social business in Washington, as most of them seem to be self-seekers, gossips and liars. Your Friend,

T. Thomas Fortune

TLS Con. 196 BTW Papers DLC.

To Whitefield McKinlay

Crawford House, Boston, Mass. December 17, 1901

My dear Mr. McKinlay: If you think it wise, I wish you would attend to the following matter for me. I do not like to have the Washington Post be taking the attitude that it seems to be doing through editorials, squibs and other kinds of articles that are appearing in its columns from time to time. I wish you would go and have a frank talk with the managing editor and let him know in the first place, that everything he has had in his paper referring to my being turned away from hotels in New England is absolutely false and that he was imposed upon in this matter. Also impress upon him the fact that in no way have I changed my attitude towards the South or my actions in the North, I am simply going forward doing the work for Tuskegee in the same way that I have been doing it for twenty years and intend to make no change. Do this if you think wise.

The enclosed is a sample of what has been appearing in The Post. Anybody that knows anything about my work knows it is impossible for me to get the money to carry on the institution without going to the North from time to time in the way that I have been doing ever since the institution has been established.

I shall be in New York at the Grand Union Hotel from the 20th to the 25th where a letter will reach me. Yours very truly,

Booker T. Washington

TLS Con. 4 Carter G. Woodson Collection DLC. Enclosure no longer attached.

To Theodore Roosevelt

Crawford House, Boston. December 17, 1901

My dear Mr. President: Your kind letter of the 12th is received. I can easily understand your perplexity in regard to the South. Taken from any point of view it is a hard situation to deal with and requires infinite patience. I hope that you will go very slow there in making appointments so that no appointments if possible will be much below the grade of Gov. Jones.

I am satisfied that the colored men holding office in Georgia are clean men and that the putting of such men in office here and there does help the race. I called your attention to Wright because I wanted you to get every point of view. Wright is honest himself, but has a mistaken point of view in this case.

You will get the Southern delegations. The whole North and West are with you, and any one who seeks delegates in the South by the old methods will lose the North and West.

I am going to have a good frank talk with Lyons next week and can find out from him just where the colored men in office stand in reference to you and what they mean to do. I will let you know.

Please command me whenever I can serve you. Yours sincerely,

Booker T. Washington

TLS   Theodore Roosevelt Papers   DLC.

From Edward Elder Cooper

Washington, D.C., Dec. 17/01

Dear Mr. Washington: Your letter of the 14th inst. came to hand and I took the crisp $20.00 bill, which you were good enough to send, and gave it to Mrs. C. as a peace offering. The town is full of darkies, Raymond[1] of Altoona, Pa. is here, Dancy of North Carolina and Rucker from Georgia, Pledger from the same state and God knows who else. Cheatham is still "scattered" and Deas,[2] he of South Carolina whom you take occasion to poke fun at when you refer to my troubles, is also here. I know you are not from South Carolina. If you were and I could get you on the "run" as I had those people, what I would do to you would be a "whole lot." The little gift came in good time and it will help me out.

I come in contact with all classes here and I know pretty well about how the pulses beat. I met old man Cook yesterday, Jno. F. Cook, the richest Negro in the District. We had a very friendly chat, and for some reason he warmed up to me and wanted to know when you were coming through again as he wants you to stop with him or to have a few of your friends to join you in a dinner with him. I think this is a good omen. It shows that you are reaching a class who have heretofore stood aloof and watched and waited to see what you would do.

I heard you were here Saturday as I wrote you in a previous letter and I didn't understand it but your letter has made it plain to me. I think Gov. Pinchback is all right but you know it is hard for the old chieftains to give away to the young leaders and they die hard even though ignominiously. Pinchback is all right, however, and I believe after all is your friend.

Don't say anything about the Fortune matter for I really blame Paul Laurence Dunbar rather than Fortune. Fortune is bright and witty and entertaining and when two live spirits get together they are apt to do most anything.

I will hold the exposition matter back for a little while and you can indicate to me just the time to spring it. A Rev. P. A. Scott[3] of Oil City, Pa. has written a most excellent article about you and I am going to print it and make him a nice cut to accompany the article.[4] It came unsolicited, but it is all right, and it is one of the best things I have read for some time on you and your work.

Old man Gibbs is tickled over the letter you wrote him and his book will really be very creditable when it comes out. You have no idea of the service you have done me by agreeing to write the review of the book. He is "apple pie" with me now and everything is lovely. I enclose the clipping from The Chronicle in this letter and if you have the letter from Prof. Councill that I gave you and it is handy, I wish you would return it. I did not get to read it. Let me know when you are coming through as I want to speak with you if only for a minute. Yours very truly,

E. E. Cooper

TLS Con. 194 BTW Papers DLC.

1 James B. Raymond was an alderman in Altoona, Pa., according to a 1902 city directory.

2 Edmund H. Deas, the "Duke of Darlington," S.C., was born in Georgetown, S.C., in 1855. He began his long and active political career in the state Republican organization in 1874 and by 1880 was elected county chairman. In 1900 Deas became chairman of the state party. By 1901 he had been a delegate to five national Republican conventions and held federal appointments as pension examiner in Washington, D.C., and in the office of the collector of internal revenue in South Carolina. Roosevelt

disliked Deas's emotionalism, and several black leaders, while agreeing with Deas's views, disapproved of his outspoken style. William D. Crum and BTW, for example, were considerably more moderate than Deas in their opposition to lynching and Jim Crow laws. (Gatewood, "William D. Crum," 301-20.)

3 Price A. Scott, pastor of the A.M.E. Church in Oil City, Pa., was born in Virginia in 1866.

4 Washington *Colored American*, Jan. 4, 1902, 6. The laudatory article referred to BTW in such terms as "the Race's most consummate flower, and the Nation's uncrowned king."

From William Henry Baldwin, Jr.

[New York City] Dec 18, 1901

Dear Washington, I have your enclosures, and am thinking.

I believe that the Prest. should be asked *privately* & *confidentially* to put the Secret Service men at work. Wire me if you have any objections.

I was threatened last winter, and hoped I would be done up, as I was sure that it would produce the results for which I was working. But I dont want you troubled.

You will stay here for a time anyway. Don't go South yet.

Will write fully after I have thought it out. Faithfully yours

W H Baldwin Jr

ALS Con. 792 BTW Papers DLC.

From Clark Howell

Atlanta, Ga. December 18, 1901

Dear Professor: Can you recommend an intelligent, competent and painstaking woman for domestic service at my house?[1]

I am anxious to secure the services of a bright, amiable woman to act as maid for my wife and to assist in the care of two children — one eight and the other ten years of age. I would want a woman who is able to go over their lessons with them each evening and to make herself generally useful in chambermaid work. A satisfactory woman would obtain a good home with room in the house.

The thought occurs to me that among your students or among those who have recently graduated from your institution, you might select some one whom you could recommend. I am anxious to get a woman who is, at least, reasonably well educated in order that she may assist the children in their studies.

Kindly let me hear from you as soon as practicable, and oblige,
Very truly yours,

Clark Howell

TLS   Con. 201   BTW Papers   DLC.

1 BTW gave Howell the name of Rosa Lee Baker of Montgomery, Ala., a junior at Tuskegee for part of the 1901–2 school year. He apparently did not personally endorse her, however, since Howell's wife, Annie Comer Howell, wrote BTW that Rosa Baker "was from the first a decided disappointment not having come from you with your personal endorsement." (May 3, 1902, Con. 230, BTW Papers, DLC.) Rosa Baker quit her job in Apr. 1902. (See Baker to BTW, Apr. 28, 1902, below.)

From Timothy Thomas Fortune

Red Bank, N.J. December 19, 1901

My Dear Mr. Washington: Your letter of the 17th was received.

I find that my "very best friends in Washington," most of whom drink more than I do, keep a tab on every drink I take and promptly gossip about it, while I would scorn to speak of any such thing as being beneath my dignity, and hereafter I shall cut the whole blamed shoot out.

I am having success in getting the few necessary endorsements in this State.

I am still working on the cold and the dumb chills. Your friend,

T. Thomas Fortune

TLS   Con. 196   BTW Papers   DLC.

From John Davison Rockefeller, Jr.

New York. December 21st, 1901

Dear Mr. Washington: We will be glad to have you take supper with us on Sunday night at half past six, No. 4 West 54th Street. My wife and I usually take Sunday night tea at my Father's house and my Mother has asked us to bring you with us. Therefore I give you the address of my Father's house instead of mine.

Looking forward with pleasure to seeing you, I am, Very truly,

John D. Rockefeller, Jr.

TLS Con. 709 BTW Papers DLC. Addressed to BTW at the Grand Union Hotel.

From William Henry Baldwin, Jr.

Brooklyn Heights [N.Y.] Dec 23, 1901

Dear Washington; Dinner: Xmas, at *6.15 Tuesday* evening. Come early, and have an extra stocking to hang up. Yours,

WHBJr

ALI Con. 214 BTW Papers DLC.

To Theodore Roosevelt

Grand Union Hotel, New York. 12, 24, 1901

My dear Mr. President: After my interview with you yesterday I saw our friend, Mr. Edgar S. Wilson,[1] of Jackson, Miss., and we are both convinced that it will be best for him to take one of the most important and influential offices in the state, that is, the Marshalship of the Southern District of Mississippi. This will give him an opportunity to travel through the state and inform himself concerning men and conditions and thus be able to render better service to you than by being confined to the office of Register in Jackson. I want to suggest that we think it will be well to make Mr. Wilson Marshal, and to appoint the present Marshal to the position of Register, and let Mr. Isaiah T. Montgomery, a colored man of first class order, take the position of Receiver of Public Moneys. If on further consideration, Mr. Wilson and I think that some other colored man will be better than Mr. Montgomery, we will let you know.

Mr. Wilson is not only keeping in mind the putting of first class men in office, but also keeping in mind the bringing about of such conditions as will not injure the party and the support which you should have from Mississippi. The more I see of him, the more I am convinced of his wisdom and unselfishness and his great power for good. Yours truly,

Booker T. Washington

TLS   Theodore Roosevelt Papers   DLC.

1 Edgar Stewart Wilson (1858–1935), born near Union Church, Miss., was the editor of several small-town weekly newspapers in Mississippi. For a short time in the 1880s he was clerk of the Mississippi House of Representatives, and in 1884–85 he was U.S. Senator L. Q. C. Lamar's private secretary. From 1885 to 1889 he was register of the U.S. Land Office in Cheyenne, Wyo. Returning to Jackson, he was the state swamp-land commissioner from 1890 to 1895. At the time of his appointment under Theodore Roosevelt he was manager of the Mississippi bureau of the New Orleans *Picayune.* From 1902 to 1910 he was U.S. marshal and referee for all presidential appointments in the state. As a former Gold Democrat, he gave his loyalty more to Roosevelt than to the Republican party, though he became a member. He worked closely with BTW in all political matters and spurned the lily-white faction in his state, but he was resented by many Mississippi black Republicans who thought that they and not a white former Democrat ought to be in charge of party affairs in the state.

A Poem on the White House Dinner

[Mobile, Ala. ca. Dec. 24, 1901][1]

WILL YOU WALK INTO MY PARLOR

"Will you walk into my parlor
And my guest this evening be?"
'Twas the President inviting

358

The distinguished "Booker T."
"Oh, yes thanks your Excellency,
I will take a tea and chat,
For the world will scarcely notice
While I rest my coat and hat."

But alas for good intentions,
And such democratic ways!
For there came a cry from Dixie,
And a fire was set ablaze.
"You insult us, you outrage us!
You commit an awful sin!
When you welcome to your table
That — er — man with a dark skin!

"Matters not that he is learned,
That he talks with fluent grace,
And might help to solve the "problem"
For, Sir, that is not "his place."
Foreign rulers have him honored
Statesmen, scholars make him welcome
Call him eloquent — refined,[2]

"But alas! all goes for nothing —
This outrageous, social sin!
What can ever soothe our feelings
Or can make the White House clean?
Forthwith every hungry Negro
Will demand the same high fare;
We must take them to our parlors,
Entertain them nicely there.

"Nay! By all the traditions,
By the memory of our sires,
By the help of Ancient Woden
They shall not see our hearth fires!
Down with Roosevelt! out with Booker!
At the kitchen fill your mouth,
And beware how you shall tamper
With the feelings of the South!"

Mobile *Weekly Press*, ca. Dec. 24, 1901, Clipping Con. 196 BTW Papers
DLC.

1 A. N. Johnson, editor of the black Mobile *Weekly Press*, forwarded the poem to BTW with the comment: "Dear Sir and Friend: The Press apologises for the enclosed." (Dec. 24, 1901, Con. 196, BTW Papers, DLC.)

2 Possibly a line was omitted in the newspaper version.

An Article about Portia Marshall Washington in the Indianapolis *Freeman*

[Indianapolis, Ind.] December 28, 1901

From toiling in the cotton fields to study in one of America's most aristocratic colleges seems a far cry indeed. Yet there is a family which, in the step of one generation, has thus passed at a bound the batteries of environment and social conditions. Portia Washington, the daughter of the man who has made himself the leader of his race, was this month enrolled a Wellesley girl.

When Booker T. Washington went to college he tramped as a ragged, forlorn little black boy from a Southern Negro cabin to Hampton, where he helped pay his way through the institution by sweeping the floors and working at his trade in holidays and vacations, says the North American. When his daughter commenced her collegiate education the other day he himself took her in a Pullman car to Boston and thence to the fashionable woman's college, where she was placed under the care of the dean with all the ceremony and distinction that is shown a millionaire's daughter.

And she has been as carefully reared, this Negro girl, as any of Boston's own cultured children. It is evident in an air of good breeding and a refinement of manner, which are as well marked in her as though her color were white. She is 18 years old, she says, but with her slim, straight figure and her skirt yet ankle length, she looks not more than 16. She is only a little schoolgirl in her ways, scarcely yet a college young woman, very childlike and unsophisticated. One looks in vain for the dominant qualities of independence and leadership which she might have been expected to have inherited from her mother, whose executive ability called her to the presidency of a national federation and from a father who is the founder of Tuskegee. But there is no evidence, so far at least, that the little Wellesley girl has inherited any endowment from all of this parental achievement. So far as any pride of position is concerned she might just as well be the daughter of an obscure hotel waiter or railroad porter as of the greatest colored man the world has known since Hannibal and Othello. Altogether quiet and unassuming, she has been completely overwhelmed at the attention which the newspapers have lately given her.

"You want to write me up, you say?" she replied, in a mystified sort of way to a reporter recently.

"Why, what for?" she added, while the dazed expression on her face deepened.

It was explained that the public might be interested in knowing something of her and hearing about her as about her father and her mother.

"I don't understand," she repeated. "With mamma, of course, it's different. She's a grown-up woman. But me, why I'm only a little girl," and she laughed at the suggestion that she could possibly be of any importance.

Miss Portia is a very good looking young colored girl. She is almost beautiful; some people would call her quite so in spite of the fact that her features are not as regular as they should be to deserve it. They are not characteristic Negro features, however. Her complexion is several shades removed from black, and even if the beauty of her face might be questioned, there could not be two opinions about her hair. The glory of the night is in it, and it is a crowning possession which any white girl might be proud of. It is raven black, of course, and as fine and shining as silk. It waves in pretty ripples and is parted above her smooth brow in Puritan-like simplicity and fastened in a loose knot at her neck. Her dark eyes look shyly from beneath long, drooping lashes.

Her voice, which is one of her chief charms, confirms the impression of refinement already conveyed in her bearing. It is soft and low and sweet, with all of that delicious Southern accent so musical to Northern ears, and especially to Northern ears accustomed to hearing the harsh New England nasal twang.

For college she dresses very plainly, in a gray skirt and jacket and a wash shirtwaist. All of them she could make with her own hands if necessary, for last year she devoted herself to an industrial course at Tuskegee. Besides being a practical dressmaker, she can trim a hat or bake a loaf of bread equally well, for she has also taken the courses in millinery and housekeeping. All this is in accord with her father's belief that every colored girl or boy should have manual along with mental training.

In June, 1900, she was graduated in the regular course at Tuskegee, and before that she had had four years of boarding school life at Framingham, Mass.

At Wellesley Miss Washington is studying music. That is her specialty, and all of the lovely melody of her race tingles in her finger tips. She spends two hours a day in practice on one of the pianos in the music hall. It is in a room on the third floor, like all of the others, a bare little room with not another piece of furniture in it than the piano and stool and a tiny radiator. But from the single gabled window there is such a view that rivals in splendor any wealth of luxurious furnishings or even the painter's masterpiece. Far away rise the bleak New England hills, nestling at their base in the nearer distance sparkles the clear blue water of Lake Wabau, and all around rustle the Wellesley oaks whispering in murmuring chorus to the blushing red-hued maples that lend their gorgeous hues to make the landscape scheme complete.

"It's all so pretty, isn't it?" the young colored girl from Alabama exclaims. "I could stand for hours and look from this window." But she shivered a little even as she said it, for already the November winds blew colder than the balmy breezes to which she is accustomed in the sunny South.

In connection with her lessons she has the study of harmony, German, and Biblical history. But she isn't a student in the regular course. She is a "special." That, by the way, is the reason why she has rooms in the village instead of within the college grounds.

"I don't know what people mean by talking about the 'color line,' " she exclaimed in wide-eyed wonder. "I'm sure the girls are just as nice to me as they can be."

And they are "nice" to her. They walk to college with her, as you can see them any day. They call on her and chum with her, and invite her to their receptions and social functions. Last week she was made a member of the Young Women's Christian Association at the college.

"I'm not the first colored girl here," she explains, "nor the only one now in Wellesley. There is Miss Charlotte Atwood, a junior, who lives at Stone Hall, and sleeps in the same building and eats at the same table with the other girls."

Careful inquiry shows that the "color line" at Wellesley is only the dream of an alarmist. The few Southern girls at the institution do not make friends with either Portia Washington or the other colored girl students, but their position is simply one of neutrality. As they put it, they "let the colored girls alone." But if that can be considered a slight the latter have never felt it, for the Northern girls treat them on a footing of equality that totally compensates for it.

Miss Washington lives where other special students have been accustomed to, at Mrs. B. E. Brehaut's, in Howe street, in the village. She takes her meals directly across the street at the home of Professor Coman, the instructor in astronomy. She is outside the college grounds simply because she's a special student, and the regulations of the institution do not admit "specials" to the dormitories.

To become a music teacher is the girl's ambition, and it is that for which she is preparing herself.

"I don't know how long I can stay at Wellesley," she adds. "I may never graduate, but I am here for this year at any rate."

Portia is Booker T. Washington's only daughter. For her father she has the most intense admiration. His word is law to her, and she renders him an implicit obedience that fulfills even to the letter his least command. The other two children are boys, now at Tuskegee, one of whom spent last year at Boston taking a course in physical training.

Indianapolis *Freeman*, Dec. 28, 1901, 4, 6.

From Robert Lloyd Smith

Oakland, Texas, Dec 30 1901

My dear Mr Washington, Your kind letter reached here Friday but I was away from home attending a meeting of our executive committee preparatory to our year's work and so delayed answering the same.

I want to express, as best I can, my heartfelt thanks to you for your great interest in me and the wonderful loyalty you have displayed throughout this remarkable fight.

It is the one thing that has most of all impressed itself upon me and which is a source of much pride to me.

It is something I assure you to have won the confidence esteem and *friendship* of such a man as Booker Washington.

I have been therefore the gainer by all that has happened thus far. The first thing that entered my mind in this affair was the enlarged sphere of usefulness that the tender of a first class position — a representative position would give me.

I knew if I was "recognized" by the President that I could lift my people up from the bondage of bad methods, bad homes and bad ideals by hundreds. You see what has been done already without resources and with the backing of only four prominent Negroes — yourself[,] Bishop Grant, Dr Scott[1] & Prof Kealing.[2]

I knew too that I was *the Negro* in this state that would be acceptable to the bulk of the white population and that was worth so much to the race just now I thought.

Then again, Negro office holders have generally been immoral men; they have "wasted their substance in riotous living" and too often not only brought reproach upon the race but have helped to degrade and ruin hundreds of young men by their example and influence.

Had I secured the position every colored man under me would have had to use his influence his talent to help *uplift the race* — to help to show them the foundation stones of Christian Civilization industry — economy — thrift and a *good home.*

Thus there would have been inaugurated a *new* era in politics so far as Negro office holders were concerned. A class would have arisen under Pres. Roosevelt that not only had wide spread influence among *all* the people but would have *deserved* it.

And they could be just as successful as the boodlers are now because if you remove the abuse of official patronage and corruption found *now,* I myself *without* anything can give any man a hard fight in this state. I feel immensely gratified at your assurance that the Pres is satisfied with my integrity. We have here as base a set of scoundrels to contend with as anywhere — much more so than I thought when I spoke with you in Sept about the machine in Texas.

The Hawley machine is only a thing of a few more months. We are going to get something better next fall when the state convention meets.

I am glad that he purposes to *vindicate me*. I can not walk anywhere without having forced on me by the best white and blacks, congratulations on my "success." It is in vain that I tell them I havent won or that there is serious opposition. It has gotten into peoples' minds that Pres. Roosevelt pays no attention to machine made charges when they are *false* and as they know I have proven the falsity of the charges against me and was *slated* for the place they *insist* that I have won out. God bless you dear friend. My heart goes out in gratitude to you for your *loyalty*. I have lost the collectorship but I have gained whats far better your loyal support on principle.

R L Smith

ALS   Con. 210   BTW Papers   DLC.

¹ Isaiah Benjamin Scott.
² Hightower T. Kealing.

An Advertisement for *Up from Slavery*

[1901]

HIS PATRON SAINT

Booker T. Washington says biography is his favorite reading and Abraham Lincoln is his patron saint. He claims to have read every book written about Lincoln. Perhaps this is one reason why his own autobiography, just published by Doubleday, Page & Co., is so full of anecdotes and stories, and withal one of the most interesting, helpful and solid of American biographical writings. In his single-hearted devotion to a righteous cause he is not unlike the great President.

PD   Con. 992   BTW Papers   DLC.   Page proof for an advertisement.

From C. B. Church, Sr.

Nigger Heaven was wonce New Orleans [1901]

Sir   All you have said & don for the Nigger goes to naught   hardly a day passes but you see a Nigger Lynched   shot   hung or Burned at the stake. the Nigger has brought al on them selves. Murdering and Rapeing white woman and children. the southern People are no less Law abiding or more vicious than they should be under the circumstances   you know there is a million young men grown up that was not Born when the Nigger was turned loos   Now they know who and how the nigger was turned loos and are as sower on them as the nigger   they are taking no stock in the Lost caus so called. while these men is plowing they are saying to them selves it was for the nigger that my Father Rebelled against the Government of the United States that brought about this state of afairrs. other wise I would be watching the nigger plow now   he is watching me plow in this field and every furrow he plows he gets bitter on the nigger with the rising generation and the two million Dagoes in this country

unless the Nigger attens his mooves I will giv him just two years to live in this country. the white man made niggers one becoming impudent presuming on ther being a white mans son.

Booker   The next to the w[o]rst mistake the southern people made was to let the nigger believe that Abraham Lincoln set them free which is not So   it was the first gun fired at fort sumper that led up to the fredom of the niggers

History tells you that Abraham Lincoln isued the Emancipation proclamation but failes to tell you that he isued two proclamations two years prior to that in which he implored in a beging tome to the Southern People to lay down ther armes and return to the Allgiance to the Government of the United States and they would be guaranteed in ther Person & popperty (Published in New york Herald and Tribune July 1861) What was meaned by your Propperty. was it not the Negro now Mr Nigger

if the sothern people had excepted that propposition what woul[d] be your condition to day.

Abraham Lincoln was willing to sell you in Purpetual bondage for the Presorvation of the Union. Lincoln isued the Emancipation Proclamation as a ware measure to cripple the South not for any lov he had for the niggers. The nigger was given the franchise to humiliate the southern People for Boasting of ther Rebelious acts after they had been crushed out   it was not for any love for the Niggers. There is more Nigger lovers in this town than ther is in all the yankee States in the Union. I was in the Union army & I know that if there is any thing the yankee hates wors than the Devl it is a nigger.

Now Mr Nigger who are you indebted to for your freedom is [it] not the people you are Raping   Robbing   murdering. Wo[E] Nigger the day is not far distant when you will be Swept from the face of the earth

C. B. Church Sr

PS   I can see no future for the nigger in this country   CBC

ALS   Con. 194   BTW Papers   DLC.   Written in purple ink on brown paper.

From Edgar Gardner Murphy

Concord, Mass. Jan. 1/02

My Dear Mr. Washington: The enclosed is our only copy of an interesting record and I beg that you will kindly return it to my New York address (Care, Mr. Ogden) when you have read it.

Just ten years ago (February, 1893) there took place perhaps the very first of the negro burnings for crime. I was then stationed at Laredo, Texas — a young man just beginning my active ministry in the South. The negro's crime was one of the most frightful I have ever known (upon a dear little girl of four years — he literally tore her body to pieces). The atrocity of the crime drove the people mad and made the rebuke of the punishment peculiarly difficult. Yet my whole heart cried out against the form of the negro's punishment — for I then foresaw that it would be taken as a precedent for many spectacles like it. I wrote the call for the mass meeting and then went from man to man through the town getting the names of the best men of Laredo to aid me in the public effort to *protest* against the form of the execution. I was opposed by some of my strongest church supporters, but our note was sounded — and I think if our course had been taken throughout the South there would never have been another negro "burning," with all its imbruting consequences. I had almost forgotten about it until I chanced upon something which reminded me that Mrs. Murphy had a copy of the paper.

Pardon my sending it to you — and with so much of detail about myself. I have wanted you to see this, however, in order that you may understand how long and how deeply my heart has been in this whole question. I was then twenty three; and you can easily see that it all happened long before I knew you — long before I knew one intelligent educated negro man — and before the period of my many friendships at the North. Faithfully Yours,

Edgar Gardner Murphy

You may show this to Mr. Bruce if you think he would be interested.

ALS   Con. 865   BTW Papers   DLC.

From Elizabeth Hyde Botume[1]

Whitney School   Port Royal, S.C. January 1st 1902

Dear Mr. Washington   I am very desirous to consult with you in regard to the future of my school for negro children known as "Whitney School."

The time has come when I must give up my work here. Circumstances & especially my age & increasing disability demand this.

I see by the daily papers that you are to be in Charleston to attend the Exposition. Will you not come to Port Royal & see what is doing for, & the needs of the negroes here? I live a little more than a mile from the R. R. Station at Port Royal. I shall be happy to send for you there & entertain you at my own house.

I came to this place in 1864 to take charge of the "Contraband Refugees" located here. Like so many others I came as an independent worker — a volunteer from Rev. James Freeman Clarke's Church of Disciples, Boston. I had a Certificate from the Freedman's Aid Society.

In 1865 the Whitney family of Belmont became interested in my work & adopted my school which I named "Whitney School" for them.

When the F. A. So. disbanded Rev. Mr. Clarke & Mr. Edward Whitney[2] pledged themselves to the support of my school as long as I wished to keep it up. They nobly kept this pledge while they lived.

Mine is a day school. I have a new School building which is on my own land. When I came here this was entirely an agricultural district. Since then the new town of Port Royal has been built & the Augusta & Port Royal R. R. been brought in. Phosphate Mines have been opened around me & the Naval Station on Paris Is. is in sight. Strange people quite different from those I first knew have come into my district. There is a great work to be done here, but I am not strong enough to reorganize & arrange these new people['s] methods. There are good people around me, many of my old pupils who have children to be educated.

It is my wish to put my school under the care of your board of Trustees at Tuskegee. I ask that they should send a normal teacher, —a man is needed who will teach & advise the young men & who will report to your board of Trustees.

My school has no endowment. Most of the old friends interested with me in this work have passed away. Gov. John A. Andrew, Rev. & Mrs Clarke[,] Mr. Whitney, Mrs Stearns & Miss Mary Shannon & Mr. Edward Hooper[3] & very many others who were personal friends. But there are many left who I am assured would gladly help to keep up the work here for my sake & to support a teacher from Tuskegee for their great interest in the work there. Rev. Mr. Ames, — Mrs Ednah Cheney & Miss Clarke, are deeply interested in Tuskegee. They would be happy to know my work here was affiliated with yours there.

Hoping to see you here, I am   Cordially & respectfully   Yours

Miss Elizabeth Hyde Botume

ALS Con. 221   BTW Papers   DLC.

1 Elizabeth Hyde Botume was among the first northern teachers of blacks on the South Carolina sea island of Port Royal, beginning in 1864 and continuing until 1902. She was the author of *First Days amongst the Contrabands* (1893).

2 Edward Whitney (1815–96) was a wealthy Boston merchant, with interests also

in banking and insurance. He was an active opponent of slavery and champion of the freedmen.

3 Edward W. Hooper (1839–1901), after graduation from Harvard Law School in 1861, volunteered to work among the freedmen of the sea islands without pay. He went to Port Royal in 1862, where he served as aide to Edward L. Pierce and later to General Rufus Saxton. He was admitted to the Massachusetts bar in 1868, and was treasurer of Harvard University from 1876 to 1898.

From George Eastman[1]

Rochester, New York Jany 2d, 1902

Dear Sir: I have just been re-reading your book "Up from slavery" and have come to the conclusion that I cannot dispose of five thousand dollars to any better advantage than to send it to you for your institute.

Hence please find enclosed draft on the Am-Exchange Natl Bank New York for that amount. Yours truly

Geo Eastman

ALS Con. 707 BTW Papers DLC.

1 George Eastman (1854–1932), inventor of the Kodak camera, was treasurer and general manager of the Eastman Kodak Co. and founder of the Eastman School of Music in Rochester, N.Y. Beginning with this gift, Eastman became one of the largest contributors to Tuskegee Institute.

From John H. Lewis[1]

Boston, January 2, 1902

My Dear Sir: I have just returned from a little Christmas trip to my old home at Heathville, N.C. On my way down South, I stopped at Washington a day, and spent a little time looking around among the good friends, and I heard through them that ex-gov. P. B. S. Pinchback was sadly in need of something to do, and also that he had gone thro' nearly all he possessed, and was quietly asking his friends to interest themselves in his behalf, and I had a little quiet talk with some of his friends, and they promised their level best to see if they could not get something from the government for him.

I want to beg you from the bottom of my heart to interest yourself in his behalf, as he has been a noble representative of our race, and it makes me feel badly to know that he has got to go down, unless we are able to get him something to do. It would not only do a great good to our people, but it will also be a personal favor to me, if you can help him in any way, shape or manner.

Wishing you a happy and prosperous new year, and awaiting a reply, I am   Very truly yours,

J. H. Lewis

TLSr Con. 233 BTW Papers DLC.

1 John H. Lewis was born in North Carolina in 1854.

To Theodore Roosevelt

Pittsburgh, Pa. January 5, 1902

My dear Mr. President: If you have in mind the sending in of a special message bearing upon the lynching of Italians in Mississippi, I am wondering if you could not think it proper to enlarge a little on the general subject of lynching; I think it would do good. I think you could with perfect safety, give the Southern States praise, especially the Governors and the daily press, for assisting in reducing the number of lynchings. The subject is a very important and far reaching one and keeps many of our people constantly stirred up.

Mr. Cashin,[1] the colored man who is Receiver of Public Moneys at Huntsville, Alabama, I find has a very fine reputation among the colored and white people in Alabama. As to how he has conducted the affairs of his office I am not able to state. I have talked with Mr. Thomas H. Clark[2] about him; he is also seeking information.

My address from now on will be Tuskegee, Alabama. Yours truly,

Booker T. Washington

TLS Theodore Roosevelt Papers DLC.

1 Herschel V. Cashin, born in Pennsylvania in 1854, practiced law in Alabama.

2 Thomas Harvey Clark (b. 1857) was a white Alabama lawyer who edited the Selma *Times* briefly in the 1880s before joining the staff of the Montgomery *Advertiser*. In 1887 he became recording secretary for Governor Thomas Seay, and returned to law practice in 1891. He was active in the Democratic party in Alabama.

To Emmett Jay Scott

Pittsburg, Pa. January 5, 1902

Dear Mr. Scott: After you have read the enclosed letter from the President please give it to Mrs. Washington. It relates to matters in Mississippi. There is going to be quite a shake-up there within a few days. Mr. Edgar S. Wilson, my friend, who is the correspondent from Mississippi for the New Orleans Picayune, is going to be given the whip hand in that state. He is brother in law of Gov. Longino, and is one of the finest, truest white men I have ever seen. While he is a Gold Democrat at present it will not take much encouragement for him to become a Republican. He will be made United States Marshall and Isaiah T. Montgomery will be likely to take Hill's place as Receiver of Public Moneys. Hill has made a miserable record in the conduct of his office. Yours truly,

Booker T. Washington

TLS   Con. 272   BTW Papers   DLC.

A List of the Seven Highest Salaries at Tuskegee Institute

[Tuskegee, Ala.] Jan. 14 1902

1.	Booker T Washington		$208.33 Per Mo
2.	Warren Logan	House &	125.00
3.	Emmett J Scott	do	115.00
4.	J. H. Washington	do	100.00
5.	R. C. Bedford	Board &	100.00

6. J B Bruce   do   90.00

6 [7] Lowis [Lewis] Adams   100.00

Wm H C[1]

ADI   Con. 223   BTW Papers   DLC.

1 William H. Carter was a bookkeeper and accountant at Tuskegee Institute for many years beginning in 1900.

To James Meadows

[Tuskegee, Ala.] 1, 15, 1902

Dear Sir: As much as I regret it, I am compelled to advise you that our physician has just discovered that your daughter must be withdrawn from school because of a serious mishap two years ago last April. This she has confessed to our physician, naming at the same time the physician at Charleston, W.Va., who operated on her. This is a very serious matter as you can easily understand and one of such character as to necessitate our asking you to take her from the school, and I shall be very glad if you will send the money at once so that she can leave here. This girl was highly recommended to us and it was upon the recommendations submitted that we admitted her to the school. Yours truly,

[Booker T. Washington]

TLp   Con. 282A   BTW Papers   DLC.

From Timothy Thomas Fortune

Red Bank, N.J. Jan. 16, 1902

My Dear Mr. Washington: Your letter of the 14th instant was received and I am very glad to know that if the President should send a message to Congress on the lynching of Italians in Mississippi he will have some thing to say on mob law in this country generally. It will be of great service to him in mollifying our newspaper men, and others, as some of the former have intimated that the President omitted to refer to mob law in his annual message upon your suggestion.

Talking about mob law, a man just from the southwest told me yesterday that a railroad man had told him that when you were on your recent trip in Mississippi that a mob of white men boarded your train at three stations on the road with intent to do you violence, but could not find you because you were in the sleeping car, and that the railroad people shielded you. Did you know anything about this, or have you heard anything about it?

I have been in communication with Philip Waters, and he says he will see what his senators have to say of his chances before he goes ahead. His Congressman is with him.

Mr. Durham says he has about decided to go in for a judicial position in the Insular Possessions, and that he would write to you about it.[1] I told him to make up his case and file it, as that was the only way he could find out whether he could get what he wanted.

I enclose Mrs. M'Kinley's letter, so that you can see what she says about her brother, and to see if you can place her in the way she indicates. She is a very lovable and accomplished young woman, and Mr. Scott will be glad to tell you all about her. Please return her letter.

Your telegram of the 16th instant was received. Yours truly,

T. Thomas Fortune

TLS   Con. 227   BTW Papers   DLC.

[1] See Durham to BTW, Jan. 15, 1902, Con. 225, BTW Papers, DLC. Durham wrote that he thought he would be offered a judgeship in the Philippines.

From Edgar Stewart Wilson

Jackson, Miss., Jan. 16, 1902

My dear Mr. Washington: Your telegram from Tuskegee was forwarded to me in Washington, where I had gone to look after an important matter, with the president, and which he agreed with me. I had already been saving the press comments on my appointment, and the others, which greatly pleased him. All, save from

sources from which opposition is badge of honor, have been complimentary both to the president and myself. The dispatch sent
from here to the Atlanta Constitution mentioned by you, I have
not seen, but the correspondent, was so disreputable as associated
press correspondent, that he was dismissed about a year ago, and I
was appointed, and hence his enmity to me. He was abusive of the
governor before that, and was denied access to the executive office
for the same. He has no following in this state. I will continue to
send in clippings to the president.

As to the New York telegram, I regret to state that there is only
one office deputy, and I had before I got your wire, as an act of self
defense, asked the incumbent, who is a fine book keeper and accountant, a life long young republican, to remain at least for this
year, and he had consented to do so. There is not much doing in a
marshal's office in a state like Mississippi, where there are few
distilleries, and the like breeders of crime. I fully concur with you
about places for colored men. In fact I have absolutely refused to
countenance any suggestion looking to the turning out of colored
post masters, men and women, of which there [are] a number in the
state. I shall be the same friend to the colored people that I have
all my life, and merit, will be the touchstone to my endorsement,
and not color. You will see from a clipping that I will send you from
tomorrow's Picayune, that I am working as a journalist, as well as
otherwise for the great peasantry of the commonwealth. This was
written before your letter came this afternoon.

The idea of Montgomery being a democrat is absurd. He is a
member of the republican state committee. The president spoke of
his appointment to me, and seemed greatly pleased at it.

The president is more popular in Mississippi than ever. I am
vigilant to the end you detail in your letter, and have impressed
the appointees that he must receive the delegation. I know full well
and appreciate the balance of power is held [by] colored people of
the states that you mention. I am watching everything with the
best possible care, and shall continue to do so. I agree with everything you say, fully and heartily.

I told the president in a note that I mailed him, after doing some
things there he suggested, that I was his "as ever, more than ever
and for ever."

Of course bourbons, and people whom the president have turned down, will stir up all the strife possible, and hesitate at nothing that they think will benefit them. The bourbon hates to see the wedge driven in, that will cleave two parties, and the professional office holder, wants to get back in power. I recognize to the fullest my great trust and responsibility. If I fail in my duty to country or in my devotion to my chief, may my right hand forget its cunning, and my tongue cleave to the roof of my mouth.

Please let me hear from you often. I needed no congratulations from you, because I knew how glad you must be. I have telegrams and letters by the hundred from people of the state, white and colored. Sincerely,

Edgar S. Wilson

TLS   Con. 261   BTW Papers   DLC.

To Timothy Thomas Fortune

Tuskegee, Ala., Jan. 20, 1902

My dear Mr. Fortune: Replying to that portion of your letter which refers to my trip through Mississippi I would say that, there is not the least foundation for such a report. I received a perfect ovation from the time I entered the state of Mississippi from both white and colored until I left, and I am sure that there was not the least indication of bitterness. Yours truly,

Booker T. Washington

TLS   Con. 541   BTW Papers   DLC.

To James Dickens McCall

[Tuskegee, Ala.] Jan. 21, 1902

Mr. J. D. McCall: It is my intention to have the Academic Department reorganized at the beginning of the next school year. When you took the position of Head Teacher in the Academic Department I understood that you did so with reluctance and solely with a view of accommodating the school and complying with my own wishes in the matter. I appreciate your attitude in this matter and the work that you have done as head of the Academic Department. I feel, as you have yourself several times expressed it, that your best work can be done in some branch of the physical sciences, and I write to say that it is my wish that at the end of the present school year that you resume work at the head of some branch of physical science which we can agree upon later. I should make no change in your present salary and will do everything possible to accede to your wishes in regard to the work that I wish you to do next year, especially in view of the fact that you have against your own inclination tried to accommodate the school in filling your present position. I ought to say further that it is my present plan to have Mr. Roscoe C. Bruce, who graduates at Harvard this year, take the position which you are now filling, and in several respects the department is to be reorganized, the details of the reorganization it is not necessary for me to enter into at present. It is the desire of the school to make just as few changes in teachers from year to year as possible. We want to carry out the principle of teachers settling down and feel that this is their permanent life work.

Booker T. Washington

TLpS   Con. 282A   BTW Papers   DLC.

To Theodore Roosevelt

Tuskegee, Alabama. January 22, 1902

My dear Mr. President: I wonder if it will be possible and practicable for you to defer the appointing of a Naval Officer for the port of New Orleans to take the place of Mr. Webre,[1] the colored man who died there recently, until I can have a conference with you. It is my present plan to pass through Washington on my way to New York during the second or last week in February.

One other thing. At your request sometime ago I gave you information regarding the character and ability of Mr. J. H. Bingham, the present Internal Revenue Collector for the State of Alabama. I am more convinced now than when I wrote you that Mr. Bingham in every way is all right, in any case I hope that you will not remove him before I have had an opportunity to talk with you.

There are several other matters of importance which I want to discuss with you at that time if possible. Yours truly,

Booker T. Washington

TLS   Theodore Roosevelt Papers   DLC.

1 John Webre.

To Whitefield McKinlay

Tuskegee, Ala., January 22, 1902

My dear Mr. McKinlay: I am in receipt of your letter of January 18th. I am very much interested in what you say regarding the influence of putting a white man in Dancy's place. The last time I talked to the President I went over the matter of Negroes in office very carefully and he told me that it was going to be his general policy to either keep the present men in office or wherever he thought it necessary to remove them to put other colored men in their places if decent colored men could be found. This policy has been pursued in Alabama; for example, Mr. Cashin, the Receiver of Public Money in Huntsville was reappointed, while Mr. Leftwich, the Receiver of Public Money in Montgomery, who was not a proper man, was not reappointed. In each case the matter was done promptly, and as you suggest, without giving time for a noise to be made, and as a result I have not heard the least criticism from a single paper or from a single white man in Alabama. I am quite sure that much of the difficulty occurs because of the fact that there is unnecessary delay. In the case of Morton of Athens I am sorry to say that some very grave charges have been brought against him.[1] Enclosed I send a copy of a telegram which is for the eye of no one but yourself. The man who sends this telegram is a high-toned white man, and while he may not be stating the truth I think he believes this himself. I have not acted on this telegram as I must have other evidence before I should withdraw anything that I have said in favor of Morton, but we cannot stand by our men unless they stand by themselves by keeping themselves clean and in every way in good company. I am doing what I can to see that C. C. Wimbish is retained as Naval Officer in Atlanta and DeVeaux as Collector of Customs in Savannah.

I am trying to make a plan by which some of our strong men like Durham will secure judicial positions in the Philippine Islands. When I go through Washington again I want to put matters as forcefully as I can before the President. Looked at however, from the racial standpoint alone, I do not believe that it would hurt the race if something would occur that would cause a division among our people in the pivotal states like Illinois, Indiana, New Jersey and New York.

The colored people in New Orleans are very much agitated over the matter of the appointment of a Naval Officer for that port and are doing their best to see that a Negro is retained in office. That matter I want to take up with the President very soon.

I will write you later regarding the Philippine question and the Washington meeting. Yours truly,

Booker T. Washington

TLS Con. 4 Carter G. Woodson Collection DLC.

1 Monroe ("Pink") B. Morton, the black postmaster of Athens, Ga., was a McKinley appointee in 1897. Roosevelt did not reappoint him, and Morton wrote BTW that he was frustrated in his efforts to find out just what the charges against him were. The Postmaster General had advised him that no charges had been filed. Morton wrote BTW, "I leave it to an unbias[ed] public to decide whether the race was not discriminated against in my case, or whether the president was justifiable in turning me down under the circumstances." (Mar. 10, 1902, Con. 236, BTW Papers, DLC.)

From Frederick Winsor[1]

Middlesex School Concord, Massachusetts Jan. 22, 1902

Dear Sir: I have your letter of inquiry of January 18th. The question which you ask is one which I do not feel that I can answer without consulting my Board of Trustees, as it is one which has not before come up. My personal wish, and I know it would be that of every member of the Board of Trustees, would be to admit your son without question; but we have the wishes of the parents to consider as well, and we shall have boys next year from as far south as Augusta, Georgia. The problem thus becomes complicated and the question develops into one of school policy.

I have expressed myself very frankly because I am sure that is what you wish. As soon as I can get the reply from my Board of Trustees, I will transmit their decision to you. I am extremely sorry that I was absent from the school the other day when you telephoned to me. Very truly yours,

Frederick Winsor

TLS   Con. 213   BTW Papers   DLC.

₁ Frederick Winsor (1872–1940) founded Middlesex School in 1901 to train young men for Harvard. He was its headmaster from 1901 to 1938. The school had an innovative curriculum which included, in addition to the standard college preparatory courses, classes in music, fine arts, and woodworking. Winsor originated the first private school competitive scholarship program in the United States, thus drawing students from all over the country and from many walks of life.

From Paul Laurence Dunbar

Washington, D.C., Jan. 23, 1902

My dear Mr. Washington, I have your letter and note your objections to the song.[1] In the first place, your objection to the line, "Swift growing South" is not well taken because a song is judged not by the hundred years that it lives but from the time at which it was written, and the "swift growing" only indicates what the South has been, and will contrast with what it may achieve or any failure it may make. The "Star Spangled Banner" was written for the time, and although we may not be watching the stars and stripes waving from ramparts amid shot and shell, the song seems to be going pretty fairly still.

As to emphasizing the industrial idea, I have done merely what the school itself has done, but I will make this concession of changing the fourth line of the third stanza into "Worth of our minds and our hands," although it is not easy to sing.

The Bible I cannot bring in. The exigencies of verse will hardly allow a paraphrase of it, or an auctioneer's list, and so I am afraid that I shall have to disappoint Mr. Penney as to that. I am afraid that I cannot write verse up to Mr. Penney's standard of it but I believe if you will look over "Fair Harvard" you will note that they have not given their curriculum in the song or a list of the geological formation of the country around the school. Very truly yours,

Paul Laurence Dunbar

TLS Con. 178 BTW Papers DLC.

1 See The Lyrics to the Tuskegee Song, Feb. 15, 1902, below.

From Frederick Smillie Curtis[1]

The Curtis School, Brookfield Center, Connecticut. January 23, 1902

My dear Mr. Washington, Your letter of the 18th inst. asking if I would receive your son into my school is at hand to-day. I am very sorry to be obliged to say that he is too old to come as a new scholar. I do not take anyone who has reached his fourteenth birthday, as a new boy, though we keep the boys till sixteen or seventeen.

I want to tell you, nevertheless, what my position is in the matter. Personally I should have not the least hesitation, but sh'd be very glad that a man who had done what you have done and had created such an atmosphere for his boy to grow in should be willing to entrust his son's guidance to my care. I have boys from all quarters of the country, including California, Texas, far Western States, Central and Eastern. You know as well as I that it would be my duty to consult with their parents before taking a step that would involve a question touching their sons; yet if I had to do that I am confident they would confirm my own decision. I have read with our boys the whole of your autobiography, on Sundays in the evenings as they sat about before the open fire, and we have talked together about it much. When I told them of your letter they were all very sorry that your boy would have to be excluded.

If I may modestly make the association of our interests I may say that you in your large way and I in my very small way are trying to impress youth with the same idea: that education increases our responsibilities and finds its highest application only in the improvement of our own and our fellows' condition for this world and the next; and that abundant and continued work is the right expression of it. Some day I want to find the opportunity to take your hand and thank you for what you are doing for the race, and to talk with your students as a Northern educated man who has done many kinds of hard work with his hands, in old clothes, as well as with his head. I want to give them personal encouragement that can come from such a source as from no other.

When you come North and can give yourself a day of rest such as you must take sometimes, branch off from Boston or New York and come to see us. You shall have a very appreciative welcome by us all. We remember Mr. Whittaker's[2] visit with much pleasure; remember us to him with regards.

I cannot say how sorry I am not to be able to come closer to your work through your son's education. Very sincerely Yours,

Fredk. S. Curtis

I send copy of our circular marked.

TLS   Con. 224   BTW Papers   DLC.

[1] Frederick Smillie Curtis (1850–1930) was the founder in 1875 and principal of the Curtis School for Young Boys in Brookfield, Conn. He was also a member of the Brookfield Board of Education from 1894 to 1915.
[2] John W. Whittaker.

To Timothy Thomas Fortune

Tuskegee, Ala., Jan. 25, 1902

My dear Mr. Fortune: I have received your telegram of January 24th saying that you are going to Washington and that things are in bad condition there. I do not know to what your telegram refers but hope to hear from you in detail and at length later. I have had letters from [a] party in North Carolina complaining that the colored people were being treated wrongfully there, through the influence of Senator Pritchard. In the last analysis we all must acknowledge that the President must not be blamed for paying heed to those whom the people themselves select to represent them. If

Senator Pritchard is not representing the colored people in that state as he should the colored people have themselves to blame and not the President wholly. When it gets down to hard pan, it is hard to give an individual or race influence that it does not intrinsically possess.

I am especially interested just now in the Naval Office at New Orleans and am trying to do all I can to keep this position in the hands of a colored man and have reason to believe that I shall succeed.

I am still deeply interested in your case and cannot understand why I have not heard from Mr. Leupp to whom I have written. Would it not be well for you to call and see him and see how matters stand?

I have not been doing much literary work lately but am now pinning down to it and hope to have something in the press soon.

I am sorry to hear that you have been unwell. Yours truly,

Booker T. Washington

TLS Con. 261 BTW Papers DLC.

From E. W. Whips[1]

Ensley, Ala. Jany 27th/1902

Dear Sir   I am in receipt of your letter of the 25th inst. We have not written you, heretofore, in regard to Booker City[2] for the reason that we wanted to get the "proposition" a little further along. It was our intention then, to invite you to come and visit the place. Booker City is named after Booker T. Washington and the Main Avenue is Washington Ave. Our Directors are all men who appreciate what you have done and are still doing for the good of the Southern Negro, hence the name. Booker City was not started by a few "Schemers" to get all the money possible from the negro in this section and give him as little as possible in return, but the projectors are the most conservative business men whose desire it is to let no one put a dollar in Booker City until he is throughly satisfied that he is getting value received for it. We are trying to interest the very best class of colored people and to show you how well we are succeeding, along that line, we have sold more than 100 lots since they were put on sale about the 5th of this month, and have sold to only one man who could not sit down and read his papers over and write his own name. The Company will deal liberally with churches and schools and if you can suggest anything that will help us we will appreciate it. The Co. owns over four hundred acres of fine land, with two miles of railroad frontage and it is the purpose of the Co. to let your people build a town of their own and run it to suit themselves. As you probably know, we have already located a school there, The Miles Memorial Institute. I send you, under separate cover a map of the town. Only a few lots have been laid off and we are selling those for $25. and $30. Very Truly

E. W. Whips

TLS Con. 792 BTW Papers DLC.

[1] E. W. Whips, president of the Booker City Land Co., was a white real estate agent born in Missouri in 1858.

[2] Whips's letterhead indicated that the Booker City Land Co. was capitalized at $25,000 and owned 410 acres of land eight miles from Birmingham and two and a half miles from Ensley, Pratt City, Wylam, and Adamsville.

From William H. Ferris[1]

New Haven, Conn. [ca. January 1902]

My Dear Sir: The rumpus the South kicked up over your dining with Pres. Roosevelt set me to thinking. I was somewhat surprised because if there is one man the South ought to be grateful to, ought to respect & love, that man is your self. Three things are made apparent by the incident.

First it shows that the South only cares for you in so far as it can use you as a tool or catspaw, but that deep down in their hearts they despise you as they do the most ragged worthless loafer. If the south really respected & esteemed you they would not have gone into hysterics over your dining with Pres. Roosevelt. No matter how magnificent an institution you may, by your constructive

genius & tact, erect, no matter how many nice things you may say
about the white man of the south, in his estimation you are a nigger
just the same. This may sound hard but it is true.

Second the South by that insane fury has given the lie to all the
splendid compliments you have been paying to the South. You have
in grandiloquent words eulogized the white men of the South. And
they turn around & through God, McSweeney, Dr. Richard Mc-
Ilwaine and others show that they are not the angelic beings you
have pictured them to be.

I with other colored bellboys worked for a southerner once. As
long as we worked hard for him we were fine fellows but as soon
as we displeased him we were "dam niggers." Now that is the estimation the South holds you in. They dont have any intrinsic admiration or respect for you; they pat you on the shoulder because
you play into their hands & make music for them.

Now Prof. Washington there are many colored people and a
growing number of white people who think that you kiss the hand
that smites your race too much. Now after the insulting, disparag-
ing & contemptuous things the leading newspapers and most prominent men of the South have said about you, you cannot without a
loss of respect and manhood continue to play the sycophant to the
South as you have in times past and gone. There is a time when
patience ceases to be a virtue and when love for your enemies becomes a slave's love rather than a man's love. I wish you had less
of the Christ and more of the John L Sullivan spirit.

Now I dont want you to curse the South & have your institution
burned up. But for God's sake Prof. Washington, do stop going out
of your way to throw bouquets at and grovel before the South. They
dont thank you for it nor care any more for you. This volcanic
eruption which followed your Roosevelt dinner clearly shows what
the South thinks of you.

Indeed four years ago a white lady from Atlanta told me that
Booker T. Washington was a greater man than Frederick Douglas[s]
because he didn't teach them that they were the equals of the white
man. You are only a good nigger in the eyes of the South. They
like you because you teach the negro to know his place. They only
regard you as they regarded the white men's niggers who told their
masters when their fellow slaves contemplated running away in the
good old Ante Bellum days. Hold your head erect and be a man.

The white men would respect you more. The way they have called you nigger, said you wasn't fit to sit at a white man's table, said that Roosevelt disgraced himself etc. shows how much respect they have for you. You have been casting pearls before swine.

For myself, a man who thinks I am not good enough to sit at his table can be damned and go to Hell. God dam Pres. McIlwaine. Very truly Yours

Wm. H. Ferris

P.S. I believe that Tuskegee is a monument to your genius & tact & executive ability; but I speak so frankly because I respect & esteem you so highly.

ALS Con. 227 BTW Papers DLC. On stationery of the Hart Farm School and Junior Republic for Dependent Colored Boys, Washington, D.C., of which Ferris was traveling agent.

[1] William H. Ferris (1873–1941) was a black intellectual of erratic personality who was at different times a Trotterite, a BTW supporter, and a Garveyite. He earned a B.A. and an M.A. from Yale. Then he attended Harvard Divinity School for three years, receiving an M.A. degree. After teaching for a year in Florida, he became field agent of the Hart Farm School in Washington, D.C., in 1901. The following year he was a correspondent for the Boston *Guardian* and the Washington *Colored American*. Early in 1903 he rendered a verbal attack on BTW, "The Boston Negroes' Idea of Booker T. Washington," before the Bethel Literary and Historical Association. (Washington *Colored American*, Jan. 10, 1903, 7.) At the Louisville meeting of the Afro-American Council, Ferris joined with Trotter, George W. Forbes, and other militants to attack BTW's ideas. They were a distinct minority, however, and Ferris caused an uproar when he demanded that a huge picture of BTW at the meeting hall be taken down. In 1907 he got into a personal quarrel with Trotter, a man almost impossible to get along with, and sought to ingratiate himself with BTW. The race needed, he wrote to BTW, both "the men who bring things to pass & also the men who see a vision & dream of the ideal. We don't need though such a fiery, fire-eating firebrand as Trotter." (Dec. 9, 1907, Con. 348, BTW Papers, DLC; Fox, *Guardian of Boston*, 47–48, 108–9.) In 1913, when he sought Julius Rosenwald's help in publishing his two-volume work, *The African Abroad*, BTW advised the Chicago philanthropist against aiding Ferris. In later years Ferris taught at the Berean Manual Training and Industrial School in Philadelphia. In the 1920s he was active in the Universal Negro Improvement Association and was editor and writer for several black publications, including the *Negro World*.

To Hollis Burke Frissell

Tuskegee, Ala., Feb. 1, 1902

My dear Dr. Frissell: I am very sorry indeed to hear that you are so disappointed regarding matters at Charleston. I did not know before the receipt of your letter that you did not receive the space that was promised you. I do not know to what the other portion of your letter has reference. The Exposition as a whole is far from the success that it was expected to be and in this of course Hampton will share in the general disappointment. Those in charge of the Negro Department however, are in no way responsible for the general failure of interest being taken in the Exposition. Since we had promised to go into the matter I felt that the only thing was to make a success of the Negro Department as far as it could be done and I think we have a reasonably creditable exhibit in that department. I very much fear however, that the attendance on the Exposition as a whole is going to be poor all through.

I think I wrote Miss Hyde[1] some days ago that I have advised Mr. Roscoe C. Bruce to visit Hampton during March or April with a view of seeing the work there and also with a view of selecting some teachers for next year. Mr. Bruce has spent a month here looking into matters, and I confess we were very much surprised at his very clear insight into matters and were pleased to note how well he is up on all matters in connection with the latest phases of education. He is to take charge of our academic work next year. Yours truly,

Booker T. Washington

TLS BTW Folder ViHaI.

[1] Elizabeth Hyde.

From Timothy Thomas Fortune

Red Bank, N.J., Feb. 1, 1902

My dear Mr. Washington: Your letter of the 29th ult., with the check for $60 enclosed on account of the St. Louis trip, was received today. I cannot leave for St. Louis before Tuesday night or Wednesday morning, as I have that Trenton dinner on for the third, and must get my Age work for the coming week done.

I did not care to write about the Washington situation until I had fully informed myself as to it, and it takes time and patience to do that, as the whole thing is made up red tape, selfishness and humbug. The more that I see of it the more I despise it.

I saw Mr. Leupp, and he explained that he turned the papers and suggestions over to the President with his own suggestions so that the matter could have official status, and that when Mr. Cortelyou had acknowledged the receipt of the papers his, Leupp's, connection with the matter ceased. He seemed as pleasant as when I first saw him and if there is anything wrong he did not disclose it to me.

I spent three hours in the President's reception room, where he received the rabble, watching him and the people he met, and I will talk to you about that when we meet. When he reached me he was very gracious, and as I told him I only called to pay my respects he said confidentially that he expected to see you in a short time, which I had to interpret that he would then consider my matter with you and dispose of it. Of course, it was none of my province to discuss the matter further, and after a pleasant exchange we parted. I think that matters are in good shape and that if you insist upon Hayti I can have it.

I went and paid my respects to Postmaster-General Payne, because I had worked with him in the west in the last campaign, and for him he seemed particularly gracious. He asked me how my affairs were prospering I told him I thought they were in fair shape; and he smiled pleasantly and said he thought so too.

I think the conclusion of the entire matter will or can be determined when you see the President again.

I saw all of our big men, and they are a very scared and anxious lot. They think they are clean out of the running, and so do I. I hope Deveaux will pull through and that we may not lose the naval officer at New Orleans, but I think both places are hanging in the balance.

Saturday night Dunbar went home and tried to kill his wife. He left Washington on the 12 o'clock train, and had not been heard from when I left Washington Thursday morning. He is a high class brute, and I will tell you what led up to it when we meet. His family has left his home, on the advice of friends, but I donot know their address. I am sorry, for them, as they are helpless.

The situation among our newspaper men is not satisfactory. They are dissatisfied and disposed to fight.

I wired you to-day as to St. Louis and the 25$ I asked for last month and you said you would send. I was in hopes that you would have sent it in the check for St. Louis, as I need it in my accounts here on the 10th instant. The St. Louis trip costs about $35. each way. I hope to get matters straight definitely the few hours I am there. Of course I shall put it out that I am in the West on my business. Yours truly,

T Thomas Fortune

TLS   Con. 227   BTW Papers   DLC.

An Advertisement in the Brooklyn *Eagle*[1]

Brooklyn, [N.Y.] February 5, 1902

BOOKER T. WASHINGTON

Endorses Pe-ru-na---Says "Pe-ru-na Is a Certain Cure for Catarrh."

Booker T. Washington, the famous educator, founder of Tuskegee Institute, Alabama, has done more than any colored man now living for the advancement of his race in this country. In a recent letter from Tuskegee, Ala., he says:

The Peruna Medicine Company, Columbus, Ohio:

Gentlemen—"Your remarkable remedy, Peruna, is certainly unexcelled as a tonic. I have used one bottle and I can truthfully say that I have never taken any medicine that has improved me as much as Peruna. Peruna has my hearty commendation as a catarrhal tonic and a certain cure for catarrh." **BOOKER WASHINGTON.**

What this noted man says must inspire faith. The late President McKinley said of him in an address at Tuskegee: "He (Booker Washington) has won a worthy reputation as one of the great leaders of his race, widely known and much respected at home and abroad as an accomplished educator, a great orator and a true philanthropist."

Catarrh hovers ominously over every city, and nestles treacherously in every hamlet. It flies with vampire wings from country to country and casts a black shadow of despair over all lands. Its stealthy approach and its lingering stay make it a dread to the physician and a pest to the patient.

Catarrh in some form, catarrh in some stage lurks as an enemy in the slightest cough or cold.

No tissue, function, or organ of the body escapes its ravages; muscles wither, nerves shatter, and secretions dry up under its blighting presence. So stubborn and difficult of cure is this disease that to invent a remedy to cure chronic catarrh has been the ambition of the greatest minds in all ages.

Is it, therefore, any wonder that the vast multitude of people who have been cured of chronic catarrh by Peruna are so lavish in their praise of this remedy? That the discovery of Peruna has made the cure of catarrh a practical certainty is not only the testimony of the people, but many medical men declare it to be true.

If you do not derive prompt and satisfactory results from the use of Peruna, write at once to Dr. Hartman, giving a full statement of your case, and he will be pleased to give you his valuable advice gratis.

Address Dr. Hartman, President of The Hartman Sanitarium, Columbus, Ohio.

Brooklyn *Eagle*, Feb. 5, 1902, Clipping   Con. 792   BTW Papers   DLC.

[1] William H. Baldwin, Jr., sent BTW the advertisement and advised BTW to sue the Peruna Co. if they used his name without permission. (Feb. 6, 1902, Con. 541, BTW Papers, DLC. See BTW to Hartman, Feb. 7, 1902, below.)

From Timothy Thomas Fortune

Red Bank, N.J., Feb. 6, 1902

My Dear Mr. Washington: Your letter of the 4th instant was received. I cannot see how there appears any disagreement in my letter and the Washington telegram. In Washington I wired that all was satisfactory; when I got here I tried to write you the Washington situation with the side lights on my interviews with Mr. Leupp, the President and Postmaster General Payne. The letter would naturally give a truer view of the situation than the telegram. The situation is, that there is no such hitch as I imagined might have existed, and nothing but my visit to Washington could have convinced me otherwise. As far as the matter now stands it is up to you and the President.

You can have great influence with Mr. Payne in the matter of the Alabama offices (post offices), as he evidently likes you. And he is the politician in the Cabinet. I am real glad that you feel sure that Deveaux is safe. He is a good man and should not be displaced. I am also glad that the Naval Officer at New Orleans seems safe. I have written you about Dr. Albert[1] in my letter yesterday. But the fight is getting on in earnest in our papers, as I am sure that you are seeing, over the whole Southern policy, and when it is lined up we shall have no more than five of the best papers with us. We will see that to be the case. I am being hammered by our press unmercifully for my position, and I am awaiting the whole line up to see where we are at. I have much to lose and much to gain in the next thirty days, and I am anxious. If I am going to shoulder the brunt of the fighting I want to be where I can fight best. Politics is politics.

The whole Dunbar business is disgusting and pathetic.

I return the check for your endorsement. I did not discover the omission until the cashier of my bank called my attention to it. I am sorry about the matter. Please sign and return me the check.

With kind regards, Yours truly,

T. Thomas Fortune

TLS   Con. 227   BTW Papers   DLC.

[1] Aristide E. P. Albert.

To Samuel B. Hartman[1]

[Tuskegee, Ala.] Feb. 7, 1902

Dear Sir: One of the friends of this institution living in New York has wired me of the use of my picture with testimonial of your Peruna remedy in the Brooklyn Eagle.[2] On November 11th, you will remember that I wrote you that I did not desire that this advertisement should appear in any other newspapers, and you wrote me under date of November 18th that my request should be followed.[3] The Brooklyn Eagle of Wednesday, February 5th, contains this same advertisement much to my chagrin and displeasure. I am compelled to ask you to be very sure that this advertisement is withdrawn altogether from any newspapers with which it has been placed for future publication. The statement that you have recently received a letter from me is misleading and deceptive. Yours truly,

Booker T. Washington

TLpS Con. 282A BTW Papers DLC.

1 President of the Peruna Drug Manufacturing Co. and the Market Exchange Bank of Columbus, Ohio.

2 See An Advertisement in the Brooklyn *Eagle*, Feb. 5, 1902, above.

3 A representative of the Peruna Drug Manufacturing Co. wrote to BTW that the running of the advertisement was a mistake that resulted when the Brooklyn *Eagle* repeated a poorly printed advertisement that they had run earlier. He advised BTW that all the plates had been destroyed and apologized to BTW. (Peruna Co. to BTW, Feb. 12, 1902, Con. 239, BTW Papers, DLC.)

From Whitefield McKinlay

Washington, D.C., February 7, 1902

Dear Mr. Washington: Below is a copy of a letter just received from Prof. Kealing.

"The fight seems lost. Mr. Wilford H. Smith sends me this morning a letter from Mr. Lyman,[1] Chief Division of appointments, stating, 'you are informed that the President has decided to retain the present incumbent in the said office.'

"I suppose that settles it. If the President offers Mr. R. L. Smith something else good, I favor his accepting and thus continuing the fight from a new vantage point."

The President has missed another excellent opportunity and I am afraid that it requires more moral courage in him to make such an appointment against the machine than to invite you to dinner, and I am also afraid, unless he does something very soon, he is going to meet some very severe criticism from some of our best men. There is little or no excuse for hanging up such men as Deveaux so long, when white men similarly situated are rushed through. These things will be hard to explain. Hereafter it will be good policy not to enthuse our friends about his good intentions until he does some thing to justify it. Senators Bacon and Clay[2] have been quoted in the news papers as saying that they convinced the President that a negro was distasteful to the patrons of the Athens post-office. You can readily see what capital can and will be made out of that remark. I quite agree with Sen. Chandler's recommendation; that the President ought to be relieved of appointments, and hence such embarrassments as this would not confront him. Very truly,

W. McKinlay

TLS Con. 236 BTW Papers DLC.

[1] Charles Lyman (1843–1913), born in Bolton, Conn., a Union Army veteran, served for decades in the U.S. Treasury Department. In 1873 he was appointed civil service examiner. From 1883 to 1886 he was chief examiner of the U.S. Civil Service Commission, and was a commissioner from 1886 to 1893. He later served in the Secretary of the Treasury's office as chief of the appointments division.

[2] Augustus Octavius Bacon (1839–1914) and Alexander Stephens Clay (1853–1910) were Democratic U.S. senators from Georgia. Bacon served from 1895 until his death and Clay from 1897 until his death.

To Timothy Thomas Fortune

Tuskegee, Ala., Feb. 8, 1902[1]

My dear Mr. Fortune: I am in receipt of yours of February 6th. When I go to Washington again I expect to have a conference with the Postmaster General. I have had a letter from him this week regarding matters in Alabama and he seems to rely upon me a good deal.

There is one thing in which I do not want you to misunderstand me or do any injustice to yourself. I am standing by the President solely for the reason that I believe his intentions are right and that he is straightforward and honest and means to do the proper thing by our people, the thing that will in the end result in the greatest good to the greatest number. So long as I feel this I shall stand by him regardless of whether he may confer any personal benefit upon me or not. Of course it is hardly possible for a man living in the North to see from the same point of view that many of us do in the South. The Negro sooner or later has got to take the position, and I am glad to say that many of the most thoughtful ones in the South are already doing so, that we are to reside in this part of the country, and in every manly straightforward manner we are to make friends with the people among whom we are to live for all time. You are most wise and far-sighted, for example, in cultivating and retaining the friendship of the white people in the city of Red Bank where your family lives. The Negro in the South must learn to do the same thing. I have no hesitation in asserting that the interests of the Negro will be vastly more enchanced through the recognition of such a man as Gov. Jones in Alabama, a native white man who has an honest and courageous heart and who also has such a standing in the community that he can protect the Negro and assist in securing him additional privileges. The white Republicans whom the Negro has kept in office during the last thirty years in the South in most cases not only have no interest in the Negro, but have no ability to help or protect him even if they have the disposition. Of course there are exceptions to this statement. For example, in Alabama recently, one of these old time Republicans went to Gov. Jones and congratulated him upon his selection for the judgeship and stated at the same time that he was glad of it because his being judge would mean that the court would be rid of the Negro on the grand jury and petit jury. Gov. Jones instantly called him to time· and told him that he was talking to the wrong man, that he expected to see that Negroes were kept on the juries just as long as he was judge. The recognition of such men cannot help but eventually to split the Democratic Party and end in the formation of two distinct parties in the South. Until this is done, it is hardly possible for the Negro to receive any kind of political recognition.

I should feel very awkward and uncomfortable were it apparent to me that you are supporting the President or refraining from criticising him simply because of friendship for me or because of some hoped for recognition or profit when deep down in your heart you do not approve of the President's policy. I think it would be far better for you to come out in any case openly and express your views, that is provided you have views different from those that have been already expressed through the Age. I am sure that such a course would not change my personal friendship for you. I should rather have that done than to cherish the feeling that you are refraining from expressing your honest opinion or from doing what you consider the right thing on my account or on account of recognition by the President. I am sure that in the end both of us should do what we consider to be the real straightforward, honest thing for the benefit of the race. When I had the conversation with you in New York and when I arranged to assist The Age in carrying out a certain policy I did so with the full understanding that you and I agreed and that you were going to pursue the policy from principle. I shall work for you just as hard with the President and others regardless of what your course in this matter is, but I do not like to feel in working that if you are recognized you are going to stand by him, and if you are not recognized you are going to "lay down" upon his policy. I think that we owe it to the race to stand upon broader and higher ground. I write thus plainly so that hereafter you may feel free to follow your own conscience and judgment in all of these matters.

I am very glad to hear that the Trenton meeting was so successful.

I am doing what I can to secure a judgeship for Mr. Durham in one of the foreign possessions.

I am planning to be in New York soon after the first of March and want to have a long talk with you. Yours truly,

Booker T. Washington

TLS Con. 261 BTW Papers DLC.

1 BTW wrote the letter on Feb. 8 but did not mail it until Feb. 23. He sent Fortune a cover letter stating that he delayed sending it "for fear you would not understand me, but on re-reading the letter I feel that I ought to send it. I am sure you will not misunderstand what is expressed in it." (Feb. 23, 1902, Con. 247, BTW Papers, DLC.)

From Roscoe Conkling Bruce

Cambridge Mass. 8 Feb. 1902

My dear Doctor Washington — I inclose a significant "cutting" from the *Guardian*. I really fear the paper is doing harm — it serves to organize the malcontents & to intimidate the weak. Moreover, there seems to be no immediate or even remote prospect that the paper's resources will dry up; it is supported by the malcontents whose doctrines it expresses, by the curious whose curiosity it feeds, & by the rather large lower middle class of Negroes who yearn for a lively race paper in Boston. Forbes & Trotter, therefore, aren't likely to be losing money — indeed, they have little to lose. Trotter writes, I have reason to believe, very little for the paper. He is a man with the persistent audacity of a fanatic. Forbes delights in writing the editorials. He is not so hard to deal with as is Trotter. Just one word from the Librarian would in my opinion shut Forbes's mouth. Trotter can't carry on the paper alone — & no conceivable coadjutor could equal Forbes! If something is not done, the *Guardian* may exert some slight influence over the white people here — that of course is the hope of Forbes & Trotter. Several white men of eminence have asked me how to account for the attacks upon Tuskegee of Boston Negroes; there must be other such persons.

Thank you for changing Miss Lane.[1]

I shall keep in mind all your suggestions. Faithfully,

Roscoe C. Bruce

P.S. After thinking the matter over, I agree that it would be impolitic except in the last resort to proceed against the *Guardian* for libel. At first I felt that such a proceeding instituted by Mr. Taylor[2] would be wise. But, all things considered, that doesn't seem necessary.

R. C. B.

ALS Con. 20 BTW Papers DLC.

1 Elizabeth E. Lane was transferred from the academic department, where she taught grammar, to the industries for girls department, where she became Margaret M. Washington's assistant.

2 Robert Wesley Taylor, northern agent of Tuskegee Institute, was frequently the butt of satire in the Boston *Guardian*.

From John C. Asbury[1]

Philadelphia, Feb. 8 1902

Personal

Dear Sir: Your kind invitation to become the guest of the Tuskegee Institute and attend the Tuskegee Negro Conference of the 19th and 20th inst., has been duly received. I regret very much that I shall be unable to attend and to accept the hospitality so kindly extended. I have just been absent from this office for one week attending to some business which could not longer be neglected in Virginia. I assure you that nothing would give me more pleasure than to be able to be present at this conference and witness the fruits of the great work you are doing for the uplift of our people. You have my very best wishes for a successful Conference, and the continued success and prosperity of the great institution of which you are the presiding genius. If the invitation extended holds good for the Conference of 1903, I assure you that I shall make every effort to be present on that occasion.

If I do not take too great a liberty I should like to add a word concerning a political matter in which, it is rumored here, you are interested. The rumor is, that you are using your good offices in the furtherance of the candidacy of Hon. J. S. Durham of this city, for an appointment to a judgeship in the Philippines. If this be true I am sorry, for I think you are making a great mistake and, should you succeed in the effort, will do both yourself and the President a great deal of harm. There is nothing personal in my objection to Mr. Durham nor do I question his ability or fitness for the place. As you know, Mr. Durham has married a white woman;[2] should he get this appointment through your influence, it would revive the recent contention upon the part of the Bourbon people of the south that you are endeavoring to establish social equality and are in favor of mixed marriages; it would also furnish the same class of newspapers with ammunition for their argument that [the] President has given his endorsement to the marriage of colored and white people. I am sure that the newspaper notoriety and incendiary utterances of designing politicians which would be engendered, by this appointment could not but be harmful both to yourself and the President. It would also injure you, I think, with

397

some of those who contribute most to the support of your institution. We all know that the day is not yet when even the best friend of the race looks upon mixed marriages with equanimity and if the idea becomes prevalent that as soon as a colored man becomes educated above the average of his race, he desires to break down social barriers and marry a white woman, that day will see a great falling off in the contributions of our present friends for Negro education. I do not question Mr. Durham's right to marry a white woman; that was his affair and, so far as the mere marriage is concerned, it is none of my business or yours; but a man occupying your position to the race, to the President and the nation is bound to take account of it when by endorsing and promoting the interests of the man who has contracted the marriage, you will not only do yourself and the President an injury, but, I fear, the entire race. Now, Mr. Washington, I hope you will accept these suggestions from me in the spirit in which they are offered. If in your superior wisdom you think me unduly timid and the reasons for my objections to Mr. Durham of no consequence, treat them accordingly and proceed as if you had never heard from me on the subject. I am   Very truly yours,

J. C. Asbury

TLS   Con. 219   BTW Papers   DLC.

1 John C. Asbury, editor and manager of the *Odd Fellows' Journal* in Philadelphia, was born in Philadelphia in 1862. Asbury was also a director of the Keystone Bank, a black firm, and on the executive committee of the Negro Protective League of Pennsylvania. He was a loyal supporter of BTW on racial matters.

2 Constance Mackenzie became the wife of John Stephens Durham on July 1, 1897.

To George Bruce Cortelyou

[Tuskegee, Ala.] Feb. 9, 1902

I am very anxious that Rev. Edgar Gardner Murphy of Montgomery, Alabama, a close friend of Judge Thomas G. Jones and very influential man have an opportunity of seeing the President on Friday, the 13th. Please telegraph answer and name hour.

Booker T. Washington

TWSr   Con. 225   BTW Papers   DLC.

To Whitefield McKinlay

Tuskegee, Ala., Feb. 10, 1902

My dear Mr. McKinlay: What would you think of having Dr. I. B. Scott, the editor of the Southwestern Christian Advocate, appointed to the position of Naval Officer in New Orleans? Dr. Scott I think you know. He is a man of the very highest type of character and would lift the whole service into an atmosphere where it has not been before and would present to the rest of the country an object lesson that I think would lift up Negro politics. If you can get Gov. Pinchback's idea in some way without letting him know what you are driving at on this point I should like it. Gov. Pinchback is very anxious to have the old gang in New Orleans gotten rid of. The matter will be decided pretty soon. Yours truly,

Booker T. Washington

TLS   Con. 4   Carter G. Woodson Collection   DLC.

From William Henry Baldwin, Jr.

Brooklyn Heights [N.Y.] Feb 10 1902

Dear Washington, Talcott Williams[1] of Phila, sends word through Mr. Ogden that the Southern men in Congress are mightily disturbed on account of your connection with appointments in the South.

The criticisms are reported to be very sharp. Yours ever,

W H Baldwin Jr

ALS   Con. 792   BTW Papers   DLC.

[1] Talcott Williams (1849–1928), a journalist and reformer, was a trustee of the Anna T. Jeanes Fund and one of the managers of the Pennsylvania Free Hospital for Poor Consumptives. Born in Turkey, the son of American missionaries, Williams graduated from Amherst College in 1873. After many years as an editorial writer for the New York *World*, New York *Sun*, Springfield (Mass.) *Republican*, and Philadelphia *Press*, Williams was the director of the Columbia University School of Journalism from 1912 to 1919.

From Helen Pitts Douglass[1]

Cedar Hill, Anacostia, D.C. February 11, 1902

Dear Mr. Washington: I take the liberty to send you a copy of the Frederick Douglass Souvenir, I desire also to ask you if they can be placed for sale in your book and newspaper selling room — if you approve of so doing — or wherever they will best meet the public eye.

It may be that many who honor Mr. Douglass' name will be glad to possess this little memento, especially in view of the fact that this home is, we trust, to play in the future, an important part in preserving alive those sentiments we must not let die.

These souvenirs are .25 singly, or .20 by the hundred.

You may not be acquainted with the project of making Cedar Hill a Memorial. I therefore enclose a copy of the bill as passed by Congress, hoping that all the homes reached through the influence of far-famed Tuskeegee, may, through their personal interest, be made a party to the movement, and look forward to the time when their children's children shall come to this mecca as on a pious pilgramage.

I had no thought of writing so much. My pen is always liable to run away with me. Will you kindly let me know concerning the Souvenirs.

I am, with great respect, Yours very sincerely,

Helen Douglass

ALS Con. 225 BTW Papers DLC.

1 Helen Pitts Douglass (1837–1903) was the white second wife of Frederick Douglass. Born in western New York, she graduated from Mount Holyoke Female Seminary in 1859. She first met Douglass at her uncle's house, which adjoined the Douglass home, Cedar Hill. She became the black leader's close friend and adviser when he was recorder of deeds. They were married in 1884 by Francis J. Grimké after the death of his first wife, though the families of both opposed the marriage. As BTW wrote of it years later in a biography of Douglass, the marriage "caused something like a revulsion of feeling throughout the entire country." (BTW, *Frederick Douglass*, 306.) Despite the strains of an interracial union, the marriage was happy and successful.

From Emmett Jay Scott

Montgomery Ala   Feb. 12, 1901[2]

My Dear Mr Washington: I called on Judge Jones today and had as pleasant an interview as I have ever had in my life. He was genial and kind and most cordial. He dismissed his stenographer & his door-keeper and asked the latter to hold the door against all comers. He kept me from 3:30 P.M. to 5 o'clock.

To begin with he said that he was very, very sorry to note that many newspapers are giving the impression that you are a "patronage broker" — that you are to dispense the patronage in Alabama & the South. I told him very frankly that we are fully alive to the evil that will be wrought by such mischievious publication & told him of the Chattanooga newspaper comment in re the Vicksburg postoffice fight — of your letter to the Editor and of his subsequent retraction. He seemed very glad over this and then I told him of the character of letter we write to everyone who writes you about matters political & he seemed to think this an excellent way to fight shy of the place seekers & political mendicants. He said that this was his own position, that he had not spoken of a single man to the President except at the latter's request & suggestion. We then branched off into a general discussion of matters racial and this gave him the opportunity to give utterance to some of the same strong, virile, courageous utterances made by him as Governor and as a member of the Constitutional Convention. He is one of the noblest men I ever met, & you are to be praised & commended for your offices in having him appointed to this place. He told me of many little things he has done for our people since he came to the Judgeship, not to mention his long record of loyalty to duty as Governor and as Citizen. We have in him a stalwart friend & defender (when we are right & we do not need any except when we are). We then came to the Judgeship & he asked me directly if I was not in Washington in his behalf, and asked me to tell him all about it, *and I did!* When I had finished he said it was the first time he was assured of the circumstances leading to his appointment, said he was proud of the place coming through you. He said the President told him how much he (the President) regretted his having voted for Bryan & that gave me a chance to tell him all about the negotiations & I am glad

I had the chance to tell him that it would be told him at his own request without coming from you in any way. I told him to start with that I only called to pay my respects, etc. He laughed heartily at the whole recital of the Chambers-Chandler episode, of the President's hesitation because of the Bryan voting & all![1]

He said that some of his white friends told him with effusiveness that they were proud of the appointment & awfully sorry tho that Washington had anything to do with it. His reply was characteristic, & he wound up by telling them that he liked you personally a very, very great deal, etc. etc.

He is to speak at Grant's Tomb, New York, May 30. He goes to Birmingham Mch 1 to hold court & to Huntsville April 1. He says he would so much like to talk with you, said so three times. I asked him to come to Tuskegee when President Elliot[2] is expected, but he cannot — says he would certainly do so but for the Court. He says he appreciates the delicacy that leads you not to come around him & asks me to say that he doesn't want that to stand in the way & asks that you come to see him at first opportunity. As I said at first it was a splendid interview & I am so glad I had it with him.

He is a rare soul! Yours faithfully

Emmett J Scott

ALS Con. 217 BTW Papers DLC.

1 See Scott to BTW, Oct. 4, 1901, above.
2 Charles William Eliot.

A News Item in the Cleveland *Gazette*

[Cleveland, Ohio] February 15, 1902

I. T. Montgomery, of Mississippi, as a member of the late constitutional convention of that state, voted for Mississippi's new constitution which, of course, includes the disfranchising clause, and supported his action and the measure with a speech which the Democratic press of that state applauded to the echo. Montgomery is the Afro-American that President Roosevelt recently appointed register of the land office with headquarters at Jackson, Miss., displacing that veteran republican and one of the few remaining members of the "Old Guard," Hon. James Hill, the republican leader of the state for many years. Montgomery was elected a member of the constitutional convention by the Democrats of Bolivar county, Miss. Just how much a republican he is remains to be seen. Any black man who can thus be used by democrats seeking to disfranchise his people, can hardly be either a loyal Afro-American or republican. He was recommended for the place (we are informed by leading Afro-American republicans of Mississippi) by Edgar S. Wilson (white) recently appointed to a federal position, and Booker T. Washington. The same gentleman writes us that "Wilson is a bitter democrat and Negro hater and for years was a correspondent of the New Orleans Picayune. Also that he was put in touch with President Roosevelt by Booker Washington."

Cleveland *Gazette*, Feb. 15, 1902, 2.

The Lyrics to the Tuskegee Song[1]

[Tuskegee, Ala., Feb. 15, 1902]

Tuskegee, thou pride of the swift growing South
    We pay thee our homage to-day;
For the worth of thy teaching, the joy of thy care,
    And the good we have known 'neath thy sway.
Oh, long striving mother of diligent sons,
    And of daughters, whose strength is their pride,
We will love thee forever, and ever shall walk
    Thro' the oncoming years at thy side.

Thy hand we have held up the difficult steeps,
    When painful and slow was the pace,
And onward and upward, we've labored with thee
    For the glory of God and our race.
The fields smile to greet us, the forests are glad,
    The ring of the anvil and hoe
Have a music as thrilling and sweet as a harp
    Which thou taught us to hear and to know.

Oh, Mother Tuskegee, thou shinest to-day
    As a gem in the fairest of lands;
Thou gavest the Heav'n-blessed power to see
    The worth of our minds and our hands.
We thank thee, we bless thee, we pray for thee years
    Imploring with grateful accord,
Full fruit for thy striving, time longer to strive,
    Sweet love and true labor's reward.

Tuskegee Student, 14 (Feb. 15, 1902), 2.

[1] Paul Laurence Dunbar wrote the lyrics to this song, which was to be sung to the tune of "Fair Harvard." (Dunbar to BTW, Jan. 9, 1902, Con. 195, BTW Papers, DLC.) BTW had some objections to the song. (See Dunbar to BTW, Jan. 23, 1902, above.)

To Theodore Roosevelt

Tuskegee, Alabama. February 16, 1902

Personal & Confidential

My dear Mr. President. I have just a little fear that owing to your duties in connection with the reception of Prince Henry[1] I may not be able to see you as I pass through Washington, and for that reason I write regarding the Naval Officer vacancy in New Orleans. This information is submitted to you personally and I hope it will not be filed in the Treasury Department.

All things considered, I feel rather sure that Dr. Isaiah B. Scott is by far the best man for this place. He is well educated, clean, and would lift the whole service out of the filthy atmosphere where it has been for too long in New Orleans. I think you will find that Secretary Shaw[2] is personally acquainted with Dr. Scott as he is a member of the same church that Secretary Shaw is. Dr. Scott is the kind of man that I am sure you want to recognize. He is known throughout the country and his appointment would present an object lesson to the rest of the colored people that would prove valuable.

Have you reached any decision as yet regarding our friend T. Thomas Fortune? He is anxious to go to Haiti. Yours truly,

Booker T. Washington

TLS   Theodore Roosevelt Papers   DLC.

1 Heinrich Albert Wilhelm, Prince of Prussia (1862–1929), was the brother of Kaiser Wilhelm II of Germany. BTW met him during his tour of the United States.

2 Leslie Mortier Shaw (1848–1932) was governor of Iowa from 1898 to 1902 and U.S. Secretary of the Treasury from 1902 to 1907.

To Whitefield McKinlay

Tuskegee, Ala., Feb. 17, 1902

My dear Mr. McKinlay: Be very sure that not a word escapes you regarding the appointment of Dr. Scott of New Orleans. I am not sure of course that he will be appointed, but I am very glad to hear through you that Gov. Pinchback favors Dr. Albert. Dr. Scott is the same kind of man that Dr. Albert is except that he is a much stronger and more forceful man in every way. They both belong to the same church and both are strong and clean. Dr. Scott is much more widely known and as I have stated, is much more forceful, and besides it seems that the old machine in Louisiana seeing that they could not win with any of the old time characters have rather concentrated on Dr. Scott.

What you say regarding the prevailing belief that all Southern appointments are submitted to me is interesting. Of course no such thing is true, and I would not think of taking any such responsibility had I an opportunity to do so. While all of us must strive earnestly to hold all the ground that we have gained in politics and try at the same time to gain more, we must bear in mind that in the end our real and permanent advancement is going to be in proportion to our growth in property, education, business and in the general confidence of our neighbors. Yours truly,

Booker T. Washington

TLS   Con. 4   Carter G. Woodson Collection   DLC.

To Whitefield McKinlay

Tuskegee, Ala., Feb. 18, 1902

My dear Mr. McKinlay: I think your idea of calling on the President with a few gentlemen is an excellent one, and I hope that you will prepare yourself to talk frankly and fully with the President; he is a man who does not fall out with one who differs from him, and I feel that he is honestly seeking information and I hope you will let him know exactly what the feeling of the colored people is. I have written him this morning as you suggest and I feel sure that if you call to see him after he has had time to receive my letter that he will give you a cordial reception. He may be very much engaged during the next few days in connection with the reception of Prince Henry, so it might be wiser to omit calling on him until after this reception is over.

The only thing I would suggest in connection with the composition of your committee is that you might add another gentlemen who might give a little more "color" to the delegation.

I have taken the liberty to tell the President that you are not to call for the sake of urging any individual for office or asking for office but to talk with him frankly concerning the general attitude of the race. Yours truly,

Booker T. Washington

TLS Con. 4 Carter G. Woodson Collection DLC.

To Timothy Thomas Fortune

Tuskegee, Ala., 2, 21, 1902

My dear Mr. Fortune: I wish you would take occasion to say in The Age that there was absolutely no truth in the report sent out by the associated press to the effect that some of the students in the University of Nebraska rebelled because of my selection to deliver the commencement address in June. I have just had a letter from Chancellor E. Benj. Andrews[1] to the effect that there was not a single dissenting vote and my election was hearty and unanimous. The whole thing was manufactured by the associated press. Yours truly,

Booker T. Washington

TLS   Con. 272   BTW Papers   DLC.

1 Elisha Benjamin Andrews (1844–1917), a prominent American educator, was chancellor of the University of Nebraska from 1900 to 1908.

A Letter in the Washington *Colored American*[1]

[Tuskegee, Ala.] February 22, 1902

The idea of setting aside a day by your organization to be known as Douglass Day is a very wise one, and I wish that the custom might be adopted by our people in all parts of the country. A close study of his life and teachings would prove a source of help and inspiration. Only recently I have been reviewing his life, for the purpose of informing myself more accurately upon his teachings in certain respects, and I am surprised now, as I have been in the past, to see how clearly he saw into the needs of our people. He early perceived the value of practical education, as indicated by a letter to Harriet Beecher Stowe more than fifty years ago. His were the words of a prophet and a statesman. Mr. Douglass was both, and more.

More and more, during recent years, I deplore the fact that so many of our educated men and women fail to give the race the benefit of their education by following some first-hand, productive, primary, wealth-producing occupation, such as come from the soil, the mine, the tree, or even the air and the water, instead of yielding to the temptation in too many cases of trying to live by their wits, or from productions that other brains and other hands have brought forth. The young college man who goes into a field and makes for himself a position and accumulates wealth by raising and selling vegatables is in a much more secure and enviable position, for instance, than one who depends upon the exigencies of political office for his subsistence.

I have little faith, and I am sure you have not either, in the ability of any man to take part successfully in controlling the affairs of the nation who cannot run successfully the affairs of his own family and make a success of some private business.

In the long run, when we reach the last analysis of any individual or race no President, individual, or political party can long keep an individual in a position when he has been placed there merely by artificial or temporary conditions — in the last analysis every individual and race secures and retains that to which its productive powers and business environment entitle it. In our case, the Negro will secure and hold whatever position he actually makes for himself, not the position made by others for him. When through natural and gradual processes of development, through the accumulation of wealth, commercial power, education, high character, we gain places of eminence, no power on earth can deprive us of them. No one can give an individual power which he does not inherently possess, no one can take from him influence which he has really won.

In making real, natural, and permanent positions for ourselves the outlook was never more hopeful than it is to-day. In every section of the country my observation convinces me that the race is going forward with a stride and determination that has never before been equaled, and there is nothing in the atmosphere to discourage or to cause undue apprehension.

Washington *Colored American*, Feb. 22, 1902, 4.

1 Addressed to the Pen and Pencil Club. Founded about 1900, it was composed of about forty blacks active in public affairs, including John C. Dancy, Cyrus Field Adams, P. B. S. Pinchback, and George H. White. The club met in Washington, D.C., for the purpose of celebrating the eighty-fifth anniversary of the birth of Frederick Douglass. The group later collaborated with BTW in efforts to pay off the mortgage on Cedar Hill, the Douglass home.

From Roscoe Conkling Bruce

Harvard Univ. Cambridge   22 Feb. 1902

My dear Mr. Washington — I sent you a copy of the Boston Globe containing a report of a speech I delivered at the Middlesex Club. I tried to make such a speech as would please both north & south &

emphasize the educational needs of the Negro. In the *Guardian* was printed a mud-flinging attack upon speech & speaker. Of course I paid no attention publicly to the *Guardian;* privately I consulted Doctor James L. Whitney,[1] Forbes' chief. Doctor Whitney is of course enthusiastic in his admiration for you & Tuskegee. I let him understand the situation created by the *Guardian* — I spoke as far as Doctor Whitney knew, entirely on my personal responsibility. He promised to do whatever he could to shut Forbes' mouth. Under the Civil Service rules it would hardly be possible to dismiss Forbes.

Indeed, I strongly incline to believe that for Tuskegee's purposes it is better as long as possible, to have Forbes remain at the beck & call of Whitney. If Forbes were out, he would be wholly beyond reach of anything except the law. And the more I think the matter over the more I feel that a resort to the law would be impolitic. With Forbes in the Library, we have a constantly effective check upon his audacities. As for Trotter I see no remedy except his own ill judgment & fanaticism. If we give him rope enough, he is sure to hang himself. He has already lost character in the eyes of the few white men who have heard of him. So much for the *Guardian*.

Clement Morgan is the most sensible fellow of his group. I, therefore, took pains recently to have a talk with him. At first he was inclined to talk in the air but after a while he got down to earth. Before I got through the man's whole attitude was, externally at least, transformed. I incline to feel that a word or two to him once in a while will keep him in line. If he would, after the manner of Lewis, put himself on record, it would be well.

I had a long talk with Hill.[2] He is unmistakably a man of force. He has determined, as you know, to remain at Harvard one more year, then, he would like very much to come to Tuskegee — even at a smaller salary than he could get at Lynchburg. I shall keep him in view.

Pinn is really eager to come to Tuskegee & will be at our service after the present year. He is competent to give a course in the history of education with special reference to Negro education, a course in morals, & work in English composition & literature. I feel that the work in the history of education would be a valuable contribution to the Normal department, that the work in morals would be valuable for the Normal Department & the Bible Training School. The fallacy of the Bible Training School is that it has emphasized theology almost to the exclusion of morals. Pinn is just the man to give a good rousing course in morals. (Address — Calvin Pinn   Harvard University   Cambridge)

I wrote to Miss White[3] of Oberlin; she would be delighted to come to Tuskegee were she to continue teaching; she is not to continue.

Mercer Langston[4] (3540 South Jefferson Avenue   St. Louis Mo.) is a good man; he is a graduate of Oberlin. Langston is eager to come to Tuskegee next year. Precisely what studies he is best qualified to teach I don't know; I shall find out as soon as possible. In any case Langston would be easily utilizable at Tuskegee.

I shall write to Doctor Rankin[5] of Howard in reference to Mr. Baugh[6] & to the President of Ann Arbor[7] in reference to Miss Murrell.[8]

I note with interest the resignation of Mr. Myers.[9] It is important to get a vigorous teacher in physics. I understand that Mr. J. A. Bluford, a post-graduate in science of Cornell & now a teacher in the St. Louis Sumner High School, is a good man. I'll look him up.

Will you please have Mr. McCall send me a list of all the studies pursued in the academic department with the time-allotments, & a list of the text books used in the respective studies? I should like also, to have a list of the teachers in the academic department with their subjects.

Governor Brackett[10] & Secretary Long wish to be heartily remembered to you. Faithfully

Roscoe C. Bruce

ALS   Con. 221   BTW Papers   DLC.

1 James Lyman Whitney (1835–1910) was librarian of the Boston Public Library from 1899 to 1903.

2 Leslie Pinckney Hill, a graduate of Harvard, taught education at Tuskegee Institute from 1904 to 1907. He left to become head of Manassas Industrial School, and later was president of the Institute for Colored Youth in Cheyney, Pa. He married Jane E. Clark, dean of the woman's department at Tuskegee from 1902 to 1907.

3 Viola Madeline White, later Mrs. Edward Franklin Goin (1878–1955), graduated from Oberlin in 1901.

4 John Mercer Langston taught history and geography at Tuskegee Institute from 1902 to 1904.

5 Jeremiah Eames Rankin (1828–1904) was a white Congregational minister and the author of many religious articles and hymns. He was president of Howard University from 1889 to 1903.

6 William Edward Baugh.

7 James Burrill Angell (1829–1916) was president of the University of Michigan from 1871 to 1909.

8 Margaret P. Murrell taught English literature at Tuskegee from 1902 to 1904.

9 John W. Myers taught physics and geography at Tuskegee from 1899 to 1902.

10 John Quincy Adams Brackett (1842–1918) was lieutenant governor of Massachusetts (1887–90) and governor (1890–91).

To Timothy Thomas Fortune

Tuskegee, Ala., 2, 23, 1902

My dear Mr. Fortune: I put the question direct to the President regarding yourself and the Haytian mission and I have just had a letter from him to the effect that he has decided to make no change in that place at least for the present.[1] I thought I owed it to you to get a direct answer from him on this question and to inform you. Of course while this information may not be very encouraging to you I think at the same time it will give you the advantage of making the announcement in your paper to the effect that there is to be no change and coming from you will tend to relieve the awkward situation that was brought about by reason of the publications emanating in New Jersey. Yours truly,

Booker T. Washington

TLS Con. 272 BTW Papers DLC.

1 Fortune wrote to BTW on Apr. 10, 1902: "I have it straight that President Roosevelt said that I was unreliable in politics, and that I was not popular with the leaders of the race. Why can't he keep his mouth shut? If I should open up my batteries on him and his unpopular policy at the South he would very soon find out how much popularity I have." (Con. 227, BTW Papers, DLC.)

To Warren Logan

Tuskegee, Ala., Feb. 23, 1902

Mr. Logan: At the next meeting of the Executive Council and also at the next meeting of the General Faculty I wish you would make it known that I have recently found that two of our graduates have been refused positions because when they were written to by persons wanting to employ them their letters were so poorly folded and written that they gave the impression that was anything but favorable. I wish you would take means to see that every teacher who has charge of any composition class spends some time within the next two or three weeks in teaching the writing and folding and backing of letters.

Booker T. Washington

TLS   BTW Papers   ATT.

From Addison Wimbs

Greensboro, Alabama. 3/1/[1]902

Dear Sir   I would like to have a copy of the Memorial you as Chairman presented to the Constitutional Convention. I thought it would be in the Journal, but I fail to find it. I would thank you for the same. Your Friend

Ad Wimbs

The sky looks dark for us, but I still have faith in the final good to come to us under the New Constitution. In time we will have many legal Negro voters and through them the interest of the race can be protected whereas under the Old we had in effect none. The few legal Negro voters will have, that [what] the few white voters in the black beats have had under the Old. The occupation of the ballot thief is gone and they know it.

Ad Wimbs

ALS   Con. 246   BTW Papers   DLC.

From William Edward Burghardt Du Bois

Atlanta, Ga., Mch 4 1902

My Dear Mr. Washington: I am sorry that I was detained so long in the North with lectures that it was impossible for me to attend your conference, much as I would have liked to.

I write now to invite and urge you to attend our conference May 27, Tuesday. Our subject for this Seventh Conference is *The Negro Artisan,* we are collecting data on the history of trades among Negroes, the number & distribution of artisans in the United States; the increase & decrease in various communities, the influence of trade schools, the influence of colleges. We expect Hampton, Fisk & other schools to be represented & are particularly anxious to have you.[1]

I think you will grant that I have sought in every way to minimise the breach between colleges & industrial schools & have in all possible ways tried to cooperate with Tuskegee in its work. I have not been so successful in getting you to cooperate with ours, altho' this is of course largely due to the fact that you are a busy man. This time, however, I hope you can serve us & will accept this invitation to speak to us on that occasion. Very Sincerely Yours,

W. E. B. Du Bois

ALS Con. 272 BTW Papers DLC.

[1] BTW accepted the offer to go to Atlanta. Du Bois asked him to speak for about fifteen minutes. (Du Bois to BTW, Mar. 15, 1902, BTW Papers, ATT.)

From Thomas Dixon, Jr.

Elmington Manor, Dixondale, Va. March 4, 1902

My dear Doctor: I mail you to-day an advance copy of my novel "The Leopard's Spots." It is an historical study of the Race Question from 1865 to 1900.

Frederic Harrison recently said that this is the one great problem which shadows the future of America. I hope that you will enjoy it, and if you can find time to say a word in review I will appreciate it very much. Sincerely,

Thomas Dixon Jr

TLS Con. 225 BTW Papers DLC. E. J. Scott wrote on the letter: "Just rec'd today — Told him you're away — The book has come here & will be held! EJS."

From Edmund H. Deas

Washington, D.C., March 11, 1902

Dear Sir: I wrote my friend Mr. Harry C. Smith, of the Cleveland Gazette, of your unselfish interest in matters pertaining to the race and also of your attitude in the Koester matter. He has answered it and said that he was glad to hear it and that he would let up. Mr. Trotter of Boston also wrote me asking for your attitude in this same affair, and I immediately replied and stated substantially what I did to Mr. Smith. Unfortunately these papers have put me in the attitude of antagonizing the President and yourself, and I thought in justice to you that I would write them and give the facts in the case. What I regret most of all is that both Senator McLaurin and Capers[1] should succeed in defaming me to the President as an ignorant, selfish thieving politician, whereas neither of them possess the same standing in their respective communities as to integrity and force of character as I. I can bring credentials from the best democrats in the State as to my past life. I keep two bank accounts in the State and own property in four counties in the State and hold mortgages in many parts of the State. This ought to be convincing proof that I have made good use of my opportunities and that I am not as bad as I am painted. I beg to assure you that I thoroughly appreciate what you have done for me, and in the future you can call on me at any time that I can serve you.

As would be naturally expected I am asked by private individuals as to where you stand in this Koester matter, and it gives me great satisfaction to relieve them of any false impression. Both last week and to day I severely criticised Chase, but of course in his case I do not hope to exert any influence. Very truly,

E. H. Deas

DICTATED.
P.S. Koester's matter not settled as yet. If you can help me further please do so.

E. H. D.

TLS Con. 261 BTW Papers DLC. The postscript is in Deas's hand.

[1] John G. Capers (1866–1919), of South Carolina, was a Democrat until Bryan's nomination in 1896. After actively campaigning for the Republican party he was

appointed assistant U.S. attorney in the U.S. Court of Claims in 1894. In 1901 he was appointed U.S. district attorney for South Carolina, and in 1907 he became a commissioner for the U.S. Internal Revenue Service.

The Lyrics to a Song
by John Townsend Trowbridge[1]

Arlington, Mass. [Mar. 13, 1902]

WHITE HOUSE SONG
Air—"John P. Robinson"

The shoddy-backed chivalry made a wry face:
   "The White House is asking a darky to dine!
Any gentleman, after this shocking disgrace,
   When *he* is invited will sho'ly decline!"
      But Booker T.
      Washington, he
Sat down to his soup as polite as could be.

A prince came to town, and we made a grand spread,
   In the very same mansion where Booker had dined
"A black man has been there before you!" they said.
   But the Emperor's brother remarked, "Never mind!
      Your Booker T.
      Washington, he
Is a mighty brave fellow, his friends all agree."

The guests were invited; who wouldn't forget,
   In the hope of such honor, that horrid disgrace?
But one, at a very wrong moment, had set
   The seal of his fist in a sad brother's face.
      "Tell Senator T.,"
      Says Teddy, "from me,
There'll be *no* room for him with Prince Henry at tea."

"No room, sir? and all the Ambassadors there!
   With even a German schoolmaster, they say!

They could put in a leaf and fetch some sort of chair,
And let me squeeze in between Pauncefote and Hay!"
Senator T.
Swore a word, and says he,
"The chair Booker sat in might answer for me!"

PD Page proof Con. 244 BTW Papers DLC. The song appeared in *The Independent*, 54 (Mar. 13, 1902), 616.

1 John Townsend Trowbridge (1827–1916), pseudonym of Paul Creyton, was a novelist and writer of children's stories.

To Hollis Burke Frissell

Grand Union Hotel, New York. March 14, 1902

My dear Dr. Frissell: I do not know what your plans are regarding getting aid for Hampton through the General Education Board, I hope however, that you are planning to put in an application for aid for Hampton. I very much hope that this board will feel that it is proper among the first things to help put the older and larger institutions upon their feet. For several years Tuskegee has been getting $10,000 for current expenses from Mr. Rockefeller; this matter however, has now been referred to this Board.

I was very sorry to hear about the turn affairs have taken in Virginia about taxing industrial schools. I very much hope that you have succeeded in keeping the matter out of the constitution. If it goes in I fear it will prove hurtful in more ways than one.

I was sorry that I did not have opportunity of seeing you before you went South but I did not know you were going so soon. If you are to be here before I leave I shall make an effort to see you. Yours truly,

Booker T. Washington

TLS BTW Folder ViHaI.

To Hollis Burke Frissell

Grand Union Hotel, New York. March 15, 1902

Dear Dr. Frissell: When I saw Prince Henry last Saturday he expressed an earnest wish that I might send him a volume of the plantation songs. Will you be kind enough to send me to this address one of the Hampton volumes? He said that few things in America had rested him and pleased him so much as the singing of the Hampton students, and he was very earnest in his wish that these songs might be kept up by our race and not permitted to die out. He told me that he and his wife sing them in their own home when they can get hold of them. Yours truly,

Booker T. Washington

TLS   BTW Folder   ViHaI.

From James Nathan Calloway

Tuskegee, Ala., March 17th, 1902

Dear Mr. Washington: I received your telegram of 15th inst., requesting me to see you before leaving for Africa. I had, on the day before, received a cable from the Komitee, Berlin, asking that I sail on the 29th inst.[1] I will remain at Tuskegee as long as I possibly can. I plan to leave here on the 27th. This will put me in Washington the morning of the 28th. I can meet you in Washington in the afternoon or in New York in the evening of March 28th. If you desire an earlier meeting, I will leave here one day earlier, which will give me a longer time in New York, before sailing at noon of the 29th.

The Komitee has asked that I bring four (4) young men as cotton planters: Two of them may be married. None of the young men as yet have married, but one of them plans to marry and take his new wife with him. All of these young men are under-graduates of the School, and are in the "B" Middle, Junior, and "A" Preparatory classes. I think these young men will be quite suitable for the work

417

we have planned for them. Their names are, William Drake,[2] Hiram Simpson,[3] Walter Bryant,[4] Horace Griffin.[5] You will please let me know if you wish to meet them also before they sail.

The Komitee is sending $1,200. to your order on the Macon Co. Bank; but it may be that this money will be quite late getting here. If so, I would like to draw upon the School for half this amount, so that I will not be delayed in getting off.

But I shall wait until the last minute for the money.

Many thanks for News paper articles. Yours

Jas. N. Calloway

TLS Con. 272 BTW Papers DLC.

1 For an account of the departure see the New York *Times*, Mar. 30, 1902, 8.

2 William Drake of LaFayette, Ala., was a junior at Tuskegee in 1901. He drowned in the surf off Africa in 1902. (See Calloway to BTW, May 8, 1902, below.)

3 Hiram Dozier Simpson of Hamilton, Ga., also a junior, drowned in the same accident along with William Drake.

4 Walter Bryant of Jacksonville, Fla., was a member of the A preparatory class in 1901.

5 Horace Greeley Griffin of Giddings, Tex., was in the B middle class in 1901.

From Booker Taliaferro Washington, Jr.

Rock Ridge Hall   Wellesley Hills, Massachusetts   Mar. 18, 1902

My Dear Papa; I am well and hope that you are.

I received your letter yesterday, and was very glad to hear from you.

I am getting along very well. I wish that I could see you again before you go home but I guess not.

I am trying in every way to do my best.

Papa dear, I received the money for the shirts and I thank you very much.

I will try and let you hear from me again soon. Your loving Son,

Baker

ALS Con. 222 BTW Papers DLC.

From Walter Hines Page

New York   March 19th, 1902

Dear Mr. Washington: I write this simply as a series of memoranda to get things into proper shape.

We are presently to receive from you a copy of "The Building of Character, Being Sunday Evening Talks to the Students of Tuskegee Institute." This we shall make into a book forthwith, and use our best judgment with reference to the syndicating of a part of the matter. We will take up the matter of syndicating as soon as it reaches our hands. Then, too, we shall send you a contract for this.

Concerning the French book on "The Equality of the Races," by Mr. Firmin,[1] — this we shall have looked into forthwith and give you a definite answer.

Concerning the possibility of your writing a book to be called "The Story of the Negro in America," let us say that we most heartily appreciate your kindness in not entering into a contract to do this work for another house. We think well of the plan, but we think that it would be well to have you at the present postpone it. We should be willing to take it up with you as soon as the other books, which are to come from you, have had their appropriate season. We return herewith Mr. J. B. Gilder's letters[2] concerning the matter. If you see your way clear to telling him that you prefer not to take this matter up now, and if you will let us hold it as a plan to be executed later, we shall be greatly pleased and hold ourselves very heartily at your service.

Concerning "Working with the Hands," our understanding is that we shall have the pleasure of beginning to receive these articles from you for "Everybody's Magazine" as soon as you get "Building of Character" off your hands. We are anxious to begin publishing in the magazine forthwith and to turn them out in book form in due time.

Concerning your book, which is published by Small, Maynard & Co., we are anxious to buy that and whenever you have any information from Mr. Lewis, your attorney, we shall act upon it immediately.

We shall at the same time be willing to take over Mr. Thrasher's book on Tuskegee, if it can be done on reasonable terms.

We return you the letter from Messrs. D. Appleton & Co., about the Spanish translation of "Up from Slavery," which we understand. We shall send you, simply as memoranda, forthwith, a statement of the whole matter of the translations of this book.

It gives us pleasure to inform you that the sale of "Up from Slavery" continues to be good. We need not tell you that we hardly let a day go by without trying to do our share in making it known through some new channel. Very sincerely yours,

Walter H. Page

TLS Con. 261 BTW Papers DLC. Addressed to BTW at the Grand Union Hotel, New York.

1 Antenor Firmin (1850–1911), a Haitian intellectual and general, was the author of *De l'égalité des races humaines* (1885). As an opponent of the government of General Nord Alexis, he was forced into exile, first at the French consulate in Gonaives, Haiti, then at St. Thomas in the Danish West Indies, and finally in Puerto Rico. While in Washington in the summer of 1908 in search of aid from the U.S. Department of State, he met BTW and believed that they had much in common as uplifters of the black race. When he later sought help in securing a loan of $25,000, however, BTW replied that it was impossible. The reply was misaddressed to St. Thomas, Haiti, however, and thus may not have reached Firmin. (Firmin to BTW, Oct. 16, 1908; BTW to Firmin, Oct. 31, 1908, Con. 370, BTW Papers, DLC.) In 1911, while in Puerto Rico, Firmin was reported to be urging his Haitian followers to remain calm, while the government spread rumors of an uprising of Firminists in order to justify additional funds from the treasury and the execution of political prisoners. (New York *Herald*, May 12, 1911, 9.)

2 Joseph B. Gilder (1858–1936) was a prominent New York journalist and banker. He was president of The Critic Co. from 1893 until 1901, and was literary adviser to *Century Magazine* from 1895 to 1902. Gilder was editor of the *New York Times Book Review* in 1910–11. After that date he engaged in banking and insurance until his retirement in 1929. In early 1902 he corresponded with BTW in behalf of Dodd, Mead & Co., inviting BTW to write "The Story of the Negro in America" for publication by that firm. He called BTW's attention to his article in the New York *Herald*, saying that *Up from Slavery* and Jacob Riis's *The Making of an American* "should stand side by side within easy reach of every American citizen." (Gilder to BTW, Jan. 28, Feb. 7, 1902, Con. 228, BTW Papers, DLC. See also Gilder to BTW, Jan. 24, Feb. 7, 1902, Con. 225, BTW Papers, DLC.)

From Joseph Eugene Ransdell

Washington, D.C., March 19th, 1902

Dear sir: I would like very much to have an expression of opinion from you as to the advisability, vel non, of the House of Representatives adopting the Crumpacker resolution. It seems to me that it will be productive of a very unpleasant state of feeling between the whites and the negroes of the south who are now getting along so harmoniously and prosperously. I know that in my own section (East Carroll parish, Louisiana) there never was a better state of feeling than there is now. Your people are making rapid progress along educational and industrial lines. Many of them are accumulating real estate. They live on the pleasantest terms with their white neighbors, and in general there is peace and prosperity in the land. Will it be wise to disturb these relations, and would or would not such a disturbance result from the adoption of the Crumpacker resolution and its logical result — an attempt to reduce southern representation? Would your people be benefitted by a reduction of representation in Congress? It seems to me that they have as much interest in a full representation as the whites of the south. I feel convinced that the southern states which have recently adopted restrictive suffrage clauses can not be induced to recede from their position by any reduction in their membership in the House. Congress may have the physical power to reduce their membership, but it can not compel them to change their suffrage laws, and in my judgment they will not do so voluntarily. Now the question confronting your people and mine is, what under the circumstances of the case is best? Shall we leave things as they are, and allow our people to work out their own salvation, or shall we stir the question up and bring in outside interference with its long attendant train of possibly very great evils? I regard this question as one of the most important that has confronted the southern people for many years, and I believe that all true friends to the south and her whole people are tremendously interested in its outcome.

Hoping to hear from you soon, I am, with much respect, Very truly,

Jos. E. Ransdell

TLS Con. 1 BTW Papers DLC. E. J. Scott wrote on the letter: "Told him you're away from the school. I do hope you will not allow him to quote you in any way — except by your books. 3/21."

From Emmett Jay Scott

Tuskegee, Ala., March 20, 1902

Dear Mr. Washington, I thought you would like to know that the scaffolding has been pulled from around the Library building, and that it is indeed one of the most beautiful buildings we shall most likely ever have at Tuskegee. It has won and is winning the enthusiastic praise of every stranger who comes on the grounds, as well as of all teachers and students. It is a real thing of beauty and I hope you will carry out your announced purpose of trying to get Mr. Carnegie to come to Tuskegee when the Ogden party does. As Mr. Thrasher said to me yesterday, in conversation, "if he could see this building and know that so pretentious a one could be put up for $20,000, one that is certainly far in advance in architectural beauty of any that he has given that cost as much as $50,000 I am sure he will be inclined more than likely to do even more for the school."

In my wire regarding the Huntington matter, I said that I had made no announcement of the gift here. I felt quite sure that you would care to make whatever announcement was made, and so was careful not to give out the information. I am sure it gratified you to receive this telegram. We are jubilant with you that so splendid a gift has been made to the work here. Very truly yours,

Emmett J. Scott

One of the Cubans died suddenly yesterday morning — was found dead in bed in fact — One named Miguel Marin.[1] He was buried this morning. His mother lives in New York.

TLS Con. 245 BTW Papers DLC. The postscript is in Scott's hand.

1 Of Havana, a member of the A preparatory class.

From N. P. T. Finch[1]

Birmingham, Ala., Mch. 25 1902

My Dear Sir — I wrote you at Tuskegee, asking if you were likely to come to Birmingham soon, and your private secretary replied that you would not be likely to come here soon, and that he would forward any letter I might write. And so I write.

I want you to do me a great favor. I am poor. I had considerable money but I lost it. I want very much a government place — not a great one, but one that will give me a fair income. In almost any place I can continue, either here or in Washington, to write editorials for the Age-Herald. I could so arrange here.

I have held Gov. Jelks[2] firmly up to the stopping of lynching, and if another case occurs I will demand action unflinchingly and unceasingly. The Elmore cases[3] and the St. Clair case[4] have had a wonderful effect, and I never fail to rub them in. Since you were here Gov. Jelks has been attacked, because he did not pardon the Elmore lynchers. I answered this and put an end to it.

There is another line I propose to take up. It relates to the "equitable" division of public school moneys. I know all about the robbing of negro schools, and I think it can be stopped. I will proceed carefully, but I think it can be done.

Now while I watch these two issues, can you not stretch your influence and get me a place? I see special agents for the collection of mineral statistics and the like are to be appointed by the census bureau. Some such place as that would do. It would have to be gotten by direct influence with President Roosevelt.

You can depend on me as to both the matters I have named. I can help your people, and I will help them. I am determined to stop lynching, and I believe I can find a way to stop the robbing of negro schools. The latter is contemptible — the former is villanous. Very Truly Yours,

N. P. T. Finch

Please consider our correspondence confidential, and I will do likewise.

ALS Con. 244 BTW Papers DLC.

1 N. P. T. Finch was a newspaperman on the staff of the Birmingham *Age-Herald*. Because he was from New York and because the managing editor and owners of the *Age-Herald* had a different viewpoint on racial issues, he felt that he had to be careful not to branch out too widely in his sympathetic treatment of the predicament of blacks in the state. He decided to concentrate on the evils of lynching and maldistribution of public school funds. He assured BTW that "my sympathies are all right. My powers are limited." (Oct. 20, 1904, Con. 288, BTW Papers, DLC.) He occasionally gave BTW cogent advice on racial strategy.

2 William Dorsey Jelks (1855–1931) was governor of Alabama from 1901 to 1907.

Born in Georgia, he graduated from Mercer College in Macon. Moving to Eufaula, Ala., he edited the Eufaula *Times* for twenty years. An active supporter of the Democratic party, Jelks was elected to the state senate in 1898 and became its president in 1900. When Governor William J. Samford died in Jan. 1901, Jelks became governor. Jelks took a strong stand against lynching, on one occasion sending state militia to protect a black prisoner, but his efforts did little to stop the lynching evil. On other aspects of race relations he was on the side of inequity, strongly supporting the Alabama Constitution of 1901, which disfranchised most of the black voters of the state and engrafted into the constitution the provisions of an act of 1891 that gave local school officials absolute control of the distribution of school funds and thus allowed them to discriminate against black schools. Jelks made no effort to equalize school opportunities. He urged BTW to give special emphasis to agricultural training, for leaving the farm was the cause of vagrancy, crime, and racial strife. (Jelks to BTW, Nov. 22, 1906, Con. 324, BTW Papers, DLC.) At the end of his term as governor, Jelks founded the Protective Life Insurance Co. in Birmingham and managed it until his death.

3 Two black brothers, Robert and Winston White, fled after a gun battle with a white neighbor over allegations that their chickens had eaten his vegetables. Posses separately pursued and captured the brothers near Tallassee in Elmore County. Winston White's captors took him to the county jail in Wetumpka, but a mob of about thirty persons seized Robert White from his bailiffs and hanged him. The circuit court indicted ten men for the murder of Robert White and jailed the bailiffs for contempt of court when they refused to give evidence. A jury, however, convicted only three men, and Governor Jelks pardoned all but the ringleader after a year in jail.

4 At noon on Aug. 1, 1901, near Leads, St. Clair County, Ala., a white mob hanged a black man, Charles Bentley, and then riddled the corpse with bullets. This was shortly after a coroner's jury had found the cause of death of a white man, Jim Van (alias Williams), to have been murder and had indicted Bentley.

Fredrick L. McGhee to Emmett Jay Scott

Saint Paul, Minnesota. March 25th, 1902

My Dear Sir: I have your letter of March 20th, and though it is not within my province to answer the inquiry you made to President Walters, nevertheless, having some idea what the press of business may be upon him and being familiar with the facts, I take the liberty of giving you my view on the situation though I do not wish to be understood as saying that I am altogether correct. Perhaps I should suggest that you make inquiry of the secretary, but I am afraid that you might not meet with any better success than you have heretofore for I have found it very difficult to get precise information.

You say that you wish to be advised as to what your duties are as Director of the Business Bureau of the Council. I reported the minutes of the session at Indianapolis, Ind. and I find in my copy the following reference. On Aug. 31st, the executive committee made report to the Council asking to amend the Constitution and Bylaws and the amendments created the bureaus as they now exist excepting the bureau of Vital Statistics which was created at the Philadelphia meeting. Article 5th of the amendments provides, "The directors of the bureaus shall have full charge of their respective departments and shall have power to solicit funds to enable them to properly operate their bureaus. They shall make annual reports to the Nat'l Afro-Am. Council, and semi-annual reports to the executive committee." I am of the opinion that article 5th has not been amended, and there was no section of the Constitution and Bylaws that provided what the duties of the directors of the several bureaus were. I was at the meeting of the executive board held at Washington 1899 when the question came up respecting these bureaus and when they were first created. The purpose of their creation was to have departments that would take charge of such matters as appertained to their departments and as implied by its name. Perhaps the Legal Bureau has been the most active of any of them and our method may be of some assistance to you in understanding the duties. We undertake to do whatever seems to us best for the purpose of enforcing the law as it now exists and obtaining such remedial legislation as will best enhance the good of the race. So that wherever a case is pending of which we have knowledge that we can render any assistance to, we do so, and also seek to secure briefs of counsel used in the arguments and in the presenting of questions to the Supreme court of the states and the Supreme court of the U.S. wherein is involved points that bear upon any phase of the status of our race in matters of law.

Prof. Du Bois was the first director of the business bureau, and my information is that he had made preparations to gather statistics concerning the status of business among men of the race and to employ all methods to encourage and assist in the promotion of their interest along all business lines, in fact, it was my understanding that he would have worked out through his bureau the same results that are being so well brought about through the National Negro Business League ~~and~~ unfortunately for the Council Prof. Du Bois was not re-elected at the Indianapolis convention.

I was much delighted to learn that you was made director of the Business Bureau for I feel as you do that the organizations should be brought into "close relations along its business activities," and I sincerely trust that you will find a way to bring about a most perfect harmony and co-operation between the two organizations.

I am not sure that you will be able to get a hold of the Constitution and Bylaws. I have myself sought to get copies for sometime without success. I trust that the information herein contained will be of some value to you.

I send you under separate cover, some announcements concerning our forthcoming meeting at St. Paul.

Fredrick L McGhee

TLS   Con. 234   BTW Papers   DLC.

A Tuskegee Faculty Bill of Fare

[Tuskegee, Ala.] 3-26-02

MR. BOOKER T. WASHINGTON, PRINCIPAL

THE TEACHERS HAD TO-DAY:

FOR BREAKFAST	HOW COOKED
Oat Meal	
Ham	Fried
Eggs	Scrambled
Apples (Evap.)	Stewed
Syrup & cakes	
Butter & S. Milk	
Light bread	
Coffee & tea	
Chocolate	

FOR DINNER	
Soup	
Steak & gravy	Fried
Cabbage	Boiled
Rice	"
Corn (Canned)	Stewed
Butter & B. Milk	
Light & Cornbread	

FOR SUPPER	
Oysters	Fried
W. potatoes	"
Pears (Canned)	
Syrup	
Butter & S. Milk	
Light bread	
Coffee & tea	

H. G. Maberry
In charge

ADS   Con. 204   BTW Papers   DLC.

A Tuskegee Student Bill of Fare

[Tuskegee, Ala.] 3-26-02

MR. BOOKER T. WASHINGTON, PRINCIPAL

THE STUDENTS HAD TO-DAY:

FOR BREAKFAST	HOW COOKED
Boston Beans	Boiled
Syrup	
Corn bread	
Coffee	
FOR DINNER	
Beef & gravy	Boiled
Greens	"
Corn bread	
FOR SUPPER	
Light bread	
Syrup	
Ginger "	
Blackberries	
Tea	

H. G. Maberry
In charge

ADS   Con. 204   BTW Papers   DLC.

An Interview in the Washington *Colored American*

Boston [Mar. 29, 1902]

As I understand it, the Prince asked Admiral Evans[1] to have me presented to him mainly for the reason that he wanted to talk with me concerning the work of the Tuskegee graduates who are introducing the raising of cotton in the German-African colony. The

Prince also spoke of being deeply interested in the progress of the Negro in America, about which he asked many questions. He also asked me to send him a copy of my book, *Up From Slavery*, and a volume of the Hampton Institute plantation songs. He said that few things had pleased him so much as the singing of the Hampton students, and expressed as an earnest wish that the songs might not be permitted to die.

Washington *Colored American*, Mar. 29, 1902, 2.

¹ Robley Dunglison Evans (1846–1912), a rear admiral in the U.S. Navy, was aide-de-camp to Prince Henry of Prussia during his visit to the United States.

To Hollis Burke Frissell

Grand Union Hotel, New York. March 31, 1902

Dear Dr. Frissell: I have just had a very satisfactory conference with Mr. Carnegie and he has agreed to give Tuskegee $10,000 a year, and remarked that he wanted to do something for Hampton in somewhat the same way but said that he would not promise to give it just now as he wanted to see how Hampton stood financially, but said he was deeply interested in Hampton and wanted to help it.

I write to suggest that you see him before he sails for Europe which I understand is going to be on the 30th of April. Perhaps it might not be wise for you to see him right away because he might suspect that I had given you this information. I think if you see him within ten days or two weeks you will be sure to get the same amount from him he has promised to give Tuskegee. I can see by his conversation that he is becoming deeply interested in the South and I think that we ought to educate him in every way possible. Please do not use my name in any way. Yours truly,

Booker T. Washington

TLSr BTW Folder ViHaI.

From Libbie Victoria Jennings[1]

Lose Angeles Calif. March 31, 1902

Dear Sir: I write to you, to ask why you call us, the colored race, negroes.

If a man is from England, he is a Englishman, and if he come from Italy he is a Italian, if he come from Africa, he should by right be called Afro-American.

You are called one of our best educate men, and do you call yourself a negro? you should teach the young one of the race that their are Afro-American.

Webster does not call white childrem, black childrem, but he call us negroes, and he knows it is not right, and so do you   I write this as I have read two of [your] books and see where you have said negroes. Your

Libbie Victoria Jennings

ALS   Con. 231   BTW Papers   DLC.

1 The eighteen-year-old daughter of Albert Jennings, a plasterer, and his wife, Maggie.

From Alonzo Homer Kenniebrew

Tuskegee, Ala. 4-1, 02

Mr B. T. Washington   I wish to submit the fol. report of the hygienic condition of the School.

Since my last report we have had Eight cases of Pneumonia and I am glad to say, only one death, which [was] due to exhaustion as the patient had twice before had the disease, therefore was almost impossible to recover. But even then he recovered enough to have caused me to think that he was out [of] danger and began sitting up — when suddenly his strength failed.

At this writing we have on[e] case of double Pneumonia (3-18) but is getting along remarkably well.

The morning of the 25th inst — Micheal a cuban was found dead in his room [in] O. Davidson Hall. The examination after death found general consumption of the body which brought on *disease* of the *valves* of left side of heart — hence the sudden death.

The State of his health was clearly noted last Aug. when he was brought back to the school from Tallassee very dangerously sick & allowed to enter the hospital for treatment. He had not fully regained his original health up to his death.

As soon as I found his true condition I advised the school to send him home which the school thought best not to do.

Two cases of consumption have lately been excused to go home.

Claudia Price a *special* student in millinery from ark. proved to be pregnant and was sent away.

The sickness among the girls has made a very rapid decrease since the matter of making them wear heavier clothing out at night and being inspected more closely. The average sickness drop[p]ed from 7 to 2 daily pr wk.

At present we have four patients in the hospital, & we are hoping to have it clear soon.

I am sorry to have to again state that Miss Smith Head Nurse is as yet confined to bed and for five weeks she has been disabled to work. She will not be able to do any work this term to amount to much. But with Miss Ricks[1] & Miss Washingt[o]n[2] we are going on nicely with the work — which is getting in good shape.

The light epidemic of measles & chicken pox which struck the school sometime ago has been completely stamped out.

Next Sumer promises to be a very hot one & will doubtless be followed by much fever next fall, therefore I earnestly advise (1) that no sickly students be kept over during sumer — but be excused to go out for a change of climate — localities & food and it will enable them to with stand the following year's work better.

(2) Also that a general plan of whitewashing & painting of all the needy buildings & rooms during next sumer.

(3) That the laundry hall, if it is [to] be used for girls' rooms be divided into rooms before the fol. term. As it is now it is a very undisarable place — account of its being so open, & cold.

(4) That the drainage system of the school be especially looked into & improved. That leading out from boys' closet, and that from laundry & Ala Hall. That from the last two named places has to go down in front of the hospital — hence the urgent necessity of better protection from the infection from poor condition of the present

system. The air that blows in front of the hospital at night if it is a little warm, is very heavy & foul. This in Sumer will have back [bad] effects on sick people.

(5) The closet, Ala. Hall, (girls,) is in bad shape & needs much repairing; probably that would help keep in a better condition as to cleanliness.

I wish to call attention to the matter of lighting the hospital again — When the matter of making out list & setting aside so much for hospital fixtures &c to take up the 1200 gift — we set aside $300 for electric lighting alone & you gave Mr Driver order to go ahead & purchase these things for hospital.

But it seems that some of these things are being taken up by the finance committee or some others not withstanding the fact that Mr Driver was safe to go ahead — and likewise altered. The most important interference has come in the way of electric lighting the hospital.

There are special kinds of lights & apparatus for hospitals, which can be adjusted according to demands which is not true of the ordinary light yet not much more expensive.

We made out the requisition accordingly which amounted to $211.00 which is $89.00 less than the amount we set aside for that purpose, and we are sure of a good per cent reduction on the goods. But I am informed that this order has been cancelled & a different one of ordinary drop lights substituted — which can't be found in any hospital in the country because they are not suitable. They can't be adjusted according to brilliancy of light nor appearance in wards. Yet they are a little cheaper.

As far as possible we must make our hospital look like a hospital — and we are able to do so in this respect — and for any one to visit it — accustomed to hospitals there would be severe criticisms.

I beg you to look into this matter. Since the matter has gone very far it is more easily adjusted. Yours for health,

A H Kenniebrew

ALS   Con. 232   BTW Papers   DLC.

1 Nettie Ricks was a nurse at Tuskegee during the 1901–2 school year.
2 Possibly Mayme B. Washington, who taught in the girl's industrial department from 1902 to 1905.

From Heinrich Albert Wilhelm, Prince of Prussia

Darmstadt, April 4, 1902

My dear Mr. Washington: I have just received your kind letter and the two books containing the Cabin and Plantation songs and hasten to thank you for remembering your promise.

You also kindly send me a copy of your book, "Up from Slavery," for which I thank you, though I must tell you, that Mr. Schieffelin[1] had already given me a copy at New York, after we had met at the Waldorf-Astoria and after I had told him that I was particularly interested in your person. I am reading the book now and can not tell you how deeply it touches and interests me. I have seen a great deal of your race in my time, especially during repeated visits to South America, and I may add, that I always felt great sympathy for those of your race.

I am on a short visit to my brother in law, the Grand-duke of Hesse[2] who is very musical and almost an authority on music. He asked me if I thought it possible for him to obtain the same songs which you have sent me, and I therefore venture to suggest your sending two more editions of the same songs, if this should not be asking too much of you?

Having seen and noticed something of the ways of American citizens, I hope you will not mind my asking you to treat this letter with absolute discretion, the more so, as I should like to keep up a communication with you, which naturally is impossible, should your papers get hold of knowledge of our correspondence. I am sure you will understand me and not mind this hint.

The happy days I spent in the U.S. are still fresh in my memory and I shall never forget the kindness shown me by all your country-men and let me add, that I am particularly glad to have met you and that you will always find me ready to shake hands with you, either in your or my own country, or wherever we might chance to meet. Thanking you again for your kindness pray believe me, dear Mr. Washington, Yours very sincerely,

Henry Prince of Prussia

TLSr Copy   Con. 237   BTW Papers   DLC.

1 William Jay Schieffelin (1866–1955), a wealthy New York businessman, was a trustee of Tuskegee Institute from 1907 until his death. After a Ph.B. at the Columbia School of Mines in 1887 and a Ph.D. at the University of Munich in 1889, he joined the family wholesale pharmaceutical firm as a chemist. Eventually he became chairman of the board. His ardent interest in municipal reform began as soon as he was old enough to vote. For thirty-two years beginning in 1906 Schieffelin was president, chairman, and chairman emeritus of the Citizens' Union, founded in 1884 as a New York City reform party. He and the Citizens' Union took a prominent part in starting the Seabury investigations which led to the resignation of Mayor Jimmy Walker. Generally anti-Tammany, he supported Al Smith for the governorship of New York. As a supporter of Fiorello LaGuardia he ran unsuccessfully for the city council in 1937.

Schieffelin's interest in Tuskegee probably evolved from an earlier interest in Hampton Institute, of which he was a trustee, and active membership in the Armstrong Club of New York City. As a Tuskegee trustee Schieffelin did not during BTW's life take an active part in forming policy. He generally attended the meetings of the trustees in New York City but not the meetings at Tuskegee. Every August, however, Schieffelin faithfully provided entree for BTW into the summer homes of his wealthy neighbors at Bar Harbor, Me. After BTW's death Schieffelin was a more active trustee, serving as chairman from approximately 1933 to 1940. He was also active in founding the National League for the Protection of Colored Women in 1906 and the Committee for Improving Industrial Conditions of Negroes in New York in 1910, which merged with another organization in 1911 to form the National Urban League.

2 Ludwig Ernst (1868–1937) was grand duke of Hesse from 1892 to 1918.

From Theodore Roosevelt

[Washington, D.C.] April 4, 1902

Personal.

My dear Mr. Washington: Mr. C. M. Ferguson of Texas, a graduate of Fisk University, where I believe he met you on some occasion, has been in to see me and talk over the political situation in Texas. On Mr. Ferguson's statement it really does not seem to me that Mr. Smith ought to receive recognition at my hands. Mr. Ferguson tells me that Mr. Smith came out openly against Mr. Hawley when Hawley was the only Republican congressman in Texas and the only one whom there was a chance of electing, and against whom all the Democrats had combined. Mr. Ferguson was sent by the Republican committee to try and get Mr. Smith out of the race, and Mr. Smith declined to go out unless he should receive a certain sum of money to help him work for some candidates for county offices (not Republicans, but Democrats), whom Mr. Smith had endorsed against the regular Republican organization which had endorsed the other set. Mr. Smith further insisted on having his brother in law endorsed for a post office by Mr. Hawley. Every one seems to think that Mr. Smith has done well in educational matters, but there is a very strong feeling that he is not straight in political matters — by straight, I mean not merely in a party sense, but that he is not straight because he will not work unless there is something in it for him personally. Sincerely yours,

Theodore Roosevelt

TLpS   Theodore Roosevelt Papers   DLC.

From Fredrick L. McGhee

St. Paul, Minn., April 5th, 1902

My Dear Mr. Washington: I have to write you of our very deep anxiety concerning your coming to the meeting of the Nat'l Afro-Am. Council in St. Paul next July. Recognizing how very much you will aid us (the people of St. Paul) by coming, we want to say that in a much larger way your presence will be helpful indeed to the race and to the Council, for that, men who would be actuated by personal and selfish interests will be deterred in pushing them. Our organization too needs now more than ever heretofore safe and sound guidance. The counsel of the best minds of our race alone can give this.

Aside from the Louisiana case, the Council has no well defined course. It needs to have a settled policy to the promotion of which its best energies and efforts should be spent. It is not flattery when I say we can't safely adopt that policy without the benefit of your judgment and advice.

I appreciate how that you need to be careful lest you become indirectly if not directly involved in some wrangling, but those who would cause such will hardly come to St. Paul, and what with the N.E.A. meeting in Minneapolis at the same time, you will be safe from entanglement and I am certain that the educators of the race will be here in such large numbers as that they will control.

435

We are free to arrange our programme so that you will not be placed under any embarrassment from that source. So far we have with all Mrs. M. C. Terrell and Mr. Fortune for the same night and among others Dr. M. C. B. Mason,[1] Dr. J. B. Scott.[2] Bishop Grant or Rev. G. W. Lee[3] of the District of Columbia will preside. You are free to say what will satisfy you best and also make any suggestions that may occur to you.

When you were here you indicated that you would like to bring Mrs. Washington and your daughter Portia. Let me again urge that you do so and let me add that we will be delighted to arrange a fishing party for you.

Fredrick L. McGhee

TLS Con. 234 BTW Papers DLC.

1 Madison Charles Butler Mason, born in Louisiana about 1860, was a Methodist Episcopal clergyman. A graduate of New Orleans University (1888), Mason received a B.D. degree from Gammon Theological Seminary (1891). He was the first black field agent of the Freedmen's Aid Society from 1891 to 1896, when he became corresponding secretary. He was the first black man to hold an executive position with the Methodist Episcopal Church and was one of the few black speakers on the Chautauqua circuit. Mason was active in the work of the Afro-American Council and later, from 1912 to 1914, he was an organizer for the NAACP. He was a director of the Standard Life Insurance Co. and a lifetime member of the NNBL.

2 Probably Isaiah Benjamin Scott.

3 George W. Lee was pastor of the Vermont Ave. Baptist Church in Washington, D.C., beginning in the mid-1880s.

From Emmett Jay Scott

Tuskegee, April 5, 1902

Dear Mr. Washington, Somehow I do not feel that my general usefulness to you can be of direct service unless I am at all times perfectly frank in speaking to you about the various and kindred relations of the institution. The immediate matter under discussion in the Council meeting last evening is the one to which I wish to advert now. I have loyally supported every declared policy of the school, and I know you will acquit me of anything other than what I consider eminently proper in making these criticisms: —

To start with, I think you know I thoroughly agree with you that the institution must insist upon unquestioned obedience of all direct orders given and respect to those in authority. Unless the school so insisted chaos and destruction would result. But I do not believe that it ought to contemplate the establishment of an autocracy in the matter of Miss Porter's work. I have sympathized with her and the hard work she has to do, but I honestly believe that in the effort to crush the individuality and spirit of some whom she considers not quite as amenable as others that she is allowing her own spirit of antagonism toward them to blind some of her superior judgment. I say this from many things that I have been able to observe myself. I believe that the teachers ought to be made to feel that they really have some rights, and that it is not the disposition to absolutely crush them and deny them the right of appeal to you or to the Executive Council. The right of petition, it seems to me ought to be kept very sacred, and, as the humblest student is granted permission to appeal to you, I feel that this privilege should not be denied teachers. I have said that I believe there is much to be done in bringing the school's work up to a proper standard, but out of three persons, whom I consider genuine educational experts, who have been here during the year, all of them have in many respects unmercifully scored some of the methods followed in the department, two of them I am privileged to mention to you, Dr. Albert and Col. Orville T. Bright, Supt., of the Cook County schools, the latter of whom conducts every year a large institute in Chicago for western teachers. The third one was willing for me to convey to you his criticisms but was not willing to have his name mentioned. Dr. Albert and all of them seemed to feel that much in the way of valuable time is being lost in fretfulness after little details, and that the larger considerations are being overlooked. Just what this actually meant, perhaps I do not thoroughly understand, but he and the others seemed to feel that the teachers were being coerced and browbeaten, and that the thoroughly tactless manner in which they were handled is hurting not the teacher so much as the whole student body. I do not believe that it is your feeling that a critic teacher should come into a class room and take charge of the class in the presence of the teacher and give directions as to how this teacher shall conduct a recitation, and among other things, correcting statements which have been made to the class. Numbers of questions were asked Prof. Albert as to the lesson plan form, as to teachers sitting and standing, and as to keeping various sections of the class together and in each and every instance his reply was directly antagonistic to that which is being carried out.

I do not write this letter because I hope to influence you to change your position in these matters at all but simply and solely because I feel that you ought to know that there is a disposition to believe that the teachers have some rights which are not being at all respected. All of these are serious matters and in establishing the authority of the institution, I am sure that you will not overlook purposely the rights of those whom you have employed as your teachers and I do not believe that you mean to say to a teacher that his experience and individuality count for nothing. Very sincerely yours,

Emmett J. Scott

TLS   Con. 272   BTW Papers   DLC.

From Charles William Anderson

New York, April 7th, 1902

My dear Mr. Washington: Permit me to acknowledge the receipt of your good favor of the 4th inst., and to thank you for its kindly tenor. It was a very great pleasure to both Mrs. Anderson and myself to have you with us, during your stay in this City; a pleasure we both hope to renew when you are again in "this neck of the woods."

I hand you herewith some clippings from the New York Times of April 5th.[1] Relative to your "Up from Slavery," you will notice that it received 102 votes as against 108 for the "Crisis." This is a very remarkable showing, when the fact that the "Crisis" is a work of fiction, and therefore in demand by young girls and boys who would not touch a more serious work, is taken into consideration.

Relative to the review of Mr. Dixon's romance, "The Leopard's Spots," you will notice that the reviewer brings in your book as an antidote, and states that it "sufficiently meets the arguments and rebukes the spirit of the Leopard's Spots." The Catholic World,

438

sometime ago, in a review of Mr. Hannibal Thomas' book quoted your "Up from Slavery" in rebuttal of the absurd statements contained in that wail of despair. If any man is in doubt about the beneficence of your public service, apart from your great work at Tuskegee, he has but to recall that your "Up from Slavery" is put in evidence against every book written in opposition to the negro, by the book reviewers and editors of the entire country. It seems to me that our editors ought to bring out this fact. I shall take the liberty of suggesting it to Mr. Fortune.

Will you be good enough to send Mrs. Anderson and myself your photograph with your autograph. If you will, I can assure you that it will be greatly appreciated. Yours very truly,

Charles W. Anderson

TLS   Con. 219   BTW Papers   DLC.

1 The New York State Library polled the librarians in the state for the names of the fifty most important books of the year for the use of a village library. Winston Churchill's novel, *The Crisis*, led the list with 108 votes. *Up from Slavery* with 102 votes was tied for second place with two other books. Elsewhere in the same issue was a review of Thomas Dixon's racist novel, *The Leopard's Spots*. Noting that Dixon's book treated the Negro as a "hellish brute" whom even industrial education could not elevate, the reviewer recommended *Up from Slavery* as an "antidote to its pessimism." (New York *Times, Saturday Review of Books and Art*, Apr. 5, 1902, 226, 234.)

From Jabez Lamar Monroe Curry

Washington, D.C. 10 April 1902

Dear Mr Washington — Feeble health, pressure of business, Mr[s] Curry's sickness, have kept me away from Ala. Both Mr[s] C & I are nearly restored but a very short time remains for me to prepare for a several months' absence.

I am glad your inquiry as to Mr. Graham[1] confirms my favorable judgment.

Allow me to suggest that, as one of the "Field Agents," you address a strong letter to Frissell, McIver[2] and Alderman, calling their attention to Ala. and the ripeness of the field for an advance movement. If Mr Murphy be able to act with you it is better to consult him and have him cooperate with you, Abercrombie[3] and Phillips.[4] Send the letter to Athens, as all are to attend the Conference there on the 24th

I am glad to hear that you and Prof. Thach[5] have Educational plans which promise good results. Who has been Elected President of the School at Auburn?

My going away at this time is a severe disappointment to me, in so far as it takes me temporarily from the great work inaugurated by the Southern Board and the General Board. Did I say to you that the Slater Board meets on 16th in New York to make appropriations for 1902–3d. Mr Jesup advises me not to attend, as it would be a heavy tax on me to travel there on 16th & 18th, but I shall send on my recommendations, which will include a continuance to Tuskegee of the amount given this year.

I wish I could have a talk with you. Yours very truly

J. L. M. Curry

P.S. The President, on an intimation of a wish from the Spanish Gov. has raised the grade of my appointment from "Special Envoy" to "Ambassador Extraordinary."

Thanks for Mr Fortune's article.

ALS   Con. 224   BTW Papers   DLC.

[1] Joseph Brown Graham.

[2] Charles Duncan McIver.

[3] John William Abercrombie.

[4] John Herbert Phillips (1853–1921) was superintendent of schools of Birmingham, Ala., from 1883 until his death. Born in Covington, Ky., he grew up on a farm in southern Ohio. He graduated from Marietta College and studied at the Universities of Chicago and Edinburgh. An efficient and dedicated school administrator, Phillips made the Birmingham school system one of the best in the South, with a strong esprit de corps among the teachers. Subscribing to BTW's approach to black education, he established in 1899 the Industrial High School for Negroes. He was active in the Conference for Education in the South and in 1895 was president of the Southern Education Association. (Dabney, *Universal Education in the South*, 2:402–7.)

[5] Charles Coleman Thach was professor of English at Alabama Agricultural and Mechanical College (later Auburn University) in Auburn, Ala., from 1883 until 1902 and president of the college from 1902 to 1919. Thach had an active interest in the Southern Education Board's work in Alabama and was also a member of the Alabama Education Association and the Southern Education Association.

From Solomon C. Conyers,[1] Charles H. Gibson, and John Robert E. Lee

[Tuskegee, Ala., ca. Apr. 10, 1902]

Mr. B. T. Washington, Prin. We, your committee, appointed to find the facts of case referred to us report as follows.

Miss S. May Smith appeared before the committee and stated that she with the assistance of Mary Chandler performed an operation upon Josie Gillen during the month of June, last and that there were no other persons present. That to her knowledge no other operation had been performed upon Josie Gillen.

Josie Gillen appeared before us and stated that during the month of June, last that Miss Smith assisted by Mary Chandler performed an operation upon her. That Dr. Kenniebrew was not present there and that he has never performed an operation upon her.

Mary Chandler stated to one of the committee that she was present on one occasion during the month of June, last, when Dr. Kenniebrew assisted by Miss Smith and herself performed an operation upon Josie Gillen. That she remembers another operation by Miss Smith assisted by herself when Dr. Kenniebrew was not present.

Dr. A. H. Kenniebrew appeared before the committee and stated that he had peformed two operations — one when Miss Smith and one of the nurses were present and another about the 15th or 16th of June, last, for which he charged seven dollars, when no other persons were present. That the work was done on the school grounds but that he did not remember in what room.

Mrs. Wheelis stated to one of the committee that Josie Gillen began living with her on the 26th of June, last.

> S. C. Conyers
> Chas. H. Gibson } Committee
> J. R. E. Lee

ALS   Con. 233   BTW Papers   DLC.

1 Solomon C. Conyers taught blacksmithing at Tuskegee from 1896 to 1902.

To Albert Shaw

Tuskegee, Ala., April 11, 1902

My dear Dr. Shaw: Replying to your favor of April 8th I would say that it is our present intention to have no one speak except yourself. We had invited Bishop Potter[1] to speak at the same time but he writes that he is not coming South. I think an address of fifteen minutes will be all that is necessary. We mean to have the exercises very short and very simple. Perhaps we shall have a prayer and singing of plantation songs by the school, then some introductory remarks telling something of the building, this to be followed by your address.

It seems to me that since Mr. Carnegie has given several libraries to the South, anything you might say that would bear upon libraries, especially in this part of the country, would prove valuable. I think you already understand that there are very few libraries in the South. This I believe is the only library that Mr. Carnegie has given to which colored people are likely to have free access in the South.

In case anyone else is asked to speak it will be some Southern man like Mr. Branson[2] of Athens, Ga., but in that case I shall notify you. Yours truly,

Booker T. Washington

TLS   Albert Shaw Papers   NN.

[1] Henry Codman Potter (1835–1908), a Protestant Episcopal clergyman, was bishop of New York beginning in 1887. He frequently accompanied Robert C. Ogden to meetings of the Conference for Education in the South.

[2] Eugene Cunningham Branson (1861–1933) was superintendent of schools in Athens, Ga., from 1887 to 1892. He taught psychology and pedagogy at the Georgia Normal and Industrial College at Milledgeville beginning in 1893. From 1901 to 1912 Branson was president of the Georgia Normal College at Athens, where he directed major changes in the quality of the school with funds from Robert C. Ogden, George Foster Peabody, and the General Education Board. He wrote several books on educational theory as well as textbooks on hygiene and spelling. Branson sponsored the Conference for Education in the South, held at Athens in 1902, which helped launch the work of the General Education Board in Georgia. He reisgned his duties as president of the Georgia Normal College in 1912 in order to devote his time to studies of rural economics and sociology in the South. In 1914 he organized the department of rural social economics at the University of North Carolina and pioneered in the study of the rural South until his death in 1933.

To Charles Duncan McIver

Tuskegee, Ala., April 12, 1902

My dear Sir: After corresponding with Dr. Curry and going over the matter somewhat thoroughly with Mr. Murphy and others, I write to say that arrangements are being made in this state for a thoroughly, and we hope vigorous, educational campaign, somewhat after the style of those already started in other states under the auspices of the Southern Education Board. Prof. Thach, of the Auburn College, is especially helpful and active in this matter just now. I am glad to say that the State Superintendent of Education is also deeply interested and is anxious to do whatever he can. As soon as Mr. Murphy is able to return to the state we shall get matters in a definite shape, but the outlook just now is most hopeful. Yours truly,

Booker T. Washington

TLS Charles D. McIver Papers NcGU. Mistakenly addressed to D. W. McIver.

From Estelle du Bois-Reymond[1]

Berlin, S.W. April 12th 1902

Dear Sir, I have been entrusted by the firm of Dietrich Reimer with the translation of your book "Up from Slavery." Now I have found some difficulty in transcribing the expression "Grape Vine Telegraph," chiefly because I do not know exactly what it means. I would be greatly obliged to you if you would have the kindness to explain in a few words what kind of an institution the Grape Vine Telegraph was, how it worked and how it came by it's name, so that I may be able to find not of course the equivalent in German, as that cannot exist, but still a rendering intelligible to German readers.

Thanking you in advance for any trouble which this request may cause, I am yours truly

Estelle du Bois-Reymond

ALS Con. 240 BTW Papers DLC.

1 Estelle du Bois-Reymond was the daughter of the German physiologist Emil Heinrich du Bois-Reymond (1818–96). She was the editor of her father's posthumously published works.

From Edgar Stewart Wilson

Jackson, Miss. April 12, 1902

PERSONAL.

My dear Mr. Washington: I have not only not permitted a single colored man to be turned out, where he was doing his duty, and I may add that I have not found any of them not doing their duty, but I have been the cause of putting some colored men in places. In my own appointments, at courts, I have given the preference to colored men, for the reason that there are so few places in the state, outside of post offices, to be filled I have kept in several colored post masters, and mean to continue to do so where their records are good, as shown by the department reports, and no clamor shall swerve me from the purpose to treat the colored people with absolute fairness, and just consideration. A great fight on the color line is being waged to have removed, or rather to have supplanted by appointment, Piernas, at Bay St. Louis. The pressure has been fierce, on color line. The man is absolutely competent, and his endorsements before the fight begun, which I have seen, warrant fully his re-appointment, and he shall have it if it be in my power to see that [he] has justice done him. I am also doing what I can to get some colored men on the federal juries. I do not draw the juries as you know that [is] being done by the United States commissioners. McAllister[1] collector of the port at Vicksburg, is a colored man and a fine fellow. I am being blackguarded by the Herald and Post of that city for his appointment, but it counts for naught. It was right, and I am willing to stand by the right. I recommended the appointment the day before your letter came of [a] colored man for postmaster at Dry Grove in Hinds county, not far from Jackson. Wherever they can be placed, merit shall be the test with me.

> "Come one come all,
> This rock shall fly,
> From its firm base, as soon as I."

About the Judgeship. I fully concur in your suggestions. I have cause, however, to suspect that this state may be given the place, and in that even[t] there is no republican in it fit for it, as you may know. I am not prepared to speak for the other two states. If any one in this state is to be considered, I hope it will be our mutual friend.

I am glad to know the president is pleased with me. I have tried to do the "Right," in the language of the immortal Lincoln, "as God give[s] it to me to see the right," mindful always of the interest of that unselfish, good man in the White House.

Your letters found me in bed. I hope you are well. Sincerely,

Edgar S Wilson

TLS   Con. 272   BTW Papers   DLC.

1 Noting that "T. V. McAllister, a light colored negro Republican, has been made collector of the Port of Vicksburg," the Vicksburg *Herald* remarked that "the Prince Fortunatus" of this tale was BTW, "who waved his magic wand and broke the 'six times six years spell' by steering together the President and his highly gifted referee." The editorial ridiculed the idea expressed by the New York *Evening Post* that Roosevelt's appointments were designed to promote good government in Mississippi. (Vicksburg *Herald*, Apr. 8, 1902, 3.)

A Statement in the Montgomery *Advertiser*

Tuskegee, [Ala.] April 17 [1902]

DENIED BY WASHINGTON

HAS BOUGHT NO SUMMER HOME IN MASSACHUSETTS

FAMOUS EDUCATOR HAS LEASED A
SMALL COTTAGE IN SOUTH WEY-
MOUTH IN ORDER TO BE NEAR
HIS SUMMER WORK

Booker T. Washington, in regard to the report that he had bought a colonial mansion for a summer residence in South Weymouth, Mass.,[1] today said:

"It is rather interesting to go to bed feeling that one is a poor man and to wake up in the morning and find that he is the owner, according to the newspapers, of an old colonial mansion in Massachusetts. The fact is, I have bought no house of any character whatever in Massachusetts and am not intending to do so, and am not able to buy one. For several years I have rented a small cottage in Massachusetts during the summer so that I could be near the work which I usually devote myself to during that season. A few months ago a friend of mine in New York bought a small cottage for himself in South Weymouth which he has permitted me to rent or lease for the summer in the same way that I have been renting a house for the summer for sometime. There is no truth whatever in the statement that I have bought the ancestral home of any famous Massachusetts people."

Montgomery *Advertiser*, Apr. 18, 1902, 8.

1 In a special to the *Advertiser* from Washington, it was alleged that BTW had secretly purchased the family home of Congressman Charles Quincy Tirrell in South Weymouth, Mass. In fact, it was purchased by William H. Baldwin, Jr., who made it available to BTW as a summer home until 1905.

From Daniel Alexander Payne Murray[1]

Library of Congress, Wash. D.C. April 21st 1902

My dear Mr. Washington: Your letter received and in reply I would say; I have so far as I am concerned scrupulously avoided using your name in any public manner in connection with this bill.[2] I am sure nothing has been done of the kind mentioned, if so it has not come to my notice.

The sub-committee gave us a hearing this morning which was very effective, since after hearing us they at once decided to recommend to the full Committee a favorable report.

At the hearing your name was not mentioned. I thought you would have been able to reach before the time set. Bishop Grant, Geo H. White, Gov. Pinchback, Rev. E. W. Lampton,[3] Jesse Lawson, Rev. Walter Brooks[4] and about ten others appeared. Mr. Irwin also appeared and aided the bill in every manner. There were no long speeches, Mr. Irwin met at my house on Friday night a committee and the whole matter as it was to be presented, was agreed upon and type written, the speeches were in answer to questions.

The whole matter was carefully planned and carried out without a hitch. The name of no one was used as favoring the bill, who was not present to give force to his interest. So you may thus be assured that any statements that your name was being used thus unauthorized, are not sustained in truth. The bill now goes to the full Committee with a favorable recommendation and as it has carefully been preserved from being denominated a political measure, there is a strong probability of its passage. Very Sincerely yours.

Daniel Murray

ALS   Con. 234   BTW Papers   DLC.

[1]Daniel Alexander Payne Murray (1852–1925) was assistant librarian of Congress. Born in Baltimore, he was educated in a Unitarian seminary there. He joined the Library of Congress in 1871, when there was a staff of only twelve persons, as personal assistant to Librarian Ainsworth R. Spofford. After nine years Murray was promoted to assistant librarian. Nearly all of his time was spent seeking answers to inquiries from congressmen. His principal interest, however, was bibliography of black authors. In 1900 he prepared for the American exhibit at the World Exposition in Paris a list of 1,100 titles, of which about 500 were placed on exhibit at Paris and the following year at expositions in Buffalo, N.Y., and Charleston, S.C. Over a period of more than fifty years he compiled materials that he hoped to publish as "Murray's Historical and Biographical Encyclopedia of the Colored Race Throughout the World," in six volumes. Murray was also engaged in the real estate business in Washington from 1879 to 1893. He was a member of the board of trade and president of the Washington Civic Centre. He was a delegate to the Republican national convention in 1920. Murray was a loyal supporter of BTW and kept him informed of matters before Congress.

[2] The bill introduced by Harvey Samuel Irwin (1844–1916), Republican congressman from Kentucky, was to create a Freedmen's Inquiry Commission to make "a comprehensive investigation of the condition of the people of the negro race in the United States, their educational progress, and the best means of promoting harmony between the races in the United States." The bill had originally been drawn up by Daniel Murray and approved by President McKinley but not introduced until 1902. Murray urged BTW to appear before the subcommittee considering the bill or else to send a letter which Murray might use. BTW, however, apparently did not do so nor allow his name to be used. (Copy of H.R. 12940, Mar. 24, 1902, Con. 227; Murray to BTW, Mar. 27, 1902, Con. 234; Murray to BTW, undated, ca. Apr. 21, 1902, Con. 234, BTW Papers, DLC.)

[3] Edward Wilkinson Lampton (1857–1910) was an A.M.E. minister in Kentucky, Mississippi, and Washington, D.C. In 1905 he was involved in an abortive plan to establish a pro-BTW newspaper in Washington. In 1908 he became a bishop, residing in Greenville, Miss. He became embroiled there in a controversy with the telephone

company because of his insistence that operators address black customers by courtesy titles. As a result of the furor, Lampton lost his telephone, and threats to his family forced him to move to Chicago.

4 Walter Henderson Brooks was born in slavery in 1851 at Richmond, Va. He was pastor of the 19th Street Baptist Church in Washington, D.C., beginning in 1882.

To Ethan Allen Hitchcock[1]

Tuskegee, Ala., April 25, 1902

My dear Sir: I am very much interested in the development of the Freedmens Hospital. It has already been a force for good, and if it can be further developed I am sure that it will prove of the greatest possible help to our people. We very much hope that we can retain the Freedmens Hospital so that students of color may have proper facilities for the proper medical education and for the training of nurses, and it would aid the work very materially if a modern hospital building and a nurse training school building were provided. The building if it were provided with capacity for 100 beds, reserving 20 per centum for pay patients, and a nurse training school to be first class in every particular so that young women from the South would have facilities may have an opportunity for taking post graduate courses, would greatly aid the work. I am sure the Government would make no mistake if it should support this hospital and nurse's training school, the whole management to remain now, as before, under the administration of the Secretary of the Interior. I think it would help the work if the medical faculty should serve without compensation and as there would be no salaries there would be no politics. Our people throughout the country are very much interested in this matter, and I hope you can give it your support. Yours truly,

Booker T. Washington

Dr. F. J. Shadd[2] is a colored physician of Washington in whom I have a great deal of confidence. He is entirely disinterested and I am sure would be glad to talk with you about this matter. He could give you all the information you desire.

TLS   File 327   Patents and Miscellaneous Division   RG48   DNA.

[1] Ethan Allen Hitchcock (1835–1909) was born in Mobile and reared in Nashville and St. Louis. When he was twenty-five he went to China and made a fortune in twelve years as a merchant. Returning to St. Louis, he engaged in many business enterprises, including plate glass, iron, steel, and other corporations. As Secretary of the Interior from 1898 to 1907 he aided Theodore Roosevelt in his campaign to protect the public domain. Early in 1903, convinced that the government was being robbed of valuable lands and resources, he fired the commissioner of the general land office and undertook widespread investigations into land frauds, often using secret service agents in his probes. As a result of his efforts 1,021 persons in twenty states were indicted, and 126 had been convicted by the time he resigned in 1907. He was dissatisfied with the results, and toward the end of his term he became openly suspicious of politicians, including the blacks who held posts in the southern land offices.

[2] Furmann J. Shadd, born in Washington, D.C., in 1852, was a graduate of Howard University (1875) and the Howard University Medical School (1881). He was a physician and surgeon at Freedmen's Hospital and served on the medical school faculty. He was a founder of the black-owned Industrial Building and Savings Co. and the Capital Savings Bank. He served on the District of Columbia school board for five years.

From Rosa Lee Baker

Montgomery Ala. Apr. 28, 1902

Dear Mr. Washington   You no doubt will be surprised to receive a letter from me at this point, as I was in Atlanta when I wrote you last, but on account of my refusing to wash a pair of trousers on yesterday (Sunday) Mrs Howell[1] said she did not care for me any longer.

My choice was to wash the trousers or take the afternoon train the lat[t]er I chose. Yours truly

Rosa L. Baker

ALS   Con. 221   BTW Papers   DLC.

[1] Annie Comer Howell in 1900 became the second wife of Clark Howell. She was the daughter of Hugh M. Comer of Savannah, president of the Central of Georgia Railroad, and was the niece of Braxton Bragg Comer, textile manufacturer and governor of Alabama from 1907 to 1910. She died in 1922.

From Charles Winston Thompson

Washington. April 30, 1902

Personal

Dear Sir: Replying to your esteemed favor of the 25th inst., I will be able in a few days to give you a correct list of the party who will visit Tuskegee with me on the 20th of May. We will leave here on the morning of the 19th and get to Tuskegee on the 20th. I think there will be at least thirty in the party, perhaps forty. Mr. Little-field,[1] Secretaries Shaw and Wilson, Mr. A. W. Machen, Sup't Rural Free Delivery, Mr. Crumpacker, and Mr. Merriam, Director of the Census, have all consented to come.

My object for requesting you to telegraph me a formal invitation to visit your school was to use it for the basis of an interview which appeared in the Washington Post to enable me to make public my endorsement of your work. I mailed you twenty-five copies of the Post containing the article, and hope they reached you in due time.

Our trip has excited considerable interest all over Alabama and I am to-day in receipt of a copy of resolutions adopted by the City Council of Mobile inviting us to come there. They propose, if we will come, to entertain us in their homes and take us on a trip down the bay to Ft. Morgan. We have also been invited to spend a day in Birmingham, and in arranging the itinerary of the trip, I shall endeavor to visit both of these places.

Now as to the matter of providing meals en route for the party, I hardly know just what is proper in the premises. If we furnish the meals, it will cost at least $400.00 for the meals we take on the sleeper. I propose to entertain them myself at my expense in Tuskegee and to give them a barbecue on my plantation on Tuesday. Now if you could see your way clear to bear the expenses of the meals on the sleeper, I could announce in a quiet way that you had furnished the sleeper for the trip with the meals, with your compliments, as an appreciation of the honor of having them visit your school. If you think this would be too great an expense, I can just let each member of the party pay for his own meals as he gets them.

I believe the trip will be fruitful of much good to your school. I spent Friday and Saturday in New York, and while there I invited Mr. Jas. T. Woodward,[2] President of the Hanover National

Bank, and Mr. McKesson, of the firm of McKesson & Robbins, to go with us. They both accepted conditionally, and say they will be delighted to join us if they can arrange their business affairs to do so. I had a long talk with Capt. Woodward about your school and work, and he was surprised to know of the magnitude of your institution. My object in inviting Mr. McKesson was to get him to give your school a large plantation he owns in Macon County. He is a member of one of the richest firms in New York City, and many years ago they took a large plantation near Ft. Davis for debt, and it has never been a source of much revenue to them. I told him he could not do a better thing than to go with us on the trip and while in Tuskegee donate the plantation to your school. He promised me he would talk to his partner and consider the matter. Now, if they do not donate the plantation to your school after we have visited Tuskegee, I want you to write them to know if they will sell you the plantation. It contains 800 acres of good farm lands and would be a good investment for your endowment fund, provided they will not give it to you.

General Ketcham,[3] who will be one of the party, and who is the honored Representative from the State of New York, having represented his district for thirty years, is a multi-millionaire, and I have insisted upon his giving your school 25,000 while there. I believe the trip will add at least $100,000 to your endowment fund, if not directly, indirectly.

I regret very much not being able to be with you while the Ogden party is in Tuskegee, and hope their trip will increase your endowment fund to a half million.

Please let me know if you have any special friends here you wish me to invite. Secretary Shaw and Representatives Conner,[4] Smith,[5] and Southard[6] all expect to bring their wives, and if I thought the President would let Miss Alice go with us, I would invite her, but I do not know whether to invite her when he is not to go. If you have any special friends you want to join us, you might write them that I have requested you to invite a few of your special friends to join the party, and send me a list of their names, and I will see them in person and extend an invitation also.

The papers all over the country are speaking in the highest terms of the trip, and I am sure it will be fruitful of much good both to your school and to the entire south.

Awaiting your further commands and assuring you of my grateful appreciation of your co-operation in this matter, I am   Yours very truly,

Chas. W. Thompson

TLS Con. 244 BTW Papers DLC. Attached was a note from E. J. Scott dated May 2: "Dear Mr Washington: I attach letter from the modest Congressman, I have written him that letter has been sent to you."

1 Charles Edgar Littlefield (1851–1915) was a Republican congressman from Maine from 1899 to 1908.

2 James T. Woodward (1845–1910) was president of the Hanover National Bank and director of several other New York banks. His interest in the South perhaps stemmed from his directorships of the Birmingham Trust and Savings Co. and the Southern Railway Co.

3 John Henry Ketcham (1832–1906) was a Republican congressman from Dutchess County, N.Y., from 1865 to 1873, from 1877 to 1893, and from 1897 until his death.

4 James Perry Conner (1851–1924) was a Republican congressman from Iowa from 1900 to 1909.

5 Walter Inglewood Smith (1862–1922) was a Republican congressman from Iowa from 1900 until 1911, when he was appointed U.S. circuit judge.

6 James Harding Southard (1851–1919) was a Republican congressman from Ohio from 1895 to 1907.

From Charles F. Bacon[1]

Grand Rapids, Mich., May 2, 1902

Dear Mr. Washington: We write you to ascertain if you have lent, or in any way allowed your picture and signature to be used in the advertisement of cigars or tobacco with any company in the United States.

Our town is posted with your picture and signature in the advertising of cigars, even to the slums.

It is a source of great chagrin for us to be compelled to face your picture advertising this nefarious business, the picture of one we have heretofore learned to associate with everything that is pure and ennobling.

For twelve years it has been my duty to train the minds of the youth and I have always been proud to hold up before them, Booker T. Washington as an example, and now to see your name and picture placed upon sign-boards all over the country and in the street cars where every child and passer-by cannot help but be attracted by it, causes me to feel that my work, as far as your influence has had to do with it, is turned to a source of great evil.

I am closely connected with the educators of Grand Rapids and I know that I am voicing their sentiments in this matter.

We wish that you would kindly inform us whether these companies have the legal permission to thus use your name and signature. If not we would like to take some steps to bring them to an account and to check such influences upon our youth. Most sincerely yours,

Chas. F. Bacon

TLS   Con. 221   BTW Papers   DLC.

1 Charles F. Bacon of Grand Rapids, Mich., was an agent of the Sun Life Assurance Co. of Canada in 1902 and a travel agent in 1911, according to city directories.

To Charles F. Bacon

[New York City?] May 5, 1902

My dear Sir: I thank you for your kindness in calling my attention to the display of the tobacco manufacturers who have flooded Grand Rapids with advertisements of a cigar bearing my name and exploiting same with autograph of myself. I have given my consent to no company and the unwarranted liberty taken in this matter I shall be glad to have looked into at once if you will kindly advise me as to the name of the manufacturers and jobbers of these cigars.[1] I feel very much grieved and shocked that persons have used my name in so unworthy a manner. Yours truly,

[Booker T. Washington]

TL Copy   Con. 221   BTW Papers   DLC.

1 Bacon wrote BTW that the Putnam Candy Co. of Grand Rapids was the one using BTW's name. (May 10, 1902, Con. 221, BTW Papers, DLC.)

From Granville Stanley Hall[1]

Clark University. Worcester, Mass. May 5, 1902

My dear Sir, In some address I saw of yours some time ago, you spoke of the colored race as being preeminent in feeling emotion. This seemed a very interesting, true and important contribution for a psychologist. Can you kindly tell me where I can find this address, or if you have copies of it, send one with bill?

May I also ask whether your addresses have ever been published either separately or collectively; if so, where can I get them? I know and have read with great pleasure your Autobiography.

I am, Most truly yours,

G. Stanley Hall

TLS Con. 230 BTW Papers DLC.

1 Granville Stanley Hall (1846–1924) was a pioneer American psychologist. He was president of Clark University from 1889 to 1919, and founded and edited the *American Journal of Psychology* beginning in 1887.

To Wallace Buttrick

[New York City?] 5-6-02

Dear sir: As far as it is consistent with the plan and policy of the General Education Board to do so, I feel sure the foundation for more effective work can be laid by aiding in the carrying out of the following plan:

(1) the holding of a large central mass meeting in Montgomery Alabama sometime during the present month, that shall have the endorsement of the Governor and State Supt of education and that shall be in the direct charge of Rev. E. G. Murphy and Prof. Thatch.

2 That all County Superintendents and city Superintendents education urged to attend this meeting and that they be invited by the S[t]ate Supt of Education.

3 that in the day following the mass meeting that there be a conference of all the superintendents,

4 That as speakers such men as Drs. Alderman, Dabney, or Mc-

Iver, together with one or two Alabama men and Dr. But[t]rick, be secured.

5   That all of the fore going be done largely with a view of preparing the way for a state campaign of education, for which it is hoped to secure the Hon. Mr. Graham six months in the year, but no definite [decision] is to be made toward putting a man in the field till Dr. But[t]rick can be on the ground and look the field over.

6   Estimated expenses
   (a)   Public meeting 200.
   (b)   Securing the attendance of 76 County and city superintendents, (taking for granted that 50 attend) 400.
   (c)   Pay Mr. Graham if he is put in field about $150. per month. Yours truly

[Booker T. Washington]

ALd   Con. 247   BTW Papers   DLC.

From James Nathan Calloway

Lome   Togo W.A. May 8th 1902

Dear Mr Washington   It is with deep sorrow that I am writing you that two of our young men, Simpson and Drake, were drowned while trying to land here May 2nd. Our Journey from New York had been a very pleasant one and all were in high spirits. I had landed and with many others waited to see them come on shore. When they were 50 yds out the boat capsised with passengers and trunks. Our party of five and one white man were in the boat. The White man, the woman and two of our young men were rescued. The other two were never seen again. Three days after we told the wife that her husband was lost. She wishes to remain for awhile here and when stronger to go back to U.S. She will probably go on with us to interior and remain until someone is going to America. I think the committee will be willing to send her home to her people.

On 5th inst. at request of K.W.K. I cabled you to send out two more farmers at once. I hope you are able to find them and that they will be able to reach Lome by the first of July.

455

I arrainged in Hamburg to have the pictures of the party sent to you. I suppose they have reached you before now. The Article from New York times was sent out to me by that paper. The Komitee had me to write them of your meeting with Prince Henry and you may see it again in the German papers.

The young men are all quite well at present the two just out have started for interior already.

I shall buy a small farm on coast and put one young man here. If cotton grows well here we will put gin and press here also. Mr Burks will probably come here where his health will be better.

Best regards to your family   I am yours truly

Jas N Calloway

ALS Con. 225 BTW Papers DLC. Docketed in E. J. Scott's hand: "This news is shocking!"

From Henry Hugh Proctor

Atlanta, Ga., May 10, 1902

My dear Mr. Washington: I enclose you a clipping from the morning Constitution in regard to Wimbish's case.[1] Of course we do not know how exact the account is; but from what I learn from other sources I think there is something in it. You see the President is in a quandary. The matter is in a balance. I believe a word from you at this time will turn the scales in Wimbish's favor. Will you not wire the president at once on the matter?

It is not so much an individual as a race matter. There is nothing against Wimbish, but his color. Deveaux has won out in a similar case, and I think the President can be led to see the Wimbish matter in the same light.

I enclose stamped envelope for reply. The fight is on, and if we knew just what you have done we will know better how to proceed. Yours very truly,

H. H. Proctor

ALS Con. 239 BTW Papers DLC.

1 The Atlanta *Constitution*, May 10, 1902, 2, referred to the effort of Christopher C. Wimbish (b. 1854) to retain his federal position as surveyor of customs for Georgia.

His white rival for the position was supported by Atlanta businessmen and lily-white Republicans, while the regular organization led by Register of the Treasury Judson W. Lyons supported Wimbish. The article reported that Postmaster General Payne, influenced by President Roosevelt, supported Wimbish.

Francis Jackson Garrison to Oswald Garrison Villard

The Cedars, [Lexington, Mass.] May 12, 1902

Dear Oswald: I am very sorry that you were unable to visit Atlanta University, & all the more because your fellow-travellers were so strongly — not to say bitterly — prejudiced against it. When the Ogden party visited Atlanta last year, they deliberately ignored the University. They were there over Sunday, & Booker Washington, who had charge of the programme there, arranged for three church meetings, but neither he nor Odgen (whom Dr. Bumstead had begged to include a visit to the Univy. in their itinerary, before the party left N.Y.), nor Billy Baldwin (who is bitter & contemptuous towards A. U.) meant to give any countenance to it, and it was only through Prof. F. G. Peabody's[1] going out there to give a talk or sermon that about half the party were decoyed there, & they did not stay long enough to look about thoroughly. Now if Booker Washington is insincere or playing double, I want to know it. I had a plain talk with him on the subject the last time he was in Boston, & he told me that he thought the best tribute he could pay Atlanta Univy. was to get teachers from it, as he had repeatedly; that he valued & appreciated it, & would be glad to speak at a public meeting in its behalf (as, indeed, he did, some three years ago, in Cambridge); and he repeated these statements a few weeks ago to Dr. Bumstead. However he is announced as one of the speakers at the 7th Annual Conference to be held at Atlanta the latter part of this month. As to his attitude towards Benson & Kowaliga, I know he distrusted B. & spoke slightingly of him for some time, until B. confronted him, man-fashion, when he took a different tack & professed himself satisfied with B's showing; and I thought he had since given his name & countenance to the Kowaliga school, but I may be mistaken as to this. I may be no judge of character, but I confess I believe in Benson & think him a rare young fellow, and as for

457

Dr. Bumstead, I believe no better, more devoted, unselfish, wise & farsighted laborer for the education of the blacks can be found in the country to-day. After his long years of heart-breaking, brain-wearying work to sustain Atlanta Univy.; his noble courage in refusing to draw a color line there & say that the two races should not be taught there (except as their blood is mingled in the same person!), thus forfeiting the State appropriation of $8000 a year & bringing threat of penal legislation; & with my long personal intimacy with him & familiarity with his fine traits of character, it makes my blood boil to hear of the pious Ogden calling him "a pious fraud." He is a gentleman & a scholar, of broad & liberal views, free from cant or sectarianism, & while he lacks magnetism & the cheek & confidence & push of such a man as Prest. Frost[2] of Berea, he always presents his case with force & dignity, & in a straight-forward & business-like manner. It is the simple truth that the best teachers in the Southern colored schools to-day are those trained at Atlanta Univy. and if the race is to have trained leaders, it is of vital importance to maintain such an institution, which has proved its capacity for this work. Only the other day I asked Prest. Atkins[3] of the Winston-Salem school about Atlanta, & he said with the greatest earnestness, "It is one of the very best schools we have. We draw our teachers from it, & its failure would be a calamity." I groan in spirit every time I read of a legacy or gift of $50,000 or $100,000, or $500,000 going to Harvard or Yale, or Columbia, or Chicago — universities which have scores of millionaire patrons, or thousands of wealthy alumni who are tumbling over one another to swell the treasury of their *alma mater,* and think of what the money would do for these struggling altar-fires in the South. Five-million dollars, which Harvard has just secured so easily from Morgan & Rockefeller for its medical school, would do more good if divided among Hampton, Tuskegee & Atlanta than five times five millions given to these northern universities with their splendid equipments & already enormous endowments. I marvel that no one has yet been moved to give Tuskegee a million dollars & free Booker Washington — one of the most valuable lives in the country — from the strain & wear & tear of begging money half the year. And Dr. Bumstead, if a less picturesque, is a far more heroic figure to me, undergoing from a sense of duty & from stern necessity (so long as he remains the Atlas of Atlanta Univy.) the odious task, to a refined & sensitive nature, of appealing, year in & year out for the funds to carry on his work, of telling his story a thousand & ten thousand times, of receiving rebuffs, encountering indifference, & meeting the hostility of those who ought to be foremost in sustaining his work & seeing that he does not fall exhausted by the wayside. I truly believe that I would rather go to the guillotine than take up such a cross as he has borne for the last sixteen years.

I know your father was not much interested in Atlanta, & that his one visit gave him an unfavorable opinion of it, but the reason for the first was that he thought the race unfit for the "higher education" & held the common Southern view that industrial education was all-sufficient, ignoring or failing to perceive the necessity for the higher education of the relatively small number who aspire to an equipment that shall qualify them to lead their people wisely & well. As for the second, a chance attendance at a class recitation where the text-book used had "Christian" in the title, & the matter in which seemed absurdly abstruse for the students, was sufficient to prejudice him irrevocably against the whole institution. With all respect & affection for him, I should trust your observation & judgment far more, & I wish with all my heart that you were to be at the Atlanta Conference this month with Dr. Bumstead, Prof. Du Bois & Booker Washington.

In your letter in Friday's *Post*[4] you touch the nub of this feeling against Atlanta when you say that most of the men in this Southern Education Assocn are men of Southern birth or Southern affiliation. Naturally these cling to the old prejudice against thoroughly educated "niggers" & the old fear that "social equality" is the goal of such. They believe in the negro as a hewer of wood and drawer of water, & are willing that he should be a carpenter or a blacksmith. Hence they approve of industrial & manual training schools, but stop there, please! But what gives Booker Washington his position & influence to-day is not his ability as a mechanic — nobody knows what his skill in that direction is — but his brain power & quality of leadership, and the same is true of Robert L. Smith, Atlanta's one-armed graduate, who teaches school in Texas, has organized societies & communities now numbering 3500 members to buy land & keep out of debt, & accumulate property, — and a white district (one having a large white majority) twice elected him to the Legislature.

But I must go to bed & inflict no more on you now. I hope to see you here or at Thorwood ere many weeks. Affecty.

Uncle Frank

P.S. Did you write the editorial on "The Real Enemies of the Army," in Friday's *Post?* The pressing of the accountability on the Government is all right, but you can't have an army, my dear boy, without profligates in it, or without murderers; and army officers will no more denounce or condemn one another for cruelties than "regular" medical practitioners will betray one another in cases of blunder or malpractice, or Masons their brethren who get into scrapes. My own belief is that there are very few officers or men in the Philippines who have not been guilty of torture, murder and arson. And Gen. Bell,[5] of whose "good record" you wrote awhile ago, has revealed himself a tyrant in his dealings with the Filipinos. Chaffe,[6] I hear, is a hard drinker.

P.S. 2. Since writing the above I have read the editorial in Saturday's *Post* on the higher education of the negro. It reads as if inspired by Dr. Bumstead, if I may take the extract from Prest. Eliot's admirable speech (which I heard) as an ear mark. But I fear that the recommendation at the end to "friends of colored education & the educated negroes themselves" to take up the task of supporting these institutions will seem to most of your readers to relieve their own minds of further concern on the subject, when, as a matter of fact, it should appeal most powerfully to all who have this matter of Southern education at all at heart, & especially to the Southern Education Assocn which is so deliberately turning its back to Atlanta.

Tuesday, 13th. Thanks for your note of yesterday, with clippings. I had missed your two letters from Charleston, & that on "The Southern Negro's Education" is the most blood-stirring one of the lot to me. "Not a single colored man present as a delegate or an invited guest at the Conference." What nice regard for Southern white sensibilities! And these last ready to flare up at the mere words "disadvantaged race." How gross the behavior of that Montgomery judge in discharging the white assailant of the colored woman! Martha Schofield of Aikin told me years ago that she said to one of the white pastors there, "why don't you keep your young men from corrupting my [colored] girls?" "Ah," he replied, "why do you make them so attractive?" I fear that the more money Northern philanthropy pours into white schools, the more jealous the whites will be of what goes to the blacks, & the more they will try to divert & absorb for themselves; & the tendency will be, on the part of the millionaire patrons such as Ogden is trying to corral & influence, to slight the black schools, save Tuskegee & one or two conspicuous examples, & to give to the whites.

ALS Oswald Garrison Villard Papers MH. Brackets in original.

[1] Francis Greenwood Peabody (1847–1936), a Unitarian, taught theology at Harvard from 1881 to 1913.

[2] William Goodell Frost (1854–1938) was president of Berea College from 1892 to 1920.

[3] S. G. Atkins, a clergyman and officer of the A.M.E. Church, was principal of the Slater Normal School in Winston-Salem, N.C.

[4] Villard praised the work of the Southern Education Board and said that education was the key to uplifting the South. (New York *Evening Post*, May 9, 1902, 7.)

[5] James Franklin Bell (1856–1919), an army officer, awarded the Congressional Medal of Honor for action in the Philippines, was U.S. Army chief of staff from 1906 to 1910.

[6] Adna Romanza Chaffee (1842–1914) served in the Spanish-American War and was commander of American troops that captured Peking during the Boxer Rebellion. He was U.S. Army chief of staff from 1904 to 1906.

From William Hayes Ward

New York   May 14, 1902

My dear Dr. Washington: I thank you for the clipping you sent about the negro mayors, and if possible I will make use of it.

I hope that when the next conference on colored education meets *all* the officers will be invited to attend.

I have had a communication from Mr. Wallace Putnam Reed,[1] of Atlanta, which I am afraid we cannot publish, in which he says that Mr. Gilreath accepted an invitation to take tea with you at your home and that it made a very big sensation. Is this substantially true? I know that you have generally taken great pains to avoid anything that would give offense, and that when you have entertained white people at your home you have had them waited upon separately at table. I suspect that he rather invited himself than that you gave the invitation. Yours very truly,

William Hayes Ward

TLS   Con. 224   BTW Papers   DLC.

1 Wallace Putnam Reed (b. 1849) was on the editorial staff of the Atlanta *Constitution*. Earlier he had edited a five-volume *History of Atlanta, Georgia* (1889).

From Emmett Jay Scott

Washington, D.C. May 15, 1902

My Dear Mr. Washington: I received the letter from General Jas S Clarkson too late to take with me when I went to call on the President yesterday, so I wrote the latter this morning & sent Gen. Clarkson's letter & said to him that it was only confirmatory of all I had said and I know that means the end of Mr. Ferguson. I enclose copy of Mr. Clarkson's letter. I sent it Special Delivery to the President & took occasion to emphasize again some of the remarks you asked me to say to him. I have refused to talk [of] my mission to any one tho' the brethren are all curious to know what I am here for. Even Adams with whom I am staying has not learned anything from me, nor has he tried for that matter. The old guard are for him I learn & I had to tell Cooper today quite strongly that I resented his insinuations as to my presence & his pressing inquiries and his effort to make me say I'd try to get you to support Ferguson. He has told Ferguson he'd get your endorsement I learn. Dancy and Lyons are also for him. They went to see the President yesterday after I was there & the President asked him about his St. Louis conduct I learn & also if he thought he could get your endorsement. He said he wasn't sure. The President told me without reservation that he'd appoint no man over your protest — that is when you do not think them fit. I made much of the fact that you were only seeking to get the best men in & that touched him. Leupp is disgusted that the President should hesitate in this matter at all & has about washed his hands of Southern matters altogether.

I'll write again tonight. Yours Sincerely

Emmett J. Scott

ALS   Con. 245   BTW Papers   DLC.

From Leila Usher[1]

New York   May 15th 1902

Dear Mr. Washington: The bust got here in as good condition as when it started, and is now at the plaster-cast shop being put into plaster.

The first of next week it will be ready for your friends to see it. If they will write me at the above address I will meet them at such time as they designate at 210 West 33rd Street, the plaster cast shop.

I enjoyed my stay in Tuskegee, and learned much that was interesting to me. I thank you all for your courtesy, and wish to be remembered to Mrs. Washington. I am staying in New York primarily to attend to the casting of your bust, so shall be glad to have your friends see it as soon as convenient to them.

I only hope that when a copy of your bust gets to Tuskegee it will give general satisfaction. Very sincerely yours,

Leila Usher

ALS   Con. 244   BTW Papers   DLC.

1 Leila Usher (1859–1955), a sculptor, was born in Onalaska, Wis., and moved to New York. She was best known, perhaps, for her 1902 bust of BTW. Her work won awards at the Atlanta Exposition in 1895 and at the Pan-Pacific Exposition in 1915. She did a number of busts and bas-reliefs of prominent people, including Nathaniel Southgate Shaler (at Harvard), Susan B. Anthony (at Bryn Mawr), and John Wesley Powell (at Arlington National Cemetery.)

From Emmett Jay Scott

Washington, May 16—02

My Dear Mr. Washington: I did not finish the letter I started last night & promised to write again this morning.

About Mr Leupp: He said to me that he could not thoroughly understand the President now — that he could not see why your judgement is not unreservedly followed in the South — & in this case of Smith's at any rate without reservation — that you know more of it than any one else certainly more than he or the President. I went over the whole matter with him very carefully before going to see the President. He talked over the matters at length & read each of the newspapers exposing the perfidy & duplicity of this man. He promises to talk with the President about Smith again. The whole trouble arises from the organizations stand against him, & their unrelenting hostility. He has wired for Judge Burns[1] to come here & I guess he'll be here soon. He said frankly as I wrote you that he'd not appoint Ferguson with these disclosures of his character, but he is a strange man. When Ferguson went up to see him he asked him direct questions about his St Louis conduct. As soon as Ferguson knew I was in town he knew how the President got his information — and he has had Cooper trying to call me off — or to win your support.

Mr Thompson's party seems to be attracting a great deal of attention. I have seen him again & he is elated with the way we came to his rescue to help him out. This thing is larger than he at first suspected, and he was glad to get the amount we proffered. I leave here Sunday morning for home. Yours sincerely

Emmett J. Scott

ALS   Con. 245   BTW Papers   DLC.

1 Waller T. Burns was judge of the U.S. District Court for the southern district of Texas, beginning in 1902.

Oswald Garrison Villard to Francis Jackson Garrison

New York, May 16, 1902

Dear Uncle Frank: Many thanks for your letter of 15th. I shall be very glad to see Dr. Bumstead when he calls, but I am not in a position to go into the criticisms of his institution, except in a general way.

I am glad that he feels as he does about the Athens movement; so does President Merrill,[1] of Fisk, a letter from whom I enclose. Please note the sentence in it that I have underlined. I think you are mistaken in your feeling. In fact, I am sure that you are. I am glad that Hoke Smith[2] said what he did of Shaw. The latter has asked me to write an article for the "Review of Reviews" about Benson's School.[3] That was certainly a very foolish remark of Benson's about Booker Washington.[4] Benson is, of course, young, and his danger is keeping his tongue in check. But considering the frightful situation in which he is placed, I think he has done very well so far.

To show you how this conference is enlightening and broadening the southern people, let me tell you in confidence that the wife of the Governor of Virginia,[5] who was in our party, lunched with Washington and his wife! It must not get out at present, but she did. Moreover, she was quite in the dark about the whole movement, and quite rabid when we left Richmond, so that she saw the light very quickly, and I am sure that her whole life will be changed by that experience. Her husband did not like my speech in the Executive Mansion at Richmond. I could see that. But, at least, I made it, and others liked it, I think. Affectionately yours,

Oswald Garrison Villard

TLSr   Oswald Garrison Villard Papers   MH.

1 James Griswold Merrill (1840–1920), a Congregationalist clergyman and editor, joined the Fisk University faculty in 1898, teaching logic and ethics and also serving as dean. He became acting president of Fisk from 1899 to 1901, because of the illness of Erastus M. Cravath, and upon Cravath's death Merrill became president from 1901 to 1908.

2 Hoke Smith (1855–1931), Secretary of the Interior from 1893 to 1896, was president of the Atlanta Board of Education from 1896 to 1907. He was a two-term governor of Georgia. In 1911 he was elected U.S. senator and served until 1921. Up until the time of his campaign for governor in 1905, Smith had been a supporter of BTW's approach to race problems and an advocate of education for blacks. In 1899

465

he had opposed disfranchisement in Georgia and spoken out against lynching. During the gubernatorial campaign, however, Smith became blatantly racist, partly to gain the support of Tom Watson. He condemned the "ignorant, purchasable negro vote," and declared Georgia to be "white man's country." He proclaimed that his case rested "upon the intellectual superiority of the white man; the capacity of every white boy who has a fair show to fit himself for duties the negro can never discharge, no matter what his opportunities." (Grantham, *Hoke Smith*, 148–49.)

3 See Oswald Garrison Villard, "An Alabama Negro School," *American Monthly Review of Reviews*, 26 (Dec. 1902), 711–14. Villard praised the work of the school and gave John J. Benson and his son William E. Benson the major credit for its success. Villard added: "That Mr. Booker T. Washington's influence has penetrated to Kowaliga goes without saying. Wherever there are intelligent negroes there will be found some knowledge of Mr. Washington's teachings and ideals."

4 Francis J. Garrison wrote Oswald Garrison Villard of "the secret of Washington's antipathy to Benson." He said: "Wm E. Benson told William [Lloyd Garrison, Jr.] that B. T. W.'s dislike of him was due to his having said that W. had married three of his teachers, & would marry another in a fortnight if this one should die. The remark reached W.'s ears & he was naturally incensed. It was not a nice thing for B. to say, especially as B. T. W.'s wives have been women of exceptional worth & character." (May 15, 1902, Oswald Garrison Villard Papers, MH.)

5 Elizabeth Lyne Hoskins married Andrew Jackson Montague in 1889. Andrew J. Montague (1862–1937) was attorney general of Virginia from 1898 to 1902, governor from 1902 to 1906, and congressman from 1913 until his death. A moderate progressive, Montague contributed nothing beyond rhetoric to the cause of black education, though for a brief period the Southern Education Board pinned their hopes on him.

Filipino [Wilford H. Smith]
to Ajax [Emmett Jay Scott]

[New York City] May 17th, 1902

Dear Ajax: Fearing that you will forget the name I give it to you again. Miss Maybelle McAdoo.[1]

I wish it was so that the amount could double itself at least, but small favors thankfully received etc. Very truly yours,

Filipino

TLSr   Con. 227   BTW Papers   DLC.

1 Maybelle McAdoo was Smith's secretary. Sometimes Smith's telegrams were signed "McAdoo" in order to keep his identity secret. An undated memorandum in the same container as the above reads: "In writing Filipino use Postal Telegraph Co. to McAdoo she to use same line to us. She to use Western Union in wiring Filipino and he to use same line in wiring her."

A Speech at Tuskegee Institute

[Tuskegee, Ala.] May 21, 1902

This occasion is due first to our honored member of Congress, from this District, the Hon. Charles W. Thompson, for the treat which we enjoy to-day, and we are glad to welcome Mr. Thompson together with his party to this Institution, and to let you know that we appreciate, in the highest terms the honor which you have paid us in bringing this party to see the work that this Institution is undertaking to do. I am sure that all of us are glad that Mr. Thompson overcame that characteristic modesty, which seems to cling to all Alabama people, and was good enough to accept the nomination to Congress, and finally overcame his modesty to the extent that he was willing to go to Congress after he was elected. I confess that some feared that in his modesty that he would decline the nomination; and, later on, that he would decline the election, after it was conferred upon him — almost unanimously — by the people of this District. But all of us are of one accord in thanking Mr. Thompson for accepting the nomination; for accepting the election; for going to Congress, and for bringing this delightful party to see Tuskegee. And I am sure that this Institution is not only grateful to him, but the people throughout the State of Alabama; further than that, throughout the South.

I have said more than once that what we need above all things is to get better acquainted with each other. For the best people in the South and in the North to get better acquainted with each other. We have staid far off, one from the other. Sometimes we have called each other hard names. When we got together, shook hands, had a heart to heart talk, we found out we are not so far from each other as we thought we were.

We are glad that Mr. Thompson has brought this party to the South, in order that they may see the magnificent opportunities for development in agriculture, in minerals, and last but not least the development of men in the South. At Tuskegee, at this Institution, we have bended all our energies to the building of characters, of industries. We are trying to turn them all into usefulness; into high, pure, noble citizenship; for Alabama citizenship; for our whole Country. And in trying to do this, this Institution has had no warmer, and more helpful friend, than the Hon. Chas. W. Thompson. (Applause.)

Now I have been asked what becomes of our students when they graduate. I shall not attempt to answer that question in detail this afternoon, except to say that we have followed their history closely, and, so far as we know, not a single graduate of this Institution has ever entered a State Penitentiary or the United States Congress. (Laughter.) And we should feel very much encouraged by the progress that we have thus far made; and we hope to keep up the record.

I shall not detain you longer from the treat which I am sure you all are longing for, and I shall introduce first our honored member of Congress, Mr. Charles W. Thompson, of Tuskegee, Alabama.[1]

TM Con. 244 BTW Papers DLC. Delivered at the Tuskegee Institute Chapel, 2:30 P.M.

1 Thompson gave a sentimental talk about two of the best friends he ever had, who happened to be black. They were "Old mammy Aunt Sarah Parks," who had nursed Thompson's children, and "Uncle Sam Hill," whom Thompson described as a "good man." He also told the blacks in the audience that BTW was their Moses. "Trust him; love him; obey him," Thompson admonished, "and all your efforts will be crowned with victory." (Con. 244, BTW Papers, DLC.) The day before, Thompson had entertained the white visitors at his plantation with a barbecue. That evening the students of the Alabama Female College gave a concert on the Thompson plantation. (*Tuskegee Student*, 14 [May 24, 1902], 2.)

To Frank W. Hale[1]

Tuskegee, Alabama. May 23, 1902

Personal

Dear Sir: I desire to arrange if possible, for one of my children to enter the New England Conservatory of Music at the opening next fall, and I want if possible for her to secure a room in the new dormitory. I want a single room and one that is medium in price.

I would say that my daughter has been well raised and I think you will find that she will not be in any respect offensive nor will give any trouble in any regard.

May I beg of you that nothing be said about this correspondence where the newspapers can get hold of it, and if my daughter does enter the Conservatory I wish as far as possible to guard against newspaper publicity. In regard to my public life I care nothing about such publicity but I do not like to have my family affairs discussed in the press. Yours truly,

Booker T. Washington

TLS   In possession of Mrs. Frederick C. Green, Jr., Fitchburg, Mass.

1 Frank W. Hale taught music theory and organ and piano tuning at the New England Conservatory of Music. At the time of BTW's letter he was also manager of the conservatory.

An Article in the *Tuskegee Student*

Tuskegee, Alabama, May 24, 1902

Industrial Training for Southern Women

One of the most important questions to be settled in the South is, what to do with the women in an industrial sense. This applies not alone to the colored women, but in a large measure to the white women. Slavery taught both that labor was something to be escaped — to be gotten rid of just as soon as possible.

In most prosperous countries the women are employed to a large extent in factories, shops, stores and various forms of industry, but, except in a limited way, this is not true of the South. For many decades the education of women in the South has been largely along the line of belles lettres, art and music. With the dawn of freedom, the temptation was to educate the colored girl along the same lines. Nor have many as yet seen that it is necessary to change to a large extent the education of the white women, especially of the poorer and middle classes. Art and music for people who live in rented houses and have no bank account, are not the most important subjects to which attention can be given. Such education creates want without a corresponding increase of ability to supply these increased wants. One of the saddest sights I ever saw in the South, was a colored girl recently returned from college, sitting in a rented one-room cabin, attempting day by day to extract music from a second-hand rented piano, when all about her indicated poverty, want of thrift and cleanliness.

I suppose it is safe to say that about three-fourths of the women and girls in the South have no profitable and commendable way to employ their time. The changed conditions resulting from the freedom of the slaves, have forced many white women, who have not been trained to do anything more profitable, to become various kinds of agents for cheap books, cheap periodicals, so-called silver ware, etc. The colored woman, to evade the hard work of plowing or hoeing or splitting rails by the side of men, escapes as soon as possible to the city, where she too often finds nothing that she is fitted to do, and the result is a life of shame.

It is true that in the country districts of the South the white women and girls take their places in the field by the men, but they, like their colored sisters, feel that this is not their proper place, and who can blame them?

These conditions bring us face to face with the question as to what is the best thing to be done with the millions of poor white women and girls in the South and the equally large number of colored women and girls. The recent introduction of cotton mills into the South, has given employment to a few white women in a few local centres, but this does not settle the matter.

What are some of the industries in the South that a woman can be trained to follow? I mean industries that will be creators of wealth. Among others I would name dairying, fruit-growing, small berry-growing, floriculture, poultry-raising, fruit-canning, as industries that the South is especially suited for. Work along these lines for women is infinitely better than peddling cheap books and other cheap wares, and is vastly better suited to the constitution of a woman than plowing, hoeing or splitting rails. Such work is not only more elevating, but it will pay, will produce wealth where there was none before. Such industries make a producer rather than a parasite.

The average man in education likes to do the same thing that was done centuries ago, with no other reason for it than that it has always been done thus. Why not in the South face conditions as they are and apply ourselves to the remedy?

There is room and need for a half dozen great institutions in the South where women can be taught in connection with academic studies, can be given the best theoretical and practical training in dairying, fruit-growing, growing of small berries, floriculture, poultry-raising, etc. Such institutions are needed for colored and white girls. The schools should have instructors of the highest type of intelligence and broadest culture. The instructors should possess such special knowledge of the industry taught as will result in raising it from drudgery and common labor into that which is dignified and beautiful. This result can only be secured by teaching the use of labor-saving machinery and putting brains into every stage of the work.

Besides the valuable training that such an institution would give — training that would in time result in making green many waste places in the South—such an institution would in time be in a measure self-sustaining.

Here at the Tuskegee Normal and Industrial Institute in Alabama, in connection with training three hundred girls in literary branches, sewing, cooking, laundering, millinery, general household science, fruit-canning, etc., we are gradually moving into the fields of industry mentioned in the foregoing. Next year we are planning to give a large number of girls training in dairying, and the work will be pushed all along the line just as fast as we can secure funds with which to start and pay expenses of these departments. If we had the means we could have five hundred girls receiving such training at Tuskegee. As it is, we are compelled now to refuse admission to at least three hundred girls every year.

Looking at the commercial value of such training, it can be safely said that the products of such training find a ready market, not only in the North, but in the South.

There will be those who will argue that such a course of training has too much of the utilitarian idea in view, and does not lay enough stress on the mental and moral development. Right here is where the average man blunders. You cannot give a hungry man much moral training. To secure the highest moral and religious training among the poor white and colored women in the South, we have got to get them to the point where their stomachs can be regularly filled with good, well-cooked food. Investigate the physical condition of those who compose the mobs, the lynching bees in the South, and see how many get plenty of well cooked food three times a day. A man can't read his Bible to much advantage or write poetry when he is hungry.

Then one is likely to overlook the amount of mental discipline that can be secured from such training as I have described, well systematized. One who deals with nature in the industrial world, is forced to think, or plan for the future, to investigate, to compare. Is there not as much mental discipline in having a student think out and put on paper a plan for a modern dairy building, as in having her merely commit to memory poetry that somebody else thought out years ago? I repeat that we must face conditions as they exist about us. During the next fifty years the problem that the South will be continually facing is that of "bread and butter." With this settled, the next generation of colored and poor white girls can afford to give more time to the aesthetics. When one builds a house, he does not begin by putting fine paper and pictures on the walls or carpets on the floor. The foundation and framework first, and year by year, by patient industry, the trinkets and ornaments come, but the man who begins by getting the trinkets and ornaments first, will never get the house.

In giving the training that I have attempted to outline, I do not mean to give the impression that literary or academic education should be cast aside or neglected. Far from it. The more brain training that can be mixed in, the better. An ignorant woman is an ignorant woman, no matter where placed, with all the disadvantages of ignorance.

Few movements will do more to rid the South of some of the evils that now afflict it, than the introduction of such industrial teaching. One trouble with the South is that there are so many people who have time to waste, thus they can devote time to attending to everybody's business. People whose thoughts and hands are deeply immersed in some paying business, do not bother themselves about matters that the courts and other lawful authorities should attend to. Something to occupy constantly during all seasons of the year the masses of the people in the South, will do as much as any other force to solve the Southern problem.

Production and commerce are two of the great destroyers of race prejudice. In proportion as the black woman is able to produce something that the white or other races want, in the same proportion does prejudice disappear. Butter is going to be purchased from the individual who can produce the best butter and at the lowest price, and the purchaser cares not whether it was made by a black, white, brown, or yellow woman. The best butter is what is wanted. The American dollar has not an ounce of prejudice in it.

Tuskegee Student, 14 (May 24, 1902), 1, 2, 3.

From Edmund H. Deas

Washington, D.C., May 24, 1902

Dear Sir: I have just returned from Boston, where I spoke on disfranchisement and lynching; eked out or dragged through. Notwithstanding that I was chief orator, and as they claim the drawing card, I was the last on the program to speak. I did not commence to speak until very near eleven o'clock, a time that I am required to be in bed by my physician. Though I received quite an ovation I could not do justice to myself or the paper I prepared, still I received flattering compliments from friends and the press.

While in Boston I was entertained by friends who are supposed to be unfriendly towards you, but I deemed it my duty to endeavor to convince them that they did not thoroughly understand you. I took the liberty of showing them your letter touching the Koester matter, in which was shown conclusively your sympathy. Mr. Archie Grimkie was at a dinner at which one of these discussions concerning you came up, and he will bear testimony to the stand I took. If Trotter continues to oppose and criticise you in the manner heretofore it will be only because he is unwilling to be convinced of your unselfish interest in the race.

I am in communication with Gen. Clarkson, touching affairs in my State, and as he has a high regard for me I am willing to place myself in his hands and assist in settling affairs in South Carolina. I think by this time the President is convinced that McLaurin is an over-rated man and cannot be trusted to dictate appointments in the State. Mr. F. E. Leupp told me that he had told the President that he did not have a favorable opinion of McLaurin. In my opinion the President would have had far better advice from either Judges Simonton[1] or Brawley[2] — both democrats.

I am going to use my utmost endeavor to land Col. Kaufman as the next Postmaster at Charleston, and I hope you will co-operate with me. Very truly,

E. H. Deas

dictated.

TLS Con. 272 BTW Papers DLC.

[1] Charles Henry Simonton (1829–1904), a Confederate veteran and long-time state legislator, became U.S. district judge in South Carolina in 1886 by appointment of

473

Grover Cleveland, and in 1893 Cleveland appointed him a U.S. circuit judge in the same state, a position he held until his death.

2 William Huggins Brawley (1841–1916), a one-armed veteran of the Confederate Army, a former state judge and legislator, served in Congress from Charleston from 1891 to 1894 and as U.S. district judge from 1894 to 1911.

An Extract from an Article by Robley Dunglison Evans

May 1902

NEGRO MELODIES — BOOKER WASHINGTON

The first request made by Prince Henry after being received in New York was that I should arrange to give him some of the old Southern melodies, if possible, sung by the negroes; that he was passionately fond of them, and had been all his life — not the ragtime songs, but the old negro melodies. Several times during his trip I endeavored to carry out his wishes, with more or less success; but, finally, at the Waldorf-Astoria, the Hampton singers presented themselves in one of the reception-rooms and gave him a recital of Indian and negro melodies. He was charmed.

And while I was talking to him just after a Sioux Indian had sung a lullaby, he suddenly turned and said, "Isn't that Booker T. Washington over there?" I recognized Washington and replied that it was, and he said: "Evans, would you mind presenting him to me? I know how some of your people feel about Washington, but I have always had great sympathy with the African race, and I want to meet the man I regard as the leader of that race." So I went at once to Washington and told him that the Prince wished him to be presented, and took him myself and presented him to the Prince. Booker Washington sat down and talked with him for fully ten minutes, and it was a most interesting conversation — one of the most interesting I ever heard in my life. The ease with which Washington conducted himself was very striking, and I only accounted for it afterwards when I remembered that he had dined with the Queen of England two or three times, so that this was not a new thing for him. Indeed, Booker Washington's manner was easier than that of almost any other man I saw meet the Prince in this country. The Prince afterwards referred to President Roosevelt's action in regard to Booker Washington, and applauded it very highly.

McClure's Magazine, 19 (May 1902), 34. The article was entitled "Prince Henry's American Impressions," and consisted of a series of short sketches.

To Oswald Garrison Villard

Tuskegee, Ala., June 4, 1902

Personal and Private.

My dear Mr. Villard: Replying further to your letter containing your report I would say that, I thank you very much for your frankness and for the information which your letter contains.

I am often placed in a very trying position. I am safe in saying that there is hardly a week when I am not applied to for endorsements of the work of some Southern school. If I refrain from giving the endorsement in many cases I am blamed and misunderstood; if I give the endorsement in many cases I find myself blamed also. For example, within the last month I have been more than mildly rebuked for endorsing two schools which in the opinion of other people are not worthy. In most cases where I have made the mistake of endorsing unworthy schools I have done so by yielding to the persuasion of other people rather than following my own judgment. It is very hard and trying for me not to give full and hearty endorsements to all the schools that apply to me; if for no other reason than for my own peace of mind this would be the easiest way out, besides, of course, I must realize, as anyone who comes to the South does, that there is plenty of work for all of these schools to do.

In the case of the school at Kowaliga I would say that my impressions have been formed by contact with it as a trustee and otherwise through a series of years, and you must bear with me if I cannot bring myself to the point where I can rid myself of these impressions without careful consideration. Of course I do not mean to say that my opinion or endorsement are of much concern in bearing upon the work of the school.

Of course it is human nature for [one] always, perhaps, to be more attracted to those institutions where he feels that his word and perhaps influence are respected more than to those where one has been made to feel that this is not true.

Some of the things outlined in your letter wherein a reform is to be made were taken up by me when I was a trustee, or soon after my resignation, I forget which.

I cannot cover the whole subject by letter, but I would say that some of the details where [which] are covered by your report and the facts as I came into contact with them when I was a trustee and as I have actually known them since, do not agree. This school has been the cause of more worry to me than all of the other schools combined in the South which I have tried to help. When I was a trustee, several of the matters covered in detail by your report I had rather disagreeable experience in trying to get in proper shape, and you must not be surprised if while I have this experience in mind I cannot dismiss these matters as quickly as you think I ought to, and must not be further surprised if I do not have quite as much faith in promises as you do. For example, the matter of separating the office of collector and treasurer was taken up in the same way that is now suggested by you some years ago, and a promise was made that such a separation would be made but nothing came of it.

In regard to Mr. Calloway I would say that the fact which you mention of his having asked another woman to elope with him is new to me, and I shall take that up and give it due consideration. I have no desire to keep any man in the employ of this institution who is unworthy or who is tainted too much with suspicion. The committee appointed by me did not go to Kowaliga to make the investigation for the reason that they got hold of persons in Tuskegee who had been connected with the school and seemed to be unprejudiced who gave them all the information that it seemed possible to get hold of at that time. In addition to the report of the committee, I had Mr. Calloway secure a letter of recommendation which I now hold (and which you can see if necessary) from Dr. Beard, the Secretary of the American Missionary Association by whom Mr. Calloway was employed. I saw this letter before I employed Mr. Calloway. I do not know whether in your investigation of Mr. Calloway's case you saw Mr. Calloway yourself and had him and the people who accuse him brought face to face. In my dealing with our teachers and students here I have always found this a pretty safe thing to do before passing judgment; in all of these matters I have found it rather safe to assume that there are two pretty emphatic sides, and in many cases if the accused is given an opportunity he can disprove many stories.

You must forgive me for burdening you with so long a letter. The point, however, of everything I want to say is that I am most anxious to be of service in helping forward the work of every man and every organization that has for its object the elevation of either race in the South. I want to help and not hinder, and I shall be most happy if I can get to the point where I can conscientiously and earnestly assist in pushing forward the work at Kowaliga. Yours truly,

Booker T. Washington

TLS Oswald Garrison Villard Papers MH. A signed draft is in BTW Papers, ATT.

From Henry Clay Alvord[1]

South Weymouth, Mass. June 4, 1902

My dear Sir and Brother: We here in South Weymouth have learned that you contemplate bringing your family and making a sojourn in our community.

It is my experience and observation that it is oftentimes well to say in definite terms some things which we are warrented in taking for granted.

I am sure that it is not *necessary* to say that you will find a cordial welcome awaiting you and yours, but it may not be wholly unacceptable to you for me, having no official commission indeed to represent the So. Weymouth people and yet beyond doubt essentially doing so, to say that we feel much pleased to have you come among us, and shall be glad to welcome you to our village and its pleasant interests and life. We trust that you will find it congenial and restful, both in its contribution to the renewal of mind and body, and in the sympathy you will find with you and the great work in which you are engaged. I trust you will command us — any of us — as to any matters in which we can be of service.

With best wishes for prosperity in your special work, with kind regards to your family, and pleasantly anticipating your early coming   I remain — Very sincerely yours,

Henry C. Alvord

ALS   Con. 220   BTW Papers   DLC.

1 Henry Clay Alvord, born in 1854, became the pastor of the Old South Congregational Church in South Weymouth, Mass., in 1886. A genealogist, he was the author of *The Descendants of Jonathan Gillet of Dorchester, Mass., and Windsor, Conn.* (1898).

From Timothy Thomas Fortune

Maple Hall, Red Bank, N.J. June 9, 1902

My Dear Mr. Washington: Your letter of the 5th instant, dated at Lexington, with check enclosed, was received. Please accept my thanks. It got here just in time.

I have written you that my first impression of the President's Arlington address was erroneous. We take up the matter editorially in The Age this week, and shall give the President the credit due him for the position that he takes.

The Commencement article of Tuskegee in the current Age makes a splendid showing for your work. I will keep track of the comments on the Southern Education article.

I am still inclined to get out of the race journalism and work, and devote myself to truck farming and general literary work. Referring to a conversation we had about The Age sometime ago, when the question of enlargement was under consideration, I have thought that you might care to acquire my unencumbered half interest in The Age. Perhaps Mr. Baldwin and Mr. Ogden might care to go in with you, so that the paper could stand for the joint educational work, with some such man as R. W. Thompson as the editorial director. I would contract to write a signed article every week, if it was thought that my connection with the paper was desired. If you care to consider the proposition I would be glad to hear from you.

I should want $10,000 for my interest. I am sure that no better business manager than Mr. Peterson could be desired. The paper represents my efforts for twenty years, is free of debt, and pays its way. Yours truly,

T. Thos. Fortune

TLS Con. 227 BTW Papers DLC.

From Lawrence Fraser Abbott

New York   June 13, 1902

My dear Dr. Washington: I have just returned from two weeks' absence in Maine, and have my first opportunity to acknowledge your letter of May 26th. I am sorry for my absence, because if the paragraph on lynching which you suggest could have been printed at the time of the occurrence, we should have prepared one. Such a piece of savagery as that described in the extract from the Montgomery "Advertiser" which you send, is so horrible as to be almost incredible.[1] Why intelligent white men of the South do not see that such things are far more likely to destroy the white race than the black race, I cannot understand. I can sympathize with a man who shoots down quickly and as painlessly as possible any one who violently attacks his home, his life, or the life of any individual whom he is bound to protect. That aspect of lynching under certain conditions, as, for example, in the days of the Vigilance Committee in California, can be given some explanation, if not excuse; but no possible explanation can be given of hideous and devilish torture. I think we shall find a way before long to say something of this kind in the columns of The Outlook. I thank you for bringing the matter to my attention.

Did you see Mr. Leupp's article about you and your work in a recent number of The Outlook?[2] It has brought to us an amusing and yet painful letter of protest from Dr. Merrill of Fisk University — not a protest against Tuskegee or yourself, but a defense of what he, I think needlessly and groundlessly, considers an imputation upon the teaching of the so-called higher branches at Fisk. We do not want to publish it in The Outlook, on his own account, for I

479

think it would do Fisk University a great deal more harm than good, and we have written to him telling him so. This of course is personal between you and me. As a matter of fact, if we printed all the protests that come from Fisk, I am inclined to think we should have to get out a special edition every month. If you will allow the personality, we here very much prefer the spirit in which Tuskegee goes ahead and minds its own business, and minds it well, and lets fancied criticisms sink into the oblivion which such criticisms always do when they are left to themselves. Yours sincerely,

Lawrence F. Abbott

TLS Con. 261 BTW Papers DLC.

¹ The Montgomery *Advertiser*, May 23, 1902, 1, reported a lynching at Longview, Tex., on May 22, when a black man named Dudley Morgan, accused of assaulting a white woman, was tortured and burned slowly to death. After the fire was out a few people in the crowd of several hundred persons searched the ashes for parts of Morgan's body for souvenirs.

² Frances E. Leupp, "Why Booker Washington Has Succeeded in His Life Work," *Outlook*, 71 (May 31, 1902), 326–33. Leupp praised BTW for his conservative, gradualist approach and his willingness to work on in spite of the pressures of racism in the South and indifference in the North. Leupp wrote: "His faith is firm that the negro has certain natural qualities — cheerfulness, endurance, devotion, tractability — which fit him for a place of his own in the great human mosaic, and need only a little friendly guidance to develop them." Commenting on BTW as the Negro Moses, Leupp thought the analogy had limitations, since Moses sought to lead his people to the promised land while BTW told blacks they were already in the promised land. Furthermore, Moses was a lawgiver who was often fiery and dictatorial, while BTW governed by suggestion and a masterful control of his temper.

From Warren Logan

Tuskegee, Ala., June 13, 1902

Dear Mr. Washington: I have yours of the 10th enclosing Mr. Calloway's letter. The news which it contains is indeed deplorable. I have spoken to Mr. Scott about notifying the people of the young men who were drowned about their death, and he tells me he has already done it.

I fear it is going to be somewhat difficult to get young men to go to Africa to take the places of the two who were lost. You know the matter of securing men was referred to Mr. Carver, and I find that he has not yet found any whom we would regard as suitable to go. I have asked him to make special effort to get men and I hope to be able to have them start very soon. The money for their expenses is on hand already, having been sent at the time remittance was made for expenses of Mr. Calloway's party.

I shall hold the check for the Hyde legacy until I hear from you again about the matter. Trusting you are well and that you enjoyed your Western trip, Very truly yours,

Warren Logan

TLS Con. 233 BTW Papers DLC. Addressed to the Palmer House, Chicago.

To Timothy Thomas Fortune

Washington, D.C. June 15, 1902

My dear Mr. Fortune: I have your letter of June 9th and will talk the matters covered in it over with you when I see you, which I hope will be within the next week. I shall telegraph you sometime ahead.

I also have your circular letter of June 7th asking my opinion regarding the possibility of getting 100,000 Afro-Americans to go to the Congo. I would say briefly that I feel very sure that if you could get Bishop Turner, Col. Pledger and Rev. W. H. Heard to go to the Congo and settle there that you would have little trouble in getting the remainder to follow. What do you think of this scheme? Yours truly,

Booker T. Washington
Address South Weymouth Mass.

TLS Con. 247 BTW Papers DLC.

From Filipino [Wilford H. Smith][1]

[Montgomery, Ala.] June 17th, 1902

My dear Friend: The decision of the court is purely political, with the sole purpose, in my opinion, to delay, and thus discourage the further effort to bring the case before the U.S. Supreme Court. They are calculating on the non-combative disposition of the race. I am more confirmed in this belief, since they even refused to allow me to withdraw from the files, the petition which I had spent so much time and pains to prepare; so that now, all that work must be done over.

My purpose, as you know, was to get the case out of the state court in the speediest way, and hence I started in the Supreme Court. Still, had I started in the Circuit court or the city court instead, I would not have gotten the case up to the state Supreme court on appeal any sooner than the November term, which I will still be able to do.

Appearing in the Supreme Court of the state in the first instance, has helped our case, instead of harming it. The fact that I have appeared before that tribunal and was heard in argument, will enable me to obtain far more consideration in the lower courts than I would have, had I not taken that course. It is possible that had I started in the lower courts, and there divulged my purpose, I would never have been admitted to the bar, or been allowed to proceed or be heard in any of the courts. So, to my mind, the dog-fall decision means more to us than it does to the registrars.

They have by their action, clearly convinced me that they mean to resort to every possible device permissible under the state practice, to avoid deciding the Federal question, so as to prevent our appeal being effectual in the U.S. Supreme Court. So, I have concluded not to depend upon the mandamus case alone, but to bring two other cases up to them on appeal, in which no other question will appear but the Federal question. These are my plans: To go down to the city court with the same application for mandamus, which of course will be refused, and then take an appeal from that ruling to the state Supreme court. Also to bring a suit for damages against the registrars in the city court, for refusing to register a negro, which will be decided on a demurrer, which is a question of law, and that case will also be appealed to the state Supreme court. And in addition to these, to raise the same Federal question in a criminal case, where a negro is on trial for a felony. In the criminal case, I will make no other defence for the man except the Federal question, so as to give the court no ground to release him in order to avoid the Federal question. Upon the conviction of the negro, that case will be appealed to the state Supreme court likewise. So that when the Supreme court comes in in November they will meet three cases here on appeal, all involving the same Federal question, and no other question, which they will be bound to pass on.

Knowing that the sole purpose of the court here is to avoid the Federal question, and that all the state courts and court officers are in league and conspiracy to prevent our case going to the Supreme Court of the U.S., I am not willing to trust any of them in making up the record and preparing the appeals and appeal bonds, and assignments of error, and such other things necessary to perfect an appeal to the state Supreme court; and hence my personal presence is absolutely necessary here until the appeals are all taken and filed in the state Supreme court, and even after the Supreme court meets till a decision is had. Because if they could find a way to dismiss any one or all of our appeals for some informality they would do so, and that would be no ground of appeal to the Supreme Court of the U.S. An appeal lies to that court from a state court, only when the decision involves some question arising under the Constitution of the United States, called a Federal question.

You can see by this, that the task before us is not an easy one, and is one which must take all of my time from now until November, or very nearly all of it, if we want to make a success. We have only to get to Washington on the Federal question and our case will win itself; and with the proof I shall be able to put in the record, we will knock out both the temporary and permanent sections of that odious document.

I dislike very much to inform you, that I am very much embarrassed financially, in that I am pressed by current expenses and other bills at home, and will not be able to give all the required time to this work without more ample and immediate financial provision can be made for my assistance in the way of a fee. This kind of a fight, quasi political, is entirely new to me, and I had no idea at first what such a case would require. While I would like very much to have the honor of winning the case, because it involves the right of suffrage of my people, and would hate to have to give up the fight in the face of the adverse ruling of the court, when I know it was made for that very purpose, still I am too poor to stay away from my business in the city, and perhaps fall behind and lose my little financial standing and credit, unless more ample provision can be made for me financially while engaged in the work.

I beg to suggest, that you consider that I have already received for my services $500.00, and that out of it, I will bear all my expenses; and in addition to that sum if you could let me have $1500.00 more, making my entire fee $2000.00, I could make out. This amount would enable me to arrange my affairs in the city so that I can proceed with my work here without uneasiness and apprehension as to financial troubles. It is impossible to make any of my creditors believe that my fee is not just fabulous for dangerous work like this as they term it.

There will be costs of court in the lower court, and the Supreme court of the state and of the U.S., which I feel I can get the local organization here to bear. These costs will have to [be] arranged by cost and appeal bonds, which they will get their friends to make, and they will protect the sureties from loss in some satisfactory way.

If you can let me have the sum above mentioned, I will conduct the case to its termination, and will have no occasion again to annoy you about money, and you will thereby place me on easy footing so that I can camp here and contend with these courts until I get the ruling we want. I have put the amount down to the lowest possible figure, consistent with my immediate needs and situation, and the time and work that must be devoted to the case, because I consider it quite an honor to be engaged in any work where I have the opportunity of winning your confidence and esteem, and I would not for anything but the direst necessity run the risk of having our relationship in this matter severed.

I hope that you can see your way clear to arrange this matter, and that you will let me hear from you at once, so that I may know whether I shall be enabled to stay here and prosecute this work to a successful completion. Very respectfully,

Filipino

TLSr   Con. 236   BTW Papers   DLC.

1 Smith and Scott took elaborate precautions to maintain secrecy about BTW's involvement in the case. Scott met Smith late at night at J. W. Adams's house in Montgomery. Smith typed the letter himself and gave it to Scott to hand-carry to BTW. (Scott to BTW, June 18, 1902, Con. 236, BTW Papers, DLC.)

From Emmett Jay Scott

[Tuskegee, Ala.] 6/18, 02

Personal

Dear Mr. W. Something will have to be done to repress this "beer carnival" business. You know of course of the keg ordered from Montgomery. Well, last Saturday at dinner — a man, a member of the Council mentioned that a good old time was to be had that night & he was overheard by another teacher. In addition W C Smith heard this same member of the Council invite Mr. Wheeler — who had just come — to join them at night — in his room. This was on outside & near Willow Cottage. Smith took the matter up & reported to Maj Ramsey & saw after the last bell had rung the following persons in a room together — cracking corks on bottles — he supposes beer bottles tho' it could be claimed that they were soda water bottles — if matter were brought to their attention: Mr R M Atwell, Mr. E T Atwell (both serving as members of Council) Mr Gilmore & Mr. Wheeler. Major Ramsey feels quite decidedly that these men do not bring up the Council standard — knowing of many things of which you cannot know, but he would not say so to you — but he remarked it to me & I make bold to pass it along.

I do not file this as a complaint. I only bring it to your attention that you may know some of these goings-on.

Emmett J. Scott

ALS   Con. 46   BTW Papers   DLC.

To Theodore Roosevelt

South Weymouth, Mass. June 19, 1902

My dear Mr. President: I am glad to state to you that I have learned from several sources that Mr. A. B. Kennedy,[1] the colored man in New Orleans whom you mentioned to me, is a man of high character and high ability. As between him and Dr. I. B. Scott you will have to decide. I know that Dr. Scott is more widely known throughout the country among our people and carries more weight, but I do not know how he would compare with Mr. Kennedy in the matter of being able to control the colored people in Louisiana. Both of them, however, seem to be good men and of the class that you desire to recognize. Yours truly,

Booker T. Washington

TLS   Theodore Roosevelt Papers   DLC.

1 Alexander B. Kennedy, a former postal employee, was receiver of public monies in New Orleans.

To Theodore Roosevelt

South Weymouth, Mass. June 23, 1902

My dear Mr. President: Since I talked with you about the New Orleans matter I have consulted with one or two colored men of prominence and influence, and they feel that if you still think it necessary to put a white man in the Naval Office and give a colored man some other position that it would be much wiser and would serve to stir up the colored people less if you made a colored man Surveyor of the Port instead of making one Receiver in the Land Office.

Hon. P. B. S. Pinchback, a colored man who formerly lived in New Orleans and now resides in Washington, is a man in full sympathy with your idea of making a change in the Louisiana situation, and if you can possibly spare the time I wish very much that you would send for him and have a conversation for a few minutes with him. I think he can give you some information that will be of value. He is modest and does not want to call upon you without knowing that you want to see him. A letter addressed to him at 1422 Bacon St. will reach him. Yours very truly,

Booker T. Washington

TLS   Theodore Roosevelt Papers   DLC.

To Emmett Jay Scott

South Weymouth, Mass. June 23, 1902

Dear Mr. Scott: Regarding Washington matters I wish you would watch very carefully the tone of the Southern press, and in fact the press of the whole country for that matter, in regard to my connection with Mr. Roosevelt and colored office holders. I want to help him and the race if I can, but at the same time I must be careful not to injure our institution and the work for which I am trying to stand. I had several talks with several prominent newspaper men while in Washington, men that can be trusted, and without exception they said it is perfectly understood among all the newspaper men in Washington that the President consults me freely regarding the appointment of colored men to office and there is no use to try to overlook that feature; this I think we may just as well take for granted. Now the question is whether I can go on doing as I am trying to do and not injure our cause. Yours truly,

Booker T. Washington

TLS Con. 272 BTW Papers DLC.

To Emmett Jay Scott

So. Weymouth, [Mass.] June 23, 1902

Tell Mr. Logan Filipino desires fifteen hundred to cover all costs addition to five hundred. Put request before him and telegraph me his opinion. Perhaps payments might be made in installments. Have you heard from Smith?[1] What does he say?

Booker T. Washington

TWSr Con. 541 BTW Papers DLC.

[1] Robert Lloyd Smith.

From Emmett Jay Scott

Tuskegee, Ala., June 23, 1902

Dear Mr. Washington: I shall write Judge Terrell at once, asking him to speak at Business League meeting.

I have your wire anent Filipino matter, & have wired you as to Mr. Logan opinion. He very earnestly feels that matter ought to be pushed — and that it should not be allowed to go by default. I will not notify *Filipino* till I have your word that he shall go on with work.

I have the copies of letters regarding Kennedy & Dr. Scott. I am sorry the President hesitates. I fear it means the former rather than the latter, but you can do no more than you have done.

All work has stopped account of having no brick. A new kiln — one of 30 eyes — with 250,000 brick in it however is to be open'd Wednesday & the work will go forward rapidly again. Two others — one of 14 eyes & the other of 24 eyes — are ready to be burnt, & with good weather these ought to assure enough brick for the summer, or nearly enough *anyway*.

I have letter from Smith jubilating. He only awaits tender of place. He is very grateful to you.

With best wishes for Mrs. Washington & all. Yours sincerely

Emmett J. Scott

ALS   Con. 241   BTW Papers   DLC.

From Emmett Jay Scott

Tuskegee, Ala., June 24, 1902

Dear Mr. Washington: The Executive Council referred to Mr. Carver the matter of securing the two men to go to Africa. Although I have taken up the matter and pressed it *every other day*, nothing has been done in the way of securing the men. I suppose Mr. Carver has done all that he could do, but the fact remains that we have nobody yet to take the place. I am able to detect a lack of sympathy with the enterprise on the part of members of the Council which may have communicated itself to the young men at the school. At the meeting yesterday it was learned that nobody has yet been secured, although Mr. Carver is still trying to get some one, he says. It seems to me the only thing to do is to notify the Kolonial Komitee that we can get no one since the kind of men that ought to be sent cannot be secured.

The agreement that the young men must enter into is not a very desirable one, either. By analyzing the contract, you will note that the man who goes is to have his passage paid to Togo. His return passage he is to pay himself and he is to remain five years. During the first year he will receive for himself only forty marks a month, or $9.20. The balance of the total which he is to receive during the year is to be paid for laborers and for building house and for implements.

This is absolutely no inducement at all since even the land remains the property of the Kolonial Komitee. Whatever cotton is harvested must be sold to the Komitee, but it is perhaps easy to determine that there will be no great amount of this considering all things.

Although the correspondence has been held a long while, I have not yet notified the Komitee that we are not able to secure any one, for the reason that we want to be sure first whether we have anybody in mind.

I shall be guided in my reply by your instructions. Very truly yours,

Emmett J. Scott

I think members of the Council are lukewarm is because of the small amount paid the young men.

TLS   Con. 241   BTW Papers   DLC.   Postscript in Scott's hand.

Francis Jackson Garrison to Oswald Garrison Villard

Boston, June 27, 1902

Dear Oswald: I return Booker Washington's letter herewith, and quite agree with you in your estimate of it. It is not a manly or straightforward letter, and moreover it betrays a weakness against which I hoped he was proof, of saying more than he really means in order to conciliate or not to offend. If he thinks a school is unworthy, he ought not to endorse it on anybody else's testimony. His own personal judgment and personal knowledge are what is expected, and if, on the other hand, he has any fault to find with another school, he ought not to hesitate to speak with entire frankness and definiteness to a friend like yourself. As it is now, he deals in vague generalities for the most part. What he says about his securing a letter of recommendation of Calloway from Dr. Beard reads to me rather as if he desired to be fortified against future complaints about C. than as if the letter itself carried complete conviction to his own mind. Above all, he ought to realize that in employing teachers he is bound to take only such as are above suspicion so far as their moral character is concerned.

I hope your ankle has improved since your return, and will soon be giving you no further trouble.

Of course you have read Roosevelt's speeches in Boston on Wednesday. I note that the Post, like the Springfield Republican, has taken up his eulogies of Wood and Root, but did you notice his assertion at the military dinner here that "a good soldier must not only be willing to fight, but he must be *anxious* to fight. I don't want to have anything to do with him if he is not."

I heard Bourke Cockran last night for the first time, and was disappointed in him as an orator. He has a deal of rant, and wears his voice to the bone, if I may use such a mixed metaphor. He said many good things, but he has a touch of the demagogue, and there were two or three false notes. Yours affectionately,

Uncle Frank

TLS   Oswald Garrison Villard Papers   MH.

To Theodore Roosevelt

[South Weymouth, Mass.] June 30, 1902

My dear Mr. President: In addition to what I have already written you and telegraphed you regarding R. L. Smith, I want to add that since looking further into the matter, I find that Judge Burns offered Smith a minor position in the Internal Revenue department in Texas not very long ago. If Smith was worthy at that time to be given a minor position he is also worthy I think you will agree with me, to be given a higher position at the present time.

The charges sent you by various parties in Texas recently are the same old charges made months ago, they were merely re-dated.

Smith, on my advice, has agreed to make an earnest effort to bring about peace and harmony in Texas between the different elements, and I believe that if he is given this appointment that it will go a long ways toward settling matters in that state.

I am watching matters closely in Mississippi, and I believe that Mr. Wilson will soon have things in that state in a shape for proper delegates to be secured. Yours truly,

B.T.W.

TLIr Copy   Con. 245   BTW Papers   DLC.

From Emmett Jay Scott

[Tuskegee, Ala.] 7/1—02

Dear Mr. Washington: I have kept track pretty well of newspaper comment with reference to your relations with President Roosevelt. I do not seem to notice anything that is ominous, or to be feared. It seems to me — and I have tried to think of the matter in an entirely judicial way that you need *only* & *most* to have it understood that you are serving your race — and the President when you help him to select colored men of worth for places to which he intends appointing black men. Of course there are going to be some people who are antagonistic to *any colored man* for any place — whether he be a man of character, or not; with these I do not think you need unduly concern yourself. I do not believe that the work of the school is going to be damaged by reason of the President's dependence upon you for advice regarding these appointments. You have friends among the newspaper correspondents at Washington. If you could talk to one or two of them — *Ohl*[1] for one if he can be reached — and have them strongly urge that your audiences with the President are at *his* request & that your relation has nothing to

491

do with the "brokerage" feature of office filling but only & decidedly with the character of colored men whom the President is considering in certain particulars, it will be well. I attach editorial from the Atlanta Constitution.[2] If Mr. Howell should be written to *he will be sure* to print your letter and so it will be better if you can have some friend like Mr. Leupp prepare an authoritative statement & give it out from Washington. I am sure he could reach the best & most serviceable of the Correspondents. I do not see how you can refuse to serve the race & the President in these matters. To get good men, who will reflect credit upon all concerned, is a great step forward & we can not go back to the old condition. I hope you will not feel that you are jeopardizing matters here. I do not believe you are & I know & all fair men know that your disinterested service is of incalculable service to the race & to the nation as well. Yours sincerely,

Emmett J. Scott

ALS   Con. 46   BTW Papers   DLC.

[1] Josiah Kingsley Ohl (1863–1920) was the Washington correspondent of the Atlanta *Constitution*.

[2] The Atlanta *Constitution*, June 23, 1902, 4, said: "The Constitution as much as any one anywhere would regret any false step on the part of Booker Washington that would sacrifice his standing and potentiality in the chosen sphere and work that he professed is the heart of his life." The editorial reported that it was rumored that BTW was acting as an adviser to President Roosevelt on black appointments in the South. The *Constitution* hoped the reports were not true and added: "It is up to Booker Washington to elect whether he will be a negro political boss and so lose the respect and support of the heretofore friendly white leaders of the south, or whether he will be true to his promise to let politics alone and continue the truest and safest Moses his people have ever known in their emancipated condition."

From Peter Jefferson Smith, Jr.

Boston   July 3d-02

My dear Doctor: From what I can learn the "Guardian" folks are going to use every effort to have the Afro American Council *Denounce* you at their meeting soon to be held, and from what Bishop Walters said they have got their plans pretty well in hand and purpose to capture the convention for that end.

As you do not intend to be there why not have a good reliable man to keep his eye on the resolutions that are to be presented and take care of the Associated Press news.

Be careful to whom you write on the subject and not one word to the "Colonel." You know him.

I speak advisedly. You had an experience with him at Chicago last year as you also had at Indianapolis a few years ago. I am sorry you can not be there.

May be Mr. Napier is to be there.

A good friend of yours I think is Adams. Cyrus Field Asst. Register. Faithfully yours,

P. J. Smith

ALS Con. 241 BTW Papers DLC.

From Isaiah Benjamin Scott

New Orleans, La., July—3—1902

Dear Mr. Washington: I guess at your distance from these parts you can have no idea what a dust has been raised here among the politicians. Gov. Warmoth[1] who is a leader among the Lilly Whites came to town and led the fight. He even organized the disgruntled Colored troops and they sent forward a petition against me declaring me to be a bitter writer in denouncing the southern whites. Think of that in face of the fact that what the people generally and my church in particular commend me for is my "conservatism." Not only so but northern editors who have written me for articles, some of them on your recommendation, have given as a reason that they believe me to be a conservative writer. Well it is all right, if these things frighten the President, in face of the factional fights in this community, I can only submit. I sent conclusive evidence of my citizenship and the fact of my being a tax payer and the papers are on file in Secretary Shaw's department.

Now, Mr. Washington, dont you worry on my account; I feel greatly honored to have had the endorsement of the man whose standing and ability are recognized the country over — north and south. If you deem it wise to do so you can for my part write and release the President; that is, so that he may not feel that not to name me will be considered by you a slap in the face. Do whatever you think is best.

I leave Saturday morning for St Paul, Minn. to attend the National Editorial Association, and will be there a week. Should you find it convenient to write me address in care *The Appeal, Union Block.* I am as ever, Yours truly

I. B. Scott

ALS Con. 241 BTW Papers DLC.

1 Henry Clay Warmoth (1842–1931), the brilliant but opportunistic carpetbagger governor of Louisiana from 1868 to 1872, remained in Louisiana to become a large sugar planter, railroad president, and leader of the lily-white Republican faction in the state. From 1890 to 1893 he was collector of customs at New Orleans. Throughout the Roosevelt-Taft era, Warmoth's faction fought a bitter contest with the largely black faction led by Walter L. Cohen and James Lewis for recognition by the national Republican party as representative of the Republican party in the state. During Roosevelt's period of leadership, the issue was usually settled by compromise, both at the national conventions and in patronage matters. During the Taft administration the lily whites gained the upper hand.

To Warren Logan

South Weymouth, Mass. July 14, 1902

Dear Mr. Logan: I do not feel we ought to give up the idea of getting two good men to go to Africa. I wish you would make another effort to find two good men. I very much fear that the success of the movement will be crippled if we do not send these men, and I think that even at considerable cost and extra time we ought to find them. Yours truly,

Booker T. Washington

TLS BTW Papers ATT.

From Emmett Jay Scott

Tuskegee, Ala., July 17, 1902

Dear Mr. Washington: First of all, I want to thank you for affording me the opportunity of being present at the recent session of the

Council. I had no idea that I should be able to get off, and, in fact, felt that I should not be able to go because of the coming meeting of the Business League. I enjoyed being present very much and hope that I was able to be of some assistance.

I talked quite fully with Pledger, both on the train to Chicago and after reaching there. The whole business in his mind was this: Some one told him that the reason Crossland got the Liberian mission was because you supported him for it. He could not understand how you could support Crossland when he understood you to be committed to him, and he felt that Crossland had never been any assistance to you and that he had been your staunch and loyal friend. Much of this kind he had to say. I told him that he was entirely mistaken; that you did not endorse Crossland for the Liberian mission and that you did not know he was a candidate for that place; that you understood Crossland was after Cheatham's place and that you were wired to by the Secretary of the Interior asking as to his general character and all with no reference whatever as to the position which he sought. I think I reached him, in fact, I know I did, as he told me that that put a new explanation on the matter altogether. The President himself, or some one, said that you had endorsed Crossland and of course Pledger thought that that meant that he had been endorsed for the Liberian place.

Another matter I was able to worm out of Deas and Pledger which I thought ought to be brought to your attention: They, together with Fortune, have been very strongly approached by some of the older politicians to join in a movement to directly approach the President decrying your influence with him and seeking to undo you with him. I told them to start with that I did not believe any such thing as this could happen, but from what I was able to get from them, (though I could not get the names of those who head the movement — I suspect Hill is one of them), there is something of this kind in the atmosphere. The fact that the President told Ferguson directly that he would not even consider him for a position without your endorsement has scared these old fellows as they never have been scared before. They feel that, like Othello, their occupation is gone, and that in a last desperate stand they must discredit you, if possible. Of this I have no fear, though I want to place the facts before you for your guidance and information. I do not know what to say as to some of these men.

495

Pledger and Deas, for instance, are potential characters. Pledger is Chairman of the State Executive Committee, Chairman of the District Executive Committee, and Chairman of the County Executive Committee. He has thus buttressed his position at every point. Deas is Chairman of the State Executive Committee and an influential character, as you know. These men, I was able to gather from them, feel particularly affronted that they cannot even reach the President for consultation when their states are in question. In my talk with Pledger I found that he desired among other things that you should try to place him right with the President. I told him frankly that you would not do anything more, *if anything*, than to write the President suggesting his political influence and asking that he (the President) confer with him (Pledger), when matters of Georgia were in question. This I suspected you would be willing to do because you had done so in the case of Deas.

There can be no doubt of the fact that Fairbanks[1] is at work. There can be no further doubt of the fact that these men are in communication with him. They can be won away now as they cannot be perhaps later before they are definitely committed. Whether the President will at all care to conciliate them, or to in any way advise with them, is something I do not know, but if he should feel inclined to do so, now, it seems to me, is the proper time for him to commit these men.

I do not mean by this that the President should himself do so, but that they should be seen by his agents.

I hope you will not fail to see General Clarkson when next in New York. I know that the General will talk to you freely and frankly and he will tell you how most of these men are standing as they undoubtedly have been to see him, or he has had them seen.

In the Mississippi matter, after talking with Mollison fully, I feel that Mollison's anxiety to land the place overtops and forces his optimism. My own impression, as I talked with him, was that matters in that state were not quite what he would like to have them.

Smith writes me that Burns has written him that he has been nominated by Houston[2] of the Northern district to an office deputyship carrying a salary of $2500 a year and that as soon as matters are straightened out he will take the place.

In New Orleans I do hope for the general cause that Dr. Scott will not be turned down. His appointment during the period of uncertainty and all would do much to reassure our people that the President only seeks the best interests of the race, and that he is willing to appoint our best men to these places. You cannot do anything further in the matter than you have done, but I make the suggestion for what it may be worth.

There is no special news at the school. The work on Rockefeller Hall and the Office Building seems to be proceeding satisfactorily. Heavy rains have fallen during the past week and have added much to the cheerfulness of everybody in this section.

I met Congressman Thompson on my return to the school and he particularly inquired as to your address which I furnished him. I thought that there would be no objection to this on your part.

Reverting again to matters political, it is not hard for you to understand that we control the Council *now*. Fortune is President. Pledger, whom we can hope to hold, is 1st Vice President. Bishop Walters is Chairman of the Executive Committee. Adams[3] is Secretary, and you and I are first members representing Alabama on the Executive Committee. Most of our friends compose the Executive Committee. Steward,[4] of course, will be a dominating factor at Louisville and is one of the Vice Presidents and a potential character.

It was wonderful to see how completely your personality dominated everything at St. Paul. From the moment that you reached there you were the one center of interest, much to the chagrin and regret of our friends, the Barnetts — especially.

I stopped in Chicago to see our men regarding the Business League meeting. I found them hustling and fully alive to the importance of the coming gathering. Howard[5] and Stevens[6] are pushing matters and I am sure we shall have a splendid delegation from there. Very truly yours,

Emmett J. Scott

TLS Con. 46 BTW Papers DLC.

1 Charles Warren Fairbanks (1852–1918) was U.S. senator from Indiana from 1897 to 1905 and U.S. Vice-President from 1905 to 1909.

2 Andrew Jackson Houston (1854–1941), the son of Samuel Houston, was a Texas lawyer and politician. Theodore Roosevelt appointed him a U.S. marshal in Texas, a position he held from 1902 to 1910. He ran unsuccessfully for governor of Texas on the Prohibition ticket in 1910 and 1912.

3 Cyrus Field Adams.

4 William H. Steward of Louisville was for many years editor and publisher of a black weekly newspaper, the *American Baptist*, and a leader in the National Baptist Convention. When T. Thomas Fortune resigned as president of the Afro-American Council in 1904, Steward was a vice-president. He succeeded as head, but the organization from that time on ceased to be a powerful force in black affairs.

5 James W. H. Howard, born in Canada in 1859, published *Howard's Negro American Magazine* from 1880 to 1885, the *State Journal* from 1885 to 1890, and *Howard's American Magazine* from 1897 to 1904. A business entrepreneur with several firms in banking, advertising, produce, and shirt manufacturing, he was an active member of the NNBL. A Democrat, Howard was a member of the Harrisburg (Pa.) City Council from 1885 to 1888 and held several clerkships in the Pennsylvania state government.

6 Andrew Frazier Stevens, Jr., a black insurance and investment broker, was born in Philadelphia in 1868. Active in black affairs and politics in Pennsylvania, he was a delegate to the Republican national convention in 1912 and was chairman of the Republican state committee in 1912 and 1914.

To Emmett Jay Scott

South Weymouth, Mass. July 26, 1902

Dear Mr. Scott: I have been thinking about the fictitious names, "Filipino," etc., used by you in correspondence with Mr. Smith. It seems to me in case any of these communications were found, it would be less suspicious should some real name, such as "John Smith," be found on the letters. Yours truly,

Booker T. Washington

TLS   Con. 247   BTW Papers   DLC.

To Emmett Jay Scott

South Weymouth, Mass. July 29, 1902

Dear Mr. Scott: I was rather surprised to see in the last issue of the Colored American a comment on my receiving a letter from Prince Henry.[1] I wish you would guard that matter as closely as you can in every way possible. I rather think this matter got out by showing one of the letters to either Cooper[2] or Thompson.[3] I am sure I impressed upon them, however, the importance of saying nothing about it. Yours truly,

Booker T. Washington

TLS Con. 272 BTW Papers DLC.

[1] Washington *Colored American*, July 26, 1902, 7.
[2] Edward Elder Cooper.
[3] Richard W. Thompson.

From Theodore Roosevelt

Oyster Bay, N.Y., July 29, 1902

Personal.

My dear Mr. Washington: I had a very nice note from Smith, who I think is really pleased with his appointment. With Deas I have had some talks, but they were not satisfactory, because somehow our ideas did not "gee." Do you know, I often feel as if I really were hardly fitted to encounter certain classes of politicians. Of course I must, for it is my business. It will be a pleasure to see Mr. Murphy if there is anything I ought to know from him, but I do not want to see him unless he has something definite to say, as I am trying to get a rest. Sincerely yours,

Theodore Roosevelt

TLS Con. 16 BTW Papers DLC.

To Robert Curtis Ogden[1]

South Weymouth, Mass. August 6, 1902

My dear Mr. Ogden: I have received the check for the monthly payment on account of the Southern Education Board for which I thank you.

499

I cannot get the consent of my conscience to continue receiving this monthly payment under present conditions. When this proposition was made and when I first began receiving it, I was under the impression that I was to see the Southern members of the Board and that some kind of definite, systematic and organized plan was to be agreed upon by which I could work, but this has not been done. I cannot see that I am doing anything now for education in the South which I was not doing before I began receiving this money, and under these circumstances I cannot feel that it is right, I repeat, for me to continue receiving it. I do not mean to intimate that there is not plenty of work to be done in the South in connection with my race to consume this amount and many times more. Everything possible ought to be done to keep the colored people intelligent and enthusiastic concerning the work being led so finely by the Southern Board, and the race ought to be kept in close and vital touch with it. The colored people can do much to help themselves and to help make the burdens of others lighter. Whatever I do should be done according to some plan and with the cooperation and approval of the Southern members it seems to me. Yours truly,

Booker T. Washington

TLS Con. 792 BTW Papers DLC.

1 BTW forwarded this letter to William H. Baldwin, Jr., who advised BTW not to send it to Ogden. (See Baldwin to BTW, Aug. 11, 1902, below.)

From William Henry Baldwin, Jr.

[New York City] August 11th., 1902

Dear Mr. Washington: I return herewith the letter addressed to Mr. Robert C. Ogden. I had a talk with Mr. Ogden about the matter; did not show the letter or send it to him, because it would seem like a criticism, whereas the whole matter is thoroughly understood and the feeling is all right. Mr. Dabney is spending all his money in his work, and Mr. Alderman the same. I think that the money you receive should be kept for that purpose, and when the time does come to use it we will have an amount that will be sufficient to do something. Yours very truly,

W H Baldwin Jr

TLS   Con. 792   BTW Papers   DLC.

From Frances Benjamin Johnston[1]

Atlantic City, N.J. Aug 11 1902

Dear Mr. Washington. I am in receipt of your recent favor in regard to making photographs of Tuskegee and I regret that I have been prevented from giving it earlier consideration owing to the fact that I found my mother seriously ill on my return from New York and have since been busy with the preparations for getting her out of town and comfortably located at a sanitarium.

In the absence of any definite understanding as to the extent of the work you wish done at Tuskegee I can give you as a basis of calculations the cost of the Hampton pictures.

I received from them $1000.00 and the living expenses of myself and my assistant during a period of about six weeks.

In return I furnished 150 8x10 negatives and 450 prints (3 from each plate) for the $750.00, the additional $250.00 covering the expense of an almost complete set of duplicate negatives and many extra prints. The plates, of course, remain the exclusive property of the Hampton Institute.

The season was most unfavorable and afterwards at Carlisle I did nearly the same amount of work in about half the time. As to Tuskegee, I assume that you wish to cover every phase of the life and training there; that you will require prints both for exhibition and publication and that you desire absolute ownership of the negatives. On this assumption I will make you a tentative offer of the same terms as I received at Hampton. For $1000.00, the living expenses of myself and assistant, with our transportation from Washington to Tuskegee and return I will fully cover your Institution and its work estimating 150 to 175 8x10 plates for it and furnishing you four complete sets of prints, one set on platinum paper mounted for exhibition.

Incidentally I will leave your negatives filed and catalogued, and doubtless during my stay I could train some of your young assistants to make such prints as you might require in future.

This gives us a definite proposition to discuss and in the meantime I should be glad to have your views in the matter.

I expect to be here until the early part of Sept. Thanking you for your favor   I am sincerely

Frances B. Johnston

ALS   Con. 231   BTW Papers   DLC.

1 Frances Benjamin Johnston (1864–1952) was a prominent Washington, D.C., photographer whose long career covered many aspects of the field including documentary, portrait, and architectural photography. From her studio in the nation's capital, she photographed many of the famous people of the period including the Theodore Roosevelt family, and she earned the title of "photographer of the American court." Her photographs of Hampton Institute in 1899 were so successful that BTW hired her twice, in 1902 and again in 1906, to capture Tuskegee Institute and its people on film. In 1902 BTW also commissioned her to take photographs of some of the small Alabama black schools that represented "little Tuskegees," such as the Mt. Meigs Institute, Snow Hill Institute, and the Ramer Colored Industrial School. At the Ramer school, a racial incident occurred when the white woman photographer was seen late at night in the same buggy with the school's black teacher, N. E. Henry. An outraged Ramer citizen fired several shots at Henry, and both he and Johnston were forced to flee for their lives. (See G. W. Carver to BTW, Nov. 28, 1902, below; Daniel and Smock, *A Talent for Detail*, 116–17.)

Edwin B. Jourdain[1] to Emmett Jay Scott

[New Bedford, Mass.] August 19th, 1902

Dear Sir: I owe you an apology for my unintentional delay in answering your courtesy of several weeks ago; I have just unearthed your letter from a pile of papers on my desk. I was very busy at the time of its receipt, and delayed answering, thinking I would turn your letter over to some one else. I spoke to several business men, but found no one who had any idea of going to Richmond to attend the Business League. Most of them expressed sentiments identical with my own, viz.: that the reception accorded the New Bedford delegation at the Boston meeting in 1900, demonstrated that we were an undesirable quantity to the powers that governed the Business League.

We attended that gathering in response to the published invitations to Negro business men, and the suspicion and opposition which met our attempt to render our report was as little in keeping with those published calls as it was unexpected. We were all well known to the Boston Committee, and no one will for an instant question that the men composing our delegation were of unquestioned character, and two of them, Messrs Bush[2] and Douglass,[3] at least, were business men of this city, respected by white and black alike. We have always believed that Mr. Washington's adherents were afraid our report would deal with topics which were forbidden at that gathering. Topics of manhood and those rights and privileges which every true man holds dearer than all the wealth or traffic of the world.

They knew we were all members of the Union League, an organization devoted to the protection and advancement of our race, and they knew we were accustomed to speak out. But their fears and suspicions were unjustified, not a word in our report but dealt with business pure and simple. We did not agree with Mr. Washington's fiat (with the New Orleans horror and the Georgia outrages still burning in our memories) but we respected the wishes of the callers of the meeting and laid supreme questions of manhood by, for the sordid materialism of business, although our hearts throbbed in unison with that lofty, manly sentiment of Emerson's

"For what avail the plough or sail,
Or land, or life, if FREEDOM fail."

We respect Mr. Washington's devotion to the educational interests of the race; we admire his genius in rearing such a beacon-light as Tuskegee, in the dismal swamp of ignorance and degradation, the great black belt; but we cannot follow his lead when he counsels *"nolo contendere"* in the matter of manhood and citizenship rights. We doubt not his sincerity in the belief that he but "stoops to conquer" but we don't admire, agree with, or respect his position of *passive surrender* of all rights in order to win them. All history of every people in every age is against such a position.

We know our race, in point of attainment, is far below the Caucasian; but we know that the responsibility, and the blame, and shame, for the low estate of the Negro in America today, rests not on him but on his pale faced brothers; and with Frederick Douglass

503

we don't believe in allowing them to forget the fact, and ease their consciences for wrongs done the Negro by hugging to their hearts the idea that his low development and backward condition make him unable to appreciate better treatment and unworthy of it.

The Negro is not alone on trial. For while our white American brethren are marking and mocking the Negro's deficiencies, the civilized world looks on with a cynical sneer to see how America makes good her boast of American love of personal liberty and of fair play; to see whether those who have oppressed the Negro, robbed him of the proceeds of his toil, and barred the gates of knowledge against him, will like men acknowledge their wrong doing, and strive to "undo the accumulated wrongs of two centuries; to remake the manhood that slavery well nigh unmade; and to see to it that the long oppressed colored man has a fair field for development and improvement," before passing judgment on him and condemning him because he has not achieved in less than four decades an altitude which the Anglo-Saxon has been one thousand years in reaching.

> "They must give him wings ere they bid him to fly,
> They must set the example and bid him try.
> Let the white man pay for the white man's crime,
> Let him work in patience and bide God's time."

We appreciate the necessity for material advancement, we recognize that as a very safe measure of the industry and ability of any people; I think that no one can charge that our people in New Bedford under estimate this phase of the question, for while we number only about 1700, we pay taxes on real estate the assessed valuation of which is $330,000.00; and our percentage of men in business for themselves averages well with other races.

We are convinced however that any people who attempt to build a noble structure of lofty manhood and womanhood with sordid materialism as its chief corner-stone will fail of success. "Not failure, but low aim is crime."

If we would reach those lofty heights of thought and action where true men hold communion, we must incorporate the highest, noblest ideals of manhood and womanhood into the very base of our structure and build on them. We don't interpret humility to mean asininity.

Love of personal liberty, a jealous defense of their rights and liberties, have been the dominant traits of every people who ever achieved anything admirable, and we believe those traits to be prime essentials of the Negro American today.

I think I have made it clear why the business men of this city do not "enthuse" over the League, although we can see that such an organization can be made a powerful factor in uplifting the race, and sincerely trust that it may become such. Very truly

Edwin B. Jourdain

TLS Con. 231 BTW Papers DLC.

1 Edwin B. Jourdain, a lawyer of New Bedford, Mass., was born in Massachusetts in 1865. He was apparently of light skin color and was reported as white in the 1900 census. Jourdain admired BTW's work at Tuskegee but was critical of the Tuskegean's conservative public utterances and his failure to be more outspoken on matters of civil rights. (Jourdain et al. to BTW, Dec. 17, 1903, Con. 261, BTW Papers, DLC.) He was a founder of the Niagara Movement.

2 Andrew M. Bush, a black merchant tailor of New Bedford, was born in the District of Columbia in 1838.

3 Frank M. Douglass, a black New Bedford druggist, was born in Massachusetts in 1855. The census of 1900 reported him as an Indian.

From Amanda Ferguson Johnston

malden, W.Va.   Aug. 22 1902

Dear Brother   Ben is very sick   We Have not Had Our Clothes off Since Sunday night. He is very sick   We hafter lift him as a baby. We thought it best to write yu all   He gross warse all the time. Hope yu all well.

Let Brother John know   from your sister

Amanda Johnston

P.S. i[']ll Write thur Day to Albert

ALS Con. 1 BTW Papers DLC.

To Bliss Perry[1]

South Weymouth, Mass. August 23, 1902

My dear Mr. Perry: I have received your letter. I have noted with deep interest the controversy over the Sledd[2] matter in Georgia. Looked at in the broader way I can see nothing in this controversy to be discouraged. It shows that Southern men of influence and standing are beginning to speak out, and they will do so more and more in the future. By this mail I send you a marked copy of the Atlanta Constitution which has a rather significant letter in it from a Southern white man.

By the way, do you know that Mr. Sledd is the son-in-law of Bishop Candler and is the nephew of the present Governor of Georgia I think. Yours truly,

Booker T. Washington

TLS   Walter Hines Page Papers   MH.

1 Bliss Perry (1860–1954) was professor of English at Princeton from 1893 to 1900 and taught at Harvard from 1900 to 1930. He was editor of the *Atlantic Monthly* from 1899 to 1909, and he wrote numerous books on American literature and literary criticism.

2 Andrew Sledd, professor of Latin at Emory College in Georgia, wrote a mildly heretical article, "The Negro: Another View," *Atlantic Monthly*, 90 (July 1902), 65–73. He accused the South of persecuting blacks, and particularly deplored lynching. He urged that blacks be treated with courtesy and equality in public places. Sledd was the son-in-law of Southern Methodist Bishop Warren A. Candler, a former president of Emory College. Rebecca L. Felton, later to be the first woman U.S. senator, launched an attack on Sledd in the Atlanta *Constitution*, and it was quickly taken up in other newspapers. Sledd precipitately submitted his resignation, and with alacrity the executive committee of the college's board of trustees accepted the resignation, though in 1914 he returned to a position in the theology school at Emory. Bliss Perry, whose magazine had published Sledd's article, had written that he was "thoroughly indignant" at the local outcry against Sledd. Perry helped Sledd secure a scholarship to study at Yale the following year. (Perry to BTW, Aug. 16, 1902, Con. 1; Francis J. Garrison to BTW, Oct. 23, 1902, Con. 228, BTW Papers, DLC.)

From Henry Francis Downing[1]

[London, England] 2nd. September 1902

Dear Sir, New Cotton Fields Ltd., of which I am Managing Director, is on the eve of inaugurating the growth of the Cotton plant in West Africa, where there is reason to believe the Egyptian and American plants will thrive and produce a fibre suitable for the manufacturer.

The Company desires to secure the services of an expert who would be able to locate areas suitable for the Company's operations. I had occasion to speak of this matter to my friend Mr. Calloway who is now in Togoland, and he advised me that you would be able to nominate the expert we require. We would wish to enter into an agreement with whomever may be selected, so that we may be certain of his services for one year at least. It may be taken that he would be retained in the Company's employ in one way or another, just so long as he serves the Company faithfully.

We would like to know what salary he would require; of course all his expenses, transportation, subsistence, etc., would be met by the Company.

It may be interesting to you to know that the Company in carrying out its operations has in view the locating on its properties in Africa of American families (coloured) experienced in Cotton growing. The methods the Company may adopt in order to carry out this part of its scheme, have not been fully formulated, therefore it is impossible now to advise you what they may be. It is my personal belief that the removing from the Southern States of even a small proportion of its skilled labour, will have a beneficial influence in the way of helping to bring about a better understanding between the various peoples in the Southern States.

I take it that you will be concerned to see the result of this endeavour and I hope that when the moment arrives for active work, to have your co-operation.

Trusting to receive from you a response at an early date as will suit your convenience. I remain with respect, Yours faithfully,

Henry F. Downing

TLS Con. 225 BTW Papers DLC.

1 Henry Francis Downing (1846–1928) (see above, 3:84) was born in New York City. He served in the U.S. Navy from 1872 to 1875. In 1887 he was appointed a U.S. consul in West Africa but resigned the next year. Downing maintained a lifelong interest in Liberia. He was a delegate to Henry Sylvester Williams's Pan-African Conference in 1900 and was appointed to the executive committee of the Pan-African Association. For several years beginning in 1902 Downing was manager of New Cotton Fields Ltd., a London company that promoted cotton-raising in West Africa and encouraged black American farmers to migrate to West Africa.

Downing remained in London until 1917. He wrote several plays and a novel, *The Black and White Tangle*, which was serialized in Duse Mohammed Ali's journal, *The African Times and Orient Review*. He also wrote about life in Liberia in *The American Cavalrymen* (1917). For the last eleven years of his life he lived in Harlem, where he continued to write about Liberia.

From Amanda Ferguson Johnston

malden. W.Va. Sept. 4. 1902

My Dear Brother I recived yur very kind Letter was glad to Here fom yu. This is the first Letter Ive tried tu Write am not Well trying to Stay on my feet. Clara is trying tu rase Some Chickens. Well Br i[']m alone in this world. if I keep Restrant. i[']ll not get up all Hours of the night & i[']m afraid that Will Caus trouble I dont know what to do

Will Write you again you Herd of the Deth of father rice the Same Day Ben died Clara Has thirteene yung Chickens Sad they are fine Hope we Can Do Well With them. if yu Can Send me 20.00 twenty Dollars tu finish the expense of the Burel ill [burial]

Yu Can teake it out When I get mine. yu are So kind & good tu me

Brother the 24 of Janry I Had Bens Life insured at His own Will for five Hundred Dollars face valure So I Spoke tu Alber if I get it & Send What is Left after Paying my Dets for Him tu Put in Something that Will Bring me intrus if yu think that is best Let me Here We Have a nice Crop of Corn Will Hafter get it in tell me What tu do.

Sister Amanda

ALS Con. 231 BTW Papers DLC.

From Adam Clayton Powell[1]

New Haven, Ct., Sept. 13th 1902

Dear Sir: Is it possible, either this or next month, when passing, to stop off one or two hours to address a meeting of colored citizens in New Haven?

The Boston Guardian is widely circulated here and many white people think that its editorials about you and your work represent the sentiment of New England colored folks. We wish to demonstrate that we, at least, know enough to recognize and appreciate the leading man of our race. It will not do, as you know, to charge an admission fee, but suppose we guarantee a donation of $50. to your institution to be presented on that evening. Perhaps it can be made more.

I am from Wayland Seminary and have been here nine years trying with a few others to teach our people that Christianity is a set of moral principles to be translated into their every day life. Your presence here for one hour with a colored audience would be a stimulus to the few of us who are working on the knotty Negro problem in New England.

Will you write what date you will be passing through if you can stop long enough to speak for us. Sincerely yours

A. Clayton Powell

ALS   Con. 239   BTW Papers   DLC.

1 Adam Clayton Powell (1865–1953) was born in Franklin County, Va., of mixed white, black, and Indian ancestry. When he was ten years old his family moved to Malden, W.Va., near BTW's childhood home. After Howard University Law School rejected his application for admission, Powell enrolled in Wayland Seminary in Washington, graduating in 1892. He was pastor of the Immanuel Baptist Church in New Haven from 1893 to 1908, when he became pastor of the Abyssinian Baptist Church in New York. Powell revitalized the hundred-year-old church through a crusade against the brothels that surrounded it. After Harlem became the city's black ghetto, Powell moved his church there. It became known as the best-organized black church in America, devoted to social justice. After Powell resigned his pastorate in 1937, he wrote three books, including *Against the Tide: An Autobiography* (1938) and an account of the Harlem race riot of 1943. At first a critic of BTW's race leadership, Powell by 1911 had concluded that BTW's critics were motivated by jealousy. After BTW was assaulted in New York, Powell wrote him: "While the outrageous experience of Sunday night must be unspeakably embarrassing to you, in my humble opinion it will serve to unite the race as no other single occurrence since the Emancipation." (Mar. 22, 1911, Con. 435, BTW Papers, DLC.) Powell continued to criticize BTW's industrial education program until he built his new church in 1920. Though there were many unemployed professional people in his congregation, the contractors for the church could find no black carpenters to employ.

From John D. Powell, Jr.[1]

Boston   Sept 14th, 1902

My Dear Sir, Since the re-establishing of the Boston Advocate I have endeavored to do what I thought was right in advocating the best thought and sentiment that exists among the race. It has been a pleasure to me [to] work early and late in championing your cause.

I will be brief by saying that last Friday witnessed the starting of the engine and machinery at the Boston Advocate office.

The first paper run off was at 3 P.M.

The accompanying is an editorial in that issue.[2]

Can you help us in our struggle to the amount of $100.00 and let us repay you on instalments of $8.33 per month.

I have an option on another outfit which will greatly assist in facilitating our work.

The party is hard up and wants $100.00 cash for an $800.00 outfit.

Incidentally if you can do me the favor to send a letter of indorsement of the work we are doing which has been made possible through the energy displayed by you it will greatly aid us in our work both in the matter of ads and subscriptions.

The articles the Boston Guardian are publishing from time to time are done to bring cheap notoriety to the managers of that paper who have ever since the incipiency of the National Business Mens League first meeting been jealous of your great success.

We will virtually drive them out of the field of journalism.

Your friend Morse[3] is an apt student and worthy of Tuskegee.

I suppose you are aware that the paper issued during the week of the convention was the premier journal ever published in Boston and the writeups emanated from the typewriter and the brain of your humble servant.

Hoping to have a ready response to this communication and a wish for your success, I am   Respectfully,

John D. Powell, Jr
Business Manager and founder of the Boston Advocate

P.S. Cannot we get you interested as a silent partner. Moss[4] is treasurer and you know the investment is a safe one. We are doing a corking Job Printing business.

TLS Con. 239 BTW Papers DLC.

1 John D. Powell, Jr., was born in Maryland in 1857 and moved to Massachusetts with his family when he was a young man. The 1900 census reported his occupation as clerk. He was business manager of the short-lived Boston *Advocate*, designed to be an anti-Trotter newspaper. This was the first of three halfhearted secret efforts by BTW to subsidize Boston newspapers to counteract the influence of the Boston *Guardian*. In 1903 the *Enterprise* appeared in Boston as a pro-Washington paper, and later that year Peter J. Smith, Jr., and J. Will Cole started another paper with BTW's help, the Boston *Colored Citizen*.

2 The editorial was a defense of BTW against charges made by the Boston *Guardian*. Referring to the *Guardian* as a "wall paper sheet," the editorial stated: "The abuse these little picayunes of journalists are trying to place on our great leader should be treated with supreme contempt." (Boston *Advocate*, [Sept. 12, 1902?], Clipping, Con. 239, BTW Papers, DLC.)

3 Probably William James Morse, of Waco, Tex., a member of the B middle class of 1898–99.

4 William H. Moss, a black entrepreneur of Boston, Mass., was born in Colorado in 1870. Moss's principal occupation was manager of the Moss Cleaning and Building Care Co., which he founded in 1892. The company provided a combination of services involving the rental and sale of properties as well as janitorial services. Moss also was president of a drug company in Birmingham, Ala., and served as an agent for a barber-supply company and several railroads. He was president and treasurer of the Boston *Advocate*, but he probably did not invest much money in the enterprise. He was an active member of the NNBL in Boston.

From William Henry Baldwin, Jr.

N.Y. [City] Sep't. 15th., 1902

Dear Mr. Washington: Mr. Villard is very sore about the Kowaliga School matter. The next time you are here, if you remember it and have the correspondence at hand, I wish you would talk it over with me. It would be a good thing for us to satisfy Mr. Villard, if it is possible to do so without compromising ourselves in any way. Yours very truly,

W H Baldwin Jr

TLS Con. 792 BTW Papers DLC.

To James Sullivan Clarkson

Tuskegee, Ala., September 15, 1902

Private and Confidential.

My dear Colonel Clarkson: The time has come when some of our friends in influential positions will have to stand up straight and be counted in favor of honesty and justice. We are now, as a race, passing through a rather peculiar crisis. Take, for example, in Alabama. While practically, as you know, the bulk of the colored people have been cut off from voting by the democratic party, a few in almost every county have secured certificates to vote, in spite of the scrutiny of a democratic registration board in each county and state. These colored people stand so high in education, character and property, that even the democrats say they are entitled to vote. Now, in the face of this, what are the republicans doing, republicans who for thirty-five years have associated with the mass of ignorant colored voters? These same republicans all at once have become so righteous and pure that they now say that they cannot permit even a dozen or a dozen and a half of Negro representatives, and these of the highest type, to appear in convention with them, when for nearly forty years these hypocritical republicans have been assembling in convention with hundreds of colored people and they of the most ignorant type. You can easily understand that the class of men who would act in this way are weak and hypocritical. A word from you at the right time and in the right manner would go a long way towards bringing them to their senses. I do not mean to say that all the white republicans in Alabama are acting in this way, but the tendency is very fast in that direction. Unless something is done to stop what is being done by what is known as the "lily whites" in such states as Louisiana, North Carolina and Alabama, you will find that when the next national election comes, the colored voters at the North, through their ballots, are going to resent what is being done to the colored people in the South. It should be borne in mind that in Indiana, New Jersey and Illinois, the colored voters hold the balance of power and every vote, by whomsoever cast, is counted as it is cast. In many cases these so-called republican leaders are trying to make it appear that the President is back of their diabolical schemes. This, of course, both you and I know is not true for President Roosevelt is in favor of the straight, honest thing, and I know that it has been his wish from the first to encourage the Negro who is intelligent and possesses property and character. Very truly yours,

B. T. Washington

TLS   Theodore Roosevelt Papers   DLC.

To Timothy Thomas Fortune

Tuskegee, Ala., Sept. 15, 1902

My dear Fortune: Enclosed I send you copy of letter which I have just written to Colonel Clarkson. It is very hard to understand what is taking place in some of the southern states just now. I confess that I thought I knew something of the meanness and rottenness of the average southern white republican, but their actions during the last few weeks have taught me that I did not understand them by long odds. We are now passing through a rather interesting and serious crisis in reference to the Negro vote and representation in conventions in the south. I very much fear that the Negro in the doubtful states in the north will have to be called upon in no uncertain tones to come to our rescue. The most encouraging thing that has occurred in this state for a long while is the removal of Vaughan by the President. That has gotten all the politicians guessing and they do not now know, it seems, whether to line up with the "lily whites" or not.

I may have something to say about who Vaughan's successor will be, and in case I do, I cannot bring myself to the point where I feel like recommending any white republican in the state as practically all of them are more or less tainted with "lily whitism."

I hope that your hand is much better. I have not written you lately because I have been much of the time on the road, and again, have been closely engaged in getting ready for the new year's school work.

I am hoping to be in New York some time in October for a few days and shall want to see you. Very truly yours,

Booker T. Washington

TLS   Con. 272   BTW Papers   DLC.

J. C. May [Wilford H. Smith]
to R. C. Black [Emmett Jay Scott]

New York City, Sept. 15th, 1902

My Dear Friend: Yours containing *C.* addressed to Miss McAdoo was delivered to me. Many thanks. I was disappointed however, because I needed the entire October payment now, to carry out my plans in the work. I shall be unable to enter upon my plans until you can make sufficient remittance to cover the deficit.

There is every reason why matters should go to Washington at the earliest possible moment. The last papers can go directly to Washington by the October term. A victory in that will settle every thing, and will save the trouble and expense of the cases in the City Court.

I am so situated that I can make no demands upon the committee at Montgomery further than for necessary expenses, while I am sure if their plan succeed they will come to the rescue; still, it would be very improper and embarrassing to demand much until a victory has been secured.

You will understand that I am under no contract with them whatever, and was not selected by them, and must maintain the position which I took in the beginning. I am very anxious to get the matter out of the way as soon as possible so that I can get down to my work here without these long absences.

I think if I can get the present case to Washington, the matter will be settled. I appreciate what you say about the pressure at that end, and will be under obligations if you will come to my relief as early as possible. Very sincerely yours,

J. C. May

TLSr Con. 236 BTW Papers DLC.

Tuskegee Institute in 1902

A Selection of Photographs by
Frances Benjamin Johnston

from the
Frances Benjamin Johnston Collection
Library of Congress

Booker T. Washington in his office.

Booker T. Washington and Emmett J. Scott.

The Emmett J. Scott family. Left to right:
Horace Scott, Emmett J. Scott, Evelyn B. Scott,
Eleonora J. Scott, and Emmett J. Scott, Jr.

Residence of Emmett J. Scott on the Tuskegee campus.

Tuskegee Institute Executive Council. *Left to Right, top row*: Robert R. Taylor, R. M. Attwell, Julius Ramsey, Edgar J. Penney, Matthew T. Driver, Henry G. Maberry, George Washington Carver. *Left to right, bottom row*: Jane E. Clark, Emmett J. Scott, Booker T. Washington, Warren Logan, John H. Washington. *Not shown*: Roscoe C. Bruce, Charles H. Gibson, and Margaret M. Washington.

Tuskegee Institute grounds.

Construction of Collis P. Huntington Memorial Library.

Students working on a road on the Tuskegee campus.

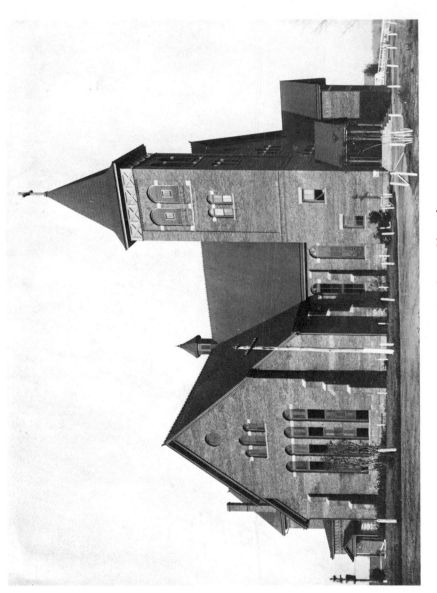

The Tuskegee Institute Chapel.

Dorothy Hall.

History class.

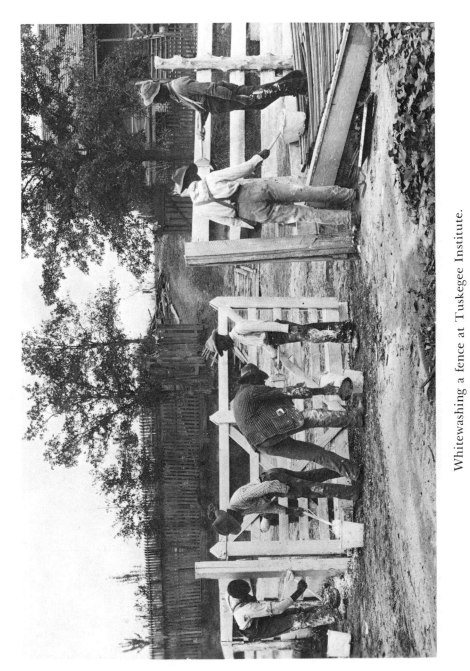

Whitewashing a fence at Tuskegee Institute.

A class in mattress-making.

The blacksmith shop.

Student carpenters.

Hoeing cotton.

A class in beekeeping.

Making brick.

Anatomy class.

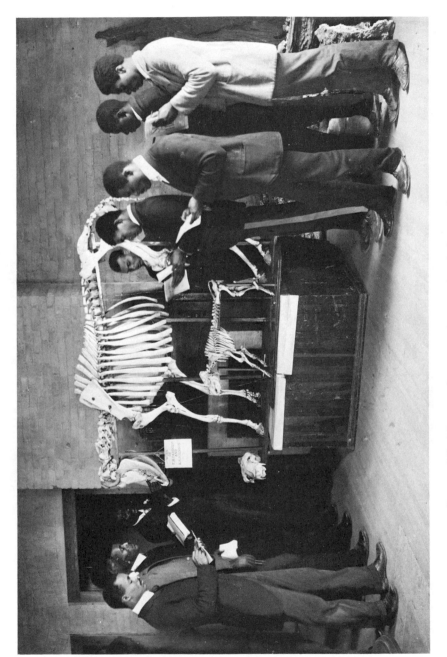

George Washington Carver points to the skeleton of a cow.

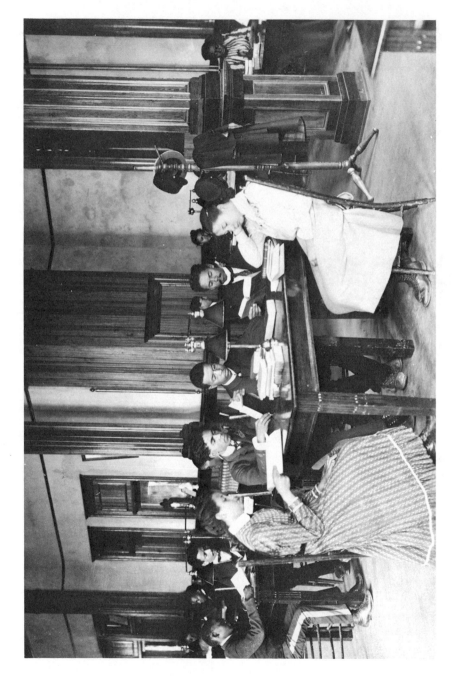

In the library.

In the barnyard.

Sewing class.

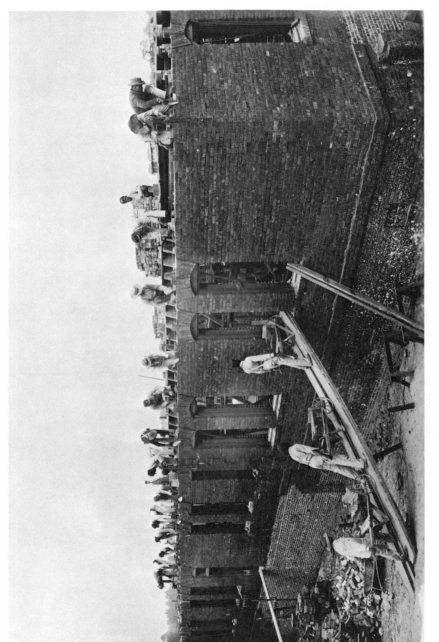

Student brickmasons.

Students in the dairy.

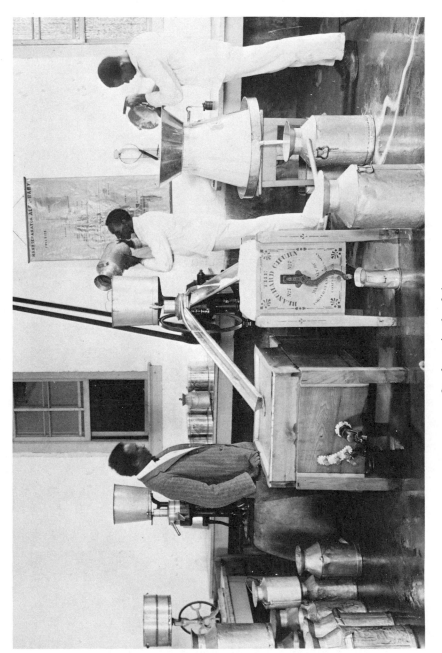

Students in the dairy.

Stacking hay.

Cooking class.

The student dining hall.

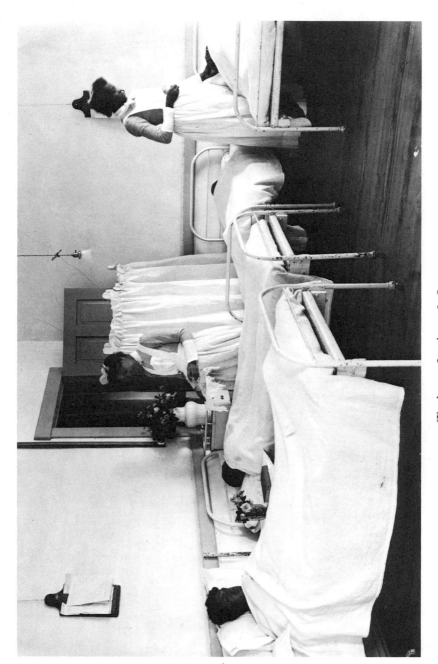

Tuskegee Institute Infirmary.

Student military corps.

To James Sullivan Clarkson

[Tuskegee, Ala.] September 16, 1902

Private and Confidential.

My dear General Clarkson: In addition to letter which I sent you
yesterday, enclosed I send you a marked copy of the Montgomery
Advertiser which contains the action of the state executive committee.[1] The direct question which is presented by this action is
whether or not the national republican party will recognize a party
in any state based upon color. There is no getting around this point.
The question will have to be faced. The executive committee in this
state has not tried to hide the fact that it has refused admission to
colored people solely on the ground of color. For example, in one
county where a convention was held and elected four delegates,
two white and two colored, the two colored were refused admission
and the two whites admitted. In Montgomery County, the law laid
down by the state executive committee which provided that the
election of delegates to the state convention be held August 30th,
was complied with in every respect, and in that case a number of
colored men were elected as delegates and a number of white men.
It was a regularly delegated convention at which they were all
elected. The white men were admitted and the colored men refused.
In every case where colored men have been thus refused, they have
been men of intelligence and high character, men, as I stated in my
last letter, whom even the democratic registration board could find
no objection to.

If this thing goes on, you will find that it is going to have a very
far-reaching effect on the colored people in the northern states
where their votes are counted. Aside from all this, there is a question of pure and simple justice which I believe with men like you
outweighs all matters of mere vote getting. Very truly yours,

B. T. W.

TLIr Copy   Con. 272   BTW Papers   DLC.

[1] Under the headline "Cut Out the Black Man," the Montgomery *Advertiser*
reported from Birmingham that the Republican state executive committee had met
on Sept. 15 and after considerable discussion decided to eliminate the blacks from
the party. Supporters of the move argued that the black man had been "a mill stone

about the party's neck; that they had dominated Republican conventions and then gone out and reported to the Democrats for duty." J. O. Thompson of Macon County and the blacks Nathan Alexander of Montgomery and Ad Wimbs of Greensboro were the leading critics of the move. Nathan Alexander said that the question of human rights was superior to any question of policy, that it would violate the state constitution to throw the black man out bodily, and that a decent Republican party could only be built up by decent methods. Ad Wimbs said that he supported the new state constitution, but the Republicans were going one step further and requiring all voters to be white. The vote on the resolution was 17 to 10, and thus the black delegates to the state convention the following day were not allowed to vote on the question of their exclusion. (Montgomery *Advertiser*, Sept. 16, 1902, 1.)

From Matthew Anderson[1]

Philadelphia, September 17th, 1902

My dear Mr. Washington: I promised myself, some time since, that my first duty on returning from my vacation should be to send you my impressions of Tuskegee, Tuskegee Institute, your magnificent work and the future of the Negro in this country. Let me say here, for several years it has been the desire of my life to visit Tuskegee and Tuskegee Institute. I say Tuskegee, because I was quite as anxious to see Tuskegee the town as Tuskegee the Institute. This desire arose from the knowledge of your successful work there, as an educator; for, being a sociological student, I was anxious to see the effect which your Institute was having upon the town and the white citizens of the immediate community. I knew only the most meager impressions could be had in few hours' time, which impressions must be more or less faulty. But, correct or false, they would be my first impressions, and as such they would not easily be effaced. Having been South, I now desire to give you my impressions.

Now, as to the town Tuskegee, my conception of this place is that it is a small, unenterprising and uninviting place; that its inhabitants are unhappy, dispirited and envious; and that which excites their envy is Tuskegee Institute, and especially its founder and intrepid Principal, Booker T. Washington.

I was surprised, too, at seeing Negro cabins of the ante bellum type in the town of Tuskegee, in the very sight of the Institution, having about them all the marks of the days of slavery, viz: one story, one room (so far as could be seen in our rapid transit), one door, no window panes, unpainted, unkempt, fences down or pailings off and uneven; the whole presenting a miserable contrast to the magnificent Institution which bursts upon the view of everyone visiting it for the first time as soon as he crosses the line which separates the town from the Institution. The effect is indescribable, presenting a most fearful commentary upon the ghastly effect of slavery. I impulsively exclaimed, in my heart if not audibly, in one breath, "How wonderfully hath God wrought," looking towards the Institution: and "How terribly hath sin wrought," looking back to the town and its sin-cursed people.

In one glance I took in the whole panoramic view of Tuskegee Institute, even to its pig sty and hennery. There was not anything that escaped my view, so far as the general effect is concerned — the array of buildings, their respective size and order; the configuration of the ground on which the buildings stand; the horticultural and artistic display in landscape gardening, and ornamental walks, even to the splendid cattle, three hundred, I was told, grazing on the hillside; all these made an indelible impression upon my mind so that while I write, a thousand miles away, I see them all as plainly as I did when they first burst upon my view. And I am sure the impression then made will be lasting.

I said when addressing the students in the chapel that "the half had not been told"; which was literally true, but not true, I fear, in the sense in which this expression is generally employed. It is not true that the half had not been told so far as the material extent of the Institution was concerned, for I had seen pictures of the Institution frequently, indeed, I have had one hanging in my study for over a year, which give rather an exaggerated impression, so far as the quality of the buildings and the artistic display of grounds are concerned. Judging from the lithographs of the Institution, one would be led to think that the buildings are all substantial and handsome appearing, the grounds beautifully laid out, the highest skill of the landscape artist having been employed. This would have been my impression had I not been correctly informed by those who had frequently visited the Institution. No! the whole had been told, and correctly told, so far as the material display was concerned. But the half had not been told in regard to the influence that Tuskegee is exerting as to the worth of the Negro. There is nothing that the American people need to know more than that the Negro whom they have so long despised or looked upon with pity is destined to become one of the most potent factors in developing the natural resources of the country of any within its reach. Tuskegee, with its different departments pulsating with life and activity, is rebuking the American people more loudly than words for the low standard of worth which has been placed upon these sable sons of toil within their midst. From the boy in the dairy to the workman in the shop, the students at Tuskegee are hard at work that they may accomplish the very most for themselves while there [so] that they may be of the greatest possible help to their people in the future.

The spirit which seems to pervade the entire Institution is that which impresses every student with a sense of his or her personal responsibility. Every student seems to be imbued with the thought that he is fitting himself for a responsible work, and hence it is incumbent upon him to put forth every endeavor. It has never been my pleasure to see happier students anywhere, if as happy, not even at Hampton, as at Tuskegee. That dull, don't-care, lifeless spirit, which is so often to be seen in schools for the higher education of colored youth, especially where the Management and Faculty are almost wholly white is entirely wanting there, so far as my observation went. Now, the effect which such teaching, going out from Tuskegee, will have for good upon the colored people of this country and the American people generally cannot be estimated. This is just the kind of teaching that is needed in this country. The Negro must be made to have confidence in his own native resources. He must be made to feel that he is endowed with all the qualities of heart and mind of other men, and that by an assiduous, faithful and persevering effort there is no power on earth that can keep him down. Such teaching is to be commended, because when properly understood it does not excite the envy of any. Its object is not to educate the black man at the expense of the white man, the red or the yellow man, but to so educate him that he will be an element of helpfulness to all men, wherever his lot may be cast, in whatever community, or among whatever people.

It was because I saw and felt this spirit, which pervades the entire place, possessing both students and teachers, that I said in my address when there, "the half has not been told."

Should I venture any criticism of your magnificent work it would be in the spirit of the greatest kindness and with the hope of protecting you against certain evils which, in my judgment, will affect seriously your work at no very distant future, unless averted. Taking in the whole scope of your work in this hasty review, it would seem to me that you are making two most serious mistakes. One is your seeming to make common cause with certain disappointed politicians who, for years, have been your bitterest and most outspoken enemies, but who now, because of your eminent standing in the country, especially with the Administration, are falling over each other to do you honor and to sound your praises. These men are ready to go to any length and to stoop to any low cunning in order to secure your influence to further their selfish ends. This was most strikingly seen during the meeting of the Negro Business League, which convened at Richmond, Va., last month. The acclamations, the high-sounding praises that each tried to excell in heaping upon you, together with their recriminations of each other or denunciations of any who may have been or are now opposed to your methods were, to say the least, disgusting to behold. As I sat observing their zeal to win your favor, I could but ask, as did the Apostle Paul: "What fellowship hath righteousness with unrighteousness, and what communion hath light with darkness; and what concord hath Christ with Belial; or what part hath he that believeth with infidels?" Your course as an educator has been directly opposite to theirs, as is all educational and Christian work, and I am sure that you are not in sympathy with them. And yet, the fact that you are being surrounded with them, many of them taking the most prominent parts in the League, the question is being seriously asked by many of your best friends of both races, "Is Mr. Washington, after having met with such eminent success without the aid of politicians going to allow them to influence him now?"

The other criticism I have already referred to in my address to the students at Tuskegee, on the 11th of August last, namely, the impression you are making throughout the country that you are opposed to schools for the higher education of colored youth. You may not be doing this now, but the impression has certainly gone out and you are being referred to generally as being thoroughly opposed to schools such as Atlanta, Fisk, Howard, Lincoln, Biddle and Scotia — schools which have been and are doing a mighty work in the way of preparing leaders for the race. I do not believe that you are at heart opposed to them. The fact that you have teachers, graduates of some of the best colleges in the land, and, too, that you are sending your daughter to one of the best New England colleges, proves, to my mind, whatever you may have said in your early speeches to the contrary, or that you may even now be saying, that at heart you are not opposed to schools of this grade. But the impression has gone out, and the consequence is, these schools, which have been established by the best friends the Negro has in this country, men and women who have made every sacrifice in order to assist in elevating the race, are being boycotted by the philanthropy of the country because of the fad that the only education suited for the Negro is an industrial education, which they say is the teaching of Booker Washington.

Now, I think you should set yourself right in regard to this, for I am sure you don't believe it. You believe, with me, that industrial education is the education for the masses; but where one has the capabilities and the opportunity to secure a higher, or the highest, education, he should be encouraged to do so. The Fathers of this country did not bring with them charters for the establishing of Manual Training Schools, but such as Harvard, Yale and Princeton. They would have leaders made first, and manual and industrial trained men after — exactly the course which has been taken in the education of the Negro in this country.

Aside from this, your work is incomparable, and my prayer is that your life may be long spared to do a greater, grander, nobler work for God and humanity than you have yet done.

In regard to the future of the Negro, permit me to say that your work at Tuskegee and elsewhere, the late Educational Congress at Atlanta and the Negro Business League at Richmond, have greatly strengthened my faith in the glorious future which awaits the Negro. I have long believed that in some way, I know not how, and at some time, I know not when, the Negro is going to become a mighty power for good, under God, in this country. For I do not believe God designed that that brawny arm, cheerful life, fertile brain and productive power of the Negro were to be employed for no other purpose than the hewing of wood and drawing of water. God is too wise to employ His instruments in this way. The mind that has within it powers which when drawn out and developed will be able to weigh the stars, map out the heavens and read the destinies, was not designed to forever be a digger in the ditch or a fawner at table. The trials through which the Negro is now passing; the prejudice, the slanders, the misrepresentations, the injustice and the hardships are employed simply as correctives to fit him for this great future. But in saying this, I do not mean to imply that the Negro is designed to supplant the white man, or any other man. He has not been, nor never will be, a supplanter. His mission shall be, as it ever has been, that of a teacher of the great fundamental truths of the Bible, namely, the Fatherhood of God and the brotherhood of men, Christ Jesus the hope of the world, and the right of all men to life, liberty and the pursuit of happiness. These truths the Negro is teaching now by his remarkable patience, perseverance, endurance and faith, though by few recognized and acknowledged. Then it will be acknowledged by all and he will assume his place as the great teacher and evangelizer of the world.

This is, my dear sir and friend, my impression of Tuskegee the town, Tuskegee the Institute, your work as an instructor and the future of the Negro of this country. I hope that you will pardon me for writing you at such length and thus taking up so much of your valuable time; but I could not express myself in fewer words and say what I wanted. You have now an honest expression of myself towards you and your work and of the estimation in which I regard the Negro race in this country, and hence you will know where to place and measure me in the future. I had once thought of sending you an open letter, and may yet publish this letter, if you offer no objection. I would be glad to hear from you at your earliest opportunity.

Hoping that you and your family are well and happy and that Tuskegee is meeting with every encouragement, I am as ever, Yours in His name,

Matthew Anderson

TLS Con. 272 BTW Papers DLC.

1 Matthew Anderson (1845–1928), a graduate of Oberlin (1874) and Princeton Theological Seminary (1877), was pastor of the Berean Presbyterian Church in Philadelphia from 1880 until his death. Anderson organized the Berean Building and Loan Association as part of the church's work. It was the largest organization of its kind among blacks in Pennsylvania. The church also conducted a kindergarten and a medical dispensary. W. E. B. Du Bois praised the social work of the church in his study *The Philadelphia Negro*.

In 1889 Anderson founded and was principal of the Berean Manual Training and

Industrial School. He wrote *Presbyterianism: Its Relation to the Negro* (1897). He was a believer in black self-help through black-owned business and industrial education as a means to solve race problems.

From James Sullivan Clarkson

New York, September 17, 1902

My dear Mr. Washington: I received the other day your letter about Alabama matters, and the President has also today sent me your letter to him of the 12th, asking me to communicate with you, and if possible, for us to agree upon some definite recommendation in these matters to him.

You and I would have no trouble agreeing, I think, if we could have a personal conference. If you are coming North soon, I shall be very glad to take it up at length with you, as you suggest. If you cannot come for two or three weeks, I wish you would give me your views in brief, so that I may be thinking them over. It would be a great pleasure to me to work with you on these lines of human interest. I hope to hear from you before long. Sincerely yours,

James S. Clarkson

P.S. Since the above was written, your letter of Sept. 15th has arrived. I am heartily with you in the position you take. I received this morning a despatch from A. D. Wimbs, a delegate in the Republican State Convention of Alabama, telling me that legal negro delegates had been expelled from their seats arbitrarily, and I sent the following despatch in reply: "Despatch just received; I can speak only for myself, but I have no sympathy or patience with any movement, new or old, that would expel a legal negro delegate from any Republican Convention." If I knew the whole situation, I would have made it much more positive and definite, but he simply stated the facts without any particulars. I will take pains to make my views known at the first opportunity in this matter. This is now a Northern question even more than a Southern, and while the Southern negro has been eliminated practically from present politics, the Northern negro is more actively in politics than ever before. But aside from the policy of party interest, the great question that presses on my conscience, and that of every other person of conviction and human feeling, is to protest in every way possible against this new idea that came creeping into the Republican party from Democratic sources and now has grown so large that it is dominating the Republican party in several of the States. It should be met, and met on the same broad lines that the negro was emancipated and afterwards enfranchised. It is just as impossible to have negro delegates in the North and refuse legal negro delegates seats to which they have been elected in Republican Conventions in the South as it was to have in the old days men free in the North and slaves in the South. It is a question of conflict, and must be met with all the courage, conscience and wisdom of this generation.

I have taken the liberty to send this letter of yours to the President. Sincerely yrs.

James S. Clarkson

TLS   Con. 223   BTW Papers   DLC.

From Timothy Thomas Fortune

Maple Hall, Red Bank, N.J. September 18, 1902

Dear Mr. Washington: Your letter of the 15th instant was received, with copy of letter to Gen. Clarkson, and I am very glad to hear from you and to have the copy of the letter. The latter is one of the things that will stand to your credit, and which I approve, every word, and I shall say as much to Gen. Clarkson. I had a talk with him along the same lines ten days ago, and he asked me to write it all out for him, but I have not done so before to-day, as I wished to get a fuller expression from the friends on the situation.

I have told Mr. Scott, and I shall have an editorial on it next week, that our men should hold conventions in North Carolina and Alabama, open to all Republicans in good standing, and let the National Republican party decide as between the regularity of the two, and draw the color line if it dare. What do you think of it? I also suggest to Gen. Clarkson in my letter to-day that he and Gen. Payne should have a conference with a few of our men and reach an understanding, as they have no right to leave us in the dark and expect us to stand fast. What do you think of it? Would you consent to be one of the conferees? I have named a dozen of the best.

I know how busy you are, but I hope to see you soon.

My health continues to improve. Yours very truly,

T. Thomas Fortune

TLS Con. 227 BTW Papers DLC.

From Robert Elliott Speer[1]

New York, Sept. 19th, 1902

Dear Mr. Washington: I think you will be interested, and I hope encouraged to know, how your influence is extending even to the foreign mission field. There are frequent references in letters that come to us from our missions to your work, and frequent expressions of appreciation of the value of your example and methods to missionaries. I venture to quote two such expressions from recent letters. One is from a missionary in Nanking, China, who has charge of a boys' school in that city.

"The practical wisdom and sagacity which Booker Washington has brought to bear upon the education of the Negroes is the same that is largely needed in dealing with the poorer classes in China. The better class of the Chinese in the Student Class are coming to realize this.

"Three men of this class called upon me just before leaving Nanking to know whether we would open an industrial annex to our school if they could secure funds for all the running expenses besides the foreigners' salary — their idea being to make it possible for poor boys to earn their own education — much as is done in Park College, Mo. I should judge such expressions are valuable as showing their great change of mind with regard to Western education."

The other quotation is from a letter from a missionary in Kobe, Japan.

"This summer we have been reading a little aloud and have just finished the autobiography of Booker T. Washington. I have not read a book in a long while that has so impressed me. Truly he is an exceptional man. It is like a fairy tale to think of a man who does not know even when he was born with any certainty, or who was his father, and to read how he finally came to take afternoon tea with the Queen of England and dinner with the President of the United States. One recalls his childhood's stories of Aladdin, and others, who rose to fame and fortune. I am a Southerner of the Southerners yet I have a feeling of justifiable pride in recalling that I am a fellow-statesman of Booker T. Washington, also of William H. Sheppard that noble missionary on the lower Congo. His old mother used to be our bath-woman at the Warm Sulphur Springs back in old Virginia. When the negro race is capable of producing such high types as these truly there is great hope for it, is there not?"

I am sure you will be glad to know of the way in which the good influence of your sincere life and sensible work is reaching out even into Asia. Very truly yours,

Robert E. Speer

TLS   Con. 1   BTW Papers   DLC.

[1] Robert Elliott Speer (1867–1947) was secretary of the Presbyterian Board of Foreign Missions from 1891 to 1937.

To Theodore Roosevelt

[Birmingham, Ala.?] 9, 20, 1902

Our people are most grateful to you for your words of sympathy in the matter of the terrible calamity which has befallen so many of our race.[1] Everything possible is being done by white and colored to help. The crowd at the meeting was very large but was perfectly orderly. The disaster grew out of one of those incidents which it was almost impossible to foresee.

Booker T. Washington

TWSr   Con. 541   BTW Papers   DLC.

[1] BTW spoke to a group of between 2,000 and 3,000 blacks at the Shiloh Negro Baptist Church in Birmingham as part of the National Baptist Convention. BTW had just finished speaking when an altercation broke out between two men over a vacant seat on the stage. Apparently a woman in the choir yelled "fight," but the

congregation thought she had said "fire," and started a stampede for the doors. About a hundred persons lost their lives in the melee. In an interview after the incident BTW said, ". . . one good sister whose name I did not learn, caught me firmly by the waist and held me throughout the excitement, saying 'Keep still.'" (Birmingham *Age-Herald*, Sept. 20, 1902, 1.)

Emmett Jay Scott to Charles William Anderson

[Tuskegee, Ala.] Sept. 21, 190[2]

One whom you know earnestly requests that you make effort to have inserted in platform New York Republican Convention resolution deprecating action of North Carolina and Alabama Republican Conventions in excluding legally elected delegates from participation therein on grounds of race and color.

Emmett J. Scott

TWSr Copy   Con. 541   BTW Papers   DLC.

From Wilford H. Smith

New York City, Sept. 22nd, 1902

Dear Mr. Washington: I wish first to congratulate you on your escape from the sad calamity at Birmingham. It seems to be the fate of you and the President to have narrow escapes here of late. It is my sincere wish that you may continue to escape.

Enclosed please find contract with the Palisades Park Company, in the name of John J. Lordan,[1] for two lots marked on the map which I sent you. I have seen the property, and am well satisfied with the investment. If you could take all the lots out to the next corner, it would make the investment still better.

You will also see from the enclosed receipt, that I paid Mr. Lordan $25.00 for his services in full; that will leave a balance of $30.00 of the money which you left in my hands to cover costs. Very respectfully,

Wilford H. Smith

TLSr   BTW Papers   ATT.

1 A New York lawyer, born in Texas in 1874.

To Theodore Roosevelt

Grand Union Hotel, New York, N.Y., Sept. 27, 1902

Dear Mr. President: General Clarkson and I have had two interviews recently. The General, I think, understands the Alabama situation well; (that is, as well as any one can, for no human being can understand the Southern situation thoroughly), General Clarkson and I can work together, and I very much hope that you will let him assist you in any way possible. I will not go into details, as the General will place those before you soon. I believe that the General can help in the Alabama matter just as he did in straightening out matters in Texas.

The complete throwing down of the few decent, property-holding Negroes — just the class that you wanted to have come to the front — by the Republican leaders in Alabama, is a thing that I hope you will rebuke in no uncertain manner. Aside from the moral wrong, the effect on the Negro voters in the North will be serious if not checked.

I shall remain here until after General Clarkson has seen you. Yours sincerely,

Booker T. Washington

TLS   Theodore Roosevelt Papers   DLC.

From William Demosthenes Crum

Charleston, S.C., Sept 27 1902

My dear Mr Washington: I am in receipt of a letter from our mutual friend Fortune who tells me that you failed to receive my letter mailed to you at Richmond. I regret this very much, in that letter I told you of the condition of affairs in South Carolina and that there would probably be a vacancy in the office of Collector of Customs for this Port, and I desired your advice as to my standing for the place. It seems to me to be the policy of the Administration to eliminate our people entirely from politics. I wish to test this question if you think it advisable. Fortune, Pledger, Deveau[x],

Lyons, McKinlay and many strong men in my own State both white and colored are backing me for the position. I am sorry that I am forced to approach you at this time knowing how very busy you must be putting the affairs of Tuskegee in motion, I believe that if the President would appoint a colored man to an office of respectability it would largely tend to settle the dispute between Messrs Deas and Capers. Any suggestions or advice you may give me will be greatly appreciated.

Hoping that Mrs Washington and yourself are well   I am   Very truly Yours

Wm. D. Crum

HLS   Con. 224   BTW Papers   DLC.

From Richard Price Hallowell

Boston, September 30, 1902

Dear Mr. Washington: The question of the merits of the Kowaliga Academic & Industrial Institute, Kowaliga, Alabama, has again presented itself to me. A few years ago you withdrew your support from Mr. Benson, but in April, 1900 you renewed your endorsement of his school. Since then I have not heard from you in regard to it, but from other sources come discouraging reports. I have recently learned that Mr. Clinton J. Calloway, principal of the school, was dismissed by Mr. Benson for immoral practices and that the American Missionary Association withdrew its support from him.

Notwithstanding these damaging facts, I am told that though you are entirely familiar with them, Mr. Calloway fills a responsible position at Tuskegee. I dislike very much to trouble you and only do so because of my appreciation of the immense importance to the best interests of the colored schools in the south involved in the condemnation of undeserving schools. Mr. Benson, it seems to me, has had a hard struggle. He impresses people here very favorably, and were it not for his relations with you I am sure he would have a much easier task. Will you kindly explain this matter of Mr.

Calloway, and at the same time state to me very definitely whether or not you still endorse the Kowaliga institution and Mr. Benson. Very truly yours,

R. P. Hallowell

TLS   Con. 261   BTW Papers   DLC.

An Article in *Everybody's Magazine*[1]

September 1902

WORK WITH THE HANDS

The Moral Value of Manual Training and Labor

A New Educational Epoch

An Autobiographical Example

My attention was first attracted in an emphatic manner to the value and elevating power of hand-work when I was a student at the Hampton Normal and Industrial Institute, at Hampton, Virginia, then under the direction of the late General S. C. Armstrong. But back of my Hampton training I recall with interest and profit an earlier experience which came to me when I was only a child, and soon after I was made a free child by the proclamation of Abraham Lincoln. Soon after I had an opportunity for the first time to attend a free public school, at my home in the State of West Virginia, I heard the teacher say that the chief object of education was to enable one to speak and write the English language correctly.

While at that time I could not formulate my ideas well enough to express disagreement with my teacher, I must confess that, although I was a mere child, this definition grated rather harshly upon my ears, and did not seem satisfactory to my reason. I felt that education ought to do more for a boy than merely enable him to write and speak correctly. At the very moment when I had heard this definition my mother was living in the most abject proverty and want; and one of my objects in going to school was to enable me to get to a point where I could make life a little more bearable

529

— and, if possible, even attractive — for her. My mother was then working night and day to afford me an opportunity to spend two or three months of the year in school. I wondered if my ability merely to speak and write correctly was going to fit me to help very much in relieving the condition of our family.

I had already observed that there were several boys who lived in our neighborhood who had had superior advantages for going to school, and who in some instances had arrived at a point where they were called "educated" — that is, they could write and talk correctly. But still the parents of these boys were not far removed from the condition which I was living in.

Young as I was, too, in some indescribable way I had come to have the feeling that to be a free boy meant, in a large degree, that one had reached a position in life where work with the hands would not be necessary. As a child in Virginia, going from one plantation to another as opportunity offered, I had naturally noted that young white boys whose fathers held slaves did not, as a general thing, work with their hands. I had further observed that the feeling was pretty general that a free boy and an educated boy should not work with his hands. The Negro boy immediately after the Civil War was confronted by — or at least it seemed so to him — two propositions which in many cases were liable to exert a serious influence upon his life. One of these was that freedom from slavery brought freedom from hard work; the other was that education of the head would bring further freedom from hand-work. The Negro, I ought to add, was not directly responsible for either of these ideas, but the fact remains that in a large degree they prevailed.

Soon after I began to think as seriously as perhaps a boy could think about some of these things, a rather important event came to pass in my life. There lived not far from my mother's cabin a wealthy woman[2] who had been born and educated in Vermont, although she had then lived for many years in the South. This woman not only had the greatest respect for all forms of hand labor, but also, notwithstanding her wealth and education, was not ashamed to use her own hands. Among the people of the neighborhood she bore the reputation of being one whom it was exceedingly hard to satisfy in the performance of any kind of manual labor. Her reputation among the boys of the village was that she was a hard person to get along with. There were, I think, at least a half-dozen boys who had gone at one time or another to live with her, but in almost every case a boy's stay with her had been exceedingly short. I think a week constituted the average time. This was true in spite of the fact that this household had one redeeming quality which was widely advertised among the boys of the neighborhood. That was that it was a place where one would always get something good to eat. In addition to pies and cakes, something that at that time the boys in a community like ours seldom got sight of in their own cabin homes, the orchards about the house were heavily laden with fruit of the best varieties. Each boy, however, who went into the service of this woman, soon returned to the village with the same story — she was too strict, too hard to please.

After a considerable number of the other boys in the village had endeavored to satisfy this mistress, my turn came. When I came home one night I was informed by my mother that she had sent to ask me to come and live with her. She said that I should be paid six dollars a month for my work. After talking the matter over seriously with my mother I decided to make an effort to serve this woman, and a few days afterward, with my clothes in the best condition I could get them, and with fear and trembling in my heart, I reported for duty.

I had heard so much about her wealth and about her fine house and costly surroundings, and above all about her strictness, that I feared to meet her, with a fear that it is now hard for me to describe. My life had been passed in a cabin. Now I was to labor in what seemed to me a great mansion.

As the time of meeting her drew near, I summoned all my courage and determined to pass through the ordeal as best I could. She talked to me in a kindly way and very frank manner. She rehearsed the difficulties that she had encountered with the other boys, and explained to me what their points of weakness had been. She told me in plain language that I would be expected to keep my body clean and my clothes neat, and that above all else she would require cleanliness in connection with all my work. She said that she wanted to have everything done systematically, and she made me realize that she would expect me to tell the exact truth at all times, regardless of consequences. I remember, too, that she placed especial emphasis upon the necessity for promptness, and said that excuses and explanations would not be taken by her in the place of results.

This, at the time, seemed to me a pretty hard programme to look forward to, and I was becoming almost discouraged when, toward the end of the interview, she told me that if I remained with her and pleased her she would permit me to attend school at night during the winter. This latter suggestion so gratified my ambition that it went a long way toward helping me to decide to make the effort of my life to remain with her and to please her.

My first work at this place, as I now remember it, was to cut the grass in the yard and give the yard itself a thorough cleaning. In those days there were no lawn-mowers. I had to get down on my knees and cut much of the grass with a little hand scythe. I soon found that my employer not only wanted the grass cut, but wanted it cut smoothly and evenly. Any one who has tried to mow a lawn neatly with a little dull hand scythe can appreciate the task which I had before me. I am not ashamed to say that I did not succeed in giving satisfaction the first, or even the second or third time; but I finally did succeed in making the turf in that yard look as even as it could now be made to look with the most improved lawn-mower. When I had once done this my own sense of pride and of satisfaction began to manifest itself in a slight degree. I found, however, that the cutting of the grass was not all. The yard was to be made perfectly clean. Every weed, every tuft of dead grass, every bit of paper or scrap of dirt of any description was to be removed. I did not succeed in pleasing my employer in this the first time, either, but I finally did succeed in making the yard so clean that I did not believe that so much as a bird's feather remained on it.

But even then that was not all. I was told that the edges of the walks must be made straight, and the walks themselves made free from grass and weeds, that the weeds and grass must be taken from the flower-beds, and the edges of the beds themselves straightened and put in order. Need I say that so far as these last-named details were concerned I tried to give satisfaction at least half a dozen times before I succeeded? Need I say that many times while trying to put this yard in order, tired and hot, I became heartsick and discouraged, and almost determined to run away and go home to my mother? But I kept at it, and after a few days, as a result of my efforts under the strict guidance of my employer, I looked out upon a yard where the grass was green and almost perfect in its smoothness, where the flower-beds were clean, the edges of the walks orderly and clean cut, and where there was not the least sign of dirt to mar the almost perfect appearance.

When I looked upon this creation of my hands, my whole nature, it seems to me, began to change. I felt a sense of self-respect, of encouragement and satisfaction that I had never before enjoyed or thought possible. Above all else I had acquired a feeling of self-confidence in my ability actually to do things, and to do them well, which it is hard for me to describe. Further, I found myself, through this experience, getting rid of the idea which had gradually become a part of me, that the head meant everything, and the hand little, and that to labor with the head was honorable, but to labor with the hands dishonorable. Added to my other sources of satisfaction came the warm and hearty commendation of the good woman who had given me what I now consider my first chance to get a touch of real life.

As I now recall this experience I find that then and there my mind received an awakening and strengthening. I began to get satisfaction out of my hands. I found myself planning over night how to go to work so as to insure the success of the next day's efforts. I found myself imagining how the yard would look when completed, and studying over the best curves for the flower-beds and the proper width of the walks. I soon became more absorbed in this work than in finding mischief to do with the village boys to occupy my time.

While I would be among the last to underestimate the awakening power of strictly mental training, still I cannot escape the feeling that this visible, tangible contact with nature gave me an awakening which could not have come to me in any other way. I favor the most thorough mental training and the highest development of mind, but I want to see these linked to the common things of life about our doors.

I remained in the family of which I have written for several years, and the foregoing is but one of the many lessons that I learned. The longer I was employed there the more satisfaction I got out of my work, and later on, so far from fearing the woman whom the other boys had found so formidable, I learned to think of her always, and think of her now — for she still lives — as one of my greatest teachers. Later, whether working in the coal mines or at the salt furnaces, I learned to get something of the same satisfaction out of everything that I did. If in sweeping or dusting a room, or in weeding a bed of flowers or vegetables, there remained the least imperfection in the shape of dust or weeds, I was unhappy, and felt that I was guilty of dishonesty until the imperfection in my work had been removed.

I think that it was this experience in using my hands that led me, in spite of all the difficulties in the way, to go to the Hampton Institute, after I had learned that this was a school where the pupils were not only educated by the use of books, but were also educated in the use of their hands. At the time that I entered the Hampton Institute the industries taught there were but few, but those few were fundamental. The hand-work at Hampton began with that which had the most direct and natural relation to the life of the students — the making of our own beds, the cleaning of our rooms, the care of the recitation rooms, the keeping neat of the grounds, the proper cooking and serving of food. Then there were the lessons in raising our food on the farm. The lessons in iron and wood work in the earlier years of the institution were given principally in the form of making and repairing farm implements, and in helping to keep the buildings in proper repair.

But all this work had great educational value. How well do I remember the uplifting and strengthening influence that the sight of a perfectly made bed had upon me, with the pillow always placed at the proper angle, and the edges of the sheets turned over in a neat and systematic manner. The work on the farm had the same influence upon me. I soon learned that there was a great difference between studying about things, and studying the things themselves; and further, that there was quite as much difference between studying in books about doing things, and doing the same things themselves.

All these experiences to which I have been referring served as preparation for the work in hand, head and heart training which, later, I was to undertake at the Tuskegee Normal and Industrial Institute in Alabama. When I went to Alabama to begin this work I spent some time in visiting towns and country districts in order that I might, if possible, get to understand the real conditions and needs of the people. It was my ambition to make the little school which I was going to start of real service in awakening and enriching the life of the most lowly and unfortunate. With this end in view I not only visited the schools, churches and farms of the people, but slept in their one-room cabins and ate with them at their meals, of cornbread and fried pork.

Often while making these visits, both in the towns and in the plantation districts, I found individuals who had received considerable education, so far as memorizing certain rules in grammar and arithmetic were concerned. Indeed, more than once, I found those who had studied to a considerable extent in the dead and modern languages. I found some who could solve problems in arithmetic and algebra which I could not master. It seemed to me that the more abstract and senseless these problems were, the further that they were removed from the life that the people were then living, or were to live in the future, the more stress these people seemed to place upon them. One of the saddest things was to find here and there cases of those who had studied what was called "art," or instrumental music, in other words what were called "the accomplishments," living in houses where there was not the least sign of beauty or system. There was not the least indication that this "art" or these "the accomplishments" had had any influence, or ever would have any, upon the life in these houses. Indeed, it seemed not to have occurred to these people that such things should have any connection with everyday life in their homes. In some cases I found young men who could solve the most difficult problems in "compound proportion," or in "banking," or in "foreign exchange," but who had never thought to try to figure out the reason why their fathers lost money on every bale of cotton they raised, and why they were constantly mortgaging their crops and going in debt. I found girls who could locate with accuracy the Alps or the Andes on the map, but who had no idea of the proper location of the various knives and forks and dishes upon an actual dinner table. I found those who remembered that bananas were grown in certain South American countries, but to whom it had never occurred that bananas might be a good and healthful food to sharpen the appetite at the breakfast table, supposing their work had been such as to allow them to buy such food. In a country where pigs, chickens, ducks, geese, berries, peaches, plums, vegetables, nuts and much other wholesome food could be produced with little effort, I found even school teachers in the summer eating salt-pork brought from Chicago and canned chicken and tomatoes obtained in Omaha.

I found that while the country abounded in all manner of beautiful wild shrubbery and fragrant flowers, few flowers ever found their way into the houses, or their place upon the dinner table. Further, I found that while in many instances the people had always lived in the country, and perhaps always would do so, what few text-books I saw in their cabins were full of pictures and text relating to city life. In these text-books I saw pictures of great office buildings, great ships, street cars and warehouses, but not a single picture of a farm scene — a large spreading apple tree, a field of grass or corn, a flock of sheep or a herd of cows. In one case I heard of a girl who, when asked to become a cook in a family, replied very seriously that she was sorry, but her diploma was for music and embroidery.

Everybody's Magazine, 7 (Sept. 1902), 297–300.

1 This was the first of a series of articles in *Everybody's Magazine* that was eventually published, with some editorial changes, as *Working with the Hands* (1904). This appeared as chap. 1 of the book.

2 Viola Knapp Ruffner.

A Draft of a Letter to the Editor of the
Montgomery *Advertiser*

[Tuskegee, Ala., ca. September 1902]

Editor Advertiser: There are some events occur[r]ing just now in Alabama that are of such moment as to demand more than passing notice. The writer calls attention to them not because he has anything to gain or lose, nor because he has any interest in any political office or in any individual.

What the writer has in mind however is more far-reaching and fundamental than mere office-holding jugglery. During a period of more than thirty years several scores of Southern so-called white republicans have been kept in places of profit and power mainly through the votes, influence, and activity of Negro voters. The Negroes have kept these white men in power in many cases at the cost of alienating themselves from their friends and neighbors, the local white people. In many cases the Negroes have stood by these white republicans at the cost of their lives. During the whole time that the colored people were thus following and supporting these white republicans, they were told and the whole country was told by the Southern white people that these pretended republicans, with few exceptions had no real interest in the Negro — that they were simply using him as a cats-paw, and that whenever it got to the point where the Negro was of no more value to them that these so-called republicans would be the first ones to throw the Negro down and put their feet upon his necks. To all of these charges, these white republicans plead not guilty with the utmost strenuousness; they protested that they were interested in the Negro from principle and that they stood by the Negro because he was abused and oppressed by white democrats. What are these same republicans now engaged in doing? When the mass of ignorant Negroes were permitted to vote, and when these white men could use the Negro as a tool they were not ashamed to associate in conventions and elsewhere with the most ignorant and depraved class of Negroes. Within the last few months the great bulk of ignorant Negro voters has been eliminated from politics, the Negro voting list has been purified as by fire to such an extent that there are not more than 3000 registered Negro voters in the whole state, and these 3000 are men that own property, have education, and character — so much so that they have passed the scrutiny of even a democratic registration board. In the face of this fact these pretended republicans, who have for nearly forty years been assembling in conventions with the representatives of quite a hundred thousand Negro voters, have all at once grown so holy, pure and exclusive they cannot associate in conventions with the representatives of even 3000 Negroes and those representative of the highest type of Negroes in the South? What hypocrisy? What base ingratitude? We would think that not one of this class of white man could ever again look a Negro in the face. What the democrats have been accused of doing in the past is not to be compared with the meanness that these white republicans are now practicing. But what explanation are these white republicans giving to the Negroes and others privately. It is this: they are saying to the Negro you lay "low" for awhile; keep out of sight. We are now trying to induce some democrats to enter the party and as soon as we have gotten these democrats "caged," and we get control of things in Alabama we will again recognize you and bring you to the front. What rot! Are the white democrats of Alabama fools? Do they not observe; do they not reason; do they not know that if these republican leaders have been leading a life of deception with the Negro for nearly forty years that these same men will deceive the white democrats in the same way? Do not the decent white men in Alabama reason that these renegade republicans cannot be dishonest for 40 years and turn to be honest men all at once merely by assembling in a convention and passing a set of resolutions. Do these republican leaders by such methods hope to deceive such honorable and straightforward democrats as Judge Thos. G. Jones — a type of man who has more real interest in the Negro in [a] day than these pretended friends had during their whole lives. Further, these so-called leaders are not only trying to deceive the Negroes and the white men of Alabama but they are trying to deceive the outside world and the President of the United States by pretending that they want to increase membership in the republican party. They want to [do] no such thing. They know the fewer white men there are in the party the more nearly will the offices go around. They also know that if they can get rid of the few Negroes now holding office that there will be that many more offices for these white republicans.

Do these pretended leaders imagine for a minute that their [these] persons hypocritical actions could have for a minute the indorsement of a high, pure character such as President Roosevelt. Can honest men anywhere indorse the actions of a portion of the white republicans of Montgomery County, Alabama, in making an effort to bodily steal the few places held by the three Negro delegates elected to the state convention? Was ever such high-handed robbery committed even by democrats? Within the last few weeks the writer has heard dozens of intelligent Negroes express regret that while he was at it that President Roosevelt did not fill more of the federal offices in the South — and in Alabama, with pure, high-minded, clean democrats like Judge Jones — men vitally interested in the welfare of both races from principle. The writer does not want to be misunderstood. He does not indict all white republicans in the State. Among them there are some that always act from principle and are actuated by the highest motives. The Negro now knows his friends and he means to mark every man who deserts him in the present crisis. A day of recogning will come — & soon, too.

ALd   BTW Papers   ATT.   Modifications in E. J. Scott's hand.

From William Demosthenes Crum

Charleston, S.C. 10/5/02

My dear Mr Washington: I wrote you about a week ago in reference to the situation in South Carolina and particularly the vacancy in The Collectorship of the Port of Charleston.

I have satisfactory assurances from Mr Jno G. Capers that if the President will appoint a colored man that he will endorse me for the position not that I believe Mr Capers wants a colored man appointed, but that if the Administration sees the advisability at this time, in view of the strained political relations of our people, of appointing one of our people to this office, he will endorse me in preference to any other candidate.

I am satisfied that the people of Charleston would soon become reconciled to my appointment on account of my past services to the community and that there would be less objection to my appointment than to any other colored applicant.

President Roosevelt feels a sentiment of gratitude toward the good people of this city for the royal way in which they entertained him during the Exposition, but I am strongly inclined to think that justice to the people who have upheld him in the past and can sustain him in the future will be the criterion by which he will make this appointment.

To my mind if the President should appoint a colored man to be Collector of this Port, [it] would offset to a large extent the bitter feeling existing throughout the country against the Administration among our people while the appointment of a white man would mean the endorsement of the actions of Alabama, North Carolina and other States that are trampling upon the rights of our people.

I feel sure that Mr Capers has selected a white man of Democratic proclivities, who will turn Republican for the occasion and that very shortly he will present his name to the President unless we can get in some good work very shortly but on the other hand should the President manifest a desire to appoint one of our people I am assured of his support as he fully realizes the situation.

Hoping that you will give this matter your most serious consideration and immediate attention, and hoping also that you and Mrs Washington are well   I am as ever   Very truly Yours

William D. Crum

HLS   Con. 224   BTW Papers   DLC.

To James Sullivan Clarkson

Tuskegee, Ala   Oct 7 1902

Scott advises whites attempting to delay Roulhac appointment am sure they will not succeed as President has promised to appoint Roulhac at once.[1] I have not wired President for that reason. Parties now urging delay have most shamefully humiliated our people and every negro newspaper is aroused. Am keeping them in line on strength of promise something will be done. Any other course will greatly embarrass me. I am sure you feel with me that human rights and justice are more important than promise of a few uncertain votes.

Booker T. Washington

TWSr   Theodore Roosevelt Papers   DLC.

[1] Clarkson wrote BTW that about a half-dozen lily-white Republicans from Alabama tried to block the Roulhac appointment, but on President Roosevelt's instructions Clarkson told them of the President's "displeasure and disapproval over the attempt to form a white man's party in their State." When the group threatened to deny Roosevelt the support of the Alabama delegation in 1904, Clarkson replied that he doubted that a delegation "representing a mongrel or bastard party based on color" would be seated. (Clarkson to BTW, Oct. 11, 1902, Con. 1, BTW Papers, DLC.)

From Matthew Anderson

Philadelphia, October 8th, 1902

My Dear Mr. Washington: Your letter of the 6th inst. has been received and I hasten to reply. I have read with no little interest your kind reply to my letter of the 17th of Sept. and I am free to admit that your statements concerning the friendly feeling of the white people of Tuskegee towards you and your work has quite changed my views in regard to them. Let me say here, the impression I had formed was not based upon anything that had been told me while there, but wholly on general appearances. I felt when I saw the character of many of the dwellings in which the colored people lived in the town, not only in the neighborhood of the depot but in the very sight of the Institution, that this condition was due to the fact that the owners of these properties were white men who were unfriendly or inimical to you and your work, as is too often exhibited towards those who are earnestly and honestly trying to lift up the degraded and oppressed; this is especially true of many owners of property in which colored people live. I was confirmed in this thought, too, when told by one of your friends on my return to Phila. that you had been anxious for a number of years to secure a large tract of land near the Institution on which many cabins of Ante-bellum type are situated, but that the owner has persistently refused to sell you a foot of it, simply because he is not in sympathy with the improvement of the Negro. You see, Mr. Washington, I was not criticising the influence of your work at Tuskegee; far from it, but the white people of the town. So far as your work is concerned, I am free to say that its good effect is felt throughout the nation, upon all classes, especially upon the Negro element of the South. I need not go out a few miles in the country from Tuskegee to see the influence of your School upon the colored people in the improvement of their homes. This is seen all over the South, wherever the Negro is free to think and act.

Up to this writing I have not heard from you through your Secretary in regard to the engagement. As I wrote last, one of our best Halls has been secured for the 10th of November, and a strong Committee selected to secure for you a large and select audience.

This Committee is headed by Mr. John H. Converse,[1] LL.D. President of Baldwin Locomotive Works.

Thanking you again for your kind letter and hoping to see you soon, I am, Yours respectfully,

Matthew Anderson

P.S. When you come to Philadelphia I want you to stop with me. Prof. Hugh M. Browne, who has come to take charge of the Institution of Colored Youth, is a guest in my house.

TLS   Con. 219   BTW Papers   DLC.

[1] John Heman Converse (1840–1910) was the president of the Baldwin Locomotive Works of Philadelphia, director of the Philadelphia National Bank and Franklin National Bank, a trustee of Princeton Theological Seminary, and a leader of many philanthropic enterprises.

From William Demosthenes Crum

Charleston, S.C. Oct 9 02

Personal

My dear Mr Washington: I received this morning a letter from our mutual friend Fortune in which he says, "I am surprised at what Mr Washington told me of your conduct while in Richmond in attendence upon The League Convention."

I would state with great sorrow that I came in contact with men who could stand up under great alcoholic pressure. I am not given to drinking and I think the testimony of my friends at home will bear me out in this assertion.

I value your friendship greatly and I cannot allow myself to be separated from you and I pledge you my word of honor that henceforth *Drink* and I shall be strangers.

Hoping that you and Mrs Washington are we[ll]   I am   Very truly Yours

Wm. D. Crum

HLS   Con. 272   BTW Papers   DLC.

From Charles Patrick Joseph Mooney[1]

Memphis, Tenn   10/9/1902

My dear sir: It seems that my little conversation with you and your conversation with me was a benefit to both of us, in so far as it set me to thinking and caused you to remember me after our short but very agreeable acquaintance. I have both of your letters. I also desire to thank you for the book, and I want to say this that I may have to charge you with causing me to be guilty of dereliction of duty. I began the book yesterday afternoon on coming to the office. I read it during the entire afternoon; went out to supper, came back and finished it before 11 o'clock. To me it was intensely interesting. Just how a human being could overcome the obstacles that were in front of you at every step is to me a marvel. Men conquer other men at the head of great armies. Nations destroy other nations, but after all some of the supreme triumphs of life are those where the individual wins his way. The book, indeed was helpful to me. Every white man interested in the South should read it, and every negro man should study it as an inspiration. I am going to ask you a question, and I do it with the utmost frankness, but also realize that it is a delicate one. Possibly the question may suggest a thought to you. If you had been entirely black do you believe you would have had that quality which made it possible for you to succeed? I am now referring to your early struggles. In other words is there in the pure African that element which made it possible for you to become the President of one of the most famous educational institutions in the country rising from the condition which made you sleep under the side walk? If there is, then there is great hope for your race. I am struck also by your suggestion of work. Let me make an additional suggestion. Impress on each person the necessity of owning a little property. I believe that as soon as the negro man gets his name on the tax book he becomes entirely a changed being. He begins to hold up his head and to stand squarely on his feet. Not arrogant but manly. I also am struck at a hint you make of a condition, that I have already profited by thoroughly. That is as to the honesty of the negro. I have long ago found the greatest incentive to honesty is this: To get the best there is in the negro man the white man must trust him absolutely.

I have a negro man, to whom when I left for Europe I turned over the keys of my house. He was not placed partially in charge with some one else to share the responsibility. No valuables were hidden, but I told him that he and he *alone* was trusted with everything. Now if I had shared the responsibility with others my man might have failed me. Of course when we are discussing the problem we have in view those who have not yet reached the condition where they can act for themselves. You have a great work before you. I think you are following the correct line, and when we get rid of some of the bad people of our own race and you and others like you improve and make better the bad members of your race things will look brighter. The fact is that we are all weak and frail and are susceptible of a little improvement. Yours very truly,

C P J Mooney

TLS Con. 236 BTW Papers DLC.

1 Charles Patrick Joseph Mooney (1865–1926) was editor of the Memphis *Commercial Appeal* from 1896 to 1902. Moving northward, he was managing editor of the New York *Daily News* (1902–3), the New York *American* (1903–5), and the Chicago *Examiner* (1905–8). He then returned to the editorship of the *Commercial Appeal* in 1908.

From Judson Whitlocke Lyons

Washington   October 13, 1902

My Dear Sir: Your favors to hand and noted. It is well to advise our folk in Alabama that as we understand it the Republican party is neither a white man's party, nor is it a black man's party; but a party for all people who believe in right and justice before the law, and who believe in the glory and welfare of the nation as the one paramount thing worthy of the supremest efforts. Hence, notwithstanding the "lily whites" they should not regard all white men in the state who claim to be Republicans, as sharing in and harboring such heretical political views, unless they have done some overt act showing that they would change the meaning of Republicanism as it has been handed down by Lincoln, Grant, Arthur, McKinley, and now is interpreted by Roosevelt. The colored man must not draw the color line. He must not allow the mistakes of the "lily whites" to lure him into an erroneous and untenable position. In short, every man regardless of race or color who believes in Republican principles as we understand them and as the great masters to whom I have referred, have expounded them, should always be welcome to the council board.

The colored man's position now is a very delicate one and requires the exercise of the broadest wisdom and the coolest judgment. They must not spoil a good case in their appeal for fair play to the old party by the exasperation produced by the injustice of the lily whites. There are a great many good and true white Republicans in Alabama who saw the folly of the "lily whites" convention, and entered their earnest objection. Those men are entitled to all praise, and the party will show it by treating them with all possible consideration.

Then, too, if any of the "lily whites" should have the scales of darkness drop from their eyes and come back to the faith, I would treat them with all fairness also. I think Mr. Roulhac would do a graceful and wise thing should he appoint Republicans to all of the places in his office as assistants etc. We must hold the party together and it is the duty of all of us to endeavor to so manage affairs as to give the opposition the least grounds for criticism of the Administration. I have always thought the best thing to do in all cases is to search diligently for a fit and proper Republican to fill all places, first, then if he can't be found we are warranted in going outside and take up somebody else. This policy will enable us to always win before the country, as there is never much room to experiment with practical politics, experience has taught me that the safest rule is to hold on to what we have got among party men and if there is to be any experimenting, do that with the enemy. Very truly,

Judson W. Lyons

TLS   Con. 233   BTW Papers   DLC.

From Whitefield McKinlay

Washington, D.C., October 13, 1902

Dear Mr. Washington: Yours came to hand. I spoke to Taylor concerning Dancy, who said that he would urge him to stand firm. Gov. Pinchback agrees with me that Dancy would not dare show the white feather in this fight.

I think that we are now in a position to get a colored man appointed Collector of Customs at Charleston. I personally know that there would not be any serious opposition on the part of the business element, and as Crum is the most available man I am urging his selection notwithstanding the weakness he displayed at Richmond, and I am further satisfied that it will serve as a good lesson to him as such breaks are not characteristic of him, for in all the years that I have known him it is the first instance of which I have ever heard.

Mr. H. L. West,[1] whom we bitterly opposed, was appointed Commissioner of the District to-day. The President told him he wanted him to see me as he regarded my opposition as giving him more serious concern than all others, hence he immediately called and explained his letters to the Post which led to my opposition. We talked the situation over as in regard to the colored people of the District for more than an hour, and I hope that some good might come of it especially as it may give our best colored men standing with him.

How about Durham's appointment? It strikes me that now is a good time to press it. Very truly,

W. M.

TLI Con. 233 BTW Papers DLC.

[1] Henry Litchfield West (1859–1940), a newspaperman and a commissioner of the District of Columbia from 1902 to 1910, was the only commissioner of the period willing to appoint blacks to positions in the local government. (Green, *Secret City*, 159.) In 1910 he became part owner of the Washington *Herald*. West was chairman of the District of Columbia Electric Railway Commission from 1909 to 1912 and executive secretary of the National Security League from 1915 to 1921.

To Francis Jackson Garrison

Tuskegee, Ala., Oct. 14, 1902

My dear Mr. Garrison: We shall be very glad indeed to use the copies of the "Hymns of Faith" referred to [by] you in your letter of October 9th, and can put them in proper shape in our printing office. You can send them by Adams Express or by freight. I do not know how large a package it will be. In case it is not very large I think it will be best to send the package by express.

A most interesting and unexpected thing has taken place in North Carolina and in this state. The registering of voters has been going on for sometime under the restrictions of the new constitution. Notwithstanding the registration boards were composed in every case of white Democrats over 3,000 colored people have so far been successful in securing life certificates entitling them to vote without further trouble for all time. In the face of the fact that the Democrats had passed upon these colored voters, the Republican convention which met a few weeks ago kept these registered colored voters from being represented in the state convention. You will be interested to know that when the matter was put before the President he sat down on the whole movement in a way which I think will stamp out any such drawing of the color line in the future. This proceeding on the part of these Republicans shows that when the majority of the colored people were ignorant and in many cases vicious, and could be controlled by the politicians, they were willing to associate with them in conventions, but as soon as those attending the Republican conventions were an educated, property holding class who could not be bought these pretended Republicans did not want to associate with them. Of course what I have said does not apply to all the white Republicans in the state by a good deal; there are many who are manly and have stood by the colored people in a courageous way.

I see by the morning papers that the senior class at Emory College has just unanimously adopted resolutions expressing faith in Prof. Sledd and regretting his departure from the college. I presume this must make the trustees feel a little ashamed of their cowardice. Yours very truly,

Booker T. Washington

TLS Francis Jackson Garrison Papers MH.

From John Grier Hibben[1]

[Princeton, N.J.] October 14, 1902

Dear Sir: Delegates and guests invited to take part in the procession on the occasion of the Inauguration of President Wilson are requested to appear in full academic costume.[2]

Should you not be provided I would suggest that you communicate with Messrs. Cotrell & Leonard, outfitters to the University, 472 Broadway, Albany, N.Y., who will give you any information you may desire. Sincerely yours,

John Grier Hibben
For the Committee

TLS Con. 230 BTW Papers DLC. On stationery of the Inauguration Committee of Princeton University.

1 John Grier Hibben (1861–1933) taught logic and psychology at Princeton from 1891 to 1912. He was president of Princeton from 1912 to 1933.

2 BTW marched in the academic procession on Oct. 25, 1902, when Woodrow Wilson was installed as president of Princeton. His hood lined with the colors of Harvard and Dartmouth, which had awarded him honorary degrees, BTW attended with about 150 delegates from universities, colleges, and learned societies. During the procession BTW was singled out by Mrs. Grover Cleveland, who shook his hand. Many years later one of Wilson's daughters recalled that BTW's presence so scandalized her unreconstructed aunt from Georgia that "she said if she had known he was to be there she wouldn't have gone (which scandalized us) and father said that Booker T's speech was the very best at the dinner afterwards bar none 'not than *yours*, Father.' 'Oh yes no comparison between them' — our incredulous 'oh's' and mother's sweet smile equally incredulous." (Jessie W. Sayre to Ray Stannard Baker, Apr. 25, 1927, Ray Stannard Baker Papers, DLC.) BTW was the only one of the visiting dignitaries not housed with a family of a Princeton faculty member, and he had to reside at a black boardinghouse in the town. The Wilsons did not invite him to either of the dinners they gave during the festivities, though it is remotely possible he attended the class of '79 dinner at the Princeton Inn the night of the inaugural. He did attend a luncheon held by the Henry Gurdon Marquands, donors of the Marquand Chapel at Princeton. (*Tuskegee Student,* 14 [Nov. 1, 1902], 2, 3.)

To Julian La Rose Harris[1]

Tuskegee, Ala., Oct. 16, 1902

Personal and Private.

Dear Sir: First I want to thank you for your kind consideration in calling to my attention the report sent out from Boston bearing upon my daughter. It is very kind and thoughtful of you to do this.

If you do not feel that, as a newspaper, you have no right to refuse to use this matter, I very much prefer to make no statement in connection with it. I am perfectly resigned to having my public words and acts discussed, but I think you will agree with me that I ought not to be called upon to discuss in public print my family affairs. I want to state, however, for your private information, that the facts bearing upon my daughter are these: In the first place, she has finished the regular normal and industrial course at this institution, and friends of mine were anxious to have her take additional studies in order that she might further prepare herself for work here and for this reason gave the money for her to be further educated, and we at first decided to have her take a special course in music at Wellesley. She stayed there for a year taking this course and was treated with the greatest consideration and kindness by every one connected with the college. She did not, however, board in the college halls as no student who is not taking the regular course is permitted to board there. At the end of the college year at Wellesley Mrs. Washington and I decided to have her take a regular seminary course and for this reason withdrew her and sent her to Bradford Academy. The whole matter that has been sent you had its [origin] in the office of The Guardian, a colored paper published by a little clique of colored people in Boston who have always opposed my idea of industrial education and have always opposed my attitude towards the Southern white people.

Another reason why I do not want to make a statement unless it is absolutely necessary is that it would please the editors of the Guardian to have me do so. For over a year they have been trying in all kinds of ways to force me to note the mean things that they have said, but thus far I have been silent and that has hurt them worse than anything I could say. I think if you will examine the

Boston papers you will find that none of them have used this matter.

Of course before my daughter could enter another school she had to secure a letter of recommendation from the authorities at Wellesley which the authorities there were glad to give. Yours truly,

Booker T. Washington

TLS Julian Harris Papers GEU. A carbon copy is in Con. 272, BTW Papers, DLC.

1 Julian La Rose Harris (1875–1963) was the editor of the Atlanta *Constitution* from 1897 to 1904. The son of Joel Chandler Harris, he had a long career as a newspaper writer and editor. He won a Pulitzer Prize in 1926 for his articles on the Ku Klux Klan.

From James Sullivan Clarkson

New York, N.Y., October 16th, 1902

Confidential

Dear Doctor Washington: I have your letter of 13th. You will have received before this my letter giving you pretty much in full the details of my visit to Washington and the interviews there. There is left only the matter of making an appointment or two in the North of some well known colored man, as a notice of the President of his loyalty and the equality of all men under the Republican party. I took him a list of Negroes holding office under national appointment, and he was surprised to find that there was no New Yorker at all in the list, so he instructed me to try and ascertain one, and if possible two worthy men to recommend to him, and also to find such men as would be agreeable to Senator Platt, as they would have to be charged up to New York State and would have to depend on the New York Senators for the certainty of their confirmation. I have now spent nearly a week in traversing the subject and trying to find some men whose appointment would be hailed by all the people of their race as the recognition of men of usefulness and high deserts. I am surprised to find this State with its large colored population possessed of very few men in it in the number who are known all over the country. I am also obliged to find men who will be agreeable to Senator Platt, as well as to the President. I feel too that the appointment of one of your people at this time should be preeminently fit and as much for the vindication of the intelligence of the race as for the recognition of it by the President. Charles W. Anderson seems the most fit of all and is certainly the most agreeable to Senator Platt; when I went to him to confer about it before I started in, he suggested Anderson at once. You know Anderson without my telling you what he is. He has held important places in this State and rendered great credit to himself and his people in doing so. He holds a $3000 office now, but says he can secure the position for another man of his race. Consequently, I am going to send him over to Washington today, with a letter to the President telling him that Senator Platt desires Anderson's appointment and that I recommend it. The President himself, when he gave me the commission to find men to appoint, said he would prefer Anderson, so I think the matter will go through if they can find a place that will be agreeable all round. I shall try and find some one else to present to the President, although I feel that if he should appoint Anderson now that would probably be enough for the present.

T. Thomas Fortune has been in to see me, and I could see he was quite irritated because he was not invited into the conference at Washington. He seemed to take it for granted that I had met people there by arrangement and by appointment, and also accepted the newspaper statement that I presented Bishop Walters, Bishop Clinton and Rev. Dr. Carruthers[1] to the President, whereas they were with the President when I went to his room and I had no previous knowledge of their movements. He also seemed dissatisfied, as I had seen by the last issue of his paper, over the appointment of Judge Roulhac. I told him yesterday that you had recommended this and I was satisfied that under all the circumstances it was the best thing to do, and that subsequent developments had proved this.

I had a long visit day before yesterday from Revenue Collector Bingham of your State. He came on the strange errand of trying to persuade me that the course of the Alabama Convention was right, and he went away with a totally different opinion.[2] He is very smart and very plucky, but I told him that he and his associates could never make this course of folly win anything but disaster. He wanted to see if he could not induce me to take their side of the question and endeavor to prevent the President from making any more removals. I told him that I did not know what the President would do, but that if I were in his place I would remove every man from office in Alabama who helped to set up this attempt to undermine the foundations of the party and to repudiate the cardinal doctrines of the faith. I asked him if he and his fellows had never thought it would be a decent thing to do to advise with the Republicans in the North before taking this course of folly in the South; he said it never had occurred to them; I said this was strange inasmuch as they had done nothing to help elect a Republican President by which they got their offices, and that it would be the part of wisdom and gratitude that if they could do no good they should certainly do no harm to the party in the North. He said they did not care for that and that they would persist in their course.

I will let you know as soon as I learn of further developments. Sincerely yours,

James S. Clarkson

TLS   Con. 272   BTW Papers   DLC.

1 Samuel Carruthers was pastor of the Galbraith A.M.E. Church in Washington, D.C.

2 Charles W. Anderson reported to BTW: "I thought you might be interested to know that Mr. Bingham of Alabama, spent most of the day on Monday in the office of Gen. Clarkson. I was in the General's office three times that day and found him there each time. He looked a trifle careworn, and I thought I detected the stench of decaying Lily-Whiteism while he was in the room. I am sure he received but cold comfort from the General." (Oct. 16, 1902, Con. 219, BTW Papers, DLC.)

From William Henry Baldwin, Jr.

N.Y. [City] October 17 1902

Dear Mr Washington   Mr Villard is still rampant on the subject of "Kowaliga," and he told me of some one who had written you a long letter from Boston and also that others were disturbed about your continuing Mr Calloway with you. I said there was absolutely no use in writing you letters on that subject, that I hoped when you next came to New York we might have a conference, and see if we cannot understand each other. Yours truly,

W H Baldwin Jr

TLS   Con. 792   BTW Papers   DLC.

From Joseph E. Wiley[1]

N.Y.[City] October 17 1902

Dear Mr. Washington: Pardon my delay in answering your very kind letter. I had thought to comply with the suggestion made therein, by calling upon Col. Kingsley and inviting him to go over and inspect our Mill, but in two calls at his office I have not been able to meet him, and will not longer delay writing you.

The New Century Cotton Mill is fast nearing completion. We have completed the brickwork and Buildings providing nearly 20,000 square feet of floor space. We have bedded and set one 125 H.P. Corliss Engine, and one 75 H.P. High Speed Buckeye Engine. Have set one 130 H.P. Manning Boiler making all Steam connections, putting in Pumps, Steam Heater, 10,000 Gallon watertank elevated above the buildings, etc.

We have put in all Shafting, Pullies and Hangers, and have the entire Power Plant operating perfectly. We have also received from the Factory Five Cars of the Textile Machinery which is set up and running beautifully. The entire balance of our Texile Machinery 6 cars (making 11 cars in all) is now enroute to our Mill, and will no doubt be fully received by the end of this Month. We had hoped to be in full operation before this time, but the Factories could not complete the construction of our Machinery and ship it sooner.

I can not close without stating one other fact to you, namely; "That we have completed the entire work done, of every character, without calling in the help of a single Machinist, or other Mechanic except our own People." In other words the work has been done by "Colored Labor exclusively" under the direction of the Mill Officers. And this same force of Labor will be largely retained in the operation of the Mill. I do not doubt our ability to succeed

553

with this Labor for a single moment. Our Superintendant Mr. J. G. Fish of Boston is as confident as I am.

I wish to congratulate you on the splendid showing made in your published Report of last years work at Tuskegee. May this years work be as brilliant.

I shall be glad to hear from you again when your time permits.

Again thanking you for your kind suggestion, I remain   Very Truly Yours,

Joseph E. Wiley

TLS   Con. 261   BTW Papers   DLC.

1 Joseph E. Wiley was secretary of the New Century Cotton Mill, according to a 1902 city directory. BTW maintained a lifelong interest in the mill as an example of black business enterprise and as an effort to break the labor monopoly of whites as operatives in the southern cotton mills. He aided Wiley in securing northern capital investments.

A Dedication Speech at the Armstrong Manual Training School

[Washington, D.C., Oct. 24, 1902]

No name could more fittingly have been given to this new school, whose purpose it is to train the hand as well as the head and heart, than that of "Armstrong." Few are there in this country who doubt the fact that General Samuel Chapman Armstrong did more to teach American educators, North and South, and the men of all races, the value of hand training, than any other American who has ever lived.

In behalf of my race I thank the public school authorities of the District of Columbia for their foresight in providing for the black children of Washington this attractive, this substantial manual training building, and for its elegant equipment. In doing this I am sure that I voice the sentiments of the Negro people of the District. I would also especially thank Dr. W. Bruce Evans[1] for the energy, courage and faith which he has shown and which are responsible largely for what we now see here.

This building, with the spirit and good will of all classes of your citizens back of it, is the highest proof that we are learning to build from the bottom upward.

EDUCATION OF THE NEGRO

An analysis of the present occupations of the Negro race shows that a very large percentage is engaged in agriculture, in different trades, or some form of domestic service. While I would not by any means limit the occupations of the race to the industries named, yet since we must face the hard fact that these must constitute the industries of a very large proportion of our race for a number of years to come, we should face these conditions bravely, and prepare the race to perform the very best service. If we lay the foundation securely in these fundamental occupations, others and higher ones will come to us as a result. If the students who graduate from our schools are to live in agricultural communities, let us teach them all that they can learn about agriculture. If they are to become mechanics, let us help them to become the very best mechanics. If they are to engage in some form of house service, let us teach them to perform that service so well that no one else can improve upon it.

It seems to me that in a large degree the whole future of the race hinges upon the question as to whether it will make itself of such industrial value in the community where it is that the people will feel they cannot dispense with the services of the race.

HONOR AND HONEST WORK

Let us teach our children that it is more honorable for the Negro boy to become a first-class truck gardener in his community than to become a third-rate lawyer or school teacher, and that the time has come when a larger proportion of the educated men and women must learn to use their hands as well as their heads; that the time has come when every man who gets an education must not expect to live by preaching or by teaching. A large number of us should become creators of positions rather than mere seekers after positions already created by others.

In the present condition of our race it is very important that our public schools produce more workers and fewer talkers. There are some, I fear, who feel that the problems confronting the race can

555

be solved by a series of talks or orations. One thousand bushels of the best quality of potatoes produced by the hands of an educated Negro is worth more in solving our problem than dozens of abstract orations or newspaper articles. The Negro child, like the white child, is never safe until he has been taught a trade, until he has been taught that all forms of idleness are a disgrace, and all forms of labor, whether with the head or hand, are honorable.

At the Tuskegee Institute we teach the students, so far as possible, that it is a privilege for them to work and not a punishment. I pity the man or woman who has never learned to thank God at the beginning of each day for the opportunity of performing some service.

FOREIGN LABOR MENACE A SPUR

No one who keeps his eyes open to present conditions in this country will deny the fact that more money is being spent for the technical and industrial education of white boys and girls in every one of our states, with one or two exceptions, than is being spent for the same object for the education of colored people. If we do not wake up to our opportunities, do not put brains and skill into common occupations by whatever name called that are immediately about our doors, we shall find that a class of foreigners will come in and take our places, just as they have already done in relation to certain industries which I could name.

I believe that those who have been instrumental in securing this magnificent plant for manual training will find that it is one of the best paying investments that the District has ever made; that it will pay in added wealth, in added moral character to the community.

NO CAUSE FOR DISCOURAGEMENT

Speaking in a broader sense, no one can shut his eyes to the seriousness of the conditions which surround and confront my race in this country. These conditions are serious for the white man, serious for the black man. There is one law, however, which is universal and unchangeable, and that is that no man can injure another man or another race without degrading his own race. On the other hand, no man or race can lift up in the slightest degree the meanest member of another race without that individual or that race itself being broadened and strengthened and made more happy. I see nothing, notwithstanding the serious work that is to be done before our problem will be solved, I see nothing for discouragement, but everything for hope and for added energy and devotion.

THE WHITE MAN'S OPPORTUNITY

When I am asked as to the prospects of the race I put this question, and I put it here to-day with renewed emphasis: Can there be found anywhere in America any considerable number of men of my race who have received through education of head, of heart, and of hand, who have in any manner disgraced themselves or become criminals? So long as this three-fold education continues to make men of our race instead of brutes, I shall have the strongest hope for the future. No set of people ever had a greater opportunity to lift themselves up, and at the same time render service to a weak race, than is before the white people of America to-day.

Tuskegee Student, 14 (Nov. 1, 1902), 1.

1 Wilson Bruce Evans, born in Oberlin, Ohio, in 1867, moved to Washington, D.C., at the age of eight. He became a teacher in the District of Columbia schools in 1885. The son of a carpenter, he learned the carpenter's trade and cement work in the summers. After serving as principal of several elementary schools, he became the first principal of the Armstrong Manual Training School in 1902. The object of this school was to provide for black students a vocational alternative to the college preparatory program at the M Street High School, later called Dunbar High School. Evans was an admirer of BTW and frequently invited him to speak at his school.

From Alexander Walters

Winfall, N.C. Oct. 24th, 1902

Esteemed Friend: Your telegram of recent date has been forwarded to me.

Accept my most sincere thanks for its expressions of confidence etc.

I was of the opinion that the time had arrived when the country should be informed of the attitude of the President towards the actions of the Republican conventions of North Carolina and Alabama in excluding the colored delegates. While some of us were aware of the fact that the President did not endorse the formation of a white Republican organization in the South, the masses did not know it. I consulted our mutual friend, Mr. Thompson as to whether my visit to the President would interfere with any of your plans and he said that he thought not.

This will give you an idea why your telegram was so highly appreciated. Mr. Fortune and I find it utterly impossible to work harmoniously with Hon. Geo. H. White and Mr. Lawson, chief factors in our Legal Bureau located in Washington. What do you think of the following as a "Ste[e]ring committee!"

Judge Robt. H. Terrell, C. F. Adams, Geo. W. Lee, Bishops A. Walters, A. Grant, T. Thos. Fortune, W. H. Pledger, R. W. Thompson, Judson Lyons, & J. C. Dancy with yourself as chairman. Such committee can be gotten together by you in case of emergency, on short notice. If you favor the idea, but know of some persons who have more influence with the Administration than any of these named, why suggest them — it will be alright with me. Let it be understood that the whole affair be kept as secret as possible. Hoping to hear from you at your earliest convenience, I remain sincerely yours,

A. Walters

ALS   Con. 246   BTW Papers   DLC.

From William J. Stevens

Anniston, Ala., Oct., 24/02

My Dear Sir: I have just heard that you are on your way to Washington, and rumor has it for the purpose of getting Mr. Joe. Thompson appointed Collector of Revenue for this State. The appointment of Mr. Thompson would be a grave mistake, for the reason that he is not competent to fill this office. He has no following among the white people of the State, and a very small following among the colored people. He has not the ability to organize, and conduct successfully a political campaign. Such a campaign as we have in front of us. And in addition to this the negroes of this State would not be pleased with his appointment. You have made no mistake, and we do not wish you to make any, in your advices to the President. The rise or fall of the negro in Alabama depends in a great measure upon this one appointment. The Collector of Internal Revenue place, is the most powerful, political position in the State. Rumor has also reached me that Colonel Youngblood has been considered in connection with this appointment. Every colored, and almost every white man has absolute confidence in his ability, and power to conduct our interests. He is a friend of our people; refused to go into the Lily White Convention, advised Mr. Bingham and others against their political proceedings. I do not know that Colonel Youngblood would accept this position, nor do I speak for him, or by the suggestion of any one, save and except the consultation with some of the leading colored men of the State. Colonel Youngblood by his course has retained our confidence, and has not driven from himself any of the old political friends and associates. We will need his sort of men; men of his brain and capacity. I beg you to consider well what I say. The negroes of this State were never so firm, or united as they are now. Yours very truly,

Wm. J. Stevens

Confidential   This is for you and no one else.

TLS   Con. 244   BTW Papers   DLC.

From Portia Marshall Washington

Bradford, Mass.   Oct. 25 02

My dear father: I have been a very busy girl for the last week or two. My work is so interesting and I seem to be getting a long so well. Miss Knott[1] is very kind to me and has me up in her room so often to play to her. One night she asked me to play her to sleep. She is so fond of music and I am so glad to do this for her.

I had a very nice letter from Booker the other day. He seems to be fond of his school and I think he will improve by being with

Mr. Benner.[2] You remember, this school was near the place where I boarded.

I was so glad to see mamma — and was so sorry that she could not stay longer.

Last night, I talked to the girls about the work at Tuskegee — and every one seemed so interested. They educate a girl there — whose name is Martha Fairfax — I met her at Mr. P. J. Smith's house in Boston and she is a very nice girl. One of the teachers said she thought it wonderful the — com[m]and of language I had — I was some what amused because I have never done this before — altho — I have always known that I could do it. I hope that some day — you will let me do more of it. I used quite a number of your stories — but I told them that they were yours.

I like Bradford more and more and the girls too. *Every one* is nice and friendly. I have some very good friends among the *best* girls here.

Hoping to see you very soon — Believe me   Your loving daughter

Portia

ALS   Con. 245   BTW Papers   DLC.

[1] Laura Anna Knott (1863–1949), educated at Hamline University in St. Paul, Minn., and Radcliffe College (M.A., 1897), was principal of Bradford Academy from 1901 to 1918.

[2] Edward Augustine Benner was principal of the Wellesley School for Boys in Wellesley, Mass.

From Michael Ernest Sadler[1]

London, S.W. October 28th. 1902

Dear Mr. Booker Washington, I am much obliged to you for kindly sending me a copy of your 21st. Annual Report of the Institute. A week next Saturday I am going to give a lecture on the work of the Institute to the Sloyd Association of Great Britain & Ireland and shall be exceedingly glad if I can in any way communicate to other students of education in this country my own strong feeling of admiration for the work which is being done under your care.

In a forthcoming volume of Special Reports dealing with Industrial Education, one chapter will be devoted to the work at Tuskegee and Hampton, and I am doing all in my power to bring under the notice of educational administrators in different parts of our Empire the valuable guidance which they would obtain from the study of your methods. I have already written to educational friends in India, the West Indies and South Africa on the subject, and once again thank you for the opportunity you gave me of seeing so much of the life and work of the Institute.

Will you be so good as to remember my friend Mr. Heape[2] and myself to Mrs. Washington, and, Believe me, Yours sincerely,

Michael E. Sadler

TLS Con. 222 BTW Papers DLC.

1 Michael Ernest Sadler (1861–1943), a prominent and influential English educator, was professor of history and administration of education at Victoria University from 1903 to 1911 and vice-chancellor of Leeds University from 1911 to 1923. From 1895 to 1903 he edited and wrote a number of important reports on secondary education affecting England, several European countries, and the United States. In the 1930s Sadler warned of the overcrowding of universities and argued that the leadership of a country should come from a college-trained elite, which was being diluted by the growth of universities.

2 Possibly Walter Heape (1855–1929), who taught at Cambridge and published in the fields of embryology and physiology.

To Thomas Ruffin Roulhac

Tuskegee, Ala. Oct. 29, 1902

Dear Sir: I am very sorry to have to trouble you about any matter and also sorry that I did not have opportunity of seeing you before you went to Washington. I was in Washington on Friday and had a long talk with the President, and he told me rather fully about his having sent for you and the matters that he was going to place before you. The President doubtless has already told you, or will tell you, that it is his intention to place matters in this state pretty generally in the hands of Mr. J. O. Thompson and yourself. I told him that this would be perfectly agreeable to me and I had enough confidence in you to know that anything you and Mr. Thompson

do would be in the right direction. There are one or two suggestions of a practical nature which I want to suggest; First, it is of the
utmost importance that the Lily White movement in this state be
crushed out at once; any dilly dallying with it will prolong the
disease and permit it to spread in other states. I have given my personal pledge to the colored people throughout the country to the
effect that this movement will be crushed out. If it is not done when
the more important campaign two years from now comes the
colored people will have no faith in what I say. Second, it is important that no consideration be shown the present leaders, notably
Mr. Wellman[1] and Mr. Dimmick,[2] in the way of patronage until
they have renounced or cut loose from this movement. Anything
in the way of patronage will enable them to keep people thinking
that they represent the views of the President. Third, Mr. Wellman,
Mr. Dimmick and Mr. Bingham are now spreading the report over
the state to the effect that just as soon as the election is over and
there will be no immediate need for the Negro vote in the North
that the Lily Whites are going to be recognized. If there is the least
move in this direction after the election the results will be most
disastrous. Fourth, I very much hope that action will be taken before Congress meets and as soon after the election as possible. If
matters are delayed until Washington is full of senators and representatives there will be no predicting the amount of trouble the
President will be given, and besides the Lily White crowd in this
state are planning to make an onslaught on the President for recognition immediately after the election. Fifth, Knowing what the
President's intentions are regarding Mr. Thompson and yourself,
I take the liberty of urging him to go at once to Washington in
order that he and you may at some period during your visit have a
conference together with the President.

If you desire it, Mr. Thompson can go over with you pretty fully
the matter of the President's conversation with me. Yours truly,

[Booker T. Washington]

TL Copy Con. 272 BTW Papers DLC. Addressed to the Ebbitt House,
Washington, D.C.

1 W. I. Wellman of Huntsville was chairman of the Republican state executive
committee and a lily white.

2 Joseph W. Dimmick, born in Illinois in 1838, was a Union soldier mustered out
in Montgomery, Ala. He remained there and took a prominent part in Republican

politics. In 1869 President Grant appointed him postmaster of Montgomery. Captain Dimmick, as he was called, also had many business interests, including the First National Bank of Montgomery, of which he was president, and several iron works. He was a leader of the lily-white faction.

From Jefferson Manly Falkner

Montgomery, Ala., October 29, 1902

Personal.

Dear Sir: Your favor of October 28th, enclosing check for $100.00, to be used in building and maintaining the Confederate Soldiers' Home at Mountain Creek, is received, and for which I most heartily thank you. I will carefully observe the request made, and will avoid publicity, although, so far as I am personally concerned it would afford me pleasure to let your generosity and good will in the matter be known, & to show my appreciation of the same, but I appreciate what you say.

I have long since had the idea that all old differences, bitterness of any kind, feuds, quarrels, prejudices etc., should be treated as fossils of a different age. Such things have no place in the progress that is being made in this age. I believe that all good men are working for the same general purposes, the up-building of the country, and of all people, and to make life brighter and better in every way possible. I have no more sympathy or prejudice against the colored man than I have against the white man. The fact is I don't believe in prejudices. I don't believe in condemning one man for the fault of another individual. I don't believe in condemning a great race of people for what a few misguided people might do. I have always had the idea that those possessing sufficient intelligence and cultivation, and other blessings of life, to give them a firm footing and standing in this world, should always be ready to reach down a helping hand to those less fortunate, and pull them up, if need be, into a higher and purer atmosphere, thus performing the part of the good Samaritan. In other words, I believe in bringing the level upward and not downward. God in His wisdom and in His own way is working out a great problem among all the people, and in the end His plan will succeed, and there is no question in the minds of

the best element among us but what He is using you as an instrumentality not only for the betterment of your own race, but for the
upbuilding of the entire country. Again thanking you, I remain
Your friend,

J M Falkner

TLS   Con. 1   BTW Papers   DLC.

From John Stephens Durham

Philadelphia   Oct 30, 1902

Dear Doctor Washington: I saw the President last evening. I think
that he gave me quite a half hour. He spoke of the difficulties in the
way of making a place for me, assured me of his desire to do so and
gave me the impression that the matter is fixed in his mind.

I waited all morning in vain except that Mr. Cortelyou let fall
that the President had taken up my case with two Departments.
About two o'clock, the President came out and bade me return at
half past six in the evening. He was very cordial and in exuberant
spirits after his outing in the saddle. I gave him the Quay & Penrose[1] letters. He read them over and then said: "These letters are
all I wanted to settle your case. I am glad that you have brought
them. Mr. Washington has spoken to me about Mr. Anderson and
yourself. You know Mr. Anderson? Well I know him. I had occasion to look into his work as Racing Commissioner. He could not
get on with another Commissioner. I went into their differences
with thoroughness. I found that Anderson was right; but, what is
more important, I saw, in the course of my investigation the splendid efficiency with which Anderson was doing his work. I mean to
place him. Mr. Washington has indicated to me his preference for
you in the matter of selecting a responsible place for you two men
and, from your wider experience and Mr. Washington's confidence
in you, you are entitled to the preference."

I was deeply gratified to hear him speak so well of Anderson's
work and told him so. I thought that he had left nothing for me to
say further and I started to go. He detained me, however, and we
talked at length about tropical conditions, our foreign relation-

ships and growths and our national attitude towards these matters. When I left him, he asked me to accept an autograph copy of his book.

I told McKinlay and Terrell that I had had a charming reception, that the President had promised nothing more definite than that he was looking around to see what he could do; that he spoke well of Anderson and that he was going to send me a copy of his book.

Enclosed, please find copies of the letters written by Senators Quay and Penrose and a copy of my letter on the Roulhac appointment. Very truly Yours

John S. Durham

I think that I will write Mr. Ogden telling him of my visit to the President.

ALS Con. 225 BTW Papers DLC.

1 Boies Penrose (1860–1921) was U.S. senator from Pennsylvania from 1897 until his death.

From Timothy Thomas Fortune

Maple Hall, Red Bank, N.J. October 30, 1902

My Dear Mr. Washington: Your favor of the 28th instant was received, and I am surprised to find that you are back at Tuskegee, as I understood by a publication in The Student that you might be in the North for some time.

I am sorry that the editorial note to the Wimbs outgiving puzzles you as to my position and that you appear to think that it conflicts with the understanding we reached in the Roulhac appointment. I think you are mistaken in the latter matter and the former is stated clearly in the note. I do "understand and sympathize with your position" in the Roulhac matter, which I acquiesced in because it was represented that there was no Republican in the State capable to be appointed who was not tainted with Vaughanism; but while acquiescing in the Roulhac appointment I distinctly urged that a Negro be appointed at the same time to succeed Bingham, which you did not think well of and subsequently wrote me you had hit upon a Tuskegee Gold Democrat for the position. I stated clearly in your presence and that of Mr. Wimbs that I am opposed to the appointment of Gold Democrats to office, or any other sort of Democrat, as in the main they all think and act alike on the race question.

You will observe, outside of the Alabama reference, all of Mr. Wimbs' statements of facts are based upon National conditions, and that as I show in the note he is in error in each one of them. I stand by the note, and the explanation of my attitude towards Democratic appointments, and the race and the race press are with me. When I sought a conference with our men and Gen. Clarkson and Gen. Payne so that we could reach a definite understanding as to the policy of the party to be pursued in the South and the measure of appointments that would be conceded in the North and West, the matter was side tracked, and we are as ignorant as we ever were on those points.

Under the circumstances I am not endorsing editorially or otherwise the President or the Southern policy so far as it has been unfolded in North & South Carolina, Alabama, Mississippi, Louisiana and Texas. I am not fighting the battles of white men in the South but of black men, and I see nothing but humiliation in the systematic side tracking of our men for Democrats; and I shall hold myself in reserve up to the nomination of the next President, if the present condition of affairs continues, and then decide what the logic of the situation seems to dictate.

Personally, the President appears to have a grudge against me, although I have been faithful to him in all his public career, and was not responsible for the failure of the public meeting when he was a candidate for Governor, which he harps on whenever my name is mentioned, and if the situation on this point remains unchanged, we shall try conclusions at the proper time as I tried them with Blaine[1] in 1884. I am the least selfish of men, but when others try it on me, as the President has done for four years, I know well when and how to make my selfishness effective.

I desire to work in good sympathy and understanding with you, and I seek always to make myself plain to you in any matter we are concerned in and to live up to the conditions of any understanding we may reach in a given direction. I am sure I have lived up to all that was understood between us in the Roulhac appointment. Yours truly,

T. Thos. Fortune

TLS Con. 227 BTW Papers DLC.

¹ James Gillespie Blaine (1830–93).

From James Merville Pyne[1]

Gen'l. Del. St. Louis, Mo. Oct. 31, 1902

Dear Sir: My lot in life is to live by the sweat of my brow.

Like a good fellow, I volunteered to fight the Filipinos, but, be assured, it was no desire to kill Filipinos that led me to volunteer. "Right or wrong, my country," and this Filipino oppression is another instance where my country is wrong.

I made the trip around the world *via* Japan, Phil. Isle, Australia, So. Africa, and Europe in order to broaden my views. Like yourself I was born and reared in a lonely nook in Va. (Monroe Co. W.Va., I call it *Va.* because W.Va. has no right to existence as a sovereign State, if we are to go back to the Constitution). Like you, too, I *worked* my way in school. First, at Park College, Mo. and then two years at Columbia, Mo. The Mo. State Univ. is as dear to me as Hampton is to you.

My country has been wrong ever since Africans were sold into slavery at Jamestown, Va. in the year 1619. I say fundamentally wrong, sir, ever since that time.

The Fathers, in framing our Constitution, neglected to do their whole duty to mankind. As Mr. Jefferson said, the Negro was bound to be free.

The Negro was *not freed* by the Lincoln Eman. Procla. altho *that was* a beginning.

This is the broad assertion I wish to make to the world: The Negro will yet have his *country*, his *flag* and his *freedom* in truth and not in name only.

After looking about the world carefully, I find that a sort of immoral leprosy is fast tearing down the White race. In *my* country there are too many drones in the hive. The working bees will sooner or later sting them to death.

The Negro and the *poor* White man made the South rich; the North fell upon the South and stript her of her wealth. The North has the wealth to-day. Every dollar on earth represents *labor*. Who made the millionaires? The laborers, the Negroes, and the poor whites.

If I had all the dollars that I have earned at labor I would be well to do but, my dollars are in the hands of others — they are scattered 'round the world.

I was robbed by the legitimate thieves of the world. The capitalists, the brutish men. No individual that was ever born into the world has use for more than $50,000. Yet $500,000,000. will not satisfy some.

This class of men would perpetuate their kind, but *Nature* abhors them and they must perish.

A revolution, as you must have seen ere this time, is coming.

I pray that ballots and reason may suffice in this revolution, but, if bullets be necessary, let them come. We *ought* to be, I believe we *are*, brave enough to *fight* to regain our liberty.

Every *thinking* man knows that we, the majority, are industrial slaves to day; and, what a pity, the Republican party would draw the oriental people into this state of serfdom against their will. But, the Republican party has outlived its usefulness. It is, and has been for years, "sowing to the wind." The whirlwind is coming. The Republican, nor no other party that may spring up in this land can start, to "free the Negro, to act in the name of humanity, to benevolent[l]y assimilate" and then wind up by re-enslaving the great majority of both Negroes and Whites in this country, forcing the Cubans to come in, and oppressing the Filipinos because they resist, can ever, I say, survive as a party.

When I turn to the Democratic party I find it bound hand and foot by party dissentions. The majority in the Democratic party are controlled by the minority.

There is *one* great God some where. *He* is infinite. *We* are finite beings — "such stuff as dreams are made of." Darwin and the Evolutionists are right.

The God, and the Bible of the Jews has been tested and found insufficient to meet the demands of *our* day and age of the world. Why, sir, I wouldn't believe a Jew if he told me a pair of breeches was all wool. Much less would I select him to choose a God for me. Please don't misunderstand me. I reverently bow to the "Unknow[n] God" of the Greeks, to the "Great Spirit" of the Red Men. I am religious, but I can't comprehend the *infinite* and I refuse to guess or to allow the Jews to guess for me concerning my future state. Not one word, in my most sincere and honest judgment, of the Jewish Bible — Old & New Testaments — was written by inspiration of Almighty God. Let us accept all that seems reasonable and just and throw the rest to the wind.

I rather like the character of a Washington, no matter whether it be George or Booker.

George founded a great Nation for White men. I am wondering if Booker will not found a great Nation for Black men. The time is ripe.

Roosevelt is apt to do the unexpected, he might be your ally in this work.

You have the opportunity that comes to but few, very few men. Be courageous. Use this chance. Make use of this great opportunity and the world will applaud you.

Where shall I start, you ask? Right at Tuskegee, Ala. The southeast part of the U.S. and the West India Islands will make a good nation — a splendid home for the "Colored" race.

Whites and Blacks will no more mix and become one homogeneous people than cattle and hogs will.

We havn't reached that stage in our evolution yet, though there are rare creatures amongst us. I'm proud to say that I never had any trouble with a Negro in my life.

All my relations with them have been most friendly and I hope to continue in the same good way. I have seen the oppression of my fellow-men and noted it. I have seen the Filipino kicked, I have heard him called "nigger" and noted it. I do not measure men by religion or race but by their virtues, and I use virtue in the highest sense — the Roman sense. In Australia this cry has been started by the Whites: "Australia the White man's country"; and I hope Aust. may be made the White man's country.

I would rather live in a country where all are white because *I* am white. If I were Black I'd rather live where all are black.

Of course, we sometimes enjoy the fellowship of one another. I like to hear the "darky" songs, I like to see them dance, etc. I *hate* the hypocrisy at the North. There, they pretend to love the Negroes. For what? To get his labor cheap, and to get his vote in a few close states, that is all.

You know all about these things. It is useless for me to mention them.

The Negro has been accused of being ashamed of his race. Why should he be *ashamed* of his race? Mongolians, Indians, Malayans are all proud of their respective races. Negroes must grow out of this shame, if it be true that they are ashamed of their race.

One man in St. Louis doesn't believe a Negro has a *soul*. Well; that man can't prove that *he* has a soul.

The closest study and observation has left me, at the age of 33 yrs., to believe that neither Whites nor Blacks have souls, but that *all* are simply matter and go the eternal round like the water of the Sea. Look at the vegetable kingdom, then at the lower animals, then at man — the self-styled lord of creation.

From boyhood days when I used to swing in a grapevine swing on the side of those Virginia mountains I have been studying these things.

I think more, much more, than I can tell and I hope you will excuse this jumble of thoughts. I have just come in from a hard day's work handling freight for the Terminal R.R. Association of St. Louis at $1.50 per day and I am writing you for pastime. However, I have not intentionally expressed an erronious thought or belief entertained and I also hope that you, sir, will find a thought or two worthy of your consideration.

In truth I am the Negros' friend. That *one* great God has created me with a good heart, and a mind that would not knowingly entertain any kind of injustice.

I dislike to see two dogs fighting. I don't want to see the people of this country fighting unnecessarily, but I'm afraid a fight is brewing.

If you have time I would like to have your views briefly stated on the so-called "Negro Problem."

What, in your opinion, will the outcome be?

Will we amalgamate?

Will the wicked of both races perish? I am conscious of the fact that we, you and I, are the frail insects of a moment. Soon we'll be gone. Evolution will do wonders. Yours sincerely,

J. M. Pyne

ALS Con. 239 BTW Papers DLC.

1 James Merville Pyne (1868–1927) was originally named Payne but changed his name at the time he was commissioned a captain in the First West Virginia Volunteer Infantry at the beginning of the Spanish-American War. He was discharged in 1899 but enlisted a month later in the regular army as a private. He reached the rank of sergeant but was dishonorably discharged as a private in Aug. 1907 because of proof that he was a bigamist and a "dissolute" man. (Pension file, XC 3–023–223, DNA.)

From Timothy Thomas Fortune

Maple Hall, Red Bank, N.J. November 3, 1902

Dear Mr. Washington: I enclose a clipping from the Sun this morning,[1] a similar publication having appeared in several other New York daily papers during the past week. The publication, or the present version of it, appeared first in Trotter's paper in Boston several weeks ago. The facts as stated in the article donot tally with the version of the matter given to me by Portia at South Weymouth. She said to me that her failure to return to Wellesley was due to the fact that as she intended to go to the Boston Conservatory she did not make her application to the former in time to be accepted, and did not go to the Conservatory because restrictions imposed on her in the matter of domiciliation were objectionable. I have said nothing about the matter one way or the other, because I believed that it was started maliciously by the Boston skunk.[2] As it appears in the daily papers the publication does no good, and if it is incorrect, and Portia's statement to me is the correct one, a correction should be made authoritatively. If Portia's version is the correct one, and you desire me to make a correct version of it and furnish it to the New York Press, Associated and other, wire me to that effect early Wednesday morning, at the New York address and I will do it.

I have a short article on the editorial page of the Sun to-day on the wisdom of employing Afro-American labor in the Philippines, but can't send it as I have but the one copy here. I told Gen. Clarkson that I would go as a commissioner on the part of the Government to study the labor and trade conditions in the Philippines and the far East, and had in mind the shunting of our surplus labor to the Orient if I found the conditions such as to warrant such recommendations. In reply (Oct. 22) he said:

"I have your letter of yesterday with its suggestion as to yourself, which I think is practical. As soon as I go to Washington I will ascertain what can be done on this line."

I want to get out of the country for awhile because I donot care to get out of plumb with the party during the next twelve months, and I shall do this as things are now tending, and because I want to make enough money to pay my debts and start fresh in purely literary work.

I have not told you that I have not drunk anything for a long time and feel safe in saying that I never shall drink anything again. I was fortunate to find in my doctor here a friend who gave me [a] remedy that destroyed the taste for liquor of any sort. You need have no further fears on that score. I have none, I am very glad to say. Yours sincerely,

T Thos. Fortune

TLS   Con. 227   BTW Papers   DLC.

1 The article headlined "Miss Washington's Failure" stated that Portia Washington had failed her examinations at Wellesley College the previous year and was presently enrolled at Bradford Academy. The *Sun* reported that the faculty would only say that she did not qualify in music, but the students spoke of her presence having caused southern and northern factions among them. "Miss Washington proved to be a thorn in the flesh to the faculty," the article concluded, "on account of the newspaper notoriety which she gained. Articles signed by her and interviews on her reception at the college did not meet with the approval of her teachers." (New York *Sun*, Nov. 3, 1902, 1.)
2 William Monroe Trotter.

From James Sullivan Clarkson

New York, N.Y., November 3rd, 1902

Dear Doctor Washington: Your letters of the 30th and 31st received. It would be the very crown of folly for the colored men of

Alabama to go to work and, by organizing a colored party, justify the action of the Vaughan-Bingham crowd in organizing a white party. It would be almost hopeless to try and befriend people who would be so utterly blind to the truth as that action would involve.

I have also your letter giving copy of letter to Judge Roulhac. After the election I shall be in Washington for two or three days, and no doubt these matters will all be talked over. I should doubt a little whether Roulhac and Thompson would cover enough ground in the line of political sagacity and experience to constitute them sufficient advisers. Why should not W. F. Aldrich (from whom I have a very strong letter) be added to the advisory board? You should write me about this at once. If not Aldrich, then some other man of high standing and with the business elements and with the Republican party. I have no fear of any return of the "Lily Whites" to favor after the election. Indeed, what was told to you as to the displacement of Bingham is the amplest guarantee of that. Sincerely yours,

James S. Clarkson

TLS   Con. 261   BTW Papers   DLC.

From Mary McLeod Bethune[1]

Palatka, Fla., Nov. 3rd 1902

Honored Sir: I hope a note of this kind may not greatly surprise you, as a man in your sphere must expect such.

I am engaged in a Mission work in this town and I greatly desire your interest in it. It is an Interdenominational work therefore has no support. It is a work that is most sadly needed to be done, and it takes great sacrifices to get it in shape. I have a rented room where I gather the poor an[d] neglected children and teach them daily. Aside from this I do general city mission work, the jail work included. I have no support what ever save some few of the children who are able to pay a little tuition. Now I would like to ask you, would you recommend this humble work to some friend asking their assistance? Would you yourself make a donation toward helping us secure an organ for the Mission room? Do you know any friend who would even send a few clothing to be used for the poor? God has wonderfully blessed you and used you and I know He will be pleased to have you lend your influence towards the sustenance of this work.

I trust you may consider well before answering. Very respectfully,

(Mrs.) Mary McLeod Bethune

ALS   Con. 222   BTW Papers   DLC.

1 Mary McLeod Bethune (1875–1955), born on a farm near Mayesville, S.C., secured an education at a Presbyterian mission school and at Scotia Seminary in Concord, N.C., and spent a year at the Moody Bible Institute in Chicago on a scholarship. After teaching at several small institutions, she founded Daytona Normal and Industrial School for Negro Girls (later Bethune-Cookman College) in Daytona Beach, Fla., in 1904. Running the school remained her principal activity until the late 1920s, but she was also a leading Negro clubwoman. She was president of the National Association of Colored Women from 1926 to 1930, but she later became discouraged about the inadequacy of the organization's response to the Depression crisis and organized a rival group, the National Council of Negro Women, in 1935. At about the same time she began to play the role of gadfly to the New Deal administration. President Franklin D. Roosevelt appointed her director of the Office of Minority Affairs (later Division of Negro Affairs) of the National Youth Administration. She sought through this position to secure federal aid to improve the educational opportunities of black students. She also sought, through the Federal Council on Negro Affairs (also known as the "Black Cabinet"), through the National Negro Conference, and through her friendship with Eleanor Roosevelt, to influence New Deal policy toward blacks. By temperament an activist, Bethune picketed stores in Washington that would not hire blacks, testified in behalf of the Fair Employment Practices Commission, helped select officer trainees for the Women's Army Auxiliary Corps during World War II, and was called a Communist by Representative Martin Dies for her participation as an officer in the Southern Conference for Human Welfare, a charge she contemptuously dismissed. A warm, earthy woman with a rich southern accent, she was a persuasive advocate of racial justice. Lester B. Granger of the National Urban League said of her: "Mrs. Bethune had the most marvelous gift of affecting feminine helplessness in order to attain her ends with masculine ruthlessness." (Holt, *Mary McLeod Bethune*, 216.) Bethune frequently said that she had built her school on the Tuskegee model, and BTW visited the institution at least once, about 1912.

To Francis Ellington Leupp

Tuskegee, Ala., Nov. 4, 1902

My dear Mr. Leupp: When I last saw the President a little more than a week ago, he suggested that some of my friends had the feeling that it was not wise for him to consult with me about matters in the South as much as he does. Of course the whole matter has been more or less mooted in the Southern papers. Since seeing the President I have talked frankly with several level headed Northern men such as Mr. Wm. H. Baldwin, Jr., and several Southern men about the matter, and all have agreed that the proper thing is to face the matter frankly and give out such a statement as the one which I enclose to you.[1]

My special object in writing to you is to ask if you will not be kind enough to see the President and place this statement before him at a time when he can read it and give it some consideration and find out if there is anything in it to which he objects, if there is not I am going to give it out to the Southern papers. This statement I think will clear the whole atmosphere and really place me in a position to be of more service to the President in the future than I have been in the past.

It is my purpose to give the matter out on the same day to about a dozen papers scattered through the South. Yours truly,

Booker T. Washington

TLdS   Con. 261   BTW Papers   DLC.

[1] See To the Editor of the Birmingham *Age-Herald*, Nov. 24, 1902, below.

To Theodore Roosevelt

Tuskegee, Alabama. November 5, 1902

Personal.

My dear Mr. President: Some days ago I sent you a letter recommending Mr. W. Frank Russell[1] for the position of Postmaster at Tuskegee in case Mr. J. O. Thompson, the present Postmaster, was appointed to the position of Collector of Internal Revenue.

I now wish to withdraw my recommendation of Mr. Russell for good reasons and to recommend Mr. John S. Webb[2] in his stead. Mr. J. O. Thompson unites with me in this action.[3]

Mr. Webb is a good strong man and will be of much help to us and the party in the future. Yours truly,

Booker T. Washington

TLS   Theodore Roosevelt Papers   DLC.

1 W. Frank Russell, a white farmer, was born in Alabama in 1852.
2 John S. Webb, a white Tuskegee businessman who sold furniture, coffins, buggies, and harnesses, was postmaster of Tuskegee from Nov. 11, 1902, to Jan. 1906.
3 See Thompson to BTW, Oct. 6, 1902, Con. 243, BTW Papers, DLC.

To Theodore Roosevelt

Tuskegee, Alabama. November 6, 1902

Personal.

My dear Mr. President: I sent you a telegram this morning suggesting that you not commit yourself to Judge Roulhac or give him instructions regarding political matters in this state until after Gen. Clarkson and I have had opportunity to confer. The matter of an advisory board in this state is of the greatest importance, and I am rather confirmed in the opinion that while Judge Roulhac is going to make a fine District Attorney and is a high clean man, he does not possess that temperament of mind to enable him to do the kind of work that is needed to be done in this state; he does not know the persons that are to be touched and influenced, and besides, there are many influential Republicans who rather resent the idea of a Democrat being made in any sense a referee. I have a solution for the whole matter which I can suggest to Gen. Clarkson and afterwards the General will see you.[1]

I was in New Orleans a few days ago and had a long conference with Mr. Edgar S. Wilson. He is planning to see you in regard to several important matters soon. Every time I see him I am the more convinced of his sterling integrity and hard work and supreme devotion to your interests. It is only a matter of a short while, I think, before he will have matters wholly in his hands so far as the Republican Committee is concerned. If he can have the appointment of two colored men as Deputy Revenue Collectors and if later on Mr. Mollison can be taken care of, matters will be in fine shape in that state. Yours truly,

Booker T. Washington

TLS   Theodore Roosevelt Papers   DLC.

1 In a draft BTW wrote on Nov. 4 but did not sign and apparently did not send to Roosevelt, he said: "I believe that the more you can *concentrate matters in Mr. Thompson's hands the better will be the results.* If you want some one else to act with Mr. Thompson, I would advise you to look into the qualifications of Mr. Oscar R. Hundley, of Huntsville, Ala., for this purpose." (Con. 281, BTW Papers, DLC.)

To Timothy Thomas Fortune

Tuskegee, Ala., Nov. 6, 1902

My dear Mr. Fortune: I have your good letter of recent date and have sent you a telegram reading as follows:

"Unless you feel that as a newspaper man you must notice the matter in your paper, I prefer to make no statement regarding the matter as it was started by those Boston people mainly for the purpose of drawing me into a controversy. I dislike exceedingly to discuss private affairs in the papers."

Perhaps you did not know that the substance of this dispatch was sent to the South through the instrumentality of these same parties two weeks ago and several of the Southern papers used it, but the more friendly ones such as the Atlanta Constitution and the Montgomery Advertiser, refused to use it and telegraphed me about it. I state the matter as it stands for your own personal benefit. My daughter went to Wellesley for the purpose of taking a special course in music. No students are admitted into the boarding halls unless they are in the regular college department and taking the regular college course; of course she could not board in the hall, and partly on that account and partly for the reason that we later decided to have her take a regular seminary course we decided to send her to Bradford Academy where she is taking the regular seminary course and is having excellent success in her work. I have such a dislike of discussing my private matters in the newspapers that so far. . . .

[Booker T. Washington]

TLf Con. 225 BTW Papers DLC.

To Timothy Thomas Fortune

Tuskegee, Ala., Nov. 6, 1902

Dear Mr. Fortune: In addition to what I said today in my letter in regard to my daughter, I forgot to say that I understand some of the papers have given the impression that she was at Wellesley during the present term and was turned away. The whole matter relates to the last school session and not to this school session. She was there during the whole of last school session. Yours truly,

Booker T. Washington

TLS Con. 225 BTW Papers DLC.

From Timothy Thomas Fortune

Maple Hall, Red Bank, N.J. November 6, 1902

My Dear Mr. Washington; Your telegram of yesterday was received here this morning. I have no disposition to have anything to say about the Portia matter, and I quite approve your disinclination to discuss your private affairs in the newspapers. But the publications have been so at variance with what Portia told me that I thought it might well be good to state the facts. But I see she has a statement in the Sun yesterday which does not tally with any of the other publications or with what she told me. Of course I shall have nothing to say about the matter not authorized by you.

I took Mr. A. C. Kaufman of Charleston to see Gen. Clarkson yesterday and he put in some strong work for Crum and laid out

Capers in awful shape. He gave a good statement of the situation in South Carolina. Yours truly,

T. Thos. Fortune

TLS Con. 227 BTW Papers DLC.

From Francis Jackson Garrison

Boston Nov. 6, 1902

Dear Mr. Washington: I am much obliged to you for sending me a copy of the Atlanta Journal containing the resolutions on Prof. Sledd by the senior class at Emory College. I cannot help smiling at the fact that Prof. Sledd seems to have won their hearts especially because he was with them in athletics, and coached the foot ball team, which goes to show that the affections of the Southern college boy are reached no less surely than those of the Northern boys through their love of sport!

You seem to keep as closely in touch with the Southern press, and as close an eye upon it, as if you were an editor. I am constantly surprised by the way in which you sweep the field and the horizon North and South with your telescope, and keep in touch with events affecting the great question. Yours very truly,

Francis J. Garrison

TLS Con. 228 BTW Papers DLC.

From George Bruce Cortelyou

White House Washington DC Nov 6 [1902]

Telegram received. Do you desire Thompson appointment in place of Bingham held up. What does Charleston protest against Crum mean it is impossible to get any respectable white Support for him in Charleston.

Geo B Cortelyou
Secty

HWSr Con. 225 BTW Papers DLC.

To George Bruce Cortelyou

[Tuskegee, Ala.] Nov-7-1902

Do not want Thompson appointment held up. Hope it can be made at once. Do not forget to appoint Mr. John S. Webb at same time as postmaster at Tuskegee. My telegram regarding Judge Roulhac related to making advisory committee in this state stronger and more useful. Will advise fully in this matter after seeing Gen. Clarkson. Am sorry about opposition to Dr Crum. Think it based on color and not character. His case would be greatly helped with some white support.

Booker T. Washington

TWSr Con. 225 BTW Papers DLC. Second sentence added in E. J. Scott's hand.

From James Sullivan Clarkson

New York, N.Y., November 7th, 1902

Dear Dr. Washington: Just as I have a call to go to Washington to meet the President tomorrow afternoon, I have your dispatch of last night and your two letters of 5th, one about Judge Roulhac's inexperience as to politics and suggesting Mr. Hundley as a desirable man in his place, the other about Wilson and Mississippi. I agree with you that Roulhac may be entirely competent as a Judge and yet not be a good politician. He also lacks experience and acquaintance in the Republican party. My own opinion is that no one man should be left to decide things for a whole State. In the first place, no man is broad enough to cover a whole State; in the second place, a public official could not attend to all the details without taking his attention from official matters; and in the third place, it would excite opposition and create jealousy. I should say that Captain Scott[1] and W. F. Aldrich, as well as Mr. Hundley, should be taken into a sort of conference, letting Thompson have the initiative of advising with these men. I have an exceedingly strong letter from Mr. Aldrich, giving his adhesion to the President beyond any recall. It seems to me that Aldrich represents such a large number of necessary men in Alabama and such large interests, that he ought to be given this consideration, and I believe that his friendship and advice would be valuable and satisfactory.

I have just wired you of my visit to Washington tomorrow, saying you could wire me at the Richmond Hotel if you have anything further to suggest immediately. Sincerely yours,

James S. Clarkson

TLS Con. 261 BTW Papers DLC.

[1] Charles Herrington Scott (b. 1870), a Republican politician from Montgomery, was a partner with his father in a mineral and timber land business. He was a captain in the Third Alabama Volunteers during the Spanish-American War. In 1903 Theodore Roosevelt appointed him referee for Alabama. He served on the Republican national committee in 1904, and ran unsuccessfully for governor of Alabama on the Progressive ticket in 1910.

From Timothy Thomas Fortune

Maple Hall, Red Bank, N.J. November 7, 1902

Dear Mr. Washington: I enclose you Mr. Smith's letter and one from Mr. Brown. I have written Mr. Smith that I would not proceed further in the matter until I had consulted you. In view of the situation as Mr. Smith and Mr. Brown present it, what course do you suggest that I shall take?

Your letter of the 5th instant was received, and I have read the enclosure with a great deal of interest. It seems to me to be in proper taste and to be justified by the condition of affairs. As I have come to understand your position, you donot offer the President any advice or suggestion unless he first invites such. If that is the case you cannot state it too plainly and bluntly, as the contrary opinion very generally prevails among our men and the white press and people as well; so that your present position is a false one and highly prejudicial to you, as responsibility for most Southern appointments and all Afro-American appointments is charged against

your account, whether good or bad. And most of our men all over
who want positions under the Government and fail to succeed
place responsibility for the failure upon you. I advised you, at the
Grand Union, after the White House dinner, to stand to your guns
in the political relation with the President which had developed up
to that time, but I donot believe that such course has strengthened
you in your educational work or with the race at large or with the
Southern white people, the latter naturally resenting the belief that
you are the dispenser of political patronage in the Southern States,
and this belief is very general among all classes of the people.

Under the circumstances, therefore, it seems to me that your
proposed outgiving is in the right direction. Yours truly,

T. Thos. Fortune

TLS Con. 227 BTW Papers DLC.

From Francis Ellington Leupp

Washington, Nov. 9. 1902

My dear Mr. Washington: I took your proposed newspaper publication to the President as soon as I received it, but have not written
you because I made up my mind from his manner that his first decision would not prove conclusive, & I knew you wished to follow
his ideas in this matter.

The sequel showed I was right. He sent for me last night, and
asked me to say that, while he approved the matter, purpose & style
of your card, and had passed the whole of it at the first reading, the
longer he thought of it the more convinced he was that it would be
a mistake to say anything about your "dictating" appointments to
him. "There are some things," he added, "that are to be *assumed*,
like a reputable man's honesty, and it is just as well to ignore the
possibility of anything else." I am not wholly of his opinion, in
view of the fact that the charge has been made, & that your card
simply rules it out as absurd; but of course his wish must govern.
He thinks that you had better lay your whole stress on the fact that

you do not *thrust* advice upon him, but merely respond when called into consultation, & that, after you have given him your judgment, he makes up his own mind independently. Hastily yours

Francis E. Leupp

ALS Con. 232 BTW Papers DLC. E. J. Scott wrote in the margin beside the last sentence: "Here is the gist of the letter! E J Scott 11/11."

From Belton Gilreath

Birmingham, Ala. Nov., 10th., 1902

My Dear Sir: Referring to our recent conversation in Tuskegee, in regard to the political situation.

I have been some-what interested in the out-come of our state election, for the Governor-ship. I did not expect to see the republican candidate elected but I was some-what interested as to how many votes he was going to receive.

I have been anxious to see our people get rid of prejudice, and be in a position where they could vote according to their convictions.

As far as I am concerned I suppose that I am an independent in politics. I have not voted but once in five years, and that was for Senator Morgan, whom I know well personally. I was not ready to vote the republican ticket, and I could not conscientiously vote the democratic ticket on account of their free silver and free trade tendencies.

I had hoped some-time ago that I would be able to vote for some clean strong republican for Governor; but the lily white movement so called drove me away.

I understand that the republican candidate Mr. Smith[1] was a good reliable man; but with the conditions surrounding him and the present status of the republican party in this state, I did not see how he could succeed.

Their effort to put the negro out of the republican party in the South was so unjustifiable, and so unwise and has done so much harm that I do not see how they can recover from its bad effects soon. It seems to me that they will have to rub out and start over again; and "that time also with its softening influences will have to intervene."

As far as I am concerned, I look on the negro as the most sincere republicans that we have in the South, and that they represent the most noble and self-sacrificing part of it. And I might state also that I look on the Southern republicans who went into the republican party years ago to get office, the most insincere, and the most ignoble part of it.

This being the case I do not see how a staunch republican party can be formed in this state with the latter class, as leaders, or in control.

In looking back over our troubles since the war, I am inclined to believe that the most of the trouble and bitterness among the best white people of the South and the negroes, was caused by the renegade republicans, of the north who came south, and the renegade southerners of the south who joined them, after the war to get office. These two classes in their scrambles for office and spoils after the war, brought about I think the most of the bitterness, that existed between the best white people of the south, and the honest negroes, as above stated.

Now I expect to see in the future some of the negroes of the south voting, at times with the democrat, as well as some of the southern democrats voting with the republicans.

Whenever we get so we look at issues and the character of the men representing them, as well as the party advocating them; then I will begin to feel as if we are growing. And I believe that the recent split between the Lily whites, and the negroes will finally be productive of good, for the reason that it will bring about such a diagnosis of the case, as will enable us to know what to do.

And I think if President Roosevelt will be as careful of his appointments, in the south, in the future, as he has been in the past, that it will result, in putting the republican party on such a basis, as our best people will be justified in supporting it, whenever their convictions point that way. Very truly yours,

Belton Gilreath

P.S. I write my views to you very hastily this morning, in order that you might know how the minds of some of our business men are operating, thinking that it might be of some value to you, in forming your conclusions on such political questions as may confront you, in future.

B. G.

TLS Con. 228 BTW Papers DLC.

1 John Antony Winston Smith, a Birmingham lawyer, was the son of the Reconstruction governor William Hugh Smith.

To Emmett Jay Scott

Wilkes-Barre, Pa., Nov 12th. [1902]

Telegraph me Philadelphia what effect use of my name in Thompson case has had in southern papers.

W.

TWIr Con. 541 BTW Papers DLC.

From Emmett Jay Scott

Tuskegee Ala   Nov 12th 1902

Matter already attended to will send you papers with announcement am unable to discover any untoward effect from publication, was montgomery yesterday and found no unfavorable sentiment will keep you advised.

Emmett J. Scott

HWSr Con. 541 BTW Papers DLC.

To Edwin Anderson Alderman

New York City, N.Y. November 16, 1902

My dear Dr. Alderman: I thank you for your kind letter of the 10th and for what you say concerning my address.[1] More and more I believe that if the best white people and the sensible colored people will hear each other's views face to face many of the seeming difficulties will disappear. All of us are very grateful to you for the movement which you have started in New Orleans.

I have directed my secretary to send you the notes of the meeting which was held at Straight University.[2] On reading these notes I find that they are not as full and accurate as I should like them to be; evidently the reporter was not quite up to his business, but I think you can get some information from these. Yours truly,

[Booker T. Washington]

TLc Con. 245 BTW Papers DLC.

[1] On Oct. 31, 1902, BTW spoke in New Orleans under the auspices of the Southern Education Board to overflow audiences of whites and blacks in two separate meetings and then spoke a third time to an interracial audience. He also conducted a meeting of Louisiana black teachers held at Straight University later the same day. Edwin A. Alderman of the Southern Education Board had been worried about the success of the meetings and feared that southern social conventions might be broken that would lead to a racial incident. The fact that Alderman introduced BTW to the mixed audience caused some people in New Orleans to refuse to send their sons to Tulane, according to William H. Baldwin, Jr. (See Baldwin to BTW, Aug. 10, 1903, below.) The meetings, however, were highly successful, and Alderman wrote BTW praising him for his speech, which he described as "flawless in its tact and wisdom." (Nov. 10, 1902, Con. 219, BTW Papers, DLC.)

[2] Notes on a Conference of Black Teachers, Oct. 31, 1902, Con. 242, BTW Papers, DLC. BTW urged blacks to get school officials to upgrade school buildings, lengthen school terms, and hire the best possible teachers. He also encouraged black parents to take a greater interest in school affairs.

From James Sullivan Clarkson

New York, N.Y., November 17, 1902

Dear Doctor Washington: I have your letter of the 16th. It would have been a pleasure to have had a short visit with you as you passed through, but I fancy that the Alabama cause is now committed largely beyond our hands, except as those to whom the whole matter has been confided may deem it best to consult with us at intervals. I have had two or three nice letters from Thompson, by which I see that he is guided by the right spirit in taking up his work. He and Aldrich and Scott now have such an opportunity as few men have to create the right condition in an important State. It will require tact, industry and skill, for they should and no doubt will bend every effort to harmonize the party in order to get thorough control of it. The plan to work with the State Committee and [in] putting the party back on its proper footing is, I think, the right one, but it should be carried out with great discretion and a constant desire to heal up things rather than to create new factions. You and I are responsible to the extent of having recommended the President to his emphatic action and also in having recommended the men whom he has accepted as advisers. I covet very much the success of the movement, for I feel keenly the sense of my responsibility, and mine is not nearly as large as yours. Sincerely yours,

James S. Clarkson

TLS   Con. 252   BTW Papers   DLC.

From William Henry Baldwin, Jr.

N.Y. [City] November 18, 1902

My dear Mr. Washington: I send you herewith a copy of the original paper which you wrote, together with the final copy suggested, after a conference with certain of your friends last evening.[1]

Dr. Buttrick has just returned from the South. He reported to me that there is a great deal of criticism on account of your alleged political activities. I went to Mr. Ogden's office and there met Mr. Peabody, Dr. Frissell and Dr. Buttrick, and I took the liberty of showing them the paper that was written by you on Monday morning. All agreed that a statement should be made, and all agreed that the draft which I enclose would do good and could do no harm.

You will notice, first, that this is now not too long for anybody to read; second, there is nothing apologetic in it; and third, that although it is a good statement and safe, it may lack some of the sharpness of style which you show in your writings; but I do not believe that, under the circumstances, you could afford to put out a statement like the first one which you submitted to me. I also believe that the advice of your real friends is a good thing to take at this time. You may wish to add something to this statement, or perhaps change it in some respects, but I should be very cautious in any changes that you may make. There is a clause in parenthesis on the second page which might just as well be left out, but you use your own judgment in all these matters.

I am sending a copy of this letter to both addresses, care Dr. Washington Gladden, Columbus, Ohio, and also care President C. F. Thwing,[2] Western Reserve University, Cleveland, Ohio. Yours very truly,

W H Baldwin Jr

TLS Con. 792 BTW Papers DLC.

1 Baldwin edited BTW's statement on political involvement and returned a draft with this letter. This was the version that BTW released for publication with only a few minor changes. (See To the Editor of the Birmingham *Age-Herald*, Nov. 24, 1902, below.) The one sentence that Baldwin objected to, that BTW omitted before publication, was: "A great part of my life has been devoted to teaching our people that industry, intelligence, and sensible relations with the white race will always be rewarded."

2 Charles Franklin Thwing (1853–1937) was president of Western Reserve University from 1890 until 1921.

From James Sullivan Clarkson

New York, N.Y., November 20, 1902

Dear Doctor Washington: I have your note as to Mr. Aldrich having received no notification of his appointment on the Advisory Committee of Alabama, and I have had a similar letter from Captain Scott. I do not know how notification would be given in this matter except that Scott and Aldrich would be notified through Thompson. Probably the first notification they would have would be on having something referred to them. That used to be the way under President Harrison, and I presume the practice is the same now. I have replied to Mr. Scott in the same tenor as this. I think there is no doubt about the matter, as the Postmaster General refers to it and it has also been mentioned in the public press.

I presume you have heard that I was able to secure for T. Thomas Fortune a Special Agency, a mission to the Philippines and Hawaii, which he desired. He has been in to see me, and, for once, his face has shown happiness. The President seemed not only willing to accept of this opportunity to show consideration to Fortune, but even eager to do it and said it was a mission that might result to the great good of the country. Some one who has the nearness and also the courage, should make Fortune understand that this is his opportunity and that he must keep himself strictly in the middle of the road; if he does and uses the fine ability that he possesses, he will build up a place for himself at the head of some bureau; and I have tried to impress him with this fact, but it needs some one to talk to him more plainly than I have any license of friendship to do. The President and I discussed the matter of his habits, and he asked if I was willing to help take the responsibility in giving him this chance to show how he could bear himself, and I said I was. He must realize that in standing sponsors for him, we have taken such a responsibility as he will take a gentleman's delight in honoring. Sincerely yours,

James S. Clarkson

TLS Con. 223 BTW Papers DLC.

From Francis Ellington Leupp

Washington, Nov. 21. /02

My dear Mr. Washington: I am very much alarmed lest the President make a costly tactical mistake by not appointing Crum after all that has been said about it. If *Crum* does not go in, *no* colored man does, and the moral which the President has tried so hard to expound is dead lost!

The scandal of 1892, that Crum went to Minneapolis a Blaine man & was brought over by a promise of the post office to vote for Harrison, has been hurled at the President & is shaking his purpose. I told him, a week ago Saturday night, that this could be raised against Crum, but he did not seem to "sense it" then.

As Crum is your candidate, in the sense we both understand, I assume that you sifted this story enough to convince you that it was false. Crum starts tomorrow from Charleston, for an interview with

589

the President here. I have told McKinlay to wire him to bring in everything he can in the way of disproof of the scandal. Do whatever *you* can, if you are convinced that the man is all right.

No matter how good the President's motive, such a withdrawal at this stage, & following his trip through the South, could be interpreted everywhere there as a backdown; and if he once yields now on the principle he has espoused, no amount of printed explanation will set him right. It is for *his* sake that I want to see him stand firm, both actually and in appearance. Hastily yours —

Francis E. Leupp

ALS Con. 233 BTW Papers DLC.

From William Edward Burghardt Du Bois

Atlanta, Ga., November 22, 1902

My Dear Mr. Washington: We have at last got a permanent committee formed here and our first work is to push the sleeping car matter before the inter-state commission. I think that we had better get Smith of New York to take it up. We are going to raise money here and are going to do three things:
1. Present personally a signed petition to Lincoln of the Pullman Co.
2. Push case before the Inter-state Commission.
3. Go to courts.

Are you still disposed to stand part of the expense, and if so, what part? What is Smith's address? Sincerely yours,

W. E. B. Du Bois

TLS Con. 225 BTW Papers DLC. E. J. Scott docketed the letter with the remark: "Gave him Smiths address. Said you'd write. EJS 11/25."

To the Editor of the Birmingham *Age-Herald*

Tuskegee, Alabama   November 24, 1902

I notice that several newspapers have recently connected my name with political matters in such a manner as to show that my position is misunderstood. I desire, therefore, to make the following statement:

My life work is the promotion of the education of my race. It is well known that I have always advised my people that it is of supreme importance, at this period of their development, that they should concentrate their thought and energy on the securing of homes, the cultivation of habits of thrift, economy, skill, intelligence, high moral character, and the gaining of the respect and confidence of their neighbors, white and black, both in the south and in the north. From such teaching and counsel, no influence can ever divert me.

Whatever conferences I have had with the President or with any public official have grown out of my position, not as a politician, but as an educator. It should be borne in mind that there are about nine millions of negroes in the United States, who are liable under the law for taxes and military service, and who are punishable for infraction of the law. These people at present have no member of their race in the national law-making body, and it is right that those charged with making and executing the laws of the land should at times seek information directly from members of the negro race when their interests and their relations with the whites among whom they live are concerned.

Under no circumstances could I seek to promote political candidacies or volunteer information regarding men or measures, nor have I done so in the past; but because of the importance I have always sought to place upon education and industry among my people as the bases of friendly relations between the races, there may be occasions in the future as there have been in the past, when, if I am so requested, I can give information about men and measures, which would tend to promote such friendly relations between the races, such information it is my duty to give when it is asked for.

At every proper opportunity I say to the youth of our people that they will make a mistake if they seek to succeed in life by mere political activity or the hope of holding political office. Now and then, however, public questions affecting our interests arise which are so fundamental and far-reaching that they transcend the domain of politics. When such questions present themselves, in justice to my race, I make my position known and stand for what I see to be the right.

We cannot elevate and make useful a race of people unless there is held out to them the hope of reward for right living. Every revised constitution throughout the southern states has put a premium upon intelligence, ownership of property, thrift and character.

As an educator, and not as a politician, I strive in every honorable and rational way to encourage the wise and enduring progress of my people; for if all inspiration and hope of reward is to be denied them, they will be deprived of one of the greatest incentives to intelligence, industry, and righteousness. On the other hand, if they are encouraged in sensible and conservative directions they will grow year by year into contentedness and added usefulness.

Booker T. Washington

Birmingham *Age-Herald*, Nov. 28, 1902, 1. The statement appeared in major newspapers throughout the country. It also appeared in the *Tuskegee Student*, 14 (Dec. 6, 1902), 1.

J. C. May [Wilford H. Smith] to R. C. Black [Emmett Jay Scott]

N. Y. C. Nov. 24th, 1902

My Dear Friend: Your valued favor containing six C's came duly to hand for which I thank you many times. I am momentarily expecting the vacuum to be filled by the Association. As soon as that is arranged I will move on the enemies works as rapidly as possible. Very truly yours,

J. C. May

TLSr   Con. 236   BTW Papers   DLC.

From Richard Theodore Ely[1]

Madison, Wis. Nov. 25, 1902

My dear Sir: I have often wished that I could give some financial aid to your school, but even at the best a professor's salary is very limited in proportion to the demands made upon it, and I have not been able to do so. It has occurred to me that perhaps I could render some assistance to two of your girls, by offering them an opportunity to work at larger wages than they would receive in the South, and to lay up some money. At the same time, it would be an assistance to me, that is, it would be mutual. I could give employment to a competent cook, and a second girl who could help take care of two children, paying their transportation to Madison, Wisconsin, and paying the second girl \$12 and the cook \$14 a month to begin with, and increasing somewhat the remuneration as time goes on. The girls would be kindly treated, and we would desire those who would respond to such treatment. They would have a very pretty room, heated, with a beautiful view, also heated bath-room. Each one would have an entire afternoon and evening each week, that is from about 3 P.M. on, and each one would have every other Sunday afternoon. The girl who stays in Sunday afternoon has the privilege of going to church in the morning. I think if the girls were studiously inclined that they would find some opportunity for study. If I have not made everything perfectly plain, I shall be glad to answer any questions. I may say that I would like the girls at once, and should rely upon your judgment. We could not have those lacking experience. When I was connected with the Johns Hopkins University we had colored people with us, and we understand them, and I think that they liked us.

I do not know whether such arrangements as I have outlined are made by you, or cared for. At any rate, I venture to write to you about this matter, and should be glad to have the favor of an early reply.

With best wishes for success in your work, I remain, Yours very truly,

Richard T Ely

TLS Con. 226 BTW Papers DLC. E. J. Scott docketed the letter with the remark: "Mrs. W. This man is one of the great *ones* of the country! Can you do anything for him. EJS 11/28."

1 Richard Theodore Ely (1854–1943), an economist, was a professor at the University of Wisconsin from 1892 to 1925.

From Joseph Oswalt Thompson

Tuskegee, Ala., Nov. 26, 02

Dear Sir, Your letter and the marked copy of the "Outlook" received; for which please accept my thanks.

I turn the Post Office over to Mr. Webb tomorrow and go to B'ham Friday, where I will meet Messrs. Aldrich and Scott and dispose of all matters now pending which require our attention as Referees.

I called to see Mr. E. J. Scott this afternoon and we have an understanding as to the policy to be pursued as to the appointment of some of our friends under me.

I have not yet decided as to whom I shall appoint as Chief Clerk but have fully determined to give Mr. Wimbs a desk in the office as soon as he cares to accept it, which he says will not be earlier than Jan 1st.

I shall put Jno Jones in the Mobile Deputy Collectorship as soon as I assume charge of the Collectors Office. I find several colored men already Store Keepers and guagers but are without assignments which is in effect being without employment.

I shall make places for them from time to time, as the opportunity offers.

I shall give out an interview in which I shall say among other things, "As to persistent rumors that Mr. Thompson will appoint colored men in his force he said that negroes had been in the Revenue Service under every Rep. Administration ever since he could remember and that there would be no exception in his case." "Mr. Thompson expressed surprise at the very few colored men who had applied to him for officers, saying that it was an indication to him that the negroes who were qualified electors in Alabama, had a higher motive in wanting to vote, than to merely hold office. The idea that the President and his friends in Ala. oppose the high suffrage standard of the new Constitution is absurd but the test should be administered to all alike. The meaning of Republicanism will not be changed but shall stand as handed down by Lincoln, Grant, Arthur, McKinley and now is interpreted by Roosevelt. It should be understood that the Republican party can hardly afford

594

to have one set of principles in one section of the country and an entirely opposite set in another section."

I will send you a copy of the paper. Your friend

Jos. O. Thompson

ALS Con. 243 BTW Papers DLC. Addressed to BTW in Boston.

From George Washington Carver

Tuskegee, Ala., November 28, 190[2]

Dear Mr. Washington: I have just returned from a trip to Ramer, Alabama, where Mr. Henry is located, and I feel that you ought to know the exact condition there as it is the most distressing of any that I have ever seen in any place. In fact, I had the most frightful experience of my life there and for one day and night it was a very serious question indeed as to whether I would return to Tuskegee alive or not as the people were thoroughly bent upon bloodshed. In all probability they have broken up the school. Mr. Henry was obliged to leave Ramer between the suns and the other teacher became so very frightened that she left also. The occasion of the disturbance was Miss Johnston, who went down on the same train that carried me down. The white people evidently knew that she was coming. The train was late in getting there but a number of people had gathered at the station to see what would happen. I took Miss Johnston's valise and put it in the buggy for her. Mr. Henry drove her to his house and put out her valise and started to the hotel, then he was met by parties and after a few words was shot at three times. Of course, he ran and got out of the way and Miss Johnston came back to the house where I was. I got out at once and succeeded in getting her to the next station where she took the train the next morning. The next day everything was in a state of turbulency and a mob had been formed to locate Mr. Henry and deal with him. They did not pay a great deal of attention to me as I kept out of the way as much as possible, but it was one of the worst situations that I have ever been in.

As things are now, the school is broken up and there seems to be no way of settling the difficulty. They say that what they want is to get hold of Mr. Henry and beat him nearly to death. I spoke to the people on Wednesday and they were — of course — very much disturbed. I quieted them down as much as I could — which was very little. I had to walk nearly all night Tuesday night to keep out of their reach. Wednesday night I stayed four miles from the place and took the train six miles from Ramer next morning. On Wednesday the place was patrolled by a white man walking up and down in front of the school house armed with a shot gun. I went down on Wednesday morning to see just what the situation was and I saw twelve horses saddled and tied to the fence of one of the chief promoters. He saw me coming down the railroad and at once mounted his horse and came down to meet me. I stepped aside to examine some plants — just to see what he would do — and he came up and eyed me closely and spoke rather politely. He evidently thought I was Mr. Henry. One of the gentlemen went down town that night to see what was being done and found that a mob was being made up for the night to take Mr. Henry. I succeeded in getting word to Mr. Henry to flee for his life, which he did. He is now in Montgomery.

Mr. Henry gone, they then telephoned over to the next station to see if Miss Johnston took the train next morning. They wanted to know who took her to the train, and everything in detail. A telegram was handed to a gentleman, which was evidently a fake — at least appeared so. It was purported to have come for Mr. Henry to induce him to come to the station. It was simply to find out where he was. I have never seen people so enraged.

Mr. Henry was doing a great work there and it grieves me to know that he must give it up. Miss Johnston was thoroughly grieved. I might say that she is the pluckiest woman I ever saw. She was not afraid for herself but shed bitter tears for Mr. Henry and for the school which is in all probability broken up. They were preparing to have a splendid exhibition. In fact, the material was there and promised to be one of the best exhibitions that I have had the privilege of attending. The exhibits were large and fine and the people seemed very much encouraged. Now as to the outcome, it is impossible to say. It stands just as I have related it to you. Mrs. Washington and I have talked the matter over here and we think it wise to say just as little as possible about it here. The people seem to be intensely bitter against any one who comes from Tuskegee.

Trusting you are quite well and that you had a pleasant Thanksgiving, I beg to remain, Yours most sincerely,

G. W. Carver

TLS   Con. 261   BTW Papers   DLC.

From Emmett Jay Scott

Tuskegee, Ala., Nov. 28, 1902

Dear Mr. Washington: We have just heard that Miss Johnston suffered indignities at Ramer where she went to take pictures of N. E. Henry's school. I have telephoned to Montgomery to-day asking Henry to come up here so that we can get a clear statement as to conditions at Ramer. We understand that after the pictures had been taken of his work, he accompanied Miss Johnston to the hotel where she was refused accommodation, and that Henry was fired at three times before he could get out of range. Miss Johnston went through the country and Henry has been in Montgomery since. We have not heard from Miss Johnston though I am sure she will write in a day or two. Very truly yours,

E J Scott

TLS   Con. 241   BTW Papers   DLC.

To William Edward Burghardt Du Bois

Crawford House, Boston, Mass. November 28, 1902

Personal and Confidential.

My dear Dr. Du Bois: I have your letter of recent date, and if you will let me know what the total expense will be I shall be willing to bear a portion of it provided I can hand it to you personally and

597

not have any connection with your committee. I do not want my name to go before the committee in any shape or to be used publicly in connection with this matter. I am very glad indeed to hear that you are moving in such a sensible way. Smith is a fine and able man. Yours truly,

Booker T. Washington

TLS   W. E. B. Du Bois Papers   MU.

A Press Release by Emmett Jay Scott

Tuskegee, Ala., Nov. 29, '02

"Standing in this presence, and measuring well my words, with the fear of God upon me, I declare to you that the Southern white man is the best friend the Negro in the South has." Such was the deliverance of Gen. Jno. B. Gordon under dramatic circumstances before the teachers and students of the Tuskegee Institute, Booker T. Washington's school, at this place last night. The General, accompanied by Former Congressman Jas. E. Cobb and Hon. C. W. Hare, had but a moment before entered the spacious auditorium of the school and had received a welcome as warm and as hearty as any he has ever received from any audience of his own race. With one accord as he entered the door, the 1800 students and teachers and citizens from the town of Tuskegee jumped to their feet and made the welkin ring with salvos of welcome, interspersed with the college yell of the male students as a huge American flag was hoisted to the rafters. In a voice trembling with emotion, the battle-scarred veteran of the Civil War, a commander of Confederate troops, faced his audience of black students to deliver his famous lecture, "The Last Days of the Confederacy." He paid an unstinted word of praise to the faithfulness of those of the Negro race who with so much of faithfulness befriended and cared for the wives and sisters of the Confederate soldiers who went to the front in a war having for its issue the continuation of slavery. "Such a record," said the General, "stands to the credit of no other race on the face of the globe." He also paid a beautiful tribute to the old plantation songs sung with much power and beauty by these Tuskegee students, and thanked them and the Principal of the school, for their preservation.

After the lecture General Gordon remarked that he was altogether unprepared for the heartiness and cordiality and unusualness of the reception tendered him by the students of Booker Washington's school.

Emmett J. Scott

TMcSr Con. 241 BTW Papers DLC. An autograph draft is in Con. 228, BTW Papers, DLC.

From Whitefield McKinlay

Washington, D.C., 11/30/02

Dr Mr W. To me Crum's appointment would be of transcendent importance to us as it would emphasise the principle that Color should not be the bar to official recognition; and because of this I practically dropped my work & devoted my attention to his case. In this I have been ably assisted by Mr. Leupp, who told the Presdt that he might as well drop his southern policy as to flinch in this fight, for he would make himself the laughing stock of the Country.

After receiving yr telegram, I saw Leupp, who said that he had just heard from the Presdt & that nothing would be done until he, L., had returned to the City, when he would go over the case with him. Sen McComas[1] & Genl Michener,[2] who were in charge of the Harrison forces, have written the Presdt, denouncing the charge. Genl Smalls[3] gave a detailed acct of C.'s actions from his election in April till June. Gov Pinchback stated that he as a Blaine man tried to persuade C. over to his side & failed. L & myself think we have satisfied the Presdt on that charge, but as there are evidently others, we are anxious to know them. L. says further that it is either C. or a white man, & hence you can thoroughly understand my nervous strain to see that the Presdt stick to his original text as the appointment either of another col'd man or a white man would be hailed as a victory for the opposition. L. is further satisfied that the race has some secret enemies who are in the confidence of the Pres.

Enclosed find clippings. Very truly

W. McKinlay

ALS   Con. 236   BTW Papers   DLC.

1 Louis Emory McComas (1846–1907), a delegate to the Republican national convention and secretary of the Republican national committee in 1892, was U.S. senator from Maryland from 1899 to 1905.

2 Louis Theodore Michener (1848–1928) was Benjamin Harrison's political manager from 1884 to 1892 and was chairman of the nominating committees of the 1888 and 1892 Republican national conventions. He was attorney general of Indiana from 1886 to 1890. After 1899 he practiced law in Washington, D.C.

3 Robert Smalls (1839–1915), born a slave in Beaufort, S.C., was the son of a Jewish slaveowner and a black slave woman. Trained by his father to be a sailmaker and helmsman, he hid his family and a few chosen companions on his master's vessel, the steamship *Planter*, early one morning in 1862, sailed it out of Charleston harbor, and delivered it to the federal fleet. He remained in command of the ship, gained a rudimentary education, and returned to Beaufort as a Reconstruction political leader. He served in the 1868 constitutional convention, in both houses of the legislature, and in Congress from 1875 to 1879 and from 1882 to 1887. From 1889 to 1893 and from 1898 through 1913 he was collector of the port of Beaufort. Never a general, he sought unsuccessfully for years to get the U.S. Navy to give him the rank of captain in recognition of his Civil War services.

BTW was never a close friend of Smalls, but when the latter was removed by the incoming Wilson administration, BTW wrote to Franklin MacVeagh, Taft's Secretary of the Treasury: "The colored people are very much disappointed and almost embittered because of the displacement of Robert Smalls. Most of the colored people thought that he at least would be permitted to retain his position. I was in Beaufort, S.C., a short while ago, and it was most pleasing as well as interesting to see how highly he is regarded by white and colored people in Beaufort. The white people look upon him as a kind of godfather, and there is not the slightest trace of bitterness against him because of the office he has held so many years." (Apr. 17, 1913, Con. 762, BTW Papers, DLC.)

To Theodore Roosevelt

Crawford House, Boston, Mass. December 1, 1902

Personal.

My dear Mr. President: First I want to thank you for your strong and clear letter on the subject of appointing Negroes to office. It seems to me that this letter states the whole matter for all time so far as you are concerned. Even Professor Norton of Harvard commended your letter to me yesterday without reservation.

Now in regard to Dr. Crum. I have no means of knowing just what the nature and strength of the protests are which you have received from the white people in Charleston, neither do I know very definitely the source and strength of the charges urged against Dr. Crum's character. I have been seeking information as best I could since these charges were made and I have not been able to get hold of anything that would cause me to change what I said to you when you requested my opinion regarding Dr. Crum when I saw you some weeks ago. I have known him for fifteen years and he is as far different, in my mind, from the old irresponsible and purchasable Negro politician as day is from night. When the white people of Charleston were seeking some one to take the active head of the Negro Department of the recent Charleston Exposition, some one who could command the respect and confidence of both white and colored people, they selected Dr. Crum, and whenever a position of responsibility is to be filled both races usually turn to him in that city. In regard to his bargaining away his vote in the National Convention I repeat I have no definite information, except I do know that it is hardly possible for any man from the South to go to one of these conventions without some stories being circulated regarding his vote. I regarded these stories of such little consequence that I did not think it worth while to mention them to you. I should be the last man to recommend Dr. Crum or anybody else for office at your hands who is unworthy or has the least connection with dishonest acts. The only one I have recommended about whose character I was not sure is Dr. Crossland, Minister to Liberia.

The appointment of Durham and Fortune has given the greatest general satisfaction.

This will be my address for ten days.

If I can serve you further please be kind enough to let me know. Yours truly,

Booker T. Washington

TLS   Theodore Roosevelt Papers   DLC.

From Robert Charles Bedford

Tuskegee, Ala., Dec. 3 1902

Dear Mr Washington   I presume Mr Scott has written you the details of the unfortunate occurrence at Ramer. Miss Johnston went to Montgomery with me yesterday. She feels very deeply and of course we all sympathize with her. We saw Capt Faulkner. He was very emphatic in his condemnation of the act and advised putting the case into the Solicitor's hands at once. But on further talk considering the interests of the school as well as the feelings of Miss Johnston he agreed it would be well to lay the matter before the Gov. We took Mr Henry and went up there. The Gov condemned the act but said we must face the facts and consider the locality and people we were dealing with. He thought Miss Johnston ought not to have gone there at night without knowing just where she was to stop and that Mr Henry made a mistake in not asking the white people to entertain her and especially in bringing her back to the white people after they supposed she had been with a colored family whereas when she started away from the Depot she did not know where Mr Henry was going to take her but on finding it was to a colored family and 4 miles away she wished him to bring her back to the white people. It was about 11 oclock by this time and there was no one around except Postmaster Turnipseed's son and his brother in law a young fellow about 20 yrs old and a stranger. The young fellow seemed to feel that the insult lay in first proposing to go with colored people and then presuming to come to his sister. The Gov gave us a letter to the Solicitor and assured me that Mr Henry should go on with his school. He said he would communicate at once with the Sheriff and that he would have him meet us at the Solicitor's office. We met both of them there. The Sheriff said he would go to Ramer today and would have matters settled so far as the school was concerned. They agreed to prosecute a suit in whatever way Miss Johnston might wish. They assured her that young Turnipseed and the Armes boy did not represent the community and that Turnipseed Sr the Postmaster would in no way approve of what had been done. I am very glad Miss Johnston agreed to leave the matter of the suit till after conferring with you. I made an appointment to meet the Sheriff with

Mr Henry later in the day. We met in his office. The Sheriff talked very freely and fairly. In questioning Mr Henry it came out that at least 3 of the leading colored men besides himself came out to meet Miss Johnston. This with her getting into the buggy with Mr Henry and riding off then coming back to stay with them was wrongly construed and led to the trouble. If it had not been so late and other stores had been open and other people around I doubt whether the trouble would have occurred. The Sheriff said he knew and respected Mr Henry. He said he owned a plantation there and his children went to Mr Henry's school. He said Mr Milligan one of the leading citizens was his son in law and they would listen to him. He could plainly see that the whole trouble had come from a misunderstanding, that he would put everything right and communicate with Mr Henry tomorrow morning. I suggested that I go with the Sheriff but he thought I had better wait till he had been down. Mr Henry will call me up tomorrow and I will write you again after that.

It seems a pity that there could not have been a presumption on the part of those men that whatever appearances might be, her motives were perfectly right. It does not seem as if it would require an over amount of chivalry to accord innocence to a woman and a stranger without protection at midnight. Capt Faulkner the Gov the Sheriff and the Solicitor think the community would have done it but unfortunately most of them were in bed and only these 3 men in sight the one who did the shooting brought up an orphan and recognized among white and colored as something of a desperado.

Miss Johnston was fully warned against going to Ramer at night. She had traveled so much she could not conceive the possibility of any one molesting her or mistaking her motives. This lesson shows us that we have not yet got to the point, everywhere, where we can act without great prudence and forethought and in view of the actual conditions in a given community. I think hereafter those who go out in any way as representatives of the school must be guided by its judgment or go out on their own responsibility.

Ramer is in a bad way. This Armes drove out the white teacher with a revolver not long ago. Mr Henry teaches 8 months each year and has when his school is full about 175 children but tells me he only gets $36 per year public money. He told me it was no uncommon thing for planters to whip the people employed by them.

We must stand by Henry and all these out of the way places. They constitute the problem in its most grievous form. I hope the Ed Board will realize this and help Mr Henry and other places like his. I shall see Mr Henry and go with him to Ramer when he returns and will look into the matter of the $36. I saw Miss Hannon, Ada, who is assisting Mr Henry and she said she would go back if matters were arranged. I think it would be a great mistake to have the school broken up. I wish you could write Mr Henry a line in C of Mr Adams. I believe good will come out of this. I will try to be wise and let you know as matters develop. Mr Logan Mr Scott and Mr Carver are good and earnest men and you may place great reliance on their judgment.

I send you McLain Birch's[1] letter which I am sure you will be interested in. Yrs

R C Bedford

ALS Con. 221 BTW Papers DLC.

[1] McLane McClellan Birch of St. Francisville, La., graduated from Tuskegee in 1901 and began teaching in Frierson, La.

To Emmett Jay Scott

Crawford House, Boston, Mass. December 4, 1902

Dear Mr. Scott: If Miss Johnston is still at Tuskegee I wish you would ask her not to do anything definite about that Ramer matter until I have had an opportunity to see her. If she has not done so, I hope she will not fail to go to Snow Hill as she will meet with no difficulties there. In case she goes I wish you would write Mr. Simpson. Perhaps Mr. Bedford might go with her. Yours truly,

Booker T. Washington

TLS Con. 245 BTW Papers DLC.

From William Edward Burghardt Du Bois

Atlanta, Ga., December 4, 1902

Dear Mr. Washington: Mr. W. H. Smith wrote me December the First in part as follows: "I have examined that law, and am of the opinion that it is absolutely void in its application to passengers taken up in the state and destined for points out side of the state, or passengers coming into the state from points out side of the state. I am also inclined to the belief that the law is void for all purposes." "I have not examined the extent of the jurisdiction of the Inter-State Commission where the sleeping car companies claim to act under a statute such as this. But, my idea would be to make a case before the United States Circuit Court, and have it come directly to Washington, so as to test the validity of that law." "I could not afford to give the time required from my business for less than $2,500 and I pay my own expenses, or $2,000 and the committee pay all my expenses. I mean either proposition that the committee will take care of the court costs."

I am replying to Mr. Smith asking what he thinks of a preliminary case simply before the Inter-State Commerce Commission.

I presume that he is right in preparing for the courts from the very first. What do you think of the fee charged? It's very high and I am not sure how much we can raise. Sincerely yours,

W. E. B. Du Bois

TLS Con. 225 BTW Papers DLC. Docketed in E. J. Scott's hand: "Referring to above — There is no trouble now about passengers who purchase tickets out of State & ride into it & through it! EJS 12/6."

From Nelson Edward Henry

Montgomery Ala. 12/4, 1902

Prof. B. T. Washington   You have doubtless heard of the incident at my school 25th. ult. on account of Miss Johnson's coming to take pictures for us. It is indeed a sad event to me after having labored so very hard for six years. But under conditions at Ramer, Something would have croped out at some time and Miss Johnson's trip only brought it out. Though none of us expected it. No one can be more sorry than I, for all of my energy and strength has been put on that work. Mr. Bedford and Mr. Adams are doing every thing possible to settle matters in which I hope they will succeed. But I can not spend any more time there. First I have no means to carry on the work. Second I should not ask for any help for the people now are unsettled. So you see there is nothing which offers any inducement for me to go back. I will write you later. Yours truly

N. E. Henry

ALS Con. 272 BTW Papers DLC.

From Emmett Jay Scott

Tuskegee, Ala., Dec. 4, 1902

Dear Mr. Washington: Alberto Roja,[1] one of the Cuban students, a very small boy, about 13 years old, last week stole from Mrs. J. B. Washington a watch. He and Julian Valdes proceeded to town and sold the watch to a Jew for Five Dollars, dividing the proceeds. Mr. J. B. Washington had the boy arrested, and he was in jail, but Major Ramsey was able to secure his release and the return of the watch by returning the $5.00 to the Jew. The Sheriff suggests that it will be best for the boy to go home and on account of the flagrant action, the Council concurs in the belief and has expelled him subject to your approval. Julian seems to be equally guilty, and the Council desires your information as to whether you approve their action in the matter, or not.

Miss Frances B. Johnston, the photographer, is planning to leave Tuskegee not later than Saturday night. She has blue prints of all the pictures she has taken here and they are far and away beyond anything of the kind we have ever had made. I am sure you will be greatly pleased with them. I have told her of your being at Philadelphia December 11th, and she desires to see you for a conference regarding pictures and other matters as well if it will be agreeable to you. Please send her word at her studio, 1332 V. St., N.W., Washington, D.C., on receipt of this letter, so that she will know what to depend upon as soon as she gets to Washington.

Mr. Gibson is very anxious to secure a new Boston and vicinity Directory. The one we have here is 1899. If Mr. Hunt can secure one from some bank, or interested friends of the school, it will save the expenditure of from $5.00 to $7.50. Very truly yours,

Emmett J Scott

TLS Con. 241 BTW Papers DLC.

¹ Alberto Rojas, from Remedios, Cuba, was a member of the C preparatory class during the 1901–2 school year.

To Warren Logan

Crawford House, Boston, Mass. Dec. 7, 1902

Dear Mr. Logan: I have received a letter from Mr. Scott regarding the expulsion of two Cuban students. At this distance it is very difficult for me to give any advice that would mean very much regarding them. I must say however, in this connection, I regret very much that anybody connected with the school should have had these students or any other students arrested by the town authorities without the approval of the school officers. We gain nothing except in very exceptional cases by appealing to the town people to settle affairs that we can settle ourselves.

It seems to me that the only thing I can say is that I would advise the Council to consider the ages and the past history and the future environment of these students, and after taking all these matters into careful consideration reach whatever consideration is thought wise. We will have to exercise a great deal of patience and forbearance with these students. Yours truly,

Booker T. Washington

TLS BTW Papers ATT.

From Robert Charles Bedford

Tuskegee, Ala., Dec 8 1902

Dear Mr Washington   The Sheriff went to Ramer according to promise and reported to Mr Henry that all was settled and he would go down to Ramer with him Sat morning Dec 6. Mr Henry consented to go and all seemed settled but during the day a colored man came up from Ramer and advised Mr Henry not to return fearing some irresponsible person might injure him. This unsettled Mr Henry and without waiting to see me he started for Evergreen where he had already been promised work. I went down Friday morning and saw the Sheriff and he said the boy who did the shooting was "mighty near scared to death" and since they have found out the facts they were all anxious to have Mr Henry come back and he was sure there would be no trouble. I went to Ramer at 6 30 Sat morning. I met Mr Jeff Harris one of the Registrars the Turnipseeds father and son, the boy who did the shooting, the Watley brothers, Rushton brothers   Dr McCrummin Pres of the Board of Revenue   J A Booth a Ramer merchant and other white people whose names I do not recall. Not one had any thing but praise of Henry even the boy who shot at him and he seemed more anxious than any of the rest for Mr Henry's return. All urged his return and said he should have protection. I then went over to the school house and looked after the property the best I could and met the colored people one by one as they came around and talked with them and then in the afternoon met about 30 of the leading ones at the school house where a free expression was had from all. They seemed to be much discouraged and the sentiment of nearly all was that in the ordinary course of things Mr Henry would be perfectly safe but they feared for his return and thought it would be unwise for him to do so. There seemed to be a determination to carry the school right on. A committee was appointed to correspond with Mr Henry and Miss Hannon to ask their judgment in the matter telling them just how they felt and promising to do their best for them if both or either of them would return. If Mr Henry would not return they were to ask his judgment as to his successor and if he could not name any one they were to write Mr Carver and he Mr C W Greene and myself would do the best we could to get a proper successor. I shall write at once to Mr Henry and Miss Hannon and I think the people will act promptly as now is the children's opportunity.

I can see the school is unfortunately located. Ramer is older than Montgomery. About the village they are nearly all white. They do not allow any colored to live in the village limits. There is an excellent locality about 2½ miles from Ramer on land owned by colored people about ½ way between Ramer and Grady so that either place could be the P.O. I think all are agreed that after this year it would be well to locate the school at this place. Whatever may be the future of the school at Ramer the good work done by Mr Henry will not be lost. He has left a splendid record there. He owes just $5.00, $3.40 to one man for some furniture he had just bought to fit up a little dormitory for some boys who had come from the prairies and $1.60 for sawing some lumber. These are not really debts but balances which he would have paid at the first opportunity. The boy who shot at him said he never had any trouble with him. They just seemed to be inflamed at the sight of 3 Negroes meeting a white woman at that hour of the night and helping her into the buggy and riding off with her and then bringing her back to stay with this boy's sister. If she had not come back I doubt whether they would have noticed it again, and it is doubtful whether it would have occurred if it had been in day light or even earlier in the evening. I was treated most cordially by every one and Tuskegee was referred to most respectfully. I shall keep close watch of things and whatever may seem best to do shall try to do. I have conferred freely with Mr Logan Mr Carver and Mr Scott. We are in perfect accord and will try to act wisely and kindly. Naturally Miss Johnston and Mr Carver are some what enraged and I think see some things that did not actually occur. I could not find from white or colored any inkling of a man patroling the grounds with a shot gun or of a purpose on the part of any of the people the next morning to do any thing but to stop further trouble. I may be wrong but I am fully convinced that I am right. It occurred so late that almost no one knew of it till the next morning and then there was a feeling of shame at what had been done. Of course the people there are provincial and have not had many opportunities and both white and colored are not of a high order. I believe with the Sheriff good will come out of this and I hope the spirit of gentleness and pity will prevail in all that is done at least unless some different phase of the matter from any thing I now see develops. I shall be glad to answer any question you may ask on which I have knowledge. Yrs

R C Bedford

ALS   Con. 221   BTW Papers   DLC.

From Timothy Thomas Fortune

San Francisco, Cal., December 10, 1902

My dear Mr. Washington: I arrived here in fine shape on the 7th and have not had opportunity to send you a line before, as the people here organized a committee to take charge of me on my arrival and have had charge of me every since. The public reception to me Monday night was one of the finest I have ever had and the newspapers and friends say that I made a splendid address and I am satisfied with it.

You have no enemies here among our people and when you come here in January you will get a warm reception from everybody.

I shall sail for Honolulu tomorrow afternoon at 1 pm reaching there Dec. [1]8 and shall leave there Jan 3 and reach Manilla Jan. 24. My health is good, with the exception of a heavy cold, caught on the train, and I am living absolutely up to your parting advice at the Grand Union.

I will have sent you a batch of San Francisco newspapers with references to me.

I miss you and word from you very much and I shall be glad when we meet again. Your friend,

T Thos Fortune

ALS   Con. 227   BTW Papers   DLC.

Emmett Jay Scott to Richard W. Thompson

[Tuskegee, Ala.] Dec. 11, 1902

Dear Thompson: Your suggestion that we consider you for a position at Tuskegee has my attention. We have already done so more than once, and I wish to write you in this letter in the most kindly and frank way as to the reasons which have operated to prevent your employment. I think you understand me as friend and brother and know that I have set down naught in malice. Washington, as you know, abounds in mockers. Many of these people have represented you to the Wizard as a man who indulges in drink to a greater or less extent; also, that your relations with women have brought you discredit from time to time. He has to be so very careful in the employment of those who are to come to the school that he has been compelled to pay some attention to these rumors, even though he has not already accepted them fully. Another matter about which I am sure he would not want me to especially write you is what he was able to observe himself when you went with him to Virginia two years ago. I think you did yourself a very serious injustice in drinking in Mr. Washington's presence and in permitting him to know that you do drink.

I am at this time without any competent helper and I have been left to secure some one to do this work. I have been seriously thinking of bringing your claims to the Wizard's attention again and of offering you the work. I could not do so, however unless I could have him feel that there was no basis for the rumors which have reached him.

If you will have sent me from those whose opinion is worth the having statements in denial of the above, I shall hope to be able to arrange matters.

What the salary would be to begin with I cannot at this time say, though Mr. Washington would try to make it as liberal as the resources of the school would permit. Very truly yours,

[Emmett Jay Scott]
Private Secretary

TLc Con. 241 BTW Papers DLC.

To Theodore Roosevelt

Crawford House, Boston. December 13, 1902

My dear Mr. President: In presiding at a meeting in Philadelphia this week where I spoke, the Hon. Grover Cleveland spoke out so bravely and sensibly in regard to the colored people that I take the liberty of sending you a marked copy of his address mainly for the reason that much of what he said is in keeping with your own letter addressed to the party in Charleston. Yours very truly,

Booker T. Washington

TLS   Theodore Roosevelt Papers   DLC.

From George Bruce Cortelyou

Washington D C   Dec 13th. [1902]

(Personal)
The President wishes to know if you are personally sure of Crum's probity and Character. Very important that no mistake should be made.

Geo. B. Cortelyou

TWSr   Con. 541   BTW Papers   DLC.

To Theodore Roosevelt

[Boston] Dec. 16, 1902

Personal and confidential. At your suggestion I have again gone thoroughly into character and probity of Dr. Crum with persons who have known him all his life, and basing my judgment upon what they say as well as upon my personal acquaintance of twelve years I have no hesitation in saying that my opinion is that he is a clean upright man.

Booker T. Washington

TWS   Theodore Roosevelt Papers   DLC.

From Timothy Thomas Fortune

Royal Hawaiian Hotel, Honolulu, T.H., Dec. 22, 1902

Dear Mr. Washington: All goes well with me. I send you under separate cover a batch of newspapers which will interest you. I have reached no conclusions, of course, as I am devoting my time to investigation. Because of the difficulties of the situation and the importance of the interests involved, I am [have] been persuaded to devote a longer time to this Territory than I had allowed myself. I may not therefore be able to leave for Manila before Jan. 17.

I have met Gen. Armstrong's brother and sister and am to spend an afternoon with them. All the people out here know about you and take a great interest in. I dined at the Pacific Club with Mr. Carter[1] and Gen. Hartwell[2] who says he once met you on the train. Mr. Carter who is one of the wealthiest and most influential men here, asked me to say to you that he is one of your disciples. He is a Yale man and President of the Hawaiian Trust company.

I am being assisted in my work by all the forces in the Territory, and have declined invitations to address the Chamber of Commerce and the allied Trades unions, on the theory that I am seeking information and not imparting any.

I shall make a trip through the Islands under the conduct of a representative of the Planters' Association and the Chamber of Commerce. Yours Sincerely,

T. Thos. Fortune

ALS   Con. 258   BTW Papers   DLC.

[1] George Robert Carter (1866–1933) was a member of the Hawaiian territorial senate from 1901 to 1903 and governor from 1903 to 1907.

[2] Alfred Stedman Hartwell (1836–1912) was one of the white officers of the 54th Massachusetts Infantry during the Civil War. He served also for a time with another black unit, the 55th Massachusetts Infantry. He settled in the Hawaiian Islands in 1868 and became a prominent lawyer, sugar planter, and jurist. He was associate justice of the supreme court of Hawaii from 1904 to 1907 and chief justice from 1907 to 1911.

From William Henry Lewis

Boston, December 29, 1902

My dear Mr. Washington: I simply drop you this note to inform you of the present status of my case at Washington.

You may probably know that I called to see the President on the 18th inst at Washington. He received me very graciously and cordially and gave me nearly three-quarters of an hour. He said, among other things, he was very glad that I was more in unison with you than formerly. I told him, of course, there were many things about which we might differ, but that we had the same aims and the same end in view. He used a very happy illustration when he replied, saying, "Of course, Mr. Lewis, if another man and myself are working in the same field, whether ploughing or hoeing or reaping, I had much prefer to have him work my way, but it did not matter so much as long as he was working and working toward the same end."

He said very little with regard to an appointment for me, except in the last few moments of his conversation, when he said that he wanted to do something for me and something here in Boston, having the same idea in view which he expressed to you, and suggested that I see Senator Hoar[1] and Senator Lodge with reference to the same.

I was fortunate enough to see Senator Lodge and Senator Hoar together at the Committee Room of the Senate Judiciary Committee. They both seemed to take a very lively interest in the matter, and Senator Hoar suggested that I ought to have something in the line of my profession, either in the Department of Justice at Washington under the Attorney-General, or in Boston under the United States District Attorney for Massachusetts. Senator Lodge said that he thought that a place might be made in the United States District Attorney's, or that possibly the post of First Assistant District Attorney now held by Mr. Casey might be available for me.

I have heard nothing from the matter since I left Washington, either directly or indirectly. *I should like very much to have the place of First Assistant District Attorney.* I feel confident that I can fill the bill. The place is now held by a Democrat and there is no reason why he shouldn't get out. So, that if you see the President you can say that that is the place which I should like above all others. Anything that you may do will be greatly appreciated. Sincerely yours,

William H. Lewis

(Dictated W.H.L.)

TLS Con. 233 BTW Papers DLC.

¹ George Frisbie Hoar (1826–1904) was a Republican U.S. congressman from Massachusetts from 1869 to 1877 and a U.S. senator from 1877 until his death.

A Speech by Emmett Jay Scott

Houston, Texas, December 29, 1902

Mr chairman, & you, men & women of Texas: My part in the proceedings of this evening is a simple & agreeable one. This cordial welcome, this mighty outpouring, fittingly crowns the pleasurable stay of fifteen hours, it has been the happy good fortune of my distinguished chief & myself to spend in your midst.

The hours have been a little crowded, function has succeeded function, but I think your reception committee will agree that we have proved ourselves pretty good "stayers." We have allowed nothing to pass!

For my part, I wish to prove my sincere appreciation of all of the kindnesses of the day, by heeding the proprieties of the occasion, & by not keeping you from the feast you have gathered to enjoy.

Five and one-half years ago, it was my pleasure to meet for the first time, here in this hall, and to introduce from this same platform to his first Texas audience the distinguished gentleman who is now your guest. Long before I had met him, I had hailed him as the successor of the mighty Douglass & had sworn allegience to him as Safe Counselor and Leader! During the years since I met him here, I have been in closest touch with him in all of his work, & I declare to you that the admiration I then cherished has not waned, nor wavered. His courage, his foresight, his deep interest in all that concerns his people, his anxieties, his hopes, his fears — all of these I have known of — & tho' it has been said that a man can be really great to all save his valet & his secretary — in this case, at least, refutation & denial are offered.

The boy starting ragged and unkempt, from a West Virginia coal mine, but courageous, full of hope, and the spirit that conquers all, has come now into his own, & to be as Former President Cleveland declared a few days ago, "one of the first citizens of America." He has given to the world Tuskegee, an instrument of good, which, in various ways, through its students & other well directed agencies, is a permeating influence throughout the Southland, working out, as nothing else can, the regeneration of the Negro people & the solution of the racial problem in the South. To this modest teacher, more than to any other, is due the credit for the impulse of the movement that promises deliverance from the ills of the past.

Regretfully, it must be confessed, constitutions & laws have thus far availed the Negro people but little, & the political strife which their cause has engendered has conferred upon them hardly anything more than the ill will of those, without whose friendly interest & sympathy & help, they cannot realize the hopes they now so fondly cherish.

It seems like a stroke of destiny, a Providential event, that all at once after years of sectional strife and bitterness & after their vain appeal to the nation that conferred upon them the rights of citizenship & to the States which gave them birth, when the hands of one seemed too palsied to assist & the spirit of the other not disposed to heed, there should arise out of the very darkness of these conditions, out of the very race itself, one who should grasp the situation with the ful[l]ness of its significance & by the genius of his common sense furnish a plan & a theory for the betterment of his people so harmonious with existing conditions, as not only to secure the unreserved endorsement of the North, but to elicit, at the same time, the most enthusiastic commendation of the South.

When his policies have been worked out to their full fruition, he will have done more than political parties, or partisan politics, commerce or art, to bring about the independence of his people, to wipe out sectional animosities & cement into good feeling & mutual confidence & respect the two races in the South!

And now, ladies & gentlemen, I present to you him of whom I speak, Booker T. Washington, friend & counselor of his people, benefactor of his section, worthy citizen of the Republic!

AMd   Con. 241   BTW Papers   DLC.

An Article by Byrd Prillerman

[December 1902]

BOOKER T. WASHINGTON AMONG HIS
WEST VIRGINIA NEIGHBORS

When a man becomes great and famous, everybody is curious to know how he is regarded among the neighbors of his childhood and youth. There is probably no saying of Jesus better known than this one: "A prophet is not without honor, but in his own country, and among his kin, and in his own house."

The educated and professional people of West Virginia honor and admire Mr. Booker T. Washington as a great orator, the leader of his race and one of the foremost educators of America; but those who knew him best in childhood and youth delight to think of him as the chubby baby, the quiet boy, the thoughtful lad, and the diligent school boy. Many remember him as an industrious Sunday school teacher, a careful church clerk, a successful school teacher, a ready debater and a Christian young man.

Booker T. Washington has ever been a unique character. I one day met an old woman who lived at the place of his birth when he was born. How delighted she was to tell of his early life. She said that "Booker" was not like other children on the slave plantation; that he would not play with the other children, but would stand around and watch them play. His frequently standing in one place and looking "North" was a curious omen to many of the old slaves. When quite a small boy he and a bag of corn were tied on to an old gray horse and sent to mill. His first teacher,[1] now teaching in Charleston, loves to tell what a diligent pupil Booker was. Some of the old miners like to tell how he used to haul coal from them in the mines.

The minister, who is now pastor of Mr. Washington's church in Malden, relates with much interest how "Booker T.," when a mere boy, was brought to Charleston by the Malden Debating Club to speak against the Charleston Club. The latter club had defeated Malden in a previous debate, but this time Malden bore home the laurels. The Charleston Club was composed of grown men, but they conceded that "Booker T." was the force which gained the victory for the Malden Club.

Some like to tell how Miss Fanny Smith, one of the purest and best young women in Malden, became his sweetheart in youth and his wife in manhood.

One of his old pupils, now one of the most successful teachers in the Charleston public schools, tells how Mr. Washington would stop teaching arithmetic and grammar to lecture his pupils on the care of their nails, hair, teeth and clothing, and on the importance of the formation of right habits. The traces on the life of this woman can be seen today. She lives in a two story house of her own, on one of the principal streets of Charleston.

Before Booker T. Washington came to manhood he was great in Malden and great in West Virginia. The first time I saw him he was speaking in the court house in Charleston. I saw him acting clerk of the leading church association in the state. I saw him again when he was invited to address a teachers' institute in Charleston, he being the only colored man to receive this recognition in Kanawha county.

One can but admire Mr. Washington's simple devotion to his sister and other friends in Malden. I have seen old "Uncle" Washington Ferguson hobbling about on his cane, delighted to welcome this stepson to his old home. Then I have seen Mr. Washington walking about Malden, looking up old friends. I have seen him sauntering in the garden of the old Ruffner house, viewing the old vineyard, and inspecting the old kitchen in which he used to study. Here he was received most cordially by the daughter and grandchildren of Mrs. Viola Ruffner, the woman for whom, as a boy, he worked.

On June 15, 1898, Mr. Washington delivered the address to the graduating class of the West Virginia Colored Institute, in his old county of Kanawha. A large audience from various parts of the state and from Ohio, came to hear him. Hundreds of people came from Charleston. The audience was anxiously awaiting the appearance of the speaker, when Mr. Washington, in passing through one of the halls to the platform, saw an old minister[2] whom he had known years before waiting to greet him. He gave the old man a hearty greeting and invited him to sit with him on the platform, and in addition to this, before they reached the hall, gave the old preacher some money and told him if he ever came to need help to let him know.

When the great educator was introduced, he began his address by telling how much pleasure it gave him to be back among the friends of his youth, and to have seated with him on the platform the man who had baptized him and received him into the church. He spoke most eloquently for two hours. But I thought what he did was even more forceful than what he said.

In May, 1899, when Mr. Washington was planning for his vacation in Europe, he decided to bring his wife to Malden, on her first visit to West Virginia. When they reached Montgomery, Alabama, however, he received a telegram urging him to come to Boston immediately. As he always puts business before pleasure, he let Mrs. Washington take one route for Malden and he took another for Boston. When Mrs. Washington arrived at Charleston, West Virginia, she was startled to find her husband there awaiting her. On reaching Charlottesville, Virginia, he had learned by telegraph that he could defer his trip to Boston until Monday. That being Friday night, he had come immediately to Charleston, arriving there one hour before his wife. They drove to Malden, where they spent the day with Mrs. Amanda Johnston, his sister. Mr. Washington spent much of the time in visiting the scenes of his boyhood, and in talking with old friends on the streets.

That evening, accompanied by one of his Malden friends, he drove to Charleston to catch a train for Boston. On arriving at Charleston he asked to be driven to the home of an old friend who was confined to his room by a protracted and fatal illness. This room, made dark and dreary by the shadow of death, seemed to those present to become illuminated by the Christian spirit of the visitor, and for the time the patient forgot his suffering. Both of these men had been born in Franklin county, Virginia, and had played together and worked together in Malden, but now they must part to meet no more in this world. Having been detained in this home until almost time for the train, the driver went dashing down the street with his passenger, when they met one of the most prominent white physicians of Charleston. Mr. Washington and this physician are intimate friends, having taught school in Malden at the same time. They recognized each other as they passed, but their drivers were going so rapidly that their carriages were nearly a square from each other before they could be stopped. Mr. Washington and the physician each ordered his carriage back. When they approached each other they alighted and grasped each other's hands in the middle of the street. Both of them had risen from poverty, and they congratulated each other on the success achieved. "We are all proud of your achievements and feel honored by them," the physician said.

Mrs. Washington spent the next day in Malden, and he came to Charleston and spoke to a large audience in one of the principal halls of the city. She left Charleston on the evening train to join her husband in New York to take a steamer for Europe, but stopped at Handley, West Virginia, to see Mr. Washington's only surviving aunt.[3] I met this aunt afterward, and she was delighted to talk of the childhood of her relative who had attained such renown.

On his return from Europe Mr. Washington was given a reception by the citizens of Charleston, the invitation having been sent to him at Paris by the city council. On this occasion he spoke to the people of Charleston in the Opera House. He was introduced by ex-Governor MacCorkle, and Governor George W. Atkinson presided. The notable feature of this visit, however, was the public reception given to Mr. Washington in the Capitol by Governor Atkinson. The reception was largely attended by men and women of both races.

This distinguished son of West Virginia has returned to this "Mountain State" many times since he went to Tuskegee twenty years ago to begin his life's work, but his vacation here in the fall of 1901 was the most interesting of all his visits.

As soon as it became known that Mr. Washington wished to spend his vacation among the "West Virginia Hills," great efforts were put forth by his old neighbors to give him a quiet and profitable rest among them. He spent two weeks in camp on the Gauley river, where, when he would return from hunting or fishing, he often found an old friend or former pupil awaiting him.

At this time he had many invitations to speak in the state, but he declined them all except at Charleston, Malden and Montgomery. After his address at Malden he attended a festival in the old church of which he is a member. There, surrounded by so many friends of his youth, he must have felt a boy again.

When Mr. Washington and his party returned to Charleston at five o'clock in the evening, they heard that President McKinley had been shot. As Mr. Washington waited at Charleston depot for the Malden train, he anxiously watched the people as they spoke to one another in subdued tones, but he could not believe the report. Soon after reaching Malden, however, he became convinced that the sad report was true, and he immediately telegraphed a message of sympathy to Mrs. McKinley. The old citizens of Malden came around him in great numbers to get his opinion of the tragedy. Some of the white men asserted that the assassin should be lynched, but Mr. Washington insisted too much of that had already been done.

Mr. Washington may not be pleased that I have made public these private facts of his Christian life, but it has been through these that his neighbors have seen into the man's soul and have learned to respect, trust and love him.

National Magazine, 17 (Dec. 1902), 353–56.

1 William Davis.
2 Lewis Rice.
3 Sophia Agee.

An Introduction to *Shadow and Light*

1902

It is seldom that one man, even if he has lived as long as Judge M. W. Gibbs is able to record his impressions of so many widely separated parts of the earth's surface as Judge Gibbs can, or to recall personal experiences in so many important occurrences.

Born in Philadelphia, and living there when that city — almost on the border line between slavery and freedom — was the scene of some of the most stirring incidents in the abolition agitation, he was able as a free colored youth, going to Maryland to work, to see and judge of the condition of the slaves in that State. Some of the most dramatic operations of the famous "Underground Railroad" came under his personal observation. He enjoyed the rare privilege of being associated in labor for the race with that man of sainted memory, the Hon. Frederick Douglass. He met and heard many of the most notable men and women who labored to secure the freedom of the Negro. As a resident of California in the exciting years which immediately followed the discovery of gold, he watched the development of lawlessness there and its results. A few years later he went to British Columbia to live, when that colony was practically an unknown country. Returning to the United States, he was a witness to the exciting events connected with the years of Reconstruction in Florida, and an active participant in the events of that period in the State of Arkansas. At one time and another he has met many of the men who have been prominent in the direction of the affairs of both the great political parties of the country. In more recent years he has been able to see something of life in Europe, and in his official capacity as United States Consul to Tamatave, Madagascar, adjoining Africa, has resided for some time in that far-off and strange land.

It would be difficult for any man who has had all these experiences not to be entertaining when he tells of them. Judge Gibbs has written an interesting book.

Interspersed with the author's recollections and descriptions are various conclusions, as when he says: "Labor to make yourself as indispensable as possible in all your relations with the dominant race, and color will cut less figure in your upward grade."

"Vice is ever destructive; ignorance ever a victim, and poverty ever defenseless."

"Only as we increase in property will our political barometer rise."

It is significant to find one who has seen so much of the world as Judge Gibbs has, saying, as he does: "With travel somewhat extensive and diversified, and with residence in tropical latitudes of Negro origin, I have a decided conviction, despite the crucial test to which he has been subjected in the past, and the present disadvantages under which he labors, that nowhere is the promise along all the lines of opportunity brighter for the American Negro than here in the land of his nativity."

I bespeak for the book a careful reading by those who are interested in the history of the Negro in America, and in his present and future.

Booker T. Washington

Mifflin Wistar Gibbs, *Shadow and Light: An Autobiography with Reminiscences of the Last and Present Century* (Washington, D.C.: privately printed, 1902), v–viii.

BIBLIOGRAPHY

This bibliography gives fuller information on works cited in the annotations and endnotes. It is not intended to be comprehensive of works on the subjects dealt with in the volume or of works consulted in the process of annotation.

Dabney, Charles W. *Universal Education in the South.* 2 vols. Chapel Hill: University of North Carolina Press, 1936.

Daniel, Pete, and Raymond Smock. *A Talent for Detail: The Photographs of Miss Frances Benjamin Johnston, 1889–1910.* New York: Harmony Books, 1974.

Evans, Robley Dunglison. "Prince Henry's American Impressions," *McClure's Magazine,* 19 (May 1902), 27–37.

Fox, Stephen R. *The Guardian of Boston: William Monroe Trotter.* New York: Atheneum Publishers, 1970.

Garraty, John A., ed. *The Barber and the Historian: The Correspondence of George A. Myers and James Ford Rhodes, 1910–1923.* Columbus: Ohio Historical Society, 1956.

Gatewood, Willard B., Jr. "William D. Crum: A Negro in Politics," *Journal of Negro History,* 53 (Oct. 1968), 301–20.

Gibbs, Mifflin Wistar. *Shadow and Light: An Autobiography with Reminiscences of the Last and Present Century, with an Introduction by Booker T. Washington.* Washington, D.C., privately printed, 1902; reprint, New York: Arno Press, 1968.

Grantham, Dewey W., Jr. *Hoke Smith and the Politics of the New South.* Baton Rouge: Louisiana State University Press, 1958.

Green, Constance McLaughlin. *The Secret City: A History of Race*

Relations in the Nation's Capital. Princeton: Princeton University Press, 1967.

Hackney, Sheldon. *From Populism to Progressivism in Alabama*. Princeton: Princeton University Press, 1969.

Harlan, Louis R. *Booker T. Washington: The Making of a Black Leader, 1856–1901*. New York: Oxford University Press, 1972.

———. "Booker T. Washington and the White Man's Burden," *American Historical Review*, 71 (Jan. 1966), 441–67.

———. "The Secret Life of Booker T. Washington," *Journal of Southern History*, 37 (Aug. 1971), 393–416.

Henson, Matthew A. *A Negro Explorer at the North Pole*. New York: Frederick A. Stokes Company, 1912.

Holt, Rackham. *Mary McLeod Bethune: A Biography*. New York: Doubleday and Company, Inc., 1964.

Johnson, James Weldon. *Along This Way, the Autobiography of James Weldon Johnson*. New York: Viking Press, Inc., 1968. Originally published in 1933.

Lane, James B. *Jacob A. Riis and the American City*. Port Washington, N.Y.: Kennikat Press, 1974.

Leupp, Francis E. "Why Booker Washington Has Succeeded in His Life Work," *Outlook*, 71 (May 31, 1902), 326–33.

Meier, August. "Booker T. Washington and the Negro Press: With Special Reference to the *Colored American Magazine*," *Journal of Negro History*, 38 (Jan. 1953), 67–90.

———. *Negro Thought in America, 1880–1915: Racial Ideologies in the Age of Booker T. Washington*. Ann Arbor: University of Michigan Press, 1963.

Peary, Robert E. *Northward over the "Great Ice."* 2 vols. New York: Frederick A. Stokes Company, 1898.

Spear, Allan H. *Black Chicago: The Making of a Negro Ghetto, 1890–1920*. Chicago: University of Chicago Press, 1967.

Thomas, William Hannibal. *The American Negro: What He Was, What He Is, and What He May Become, a Critical and Practical Discussion*. New York: Macmillan Company, 1901.

Thornbrough, Emma Lou. *T. Thomas Fortune: Militant Journalist*. Chicago: University of Chicago Press, 1972.

Villard, Oswald Garrison. "An Alabama Negro School," *American Monthly Review of Reviews*, 26 (Dec. 1902), 711–14.

Washington, Booker T. *Frederick Douglass*. Philadelphia: George W. Jacobs & Company, 1907; reprint, New York: Greenwood Press, 1969.

———. *Working with the Hands: Being a Sequel to "Up from Slavery" Covering the Author's Experiences in Industrial Training at Tuskegee*. New York: Doubleday, Page and Company, 1904; reprint, New York: Negro Universities Press, 1969.

Woodson, Carter G., ed. *The Works of Francis James Grimké*. 4 vols. Washington, D.C.: Associated Publishers, Inc., 1942.

INDEX

NOTE: The asterisk indicates the location of detailed information. This index, while not cumulative, does include the major identifications of persons annotated in earlier volumes of the series who are mentioned in this volume. References to earlier volumes will appear first and will be preceded by the volume number followed by a colon. Lyman Abbott's annotation, for example, will appear as: *3:43–44. Occasionally a name will have more than one entry with an asterisk when new information or further biographical detail is presented.

DATE DUE

HIGHSMITH 45-220